Indigeneity and the Decolonizing Gaze

Indigeneity and the Decolonizing Gaze

Transnational Imaginaries, Media Aesthetics, and Social Thought

Robert Stam

BLOOMSBURY ACADEMIC
LONDON • NEW YORK • OXFORD • NEW DELHI • SYDNEY

BLOOMSBURY ACADEMIC
Bloomsbury Publishing Plc
50 Bedford Square, London, WC1B 3DP, UK
1385 Broadway, New York, NY 10018, USA
29 Earlsfort Terrace, Dublin 2, Ireland

BLOOMSBURY, BLOOMSBURY ACADEMIC and the Diana logo are trademarks of
Bloomsbury Publishing Plc

First published in Great Britain 2023

Copyright © Robert Stam, 2023

Robert Stam has asserted his right under the Copyright,
Designs and Patents Act, 1988, to be identified as Author of this work.

For legal purposes the Acknowledgments on pp. viii–xiii constitute
an extension of this copyright page.

Cover design: Jess Stevens
Cover image: Photograph © REUTERS / Alamy Stock Photo

All rights reserved. No part of this publication may be reproduced
or transmitted in any form or by any means, electronic or
mechanical, including photocopying, recording, or any information storage
or retrieval system, without prior permission in writing from the publishers.

Bloomsbury Publishing Plc does not have any control over, or responsibility for,
any third-party websites referred to or in this book. All internet addresses
given in this book were correct at the time of going to press. The author and
publisher regret any inconvenience caused if addresses have changed or sites
have ceased to exist, but can accept no responsibility for any such changes.

A catalogue record for this book is available from the British Library.

A catalog record for this book is available from the Library of Congress.

ISBN:	HB:	978-1-3502-8236-0
	PB:	978-1-3502-8235-3
	ePDF:	978-1-3502-8238-4
	eBook:	978-1-3502-8237-7

Typeset by Integra Software Services Pvt. Ltd.
Printed and bound in Great Britain

To find out more about our authors and books visit www.bloomsbury.com
and sign up for our newsletters.

To Deana Bowman Stam, Marcelo Fiorini, and Rafaela Vargas

Contents

Acknowledgments	viii
Introduction	1
1 From France Antartique to Shamanic Critique: The Tupinization of Social Thought	53
2 The Indigenous *Cunhã*: The Metamorphosis of a Gendered Trope	115
3 The Transnational "Indian"	169
4 Cross-national Comparabilities: The Indigenization of Brazilian Media	213
5 Triumphs and the Travails of the Yanomami	277
Conclusion: The Theoretical Indigene: Becoming Indian and the Elsewhere of Capitalism	315
Bibliography	367
Index	388

Acknowledgments

Although I have been contemplating writing a book like this for at least four decades, only recently have I had the time and courage to complete it. I write this text in the conviction that when one begins to consider fundamental issues from an indigenous point of view, that view, however inadequately grasped, changes one's thinking in a way that is both humbling and exhilarating. I see the book not as an issue of "speaking for" but rather of "listening to" and "heeding" indigenous thought.

Although I have touched lightly on indigenous-related issues since the 1980s, and although I have long been writing critically about colonialism, genocide, and anti-indigenous racism, as well as about indigenous media, I have never done so at such length or as my sole focus. The critique of racist and colonialist imagery, on the one hand, and the celebration of indigenous culture and media, on the other, held a central place in the book co-authored with Ella Shohat, *Unthinking Eurocentrism* (published in 1994, with a second edition in 2014 having a new Afterword, which included updated material on indigenous issues). The original version was written in the context of the anti-quincentennial protests in 1992. I organized a film series and taught an anti-quincentennial course at NYU, while Ella, together with Annette Jaimes (Juaneno/Yaqui), organized a "Goodbye Columbus" Conference at Cornell featuring Jaime Barreiro (Taino), Ward Churchill (Creek, Cherokee, Metis), and Terry Turner. Much of the writing and thinking here on Columbus and colonialism goes back to that period but here recast in the light of new scholarship and a new situation.

The current book, like most of my books, reflects my academic and personal entanglement, for most of my adult life, with the places and cultural zones where I have lived and taught: the United States, Brazil (and to a lesser degree Portugal), France, North Africa (Tunisia), and the larger Arab World (Abu Dhabi). Living and working in those places has deeply affected my research and thinking and my realization that the history and social thought of the native peoples of the Americas are of central importance not only to the history of the Americas but also to the history of Europe and the world. My work takes place along the interface, the shifting borders between indigenous thought/art, and what we broadly call the radical left, a left whose limitations become obvious when one considers issues from an indigenous point of view.

This project crystalized over the years thanks to a number of people and institutions linked to pro-indigenous arts and activism at NYU and elsewhere. The earliest connection and longest collaboration has been with Faye Ginsburg and the Center for Media, Culture, and History at NYU and the various symposia, panels, and film festivals that she has organized in support of indigenous media. Faye has played an indispensable role not only in advancing the indigenous media cause but also in theorizing the movement through her influential concepts of "embedded aesthetics" and the "Faustian dilemma." Although I had already encountered indigenous media makers from Brazil, thanks to my innumerable stays there and Faye's various programs, I was able to see countless indigenous films and meet many indigenous directors, intellectuals, and curators such as Rachel Perkins, Loretta Todd, and many others. Faye's energetic support for indigenous projects has had a major impact on the film world. A number of indigenous filmmakers were nurtured by her program, such as Jacob Floyd (Muscogee [Creek] Cherokee), whose film *Tonto Plays Himself* (2010) is discussed in this book, and Teresa Montoya (Diné), who directed *Doing the Sheep Good* (2013), which revisits the Sol Worth "Seeing through Navajo Eyes"; and Angelo Baca (Diné/Hopi), whose film *Shash Jaa'* (Bears' Ears, 2016) discusses the anti-extraction efforts to protect a huge area of wilderness sacred to five tribal nations (Navajo, Ute, Ute Mountain Ute, Hopi, and Zuni).

I also want to thank Diana Taylor not only for her brilliant scholarship but also for her role in creating the trilingual Hemispheric Institute of Politics and Performance, which has often focalized indigenous issues and performance, leading to numerous events and performances and an archive of colonial and indigenous materials. The Hemi's "Encuentros" in Lima, Peru, Monterey Mexico, Rio de Janeiro, and New York offered the participants unforgettable experiences and new forms of knowledge.

I also want to thank Cornell's School of Criticism and Theory, which invited Ella Shohat and me to co-teach in their summer program in 2006. Although our course had to do with colonialism in general, our public lecture, entitled "Tupi or not Tupi a Tupi Theorist," contained the kernel of what was to become Chapter 1 of this book. We thank Valery Velejo for introducing our talk. We also learned from Verona Monja and Brent Hayes Edwards as fellow participants in the program. And thanks to Dominick la Capra not only as Director of the Program but also for his irresistibly carnivalesque parodies of academic discourse.

I also want to thank Princeton's Shelby Cullom Davis Center for Historical Studies and its then director Daniel T. Rodgers for granting me a fellowship in 2009, which allowed me to expand on the ideas first developed in the talk at Cornell, entitled "The Red Atlantic: Tupi Theory and the Franco-Brazilian-Indigenous Dialogue."

I would like to thank Sandy Grande for giving Ella and me the tremendous honor of dialoguing with her groundbreaking work on *Red Pedagogy* in the 10th Anniversary Edition of the book.

Finally, I want to thank the Wissenschaftskolleg zu Berlin (WIKO) for granting my partner Ella a fellowship in Berlin for 2020–21, giving her a year to write up her research on Arab Jews, and as a glorious by-product, allowing me to take advantage of a sabbatical and a leave to write up this project. I am especially grateful for the generous help of WIKO's amazing library services, which, despite Covid, was capable of finding the relevant books in English, French, Spanish, and Portuguese, all done with remarkable speed and goodwill. I could not have completed this project without the time allowed to me by that grant. Special thanks go to Vera Pfefer, Anja Brockmann, and Dunia for the immense kindness and hospitality they offered us while we were there.

I also owe a great debt to my former PhD advisee/now friend Amalia Cordova, the kind of student from whom one learns as much as one teaches. A much-beloved figure in many different communities, Amalia is admired for her intelligence, courage, writing, and tireless activism in the cause of indigenous media and culture.

The intellectual conversations promoted by various centers at NYU have been an endless source of stimulation and inspiration. Here I would like to thank Frederic Viguier from La Maison Française; Juan Fernandes, Omar Alejandro Dauhajre, and Ana Dopico at the Juan Carlos of Spain Center; Jill Lane from the Center for Latin American and Caribbean Studies, Culture and History, along with the Comparative Race Studies Group led by Pamela Calla.

I am dedicating this book to two people who for me embody living breathing love art, and activism: Marcelo Fiorini and Rafaela Vargas. Marcelo and I have been close friends ever since he prepared *caipirinhas* for the students in my Brazilian cinema course many decades ago. The friendship began in New York when he was completing his doctorate at NYU, but it continued and flourished in France and Brazil. Wherever Marcelo and Rafaela go, they bring joy, love, activism, and a festive spirituality, creating an atmosphere where friends become friends of other peoples' friends, and where people fall in love and meet fellow activists, creating transnational circles of socially engaged people. Marcelo lived with the indigenous Nambiquara for five years and speaks two dialects of the language fluently. For 35 years, he has been a risk-taking advocate of indigenous causes in Brazil, actively working for the demarcation of indigenous lands, including the first sacred (Nambiquara) territory in Brazil, which guards important Amazon sources and is crucial to their cultural reproduction. Among his many films is the feature-length documentary *Levi-Strauss: Aupres de l'Amazonie* (Lévi-Strauss, Close to the Amazon, 2008), which is discussed in this book and shown in more than twenty international film festivals. Today Marcelo and Rafaela work as activists supporting social and environmental projects for indigenous associations as well as international nongovernmental organizations. Marcelo is currently collaborating on a book with Ashininka shaman and activist Benki Piyãko.

Rafaela Vargas is one of the most talented people I have ever known. Her ancestry is indigenous and African on her mother's side, and Italian and Spanish gypsy Calon on her father's side. What is more unusual is that Rafaela is deeply familiar with all the cultural repertoires—including dancing, singing, and sacred plants—associated with those identities. To give an inkling of Rafaela's talents, after a trip to India, she offered a birthday gift to Marcelo and guests—a Kalbelya gypsy dance that she learned in Rajasthan. As a psychologist, Rafaela lived with the Xavante and riverside people in the Brazilian Pantanal, where she created programs to combat alcoholism and drug addiction. As an actress and anthropologist, with an anthropology degree from Paris, she researches ritual theater, healing rituals, and female shamanism among indigenous peoples, especially the Wauja of the Upper Xingu. Today, she directs social environmental society actions and campaigns against the destruction of the environment and for the preservation and dissemination of indigenous cultures, especially with regard to women's struggles. In close friendship and collaboration with many indigenous leaders, some living under death threats, the activism of Marcelo and Rafaela has been unending and has taken many forms—filmmaking, writing, fundraising, and actions on the ground for the indigenous cause.

I also wanted to salute a remarkable panel for the Society for Multi-Ethnic Studies: Europe and the Americas (MESEA) 8th Biennial held in Barcelona, Spain (June 13, 2012). The panel was entitled "The Crow Commons: American Indian Poetry—Ways of Saying, Ways of Knowing: Indigenous Poetics as Epistemological Mediation Chair," with Gordon Henry, Gwen Westerman, Glenn Wasicuna, Jane Hafen, and Patrice Hollrah. For me, the panel was a model of what the academe should be: generous, collaborative, funny, non-competitive, and performative. Their high-flying "Crow Commons" panel, for example, gave dynamic expression and lively form to what is often an abstract ideal—an indigenous-led academic commons. Framed by the playful drumming of Gordon Henry, the panel consisted of artfully interwoven poems, citations, and reflexions, some tragic and some wryly humorous. Playing every possible change on the avian theme by speaking of "strutting crows" and "soaring spirits," scholarly "migrations," "roostings," and improvisational "winging it," the panel modeled an inspiringly vibrant and dialogic alternative to academic conferences that too often form exercises in scholarly "enclosure" and a competitive search for "distinction."

I am also dedicating this book to the memory of my mother Deana Bowman Stam, mother of seven and the person who grounded our normativities. She was the daughter of a working-class Dutch immigrant from Rochester, New York. Despite an eighth-grade education, she was brilliant. She gave birth to seven children, and I was the "seventh son." She embodied love, not Hollywood air-kiss love but practical, total, unrelenting love.

I want to thank the wonderful Rebecca Barden, previously an editor for our *Unthinking Eurocentrism*, and Jayne Fargnoli, another beloved editor, for suggesting that I contact Rebecca.

I am also grateful for the help of various assistants over the period of gestation, notably along with the indispensable technical assistance I have received at various stages from the digital genius (and geniality) of Joseph Modirzadeh, and the general all-purpose genius and warm, gracious, and extremely efficient work, both in New York and Delhi, of Revantika Gupta.

I would also like to thank the following for their support and friendship over the years: my wonderful colleagues Zhen Zhang, Marina Hassapopoulou, Josslyn Luckett, Feng Mei Heberer, Dan Streible, Anna McCarthy, Chris Straayer, Dana Polan, and Juana Suarez. Also, in no particular order, a shout-out to Chris Dunn, Patrick Erouart, Alessandara Santos, Arturo Escobar, Robert Young, Esther Hamburger, Fabio Andrade, Joao Luiz Vieira, Luiz Antonio Coelho, Gustavo Furtado, Leo Cortana, Ze Gatti, Ismail Xavier, Livia Perez, Mary-Louise Pratt, Renato Rosaldo, Awam Amkpa, Manthia Diawara, Ed Guerrero, Marc Michael, Nezar Andari, Fawzia el-Khan, Gayatri Gopinath, Dale Hudson, Sheetal Majithia, Joana Brandao, Mari Correa, Marcelo Fiorini, Jose Gatti, Vincent Carelli, Ivone Margulies, Divino Tsweharu, and Monica Frota.

Finally, I want to express my undying love and appreciation for my son Gilberto (Giba) in São Paulo. We have been separated during this Covid period, but Giba has constantly been sending me news items and announcements about indigenous issues in Brazil. Just as I was writing about the Amazon and the Yanomami, coincidentally, Giba was writing about the Amazonian biome for science journals.

And to Ella. As always.

Although most of the material in the book is new, it does inevitably revisit earlier work, as noted in the endnotes, but almost freshly milled, within new frames, with new inflections and changes in emphasis, in relation to altered landscapes and morphing issues and discourses. The book revisits some of the issues raised in a different way in *Unthinking Eurocentrism: Multiculturalism and the Media* (Routledge, 1994) but now from the perspective of the present of 2021, in the light of new interests and new scholarship. The material on the Franco-indigenous interaction builds on, modifies, and supplements an essay (with Ella Shohat) "Postcolonial Studies and France," published in *Interventions* (Spring, 2012) and subsequently included in *Race in Translation: Culture Wars in the Postcolonial Atlantic*. Some of the material on the Red Atlantic and indigenous thought appeared in very different form in the essay "The Red Atlantic Dialogue: Response 1" (with Ella Shohat), our dialogue with the 10th Anniversary Edition of Sandy Grande's seminal book *Red Pedagogy: Native American Social and Political Thought* (Rowman & Littlefield Publishers, 2015).

During the long gestation of this book, much of the work was first presented in the form of keynotes and visiting lectures, including a 2006 lecture in Portuguese on "*O Indio Brasileiro e a Cultura Popular*" at the Seminario Internacional de Cinema e Audio-Visual/Salvador/Bahia (Salvador: SEMCINE); a 2006 (October 16) lecture on "What Cultural Studies Can Learn from Tropicalia" at BRASA (Brazilian Studies Association), held at Vanderbilt University; a 2006 (November) lecture on "Tropicalia and Brazilian Cinema" at the Americas Society in New York City; a 2008 (December 5) lecture in French on "Critical Representations of First Contact" at L'Institut d'Amerique Latine in Paris; a 2008 (August 29) keynote "Globalization and Aesthetics from Below" in Puebla, Mexico; a 2008 (June 5) lecture on "The Aesthetics of Brazilian Documentary" at Monash University, Melbourne, Australia; a 2008 (May 12–15) keynote "Tupi or not Tupi a Tupi Theorist" at the Europe in Black and White conference, University of Lisbon; a 2009 (April) lecture on "The Red Atlantic" at the Casa de Saber ("house of knowledge") in Rio de Janeiro; a 2009 (April) presentation of "The Red Atlantic: Tupi Theory and the Franco-Brazilian-Indigenous Dialogue" at the Shelby Cullom Davis Center, Princeton University; and the "The Franco-Indigenous Dialogue" lecture at the Maison Francaise, NYU (April 22, 2008).

I would like to thank Vinzenz Hediger and the Goethe University, Frankfurt, Germany, for inviting me to offer a keynote for the conference "The Other 1968" at the Museum Angewandte Kunst in Frankfurt (May 2018); Pamela Calla for her invitation to present "Protocols of Eurocentrism" for the "Comparative Race Study Group" in CLACS at NYU (May 2018); Stefan Solomon and Lucia Nagib for inviting me to form part of a Panel-Presentation on the Tropicalia Movement at the Tate Modern, London (November 2017); Consuelo Lins and Denilson Lopes for my lecture series (in Portuguese) on "Aesthetics and Politics" in the School of Communications at Federal University of Rio de Janeiro (April 2017); Esther Hamburger for a lecture series (in Portuguese) on "Aesthetics and Politics in the School of Communications" at the University of São Paulo (March 2017); Sergio Costa for inviting me to present "Variations on a Transatlantic Theme" as opening lecture for the series "Minor Cosmopolitanisms"; and for conducting a graduate seminar with the Minor Cosmopolitanisms Research Training Group, University of Potsdam, Potsdam, Germany (October 28, 2016), as well as for inviting Ella Shohat and me to participate in a book launch panel on the occasion of the German translation of our *Race in Translation* at the Freie Universität Berlin, Germany (October 27, 2016); Messias Bandeira for inviting me to offer a lecture series (in Portuguese) on "Alternative Media at the School of Communications" at the Federal University of Bahia, Brazil (June 2015); Ismail Xavier, Christian Borges, and Esther Hamburger for an invitation to present a lecture series (in Portuguese) on "Aesthetics and Politics" at the School of Communications at the University of São Paulo (June 2014); and Ilda Santos for inviting me to offer a lecture in Portuguese on "Lusophone Red Atlantic" at the Sorbonne Nouvelle, Paris III (April 2012).

Introduction

A video message, entitled "Message from a Shaman," goes out on the internet. The slick, fast-paced clip begins with cascading images of maps, paintings, animals, plants and faces, and concludes with images of pollution, wreckage, and devastation. The pithy intertitles summarize the point: "We warned you about the climate crisis. We asked you to protect the forest. You didn't listen. And now it may be too late."

The shaman in question is Davi Kopenawa Yanomami, renowned spokesperson for the Yanomami people. One of the best-known forest-dwelling tribes, the Yanomami of Northern Brazil and Southern Venezuela form the largest indigenous nation to have survived more or less autonomously into the mid-twentieth century. Seen in the 1960s as the most isolated tribe in the world, they were the subject of a best seller by anthropologist Napoleon Chagnon, entitled *The Fierce People*.[1] The book, which portrayed the Yanomami as a violent species of "primitive man," was accepted as gospel by millions of readers. Other anthropologists responded that the Yanomami were more the victims of violence than its perpetrators, but the Yanomami voice remained absent. Five decades later, the Yanomami are speaking for themselves and have become valiant defenders of the forest in the world at large. Kopenawa's collaborative book *The Falling Sky* was published in 2013 by Harvard University Press and by prestigious presses in France and Brazil.[2] At the epicenter of struggles over climate change, the Yanomami are now making films and active on the internet.

How did a situation where indigenous peoples were spoken for by others become one where they are speaking for themselves? How did the Yanomami go from being unaware of the existence of cinema to making videos and films that travel far beyond his homeland forest? How did the group move from minimal technologies to embracing cell phones and drones, while staying radically faithful to their cultural codes and to their critique of capitalist "progress"? How did indigenous people, with the legal status of children, become the ones accusing the West of behaving like spoiled children, at a time when indigenous leaders appear in Netflix features and programs like Hasan Minhaj's *Patriot Act* and Amy Goodman's *Democracy Now*? More generally, how did we go from a time when Hollywood stars were gleefully murdering hordes of war-whooping Indians to a point where indigenous people are themselves making feature films and TV series like *Rutherford Falls* and *Reservation Dogs*, while founding TV stations and, more generally, speaking in their own voices?

More broadly, how can we explain the transition from a situation where the postwar United Nations recognized only nation-states to where it makes declarations about the rights of indigenous peoples? And how did we go from native peoples having minimal participation in governments in the Americas to a situation where Evo Morales (Aymara) becomes the first indigenous president of Bolivia, and where Deb Haaland (Laguna Pueblo) is named Interior Secretary of the United States? (An earlier interior secretary, Alexander Stuart, had pondered whether to "civilize or exterminate" native people).[3] How did a situation where indigenous reflections were barely recognized as legitimate forms of thought give way to a situation where indigenous thinkers form the cutting edge of the interface of Western theory and indigenous critique, for example by relationalizing settler-colonialism and gendered heteropatriarchal violence and questioning the ideological foundations of western nation-states. For centuries, Indigenous thinkers have been offering alternative social theories rooted in native culture that are relevant to a dominant world beset by superimposed crises—the ecological crisis of climate change, the health crisis of a pandemic, the social crisis of inequality and the economic crisis of exhausted resources, the racial crisis of systemic oppression, and the political crisis in the theory and practice of liberal democracy. Indigenous thought, I will be arguing, can help us reenvision the origins and the antidotes to all these crises.

The trajectory of the Yanomami from "most remote tribe" to active presence in the contemporary debates forms a *mise-en-abyme* for the structure of this book, which moves repeatedly from nonrepresentation and misrepresentation to self-representation and self-performance, or better stated, from survival to "survivance" (Vizenor) or from the denial of agency to agential expression and self-creation. The story is not one, however, of a triumphal entry of indigenous peoples into a globalized modernity. The story has no Hollywood happy ending or even a Sundance-style bitter-sweet finale. For indigenous peoples it is the best of times—an explosion of creativity and visibility in the fields of art, politics, social theory, and activism—and the worst of times, with indigenous peoples in a terrible state of land-loss, cultural dispossession, and Covid, and in Brazil of constant murders of indigenous leaders. Yet at the same time, thanks to the internet and social media, as indigenous activist/writer Ailton Krenak dryly reminds us, genocide is less likely now, not because the powerful have learned their lesson, but because, unlike earlier genocides, it would be widely and instantly reported on social media.

Against the historical backdrop of 1492, Columbus, and the Conquest, *Indigeneity and the Decolonizing Gaze* sketches out this broad trajectory from the denial of agency and the paternalistic tutelage of "dependent domestic nations"[4] to the adulthood of "visual sovereignty" (Michelle Rajeha). To reassure the reader, the book does not try to recount the history of the world since 1492. Nor does it survey the evolving technologies and social conjunctures that made these changes possible. Nor does it survey indigenous media around the world. Nor does it offer immediate practical solutions to the problems raised. Rather, the book reflects on crucial discursive flashpoints through a historicized analysis of symptomatic texts of all kinds. Rather than offer answers and solutions, it raises questions that might indirectly point to solutions, to be led by indigenous peoples themselves. Transnational and transdisciplinary, the book shuttles constantly between South and North America, and more precisely between indigenous issues in the United States and Canada (aka *Kanata*, Huron for "village") and similar issues in Brazil (named after the country's first export product), with a few side excursions to Europe and beyond. The book offers a conversational journey through overlapping terrains of political philosophy, literature, history, and popular culture. The recurrent themes include: the critique of settler colonialism; the reverence for land; the aesthetic contribution of native Arts and media; the limitations of "positive images"; the questioning of private property and possessive individualism; the deployment of irony, humor, and parody; and, underlying everything, the relation between embodied and expressed indigenous social thought and what can broadly be called "the left." Why is it that whenever socially radical ideas have appeared over the horizon since Columbus, indigenous social thought has so often catalyzed radical thinking? What explains this haunting co-presence? And how are such concerns reflected and refracted in the media arts?

In a sense, the book continues the project begun by Ella Shohat and me in *Unthinking Eurocentrism* (1994), as a work of decolonizing audiovisual pedagogy that relationalized colonial and decolonizing perspectives. In the present book, every chapter tells a similar story, but in relation to a different topic and through a different corpus and grid. Moving through and beyond the fiction feature film, the corpus includes a wide array of cultural productions—documentaries, TV programs, music videos, stand-up comedy, activist videos, internet remixes, and theoretical writing. Rather than offer an impossible "coverage," my goal is to highlight the urgent social and artistic relevance of specific cultural productions and the social thought they embody. The discussion will be literally, and deliberately, "all over the map"; like a magic realist novel, it will zig-zag in space across the Western Hemisphere and beyond while jumping in time from Montaigne to Lévi-Strauss and from philosopher Thomas Hobbes to anthropologist Napoleon Chagnon. In this text, I will constantly move between historical periods, geographical regions, and media, going from Benjamin Franklin to a twenty-first-century shaman, or from a historical event in 1550 in France to a carnival reenactment of that same event in Rio de Janeiro four centuries later, or from October 12, 1492, to January 6, 2021.[5]

The book is about how Brazilians, United Statesians, Canadians, Europeans, and others have seen and thought about "Indians," but more importantly about how indigenous peoples have seen those others and presented and performed themselves in art and theory. The book orchestrates a virtual polylogue among disciplines and discourses and media revolving around indigenous social thought and artistic practice. It acknowledges what Linda Tuhiwai Smith calls the presence of the indigene "in the Western imagination, in its fibre and texture, in its language, in its silences and shadows, its margins and intersections."[6] My goal is not to idealize indigenous societies, but only to point out that many western thinkers, along with many indigenous thinkers, have been praising certain native social arrangements for a long time, and recently with even more force and urgency. My argument is less historical than discursive, less about historical causality than about discursive transtextuality. Although my text invokes many historical issues, it is not a work of history per se; rather, it performs an active reading of texts that unavoidably touch on historiographic issues. I am not "doing" history in the conventional sense of performing archival research aimed at asserting causality. I am not claiming that a conversation between Montaigne and a few Tupinamba caused the French Revolution, but only that important figures from various countries, over centuries, in line with indigenous peoples themselves, have argued that indigenous thought has been a generative force in revolutionary thought and practice. Is it not significant that Davi Kopenawa, a Yanomami shaman unfamiliar with western writings, and Luther Standing Bear, a Native American who had been a star in Buffalo Bill's "Wild West Show," should make similar affirmations about land, about writing, and about social equality, and that so many indigenous and non-indigenous writers, from many different parts of the world, countries, unknown to one another, have for centuries been echoing similar sentiments?

The title *Indigeneity and the Decolonizing Gaze* implies a meeting of (at least) two gazes, the colonizing gaze *on* the "Indian" and the decolonizing gaze *of* the native as encountered in literature, film, media, the arts, and social theory. Art can promote a dialogue between indigenous self-telling and world-making and the telling and world-making of others. The gazes are obviously asymmetrical and power-laden. Maori filmmaker/theorist Barry Barclay contrasts the standpoint of the First Cinema camera on the deck of the colonial ship, and the Fourth Cinema camera placed on the shore, siding with the people for whom "ashore" simply means being at home. For five centuries, Vine Deloria Jr. points out, "whites have had unrestricted power to describe Indians in any way they choose."[7] Of course, there are more than two gazes since each gaze exists at the intersection of other gazes; given colonial histories, the gazes are inevitably mixed and multiple, informed by contradictory desires, discourses, and affiliations. One of the gazes, of course, is my own non-indigenous gaze, doubtless blinkered and near-sighted at times, but trying to see clearly and ready to learn as I sit spellbound in darkness. The challenge is to be able to see one's own blind spots, by definition invisible to ourselves, but which may be clear to others through what Bakhtin called "excess seeing," or the complementarity, but also sometimes the incommensurability, of diverse perspectives.

The indigenous here forms both the privileged object of study and a subject in the sense of the producer and generator of discourse. The word "gaze" in my title evokes a long history of twentieth-century philosophy, cultural analysis, and film-theoretical reflection privileging the gaze, whether the *regard d'autrui* of Jean-Paul Sartre; the female gaze of Simone de Beauvoir; the panopticon of Foucault; the voyeuristic gaze of Metzian psycho-semiotics; the (internalized) "male gaze" of Laura Mulvey; the "downcast eyes" of Martin Jay; the "seeing like a state" of James C. Scott; the critique of the homophobic gaze of queer theory; and the returned imperial gaze of postcolonial critique. In the influential "Orphee Noir" essay that introduced Senghor's *Anthologie de la Nouvelle poésie Nègre et Malgache de Langue Française* (1948), Jean-Paul Sartre described negritude, and here we might substitute "indigeneitude," as a turning back of the gaze, by which the French colonizers were obliged to see themselves as others saw them. "For the white man has enjoyed for 3,000 years the privilege of seeing without being seen [but] now our gaze is thrown back in our eyes."[8] In *Wretched of the Earth*, Fanon casts colonialism itself as a painful crossing of looks, where the colonizer trains on the colonized a look of superiority, surveillance, desire, and appropriation, and the colonized return a look of resentment, envy, and righteous anger. The colonialist's greatest crime, meanwhile, was to make the colonized see their own selves and societies through colonizing eyes. In the context of indigenous media, meanwhile, Faye Ginsburg speaks of the "parallax view" to evoke the multi-perspectival situatedness of the gaze on the object "indigenous film." In such a conflictual situation, optical metaphors are inevitable; more important than the brute facts are the interpretative grids and prisms and perspectives through which the facts are seen.

The reader might question the wisdom of mixing discussions of Indigenous Media Arts with social philosophy. But philosophy and media, in my view, are closely related arenas of contestation. The crossed gazes toward and from the "Indian" operate isomorphically in many different spheres, from philosophy to art and activism. What Jerry Mander and Victoria Tauli-Corpuz call the "paradigm wars" are also worldview wars that flare up both in the media and in social philosophy.[9] Racism toward indigenous people, and respectful alignment with indigenous people, co-exists within the history both of philosophy and of the media. The mutual illumination and reciprocal relativization of social theory and media theory benefits both; social theory can illuminate the media, and the media can flesh out and remediate social theory. The encounter of gazes is also an encounter of disparate ways of thinking. The racial/chromatic hierarchies that inform Hegel's *The Philosophy of History*—placing "Whites" at the top, "Yellows" next, and "Blacks" and "Reds" competing for the bottom—parallel those undergirding classical Hollywood films. The Indigenous media arts movements, meanwhile, are joined at the hip with the resistance thinking that shaped them and made them possible.

Philosophical thinking is not a white European monopoly. In *As We Have Always Done,* Michi Saagiig Nishnaabeg writer, musician, academic, and theorist Leanne Betasamosake Simpson states that "indigenous peoples have always been theoretical people. We've always thought in complex ways about the nature of our worlds. We've always sought out explanations and deeper meanings [but] our theoretical understandings were constructed differently than Western theory; they are woven into doing, they are layered in meaning, they can be communicated through story, action, and embodied presence."[10] M. Nakata, in *Disciplining the Savages: Savaging the Disciplines*, speaks of "indigenous standpoint theory" concerned with the validity and coherence of indigenous knowledge within the cultural interface.[11] Scott Pratt speaks of a "native pragmatism" born out of the intersection of Western and Native American thought. Jeanette Armstrong (Okanagan) unpacks the complex and layered meanings of the word "Okanagan" (roughly "dream") as "the unseen part of our existence as human beings," pointing to three levels of meaning—the physical realm, the imaginative mind, and the weaving of strands into one string.[12] Paula Gunn Allen writes: "[W]e like to think our god is a woman, and her name is Thought."[13]

One of Deleuze's signal contributions, meanwhile, has been to show that cinema is philosophical, in that it can generate concepts through movement. The same is true, by extension, of music, dance, body painting, totem poles, and shamanic practices: any cultural activity can generate concepts, which help us see "other-wise." What the West called shamans were also thinkers, whose thinking took the forms of poetry, songs, stories, and prayers too easily seen as non-philosophical. Taiaiake Alfred's "Indigenous

Manifesto," meanwhile, was inspired by the ritual songs of the Rotinoshonni condolence ceremony.[14] Of course, for a professional philosopher, this equation of music and ritual with philosophy would reflect a "dumbing down" of philosophy, but it might better be considered as an "opening up" and "airing out" and "grounding" of philosophy.

A crossed gazes approach counterpoints celebration and critique, in full knowledge that celebration can embrace critique, just as critique can encode celebration. This "Introduction" unpacks key terms such as "colonialism," "indigeneity," and "indigenous media arts." Chapter 1, "From France Antartique to Shamanic Critique: The Tupinization of Social Thought," demonstrates that indigenous social theory has been a crucial but submerged presence within Western philosophy. More specifically, the chapter traces the 500-year "dialogue," often literal and direct but more often mediated and figurative, between French writers, indigenous people, and Euro-Brazilians, and more broadly between native thought and the West, always foregrounding the "Indian" as the exemplar of freedom and equality. After exploring this discursive lineage within French philosophy and Brazilian Modernism, the chapter moves to the impact of indigenous social thought on the French and American revolutions. The chapter ends with a discussion of Davi Kopenawa's *The Falling Sky*, a paradigm-shifting book and late entry to the ongoing franco-indigenous dialogue, a subject to which we will return at various points.

Chapter 2, "The Indigenous *Cunhã*: The Metamorphosis of a Gendered Trope," begins and ends in Manhattan but centers on the image and agency of the indigenous woman in Brazilian film, art, and activism. After a close analysis of a song/poem by Brazilian singer/artist/writer Caetano Veloso, the chapter traces the metamorphoses of the indigenous woman in Brazilian literature, cinema, popular culture, the media and activism. Chapter 3, "The Transnational Indian," after an analysis of the role of land in the frontier Western, undertakes a comparative/relational study of the "White Indian" as fashioned by various national imaginaries, including in the United States, Venezuela, Mexico, France, and Germany. The discussion then moves to transnational indigenous responses to the dominant imagery, coming largely from native groups located in Canada, in various art forms such as poetry, stand-up comedy, painting, and music video.

Chapter 4, "Cross-national Comparabilities: The Indigenization of Brazilian Cinema," begins with a comparative study of the Hollywood and the Brazilian "Indian." The chapter compares "first contact" films from the two countries; the mediatic response to two quincentennials (Columbus in 1992, Cabral in 2000); the differences between Hollywood Westerns and Brazilian "Northeasterns"; followed by an account of the swelling strength of Indigenous Media and popular culture in Brazil from the 1980s up to the present. Chapter 5, "The Triumphs and Travails of the Yanomami," is devoted to the debates swirling around the Yanomami as a kind of test case for discussions of a supposed indigenous "state of nature" and as an example of multifaceted resistance to colonial domination. After an overview of international films about the Yanomami, the chapter discusses the films created about and by and with the Yanomami. The chapter concludes with an in-depth analysis of Davi Kopenawa Yanomami's *The Falling Sky*.

The final chapter, "Conclusion: The Theoretical Indigene: Becoming Indian, and the Elsewhere of Capitalism," brings to the surface what had been implicit—

the indigenization of social theory. At a historical moment characterized by horrific interrelated crises, a point where capitalist "progress" and liberal democracy are straining against their limits, more and more non-native people are beginning to pay attention to indigenous social thought. Completing the trajectory that began with Montaigne and the Tupinamba, the discussion moves to a present-day resurgence of indigenous artistic and intellectual creativity, along with some rare glimpses of what a modicum of reciprocity between indigenous and non-indigenous social thinkers might look like. In an era where it has often been said that "we now find it easier to imagine the end of the planet than to imagine the end of capitalism," indigenous thinking suggests ways of thinking before, beyond, and alongside capitalism and the nation-state, thus opening up alternative energies and potentialities.

The Terms of Debate

It is essential at the outset to unpack some key terms, beginning with the term "indigenous" itself. The term refers to those peoples—variously called "indigenous," "tribal," "aboriginal," "originary," "authoctonous," "native," "first peoples," and "first nations"—descended from the original inhabitants of territories subsequently invaded or circumscribed by colonial conquest and nation-state expansion.[15] The designation of indigenous peoples as "Indians" relays the errant sense of geography of Columbus as an early Orientalist. Just as no one is exotic to themselves, "Indians" before Columbus and Cabral did not know themselves as "Indian" but as Xavante or Haudenosaunee; contact itself constituted them as "Indians." In *Manifest Manners*, "postindian warrior" Gerald Vizenor finds the word "Indian" hopelessly tainted.[16] At the same time, some indigenous activists, both in North and South America, have boomeranged the term as an empowering vehicle for pan-Indigenous movements. Despite the salient differences between various indigenous nations, the term "indigenous peoples," as Linda Tuhiwai Smith points out, "has enabled the collective voices of colonized people to be expressed strategically in the international arena [and has been] an umbrella term enabling communities to come together, transcend their own colonized contexts and experiences, in order to learn, share, plan, organize, and struggle collectively for self-determination on the global and local stages."[17]

Indigenous peoples form a globally dispersive and transnational phenomenon, including, for example, the Ainu in Japan, or the "scheduled tribes" of India, comprising more than 200 communities representing 10 percent of the population. In a situation where indigenous nations outnumber nation-states, as many as 3,000 indigenous nations, with an estimated population ranging from 250 to 600 million people, function within the 200 nation-states that assert sovereignty over them.[18] Native peoples, despite their primordial importance, do not always "scan" on the global screen. A reactionary political discourse called resistant indigenous peoples "savages" and "cannibals" in an early period, and "rebels," "guerillas," "separatists," or even "terrorists" in a later period, terms that render them invisible as indigenous people. At times, they are "disappeared" into broader social categories like peasants, campesinos, rural workers, mountain peoples, migrants, and the like.[19, 20]

The challenges for Indigenous peoples, and their responses to those challenges, are thoroughly transnational. Hydroelectric dams, for example, in the dominant mindset concrete icons of "progress" and "development," flood indigenous communities and destroy the environment.[21] As a result, the dams have catalyzed transnational circuits of resistance: indigenous people in India protesting the Sardar Sarovar Dam; the Kayapo and other native groups in Brazil protesting the Belo Monte Dam; and the Nisichawayasihk Cree protesting the Manitoba Hydro Dam. Punning on the two meanings of dam/ning, Jane Griffith analyzes the Hoover Dam as a damned settler-colonial project, occupying indigenous land and waterways in order to produce energy that furthers ever-more settlement.[22] Macarena Gomez-Barris speaks of "damned landscapes" as "extractive zones where military, corporate, and state technologies of resource surveillance convert Indigenous and rural territories into a digital colony."[23]

In this text, I will use terms like "native Americans," "first peoples," "indigenous peoples," and "native peoples" more or less interchangeably to refer to individuals and groups with some connection to the originary peoples, and who self-identify as indigenous. I will usually use "Indian" in quotes to refer to non-indigenous constructions and fantasies about indigenous people, and without quotes to refer to legal statutes, or where indigenous people themselves use the term to designate activist pan-movements, e.g. the "American Indian Movement" and "Indios online" in Brazil.[24] The extremely wide spectrum of physical appearance of Indigenous peoples in North and South America sometimes triggers, in a form of epidermic profiling, the "you-don't-look-like-a-real-Indian" charge. Although colonialism is about color, it is not exclusively about color. Indigenous people come in virtually every color in the spectrum. "White" Ireland, for example, was the first colony of Britain, with the Irish, writes John Mohawk, the "English encountered their first indigenous people." The land invasions against the Irish anticipated those against the indigenous peoples of the Americas: "Acre by acre the Indians were driven by their land just as the poor in England had been."[25] Political theorist Robert Nichols speaks of the two dispossessions, first the enclosures and transformation of land tenure in Europe, which took place alongside and in relation to the second dispossession, the territorial expansion of Europe into indigenous land.[26]

The white-presenting Sami people of arctic Europe, similarly, are not "Indians," but they are indigenous. Like other indigenous people, they have led a circular nomadic life of hunting and fishing, following seasonal rhythms linked to the migrations of the reindeer that have sustained them. As with other groups, their culture and spirituality, and their survival, were grounded in the land and its fauna and resources. Their land too has been threatened by mining in lands whose ecology and biodiversity they have preserved for millennia. They too suffered from colonial-style nation-state repression, in fact from four nation-state repressions. Their feature films, such as *Ofelas* (English title Pathfinder, 1987), based on a Sami legend, have foregrounded their traditional culture. The 2008 film *Kautokeino Opproret* portrayed the historical episode of the revolt of the Sami people against Church and State domination. The Sami too adhere to a kind of shamanic spirituality rooted in communally held land regarded as sacred.[27]

Since the debates about "indigeneity" are complicated, the U.N. Declaration of the Rights of Indigenous Peoples ultimately refrained from endorsing a full-fledged definition. Most discussions begin with the working definition proposed by U.N. Special Rapporteur José Martínez Cobo in his Study of the Problem of Discrimination against Indigenous Populations (1983), which states: "Indigenous communities, peoples and nations are those which, having a historical continuity with pre-invasion and pre-colonial societies that developed on their territories, consider themselves distinct from other sectors of the societies now prevailing in those territories, or parts of them. They are determined to preserve, develop and transmit to future generations their ancestral territories, and their ethnic identity, as the basis of their continued existence as peoples, in accordance with their own cultural patterns, social institutions and legal systems."[28] The notion of "distinct societies," meanwhile, has more recently shifted from static definitions aimed at a museological "preservation" of supposedly agonizing cultures to a stress on the self-conscious production and performance of identity, seen not as a pre-given condition but rather as a constantly changing construct and a generative social force. Jeff Corntassel (Cherokee) and Taiaiake Alfred (Kahnawake Mohawk) inject a crucial political dimension by adding an "oppositional, place-based existence, along with the consciousness of being in struggle against the dispossessing and demeaning fact of colonization by foreign peoples."[29]

Before Columbus's landfall, millions of indigenous people lived in the Americas—estimates range from 50 to 100 million—but colonial invasions and occupations generally created mountains of corpses, in Todorov's term, a "hecatomb."[30] As late as 1820, indigenous peoples still controlled half of the globe, but they steadily lost sovereignty under the auspices of various imperialisms and nation-states. Indigenous peoples have also suffered alien diseases, sometimes deliberately spread by whites, and have been the targets of bioterrorism. At the present moment, Covid-19 disproportionately afflicts native peoples, whether the Dine or Oglala Sioux in North America or the Yanomami and the Xavante in Brazil, thus offering a latter-day iteration of a long-standing western-induced "Syphillization."

It would be foolhardy to posit generalizations about the world's indigenous peoples, given the diversity of those peoples. But there are shared commonalities, or better family resemblances, among groups that on a negative level experienced colonialism, and on a positive level broadly shared certain cultural, spiritual, and economic assumptions. Just as it is hazardous to generalize about indigenous peoples globally, it is similarly difficult to generalize about indigenous people living within single nation-states. Any sentence that begins with "All Indians …" or "all native Americans" or "all Yanomami" or "all Cree" is on the face of it as absurd as a sentence beginning with "All Europeans …." The "indigenous" umbrella shelters a pluriverse of differentiated commonalities, where one can emphasize the differences or the commonalities. Even when one excludes the empires like the Aztecs, the Incas, and the Mayas, indigenous societies are remarkably varied in terms of social hierarchies and in relations with native neighbors and with invading settler societies. The sheer variety of indigenous cultures contradicts any notion of a "generic Indian" as constituting a single easily categorizable unit within western taxonomies. The societies differ: (1) temporally, in time of first contact (the Tupi in 1500, the Yanomami almost a half millennium later); (2) historically, in their relation to colonialism (colonized, semi-colonized, autonomous, sovereign, postcolonized, or some combination of the above); (3) politically, in relation to their hold on their land-base and their codes of governance; (4) culturally, in language, religion, and cosmologies; (5) socially, in their intersectional stratifications and power relations; and (6) in appearance, dress, cuisine, and artistic expression.

To generalize about such diverse societies even in a positive way—to suggest that all indigenous societies operate as democratic consensus societies, that all revere nature, and so forth—would be absurd. As Tracy Devine Guzman puts it, "there is no social or political consensus that stems organically from self-identification with indigeneity."[31] The settlers entered a world riddled with small-scale conflicts among indigenous peoples. All the Americas hosted intertribal conflicts and alliances, before and after contact. In some indigenous societies in Brazil, warring was a basic social feature, linked, paradoxically, to equality within the society. But the European wars against indigenous peoples followed a substantially different and more violent pattern, in that (1) the western weapons were unprecedentedly powerful and unequally distributed between the opposing sides; (2) western killing was disproportionate, leaving natives everywhere amazed at the magnitude of the death toll; and (3) European wars in the Americas, unlike indigenous wars, aimed not just at winning a symbolic battle over prestige or a stolen bride or ritual cannibalism but rather at something far more consequential—the taking of vast amounts of land, the destruction of long-standing ways of life, and the subjugation of entire populations. Indigenous wars, in contrast, were lethal, but never ethnocidal. Killing women and children was taboo. Nor did indigenous wars aim at forming standing armies or weapons industries. Wendat "auto-historian" Georges E. Sioui Wendayete finds that

> archeology shows no conclusive proof of the existence of seriously destructive or prolonged prehistoric conflicts between [indigenous peoples and] … the so-called wars that many Wendat-Iroquoian … people waged on one another were "mourning wars" [that were] normally organized – or countered – by Councils of Ancients and Matriarchs to effect the capture of a few enemies destined either to replace some male or female member of the family, clan, nation, or confederacy lost through war or some other cause.

Such wars, Sioui concludes, "carried no notion of exterminating other human beings for profit and consequently should not be put … on a cultural par with what Europeans, Euro-Americans and others meant and still mean by war."[32] More recently, Davi Kopenawa has made similar claims about "mourning wars" conducted to assuage grief among the Yanomami (in the past) but denying anything comparable to the violence of western societies with their wars of religion, their world wars, and their nuclear catastrophes.

Brazilian anthropologist Renato Sztutman pinpoints some of the paradoxes of two divergent kinds of wars, noting that the French and the Portuguese colonizers established "peace treaties" to combat the violence of cannibalism but ended up regenerating ancient resentments and producing a more violent kind of war, aimed at occupying territory and the consolidation of the colonial enterprise: "If the indigenous wars were aggressive, virtually decreeing that peace would never come, the supposedly 'defensive' colonial nation-state wars sought 'pacification.' Yet the first native group used violence only sparingly, while the western group triggered large-scale genocides."[33] Continuing with the paradoxes, Sztutman notes that colonial "pacification" actually meant war and that the Jesuits, in order to conquer souls and deliver God's message of peace, had to first conquer native bodies by force, assuming that their minds and hearts would follow.

The French in sixteenth-century Brazil, for their part, made alliances with the indigenous peoples and armed them against the Portuguese as well as against their indigenous enemies. In what seems like a relatively rare instance of trans-hemispheric inter-nation comparison, Beatriz Perrone-Moises compares Franco-indigenous diplomatic relations in Maranhao Brasil to those obtaining around the Great Lakes in the United States. The French favored intermarriage and trade partnerships, without imposing their social systems.[34] In both the Tupi and the French Canadian cases, she notes, interaction began with welcoming committees and ceremonial dialogues. Oratory was especially valued by both groups, linked to a "foreign policy" consisting of representative delegates from the various villages. For the Iroquois, even commercial relations had to be preceded by speeches, celebrations, smoking, dancing, and messages encoded in *wampum*. This account "rhymes" with Patricia Seed's analysis of the different "possession rituals" of European powers in the Americas, with the French going farthest in striving for symbolic inclusion of the indigene. At the same time, any idealized account of Franco-indigenous harmony elides the fact that French organizations such as the Jesuits, the Sulpiciens, and the ironically named "Freres de la Charite" owned slaves, and that the French enslaved indigenous people in Louisiana, Haiti, and the West Indies. The slave trade was abolished in Ontario in 1793, but only in 1834 in Quebec.[35]

In a five-episode Netflix series, "Wars of Brazil," indigenous activist/writer Ailton Krenak makes a crucial point relevant to all the colonizing powers. Before the Conquest, he points out, the Americas hosted a kaleidoscopic spectrum of cultural differences. The Europeans arrived hungry and sick, and the indigenous people, as the settlers themselves (including Columbus) acknowledged, welcomed them, fed them, and taught them how to survive. During the early decades, the indigenous people, as the vast majority, could have easily annihilated the invaders. The Europeans could have easily joined this concert of differences as just one more "instrument" within an orchestral spectrum of differentiated human cultures and tones. Had they done so, according to Krenak, they would have been accepted, as they were in the beginning. Unfortunately, the Europeans set out with a prior intention to dominate and subordinate and enslave—such was the meaning of the Tordesillas Line and of Columbus's expressed intentions to take slaves; Europeans apparently could not accept being just "another other among myriad others." And the resulting war for domination has never ended and continues today in virtually all of the Americas. The Conquest did not begin and end with Columbus; for recently contacted people in the Amazon, 1492 is not a past event; it is today and tomorrow.

A 1492 Project: Conquest and Discovery

The legal foundation for Europeans taking indigenous land drew on a common source, to wit, the "Doctrine of Conquest and Discovery," a discursive formation that granted Europeans sovereign claim over native lands and peoples the moment they were "discovered" by Europeans. The basic axioms of Conquest and Discovery Doctrine were initially developed by the Roman Catholic Church during the Crusades to Christianize the Holy Lands in 1096–1271. Various Popes asserted a worldwide papal jurisdiction rooted in the Church's supposedly universal mandate to "care for" the entire world. Conquest and Discovery Doctrine was first applied to "infidel lands" dominated by Islam, declared by various Popes to lack "lawful dominion." A Papal Bull by Pope Nicholas in 1455 claimed an absolute right to domination by authorizing Portugal to "invade, search out, capture, vanquish and subdue all Saracens [i.e. Muslims] and pagans" [i.e. non-monotheists] and to place them into "perpetual slavery," presumably as part of the Pope's mission to bring all humankind into the tender embrace of the one true Faith.

Subsequent Papal Bulls and royal edicts extended the same right of conquest to the Americas. To appreciate the arrogance of this gesture, we would have to imagine a reverse case of the Maya, Aztec, and Inca empires declaring, in advance, on the basis of their religious and political traditions, that Europe, Africa, and Asia rightly belonged to them and should submit to their authority. (In fact, a counterfactual novel by Laurent Binet—*Civilizations*—imagines precisely that by having the Inca Emperor Atahualpa conquer sixteenth-century Spain.) The Discovery and Conquest tradition in law encoded ethnocentric ideas of European superiority over other cultures, religions, and peoples, so that Europeans "immediately and automatically acquired property rights in native lands and gained governmental, political, and commercial rights over the inhabitants without the knowledge or the consent of the indigenous peoples."[36] Thus the land of the Americas belongs to the first Europeans to loudly proclaim their ownership. The Conquistadores were ideologically well primed for a *conquista* in the Americas. Following their Iberian predecessors, England, France, Holland, and the United States legitimated their own conquests with analogous rationales. Discovery Doctrine officially became part of US Law with the Supreme Court Case *Johnson vs. M'Intosh* in 1823, which provided the legal foundations for what was already occurring on the ground, the United States take-over of Indian lands. The language of Justice Marshall's opinion reeks of Euro-American arrogance in its references to "the superior genius of Europe" and the new nation-state's "generosity" in bestowing the benefits of civilization and Christianity on and over indigenous people. (Discovery Doctrine has never been officially and specifically eliminated in international law.)

Apart from Columbus "sailing the Ocean Blue," the 1492 date forms a metonym for a series of interrelated processes, including the Edicts of Expulsion against the Jews and Muslims, the Inquisition against *marranos*, the conquest of the "New" world, and the transatlantic slave trade. As Ella Shohat and I argued three decades ago in *Unthinking Eurocentr*ism, a series of interlinked "questions"—the colonial question, the slavery question, the Jewish, Muslim, "Indian," Black, and African questions—can all be partly traced back to that cataclysmic moment. In this sense, the entire world still lives under the shadow of 1492. The old prejudices of Europe traveled to the New World with the *caravelas*. Preexisting discourses about Muslims and Jews armed the conquistadors with a ready-made racist ideology. Anti-Semitism, along with "anti-infidelism," provided a conceptual and disciplinary apparatus, which, after being turned against Europe's internal "other"—Jews and Muslims—was then projected outward against Europe's external others—the peoples of the Americas—as savages, infidels, and sexual omnivores. We note, even, a partial congruency between the phantasmatic imagery projected on to both the Jewish "enemy" and the "savage." Jews as blood drinkers rhymes with Indians as cannibals; the diabolization of Judaism corresponds to the diabolization of the indigenous *Tupa* and the Afro-diasporic *Olorum*. The indispensable 1619 Project has demonstrated the ongoing structuring role of slavery and racism within American history and society. A complementary project, which has been pursued by countless indigenous and non-indigenous scholars, might be called the 1492 Project, one which delves into the pre-conditions of both slavery and genocide prior to 1619, revealing it as a transnational world-shaping phenomenon.

The link between 1492 and the slavery-molded present is both metaphoric—a question of comparable events—and metonymic—a long continuous chain of connected events. The attack on the Capitol and the Democracy it represented on January 6, 2021, forms a latter-day milestone in the trajectory that began with Columbus, offering a horrifying reiteration of the Conquista spirit in the era of capitalist globalization and nativist populism. The objects of hatred in 1492 as on January 6, 2021, were the usual suspects: Jews, Muslims, Indians, Blacks, women, and LGBTQ+ people—the Inquisition also persecuted women and gays, after all—along with those one might call the white "heretics" who "failed" to hate those groups with sufficient passion and even expressed solidarity with them.[37] The attack was strikingly testosterone-fueled, in a dense atmosphere of ecstatic homosocial bonding. The ideology of the insurrectionists formed a witches' brew of all the racist, religious, misogynistic, and homophobic hatreds that coalesced over centuries in the slipstream of 1492, conquest, and enslavement, including frontier-style "regenerative" violence, Confederate flags connoting a love of slavery, religious banners reminiscent of the Crusades, medieval-sounding conspiracy theories reminiscent of the Blood Libels against Jews, with rumors of Jews poisoning rivers and George Soros financing "Jewish rays" to start forest fires. Even Satan made a comeback, as the diabolization of Judaism, of indigenous and Afro-diasporic religions in the past gave way to the demonization of the left and liberals, accused, in what might have been a projection, of "satanic pedophilia." The visuals too were archaic: horn-wearing fake shamans, jousting with flagpoles, confederate flags, hand-to-hand combat, battering rams, and the barbaric yawps of a "fierce," well-fed, and bloodthirsty hoard actually calling for Civil War. And in a literal return to the events of 1492, radical rightist French candidate Eric Zemmour, ironically a Jew, in a situation where both Muslims and Jews are leaving France, calls his party "la Reconquete" in a literal invocation of the eight-century campaign that cleansed Iberia of both Jews and Muslims! (Raoul Peck's film *Exterminate all the Brutes* [2021] stages these issues in dramatic form, beginning with the Conquest.)

The multiple 1492s also have implications for contemporary issues of political economy. First, western economic domination is inseparable from the stolen wealth of the Americas and the "Columbian Exchange." Beginning in 1542, enslaved indigenous workers mined the Potosi mountain in Bolivia, producing silver for the treasuries of Europe. The conquistadores melted down the gold produced by enslaved labor and sent it to Spain in the form of golden bars. "The new wealth in the hands of Europeans," according to Jack Weatherford, "allowed Europe to expand into an international market system" thus making "possible a world economy for the first time."[38] The early "companies," like the Dutch West Indies Company, and the New France Company, evolved into the corporations that now engirdle the world. The question of intellectual property rights, in this sense, exemplifies the historical "morphing" that begins with royal "patents," which referred in sixteenth-century Europe to the official royal letters (*litterae patents*) by which sovereigns conferred privileges, rights, and land titles on various members of the nobility. In the "Age of Discovery," these "letters" became associated with the literal conquest of territory; five hundred years later, they are associated with transnational corporations' conquest of economic rights in the Global South, where forest biodiversity becomes linked to the cultural knowledges of indigenous peoples as an object of transnational commercial desire. As Djelal Kadir points out, the letter authorizing Columbus's conquests, conceded on April 17, 1492, by Fernando and Isabela, was "the literal prototype" and "the *locus classicus* of its genre." Five centuries after the Conquest, the WTO rules concerning copyright constitute reformatted, secular versions of the papal bulls and regal edicts that legalized the liquidation of the indigenous commons.[39]

The latter-day enclosures that go at least as far back as Columbus and the Conquest lead all the way up to the contemporary corporations and media conglomerates, as when the Disney Corporation raids the collective imaginary and the global cultural commons—from *The Odyssey* (itself rooted in anonymous oral legends) to *A Thousand and One Nights*—in order to monopolize copyright for its "properties."[40] For Vandana Shiva, "[t]he freedom of action which transnational corporations demand today is the same freedom of action that European colonies demanded, after 1492, as a natural right over the territory and riches of non-European people."[41] Indeed, the proprietary ideology and actions of the economic globalizers in the name of "intellectual property rights" can be seen as a kind of enclosure or "locking in" of all the technological and material advantages accrued over centuries to the latter-day heirs of the New World conquerors. Colonialism, Conquest, and Capitalism thus have a symbiotic relationship. What Marx called "primitive accumulation" went hand in hand with colonial expansion and expropriation. In Marx's incandescent and bitterly ironic words: "The discovery of gold and silver in America, the extirpation, enslavement and entombment in mines of the aboriginal population, the beginning of the conquest and looting of the East Indies, the turning of Africa into a warren for the commercial hunting of black-skins, signalised the rosy dawn of the era of capitalist production. These idyllic proceedings are the chief momenta of primitive accumulation."[42] And as Sergio Costa and Guilherme Leite Goncalves point out, primitive accumulation did not end with the "Era of Discovery"; it continues to this day.[43] Indigenous (Dene) theorist Glenn Coulthard has shifted the focus of primitive accumulation from "capital relation" to a supra-historical "colonial-relation," which links the enclosure of the European commons—the first example for Marx—to the enclosure of the indigenous commons.[44]

While an embryonic capitalism existed before 1492, the Conquest constituted the grandest theft, perhaps the only theft in history of an entire hemisphere, as it literally enabled capitalist proto-modernity to reach across the seas and gain access to vast resources. Capitalism consolidated itself thanks to colonialism, just as colonialism expanded the reign of capitalism, installing a dominant transoceanic mode of production reinforced by the exploitation of African labor and the appropriation of vast resources, the most valuable being the land itself. The conquerors not only took the land but redefined its meaning. Since 1500, Brazilian territory, for example, has been endlessly stolen and abused, from the crude ripping up of forests by the *bandeirantes*, to the gold, silver, and diamond extractionism that made the well-named state of Minas Gerais (General Mines) rich in the eighteenth century (until it wasn't rich any more), to the latex extractivism of the Rubber Boom at the end of the nineteenth century that made Manaus rich and the center of luxury (until it wasn't), and in the twenty-first century, the "respectable" extractivism of corporations like Monsanto, whose patents generate royalties for "intellectual property rights." Much as Columbus "discovered" and renamed already named lands, nineteenth-century scientists, in a form of biological extractivism, would "discover" new species of plants simply by translating the long-standing indigenous names into Greek or Latin. Indigenous medicine was not recognized, even though many medicines patented and marketed by pharmaceutical corporations had long been used as medicine by indigenous peoples, but the profits have gone to corporations and not to indigenous people, now unable to afford the medicine that they themselves "invented." (Lévi-Strauss, for this reason, calls indigenous science "first science" rather than "primitive" science.)[45]

As demonstrated by documentaries such as the French film *The Seed Wars* or the American film *Bio-Piracy*, and as denounced by Vandana Shiva in her numerous books, the idea that corporations can "enclose" and "patent" nature and seeds that the world had been using from time immemorial is simply grotesque. In a resource rush, seed and drug industries are extracting and commodifying the genetic resources of native people. *The Seed Wars* film explains how pharmaceutical corporations exploit the millennial knowledge of indigenous tribes to patent medicines. Certain Amazonian tribes, in a more benign form of extractivism, for example, knew how to "extract" a secretion from the throats of a certain type of frog, knowing that one drop on a scratch could serve as a hallucinogen, that two drops could cure disease, and that three drops could be fatal. "Scientists" with ecological T-shirts would buy the frogs for a pittance from impoverished natives, send them to laboratories in the Global North to detect their biological makeup, and then patent their "discovery," thus generating vast profits. Within a regime of "cognitive capitalism," corporations "own" the patents for seeds and remedies long familiar to indigenous people, even as they disseminate faux-emotional commercials explaining how they are "helping" indigenous peoples.

Just as Columbus was seen within the Eurocentric model as "progressive" in his time, Bill Gates, who Vandana Shiva calls the "Columbus of the Digital," is "progressive-presenting" today. Shoshana Zuloff asserts a different Columbus connection in *The*

Age of Surveillance Capitalism. Columbus, in her view, established what she calls the "Conquest Pattern." Quoting Matthew Restall, she elaborates its three stages: "the invention of legalistic measures to provide the invasion with a gloss of justification, a declaration of territorial claims, and the founding of a town to legitimate and institutionalize the conquest."[46] Restall describes Columbus's encounter with the Tainos as an exchange of gazes: "When they first laid eyes on the sweating, bearded Spanish soldiers trudging across the sand in their brocade and armor, how could they possibly have recognized the meaning and portent of that moment? Unable to imagine their own destruction, they reckoned that those strange creatures were gods and welcomed them with intricate rituals of hospitality."[47] Columbus's only concern, as he wrote to Queen Isabella, is "to establish a Spanish presence and order [the natives] to perform your will. For … they are yours to command and make them work, sow seed, and do whatever else is necessary, and build a town, and teach them to wear clothes and adopt our customs." The arrogance is astonishing—how can one assume a right to subjugate millions of people, about whom one knows nothing, in the name of an alien King and religion? For Jerry Mander, all the major protocols of globalized capitalism as conducted by the IMF and the WTO—Free Trade, Privatization, Deregulation, Structural Adjustments, Export-oriented Growth, and the Free Movement of Capital—are all prejudicial to native peoples.[48] Zuboff goes on to say that capitalism, having already destroyed most of the world's forests, is now, in the form of Big Tech, gleaning with their algorithms the "last virgin forest," the teeming forests of our minds, monetized through data mining.

The Protocols of Anti-indigenism

The denial of the subterranean centrality of the "Indian" within Western social thought and the world economy forms part of the denial of indigenous agency in general. Since Native societies lacked monarchies or constitutions, they were seen as having no political institutions at all. Since many consensus-based native societies exercised no apparent coercion in the form of armies or police, they were seen by Europeans as functionally impotent. For Hegel, societies without states or recognized forms of writing were prehistoric, "outside of history." The general trend was to dismiss the native peoples as lacking in history, writing, and culture and therefore not deserving of rights. At the same time, strong anti-colonial ideas emerged from what might be called the proto-anti colonial left-wing of the Enlightenment. Abbe Guillaume Reynal, author of *Les Deux Indes* (1776), invited the philosophically inclined to debate whether the "discovery" of America was a blessing or a curse to mankind, ultimately concluding that, given the "atrocious" traffic of slaves and the destruction of indigenous peoples, "only an infernal being" would answer the question in the affirmative.[49] Strangely, many have forgotten what Reynal saw clearly, i.e. the linkages between the two "original sins" of colonialism: genocide and slavery.

The most passionately anti-colonialist of the philosophers was Denis Diderot, who in his *Supplement to Bougainville's voyage* warned Tahitians against Europeans armed "with crucifix in one hand and the dagger in the other," who would "force you to accept their customs and opinions."⁵⁰ Diderot also mocked Europe's narcissistic moralism, which refused sympathy to the indigenous peoples and enslaved Africans, the very people to whom western civilization was materially indebted. In words addressed to imperialism in Africa but that apply equally to indigenous peoples of the Americas, Diderot mocks the sentimental pieties of the spectators of European bourgeois theater:

> Europe has been reverberating for a century with the most sublime moral maxims. The fraternity of all men is established in immortal writings ... Even imaginary sufferings provoke tears in the silence of our rooms and more especially at the theater. It is only the fatal destiny of unfortunate blacks that fails to touch us. They are tyrannized, mutilated, burned, stabbed, and we hear about it coldly and without emotion. The torments of a people to whom we owe our delights never reaches our heart.⁵¹

Updated for our time, Diderot is excoriating the self-regarding channeling of empathy and "affect." Needless to say, Europeans and Euro-Americans owed, and still owe, their own "delights" not only to the "torments" of Blacks but also to the stolen labor, land, minerals, lives, and ideas of indigenous people.

Crossed gazes permeate the history of Western philosophy. One recurring polarity pits the social contract thought of the English philosopher Thomas Hobbes against that of French philosopher Jean-Jacques Rousseau. Both mentioned the Indians, in their parlance the "savages," in relation to the "state of nature," but they differed on the meaning of "nature" and on the nature of the State. Although devoid of any knowledge of indigenous societies, Hobbes saw them as characterized by a black hole of lacks: of industry, agriculture, navigation, commodities, literature, and the arts, combined with the putative omnipresence of war of each against each.⁵² But while Hobbes hypothesized the native peoples as barbaric savages, others like Montaigne and Rousseau saw indigenous societies as offering an anti-model capable of inspiring alternative conceptualizations of social norms. While Hobbes saw human society as founded on the societal repression of basic human instincts, Rousseau looked to the natural goodness of the "sauvage" as a principle of hope. But the real debate, in my view, is not between Hobbes and Rousseau but rather between colonial discourse and indigenous and indigenous-inflected critique.

Many European philosophers conveyed a withering scorn for indigenous culture. In a note to his 1772 lectures on philosophical anthropology, liberal hero Emmanuel Kant declared Indians "incapable of governing themselves" and "destined for extermination."⁵³ For the Hegel of *The Philosophy of History*, the "inferiority" of the native peoples of the Americas (about whom he knew virtually nothing) was "manifest," and for this reason he relegated them to the lower ranks of the hierarchy of humanity. For Hegel, genocide was not a crime but rather a proof of inferiority, since the indigenous culture "expired" at the touch of European Spirit: "[Native] America has always shown itself physically and psychically powerless, and still shows itself so. For the aborigines, after the landing of the Europeans in America, gradually vanished at the breath of European activity."⁵⁴ In this horrific euphemization of genocide, a non sequitur attributes causality to an abstraction—European *Geist*—rather than to the armed violence and biowarfare of the conquerors/settlers.

The interchange between Western and Indigenous thought has been both uneven and unending, with indigenous thought often operating as the unrecognized catalyst for "progressive" causes like Jacobin and socialist revolution, the US confederation and the separation of powers, class, gender, and sexual equality, communal property, ecology, anti-productivism, alter-globalization, and convivial jouissance. Of course, given the fantastic variety of indigenous cultures, it would be impossible and pretentious to claim to grasp anything as immense, subjective, and variegated as "indigenous thought" in general. Dale Turner usefully distinguishes between three philosophical projects relevant to indigenous intellectual culture: (1) indigenous thinking articulated in indigenous languages (usually orally) by those recognized by the communities as keepers of indigenous ways of knowing the world; (2) indigenous intellectuals educated in European philosophical traditions who engage it critically on its own terms; and (3) indigenous intellectual "word warriors" (Vizenor) who engage Western ideas both as a philosophical and political activity through a decolonial grid to protect Aboriginal nationhood. Since I have neither the right nor the access to the first form of knowledge, I am largely concerned in this book with the second and third types.

More precisely, I am referring only to a very specific discursive formation, at the intersection between indigenous and non-indigenous thought, which might be called "Tupi Theory," in this case traceable to sixteenth-century Brazil. This lineage emphasizes indigenous concepts of freedom, equality, and reciprocity not only as valuable in themselves but also as catalysts for a critique of western habits of thought. As a situated utterance, the conversation changes in function of historically shaped challenges, national differences, and ideological needs, as different features of what might be called the "discourse of Indian radicalism" entered European consciousness in different epochs: the critique of monarchy during the Renaissance (Montaigne), the idea of "Indian freedom" and equality during the eighteenth-century Enlightenment (Rousseau, Tom Paine), the critique of capitalism and bourgeois property relations in the nineteenth century (Marx and Engels), the valorization of societies without coercion in the twentieth century (Pierre Clastres, Marshall Sahlins, David Graeber), and the protest against ecological devastation and the anthropocene in the twenty-first century (Bruce Albert, Viveiros de Castro, Naomi Klein). At the same time, I hope to communicate the crucial pertinence of this strand of indigenous-inflected thought to such issues as climate change and the ever-more apparent crisis of a liberal democracy now on life support.

The colonialist response to indigenous civilization reveals a general pattern of misrecognition whereby native cultural agency is explicitly denied or implicitly dismissed, beginning with the issue of language itself. Because the "Indians" Columbus encountered did not speak any of the languages he was aware of, he told the Spanish monarchs that he would bring the Indians to Spain so that they might "learn to speak." Since native forms of communication did not resemble European forms but rather took the forms of glyphs, quipus, wampum, icons, and the like (as demonstrated by non-indigenous scholars such as Gordon Brotherston, Serge Gruzhinski, Miguel Lopez-Portillo, Walter Mignolo, and Diana Taylor), the Europeans falsely assumed that there was no indigenous writing. The European preference for phoneme-based alphabetic writing, and the dismissal of the symbolic writing of the Haudenosaunee, in this sense, formed part of a general denial of indigenous cultural agency. Yet the wampum has successfully communicated the basic codes of a long-lasting democratic system, registering the history and laws of the Iroqouis Confederacy, which has been guiding the societal codes of six nations for centuries.

Conventional colonial-inflected pedagogy and the dominant media convey a highly mystified version of this history. Whether praised as noble savages or demonized as cannibals, native peoples have been perceived as lacking in relation to European standards. Native knowledge of astronomy was not recognized as knowledge, yet archeologists have discovered a tropical "Stonehenge," a kind of astronomical observatory in the Brazilian state of Amapa, consisting of 127 granite blocks arranged in mathematical intervals, thought to be roughly 2000 years old.[55] This book forms part of a decolonizing discursive formation adapted and developed by legions of indigenous and non-indigenous scholars as part of the seismic anti-colonial shift that developed in the post–Second World War period. In *Unthinking Eurocentrism* (1994), Ella Shohat and I distilled Eurocentrism into an "ideal portrait" of a mental schema or field of meanings.[56] The term "Eurocentrism" in a sense misleads since it stipulates a geographical locus for a discourse now permeating the entire globe; it could equally well be called "the colonial matrix of power" (Anibal Quijano), or "occidentosis" (Jalal al Ahmad), or "European planetary consciousness" (Mary Louise Pratt), or "the homesteading world view" (Tuck and Yang), or "monocultures of the mind" (Vindana Shiva), or "the colonial mindset," or "Western hegemony," or "occidental worldview," or "the hegemonic cosmovision," or as Thomas King calls it, the "unexamined confidence in Western civilization."[57] For the coloniality/modernity project of Arturo Escobar, Enrique Dussel, Ramon Grossfugel, Santiago Slabodsky, Nelson Maldonado-Torres, and Walter Mignolo, coloniality forms the inseparable dark side of modernity, just as postcoloniality forms the dark side of postmodernity.

As the discursive/ideological precipitate of colonialism, Eurocentrism enshrines and naturalizes the hierarchical stratifications inherited from colonialism, rendering them as inevitable and even "progressive." Eurocentrism does not refer to Europe in its literal sense as a continent or a geopolitical unit but rather to the perception of European culture as central and normative. The problem, in sum, is not the "Europe"—now a relatively sane haven of a modest social democracy—but the "Centrism." Eurocentrism refers to a field of knowledge shaped by power relations (Foucault), a "mental construction" (Quijano) expressive of the experience, from above, of colonial domination. It is an analysis not of what any single individual thinks, or even of what any community thinks, but rather of the substratal axioms, the discursive tendencies, the conceptual shackles, and the epistemic algorithms and lazy habits of thought, whether conscious, semiconscious, or even unconscious, which structure notions about indigenous people. Nor am I implying that non-indigenous people automatically align with the Eurocentric side, or that indigenous people automatically align with the pro-indigenous side, a view that would make dialogue across identities and social positions impossible.

What follows is an expanded list, based on the work of countless scholars and activists working in scores of fields such as indigenous studies, postcolonial studies, critical race studies, Black studies, colonial/modernity studies, and the like. Some of the protocols of Euro-colonial discourse include the following:

1. a diffusionist narrative that sees the West as generating progressive and egalitarian ideas that spread around the world, thanks to their inherent power of persuasion;
2. a temporal discourse that develops a stagist evolutionary narrative within which the West is figured as marching "ahead" and its indigenous others as lagging "behind" when in fact the entire world lives the same historical moment, but differentially, where notions of "ahead" and "behind" are highly subjective and conjunctural;
3. a cartographic imaginary that stamps colonial power on land, centering the West while casting not-yet-dominated indigenous peoples into the moral darkness of "the land of the cannibals"; the 1493 Treaty of Tordesillas, in this sense, was a predictive map and projection of metropolitan power, contested subsequently, for example, by the "counter-mapping" of peoples like the Zuni;[58]
4. a political discourse that attributes to the West an inherent drive toward democracy going back to the Greeks (an oxymoronic slave-holding democracy), while ignoring the long-standing deeply democratic traditions of many indigenous nations;
5. a lettered emplotment that portrays literary history as emerging out of biblical Hebraism and classical Hellenism, all retroactively projected as "Western," while disqualifying indigenous orature and myths as illegitimate "pre-literate" forms;
6. a narrativization of artistic modernism whereby Western artists inject generative artistic form into the inert matter of indigenous traditions; the non-West provides crude unsigned raw materials to be extracted and refined by the named Western artists, museums, and gatekeepers who retain the power not only to own non-Western artifacts but also to adjudicate their legitimacy as "art";
7. an emplotment of intellectual history that traces philosophical thinking back to the "Greek miracle," postulating a Plato-to-Nato working out of the problematics formulated from the pre-Socratics up to the present. The result is what Boaventura Souza de Santos calls "epistemicide" or the destruction of indigenous knowledge, misrecognized as pre-theoretical and lacking in seriousness; the hegemonic powers produce theory; the indigene offer raw matter to be theorized;
8. a religious discourse that would have the entire world live within Christian periodization (BC/AD) and condemn non-Abrahamic and indigenous religions as at best animist, fetishistic, superstitious, and at worst diabolical;
9. a narrativization of nationhood that equates nations with nation-states and contrasts the older, mature, and inclusive forms of Western nation-states, with the young, irresponsible, and exclusive indigenous non-states, forgetting that indigenous nations were mature, civil, and self-governing for centuries before European contact, while also forgetting the nation-state's definitional tendency to monopolize legitimate violence (Weber) toward otherized indigenous peoples and internal minorities;
10. discursive and mediatic practices that claim a factitious "objectivity" that "always works against the native" (Fanon), while devaluing indigenous life in a media-saturated world, wherein white, Western lives are assumed to have more

intrinsic value than those of indigenous people, who, within the algorithms of devalorization, have to die en masse, both in Hollywood films and in the three-dimensional world, for the dominant media to take notice;

11. an interpretation of political economy that attributes Europe's spectacular success to its enterprising spirit, forgetting the immense advantages derived from the wealth that flowed to Europe (and to the neo-Europes of the Americas) from the indigenous Americas and other colonized regions. In its various mutations (mercantilism, free-trade imperialism, modernization, take-off theory, neo-liberal globalization) the dominant political economy develops a "trickle-down" economics on a global scale, without acknowledging that this unidirectional narrative can be reversed, that the West has always developed partially, thanks to the "trickling up" of the wealth of precious metals, fertile land, and of the enslaved and indentured labor from the indigenous world;
12. an ethnocentric portrayal of the life of small-scale low-tech "hunter and gatherer" societies as one of an immiseration mired in inert precapitalist traditions, when in fact many of these societies have been characterized by the abundance guaranteed by sufficient communal land, egalitarian social systems, and a generous nature;
13. a view that sees feminism and queer theory as enlightened Western inventions, forgetting the often more equal and less homophobic gender relations emerging from many indigenous societies. "Since we came from societies where sexual freedom and self-determination of our bodies was our birthright," Leanne Betasamosake Simpson (Michi Saagiig Nishnaabeg) writes, "the control of our bodies and sexuality became of critical importance to the colonizers."[59] Her writing proposes *kwe* (woman within a spectrum of gender variance) as an epistemological resource. Joanne Barker laments the terminological forcing of "'third genders' and 'two spirits' to fit into preexisting categories of sexual difference such as bisexuality, transsexuality, or queerness."[60]
14. a hierarchical view that erects the human over the animal, culture over nature, and places Occidental Humanity at the apex of sentient beings, thus abetting the destruction of species, performed with wild abandon and scientific precision.
15. an over-investment in the chimera of mathematical rational predictability, in short an irrational faith in a Reason that has led not only to invaluable scientific and technological advancement but also to racist science and horrific events such as the Shoah, Hiroshima, Nagasaki, and the extermination of minorities and indigenous peoples.

A final protocol over-valorizes writing as a prerequisite for civilizational status and dignity, what Luther Standing Bear calls a "blind worship of written history of books, of the written word that denudes the spoken word of its power and sacredness [creating a false] criterion of the superior man" forgetting that non-literate people could be cultivated, knowledgeable, and eloquent.[61] This last point about writing bears emphasis. As Diana Taylor points out in *The Archive and the Repertoire*, "[w]hen the friars arrived in the New World in the fifteenth and sixteenth centuries," they claimed, a la Hegel, that "the indigenous peoples' past—and the 'lives they lived'—had disappeared because they had no writing."⁶² Citing Angel Rama's "Lettered City" as a critique of the exclusivist sacralization of writing in Latin American societies, Taylor develops the concept of performance as an embodied episteme, which "decenters the historic role of writing introduced by the Conquest."⁶³ Davi Kopenawa points to other forms of knowledge: "Just because our elders did not have schools did not mean that they did not study. We are other people. We learn with the *yakoana* and the spirits of the forest."⁶⁴ The power of writing's expansionism, for Michel de Certeau, "is colonial in principle. It is extended without being changed. It is tautological, immunized against both any alterity that might transform it and whatever dares to resist it."⁶⁵

In sum, this westocentric perspective systematically upgrades one side of the civilizational ledger and downgrades the other indigenous side. As a form of hubris, Eurocentrism rigs the historical balance sheet by sanitizing Western history, constantly clearing its browser as it were, as if it had always already been modern and democratic, while patronizing and even demonizing the non-West and the nonwhite. All of which is not to say that Europe is not admirable in many ways or that European philosophers have nothing to tell us or that Eurocentrism is the only "ism" plaguing the world or that social ills cannot be found in the indigenous world, or that some other "centrism" is not lurking around the corner. This narrativization does not emphasize the "virtue" of non-European peoples, or the villainy of Europeans, but rather indigenous cultural and intellectual agency in relation to historically configured relations of power. The point is not to demonize Europe but to relativize it and relationalize it as a (multi)culture alongside and interacting with other (multi)cultures. The point is not to disqualify the Western "look" but to analyze the power relations that inform multiply crossed gazes.⁶⁶

The Sacred Land

The primordial commonality among indigenous peoples is the brute fact of colonial conquest, which reframed all indigenous people as "indigenes" vulnerable to dispossession. That colonial condition is shared by most indigenous groups, in forms ranging from the genocidal to the assimilationist. But victimization is hardly the only commonality. As sovereign or partially sovereign nations, First Peoples have traditionally practiced communal ownership of land, non-commercial cooperative agriculture, and community-based childcare and education. Most are closely tied to specific territories, and their economies and cosmologies have usually been umbilically tied to the land that sustains them. Even when displaced from their ancestral land, as occurred with the Guaraní, they often recall that lost land and try to return to it, or try to recreate it, to put it paradoxically, as a newly ancestral land, even in a tiny Guaraní *Tekoa* on a noisy highway snaking through the concrete jungle of metropolitan São Paulo.

The rationale for colonialist policies, whether exterminationist or assimilationist, or a mix of both, was formulated in a wide variety of ideological/discursive forms: in religious terms of the blessings of Christianity, in civilizational terms of saving the world from barbarism, in Hegelian terms of the superior potency of the European Geist, in Social Darwinist terms of "survival of the fittest," in positivist terms of "protection" and "pacification," or in the paternalistic discourses of "assimilation" and "development," and even in the innocuous discourse of "inclusion."[67] And, at times, the formulations were more brutally frank, colloquial, and ethnocidal: "one little, two little Indians," or "the only good Indian is a dead Indian." While the discourses varied, the result, in most cases, was the same: a swamp of diseases, a mountain of corpses, and a loss of indigenous sovereignty.

European and extra-European nation-states dispossessed the native peoples in the name of variant forms of the Discovery and Conquest Doctrine. Each colonial power, as historian Patricia Seed shows in *Ceremonies of Possession in Europe's Conquest of the New World, 1492–1640,* ritualized its domination in distinct ways.[68] Each nation had its own way of installing and commemorating colonial rule: the Spanish had the *requerimiento*, which simply decreed that the native people would learn Spanish, convert to Christianity, and become subjects of the Spanish Crown, and if they failed to collaborate, would be "done great harm." The Anglos, for their part, were less invested in ceremonial gestures: rather, they created "facts on the ground" by occupying land, farming it, fencing it, seeding it and "deeding" it, and producing crops for sale. Philosopher John Locke theorized and codified this practice in his "Second Treatise of Government," where he argued that land belongs to those who "mix it with their labor," a theory which was designed to justify the theft of land from its purportedly non-productive, non-agricultural "nomadic" indigenous peoples. Locke's theory not only camouflaged the theft of land, but also resignified the meaning of the land. Locke's theory had the additional ideological benefit of creating a propagandistic contrast with the Spanish rationale for taking land—i.e. Conquest and Christianity. The French, for their part, were given to ceremonial pageantry, royal "entrances" and corteges, modeled on those of imperial Rome, usually featuring gestures toward native consent through exhibits of collaboration, which is what we will see in the case of *les Fetes de Rouen* discussed in the next chapter.

A comparative study of the role of narcissism within intercolonial discourse would examine the various "vernaculars" or "vulgates" of the larger discursive families of imperialism, such as US militaristic exceptionalism ("Unlike the others, we crave not one inch of Korean Vietnamese, Iraqi, Afghan, Laotian land"); British free-trade imperialism ("We only care about trade, which trickles down to create wealth for everyone"); the French *mission civilisatrice* ("*Vive la culture française*"); Portuguese Luso-Tropicalism ("We're culturally mixed and love *mulatas*"); and German Indianthusiasm (Indians as imaginary friends). What is missing in the US American "we are not colonialist" account is (1) the United States, like most countries in the Americas, has always been and remains colonialist toward indigenous peoples. (2) With its victory in the Second World War and with decolonization, the United States became the heir of the European empires, now transmuted into an empire of military bases, which extended the Manifest Destiny paradigm to a world turned into "Injun Country." Thus, US "patriotic" discourse has always been Janus-faced, or better forked-tongued, in its attitudes: anti-colonial in relation to Britain, colonialist in relation to indigenous peoples, racist toward blacks, and imperialist toward Latin America. In a Canadian context, Sunera Thobani speaks of the "exaltation" that "conceals the colonial violence that marks the origin of the national subject, even as it mythologizes and pays obeisance to its national essence."⁶⁹ The perpetual temptation, in such cases, is to project repressed historical memories away from the national self onto the screen of another nation. As Nietzsche put it, "Memory says 'I did that.' Pride replies, 'I could not have done that.' Eventually memory yields."⁷⁰

Indeed, nothing divides the dominant western worldview from the indigenous worldview as much as the conception of land. Just as gold has no inherent value except as part of a system of social relations, so land is not a thing but rather a set of relations. Thomas King calls land the "defining element of Aboriginal culture," which "contains the languages, the stories, and the histories of a people [and] provides water, air, shelter, and food."⁷¹ Within settler colonialism, for Eve Tuck and K. Wayne Yang, "the most important concern is land/water/air/subterranean earth … [it is] what is most valuable, contested, required." The violence of land occupation, meanwhile, is "epistemic, ontological, cosmological" and is not "temporally contained … [it] is reasserted each day of occupation."⁷² Unlike cultures of consumption geared to accumulation and expansion, indigenous societies were for the most part geared to self-sufficiency, while using a variety of cultural mechanisms to disperse wealth and limit material acquisitiveness and centralized political power. Thus, a key commonality among indigenous peoples in the Americas has to do with a shared reverence toward the land, formulated in terms at once spiritual, mythological, practical, and political. Indeed, many activists now argue that the key to saving the planet is to restore indigenous governance to more and more land. Indeed, during the Standing Rock protests in 2016, some native activists enacted the policy of "eminent domain" by claiming that they were eminently qualified for land rights based on the 1851 Treaty of Fort Laramie.⁷³

As an alibi for a colossal land-grab, native sovereignty over land was not recognized under the pretext that it was not enclosed by fences or designated in a written "deed." The fact that a densely populated land was seen as "empty" reflected a policy of imaginary removal, a mental "ethnic cleansing." The metaphors themselves were symptomatic of differing cosmo-visions. Subliminally gendered tropes such as "conquering the desolation" and "fecundating the wilderness" acquired heroic resonances of Western fertilization of barren lands. It was to the settlers' advantage to project an already fecund land, in indigenous terminology a "mother"—in *Kuna abia ayala* ("adult," "fecund" land)—as metaphorically virgin, "untouched," and thus inferentially available for literal and symbolic "de-flowering." Although indigenous agriculture had sustained the indigenous people for millennia, it was not recognized as an organized system but only as the site of the feral foraging of "hunters and gatherers." Far from "virgin," the Amazonian forest had been carefully sustained and cared for by human beings, a vast field of trial-and-error experimentation in improving food sources. Gregory Cajete (Santa Clara Pueblo) makes a similar claim about "Native Science" in North America.⁷⁴ Yet the Amazonian rainforest, interlinked with human cultures for millennia, including agricultural societies that lasted for 2,000 years in a vast rural economy sustaining millions of people, is still referred to by journalists as "virgin." The monuments of such civilizations, in the view of Daryl Posey, are not "cities and temples, but rather the natural environment itself."⁷⁵ The devastating fires in California in September 2020, it turns out, might have been avoided had the authorities learned forest management from the "good fire" traditions of the indigenous people of the region, "centuries of expertise that could have been brought to the planning, decision-making and management process."⁷⁶

Certain indigenous topoi, expressed in similar pronouncements emerging centuries apart and from different parts of the indigenous world, circulate transnationally. All over the Americas, one encounters formulations about land similar to those of native Brazilian writer Daniel Munduruku:

> The land is not ... a good to be exploited and plundered but ... something alive, the holder of a protective spirit ... In order for life to continue, indigenous peoples learned to relate to nature with respect, and for that reason developed an entire body of knowledge regarding flora and fauna ... Indigenous organizations know that the land is sacred and that everything that is done to her today will impact everyone on the planet sooner or later.⁷⁷

In the Northern Hemisphere, meanwhile, Yellowknives Dene scholar Glen Sean Coulthard cites another Dene, Philip Blake, who stresses a personal dimension: "We have lived with the land, not tried to conquer or control it or rob it of its riches ... we have not tried to conquer new frontiers, or outdo our parents or make sure that every year we are richer than the year before."⁷⁸ From Patagonia to Alaska to aboriginal Australia, one hears variations on the adage "we don't own the land, the land owns us," or, alternatively, that we are not the owners but the guardians, the caretakers, the lovers, and even the worshipers of the land. Instead of a language of possession and rights to the land, indigenous theorists stress "dispossession" and duties to the land, as when Leanne Betsamosake Simpson writes: "The opposite of dispossession is not possession, it is deep, reciprocal, consensual *attachment*. Indigenous bodies don't relate to the land by possessing it or owning it or having control over it. We relate to the land through connection—generative, affirmative, complex, overlapping, and non-linear *relationship* ... The opposite of dispossession within indigenous thought is grounded normativity."⁷⁹

The United States and Canada (and Australia) all share similar settler-colonial structures, with their usual social coordinates—residential schools, stolen children, alcoholism, poverty, and above all, confiscated land.⁸⁰ All three are settler-colonial nation-states whose basic legitimacy is profoundly troubled by the repressed memory of the oppression of Indigenous peoples. All three practiced *terra nullius*, destroying long-existing systems of communally held land in favor of deeds of private ownership. In a decolonizing spirit, Aboriginal filmmaker Rachel Perkins has consistently worked to decolonize cinema and media in Australia by emphasizing the land. Her project constitutes a kind of cinematic nullification of Terra Nullius; in fact, one of her films celebrates a key figure in the Mabo Decision that nullified the policy. Perkins' short film *One Night the Moon* scrutinizes the crossed gazes of settler and indigene, ultimately relaying the story of colonial occupation through indigenous eyes. Based on an actual incident in 1932, the story concerns a settler family whose daughter, enthralled by the sight of the moon, gets lost in the outback. The father, out of racism and inordinate pride, refuses the help of an aboriginal tracker known for his deep knowledge of the terrain. In the end, the child is found dead, and the father, victim of his own failure to recognize indigenous knowledge, commits suicide.

In telling its story, the film hybridizes the western with the musical by showcasing the indigenous country-and-western music popular among aboriginal people in Australia. This technique reaches its paroxysm in an open-air production number wherein the song is alternately sung by the white settler and the aboriginal tracker. In an antiphony at once musical and ideological, the lyrics counterpose two views of the land. As tracker and settler stride off in their opposite ways against the arid backdrop, the settler's refrain is "This land is mine" owing to the fact that he "signed a deed on the dotted line." The tracker's refrain, which answers the settler's, meanwhile, asserts, "This land is *me* ... this land owns me," culminating in a critique of settler alienation: "You only fear what you don't understand." Voiced in direct monosyllabic terms, the production numbers stage a discursive duel in the sun, an ideological standoff between what Chadwick Allen calls "native indigeneity," or the aboriginal collective view of the land as communally owned, versus "settler indigeneity," or the western view of newly cultivated land as alienable private property.[81] The question evoked in the lyrics and realized in the setting was at the heart of colonial doctrine, which decreed that the land, a la Lockean theory, did not rightfully belong to the indigenous people unless they had fenced it off and practiced sedentary agriculture. The lyrics mention all of Locke's requisite measures to justify possession: a fence, a deed, bank payments, agricultural production, and the selling of commodities ("make it pay"). The Lockean view anticipates and advances the Anthropocene in its assumption that human beings have the right, and even the obligation, to change nature itself through labor. What is ultimately a philosophical/political/epistemic confrontation here takes the form of a subtly choreographed musical number, staged as part of a western-style genre and set against the backdrop of the very land where sovereignty is in dispute.

When non-Indians, or Indians themselves, speak in favor of "Indians," or indigenous people speak favorably of their own history and culture, critics often dismiss the claims through monotonously predictable put-downs, where the keywords are "romanticism," "idealization," and that hardy perennial—"Noble Savagism." This dismissal has its right and left versions. The rightist Social Darwinist version claims that Indians are uncivilized savages, that "we" won and "they" lost, and that our victory and their defeat are proof of our superiority, so stop whining and just get over it. The left classical Marxist version, meanwhile, speaks not in the name of racial hierarchy but in terms of historical necessity and the dialectical supersession of social paradigms. While marvelous examples of "primitive communism" inspire utopian speculations, these precapitalist societies are seen as historically condemned relics, irrelevant to the main course of world history. What the two views share is their allochronic projection of Indians as existing in a remote past, and their productivism, by which indigenous societies are considered inadequately productive of wealth and therefore destined to disappear.

The critiques of pro-indigenous discourse usually come from people who know very little about indigenous people but are nevertheless quite certain that what they have seen in the movies and have been taught to think must be true. The critique of the "noble savage" often comes wrapped in a supposed defense of the "Indian" from stereotypes and distortions. To be clear, the "noble savage" myth does exist and has highly pernicious effects. The Noble Savage ideal turns native people into impossibly pure figments of the western imagination, in supposed contrast with an improbably impure European. The inverted Euro-narcissism that posits Europe as the source of all social evils in the world ("Europe exhibiting its own unacceptability in front of an anti-ethnocentric mirror," in Derrida's words[82]) remains Eurocentric and also exempts indigenous people from all responsibility, reproducing what Barbara Christian calls the "West's outlandish claim to have invented everything, including Evil."[83] Or as Viveiros de Castro puts it, to use European discourses on non-European people only to illuminate "representations of the other" would be to turn "theoretical postcolonialism into the ultimate stage of enthnocentrism."[84]

Sankhar Muthu, in his insightful *Enlightenment against Empire*, singles out Denis Diderot, Immanuel Kant, and Johann Gottfried Herder for their anti-imperial arguments, but he constantly returns to the phrase "Noble Savage Discourse" to describe a critical discourse that might better be called "decolonial critique," or "indigenous social thought," or "alternative social model discourse." As a discursive construct, the "noble savage" goes back to a time before Rousseau to Marc Lescarbot's *L'Histoire de la Nouvelle France* (1609), with its mixed description of a native people without laws, property, or religion. In *The Dawn of Everything*, David Graeber and David Wengrow, inadvertently describing aspects of the project of this book, point out that during the first half of the eighteenth century, "the indigenous American critique of European society had an enormous impact on European thought."[85] But that impact produced a "backlash among European thinkers which produced an evolutionary framework for human history that remains broadly intact today."[86] Both parts of the phrase were problematic—there were no savages, and the word "noble" had aristocratic connotations. The phrase "noble savage" was popularized a century after Rousseau as a term of abuse, part of a right-wing denunciation of gestures toward democratization linked to an affirmation of indigenous values of freedom and equality. The authors redefine Rousseau's intervention as the "myth of the stupid savage," who was good because he was untouched by civilization. The "Indian," then, was crucial to the philosophical debates in Europe not only in the sense of the valorization of "the Indian," but also in the sense of the rightist backlash against that valorization. The more important question, then, is not about the noble versus the ignoble Indian—but rather how contact with the actual or mediated voices or the implied opinions of indigenous people both in South and North America catalyzed a profound questioning of Eurotropic political and social norms by Europeans themselves. The charges of "romanticism" carry the racist implication that there is nothing positive to be said about indigenous people and that only a misplaced "generosity" would lead one to say something positive. The accusation is also premised on a segregationist attitude, which forgets that western and indigenous cultures have been reciprocally impactive for centuries. To say what should not need saying, all peoples are radically equal in intelligence and rights (but not in power or technology) and also equal in their capacity for vice and virtue. My question, in this context, is not whether individual Indians are nobly generous or magically spiritual, but rather whether the social codes and algorithms of some societies favor equality, freedom, and "happiness" and "social well-being" more than other societies, and in what ways the social thought of such societies has opened up lines of flight out of current impasses.

What interests me is not the much-studied "noble savage" discourse, or even the endlessly reiterated critique of that discourse—both of which remain locked into the same Manichean dichotomy—but rather a discourse shared by some non-indigenous thinkers and many indigenous peoples themselves, one that stresses the long-term viability of indigenous social arrangements.[87] My emphasis will be on certain catalytic political ideas that emerged from indigenous thought and practice, ideas that have been "worked over" both by Indians and non-Indians alike. Enlightenment concepts such as "freedom," "equality," and "fraternity" clearly had European roots as well. But over time such ideas became indissolubly wed to the figure of the free, equal, and convivial Indian, as pointing to the deeply alluring ideal of a more egalitarian society. A critique of merely characterological praise of "Indians" rhymes with a critique of the overemphasis on "positive images" throughout the book. A kind of anthropocentric moralism, deeply rooted in Puritanism and in Manichean schemas of Good and Evil, leads to the reduction of complex political issues to matters of individual morality. A merely epidermic integrationism simply inserts new "minority" heroes and heroines into the old functional slots, much as colonialism invited a few assimilated "natives" to join the club of the "elite." More important than an indigenous "goodness" tethered to white middle-class norms is that indigenous characters partake of the normal agential heterogeneity, artistic capacity, and the self-reflexivity, of all human beings. Rather than deal with the contradictions of a community, "positive image" analysis prefers a protective shield of devoutly wished perfection. It is revelatory, in this sense, that the corpus of Indigenous legends in both North and South America features animal fables, which allegorically portray the full range of human behavior, including negative traits such as jealousy, greed, adultery, murder, and so forth. A cinema or theater or literature in which all the indigenous characters were impeccably noble might be as much a cause for alarm as one in which they were all villains. "There is nothing more paternalist," notes Brazilian anthropologist Carlos Fausto, "than asking Amerindians to be essentially good ... the image of natural kindness can be as corrosive as the stigma of bestiality. Both served the purposes of the colonizers: native violence to justify the war of conquest and enslavement; native innocence to encourage their conversion into members of the flock of God."[88]

A cinema of contrivedly positive images in the name of a prophylactic positivity betrays a lack of confidence in the group portrayed, which usually itself has no illusions concerning its own perfection. Here, for example, is Paula Gunn Allen's appraisal of the situation of indigenous women in 1992:

> American Indian women struggle on every front for the survival of our children, our people, our self-respect, our values systems, our way of life. ... We survive war and conquest, we survive colonization, acculturation, assimilation, we survive beating, rape, starvation, mutilation, sterilization, abandonment, neglect, the death of our children. ... Of course, some, many of us, just give up. Many are alcoholics, many are addicts. Many abandon the children, the old ones. Many commit suicide. Many become violent, go insane. Many go "white" and are never

seen or heard from again. But enough hold on to their traditions and their ways so that even after almost five hundred brutal years, we endure.[89]

Gunn-Allen's summary is clear-eyed, but without despair or self-rejection, in the assumption that the truth is revolutionary.

More important than the virtues and vices of individual characters is the orchestration of social voices and the portrayal of power dynamics: how does the film regard the land? Do the crane shots see the land or just film it? Does the Steadicam plough the plains respectfully or just display technological exhibitionism? Is the music indigenous? How does the music encourage identification and channel empathy? What discourses and voices jostle for dominance? Who speaks? Who is imagined as listening? Who is in the background, and who in the foreground? What social desires are mobilized? What discourses have the upper hand? What social contradictions are laid bare? To what extent do the images and sounds liberate narrative space to play out the contradictions of a heterogenous community?

The indigenous struggle for rights and sovereignty is consubstantial with the history of the Americas. The definitions of "indigeneity" and "coloniality" are completely codependent and interrelated; indigeneity is a by-product of colonization. Apart from the long history of indigenous rebellions going back to Hatuey and the Taino resistance against Columbus, we can leap forward to key twentieth-century moments such as the *Congresso Indigenista Americana* in Mexico in 1940, and decades later, the U.N. Declaration of the Decade of the World's Indigenous Peoples in 1994, followed by the U.N. Declaration on the Rights of Indigenous Peoples in 2007. This declaration, a non-legally binding resolution, emphasized "the rights of Indigenous peoples to maintain and strengthen their own institutions, cultures and traditions, and to pursue their development in keeping with their own needs and aspirations." It prohibits "discrimination against indigenous peoples", while promoting "their right to remain distinct and to pursue their own visions of economic and social development." Article 31 stresses that the indigenous peoples will be able to protect their cultural heritage in order to preserve their heritage from over-weening nation-states.

On September 13, 2007, the United Nations, after decades of indigenous struggle, voted for the Declaration of the Rights of Indigenous Peoples by a majority of 144 in favor and 4 against. (Indigenous people themselves had no vote.) A settler-colonial Gang of Four—the United States, Canada, New Zealand, and Australia—opposed the Declaration. Former colonies of Great Britain, they all largely practiced the Anglo-style approach to land occupation. Subsequently, the four countries reversed their position, but with many qualifications and reservations, often based on a rejection of "collective rights." These divisions correspond to Sheryl Lightfoot's distinction between "soft rights" to culture, language, religion, and "hard rights," having to do with land, territory, and sovereignty, the latter being more of a direct challenge to the international system going back to Westphalia in 1648.[90]

European powers, meanwhile, insisted on a "salt-water" addendum, which meant that the corrective measures would apply only to colonizing and colonized groups not separated by large bodies of water, an escape clause for Europe and an implied slap at countries like the United States that opposed European "external" forms of colonialism, but not the "internal colonialism" of the Americas. On the other hand, it is sometimes wrongly assumed that the "real" settler-colonial countries are only the Anglo-dominant countries, those countries where Europeans initially came to settle and take possession of the land through farming and fencing, while disqualifying the native people as pre-agricultural nomads. Yet in a broader sense, all the countries of the Americas are settler-colonial states in that Europeans dispossessed indigenous peoples in the name of the assumptions embedded in the Conquest and Discovery Doctrine that established Euro-dominant forms of social life, in terms of languages, social structures, and education systems predominantly of European or Euro-American origins, almost always privileging those of lighter-skin.[91]

In his influential book *Strange Multiplicity*, James Tully speaks of the great unsaid of Republican Constitutionalism—the fact that indigenous peoples enjoyed self-governing societies long before contact, with no desire to be subsumed into another group's laws and Constitution. Domination was not only about taking the land; it was also about disqualifying and even eliminating alternative social systems, as if to decree, long before Margaret Thatcher, that "there is no alternative." When indigenous nations demand to be recognized as self-determining nations, for Tully, they are making the momentous demand that the "prevailing references of these terms ought to be revised to include them."[92] Since native peoples, even if they signed treaties under duress, presumably did not want to cede their land or their sovereignty, American Constitutionalism had to justify to Americans themselves and to others why they had a right to take away both the land and the sovereignty, despite the reality of successful self-governance and even what Tully calls the "oldest living constitutional federation on Great Turtle island: that of the Haudenosaunee and the Iroquois Confederation."[93] The indigenous peoples of the Americas had long traditions of diplomacy and mutual recognition of nations through joint agreements even prior to the treaty alliances with an inordinately aggressive new nation called the United States. John Mohawk even speaks of a "Pax Iroquoia, which spread a system of alliances over a third of the territory that is currently known as the United States."[94] As "First Peoples," they believed that they had more experience in self-government and in mutual recognition than the Europeans and that the "second peoples" should regard themselves as less-experienced "younger brothers." The Europeans, however, regarded themselves as (Fore)fathers, and the Indians as children, and in response adopted a mixed strategy, borrowing indigenous ideas such as the separation of powers, while also seizing the land and demonizing the indigenes as "merciless savages."

The kind of indigenous sociality we are discussing here is less concerned with "inclusion" and "recognition" within the settler-colonial nation-state than with sovereignty and what Dene political theorist Coulthard calls "place-based self-recognition" and "active de-colonization."[95] Nor is Western "freedom" necessarily attractive. For indigenous consensus societies, the West was not the teacher of freedom but the pupil. The West deprived aboriginal societies of a freedom they already enjoyed and were fighting to keep. They did not see their societies as a form of passive "bare life" (Agamben), i.e. merely physiological survival in the face of the lethal death power of a state, nor as a form of immiserated subsistence. Rather than a tokenistic "inclusion," or "recognition" a la liberal theory, indigenous social theorists speak of what Coulthard calls "grounded normativity," or what Anishinaabe cultural theorist Gerald Vizenor, in *Manifest Manners*, calls "survivance," an archaic legal term resuscitated by Vizenor that fuses survival and resistance, a trickster-style outwitting of domination through native stories that enables indigenous peoples to survive while changing.[96] The indigenous challenge to liberal constitutionalism, for Tully, is one that would redeem it even for its adherents, not to come to agree on universal principles but to reach agreement on a form of association that accommodates real differences through flexible institutions. Constitutionalism should not represent a mono-vocal universe, but a plurivocal multiverse that allows for the friendship and collaboration of different cultural worlds, without subordinating one to the other. (We will return to this topic in the final chapter.)

Native Arts and Aesthetics

In this book I will try to show that the "Indian" is more a presence than is commonly thought not only in the history of Western philosophy but also in the history of Art and Aesthetics. Indigenous art has often been displayed in a specific kind of museum. In the French context, Benoit de L'Estoile in *Le Gout des Autres* traces the lines that go from the racist French Colonial Exposition in 1931, in the time of "primitive arts" to the Quai Branly in Paris installed in 2006, in the era of "the first arts," suggesting that the new-style "progressive" museums embrace a slightly modernized yet still ethnocentric universalism of "inclusion" in an attempt to move past a colonial phase that has become acutely embarrassing. In a case of *le voyeur vu.*, i.e., de L'Estoile observes the observers, whose profession it is to observe "les autres," a standpoint deeply rooted in colonial soil. What had been considered examples of ethnological science now became objects of art, resulting in "first arts" all with a commercial underside of selling colonial artifacts (including by Jacques Chirac); the colonial museums, he argues, dehistoricize indigenous cultures while surrounding them with a kind of magic and mystery. As condensations of history, whirlwind tours of human creativity and power, the classical museum has offered voyeuristic experiences of traveling around the ("primitive") world in eighty minutes or a day.

Mainstream art history has sometimes been haunted by a form/content binarism that one would have thought dismantled by Bakhtin, Derrida, and post-structuralist theorists generally. This form-content binary becomes linked to the broader binarisms of a Westocentric discourse that assumes the West as generating a clearly sequenced succession of stylistic modalities such as realism, naturalism, modernism, and postmodernism, which then spread, belatedly, to the "rest of the world," including to the indigenous world. The non-West, for its part, provides unsigned "raw" materials— like so-called "primitive" masks and artifacts—to be refined and "cooked" by named Western artists like Picasso. Western cultural institutions, meanwhile, retain the power not only to possess and exhibit non-Western artifacts but also to define what qualifies as "Art" with a capital A and what qualifies as lowercase "folklore." In strictly theoretical terms, the Core, symptomatically, generates "form," seen as the quintessence of artistic creation, while the Periphery provides mere inert "materials," that art "informs."

It is hard to ignore the extractive echoes in this notion of the formal "refinement" of metaphorical raw materials, reminiscent of the ways that the colonized world historically provided literal "raw" materials to be processed, refined, manufactured, and monetized in the Global North.

But in the domain of culture, including in oral and iconographic culture, to speak in the "raw and the cooked" of Lévi-Strauss, there is no such thing as "raw" materials; the materials, no matter how "disreputable" their origins, are already "cooked" by the preexisting intertext. To paraphrase Derrida, there is nothing outside ("dehors") the oral-imagetic intertext. Indigenous legends are no less intertextual than the most refined examples of modernist literature; both embed millennial legacies. Which is not to deny that "indigenous" art cannot be colonized or derivative. In the context of cinema, Glauber Rocha distinguished between artistic texts that offer "coconut milk in a Coca Cola bottle," as opposed to his own films as "coconut milk in a coconut," informed by a palm-tree aesthetic. It is no accident that some of the most innovative theories in visual culture and aesthetics—found, for example, in David Freedberg's *The Power of Images: Studies in the History and Theory of Response*, or Alfred Gell's *Art and Agency: An Anthropological Theory*, or in Robert Farris Thompson's *Flash of the Spirit*, and in the work of others like David Graeber, Carlos Fausto, Carlo Severi, Viveiros de Castro, and Benoît de L'Estoile—have come from scholars who had enjoyed direct or mediated contact with indigenous cultures. Carlos Fausto compares Kuikuro artistic principles to Robert Farris Thompson's concept, developed in relation to African art, of "midpoint mimesis" where the image "is not too real and not too abstract, but somehow in-between, an aesthetic practiced even by children in their drawings."[97]

Many expansions of the field of Art History have to do with the concept that art objects have agency, that they make things happen, often in work linked to the creative work of indigenous peoples in the form of charismatic images, sacred flutes, and transformative masks. In *The Chimera Principle: An Anthropology of Memory and Imagination*, Italian anthropologist Carlo Severi questions the assumptions of mainstream Art History by pointing to the conjoined Iconophobic and Logophilic attitudes implicit in what is retroactively defined as "Western." He points out that the "Religions of the Book" like Judaism, Christianity, and Islam seem to imply, in a religious version of the Hegelian view, that, given the unreliability of human memory, there can be no viable tradition without the support of books or of *the* Book. Indigenous traditions are thus seen as destined to vanish—perhaps like the peoples themselves—since they depend on the fragile human voices that speak and try to remember those traditions. Even the nonverbal arts, in this view, depend on some form of writing, such as the graphic systems of musical notation.

For Severi, the opposition between the oral and the written is fallacious. Just as indigenous societies of abundance are not instances of failed capitalism, and just as indigenous self-ruling societies are not instances of failed nation-states, so indigenous iconographies are not failed attempts to develop writing; rather they are related to practices and techniques linked to memorization. All the masks and images and *quipu* and totem poles are not striving, and failing, to become words. Severi stresses instead the cross-sense synesthetic artistry where "the animal or ancestor that is sculpted gives a face to the sound of the drum."[98] The opposition between oral and written cultures is misleading; what were seen as failed attempts at writing were in fact a functioning modality of a "path midway between orality and writing."⁹⁹ Those traditions we call oral, Severi argues, are actually iconographic, forming a "memory technique, particularly within the context of ritual discourse [that] constitutes the alternative that in many societies, has prevailed over the practice of writing."¹⁰⁰

In his analysis of the Aby Warburg archive, Severi calls attention to Warburg's formative sojourn among the Hopi in 1895–6 where he first conceived his project concerning the artistic transmission of symbols through imagery. Warburg was especially impressed by Hopi children's drawings of the lightning snake, drawings at once both imaginary and realistic, abstract and concrete, naïve and yet embedding sophisticated social meanings. The Hopi thunderbird, for Warburg, represents "an intermediate stage between image and sign" like the hieroglyph.¹⁰¹ Tired of the barren "word-mongering" of aestheticizing Art History, according to Severi, Warburg was interested in an art immersed in everyday life, where "usefulness" was not taboo. Much later, Lévi-Strauss stressed the participatory agency of masks in "The Way of the Masks," insisting that masks and painting must be seen in terms not of what they represent but rather in terms of the changes they produce, what they transform in terms of its ritual uses, of remembering, inspiring, and even provoking fear.¹⁰²

What becomes clear, in any case, is that "para-literate"—as opposed to the defamatory slur "illiterate"—indigenous cultures had techniques for preserving, transmitting, and modifying crucial bodies of knowledge necessary to physical and spiritual survival. Already in the sixteenth century, the Franciscan Diego Valades, himself of indigenous origin, compared Nahuatl pictography to western arts of memory, noting that "[t]he Mexicans, like the ancient Egyptians, had invented a method for representing abstract ideas by images."¹⁰³ Henry Schoolcraft, two centuries later, noted that the Ojibwe had managed to combine graphic signs with exercises of memory.¹⁰⁴ The Austrian archaeologist Emanuel Löwy, in the same vein, stressed the psychic processes involved in artistic perception, arguing that "primitive drawing is not rudimentary, it is mnemonic."¹⁰⁵

Before swimming in waters beyond my depth, I would refer to the elaborate analyses of the series of drawings in what is called the "Dakota Bible," including the drawings of the Sioux chieftain known by his warrior name of "Running Antelope," at once an orator and a renowned artist.¹⁰⁶ Lacking paper, native peoples have drawn on whatever materials were available, including wood, bark, rocks, tepees, and skin. The designs carry out conventions, rather like Hollywood storyboarding, embedding discernible protocols both concerning the evocation of temporal sequence or in spatial configuration, as when figures to the right of the image evoke activity, while figures on the left connote passivity and victimhood. (Astonishingly, many such drawings were the product of Plains Indians imprisoned in Fort Marion.) Robert Nichols speaks of the "ledger art" of Oglala Lakota artist Donald Montileaux as a distinctive style developed in the Plains region by indigenous people, with little access to paper, who refashioned, in vibrant and graphic form, the deeds and accounting ledgers of the settlers "into an expression of their own peoples' experiences and forms of life."¹⁰⁷ Severi, for his part, depicts a world of hybridizations and metamorphoses expressed in song and image, which he calls "chimeras," giving as an example the Celestial Jaguar of the Kuna, "a bird that roars like a jaguar and a jaguar that sings like a bird, an inextricable mosaic figure produced by shifting into the field of ontological imagining, the technique of organizing the groups of words that a shaman's pupil learns in order to memorize ritual texts."[108] Often, as we shall see later with the Kuikuro, music is essential to ritual, and Severi claims that for an indigenous shaman, singing "always signifies" an intention "not to tell a story" but to "perform an action." Shamanistic power uses a transformed "twisted" language in order to become "able to understand, see, and name the things of the world in an exceptional fashion."[109]

As the reader will see, this book is haunted by Deleuze and Guatarri's fecund yet problematic concept of "becoming Indian," developed in *What Is Philosophy*, that "the philosopher must become Indian." In the tenth plateau of *A Thousand Plateaus*, Deleuze and Guattari reach new heights as the theorists of a multitude of "becomings"—"becoming intense," "becoming animal," "becoming woman," "becoming minor," "becoming Indian," and so forth. As we shall see later, the problem in the Deleuze/Guattari formulations is not the foregrounding of becoming, but rather the insufficient recognition of the rapports de force, which structure the "becomings." At the same time, Deleuzian thought was influenced by the anthropological corpus concerning Amazonian peoples. Thus, Deleuzian concepts are strangely appropriate to Amazonian indigenous culture and especially in its love of transformations of all kinds. Kopenawa's *The Falling Sky* is replete with transformative tropes and expressions like "I became other" or "she became a jaguar." The goal of Kuikuro aesthetics, for Carlos Fausto, "is to depict extraordinary beings: humans who become jaguars, rhythm batons that become spirits, artifacts that speak, words that cure and so on,"[110] all serving as exempla of "extraordinariness as manifested in the multiplication of identities in continuous transformation"[111] The "generative impulse," for Fausto, "is to imagine the transformational flux characteristic of other-than-human beings."[112]

Trans-species concepts are not at all alien to native thinkers in North America. In the context of indigenous erotica, Melissa K. Nelson (Anishinaabe, Cree, Metis [Turtle Mountain Chippewa]) speaks of the propensity of native women to fall in love with other-than-human beings—one is reminded of the lovable sea-monster in del Toro's *The Shape of Water*—and points out that "interspecies and trans-species sex are common occurrences in Native Oral literature."[113] Some indigenous films in Brazil, similarly, feature polyandrous relations between human couples and alligators. At the same time, it would be a disservice to center this project on Deleuze and Guattari. While rich in suggestion, the concept of "becoming Indian" is also fraught, as Sara Ahmed explains in her "Phantasies of becoming (the Other)." Relating the concept to *Dances with Wolves*, she suggests that "its narrative of becoming Indian is predicated on the heroism of the white masculine subject: through hybridization, he can unmake the border between self and other."[114] The becoming is asymmetrical: Dunbar is transformed by his contact with the Sioux, but the Sioux themselves have only served as the trigger for his transformation.

Indigenous Media

The rise of indigenous media arts is inseparable from the resurgence of indigenous people in the late 1960s. In the long view, indigenous resistance goes back to 1492 and continues until today, but the more notable recent manifestations of resistance go back in North America to the AIM Red Power movement of the 1970s and to similar "pan-Indian" movements in South America. The indigenous politics at the UN, meanwhile, go back to 1977 and the International NGO Conference on Discrimination against Indigenous Populations in the Americas held in Geneva in September 1977, where the arrival of 250 indigenous delegates caused something of a stir. The anti-quincentennial protests in 1992 (and in 2000 in Brazil) catalyzed massive protests, performances, films, and other artistic responses. Indigenous Media simply constituted a new modality of resistance on a continuum with other forms of resistance over the last five centuries.

Indigenous media arts are both a reaction to oppression and an act of creative celebration. A burgeoning phenomenon in many parts of the world, the term refers to the use of audiovisual digital technologies (camcorders, VCRs, digital cameras, the internet) for indigenous cultural and political ends, in such a way as to foreground the stories, values, perspectives, and cultural politics of indigenous peoples. For anthropologist/theorist/curator Faye Ginsburg, a seminal figure in advancing and theorizing the indigenous cause, indigenous media serve as a self-conscious mode of cultural production using media for "internal and external communication, for self-determination, and for resistance to outside cultural domination."[115] The phrase "indigenous media," for Ginsburg, is oxymoronic, evoking both the self-understanding of aboriginal groups and the basic institutional structures of TV and cinema.[116] Within "indigenous media," the producers are themselves the receivers, along with the neighboring communities and, occasionally, distant cultural institutions or festivals such as the Native American and indigenous film festivals held in the Americas, Europe, Latin America, Australia, New Zealand, and elsewhere.

Amalia Cordova, digital curator and research and education director of the Smithsonian Center for Folklife and Cultural Heritage, and scholar of Indigenous Media in Abya Yala (the Americas), defines IM as

> a space of power, which leads us to the action of gathering voices and generating a conversation between them [in order to] create spaces for respectful and plural dialogue. It starts by recognizing and respecting where we stand: to recognize a colonial and dominant context, which we confront by acknowledging the original peoples from each territory where we establish ourselves, doing so through a diverse range of proposals. Not from a position of unicity, but often from a collective and collaborative stance, from a deeper temporality (that comes from an ancestral originality) and which is conceptually circular (one that is infinite and inclusive).[117]

Michelle Raheja, meanwhile, speaks of "visual sovereignty" as a "reading practice for thinking about the space between resistance and compliance wherein indigenous filmmakers and actors revisit, contribute to, borrow from, critique, and reconfigure ethnographic film conventions, at the same time operating within and stretching the boundaries created by these conventions."[118]

Many forms of Indigenous Media fit awkwardly into the ossified categories that dominate film scholarship—National Cinema, World Cinema, Auteur Cinema, Mainstream Cinema, Art Cinema, and the like—within which films are usually catalogued, curated, screened, and taught. As programmer Jesse Wente (Ojibwe) explains on the inaugural website of the 2012, "First Peoples' Cinema: 1500 Nations, One Tradition," IM defies the dominant categories and modes of interpretation. "To see these films," he writes, "is not only to discover a heretofore neglected wing of film history, but to reconsider what film itself is and can be." There is no such thing as a "good film" in the abstract, without consideration of the history of the groups that produced the film and the corpus of thought from and about the group in question. Someone accustomed to a diet of high-budget Hollywood films, or even of European art films, is not well prepared to appreciate low-budget indigenous films made in very difficult production conditions. Unlike the French New Wave with its Oedipal ressentiment against "le Cinéma de papa" and the transnational adoration of the new—*Neo*-realism, *Nouvelle* Vague, Cinema *Novo*, *New* German Cinema, etc.—many indigenous filmmakers respect transgenerational gnosis and seek the approval and collaboration of the elders, who sometimes insist on certain communal norms, for example, that the film not harm members of the community, respect the dead, and so forth.

Indigenous filmmaking is generally the product not of auteurist ambition or of profit-seeking studios but rather of a humanly dense *convivencia*, a collective process of living and working together, emerging from human relationalities developed over time. Indigenous filmmaking, in this sense, is less invested in claiming personal authorship than in "discursive practices" (Foucault). Within a kind of tribal auteurism, indigenous filmmakers often see themselves as primarily accountable to family, clan, and forest rather than to producers or sponsors. According to Victor Masayesva, native filmmakers carry a collective sense of accountability that is largely alien to white filmmakers.[119] Often, there is no script per se, and villagers voice their criticisms and desires. Ivana Bentes calls this process, à la Deleuze, the "becoming anthropological" of the Indians themselves, a performative instantiation of Rouch's celebrated "shared anthropology" but now from the other side of the colonial divide.[120]

My interest here is less in prospecting for "great films" and "true auteurs" than in creating lines of flight out of the Hollywood-industrial-entertainment complex (and its global affiliates). Wim Wenders famously said that the Yanks have "colonized our subconscious." How many of our internalized standards about quality in film, in this sense, are shaped by an addiction to Hollywood-style entertainments with its megastars and mega-budgets? Often praise for a "good film" is little more than a disguised compliment to the money that went into paying stars and achieving the sheen of "high production values." Such values short-circuit any appreciation for low-budget or even no-budget underground films that show a lot of imagination but little glitz. TV movie reviews have become budget and box office reviews. But instead of how much money went into a film and how much money it scored, perhaps we should be asking: how many concepts went into this film, and how much love, energy, friendship, and community spirit? How did the makers do so much with so little, and conversely, how does the dominant, moneyed cinema do so little with so much?

My concern, therefore, is less with "hits" as defined by Hollywood, or "masterpieces" as defined by Art Film criteria, than with what can enable marginalized groups to make films and to make them in a new way. Indigenous cinema is innovative in terms of being produced by new social actors and subjects of discourse. I have in mind indigenous organizations like Wapikoni Mobile, a nomadic training and production studio that has been traveling to Aboriginal communities throughout Québec offering training to any interested indigenous person, or more broadly to any marginalized or oppressed person, in the techniques of filmmaking, scripting, shooting, editing, and producing films, music, and other forms of artistic expression. Apart from supporting filmmaking, Wapikoni helps indigenous people cope with the many challenges of indigenous life, whether on reservations plagued with addiction and abuse, or in the cities where "urban Indians" have to negotiate the passage between two very different worlds. Wapikoni trainers set out not only to teach Aboriginal youth about filmmaking but also to learn about their dreams, frustrations, and aspirations. In this sense, they work to construct the psychic infrastructure and conditions of possibility of media-making by building relationships of trust over time, letting young creators know they can rely on an organization that believes in their potential.

Many indigenous elders, meanwhile, see film as a way to preserve, remediate, and hopefully reinvigorate the traditional corpus of tales, legends, songs, stories, and rituals, the narratological commons as it were, drawn from the shared inheritance of legends, stories, and rituals. Contrary to the assumption that the adoption of media by indigenous peoples would inevitably lead to the eclipse of traditional culture, Faye Ginsburg points out, indigenous media-making projects have found creative ways to "support the maintenance or even revival of ritual practices and local and local languages … [and to] repair fraying intergenerational relationships."[121] With IM, process trumps product, or more precisely, process and product are dialectically connected. Indigenous (Inuit) filmmaker Zacharias Kunuk describes the collective storytelling practices that inform even relatively well-funded films like *Atanarjuat* and *The Journals of Knud Rasmussen*: "We work horizontally, while the usual Hollywood film people work in a military style. Our entire team would talk about how to shoot a particular scene, from art directors to the sound man. We put the whole community to work. Costumes, props—we had a two-million dollar budget [for Atanarjuat] and one million stayed with the people of Igloolik."[122] The Kayapo and the Xavante in Brazil might easily make similar claims about putting the whole community to work, although they could never claim what for them would be a kind of mega-budget.

Springing up on virtually every continent, IM now forms a "global" movement. The proliferating centers of IM include a wide diversity of peoples and projects. Among the most active centers have been Native North American (Inuit, Yup'ik, Cree, Dine, Mohawk), Indians of the Amazon Basin (Hunikuin, Kayapó, Ikpeng), and indigenous US Americans, Canadians, and aboriginal Australians. At this point indigenous filmmakers have achieved what James Clifford, in another context, calls "global indigeneitude" through feature films, such as the Native American *Smoke Signals*

(1998), the Inuit *Atanarjuat: The Fast Runner* (2001), and the Aboriginal *Bran Neu Day* (2009), many of them very successful both in commercial and artistic terms.[123] In the context of aboriginal media in Australia, Marcia Langton defines "ab-originality" as a field of intersubjectivity "that is remade over and over again in a process of dialogue, of imagination, or representation and interpretation."[124] Indigenous films often constitute an "ab-original" form of archaic innovation in that they create what Ginsburg calls "future imaginaries" based, paradoxically, on the recuperation of a past linked to a sense of transgenerational responsibility.[125] John Mohawk, in this same paradoxical vein, calls traditionalism the "wave of the future."[126] Many indigenous films reanimate connectivities with the land, traditions, and threatened languages by tapping into the indigenous cultural commons, translating ancient genres of storytelling into a modern medium. The meaning of the word "culture," after all, goes back to *culti*vation and agri*culture*. Just as the indigenous natural world harbors much of the planet's biodiversity, the indigenous world could be said to harbor much of the world's cultural and aesthetic diversity. Since stories and legends constitute the lifeblood of native communities, one could reasonably speak of bio-narratological sustainability.

For those supposed within the Hegelian tradition to be "peoples without history," these films and videos show that history can also take the form of stories, myths, and songs as part of a transgenerational audiovisual archive. Shirley Cheechoo's *Bearwalker* (2000), the first fiction feature to be directed by an aboriginal Canadian, begins by initiating the spectator into native lore about the powerfully mischievous "darkside" spirit called "bearwalker." A voice-over adds a note of cultural counterpoint: "Christians call it the devil. My people call it bearwalker." A Kiukuro film, *Ngune Elu* (2004), tells the story, announced in the title, of "the day the Moon menstruated." Videos like Dean Barclaw's *Warrier Chiefs in a New Age* (1991) and Victor Masayesva's *Itam Hakim, Hopiit* (We, Someone, the Hopi People, 1982) give a prominent voice to elders. As Leslie Marmon Silko explains, Masayesva's films show the undiminished "power of communal consciousness, perfected over thousands of years."[127]

Some indigenous films in Brazil literalize the trope of crossed gazes. In April 2015, Kuikuro filmmaker Takumã Kuikuro traveled from his village in the Xingu Indigenous Territory in Brazil to the UK to take up a challenge from People's Palace Projects: to spend a month in London directing a film that would capture his vision of London as a "village," exploring similarities and differences between his Kuikuro culture and the Londoners he christened "the Hyper-Whites." The result is a captivating documentary about the many villages hidden under the skyscrapers of London. A prolific maker of videos for the internet, Takuma was especially fascinated by the other "Indians" in London, i.e. the people from India like the Sikhs and especially Bengali dancers. (Searching for a spiritual equivalent, Takuma compared his own community's beliefs to Hinduism since "Hindu gods also turn into animals.")[128] He compares New Age healers to the Amazonian shamans (*Pajes*) and ends the film with the music of DJ Marck playing traditional Kuikuro songs, underscoring scenes of Kuikuro cultural manifestations like wrestling, dancing, and body paintings.

The hospitable rubric of IM shelters under its umbrella an extremely diverse spectrum of peoples, situations, media, and aesthetics. The term, perhaps inevitably, homogenizes and flattens a situation of extreme heterogeneity. One runs the risk of constructing, alongside the "generic Indian," a "generic indigenous media," when in fact the indigenous corpus is extremely heteroglossic (Bakhtin's social "many-languagedness"), varying widely in topics, genres, production methods, and manifesting a wide spectrum of thematic and political options. Much of IM takes us out of the realm of entertainment, box office, production values, and what Christian Metz calls the "good object" cinema, which lures spectators with voyeuristic spectacles and striptease narratives. "There are more things in heaven and earth," to paraphrase Hamlet, than are dreamt of by Hollywood and its imitators, or even in art cinema. IM proposes a different form of excitement—this time the pleasure of a collective coming-into-voice, image, and sound of those who had been marginalized yet who are in fact collectively central to history and to the present. For the non-indigenous spectator, many indigenous films redefine filmic pleasure by prodding the spectator to enjoy, or at least learn from, seeing oneself and one's culture exotically, from the outside, in a salutary kind of "self-estrangement" that stretches one's sense of the possible. The changing character, no longer on the screen, is the spectator herself in the audience.

For Michelle H. Raheja, "Transnational Indigenous Media" rethinks Audre Lorde's dictum that "the masters' tools will never dismantle the master's house by insisting that the very foundations on which the master's house is built are indigenous and should be reterritorialized or repatriated," or perhaps "rematriated?"[129] Leanne Betasamosake Simpson takes the house metaphor in a different direction by suggesting that the real question is "not about how to dismantle the master's house, that is, which set of theories we weaponize against colonialism [but rather] with how we (re)build our own house, or our own houses."[130] A related question is how do indigenous people dismantle and reimagine the architecture of alternative aesthetic/cinematic production "houses" in order to (re)build more accommodating cinematic "houses," or for that matter indigenous *igloos, malocas, shaboni*, and longhouses.

The collective coming-into-voice-and-image can take an infinity of forms in aesthetic, generic, and narratological terms. In its extreme diversity, IM makes a striking aesthetic contribution in the variety of its themes and techniques: some indigenous films stage legends, others concern rituals, some repurpose the archive, some use re-enactment, some are political protests, some are small-bore films about the everyday. The variegated spectrum of aesthetics and genres includes the conventional genres, while often indigenizing them: dramatic realism, melodrama, science fiction, horror, docufictions, community storytelling, vision quests, the incorporation of oral tradition, trickster mythologies, communitarian production, Brechtian alienation effects, carnivalesque inversions, hip-hop actualizations, children's films, essay films, collage films, recontextualization, indigenization, shamanic invention, archaic experimentation, revisionist adaptations, and the selective deployment of classical film conventions.[131] I am reminded of Caetano Veloso's formulation of the goal of the Tropicalia Movement—not to obey the norms of taste, or to disobey the norms, but rather to transform the very criteria of taste.

A deep dive into indigenous arts can help transform the criteria of taste and the very definition of art. It is often assumed that since indigenous societies do not see Art as an autonomous realm, that they are therefore less artistic, and even that only a hawk-eyed Western aesthetic consciousness can spot and measure the artistic value of their "naïve" and "intuitive" work. The indigenous peoples may offer quaint remnants of ancient practices like handicrafts and beadwork, this view suggests, but nothing that qualifies as capital-A Art. It is as if the view of native societies as immiserated cultures of scarcity in economic terms had an artistic corollary, by which social and artistic poverty are supposed to walk hand in hand. "Subsistence cultures" presumably produce a subsistence-level art. In fact, however, the lack of a separate category of Art does not signal the absence of art but rather its omnipresence, since the arts form an integral part of the everyday pleasure in what others would call the aesthetic. In a North American context, Gitxan artist and curator Doreen Jensen says, "In my language there is no word for art. This is not because we are devoid of art, but because art is so powerful … We are replete with it."[132] Edna Ahgeak NacLean (Inupiaq) writes, "Much of our literature is interspersed with songs. The songs are powerful. There are songs to call animals. Songs that heal. Songs that harm. And songs to relate oneself to the land."[133] Art is so taken for granted, so mixed up with everyday life in many Amazonian cultures that it does not have to be named. The films by and about the Enauene people in the Amazon, such as Virginia Valadao's *Yaokwa: Banquet of the Spirits* (1995) and Vincent Carelli's *Yaokwa: Neglected Patrimony* (2009) and *Yaokwa: Image and Memory* (2020), concern a song cycle that lasts for seven months every year, which mingles multiple arts—mythic narrative, music of percussion and flutes, body painting, dance and performance, some of it carnivalesque, as when the men do what we would call "twerking" for the amusement of the young crowd. In the 2020 film, the entire village gathers around the video players happily relishing the images of their own festival.

In Brazil, a short film by Edson Tosta Materezio Filho, *Ritual Ticuna da Iniciacao Feminina* (Ticuna Ritual of Female Initiation, 2013), shows that the initiation of a young Ticuna girl undergoing her first menstruation is virtually bathed in "artistic" aspects with spiritual and social overtones. According to Matarezio Filho, the ritual celebrates the power of female energy as manifested in ritual. The first menstruation, in some Western cultures surrounded with secrecy and shame, forms a crucial moment of passage into a new state of being, a time of personal metamorphosis that affects the entire socius and therefore must be protected and nourished. The individual event has cosmic implications. One girl's menstruation exists in relation to everyone in the community. Therefore, the girl is secluded from the larger society, surrounded instead by female intimates such as mothers, grandmothers, aunts, and the like. The advice itself takes the artistic form of stories and collective singing. The event is a very public ritual performance that involves the whole village. Since menstruation brings new possibilities and challenges into a girl's life, she needs the protection of spirits or spirit-animals, who appear in the form of costumed dancers, accompanied by percussion sticks and wind instruments carved out of wood, along with stick-based percussion instruments. Another misconception is that life among the indigenous Amazonians is tedious and boring. Yet anthropologists, from Kenneth Good speaking of the Yanomami to Carlos Fausto speaking of the Kuikuro, were often surprised to find out that the opposite is the case. Here is Carlos Fausto:

> Not a day went by without some ceremonial activity; food was offered to the spirits on the plaza, quintets of flautists toured the ring of houses, young people trained to wrestle in the heat of the afternoon, women with heavy bead necklaces danced at

the end of the day, the chief greeted foreign messengers with a formulaic speech. In the Upper Xingu there were as many artifacts as one could imagine: various types of masks, effigies, musical instruments, basketry, pottery, body adornments—and, of course, all associated with stories, myths, rites, songs, and ways of making.[134]

In various indigenous Amazonian cultures, complex and gendered mythologies surround the "sacred flutes" (*kagutu*). Citing Marcelo Fiorini, Fausto points out that for the Nambikwara, "the flutes are not only bodies, they are the trachea and esophogi of spirits."[135] Among the Xinguanos, according to Fausto, the *Iamarikuma* rituals involve a symbolic battle of the sexes with mythic overtones. Although the sacred flutes once belonged to women, they now belong to men, engendering, in a kind of "vagina and penis dialogue" between two different festivals, "one male, in which the flutes are played and women's vaginas form the topic of jesting male songs, the other female, which enacts the myth of the Hyper-Women and makes the penis the target of mockery."[136] (We will return to the "Hyper-Women" in Chapter 2.)

Another leitmotif in this book is the artistic role of humor. Even prior to the installation of the colonial regime, in the early sixteenth century, European visitors to Brazil were struck by the Tupi penchant for constant laughing, kidding, and creating punning nicknames based on appearance or mannerisms. A chapter in Pierre Clastres's classic *Society against the State* is devoted to "What Makes Indians Laugh." Speaking of the Chulupi Indians from southern Paraguay, he writes:

> [T]heir sense of the absurd frequently has them making fun of their fears. Now it is not unusual for these cultures to entrust their myths with the job of entertaining the people by de-dramatizing, as it were, their existence ... [the Chulupi] narratives, going from the mock-heroic to the ribald ... are well-known by all members of the tribe, young and old, but when they really want to laugh, they would ask some old man versed in the traditional lore to tell these stories one more time. The effect never fails; the smiles at the beginning become chortles that are barely stifled, then shameless peals of laughter finally burst out, and finally it is all howls of joy. While these myths were being recorded on tape, the uproar of the dozens of Indian who were listening sometimes blotted out the voice of the narrator, who was himself constantly on the verge of losing his composure.[137]

Or here is Brazilian anthropologist Viveiros de Castro speaking about his life with the Araweté in Brazil. Some aspects of his description evoke traits that Brazilians in general probably absorbed from indigenous people, such as informality and ease with the human touch:

> Few human groups, I imagine, are as amenable in nature and as amusing in their sociality, as long as one has an ability to laugh at oneself ... Fond of touch and physical closeness, informal to a sometimes overwhelming degree ... exaggerated in their demonstrations of affection, lovers of the flesh and of the feast, free with their tongues and constant in their laughter, sarcastic and at times delirious—the Arawate ... could not be adequately described using concepts such as rules and norms.[138]

Much of the humor was directed at the anthropologist himself, as when de Castro's anthropological questions usually "prompted a shower of laughter and replies of 'Why do you want to know that?' followed by a confusing polyphony of humorous, untrue explanations or a rapid recitation of names."[139]

Given the well-known links between artistic modernism and so-called "primitive" cultures, it should also be no surprise that some indigenous and indigenous-inflected films mix realism and magic. In one sense, such films connect with a long cinematic lineage. In his call for a "shamanic cinema," Chilean filmmaker/theorist Raul Ruiz traces the origins of the cinema back to a series of "magical" events: "a caveman's hand pressed against a lightly colored surface ... simulators (half-transparent demons of the air, described by Hermes Trismegistus shadows, pre and post-Platonic; the Golem ... Robertson's Fantascope; the magic butterflies at Coney Island. All prefigure the movies."[140] Conjugating the actual realistic and the fantastical, Melies discovered that editing made possible magical substitutions and transformations, thus leaving a rich legacy of the playful manipulation of the coordinates of time and space. The cinema deploys the realism of "monstration" (Gaudreault)—objective showing without human intervention—and the magic of montage and superimposition, allowing for oneiric and fantastic temporal transformations and spatial overlays, all multiplied by the post-celluloid potentialities of the digital.[141] Film theorists have noted not only the capacity of film to evoke dreams, trance, and psychotropic experiences—all valued within many indigenous cultures—but also alerted us to the analogies between dream and the ordinary film experience, with its shared metonymic and metaphoric fusions and displacements. As a technology of performance and representation, the cinema is ideally equipped to magically multiply and mingle diverse spaces and temporalities, all of which facilitate a filmic conjuring up the connections between the natural/spiritual world.

Indigenous media arts suggest new paths for film theory and art theory more adequate to the object "indigenous art" and arguably more adequate to media arts in general. A remarkable group of film anthro-theorists in Brazil is rethinking film through concepts developed in relation to indigenous peoples and indigenous media. Riffing on anthropologist Bruce Albert's evocation of the possibility of a "shamanic critique of the political economy of nature,"[142] anthropologist Andre Brasil has spoken of a "shamanic critique of the political economy of the image." While Andre Brasil admits that it would be far-fetched to claim that cinema—a recent practice among the indigenous groups—would have been incorporated into the inter-semiotic devices of shamanism, he asks a more specific question: "What happens when the phenomenological machine of cinema meets the shamanic machine of specific Amerindian groups?" Without going into detail about the richness of Brasil's formulations, suffice it to say that he suggests that we turn our attention not only to what is framed and made visible but also to what maintains the relationship between the image itself and an invisible outside that also constitutes the image. "If the framed (screen) space is mainly phenomenological—where the visible inscribes itself in its duration—the off-screen potentially brings in a cosmological space, or even a cosmopolitical one, in which interspecies relations—not always visible (or barely glimpsed) in the frame—can be established."[143] These concepts suggest an indigenous rethinking of such issues as point of view, point of hearing, moral alignment, and subjectification, taking on board Phillipe Descola's account in "Cultivated Savagery" of the indigenous Amazonians as not making clear distinctions between nature and society, and conferring "on animals and plants the attributes of humanity." According to Descola, the Achuari see most plants and animals as having soul (*wakan*) that place them among "persons" with reflexive consciousness, intentionality, emotions, and a capacity for "extra-linguistic communication."[144]

This view of a world "peopled" with different kinds of subjectivities accords with recent scientific developments. To mention just a few instances gathered from Emma Marris's *Wild Souls*: "the neurological substrates that generate consciousness are common to all mammals and birds"; dolphins know themselves as individuals and hail their kin through a unique "call"; apes communicate through hand gestures; monkeys laugh when tickled; wolves frolic when young but become serious as adults; humpback whales engage in cross-species collaboration to capture fish; animals grieve and mourn their dead.[145] Donna Haraway talks about "multi-species storytelling," while Mary Louise Pratt writes, "Trees erupt into perfume and flower to attract the animals whose bodies are adapted to pollinating them. Life perpetuates itself through orchestrated aesthetic display. Music, color, dance, belong as much to birds as to people."[146] Or again, from the collection: *Arts of Living on a Damaged Planet*: "We are mixed up with other species … without bacteria, we cannot digest our food."[147] In ant colonies, paradoxically, despite their collective behavior, no ant tells the other ants what to do. Nor is nature necessarily "red in tooth and claw" as some forms of Darwinism would claim. For Lyn Margulies, symbiosis and collaboration among species, not unrelenting competition, are more the norm than the exception.[148]

....

By way of clarification, the "jumps" and zigzags from country to country from epoch to epoch in this text form part of what I call a "trans-methodology," which can be pithily summarized through a series of "trans" concepts, such as transnational, transdisciplinary, transtextual, transactional, transmediatic, and transhistorical. To my mind, the prefix "multi" implies addition, an additive list of cultures, while "inter" implies reciprocity and interaction, and "trans" assumes multiplication and reciprocity, but also implies transformation, with the advantage of implying movement and transition from one state to another. These trans-movements also form part of indigenous scholarship. Sheryl Lightfoot speaks of "transnational Indigenous ways of being." Chadwick Allen speaks of "trans-Indigenous research," a process that "locates itself firmly in the specificity of the indigenous local, while remaining always cognizant of the complexity of the relevant indigenous global."[149] This book emphasizes the kinds of juxtapositions that Allen advocates "across genre and media, aesthetic systems and worldviews, technologies and practices" as part of a multi-perspectival approach.[150]

The method of this book is *transhistorical*, meanwhile, not in the sense of going "beyond history" but rather in the sense of deep time and "transgenerational thinking" (Sheryl Lightfoot). Deep time evokes the temporality of the redwood trees that reach back thousands of years. Wai Chee Dimock connects Native American culture to a "deep time" of the commons closer to the life of the human species than to the

500-year history of Europeans in the Americas. She cites Leslie Marmon Silko: "Five-hundred years is not a very long time. Because for 18,000 years there is evidence of the Pueblo people being in [their] land."[151] Dimock concludes her book by talking about "geological time." Watersheds and Mesolithic dwellers, she writes, "remind us just how recent the nation-state is, how small a part it plays in the recorded life of the species."[152] The Native American term "Turtle Island," for Dimock, is not only the name of the North American continent but also a "rallying call for a new environmental ethics, one that looks back to the kinship of humans and animals in indigenous cultures."[153]

The term "transhistorical" also evokes Said's "contrapuntal readings" and Bakhtin's "historical poetics" and "mutually relativizing chronotopes" as ways to relationalize chronotopes and to haunt one set of times and spaces and histories with another set of related spaces and histories within a nonlinear understanding of temporality.[154] All these trans-methods can interface and inter-fecundate to create a multiplier effect, as when one maps issues of indigenous performance and representation across inter-/trans-sectionality, trans-sexuality, transmediality across transdisciplinarity, a crossing where indigenous queer feminists have exercised considerable force. Each art, medium, discipline, and culture offers its own "exotopy" or critical gaze, its own "excess seeing"—and another traditional shamans was "seers"—which deploys a salutary estrangement to see how a culture is seen by others and can be changed on the basis of the encounter. V. F. Cordova speaks of the mutual relativization of conflicting conceptual frameworks or matrices of thought, where native knowledges reveal the limits of dominant ways of thinking.[155] In this paradoxical moment of maximum danger for the indigene and maximum visibility of indigenous creativity, in an age where mass-mediated culture usually has little to say of interest about these crises, indigenous media and indigenous social thought, I hope to show, have invaluable things to say about all of the current crises.

Notes

***All translations mine unless otherwise stated.

1. Napoleon Chagnon, *Yanomamö: The Fierce People* (Holt: Rinehart and Winston, 1968).
2. Davi Kopenawa Yanomami and Bruce Albert, *La chute du ciel: Paroles d'un chaman yanomami* (Paris: Plon, 2010); *The Falling Sky: Words of a Yanomami Shaman*, trans. to English by Nicholas Elliott and Alison Dundy (Cambridge: Harvard University Press, 2013); *A queda do céu: Palavras de um xamã yanomami*, trans. to Portuguese by Beatriz Perrone-Moisés (Companhia das Letras, 2015).
3. Report of the Secretary of Interior, November 29, 1851.
4. Chief Justice John C. Marshall, *Cherokee Nation v. Georgia*, 30 U.S. 1 (1831).
5. Rather than a *maître a penser*, I see my role as that of a *maître de* or the imaginary host in a trans-temporal restaurant where Michel de Montaigne can meet Cunhambe, Oswald de Andrade can meet Vine Deloria Jr, and Sonia Guajajara can meet Joanne Barker.
6. See Linda Tuhiwai Smith, *Decolonizing Methodologies: Research and Indigenous Peoples* (Chicago: University of Chicago Press, 1999), p. 14.

7   Vine Deloria Jr, "Comfortable Fictions and the Struggle for Turf," in Devon A. Mihesuah, ed., *Natives and Academics* (Lincoln: University of Nebraska Press, 1998), p. 66.
8   Jean-Paul Sartre, Black Orpheus, quoted in Robert Stam, "Fanon, Algeria and the Cinema," in Ella Shohat and Robert Stam, eds., *Multiculturalism, Postcoloniality, and Transnational Media* (New Brunswick: Rutgers University Press, 2003), pp. 39–40.
9   Jerry Mander and Victoria Tauli-Corpuz eds., *Paradigm Wars: Indigenous People's Resistance to Globalization* (San Francisco: Sierra Club Books, 2006).
10   Leanne Betasamoksake Simpson, *As We Have Always Done* (Minneapolis: University of Minnesota Press, 2017), p. 58.
11   See M. Nakata, *Disciplining the Savages: Savaging the Disciplines* (Canbarra, Australia: Aboriginal Studies Press, 2007).
12   Jeanette Armstrong, "Community: 'Sharing One Skin,'" *Paradigm Wars, Mander & al. ed.*, pp. 35–6.
13   Cited in Melissa K. Nelson, *Original Instructions* (Rochester, VT: Bear and Company, 2008), p. 138.
14   Taiaiake Alfred, Peace, Power, *Righteousness: An Indigenous Manifesto* (Oxford: Oxford University Press, 2009), p. 14.
15   For a fuller definition see the "Special Rapporteur on the Problem of Discrimination against Indigenous Populations for the UN Sub-Commission on Prevention of Discrimination and Protection of Minorities," summarized and quoted in Saddruddin Aga Khan and Hassan Bin Talal, *Indigenous Peoples: A Global Quest for Justice* (London: Zed, 1987). The term "Fourth World" has been used in many different ways. The discourse of global economy sometimes uses it to mean Third World countries without major resources, while Gordon Brotherston uses it to mean the Americas as the "fourth continent" after Asia, Europe, and Africa. See Brotherston, *Book of the Fourth World* (Cambridge: Cambridge University Press, 1992).
16   Gerald Vizenor, *Manifest Manners: Narratives on Postindian Survivance* (Lincoln & London: University of Nebraska Press, 1999).
17   L. T. Smith, *Decolonizing Methodologies* (New York: Zed Books, 1999).
18   Jason W. Clay estimates that there are 5,000 such nations spread around the globe. See his "People, Not States, Make a Nation," *Mother Jones* (November/December 1990).
19   See John H. Bodley, *Victims of Progress* (Mountain View, CA: Mayfield, 1990), p. 5.
20   The definitions of belonging are not always clear. Saldaña-Portillo and Cortera speak of the "double colonization" of the US southwest, first by the Spanish and then by the United States, to complicate the inclusion of Chicana/os identity within the category of "indigenous." See Maria Josefina Saldaña-Portillo and María Eugenia Cotera, "Indigenous but Not Indian?," in Robert Warrior, eds., *The World of Indigenous North America* (Abingdon: Routledge, 2014), pp. 549–68.
21   Writing in 1995, Winona LaDuke spoke of a million indigenous people slated for relocation due to dam projects. Cited in Sandy Grande, *Red Pedagogy* (Lanham, Boulder, New York, Toronto, and Oxford: Rowman and Littlefield, 1964), p. 209.
22   See Jane Griffith, "Hoover Damn: Land, Labor, and Settler Colonial Cultural Production," *Cultural Studies ↔ Critical Methodologies*, Vol. 17, No. 1 (First pub. April 6, 2016), pp. 30–40.
23   Macarena Gomez-Barris, *The Extractive Zone* (Durham: Duke University Press, 2017), p. 96.

24 Many native peoples call themselves "the people" or "the real people," which some outside observers see as an expression of ethnocentrism, yet this tendency can also be seen as a modest statement of fact since "the people" in question expresses itself in a specific language, so it might as well be translated as "the people who speak the language in question," e.g. "Xavante." In my view, the phrase means both: we are a people like everyone else, and at the same time, we are a specific people proud of our ways. The most correct and logical choice might be to use the self-ascribed identity of the person, but even then there might be multiply hyphenated indigenous identities (e.g. a person who is Cree, Lakota, Ojibwe on the indigenous side, and Irish and German on the European side). Some of the names, moreover, began as ethnocentric slurs. The "Navajos" (thieves), so-called by the Spanish, petitioned to be officially recognized by their original name "Dene" (the people). The "Sioux," who refer to themselves as "Dakota" ("allies"), were named through a French condensation of the Ojibwa word *nadowe-is-iw* ("snake," "enemy"). Others were mispronunciations and filtrations, thus the French rendered Objibwe as "Chippewa." In North America, the non-indigenous side of ancestry is often elided. At the same time, no term is "innocent," since history itself is not innocent. Even the contemporary favorite "indigenous" is tainted by association with the French *code indigene* that regulated colonial domination in Africa and Asia. In situations of deep historical inequity, it seems, words are inevitably shaded, and shadowed, by history.

25 See Jose Barreiro, ed., *Thinking in Indian: A John Mohawk Reader* (Golden, CO: Fulcrum, 2010), pp. 134–5.

26 See Robert Nichols, op. cit., 12.

27 See Neil Kent, *The Sámi Peoples of the North: A Social and Cultural History* (London: C. Hurst, 2014).

28 *Study of the Problem of Discrimination against Indigenous Populations: Final Report submitted by the Special Rapporteur, Mr. José Martínez Cobo*, Commission on Human Rights, U.N. Doc. E/CN.4/Sub.2/1983/21/Add.8 (September 30, 1983), para 379.

29 "Being Indigenous," quoted in Jodi A Byrd, *The Transit of Empire: Indigenous Critique on Colonialism* (Minneapolis: University of Minnesota, 2011), p. xxix.

30 Tzvetan Todorov, *The Conquest of America: The Question of the Other*, trans. Richard Howard (Norman, OK: University of Oklahoma Press, 1984).

31 Tracy Devine Guzman, *Native and National in Brazil: Indigeneity after Independence* (Durham: University of North Carolina Press, 2013), pp. 1–4.

32 Georges E. Sioui Wendayete, "1992: The Discovery of Americity," in Gerald McMaster and Lee-Ann Martin, eds., *Indigena: Contemporary Native Perspectives in Canadian Art* (Vancouver: Craftsman House, 1992), p. 81.

33 Renato Sztutman, *O Profeta e o Principal* (São Paulo: EDUSP, 2012), p. 353.

34 Ibid., p. 353.

35 See Marcel Trudel, *L'Esclavage au Canada Français* (Montréal: Les Éditions de l'Horizon, 1963) and Marcel Trudel, *Deux siècles d'esclavage au Québec* (Montréal: Hurtubise HMH, 2004).

36 Robert J. Miller, *Native America, Discovered and Conquered* (Lincoln: University of Nebraska Press, 2008), p. 1.

37 MAGA ignorance about Indians was demonstrated at an earlier rally at Mount Rushmore and in Trump's notorious Pocahontas epithet for Elizabeth Warren.

38 Jack Weatherford, *Indian Givers*, op. cit. 16.

39 Djelal Kadir, *Columbus and the Ends of the Earth* (Berkeley: University of California Press, 1992), p. 66.

40 "For a clever denunciation of the Disney practices, see the You Tube Video "Fair(y) Use Tale," which, in an example of media jujitsu, deploys Disney clips to denounce the Disney abuse of copyright. A Brazilian Ph.D. dissertation by Anderson Luis Ribeiro Moreira, entitled "Poeticas da Posse: Apropriacoes de Super-Herois pelo Audiovisual Brasileiro," states the case eloquently: "The enterprise which construction its billionaire catalogue of products on the basis of public domain, has long battled to keep its own creations out of that domain" (translation mine).

41 Vandana Shiva, *Monocultures of the Mind* (London: Zed Books, 1993). Vandana Shiva quotes from Djelal Kadir, *Columbus and the Ends of the Earth* (Berkeley: University of California Press, 1992), p. 66, in her essay "Biodiversidade, Direitos de Propriedade Intelectual e Globalização," in Boaventura de Sousa Santos, ed., Semear Outras Soluções: *Os Caminhos da Biodiversidade e dos Conhecimentos Rivais* (Rio de Janeiro: Civilização Brasileira, 2005), 321.

42 Karl Marx, *Capital: A Critique of Political Economy, Vol I part III* (New York: Cosimo, 2007, originally published 1867), p. 823. Peter Linebaugh writes that North American Indians asked whether the early colonists made their long and dangerous voyage because they "lacked wood"; the Tupi in Brazil asked the French the same question.

43 Sergio Costa and Guilherme Leite Goncalves, *Um Porto no Capitalismo* Global (São Paulo: Boitempo, 2020).

44 See Robert Nichols, *Theft Is Property! Dispossession and Critical Theory* (Durham: Duke University Press, 2020), p. 66.

45 Claude Lévi-Strauss, *O pensamento selvagem* (Campinas, São Paulo: Papirus, 1997).

46 Shoshana Zuboff, *The Age of Surveillance Capitalism* (London: Profile Books Ltd, 2019), p. 196 citing Matthew Restall, *Seven Myths of the Spanish Conquest* (Oxford: Oxford University Press, 2004), p. 19.

47 Ibid., p. 12.

48 See Felipe Fernandez-Arnesto, *1492: The Year the World Began* (New York: Harper One, 2010), p. 196.

49 Quoted in Kirkpatrick Sale, *The Conquest of Paradise: Christopher Columbus and the Columbian Legacy* (New York: Alfred A. Knopf, 1990), pp. 366–7.

50 Quoted in A. Moorhead, *The Fatal Impact: An Account of the Invasion of the South Pacific* (Harmondsworth: Penguin, 1987), p. 131.

51 Ibid., p. 209.

52 Thomas Hobbes, ed., C. B. Macpherson, *Leviathan* (Middlesex: Penguin, 1968), p. 186.

53 Jack Weatherford, *Indian Givers: How the Indians of the Americas transformed the World* (New York: Fawcett, 1988), p. 127.

54 Georg W. F. Hegel, *The Philosophy of History* (Mineola, NY: Dover, 1956), p. 81.

55 Today, indigenous peoples in Brazil have come up with a compromise form of "fence" taking the natural form of planting certain kinds of trees, as a way of demarcating their land, a process shown in the Vincent Carelli film *Signs Don't Speak* (Video in the Villages, 1996).

56 Shohat and I also expand on this "ideal portrait" in our book *Race in Translation: Culture Wars in the Postcolonial Atlantic* (New York: New York University Press, 2012).

57 See Anibal Quijano, *Coloniality of Power, Eurocentrism and Latin America. Nepantla*, No. 3 (Durham, NC: Duke University Press, 2000), Mary Louise Pratt, *Imperial Eyes: Travel Writing and Transculturation* (New York: Routledge, 1992), and Vandana Shiva, *Monocultures of the Mind: Perspectives on Biodiversity and Biotechnology* (London: Zed Books, 1993). See also Ella Shohat and Robert Stam, *Unthinking*

Eurocentrism: Multiculturalism and the Media (New York: Routledge, 1994). See Thomas King, *The Inconvenient Indian* (Minneapolis: University of Minnesota Press, 2013).

58 See Adam Loften and Emmanuel Vaughan-Lee, Counter Mapping. *Emergence Magazine* (California, EUA: Kalliopeia Foundation, 2018). Accessed via: https://emergencemagazine.org/story/counter-mapping/. Accessed September 30, 2020.

59 Leanne Betasamosake Simpson, *As We Have Always Done: Indigenous Freedom through Radical Resistance* (Minneapolis: University of Minnesota Press, 2017), p. 110.

60 Joanne Barker, ed., *Critically Sovereign: Indigenous Gender, Sexuality, and Feminist Studies* (Durham: Duke University Press, 2017), p. 14.

61 From Luther Standing Bear, "The Land of the Spotted Eagle" (1933), https://www.encyclopedia.com/history/dictionaries-thesauruses-pictures-and-press-releases/excerpt-land-spotted-eagle-1933-luther-standing-bear.

62 Diana Taylor, *The Archive and the Repertoire* (Durham: Duke University Press, 2003), p. 16.

63 Ibid., p. 17.

64 Kopenawa, *The Falling Sky*, p. 373.

65 De Certeau, *Writing of History* (New York: Columbia University Press, 1988), p. 216.

66 In *Race in Translation*, Ella Shohat and I explore the intellectual trend that opposes colonialism in the academe and elsewhere, which we call the "seismic shift," to refer to the attempts in various disciplines to decolonize culture.

67 In 1907, Paul Rohrbach justified the German policy of appropriating the best Herero land: "for people of the culture standard of the South African Natives, the loss of their free national barbarism and the development of a class of workers in the service of and dependent on the Whites is primarily a law of existence in the highest degree." Quoted in John H. Bodley, *Victims of Progress* (Mountain View, CA: Mayfield, 1990).

68 Patricia Seed, *Ceremonies of Possession in Europe's Conquest of the New World, 1492–1640* (Cambridge: Cambridge University Press, 1995).

69 Sunera Thombani, *Exalted Subjects: Studies in the Making of Race and Nation in Canada* (Toronto: University of Toronto Press, 2007), p. 10.

70 Friedrich Nietzche, "On the Uses and Disadvantages of History for Life," from *Untimely Meditations* (Cambridge: Cambridge University Press, 1997, 2012).

71 See Thomas King, *The Inconvenient Indian* (Minneapolis: University of Minnesota Press, 2012), p. 218.

72 Eve Tuck and K. Wayne Yang, "Decolonization is not a Metaphor," in *Decolonization, Indigeneity, Education & Society*, Vol. 1, No. 1 (2012), p. 5.

73 Cited in Nichols, op. cit., 2.

74 See Gregory Cajete, *Native Science: Natural Laws of Interdependence* (Santa Fe: Clear Light, 2000).

75 Quoted in Julian Burger's *The Gaia Atlas of First Peoples* (New York: Doubleday, 1990), p. 34.

76 See Valerie Trouet, "What Turned California Forests into a Tinderbox? Fire Suppression, Paradoxically," *The Guardian* (September 14, 2020) https://www.theguardian.com/commentisfree/2020/sep/14/california-fire-suppression-forests-tinderbox

77 Cited in Guzman, op. cit., p. 178.

78 Cited in Glen Sean Coulthard, *Red Skin White Masks: Rejecting the Colonial Politics of Recognition* (Minneapolis: University of Minnesota Press, 2004), p. 63.

79 From Leanne Betasamosake Simpson, *As We Have Always Done*, quoted in Nichols, op. cit., 144.
80 For more, see Jimmy Chi and Kuckles, *Bran Nue Dae: A Musical Journey* (Sydney: Currency Press, Magabala Books, 1991).
81 See Chadwick Allen, op. cit.
82 See Jacques Derrida, *De la Grammatologie* (Paris: Minuit, 1967), p. 168.
83 Barbara Christian, from a paper presented at the Gender and Colonialism Conference at the University of California, Berkeley (October 1989).
84 Eduardo Viveiros de Castro, *Cannibal Metaphysics* (Minneapolis, MN: Minnesota University Press, 2014), pp. 40–1.
85 David Graeber and David Wengrow, *The Dawn of Everything* (New York: Farrar Strauss, and Giroux, 2021), p. 61.
86 Ibid., p. 441.
87 For a dense history and analysis of the evolution in the meaning of the "noble savage," see Ter Ellingson, *The Myth of the Noble Savage* (Berkeley: University of California Press, 2002).
88 Carlos Fausto, *Warfare and Shamanism in Amazonia* (Cambridge: Cambridge University Press, 2001), pp. 2–3.
89 Paula Gunn Allen, *The Sacred Hoop: Recovering the Feminine in American Indian Traditions* (Boston: Beacon Press, 1986), p. 189.
90 Sheryl Lightfoot, *Global Indigenous Politics: A Subtle Revolution* (New York: Routledge, 2016), pp. 13–14.
91 Chilean anthropologist Alejandro Lipschutz coined the term "pigmentocracy" to refer to the ethnic and color-based hierarchies of Latin America.
92 James Tully, *Strange Multiplicity: Constitutionalism in an Age of Diversity* (Cambridge: Cambridge University Press, 1995), p. 39.
93 Ibid., p. 92.
94 John Mohawk in Jose Barreiro, ed. op. cit., 271.
95 See Glen Sean Coulthard, op. cit., *Red Skin, White Masks: Rejecting the Colonial Politics of Recognition* (Minneapolis: University of Minnesota Press, 2014).
96 Gerald Vizenor, *Manifest Manners: Narratives on Postindian Survivance* (Lincoln: Nebraska, 1999), p. vii.
97 Cited in Carlos Fausto, *Art Effects: Image, Agency, and Ritual in Amazonia* (Lincoln: University of Nebraska Press, 2020), p. 2.
98 Severi, op. cit., p. 9.
99 Ibid., p. 14.
100 Ibid., p. 26.
101 Ibid., p. 52.
102 Lévi-Strauss, *The Way of the Masks* (London: Cape, 1982), cited in Severi, op. cit., p. 69.
103 Valades, cited by Severi op. cit., p. 52.
104 Cited by Severi, p. 109.
105 Severi, p. 114.
106 See Severi, 116 ff.
107 See Robert Nichols, op. cit. 160.
108 Severi, p. 201.
109 Severi, p. 206.
110 See Carlos Fausto, *Art Effects: Image, Agency, and Ritual in Amazonia* (Lincoln: University of Nebraska Press, 2020), p. 15.

111 Ibid., p. 167.
112 Ibid., p. 21.
113 See Melissa K. Nelson, "Getting Dirty," in Joanne Barker, ed., *Critically Sovereign: Indigenous Gender, Sexuality, and Feminist Studies* (Durham: Duke University Press, 2017), p. 139.
114 See Sara Ahmed, "Phantasies of Becoming the (Other)," *European Journal of Cultural Studies*, Vol. 2, No. 1 (January 1999), pp. 47–63.
115 Faye D. Ginsburg, "Indigenous Media: Faustian Contract or Global Village," *Cultural Anthropology* Vol. 6, No. 1 (1991), p. 92.
116 See Faye Ginsburg, "Aboriginal Media and the Australian Imaginary," *Public Culture*, Vol. 5, No. 3 (Spring 1993), pp. 557–78.
117 See Amalia Cordova, "Healing through Curation: A Conversation between Three Indigenous Image Curators in the Abya Yala Movement," in *Senses of Cinema* (December 2018), https://www.sensesofcinema.com/author/amalia-cordova/.
118 Michelle H. Raheja, "Reading Nanook's Smile: Visual Sovereignty, Indigenous Revisions of Ethnography, and *Artarnajuat (The Fast Runner)*," *American Quarterly*, Vol. 59, No. 4 (2007), pp. 1159–85.
119 Masayesva cited in Leuthold (1998).
120 Ivana Bentes, "Vídeo e cinema: rupturas, reações e hibridismos," in Arlindo Machado, ed., *Made in Brasil*: três décadas de vídeo brasileiro (São Paulo: Iluminuras: Itaú Cultural, 2007), pp. 111–28.
121 Faye Ginsburg, "Indigenous Media from U-matic to YouTube," in *Sociologia and Anhtropologia*, Vol. 6, No. 3 (2016), pp. 581–99.
122 Quoted in S. Baldur Hafsteinsson and Marian Bredin, eds., *Indigenous Screen Cultures in Canada* (Winnepeg: University of Manitoba Press, 2010), p. 130.
123 See James Clifford, *Returns: Becoming Indigenous in the Twenty First Century* (Cambridge: Harvard University Press, 2013).
124 Corinn Columpar, *Unsettling Sights: The Fourth World on Film* (Carbondale, IL: Southern Illinois University Press, 2010), p. xiv.
125 See Faye Ginsburg, "Australia's Indigenous New Wave: Future Imaginaries in Recent Aboriginal Feature Film" (Leiden, Netherlands: Adrian Gerbrands Lecture, May 29, 2012).
126 Jose Barreiro, ed. op. cit., 195.
127 Leslie Marmon Silko, "Videomakers and Basketmakers," *Aperture*, No. 119 (Summer 1990), p. 73.
128 Carlos Fausto, *Art-Effects: Image, Agency, and Ritual in Amazonia* (Lincoln: University of Nebraska, 2020), p. 263.
129 See Michelle Raheja, *Reservation Reelism* (Lincoln: University of Nebraska Press, 2010), p. 18.
130 Leanne Betasamosake Simpson, *Dancing on Our Turtle's Back* (Winnipeg: Arbeiter Ring Press, 2011), p. 32.
131 Kerstin Knopf, in *Decolonizing the Lens of Power: Indigenous Films in North America* (Leiden, The Netherlands: Brill, 2008), mentions many of these strategies and was kind enough to cite our book *Unthinking Eurocentrism: Multiculturalism and the Media* (co-authored with Ella Shohat) as a partial source for her fascinating catalogue of strategies.
132 *Hands of History*. Dir. Loretta Todd (1994).
133 Cited in essay by Jessica Bissett Perea, included in Joane Barker, ed. op cit., p. 127.
134 Ibid., p. 23.

135 Marcelo Fiorini "Desire in Music: Soul-Speaking and the Power of Secrecy," cited in Carlos Fausto, ibid., p. 109.
136 Ibid., p. 112.
137 Pierre Clastres, *Society against the State* (New York: Zone Books, 1987), p. 130.
138 Eduardo Viveiros de Castro, *From the Enemy's Point of View* (Chicago: University of Chicago Press, 1992), p. 9.
139 Ibid., p. 16.
140 See Raul Ruiz, *Poetics of Cinema* (Paris: Editions Dis Voir, 1995), p. 73.
141 See André Gaudreault, *Du littéraire au filmique: Système du récit* (Paris and Quebec City: Armand Colin/Nota bene, 1999, revised and expanded 2nd edition, with afterword entitled "Le cinéma: entre littérarité et intermédialité)," pp. 169–83.
142 See Bruce Albert, "O ouro canibal e a queda do céu: Uma crítica xamânica da economia política da natureza (Yanomami)" in Bruce Albert and Alcida Ramos, *Pacificando os Brancos* (Open Edition Books, IRD Editions), https://books.openedition.org/irdeditions/24767?lang=en.
143 See Andre Brasil, "Tikmũ'ũn's Caterpillar-Cinema: Off-Screen Space and Cosmopolitics in Amerindian Film," in Antônio Márcio da Silva and Mariana Cunha, eds., *Space and Subjectivity in Contemporary Brazilian Cinema* (London: Palgrave Macmillon, 2017), p. 26.
144 See Philippe Descola, "Selvageria Culta," in Adauto Novaes et al., eds., *A outra margem do Ocidente* (São Paulo: Companhia das Letras, 1999), p. 117.
145 Emma Marris, *Wild Souls: Freedom and Flourishing in the Non-human World* (New York: Bloomsbury, 2021).
146 Mary Louise Pratt, "Concept and Chronotope," in Tsing et al., *Arts of Living on a Damaged Plane* (Minneapolis: University of Minnesota Press, 2017), p. G169.
147 See Anna Tsing et al., op. cit., p. M4.
148 Ibid., p. M60.
149 Chadwick Allen, *Trans-Indigenous: Methodologies for Global Native Literary Studies* (Minneapolis: University of Minnesota, 2012), p. xix.
150 Ibid., p. xviii.
151 Wai Chee Dimock, *Through Other Continents: American Literature across Deep Time* (Princeton and Oxford: Princeton University Press, 2006), pp. 175–6.
152 Ibid., p. 177.
153 Ibid., p. 178.
154 For more on Bakhtin, see my Robert Stam, *Subversive Pleasures: Bakhtin, Cultural Criticism, and Film* (Baltimore: Johns Hopkins University Press, 1989).
155 See V. F. Cordova, *How It Is: The Native American Philosophy of V.F. Cor*dova (Tucson: University of Arizona Press, 2007).

1

From France Antartique to Shamanic Critique
The Tupinization of Social Thought

The transnational debates about the "Indian" form examples of what Edward Said called "traveling theory." Not only did European ideas travel West toward the "Indians" but also Indian ideas traveled East to Europe, and both Europeans and Indians reflected on that multidirectional yet inherently unequal traffic of ideas.[1] The discourses about "Indians" also traveled in the sense that the "Indian Question" was disputed around the Atlantic by Spanish clerics and jurists (Sepulvida, de las Casas), French humanists and poets (Montaigne, Jodelle) and philosophers (Rousseau, Diderot, Voltaire), English and Scottish social contract thinkers (Hobbes, David Hume, John Locke), American statesmen (Benjamin Franklin, Thomas Jefferson, Thomas Payne), German naturalists (Humboldt) philosophers (Hegel), novelists (Karl May), and an endless promenade of Brazilian and United Statesian (and more broadly North American) writers.

What I have called "indigenous social thought," or better a specific egalitarian strand of that thought, has been expressed in symbolic actions, in speech, and in writing, as well as in films and works of art by indigenous people themselves. What interests me is the multifaceted polylogue about indigenous social thought as it has transpired in three cultural zones—mainly the French, Brazilian, and North American. As a transnational trope, the motif of the Indian as exemplar of liberty formed part of the discursive atmosphere not only of the French Enlightenment and the American and French Revolutions but also of Brazilian modernism. And to say the obvious, the idea and practice of freedom formed a taken-for-granted part of many indigenous societies themselves, even if "freedom" and "democracy," since they were assumed as part of customary law, were not necessarily the keywords.

This chapter will pursue the concept of Indians as exemplars of freedom as it manifests at diverse points of history, and in relation to a number of historical/artistic moments, to wit:

(1) the sixteenth-century moment of the first contacts between the French and the Tupinambá, with special emphasis on the short-lived French colony in Brazil called France Antartique (1555–60) and its ramifications within France itself;[2] (2) the eighteenth-century moment of the French Enlightenment, with its frequent allusions to "*les sauvages*" of the Americas; (3) the parallel eighteenth-century moment of the American Revolution and the (ambiguously) pro-indigenous proclamations of the Founding Fathers; (4) the twentieth-century moment of 1920s Brazilian modernism,

usually encapsulated in Oswald de Andrade's boutade "Tupi or not Tupi: that is the question"; (5) the present moment of the swelling importance of indigenous intellectuals in both South and North America and increasing dialogue between indigenous and non-indigenous social thought. All of these disparate moments are historically and thematically linked in a strong transtextual chain. Thus, the writings that emerged from first contact and the sixteenth-century French colony in Brazil were constantly referenced by French Enlightenment philosophers, who in turn influenced the American Founding Fathers (who were influenced both by the French philosophers and by indigenous thought), and centuries later, the Brazilian Modernistas of the 1920s read the corpus of writing from the France Antartique period and related French philosophy to indigenous thought. All these transtextual "links" continue into the present.

France Antartique and Tupi Theory

The history of "France Antartique" has been recounted in great detail, not only in contemporaneous travel accounts but also by historians, most notably by Frank Lestringant.[3] Roughly, the story has been told as follows: In an attempt to bypass Portuguese claims and colonize the region already inhabited by French sailor-traders, Vice Admiral Nicolas de Villegagnon arrived in Brazil in November 1555 with a flotilla of three ships and 600 men in the Bay of Guanabara (site of present-day Rio de Janeiro).[4] His group occupied a rocky island where they constructed Fort Coligny, named after a patron of the colony. Presumably baffled by native cultural codes, plagued by intra-European religious conflicts, and threatened by the rebellious Norman traders given to material and erotic commerce with the native Tupi, Villegagnon asked Jean Calvin in Geneva to send Protestant pastors who could bring both desire and rebellion to heel.[5] Internal dissensions and attacks by the Portuguese ended the colony after five stormy years.

The specifically French tradition of commentary goes back to the travel writings of the early sixteenth century. The French were then trafficking in Brazilwood, used for a red dye in demand by textile makers for an elite market in France. In Brazil, the merchants relied on interpreters ("*truchements*") and trackers ("*coureurs de bois*"), who sometimes lived with and intermarried with Indians while trafficking in "Brazil wood," munitions, and other manufactures.[6] Given their status as colonial interlopers operating in defiance of the Pope-decreed Tordesillas Line, and more directly in defiance of a 1505 Portuguese decree granting a Brazilwood monopoly to Lisbon merchants, the French merchants sailing between Le Havre, Dieppe, and Honfleur and Brazil were by definition "illicit." Since so many of the authors were French Protestant, Historian Frank Lestringant refers to this body of texts as the "Huguenot Corpus." It began with French captain Paulmier de Gonneville's "relation" (i.e. report) to the French authorities about his 1503–05 voyage to Brazil, just three years after Pedro Cabral's "discovery."[7] Subsequently, a number of widely disseminated texts became embroiled in the disputes about France Antartique, notably Andre Thévet's *Les Singularites de la France Antartique* (1557) and *Cosmographie Universelle* (1575),

Jean de Léry's *Histoire d'un voyage faict en la terre du Brésil* (1578), and Hans Staden's sensationally titled *Brasilien: Die wahrhaftige Histoire der wilden nacken, grimmigen Menschenfresser-Leute* ("The Brazilians: The True History of the late Wild, Grim Man-Eaters," 1557). All of these books were immensely influential. Hans Staden's book, a best seller in Europe, was a key text in inaugurating "New World" travel literature and the cannibal trope. Jean de Léry's book came to be seen as the first in-depth work of ethnography. Thévet's *Cosmographie Universelle*, with its portrayal of Tupi, accounts about the creation of the world, catastrophic floods, and the different eras of humanity, for Lestringant, foreshadowed Lévi-Strauss's *Mythologiques* four centuries later.

While a political failure, France Antartique was a tremendous intellectual success in that it generated writing that changed world intellectual history. These "original," or in some ways "aboriginal," texts have been endlessly revisited, permutated, actualized, reinterpreted, remediated, and allegorized in function of the discursive/ideological needs of diverse actors and distinct historical moments. The Swiss scholar Alfred Metraux, the Brazilian sociologist Florestan Fernandes, the French literary/cultural theorist René Girard, French anthropologist Pierre Clastres and Brazilian Eduardo Viveiros de Castro, for example, have all tried to theorize Tupinambá rituals. The reworking of the original corpus has taken place not only within the most diverse disciplines (history, philosophy, literature, anthropology) but also within and across the most diverse media (the written word, woodprints, paintings, songs, operas, photographs, films, TV miniseries, samba pageants, and so forth) each bringing its specific potentialities of expression for "doing history" and "doing politics."

What I call "Tupi Theory" refers to the discursive precipitate, the bricolage of ideas, generated by the multifaceted Transoceanic colloquy between the native peoples of Brazil and various French, Brazilian, and later North American interlocutors.[8] This Franco-indigenous philosophical symposium dates back to the sixteenth-century exchanges between Breton and Normand merchant-sailors and the Tupi in Brazil, even before the establishment of the French colony in 1555. In their history of the port of Rio de Janeiro—which coincides with the first sites of France Antartique in the Bay of Guanabara, Guilherme Leite Goncalves and Sergio Costa discuss Rio de Janeiro as a central site in capitalist accumulation, suggesting that ever since the Portuguese navigator Gaspar de Lemos glimpsed the Bay of Guanabara in 1502, that "portion of the world was irreversibly integrated into the (pre) history of capitalist modernity."[9] The authors cite Rosa Luxembourg to the effect that the "appropriation of alien property turns into a right to property and exploitation, to the exchange of merchandise, and class domination," and to what David Harvey much later would call "accumulation by dispossession."[10] Their key insight is to point out that the phase of "primitive accumulation," whereby colonializing capitalism perpetuates itself by absorbing not-yet-mercantilized indigenous land, which provides new resources, raw materials, and labor markets, continues today.[11]

Frank Lestringant, the renowned historian of "France Antartique," argues that the "Indian" of the European Renaissance, which later entered into the French and European Enlightenment, was largely Brazilian, and specifically Tupi, and that the transnational image of the Indian was Tupi-Brazilian before it was Spanish American and North American. For Lestringant, Tupi iconographies of costume and artifact were later extended to the natives of the Americas in general, who were largely depicted, in the images of Theodore de Bry, for example, as naked, tonsured, feathered, and cannibalistic, and in the prose of a Montaigne as cannibalistic but free and egalitarian.[12] The Tupinambá, as Janet Whatley put it, provided an "all-purpose allegorical figure" for the Americas in general.[13]

The Franco-indigenous encounter did not take place only in the Americas, however; it also took place in France itself. French ships returning to France were often freighted with exotic fauna and flora and with native Brazilian "Indians." Already in 1504, Paulmier de Gonneville brought a young Carijó Indian named Essomericq, the fifteen-year-old son of the chief Arosca, back to France.[14] Essomericq was sent by his *cacique* father to learn about munitions—the high-tech technology of its time—to help his people and their French allies in their struggles back in Brazil.[15] (Essomericq was an early example of what Oswald de Andrade five centuries later called the "*indio tecnizado*" or "high-tech Indian.") By some accounts, Gonneville was so fond of Essomericq that he encouraged marriage with his daughter Suzanne (in 1521). Essomericq and his French wife had children, and their grandchild became the "Indian priest" of the Saint-Pierre-de-Lisieux Cathedral, suggesting a high degree of *metissage* a la Francaise.[16]

Another major Franco-indigenous encounter took place over four decades later when the citizens of Rouen, in 1550, offered a sumptuous spectacle in honor of King Henry II and Catherine de Medici. As part of the Franco-Tupinambá alliance, the French mounted a kind of theme park—a proto-Euro-Disneyworld—in the form of a reconstituted Tupinambá village. There, some fifty Tupinambá, who followed their tradition of painting themselves red, alongside hundreds of French people in red face, reenacted episodes from the history and rituals of Tupinambá life as part of a celebration of the Franco-Tupi military alliance. Many of the participating French had learned Tupi thanks to their close commercial, amical, and sometimes amorous relations with the Tupinambá back in Brazil. From a bridge over the Seine, the royal cortege could witness the reenactment of a battle between French and Portuguese warships, in which the French and their Tupinambá allies roundly and predictably defeat the Portuguese and Tupiniquim enemy. Given its spectacular success, the exhibition was repeated in Bordeaux in 1565, in a version featuring Indian leaders declaiming speeches in Tupi, rendered by the royal translator before the King himself.[17]

The procession in some ways illustrates Patricia Seed's analysis of the variant "rituals of possession" of European powers in the Americas. The French were given to ceremonial pageantry, royal "entrances," usually featuring symbolic gestures toward native collaboration, which exactly occurred in the case of *les Fetes de Rouen*. A surprising portrayal of the Rouen festivities came some four and a half centuries after the *fetes* themselves, in a different kind of "ceremonial possession," in this case the choreographed historiography typical of Rio de Janeiro's yearly carnival pageant, as captured in the videos showcasing the highlights of Rio's annual carnival. In a striking instance of the transAtlantic and transtemporal circuitries of popular performance, the Rio Samba School group "Imperatriz" devoted its 1998 carnival pageant to the 1550 events, in a kinetic spectacle entitled "the Tupinamba in Rouen." The pageant offered a "re-enactment of a re-enactment," in that *Les Fetes de Rouen* themselves had already reenacted the Franco-Tupinambá victories over the Portuguese. In a transhistorical fusion, the samba pageant offered (1) a staging and musicalization of the Rouen festivities, emphasizing a palette of bright dye-like colors; (2) syncretic dances mingling samba and indigenous styles; (3) indigenous-style body decorations; and (4) the brio of Rio's carnival, with its *"fantasias"* of powdery white wigs typical of the French *ancien regime* and elaborate floats (dubbed *"alegorias"*) staging specific aspects of the Rouen events. The genre of the music is the "exaltation samba," an invention of the Vargas period to designate sambas meant to extoll the beauties and achievements of Brazil. The first stanza cites the beginning of Goncalves Dias's Indianist poem "*I-Juca Pirama*" (roughly "A Worthy Death" in Tupi), with its pan-American topos of Indian bravery— *o bravo guerreiro* ("brave warrior," "braves"): "*Sou Indio, sou forte, Sou filho de Norte*" ["I'm an Indian, I'm strong, I'm a son of the North of Brazil"]. The lyrics of the carnival samba begin as follows (translation mine):

> I'm Indian, I'm strong
> I'm very lucky
> I'm natural
> I'm a warrior in the light of carnival freedom.

The next lines remind us of the red dye, extracted from Brazilwood, then a la mode with the French elite.

> Today I'll bring colour to the whole town
> I'll go with my soul painted.
> I'm a fantasy of the Crown
> Bringing the New World of Splendor

In a civilizational reversal, here it is not the natives who admire the palatial splendor *of* Europe but rather the natives who bring splendor *to* Europe.

> The magic of the Jungle
> Pure Emotion
> Simple in Passion
> Dream and Poetry in Rouen
> On the Banks of the Seine
> Brazil offers the image of nudity and courage.

The next lines refer to the carnival-style mixing of social classes both within Rio's street carnival and in the *Fetes de Rouen*, which also historically mixed classes, mingling Royalty with the sailor-friends of the Tupinambá.

> Indians and Sailors and Nobles
> Mingling in the most beautiful landscape
> And the audience at the encore
> With the Empress delirious.

The word "audience," in the context of the French monarchy, evokes an "audience" or formal meeting with a head of state (Here Henri II and Catherine de' Medici), while in the context of the carnival pageant in Rio, it refers to the cheering crowds in Rio's *Sambodromo* and the Globo audience watching the proceedings on television. The finale makes a crucial point:

> In France the Bon Sauvage taught Europe
> Equality, Fraternity, and Liberty

The song begins and ends with the theme of "freedom," thus touching on our theme of the fusion of indigenous social thought and French revolutionary ideas. The lyrics emphasize the economic/aesthetic role of Brazilwood dyes in "giving color to Rouen," but more importantly for our purposes, they claim that "[t]he Indian taught freedom to Europe"—thus forging the perennial link between the Indian and the concept of freedom, but in this case instantiated in a vibrant form of multi-art pop cosmopolitanism.

A number of historical factors account for this historically unusual equality between European and indigene. First, the festivities in Rouen took place five years before the foundation of the French colony, at a time when the Tupi and the French in Brazil enjoyed a rough equality. The situation was thus atypical in comparison with later colonial situations aimed at conquest, enslavement, conversion, and dispossession. Colonial structures were not yet in place, so the relationship was not one of colonial master and slave but rather of trade between equals. Second, the situation was one of co-dependency; the French needed native allies to protect their stay in Brazil, and the Tupi needed the French as allies against the Portuguese. Third, French soldiers, translators, and traders had been living cheek by jowl with Natives for extended periods. The French in Brazil were basically living in indigenous territory, in a situation of broad native hegemony. Fourth, there was no linguistic divide; many French traders and soldiers learned the dominant Tupi. Leila Perrone-Moises sees the Franco-indigenous encounter, especially in the area farther North near the Equator, as a case of reciprocal chameleonism involving the Tupification of the French and the Frenchification of the Tupi. Fifth, the purpose of the *truchements* was not to dominate but to translate and get to know the local people. Sixth, although the major chronicler of this period, Jean de Léry, was a Protestant, he was not embarked on an evangelizing mission. France Antartique was largely the creation not of the dominant religious group in France but rather of what was then a persecuted Protestant religious minority, soon to be the victims of what some have called the first recorded genocide in modern European history. In the case of France Antartique, the partial motivation was a refuge from persecution, although the persecuted group, like the Pilgrims, subsequently showed itself to be quite capable of persecution themselves elsewhere. But unlike what occurred with the Puritans, in Brazil, there was no religious discourse of Chosen People or of a New Israel.

We find some parallels to this situation in French Canada, where Native cultures were arguably better understood by ordinary people—the trappers, the translators, the *coureurs de bois* who lived on a day-by-day basis among native people—than by the priests and administrators who tried, often vainly, to radically rearrange indigenous ways of life. The more sympathetic "*francais ensauvages*" did not practice agriculture, did not enclose land, and spoke indigenous languages.[18] Beatriz Perrone-Moises offers a rare trans-hemispheric Red Atlantic gesture by comparing Tupi self-governance patterns in Brazil to similar patterns among the Algonquins, the Huron and the Iroquois. In a 1996 article, she points to some seventeenth-century commonalities: societies governed by councils of elders who smoked stimulants to open up throats and minds to facilitate communication. While the Iroquois council of sachems was slightly more hierarchical than its South American counterparts, she argues, both societies practiced the politics of consensus, with great value given to oratorical persuasion.[19] Brazilian scholar Florestan Fernandes, in *The Social Organization of the Tupinamba*, argues that the basic political institution of the Tupinambá was a "Council of Elders," composed of renowned and respected figures, whose goal was to produce consensus through discussion.[20] Although the French both in Brazil and Quebec often had amical relations with Indians, they also sometimes enslaved indigenous populations in Louisiana and New France, a practice which materially enriched France through their coerced labor and stolen land. (Between 1660 and 1760, French colonists in New France enslaved as many as 10,000 Native Americans, forcing them to work as farm hands, domestic servants, and construction laborers.)[21]

Europe at the time of the foundation of the French colony in Brazil was a hotbed of religious friction in the wake of the Spanish Inquisition, the exiling of Iberian Jews, and the expulsion of the Muslims in 1492. The schism within Christianity initiated by Luther and continued by Calvin, meanwhile, provoked the Counter-Reformation and repression against what was seen as a Judaizing form of vernacular Christianity. Three religions were brought into fraught relationship on that little island in Guanabara Bay: (1) the religion of the native Tupinambá, with its oracular *pajes* and strangely hospitable form of ritual cannibalism; (2) that of the Catholics, with its hierarchical Church, the Eucharist, and a belief in the literal transubstantiation of the body of Christ; and (3) that of Protestant Huguenots, for whom the Eucharist was purely symbolic.[22]

Thus, the tensions that would lead subsequently to the European Wars of Religion (from 1562 until the Edict of Nantes in 1598) became projected onto the trilateral religious encounter in France Antartique. In this context, Protestants began to see the French and Spanish Catholics as the true cannibals, the "Deophages," both because they "ate God" in the form of the Host and because they were "cannibalizing" Protestants militarily. While Catholics believed in "transubstantiation," the literal transformation of the host and the wine into the body and blood of Christ, the Protestants saw the physical elements as mere tokens of body and blood. In a sense the debate was about comparative religious semiotics, bearing on the relationship between the signifier—the wine and the bread used in the Mass—the signified, and the referent, an element which adds another semiotic dimension to Lévi-Strauss's fascination with these quarrels.[23] The Protestants regarded the Tupinambá as merely symbolic and deeply spiritual cannibals like themselves.[24]

The cultural differences between the European and Indigene, and the political and religious differences between the royalist Catholics and the insurrectionary Protestants, shaped how the two groups conceptualized the Tupi peoples. These differential readings become evident in their divergent depictions of the Tupinambá chief Cunhambebe, the leader of the Federation of the Tamoios, an aggregation of native groups fighting

Portuguese colonization. Almost all of the sixteenth-century writers, including the priests, talk about Cunhambebe. Thévet describes him as wearing elaborate regalia and "venerated by all the savages" and as the "most impetuous, cruel, and renowned of all the other chiefs of the neighboring provinces."[25] As a French ally, Cunhambebe was received by Villegagnon as a monarch, greeted with all the pomp due a head of state, much as the Tupinambá leaders had been treated in France itself at the time of "*les Fetes de Rouen.*" Yet the Catholic Thévet and the Protestant Léry, as Lestringant points out, paint very different portraits of Cunhambebe, aligned with their ideological and religious predilections. As an example of early European projections, each group had a different "Indian" in mind. The official cosmographer Thévet "royalizes" Cunhambebe with exuberant eulogies to the "King of Ubatuba," turning the cacique into a French-style monarch.[26] The Huguenot Jean de Léry, meanwhile, deeply suspicious toward any monarchy reminiscent of the one persecuting his co-religionists in Europe, resented any authority incarnated in a single person. He therefore mocks Thévet's royalization of Cunhambebe and turns him instead into a Tupinambá version of a pastoral leader of a closely knit Protestant *communitas* based on the egalitarian principle of "all souls equal before God."[27] The factual attributes of Cunhambebe, in short, are less important than the discursive and ideological prism through which he was seen. Both Thévet and Léry offer a favorable portrait of Cunhambebe, but Thévet sees him as incarnating a divinely sanctioned hierarchical society, while Léry sees him as egalitarian and communal.[28] What is perhaps surprising is the overwhelmingly positive image of Cunhambebe, and by implication of the Tupinambá social system, by representatives of both religious factions.

Filming France Antartique

Cunhambebe, or more precisely an actor playing his role, makes an appearance in Nelson Pereira dos Santos's provocative film about France Antartique, *Como Era Gostoso o Meu Francês* (How Tasty Was My Little Frenchman, 1971). The director based the film on his own research into the already mentioned corpus of texts by Thévet, Villegagnon, Jean de Léry, and Hans Staden, augmented by citations from Portuguese figures such as Mem de Sa, Manuel de Nobrega, and Jose de Anchieta, many of whom are cited in the intertitles which structure the film. The protagonist's trajectory combines the story of Hans Staden's kidnapping by the Tupinambá, with the "thick" granular detail of Jean de Léry's ethnographic account. Dos Santos opted for a French protagonist in order to accentuate the colonial dimension of the episode, since the French, unlike the Germans, actually had tried, even if ultimately without success, to found a colony in Brazil.[29]

How Tasty Was My Little Frenchman, as Richard Pena points out, subverts the conventional Indian captivity narrative.[30] The subversive use of the pronoun—"*my*" *Frenchman*—already asserts identification with the Tupinambá point of view, and specifically with that of the Tupinambá wife (Sebiopepe) shown in close-up in the penultimate shot, nibbling on the neck of her delicious French husband. More generally, the film offers a didactic lesson in cultural relativism, indirectly posing Montaigne's question: "who are the real barbarians?" Relative nudity—relative because the Tupinambá still wear the insignia of culture in the form of ornaments, body paint, and tangas—becomes the cultural norm during the film.[31] More important, the film systematically cuts off the conventional escape routes, maintaining an ironically neutral attitude toward the protagonist's deglutition. Here the European is the protagonist, but not the hero, and romantic love is less important than tribal loyalty.

How Tasty Was My Little Frenchman was made during the very repressive period of the Brazilian military dictatorship that began with the coup d'état in 1964. In this sense, the film appropriates the French Huguenot corpus in order to allegorize the Brazil of the dictatorship. The voice-over of the opening sequence relays Villegagnon's letter to John Calvin, dated 1555, denouncing the rebels who consorted with native women and rebelled against Villegagnon's rule, and who supposedly "threw themselves into the sea and were drowned." The staged scene, however, contradicts the "voice of God" narration by showing the Frenchman, attached to a heavy ball and chain, being pushed into the sea, just as Villegagnon had in fact done with three rebels in his time. The sly allusion, however, is to the military dictatorship, which at that very moment was literally throwing its "subversives" from helicopters into the same Atlantic ocean, or murdering them in their prison cells, while claiming that the prisoners had committed suicide.[32] Villegagnon's letter is dated March 31, 1557, the very same March date as the onset, some four centuries later, of the 1964 coup d'état. At the same time, dos Santos was responding to the crises provoked by the creation of the Trans-Amazonian Highway, which cut through the Amazon forest, thus exposing indigenous groups to disease, depredation, and land theft.[33]

The cinematic medium, as a synesthetic and syncretic art, offers historiographic capabilities unavailable to written history, here poignantly illustrated by the use of the actual historical locale both of the production and of the diegesis. The production team reconstituted a Tupinambá village set near the colonial town of Parati, historically part of the Tupinambá hegemony centered in nearby Ubatuba, a region full of sonorous toponyms of Tupi origin (Guarujá, Caraguatatuba). Unlike the single-track verbal medium of written history, the cinema as a multi-track medium offers the moving image, the visual mediums of photography, painting, and woodcuts, along with the movement of dance, the harmonies of music, the realism of sound, and the performance of theater. *How Tasty Was My Little Frenchman* multiplies the media of representation by featuring not only the Marburg woodcuts that illustrated the original version of Hans Staden's *True History*, but also through a cinematic style that stresses the vibrant open-air tropical colors reminiscent of Brazilian painter Guignard, a "primitive" in the style of Douanier Rousseau. Unlike the lush scores of many historical films, the music is at once indigenous in its instrumentation and chants, and avant-garde in its conception and dissonance.

How Tasty demonstrates film's capacity not so much to reproduce or reenact history—although even on that level the film achieves a fair degree of accuracy—but rather to stage the contradictory discourses and ideologies through which history is refracted. In *How Tasty*, the film's signification emerges not as a naive verist claim of "this is how it happened," but rather in the form of a double-voiced narration which counterpoints two versions of history—the contemporaneous intertitular commentaries, many of them racist, with the staged scenes on the other. Through quotations from key historical figures, dos Santos summons up the languages, discourses, and ideologies of the time. In this sense, the film constructs its meaning through an aesthetic of tension that foregrounds contradictions between sound and image, between music and performance, and between image and intertitles. Villegagnon's voice-over letter to Calvin, for example, speaks of Indians as "beasts with human faces," yet the on-screen Indians appear to be gregarious, civil, hospitable, and beautiful. Prohibited by law from hiring actual native people, dos Santos engaged mixed-race and well-tanned Carioca extras and performers, those who would normally wear tangas, modeled on indigenous apparel, on Rio beaches bearing Tupi names like Ipanema and Grumari.

Far from being intimidated by technology, the film's Indians are eager, like Essomericq, to acquire the latest models of weapons and munitions. Rather than speak a fake Hollywood-style patois, the Indians (and the Frenchman) are made to speak Tupi, the lingua franca of the period, in a film that needs subtitles even in Brazil. More importantly, the film directly subverts the standard Indianist narrative of the native heroines like Paraguassu and Iracema who fall in love with the European stranger and blithely assimilate into metropolitan culture. Here Sebiopepe prevents her French husband from returning to France by shooting arrows into his derriere, less out of conjugal fidelity than out of tribal loyalty. Later, she affectionately cues his lines as he rehearses the liturgy of his own execution. Rather than have the indigenous woman assimilate to the European husband, as often occurs in Brazil's "foundational romances," the film stages a case of reverse assimilation. Here it is the European who assimilates by learning Tupi, adopting the native manner of dress, working and warring with the natives, and participating in the celebration of his own deglutition.

A profoundly subversive film, *How Tasty Was My Little Frenchman*, has often been misunderstood due to a kind of generic/ideological inertia within the habits of spectatorship that channel empathy for European heroes. Despite Nelson's subversive intentions, many in the audience still identified with the French protagonist.[34] That said, there is much that dos Santos could not have known when he made the film. He assumed, for example, that the Tupinambá no longer existed. But thanks to the internet we are now aware of vibrant contemporary Tupinambá activists in the South of the State of Bahia, a subject to which we will return in later chapters.

The dos Santos film calls ironic attention to a common Brazilian contrast between the down-to-earth Portuguese and the high-flying intellectual French when he has the Tupinambá administer a language "test" for the captured Europeans to find out whether they represent the enemy Portuguese or the French allies. The Portuguese respond to the test with recipes, a joke not only on what Brazilians saw as Portuguese gluttony, but also on the common view of the Portuguese as literal-minded and unimaginative. The titular Frenchman, in contrast, recites a lofty gem of French literary speech—a poem by sixteenth-century Pleiade poet Etienne Jodelle—"*Ces barbares marchent tous nus, et nous marchons inconnus, fardes, masques.*" (These barbarians walk completely naked, while we walk unrecognized, with makeup, masked.) The poem embeds a proto-Rousseauist theory that foils naked "savages," easily recognized as savages, with the well-accoutered French, who go unrecognized as savages. At the same time, the sequence inverts the homogenizing convention by which Europeans perceive only generic Indians; here the Indians, blind to European differentiations, see only a generic European—"they all look alike!"

The episode points to a truth about the trilateral relation between France, Brazil, and Portugal, to wit the role of France, in an obvious snub to the colonial father Portugal, as the true cultural mentor and "great orienter of [Brazilian] culture."[35] For France, conversely, Brazil was one of the colonies that "got away," a loss that had the positive side effect of freeing the Franco-Brazilian relationship from the burden of colonial guilt, on the one side, and of anti-colonial resentment on the other. While the Portuguese physically conquered Brazil and documented their native encounters in pragmatic terms, unlike the French, they did not develop elaborate theories about the broader significance of cultural differences between the "New" and the "Old" worlds. While the Portuguese took material possession of the country, the French appropriated what Mario Carelli calls the "spaces of utopia," by linking alternative social modes to their awareness of indigenous ways of life.[36] Less successful at military conquest than the Portuguese, the French through their writings nevertheless stimulated the philosophical debates about the Indians that continue to this day.

The French dissemination of a certain rebellious figure of the "*sauvage*" incorporated both the Tupinambá and Tupiniquim of Brazil in an early phase and the Huron and Iroquois in a later phase. In the literature, these two phases sometimes became melded into a generic, atemporal, and pan-geographic "sauvage." Although one might argue for the mediated symbolic "redness" of many European countries, France provides a particularly vibrant case because of the longevity of the Franco-indigenous connection, the relatively pacific nature of the relationship, at least in Brazil, and the philosophical density of the dialogue.[37] To mention just a few links in this chain of connection: (1) France has a more than five-century-long tradition of cultural and commercial exchange with the Indians of the Americas, going back to the Brazilwood trade in Brazil (and the fur trade in North America). (2) Tupi words such as "*toucan*," "*mandioca*," and "*Tupinambo*" came to form part of the French language, linguistic traces of the intermingling of the two groups both in Brazil and in France itself. (3) Many Tupi traveled to France, whether as prisoners, free people, or as "gifts" for the King, or in the Tupinambá case, as welcome visitors, some of whom learned French, assimilated, intermarried, and had children with the French.[38] (4) Many French people in the Americas became "white Indians" by assimilating into native culture, intermarrying, learning the languages, as was the case of the "*truchements*" in France Antartique and of some fur traders in Quebec.[39] (5) Like Jean de Léry in Brazil, some French writers in Canada portrayed indigenous societies as egalitarian, rational, and praise worthy, imaging the people not as noble savages, in sum, but as members of a freer and more equal society. Such was the case of Baron Louis Armand de Lahontan in *Nouveaux Voyages dans l'Amerique Septentrionale, Memoires de l'Amerique Septentrionale*, and *Supplement aux Voyages ou Dialogues avec le sauvage Adario*. Huron scholar Georges E. Sioui cites Lahontan and Joseph-Francois Lafitau's *Meours des Sauvages Americains* as evidence for continuity between French praise for indigenous social norms and long-standing indigenous views of their own society.[40]

In addition, (6) French museums have long been exhibiting objects such as the Tupinambá capes brought to France in 1557 by André Thévet. Indeed, descendants of the Tupinambá have demanded the repatriation of such objects.[41] (7) French literature, from François Rabelais and Etienne Jodelle in the sixteenth century, through Ferdinand Denis in the nineteenth century, up to Jean-Christophe Rufin's bestseller *Rouge Brésil* in the twenty-first century, has alluded to the Franco-indigenous encounter. Flaubert's modernizing pharmacist Homais, in *Madame Bovary*, ridicules the provincial French mothers who dress up their children to look like the "Botocudos" (later called "Krenak") of Brazil. (8) Not only have multiple generations of French children played "Cowboys and Indians,"[42] but also contemporary French and Quebecois adults, called by anthropologists "*les Nouveaux Indiens*," spend their leisure time reenacting "traditional Indian lifestyles."[43] (9) Brazilian indigenous leaders have frequently met with French heads of state, going back to Villegagnon's reception of the Tupi leader Cunhambebe. Four centuries later, Kayapó chief Raoni Metuktire, together with rock star Sting, was formally received by François Mitterand in April 1989. On June 20, 1996, Jacques Chirac (a fond collector of "primitive art") feted Raoni at the Elysée Palace. In May 2000, Chirac met with Amazonian tribes seeking international support for the ecological development of the Xingu Reserve.

French anthropologists like Lévi-Strauss, Pierre and Hélène Clastres, Philippe Descola, and Bruce Albert, finally, have carried out influential work on indigenous peoples in Brazil. They form a continuum with French artists and philosophers interested in indigenous peoples, bringing to mind Marcel Mauss's fascination with the *potlatch* of native groups from the American Northwest; Paul Eluard's fascination with the Pueblo peoples; Antonin Artaud's experience with the Tarahumaras; André Breton's fascination with the Zuni, for him a people spiritually aligned with the Surrealist imaginary, and Deleuze and Guattari's references to Amazonian anthropology.[44] The French dissemination of a certain rebellious figure of the "*sauvage*" incorporated both the Tupinambá and Tupiniquim of Brazil in an early phase and the Wendat (Huron) and the Haudenosaunee (Iroquois) of North America in a later phase, often melded into a generic, atemporal, and pan-geographic "Indian." The more important point is that French writers, from the sixteenth century to the twenty-first century, have found the Brazilian Indian, to coin a phrase, "good to think with." More recently, indigenous intellectuals both in North and South America have also found French theory "good to think with," citing and debating, as we shall see in the final chapter, with figures such as Foucault, Ranciere, and Guattari and Deleuze.

As part of this reciprocal cultural romance, the French influence was especially strong in the Brazilian movement called "*Indianismo*." Gonçalves de Magalhães, who founded Brazilian romanticism with his "*Suspiros Poéticos e Saudades*," published the literary review *Nitheroy* in Paris in 1836, and in the first issue he declared Brazil, in another snub to the Portuguese, the "son of French civilization."[45] Magalhães published an epic poem—"*A Confederação dos Tamoyos*" in 1856, which celebrated the alliance between the Indian hero Aimbere and the French against the Portuguese.[46] Literary critic Antonio Candido, in *A Formação da Literatura Brasileira* (Formation of Brazilian Literature), speaks of the Franco-Brazilian roots of what was sometimes thought to be a purely Brazilian movement—literary "Indianism." It was a Frenchman, historian, and diplomat Ferdinand Denis, who during his stay in Brazil from 1816 through 1819, provided the initial impetus for the later vogue of literary Indianism. At a time when the Brazilian elite had slighted the indigenous theme, Denis urged Brazilian writers to dive deep into indigenous mythologies as a way of forging an independent literature. After encountering some Indian groups in Minas Gerais, Denis himself wrote an Indianist novel entitled *Lês Machakalis* (1823). Seeing native myth as a way to re-enchant a spiritually depleted Europe, Denis described a magical world where "the voice of God was to be found in a lightning flash"—probably a reference to the Tupã, the god of thunder—and where a "thousand spirits inhabited the forests."[47] In a kind of literary salvage anthropology *avant la lettre*, Denis recommends studying the "few vestiges that have survived three centuries of destruction" to find "primitive thoughts which strongly excite the imagination."[48] The same Ferdinand Denis who romanticized Indians also praised the mixed race *bandeirantes*, apparent disregarding for the fact "that those same adventurers had been responsible for the decimation and enslavement of the Indians."[49]

In books such as *Scènes de la Nature sous les Tropiques* (1824) and *Resume de l'Histoire Litteraire du Bresil* (1826), Denis encouraged Brazilian writers to concentrate on Chateaubriand-style local color. But the Brazilian writer Jose de Alencar, while a devotee of Chateaubriand's aristocratic exoticism, insisted that Indianism should also be nourished by homegrown native sources. Although the Brazilian Indianists usually wrote in the "noble-race-doomed-to-disappear" mode, they occasionally praised indigenous social systems. In his introduction to his novel *Ubirajara* (1874), de Alencar wrote that the basis of executive power in the Tupi social system was, "as in republics, universal suffrage." Writing fifteen years before Brazil actually became a Republic, Alencar described Tupi suffrage as "ever active and vigilant, prepared to bend to superior merit, wherever that might manifest itself."[50]

Montaigne and Tupi Theory

As avid readers of travel literature, sixteenth-century Europeans were fascinated by a "New World" culture, at once recognizably human and disconcertingly different. While one trend denied the cultural agency of indigenous people within a logic of deficiency in relation to European norms, another erected the Indian as a model to be admired. In *Histoire d'un voyage faict en la terre du Brésil* (1578), written, as he says, in "Brazilwood ink," Jean de Léry, explorer, writer, and pastor, sent to the French colony in 1556, described his experience, some two decades earlier, of living with the Tupinambá. While there, he witnessed the Tupinambá ritual cannibalization of their captives. He noted that the captive was admired for his courage, and for nine months, in a kind of desired alterity, he became an honored member of the tribe, to the point of being offered a wife. The prisoner even cheerfully joined in the spectacle of his own sacrifice, drinking and dancing with the others, an integral part of a multi-art festival complete with songs, processions, and ceremonial presentations. The prisoner became a key actor by having to remind the attendees at his execution that he had (symbolically) slain and eaten their relatives. Thus, the cannibal, as Victor Grégoire puts it, was "ultimately endogamous." In devouring me, the about-to-be executed prisoner himself is telling the Tupi, "[Y]ou are devouring your own parents."[51] Contemporary anthropologist/theorists explain that the Tupinambá required sufficient time to totally assimilate the captive to Tupi ways, in language, war, and work, to the point of making war together, working together, and having children together. De Léry relativizes the evil of cannibalism by comparing it to two greater evils, first to the "savagery" of the European Wars of religion, and second, by contrasting Tupi cannibalism, as an eminently symbolic act, with the hunger cannibalism that he had witnessed among Europeans. (During the siege of Sancerre, a Calvinist married couple was caught boiling their dead daughter in a cauldron for food.) Cannibalism, for the Tupinambá, was a highly ritualized matter of warfare rather than a standard feature of everyday life; it did not involve the hunger implied in racist missionary-in-the-pot Safari films. The process was lethal, but strangely hospitable and gregarious, and Léry never gives a sense that he was personally in danger during his stay with the Tupinambá and often expressed nostalgia for his life with the Tupinambá.

Demonstrating an incipient sense of what would later be called "cultural relativism," Léry defended some of the cultural values of the Tupi. The Tupinambá walk around naked, Léry tells us, but only to avoid changing clothes in a hot climate.[52] The nakedness of Tupinambá women, he adds, is far less provocative than the intermittently veiled nudity of European women. Anticipating by two centuries Rousseau's ideas (in *Emile*, 1762) about child-rearing, Léry proposes the practical Tupinambá manner of caring for children as a possible model for French parents. When Léry explains the European custom of leaving an inheritance for the children, an elderly Tupinambá ridicules the idea, since the same earth that feeds the parents will feed the children. While eager for trade in objects, the Tupinaba were suspicious of accumulation and the hoarding of possessions. (Davi Kopenawa Yanomami expresses similar ideas five centuries later.) De Léry finds the Tupinambá more honest and generous than Europeans and writes that he felt safer with them than in some parts of France. Yet Léry never abandoned Christianity, and never endorsed cannibalism, or the penchant for war and vengeance, or what he saw as Tupinambá sexual promiscuity.

De Léry also praised the Tupinambá for their aesthetic sense, especially in relation to music, where hundreds of people would sing and dance together for hours. In chapter 15 of his *Histoire* he reports that even though they do not know what music is—i.e. they lack musical notation—

> those that have not heard them would never believe that they could make such harmony [although] I had been somewhat afraid; now I received in recompense such joy, hearing the measured harmonies of such a multitude, and especially in the cadence and refrain of the song, when at every verse all of them would let their voices trail, saying *heu, heuaure, heura, heuaure, heura, heura oueh*—I stood there transported with delight. Whenever I remember it my heart trembles, and it seems their voices are still in my ears.[53]

(Jean-Jacques Rousseau, who was not only a philosopher but also a composer, also studied Tupi melodies.) In contrast with the European Naturalists like the Comte de

Buffon, who depicted America as a place of stunted growth and degeneracy, Léry described a robust Tupi society where people were stronger, fitter, and less prone to disease than Europeans. Léry posits a series of binary oppositions such as native nudity/European dress, and native festivity/European productive labor, but he avoids "ranking" the two cultures. Claude Lévi-Strauss called Léry's history "a masterpiece of anthropological literature," praising its literary qualities and its rigorous depiction of the milieu, material life, food preparation, kinship relations, thus furnishing, for Lévi-Strauss, a model of an ethnological essay. Michel de Certeau, meanwhile, called Léry's account seminal for a number of historiographic and ethnographic lineages, the equivalent of a "primal scene in the construction of ethnological discourse."[54]

The intellectual fallout of the early European/indigene encounter made its way into such classics as Erasmus's *In Praise of Folly*, Thomas More's *Utopia*, and Shakespeare's *Tempest*. Despite the etymological meaning of "utopia" as "no place," More's utopia had a precise location, i.e. France Antartique—in the Brazilian region of Cabo Frio. The spread of utopian ideas emerging from the New World, as Marcio Souza puts it, "generated the Folly of Erasmus, the mockery of Gargantua, and the raging complaints of the wisdom of Shakespeare's Caliban."[55] After Thévet and Léry, the utopian idea entered European Renaissance thought more directly and dramatically with a close reader of Jean de Léry—Michel de Montaigne. As an early exponent of what would later be called "cultural relativism," Montaigne condemned colonialism in two essays— "*Des Cannibales*" and "*Des Coches*." A century before the French revolution, Montaigne ventriloquized the Indian voice to criticize European civilizational hierarchies and expose the economic underpinnings of European wars. Spanish genocide of native peoples, for Montaigne, was simply motivated by greed: "so many cities razed to the ground, so many nations exterminated … for a traffic in pearls and pepper!"[56] Montaigne takes a good deal from Léry's account: the emphasis on a generous communalism, the absence of laws of inheritance, and the ideal of equality.

With Montaigne, the Franco-indigenous dialogue became literal. Not only had Montaigne's assistant lived for twelve years in France Antartique,[57] but also Montaigne actually met three Tupinambá Indians in 1562, at the court of King Charles IX, and the memory of the encounter followed him throughout his life. This reported encounter constitutes an early account of the radical questioning of western social norms by indigenous people, first by questioning the institution of the Regency, finding it "very strange that so many big men with beards, strong and armed … should submit to obey a child, and that they did not rather choose one of their own number to command them." Secondly, Montaigne added, they questioned the class system:

> [T]hey had observed that there were men amongst us, full and gorged with all kinds of good things, and that their halves were begging at their doors, emaciated with hunger and poverty; and they thought it strange how these necessitous halves could suffer such injustice, and that they did not seize the others by the throat, or set fire to their houses.[58]

Montaigne practices a rhetoric of civilizational reversals by arguing that the violence of Tupinambá cannibalism paled in comparison to that triggered by religious wars in Europe, which had people drawn and quartered in the name of a religion of love. Like De Léry, Montaigne compares European practices unfavorably to the ritualistic cannibalism of the Tupinambá:

> I think there is more barbarity in eating a live than a dead man, in tearing on the rack and torturing the body of a man still full of feeling, in roasting him piecemeal and giving him to be bitten and mangled by dogs and swine, (as we have not only read, but seen within fresh memory, not between old enemies, but between neighbors and fellow citizens, and what is worse, under the cloak of piety and religion) than in roasting and eating him after he is dead.[59]

Montaigne's unnamed Tupi interlocutors catalyzed his own thinking by asking probing questions based on their own axioms about what constitutes a good society—in this case their own. Since in philosophy as in politics questions are more important than answers, here we have a philosophy of questions, an interrogative form of social thought. The Enlightenment critique of social hierarchy and political absolutism partially traces back, then, to Montaigne's encounter with the playfully critical Tupinambá, who to all appearances were unimpressed by the pomp and circumstance of Monarchical Europe.

The Tupinambá, in Montaigne's presentation, demolished with a few probing questions the prestige of the hereditary monarchy and the class system. Indeed, Lévi-Strauss claimed in *Tristes Tropiques* that when he was doing research among the Nambikwara in the 1930s, he heard observations similar to those heard by Montaigne four centuries earlier; the "civilized countries," he notes ironically, "have shown less constancy in their political philosophy."[60] I am less interested in Montaigne himself, however, than in his Tupinambá interlocutors. What is their place in the history of philosophy? Are they the subjects of theory, or only its object? Were they proto-anthropological "native informants," or were they theorizing pre-revolutionary France as much as Montaigne was theorizing pre- and post-conquest America? And were they not the precursors of all the indigenous social critics of the future? And what form must philosophy take? Must it be expressed in writing? Can it be embodied in speech, in practice and attitude, in music and dance and performance, or in our own era, in stand-up humor and music? And in this sense, did not the Tupi refusal to be impressed by European social systems constitute a form of ideology critique? And when a contemporary indigenous non-literate person makes philosophical or political observations that are recorded or videotaped and posted on YouTube, is that not the equivalent of writing in a poststructuralist sense? Must the Indian in question actually know how to write, or only speak eloquently?

From France Antartique to the Carib Revolution

The slogan partially referenced in my subheading—"Tupi or not Tupi"—as any student of Brazilian modernism knows, comes from Brazilian modernist poet-dramatist-philosopher-provocateur Oswald de Andrade and his 1928 *Anthropophagic*

Manifesto: "Tupi or not Tupi: that is the question."[61] In a recombinant version of the most famous phrase from *Hamlet*, Oswald asks whether Brazilian artists should be proud Tupi "Indians" or be servile mimic-men parroting metropolitan culture.[62] De Andrade favored a kind of aggressive artistic gluttony, by which Brazilian artists would devour and Brazilianize the European avant-garde through a metaphorically cannibalistic process. He reverse-engineered cannibalism, along the very name of the dark diabolized other, the ultimate marker of difference in a coded opposition of rational and irrational, civilized and savage, into a metaphor for a broad cultural revolution.[63] The point was not the eating but the eating together. Cultural "anthropophagy" was proposed as a way to absorb the techniques and information of the super-developed countries in order to avoid being swallowed up by them. As shown by anthropological research, anthropophagy among the Tupinambá went beyond its literal, "cannibal" sense: here, eating the Other was imbued with powerful symbolism. To eat someone was to absorb and digest the other, to constitute oneself from alterity. To create something new, Oswald, like Deleuze's philosopher, had to adopt a point of view that led to what Renato Sztutman calls "self-metamorphosis."[64]

Just as the Tupinambá Indians devoured their enemies in order to appropriate their force, Brazilian artists and intellectuals were to digest "Western" cultural products and innovations and exploit them as raw material for a new synthesis, thus turning the imposed culture back, transformed, against the colonizer. Well-read in the primary sources in the sixteenth-century literature, de Andrade references key figures such as Villegagnon, Hans Staden, and Cunhambebe. Radicalizing the Enlightenment valorization of indigenous freedom, modernism highlighted aboriginal communalism as a past-ward looking as well as an anticipatory model for a society free of hierarchy. As had occurred with the European philosophes, philo-indigenism enabled an anthropological critique of the axiomatic foundations of the dominant civilization. Here too there is a past and a contemporary French connection, both in the sense that de Andrade was aware of the 1920s French avant-garde journal *Le Cannibal*, and a contemporary connection in that French literary theorist/cultural critic René Girard invokes cannibalism as a foundational example in his *Violence and the Sacred* (1972), where he develops his mimetic scapegoat theory about the primal source of all religions. To prove the unity of all religious rituals, Girard looks to the most notorious example of ritual cannibalism—that of the Tupinambá. For Girard, the victim of cannibalism is both loved and hated: hated as an enemy in war and loved as the source of tribal unity. Girard writes:

> Sacrifice plays a crucial role in these societies, and the problem of ritual substitution concerns the entire community. The victim is not a substitute for some particularly endangered individual, nor is he offered up to so some individual of particularly bloodthirsty temperament, rather, the sacrifice serves to protect the entire community from its own violence; it prompts the entire community to choose victims outside itself.[65]

Viveiros de Castro sees it in a different, more generous light: "what was assimilated from the victim was the signs of his alterity ... a point of view on the self. Cannibalism and the form of war with which it is bound up in a paradoxical movement of reciprocal self-determination through the point of view of the enemy."[66]

Anthropologist Carlos Fausto speaks of Tupi cannibalistic warfare as "productive consumption," and a form of "family-producing" or "familiarizing predation," in that it was a consumption "devoutly to be wished," a way of fusing the victim with the killer in order to strengthen the killer and the tribe by integrating the victim. Fausto gives various examples: the Arawate who perform "ontological devoration" and the Curripaco who transform the femur of the victim into sacred flutes to appropriate the "breath" of the devoured warrior.[67] The victim was adopted to become part of the family of the enemy, including by generating children with the "enemy," thus swelling their numbers and strength. While "modern wars" objectified the enemy, Fausto points out, indigenous warfare subjectified the enemy. Fausto hastens to add that he is not trying to justify or prettify indigenous violence crime, but only to say, updating Montaigne, that there is more harm in massacring an abstract demonized enemy than in devouring a single subjectivized individual after he has been killed.

Like Oswald, but apparently unaware of his work, Girard sees cannibalism as a religious act, whereby the victim had to completely integrated into the same group that would subsequently sacrifice him. The nine months were required to guarantee complete integration, only that way would his sacrifice reconstitute Tupinambá society as an integral whole. Brazilian literary/cultural critic and Girard's former student João Cezar de Castro Rocha elaborates on the connection between de Andrade and Girard by speaking about the "uncanny and even fascinating relationship between [Girard's] mimetic theory and the topic of cannibalism."[68] For Castro Rocha, cannibalism is a "*Weltanschauung*, a complex cultural system, anti-Cartesian par excellence." He quotes Girard: "Any consumption of meat, whether human or animal, must be interpreted in the light of mimetic desire, an authentic cannibalism of the spirit."[69] The Indianist Jose de Alencar, Castro Rocha points out, had made a similar connection: "Human sacrifice signified the signal glory reserved for illustrious warriors and distinguished men when they were imprisoned … the remains of the enemy subsequently were converted into a kind of sacramental bread that strengthened the warriors. It was not vengeance but a kind of communion of the flesh, through which occurred a transfusion of heroism."[70] In metaphorical terms, anthropophagy was a form and theory of transtextuality as a source of creativity, but in a neo-colonial situation. For Peggy Sanday, "cannibalism" is less a literal act of eating than a vehicle for "non-digestible messages which have to do with the preservation, the regeneration, and the foundation of the cultural order."[71]

In *Les Origines de la culture* (2004), Castro Rocha points out, Girard provides an even more powerful synthesis by applying the principles of mimetic theory to history, which moves "*from* ritual cannibalism *to* the Eucharist."[72] He quotes Girard's words: "Primitive cannibalism is religion, and the Eucharist recapitulates this history from alpha to omega."[73] Castro Rocha translates the equation as follows: "*from* a social order founded on scapegoating and sacrifice *to* a social order grounded on the defence of the victim and acknowledgement of the other."[74] But for Castro Rocha, an even deeper affinity links the two thinkers, related to Oswald's concept of anthropophagy as a key to understanding. As Oswald famously stated in the 1928 manifesto: "I am only interested in what is not mine. Law of Man. Law of the anthropophagite." In sum the anthropophage needs the other to shape his own self. For Castro Rocha, "the anthropophagite cannot simply *be*, he can only *become* through the constant assimilation of otherness," as "a kind of inventive appropriation of alterity."⁷⁵

De Andrade, who once signed a manifesto with the name "Marxillaire"—a combination of (Karl) Marx, Apollinaire, and "maxillary" (as pertaining to the devouring jaw), linked the derisive laughter of the Brazilian Indian to Enlightenment social critique and to the later trend of Marxism. In two manifestos—"Manifesto of Brazilwood Poetry" (1924) and "Cannibalist Manifesto" (1928)—de Andrade proposed the Brazilian native as the key to an artistic practice at once nationalist and cosmopolitan, nativist and modern, and more important for my purposes, as the key to an alternative social model. Whereas a certain ethnocentric discourse had projected the Carib as a diacritical token of Europe's moral superiority, de Andrade invoked the Tupi Indian as a revolutionary figure, linked to the French revolution but also surpassing that revolution. In short, de Andrade linked what he discerned as the political culture of the indigenous peoples both to the more radical wing of the French Enlightenment and to the European and Brazilian avant-gardes. In a witty upturning of the usual "progressive" stagism—implicit in the buried militarism of an "avant-garde" that sees the European avant-garde as "ahead" of the rest—de Andrade declared surrealism, with self-mocking solemnity, as "the most important *pre*-Anthropophagic movement," an indirect jab, perhaps, against Hegelian-style stagism in the accounts of artistic history. In short, he "provincialized" European High Art.

We need not idealize de Andrade as an unblemished hero. His manifestoes embedded some retrograde concepts such as the "pre-logical mentality," and his philo-indigenism remained that of a member of the Paulista coffee aristocracy, for whom indigenism was a cost-free provocation. (His membership in the Communist Party in the 1930s, in this sense, was more dangerous to his health.) While designed to *"epater le bourgeois Paulista,"* his indigenism offered symbolic solidarity with indigenous thought, but no concrete alliance with the actually existing Indians then being "civilized" by the Rondon expedition. (To be fair, it is hard to imagine how such an alliance could have taken place within the social conditions of 1920s Brazil.) In a sense, Brazilian modernism, despite its scorn for the romantic sentimentality about the "good Indian," remained tethered to a safely remote and symbolic Indian, made to bear, once again, the burden of allegory. The metaphor, furthermore, can be coopted into a safe provocation, a metaphor for intertextuality or consumerism. In the 1940s and 1950s, as we shall see, de Andrade deepened his relation to indigenous thought, especially in terms of feminism. And his call for a "Carib Revolution," as we shall see, is ultimately more relevant to the present.

De Andrade was not always taken seriously partly because his thought was expressed in aphoristic jokes and puns, for example by calling the issues of his journal, in line with his cannibalistic "eating" of philosophy, "dentitions" instead of "editions," or by claiming that the problems of Brazil were not "ontological" but "odontological." Yet his indigeno-modernism, a decade before Cesaire's *Cahier d'un Retour au Pays Natal*, offered the most radical version of the modernisms of the period. Some present-day indigenous activists in Brazil actually cite de Andrade's concepts. Naiara Tukano, in a lecture in London (available on YouTube), quotes his witticism that instead of the

Europeans dressing the Indians, the Indians undressed the Europeans. In other words, when the French offered the Tupinambá European clothing, they scorned it and used it only to wave like banners in the air; the Europeans, meanwhile, came to wear native tangas on beaches. Ailton Krenak, similarly, cites de Andrade's aphorism that "before Columbus discovered Brazil, Brazil [i.e. indigenous Brazil] had discovered happiness," which resonates with his own experience as a Krenak, who began as a happy child living close to the Rio Doce but then spent much of his youth fleeing with his father from white invaders.

On his visit to Paris in 1922, Oswald described the impact of the European avant-garde movements, in surprisingly racialized terms, as the "destruction of the respectable behaviour of the *white*, supposedly civilized adult."[76] After this early intuition of what would later be called "critical whiteness studies," Oswald took avant-garde ideas in completely new directions. While the European avant-gardes, with the exception of the Surrealists (and later the Situationists), were not terribly concerned with colonialism, for Oswald, colonialism was at the very kernel of his preoccupations. Indeed, in the present day, when the word "postcolonial" has been eclipsed (or better supplemented) by the term "*de*colonial" favored by the Coloniality/Modernity scholars, it is striking that Oswald anticipated this discursive mutation over six decades earlier. Oswald's manifestoes employed the very same pre-fix "*de*" in his manifestos—literally calling for "*De*-Cabralization," "*De*-Columbusization," and "*De-Vespuccization*." In this same spirit, de Andrade planned for "the First World Conference on Anthropophagy" in 1922 to be held on October 11, in memory of the day before Columbus's landfall in 1492. Brazilian anthropophagy in this sense could be seen as a precocious counter-discourse to a still regnant colonialism and neo-colonialism.

The European-indigene encounter, for de Andrade, deeply shaped the global movement of ideas in the world: "To know that on the other side of the world had been glimpsed a kind of human being, knowing neither sin nor redemption, theology nor inferno, produced not only utopian dreams … but also a general shock in the consciousness and culture of Europe."[77] De Andrade reenvisioned the Huguenot corpus through the prism of artistic modernism, Marxist critique, and pro-indigenous philosophy. In his later work, de Andrade steered away from the sensationalist metaphor of cannibalism. In *A Crise da Filosofia Messianica* (The Crisis of Messianic Philosophy, 1950), he strengthened the gynocentric dimension of his avant-garde ideas. The modernists had spoken already in the 1920s of "*Pindorama*"—the putative indigenous Tupi matriarchy—as the original native society.[78] And unlike many avant-garde movements, Brazilian modernism included some powerful women artists/activists, notably two painters, Anita Malfatti and Tarsila do Amaral. The latter often treated anthropophagic themes, as with her classic paintings "Pau Brasil" (1924) and "Abaporu" (1928), whose title combines two Tupi words "*aba*" (man) and "*pora*" (people) and "*u*" (eat), i.e. "people-eater."

In his critique of Messianism and his praise of Indian-style leisure, de Andrade, already in 1950, anticipated a number of later intellectual currents: Marcuse's ideas about a post-productivist leisure society, Baudrillard's critique, in *The Mirror of Production*, of a productivism shared by both capitalist and communist models, and Lyotard's "postmodern" diagnosis of the "end of metanarratives." But, unlike these writers, de Andrade linked his analysis to what he intuited to be a coherent line of indigenous social thought. To call Oswald's philosophy a "post-colonialism" *avant la lettre* would be to underestimate its originality, in that Oswald's conceptualizations on one level cut deeper even than the postcolonial critique movement that began in the 1980s. Postcolonial studies usually emphasized the latter-day colonialisms/ imperialisms such as the French, the British, and the American, which reached their zenith in the nineteenth and early twentieth centuries, sidestepping the foundational imperialism—the Pax Iberica that made all the other imperialisms (Pax Brittanica, Pax Americana) possible through land theft, the enslavement of native Brazilians and Africans, and the massive transfer of mineral wealth to European powers.

In comparative terms, I would argue that Brazilian modernism—often unmentioned in the thousands of books on artistic modernism—is the movement that actually has the most to say to our present circumstances, for a number of reasons: (1) in its anti-colonial thrust, Brazilian modernism was the least Eurocentric of the modernist movements; (2) seven decades *before* the UN recognition of the rights of indigenous peoples, Oswald placed the indigenous question at the center of the modernist project; (3) Oswald's emphasis on native communal ownership of land recalled Marx and Engels on "primitive Communism" while anticipating the contemporary emphasis on the "commons"; (4) Oswald questioned "progress" by suggesting that indigenous Brazil had already enjoyed a past-perfect utopia before Columbus; (5) while most European avant-gardes were highly masculinist, Oswaldian modernism was at least *symbolically*, if not always experientially, feminist. More importantly for our purposes, Oswald, like many indigenist feminists in North America, linked feminism to indigenous culture and matriarchy as embodied in what he imagined to be the Tupi Ur-matriarchy of *Pindorama*; (6) in *The Crisis of Messianic Philosophy*, in line with later feminist analyses, Oswald denounced "patriarchal Messianism" as the *primum mobile* of oppression in the world;[79] (7) Oswald was post-Marxist in his friendly critique of Marxism, which shared with capitalism its penchant for a productivism harmful to human and environmental health, thus anticipating indigenous critiques of ecocidal productivism by many indigenous critics;[80] (8) Oswald anticipated Marcuse's idea of leisure as a realm of freedom rather than necessity in his indigenously oriented praise of *sacer-docio*—etymologically "sacred leisure"—as opposed to the puritanical and capitalist angelization of productive labor;[81] lastly, (9) Oswald called for an all-embracing revolution that was at once social, political, literary, religious, and cultural. In his Anthropophagic manifesto, Oswald traces a lineage of revolutionary thought that begins with France Antartique, moves to the French Revolution, on to the Soviet Revolution, and the Surrealist Revolution, to what he calls the Caraiba or Carib Revolution:

Filiation.
The contact with caraiba brazil [i.e. the indigenous peoples of Brazil].
The place where Villegagnon landed [i.e. the Protestant founder of the French colony]
Montaigne. The natural man. Rousseau.

From the French revolution to romanticism, to the Bolshevik revolution, to the surrealist revolution to Kayserling's technized Indian.[82]

This astonishingly dense entry evokes four centuries of social and intellectual history linking indigenous social thought and praxis to progressive movements in Europe, culminating in the figure of the high-tech Indian who synthesizes indigenous social thought with western science and technology. Oswald's aphorism summarizes the trajectory traced in this chapter and in the book as a whole. In its emphasis on an aboriginal Tupi matriarchy, in its non-instrumental approach to Nature, and in its celebration of indigenous communal social arrangements, I would argue, Oswald's modernism has much more to say of relevance to contemporary society than the masculinist, elitist, and often ethnocentric provocations of an Andre Breton or a Salvador Dali.[83] De Andrade's proposed lineage offers a paradoxical temporality in that it moves through a series of progressive changes—apparently in conformity with a stagist dialectics—only to proceed to final stages rooted in a millennial past that preceded the initial events. The road to the future, paradoxically, lies in returning to the indigenous past and transmuting that past into an altered present and future. As a Maori film title—*Nga Ra o Mua*—suggests, it is a matter of *Walking Backwards into the Future*.[84]

For conservative thinkers, Oswald's dream of an indigenized utopianism seemed a kind of social and ideological nightmare. A decade after Oswald's manifestoes, Afonso Arinos de Melo Franco, a jurist, historian, journalist, diplomat, politician, and later Member of the Academy of Letters, researched European intellectual history while living in Geneva, a key city both for the history of France Antartique and for the history of religion and philosophy. (Jean-Jacques Rousseau, for example, was closely linked to Geneva.) A conservative not at all invested in "promoting" the Indian, Melo Franco discerned the same revolutionary lineage claimed by Oswald, whereby indigenous voices catalyzed what would come to be known as class struggle and social revolution. In his 1937 book *The Brazilian Indian and the French Revolution: The Brazilian Origins of the Theory of Natural Goodness*, Melo Franco argued that ideas about the Brazilian native inspired French philosophers and the French revolution.[85] Rousseau's theory of natural goodness, inspired by the Brazilian Indian, helped generate the French revolution. Melo Franco's narrative recapitulates some of what was said by the Modernistas, but from the opposite perspective, in that he was denouncing the subversive appropriation of the Brazilian Indian by the French Revolution. What is for Melo Franco a "false conception" of a natural state of indigenous goodness spread its "corrosive" influence around Europe through Enlightenment thinkers like Rousseau, Montesquieu, Voltaire, Diderot, and Abby Reynal, all very much inspired by the free and self-determining Indian from Brazil.[86] For Melo Franco, the sixteenth-century travel literature by Thévet, Jean de Léry, and Hans Staden furnished the raw materials for philosophers like Montaigne and Jean-Jacques Rousseau, who weaponized their accounts as a means of attacking European authoritarianism. Rousseau gave Montaigne's ideas political efficacy, thus helping foment the French revolution. In the French Constitutional Assembly of 1789, the representatives of the left were avid readers of Montesquieu, Voltaire, Rousseau, and Diderot, all of whom spoke of the natives of the Americas. Enlightenment concepts like "freedom," "equality," and "fraternity" became inextricably linked to the "noble savage" and "natural man" and "natural goodness," pointing to the deeply alluring, but for Mello Franco "factitious," ideal of a more egalitarian and free society.[87]

As what Sergio Paulo Rouanet calls the "seismograph" of his time, Melo Franco finds those he paternalistically calls "our Indians" everywhere in the French Renaissance and Enlightenment. While he ridicules some of the early fantastical European accounts of quadrupedes, backward-walking men, and single-breasted Amazons, Melo Franco ultimately develops a fundamentally conservative argument in which he conjoins a genre-based critique—wherein negatively connoted works like "legends," "fables," and "romance"—with a political critique, where the operative put-downs are "ideological," "revolutionary," and "socialist" to disqualify pro-indigenous thought. For Melo Franco, Indians represent a menacing excess of democracy in the form of socialism. Melo Franco's central political narrative posits a French Revolution poisoned at the root by the factitiousness of its premise—the idealized Brazilian Indian as exemplar of freedom. Rather than prove the falsity of the pro-Indian view, he simply rejects it as absurd on its face. In the end, he is not interested in the Indian per se—and as a member of the elite, quite possibly the heir to lands taken from native people—but only in speaking ill of the revolutionary uses to which the Indian had been put. In this sense, Melo Franco was aligning himself with the philosophical backlash within Europe against what we have been calling indigenous critique.

The discourse of the Indian as "exemplar of freedom" also circulated widely in North America. The writings of the creole elites of the Americas, like those of North American revolutionaries, portray Indians as freer and less oppressed than Europeans in a society where every Indian was "his own master." For Rousseau, in his "Discourses on Inequality," the Indians were never persuaded of the superiority of European culture, while the Europeans who came to know native culture preferred it and were unwilling to return to "civilization." The frequently phobic reaction toward those who "went native" and became "white Indians," in this sense, was perhaps symptomatic of a fear about the precariousness of the European conviction of enjoying a superior form of social life. In his satirical novella, *L'ingenu* (1767), sometimes translated in English as "The Sincere Huron," or "The Huron, Pupil of Nature," in English, Voltaire tells the story of a Huron "child of nature" who, after having crossed the Atlantic to England, crosses into Brittany, France, in the 1690s. Having grown up outside of European culture, he begins to see the world through Huron eyes and, like Montaigne's Tupinambá, finds French social practices cruel, perverse, and unnatural. After his first confession, the Huron insists on the basic principle of reciprocity, for example asking that the priest confess as well. Through a *reductio ad absurdam* of the implications of the Christian catechism, Voltaire has a ventriloquized Huron destroy the shaky religious foundations of dominant French society. These native-inspired ideas also filtered down to the French masses through plays like Delisle de la Drevetiere's *Arlequin Sauvage* (1721) where a young Parisian woman flees to America with her Native American lover to live in indigenous freedom. The play inspired Rousseau's operetta about the "Discovery," where Columbus, sword in hand, sings a command to the Indians: "Lose your Liberty!"

From the French *Philosophes* to the American Revolution

In French Canada, meanwhile, two centuries after Jean de Lery's *Voyage*, in 1773, Louis-Armand de Lom d'Arce, the "Baron de Lahontan," intellectual heir of Montaigne, published a two-volume set of letters about Canada and its natives, based on his stay with them from 1683 to 1694, and eventually learned to speak Huron and Algonquin. Lahontan praises the native peoples as freer than Europeans in their lives and social arrangements and as more egalitarian in social and in sexual relations. Like Montaigne, Lahontan describes Native Americans visiting France as "teasing us with the faults and disorders they observed in our towns … and [laughing] at the difference of ranks … they brand us for slaves … alleging that we degrade ourselves in subjecting ourselves to one man who possesses all the power, and is bound by no law above his own will."[88] Like Davi Kopenawa two centuries later, Lahontan describes Indians as devoid of social classes and lacking in envy because they do not believe in private property. In his multivolume *New Voyages to North America* Lahontan includes a Diderot-style "dialogue" with a fictional Huron character Adario. Lahontan plays the faux naïf who defends the metropolitan status quo, while Adario excoriates western wealth inequalities, the oppression of women, and the cruelty of the justice system, evils which have as their root the valorization of private property. Yet Lahontan's verbal advocacy of the *indigene* did not extend into his real-life choices and affiliations. In practical realpolitik terms, as Sankar Muthu points out, Lahontan argued for a French divide-and-conquer strategy which would play off the various native nations against one another.[89] In any case, Lahontan's writings about Canada, like Jean de Léry's about Brazil, became a source text for the philosophers. The Indigenophilia of the *philosophes* back in France, meanwhile, also led to encounters in the flesh: Voltaire met with indigenous North Americans at Fontainebleau in 1725, while Rousseau had a similar encounter in London around 1725.[90] Georges Sioui Wendayete's "Amerindian Autohistory" cites Lahontan's writing as additional evidence for his own views of Wendat society as deeply democratic.[91] Graeber and Wengrow discuss the figure of Kandiaronk—the source for Lahonto's character Adario, as a Wendat philosopher-statesman and key strategist of the Wendat Confederacy, a coalition of four Iroquoian-speaking peoples, who ran logical circles around European representatives "by anticipating their logic, interests, blind spots and reactions."[92]

That major European intellectuals look backward to antiquity and early modern monasticism "rather than sideways to non-Western forms of life" is for Robert Nichols "symptomatic of a studious Eurocentrism." Millions of indigenous people, he adds, "have long cultivated a deep practice of care as counterdispossession and, unlike Roman law or medieval monasticism, these indigenous forms of life endure in the present."[93] If Europeans did not learn about freedom from the native peoples, from whom might they have learned it? Ideas of freedom and equality were anticipated in the popular performance of carnivalesque overturnings portrayed by Bakhtin. "What is suspended [in carnival]," Bakhtin writes, "first of all is hierarchical structure and all the forms of reverence, piety, and connected with it—that is, everything resulting from sociohierarchical inequality, or any other form of inequality among people."[94] Greek and Roman "democracies" provided partial models, and inspired the architecture of Washington institutions, but Roman democracy was based on slavery, so their freedom was limited to a certain class. As Jack Weatherford points out, "freedom does not have a long pedigree in the Old World."[95] In the Europe dominated by monarchs, freedom usually meant "freedom from," the freedom of a tribe or nation or city *from* the domination of another group or master. But the idea of an internal, immanent, freedom, at once individual and societal, of indigenous nations was unknown to Europeans. Many European commentators, from many different countries, were amazed at indigenous notions of personal freedom that did not depend on wealth or the State. Freedom, in sum, was not a uniquely Greco-Roman concept revived by French philosophers and put into practice by American statesmen; it was rooted in the soil of indigenous critique.[96]

The motif of the Indian as exemplar of liberty also formed part of the discursive atmosphere of the American revolution, partially because the revolutionaries were avid readers of the philo-indigenous *philosophes*, but also because they "read," and literally conversed with, the natives themselves. While the French philosophes saw indigenous North Americans through an exoticizing haze and a revolutionary political agenda, the philosophically inclined American Founding Fathers had a much more direct experience of indigenous people and their social and political systems. They had diplomatic exchanges with the Indians, traded with them, and were influenced by them, even if—and this point is essential—they ultimately dispossessed them; warm affect was not accompanied by substantive policies; discourse and Realpolitik were completely out of synch.

Innumerable indigenous and non-indigenous scholars have detailed the indigenous influence on social thought in what became the United States. The revolutionary Thomas Paine repeatedly lauded the indigenous societies as a model for a social organization which avoided the central problem of western societies—the simultaneous co-dependent production of immense wealth and shocking poverty. He also objected to western notions of ownership of land, since in nature there is "no such thing as landed property."[97] Benjamin Franklin championed indigenous social systems. Charles Thomson, secretary of the Continental, recommended indigenous political institutions to Thomas Jefferson when Jefferson was writing *Notes on the State of Virginia* and was adopted as a full member of the Delaware Nation. The decision to adopt new states into the Union was modeled on the Iroquois Leagues' custom of expanding their Council to include new members. Even the idea of impeachment, inconceivable under the divine-right monarchies of Europe—one does not impeach a King or Queen—was modeled on the Iroquois system of removing incompetent rulers. In cultural terms, Washington and Jefferson compiled grammars and lexicons of Indian languages. As a publisher, Benjamin Franklin printed up the proceedings of the treaty councils between the English and the Haudenosaunee. In a letter to John Adams, Jefferson wrote of his "attachment and commiseration" for Indians, recalling that "before the revolution, they were in the habit of coming often and in great numbers to the seat of government where I was very much with them."[98]

Like many members of the creole elites of the Americas, and like some European philosophers, Jefferson erected a hierarchy of Red over Black. In contrast with his racist opinions about blacks, Jefferson professed belief in the intellectual equality of

Native Americans: "the proofs of genius given by the Indians place them on a level with the whites ... I have seen some thousands myself, and conversed much with them ... I believe the Indian to be in body and mind equal to the white man."[99] Indeed, Jefferson was on a superficial level an *avant la lettre* critic of Eurocentrism in that he lamented the fact that traditional university curricula focused only on Europe, while neglecting the natural history and cultures of the Native Americans. The curriculum he designed for the University of Virginia included courses in Native American cultures and languages, but Jefferson's expressed cultural respect for Indians and their intelligence was never matched, as we know, with a consequential real-world respect for indigenous sovereignty and land rights.

Many of the superficially pro-indigenous attitudes of some of the Founding Fathers had to do with relations with the Iroquois (Haudenosaunee) Confederacy, the political expression of a multination alliance formed by the Seneca, Cayuga, Onondaga, Oneida, Mohawk, and later the Tuscarora communities, situated between areas dominated by the French in the St. Lawrence Valley and the English on the Eastern Seaboard. In contradiction to Hobbes's racist speculations about native tribes living in a brutish "state of nature," the Haudenosaunee "Great Law of Peace" (Gayaneshakgowa) established the League's Great Council, with its fifty "*royaneh*" (male religious-political leaders), each representing the female-led clans of the confederated nations. Robin Wall Kimmerer writes of the Onandaga as a rarity, "a Native nation that has never surrendered its original government ... nor compromised its status as a sovereign nation."[100] The Iroquois League existed long before the American Revolution began—estimates range from AD 1142 to around 1650—what is clear is that the League had put into practice, in historian Bruce E. Johansen's words, "concepts of popular participation and natural rights that the European savants had thus far only theorized."[101] The "Law of Peace" formed a clear contrast with European political modes: instead of despotism, popular participation; instead of the censorship that sent philosophers like Voltaire to jail, freedom of expression; instead of masculine domination, female participation. They also practiced what Thomas Paine theorized as communal ownership of the land. In nature, as Paine puts it, there is "no such thing as landed property." Here he was echoing Rousseau's famous denunciations of private ownership of land—"You are lost if you forget that the fruits are everyone's and the Earth no one's"[102]—and anticipates the anarchism of nineteenth-century thinkers like Proudhon who asserted that "through the land the plundering of man began, and in the land it has rooted its foundations."[103]

Building both on oral tradition and on a long tradition of scholarship, native Yamasee scholar Donald A. Grinde Jr. argued in his 1977 book *The Iroquois and the Founding of the American Nation* that the authors of the US constitution partially drew the concept of a federal government from the example of the Six Nations Iroquois Confederation. In 1982, Bruce Johansen published *Forgotten Founders: Benjamin Franklin, the Iroquois, and the Rationale for the American Revolution*. Within a few years, both authors became caught up in the "culture wars" that pitted multiculturalists against the conservative right. The conservatives derided the thesis of such books, usually without reading them, as simply ridiculous, apparently unaware that even such an exalted figure as President John F. Kennedy had supported the same Iroquois-influence thesis. In a 1960 preface to William Brandon's *American Heritage Book of*

Indians, Kennedy wrote that "[t]he League of the Iroquois inspired Benjamin Franklin to copy it in planning the federation of States."[104] And on the 200th anniversary of the US Constitution, Congress passed a joint resolution affirming the League of the Iroquois as a constitutional model and acknowledged its guiding principles as indebted to the Indian founding fathers and governing mothers.[105] In a sense, this scholarship offers concrete evidence of Oswald de Andrade's poetic intuition that without indigenous people the world would not even have enjoyed the republican revolutions "meagre Rights of Man."

A decade before John F. Kennedy, the distinguished American legal scholar Felix Cohen, jurist, scholar, and chief architect of the Indian Reorganization Act in 1934, had made the same point. Cohen defended a basic right to self-determination.[106] Cohen organized and wrote much of the *Handbook of Federal Indian Law*, which consisted of 46 volumes of detailed information on tribes, treaties, and laws.[107] Cohen attacked myths such as the "Vanishing Indian" and the "Nomadic Indian," while pointing to aspects of indigenous culture adopted by non-indigenous Americans like the use of tobacco, corn, quinine, and the like. And he called attention to the unpayable debt to Indians for all the harm done in the name of land and domination. In words that still resonate, he wrote: "The Indian's hair was cut, his dances forbidden, his oil lands, timber lands, and grazing lands were disposed of by Indian agents and the Indian Commissioners for whom the magic word 'wardship' made up for any lack of statutory authority." In our hearts, he wrote:

> [W]e know that Indians are not only our fellow-citizens; we know that our land was theirs before it was ours. Because we know that we never fully paid the Indians for what we received from them, we continue to salve our consciences by offering them hospitals, educational benefits, limited tax exemptions, and other aids to better living just as we extend similar bounties to veterans whom we tore from their homes and careers and sent to fight our nation's wars.[108]

Like Oswald de Andrade, Lévi-Strauss, and Melo Franco, Cohen too expressed admiration for a long indigenous-inflected social tradition thought going back to Bartolome de las Casas, Montaigne, and Rousseau. The "distinctive political ideas of American life," Cohen argued, emerged out of a "rich Indian democratic tradition" whereby

> [u]niversal suffrage for women as well as for men, the pattern of states within a state that we call federalism, the habit of treating chiefs as servants of the people instead of as their masters, the insistence that the community must respect the diversity of men and the diversity of their dreams—all these things were part of the American way of life before Columbus arrived.[109]

Cohen was thus echoing what many Native Americans themselves had said (and still say). Chief Luther Standing Bear (Lakota, Sioux) similarly suggested that the United States rejuvenate itself by recognizing a "native school of thought," a school which had developed a sophisticated set of checks and balances to prevent any one Indian nation from dominating the others.¹¹⁰ While Eurocentric discourse often imagines that the West "rescues" native women from their cruel and patriarchal native masters, in fact Europeans were surprised by the degree of power exercised by clan women in largely matrilineal societies. Women in some native societies held pivotal positions and could nominate men for positions of leadership but also impeach them for misconduct. While the Founding Fathers borrowed some procedural features of Indian institutional life, they never borrowed its egalitarian gender codes or its reverential non-proprietary attitude toward the land, or its richly suggestive cosmologies.

What was traditional for indigenous peoples became revolutionary in a Western context. Benjamin Franklin, in 1744, had printed the words of Canassatego, the chief of the Iroquois Confederacy, who explicitly urged the colonists to adopt the Iroquois model. Speaking on behalf of the six nations, Canassatego lectured the assembled colonial governors on Iroquois concepts of unity:

> Our wise forefathers established Union and Amity between the Five Nations. This has made us formidable; this has given us great Weight and Authority with our neighbouring Nations. We are a powerful Confederacy; and by your securing the same methods our wise forefathers have taken, you will acquire such Strength and power. Therefore, whatever befalls you, never fall out with one another.¹¹¹

The ironies here are excruciatingly multiple. First, the Union did imitate the Iroquois and did acquire "Weight and Authority" but then used this same Weight and Authority to "weigh down" on the neck of indigenous nations. Second, the United Statesians did in fact "fall out with one another," in the form of a bitter Civil War. In the case of Benjamin Franklin and the Iroquois, we find a trilateral cultural encounter between France, the United States, and the indigenous Americas, analogous in some ways to the earlier trilateral encounter between France, Brazil, and indigenous Tupi. A white "American" like Ben Franklin, very much influenced by French Enlightenment ideas and a beloved diplomat in Paris, including presumably their ideas about the "natural [Indian] man," actually encounters and is influenced by Native Americans like those praised by the French philosophes, while at the same time belonging to a political formation that dispossessed indigenous people.

In 1754, Franklin presented his Albany Plan for the colonial Union, advocating a federal system and a one-chamber legislature. Iroquois were invited to Philadelphia to observe debates over the Declaration of Independence in 1775. "It would be a very strange thing," Benjamin Franklin wrote in a 1751 letter to James Parker: "if six Nations of Ignorant Savages should be capable of forming a Scheme for such an Union. And be able to execute it in such a manner, as that it has subsisted ages, and appears indissoluble, and yet a like Union should be impracticable for ten or a dozen English colonies."¹¹² Franklin observed the Iroquois Grand Council at Onondaga, noting that it was a federal republic governed by local and national councils which selected leaders by clan-based consensus. Not only did the Iroquois practice peace among its constituent nations, they also recommended the same practices of peaceful relations for a Republic about to be born. Rather than the wild fantasies that the Right proclaimed them to be, the Johansen and Grinde books about Indian influence were scrupulously researched and cautious in their conclusions. Native peoples put into practice concepts of social participation and natural rights—popular nomination, right of recall, women's suffrage, separation of powers, religious tolerance—that Europeans were only beginning to glimpse theoretically.

For Jefferson and Franklin, the "Indians," as Johansen puts it, "had what the colonists wanted: societies free of oppression and class stratification."[113] Indian leitmotifs such as the "Great Tree" and "Chain of Friendship" were absorbed into revolutionary nation-state discourse. The revolutionary hero Paul Revere cast a native Indian woman as America's first national symbol.[114] Indigenous tropes even made their way into American currency. Anticipating the "Indian-head" nickel used from 1913 to 1938, and the Sacagawea Golden Dollar minted in 2000, the image emblazoned on the US dollar bill (in use since 1876) showing the national eagle, a sacred animal and figure for protection, clutching a bundle of arrows was drawn from the Iroquois Confederacy—a metaphor for the paradox of federal unity whereby "many arrows" (i.e. many states or nations) could all fit within a single quiver. Even the eagle as a symbol associated with "foresight, prudence, wisdom, and ... sovereignty, comes from native culture."[115] But despite the careful scholarship, the thesis of Iroquois influence was rejected out of hand by conservatives as simply outrageous on its face. Imagine! Indian political thought! Imagine, Indians contributing to American political culture! Yet for many indigenous peoples it has long been, to coin a phrase, a self-evident truth.

Treaties are legally binding contracts between sovereign nations that establish those nations' political and economic relations. Article Six of the US Constitution holds that treaties "are the supreme law of the land" and the treaties mentioned in the Constitution have never been officially abrogated. (It is symptomatic that the present-day "strict constitutionalists" make no reference to the Treaties, or to Washington's hostility to "standing armies," or to the lack of any mention of corporations or of political parties.) Subsequently, the treaties were not abrogated, but they were undermined. As Thomas King points out, treaties were never gifts to the Indians; they were vehicles for the dominant society to consolidate the acquisition of land: "throughout the history of North America, every time Indians signed a treaty with Whites, Indians lost land."[116] Some indigenous activists say that if the Founding Fathers had adopted more aspects of the Law of Peace, with its 117 codicils, it might have saved the Republic from the kind of troubles that have plagued American history, for example by installing communal rather than private property.

If constitutionalism is seen from an aboriginal perspective, James Tully argues, "unnoticed aspects of its historical formation and current limitations can be brought to light."[117] Modern constitutionalism, Tully points out, developed over centuries around two forms of recognition—the equality of independent nation-states and the equality of individual citizens. But aboriginal nations have insisted that United Nations-style definitions need to be revised to take group rights and their situation into account. For thousands of years, before the arrival of Columbus, sovereign aboriginal nations had been governing themselves on the basis of their own traditions of interpretation. As Tully points out "aboriginal governments are an ancient form of direct democracy in which the people do not delegate their powers of war and peace to an institutionalized legislature and executive, as Europeans have done, they are not sovereign."[118] Indeed, republican constitutions cannot countenance the communal freedom and direct representation of native peoples, especially when those who designed the constitutions are at the same time trying to dispossess and disperse those same peoples.

The French Missions, Lévi-Strauss, and the Indian

Returning to the Franco-Brazilian-Indigenous connection, Melo Franco's book on the Brazilian Indian and the French Revolution was published in the period of the French Missions to Brazil, in a situation where the "Indian" again played a pivotal role. At the time, the founders of the University of São Paulo decided to strengthen the institution's intellectual quality by inviting prestigious French intellectuals to key positions. The result was a series of French "missions" (in 1934, 1935, and 1938). The word "mission," with its religious overtones, recalls both the early religious Jesuit missions in Brazil and the more secular nineteenth-century French "artistic missions" of 1816, when French artists like painter Jean-Baptiste Debret were invited by the court to establish the first school of arts in Brazil. From 1834 to 1839, in his *Voyage Pittoresque et Historique au Brésil, ou Séjour d'un Artiste Français au Brésil*, Debret produced many lithographs depicting, among other topics, the indigenous peoples. In the long view, the word also evokes the sublimated religiosity of the colonizing *"mission civilisatrice."* Some of the invited scholars, such as Roger Bastide in sociology and Lévi-Strauss in anthropology, were on the cusp of becoming world-renowned. The missions arrived in a situation where French culture had long enjoyed a certain hegemony among the elites—who were generally fluent in French—to the point that the visiting French professors could lecture in French without having to learn Portuguese.[119] Here, French cultural involvement was not compromised by a colonial taint, as it would have been in the context of North Africa, Southeast Asia, or even the West Indies, in the same period.

It was during this tropical *entre-deux-guerres* period that Lévi-Strauss went out in search of "Indians" and found himself in a "state of intense intellectual excitement," feeling as if he were reliving the adventures of the first European voyagers. Lévi-Strauss wrote consciously in the tradition of Jean de Léry and Rousseau, whom he called "the most ethnographic of the philosophers." Lévi-Strauss, who saw colonialism as the "original sin" of the West, wrote about both North and South American Indians, and while he did his fieldwork in Brazil in the 1930s, he did much of his reading in the "Americana" Division of the New York Public Library, where he recalled working side by side with another incarnation of the "indio tecnizado," in this case an Indian in a feathered headdress taking "notes with a Parker pen."[120]

Lévi-Strauss sketches out the same intellectual lineage as Oswald and Melo Franco, but unlike Melo Franco, he sees Indian social life as a legitimate alternative social model. Lévi-Strauss describes the indigenous people he meets as generally happy and cordial, with lively and "witty" minds. In the tenderness of couples with one another he discerns "an immense gentleness" and "the most moving and true kind of human tenderness."[121] Thus, we find a continuity of social praise from Jean de Léry to Lévi-Strauss. In *Tristes Tropiques* (1955), Lévi-Strauss claims that "it was the accounts of travellers such as Jean de Léry that began the anthropological awareness of modern times; it was their unintentional influence which set the political and moral philosophy of the renaissance on the road that *was to lead to the French revolution*"[122] (italics mine). Lévi-Strauss certainly knew about Oswald's ideas, given their wide circulation in São Paulo and especially at the University of São Paulo. Lévi-Strauss and his collaborator and wife Dina were friends of novelist/poet/ethnographer/musicologist Mario de Andrade and Lévi-Strauss called *Macunaíma* a "great novel."[123]

Much of what Lévi-Strauss says simply echoes what indigenous people had said about their own cultures as emphasizing "all our relations," to individuals, to animals, to nature, and to the earth. While Western culture, as Lévi-Strauss put it in *The View from Afar*, isolates "man from the rest of creation and [defines] too narrowly the boundaries separating him from other living beings,"[124] native culture sees all of life as part of a continuum, a point made both through the "embodied theory" of indigenous social praxis and through the expressed views of indigenous leaders and writers. While the Biblical tradition sees human beings as Lords of Creation, native thought sees human beings as collaborators rather than dominators of Nature.[125] Countless native writers and activists, both in North and South America, for example Ailton Krenak and Davi Kopenawa in Brazil and Vine Deloria Jr. in *God Is Red*, have made similar points. For Vine Deloria Jr., indigenous spiritual thought, unlike Christian doctrine, does not think of the natural world as corrupted or "beyond redemption." In formulations similar to those of Davi Kopenawa decades later, Deloria believes that "humans can change into animals and birds and that other species can change into human beings."[126]

Lévi-Strauss's hemispheric admiration for indigenous peoples extends to both North and South America, as he specifically mentions the "Hurons, Iroquois, Caribs, and Tupi whose example, through Montaigne, Rousseau, Voltaire, and Diderot, enriched the substance of what I was taught at school."[127] Frank Lestringant tells a similar story about the revolutionary role of the Indian:

> The colonial failure [France Antartique] became the point of departure for the profound shaking up of certitudes that would lead, after many detours and vicissitudes, to the recognition of the equality of individuals and peoples. Had the French colony not failed in 1560, Montaigne would not have written "Des Cannibales," nor would Jean-Jacques Rousseau have written the "Discourse on the Origin and Basis of Inequality among Men." The failure of France Antartique made possible a great success.[128]

Thus, the Brazilian conservative Melo Franco, the modernist provocateur Oswald, the French structuralist Lévi-Strauss, and the French historian Lestringant, all tell the same story, with distinct inflections, about the crucial role of indigenous freedom within socio-intellectual history.

In any case, Lévi-Strauss rejected the alienating gaze of racial superiority in favor of the affectionate regard toward the Indian that he discerned in Jean de Léry and Rousseau. In Lévi-Strauss's view, Rousseau substituted for the egocentric Cartesian "I think therefore I am" the more dialogical and empathetic "I identify with others, therefore I am." In *Tristes Tropiques*, Lévi-Strauss offered a caressing portrait of Brazilian

Indians—his photo-album-text *Saudades do Brasil* offers his own photographs of indigenous people literally caressing their spouses and their children. As a critical European intellectual and a Jew haunted by anti-Semitism, Lévi-Strauss mocked the Eurotropic mimicry of the Brazilian elite, with its passion for the latest Parisian intellectual fashions, especially when unaccompanied by any deeper knowledge about the antecedent histories that shaped the meanings of such fashions. (Brazilian academics sometimes joke that for Lévi-Strauss "*we* were the real savages.") In contrast to the hoary tradition of quasi-official Indianist sentimentality and assimilationist policies in Brazil, and in contrast to the clichés about beloved indigenous grandmothers, the French ethnographer noted quite the opposite—the aversion of the elites. The Brazilian ambassador in Paris assured Lévi-Strauss that Indians no longer existed, this only a decade or two after a time (1918) when maps of the state of São Paulo—a state as large as France itself—indicated that two-thirds of the territory had been or was currently inhabited by indigenous people. Exemplifying a purist tendency often critiqued in his work, Lévi-Strauss also registers his disappointment that the Tibaji Indians he meets are not "pure Indians." But in a later passage, he comes to terms with an inevitable hybridity, since "every society includes an element of impurity which seems incompatible with the norms which it proclaims."[129]

The Brazilian Indigene again entered the history of Western philosophy through Derrida's critiques of the logocentrism of both Rousseau and Lévi-Strauss. In the celebrated chapter of *Tristes Tropiques* on the "writing lesson," Lévi-Strauss described the irruption of writing into Nambikwara society.[130] When the chief mimicked the act of writing—reproducing the signifiers without understanding their signified—he revealed the link between writing and power in that merely appearing to write could increase one's authority or function, at the expense of others.[131] Derrida answered Lévi-Strauss's "writing lesson" with his "violence of the letter," which supposedly revealed all the fissures and contradictions in Lévi-Strauss's text.[132] Rather than try to referee this battle royale between two *maitres a penser*, I would only suggest that here again, the Indian moves close to the center of philosophical debate, at a kind of inflection point, in this case in the debate between structuralism and post-structuralism. In the end, it is a quarrel engaged by two critics of ethnocentrism, both Jewish, but who go about it differently. Lévi-Strauss deconstructs Eurocentrism through his privileging of *la pensée sauvage* and denunciations of biological racism, while Derrida accuses Lévi-Strauss of a Rousseaiste and phonocentric nostalgia for indigenous purity yet redefines writing so as to include non-literate societies, while at the same time deconstructing the logocentric Western episteme.

For European philosophers like Hegel, in contrast, a people without writing, and significantly without a Bible or any sacred revealed text, were by definition without history and without laws and social principles. Although empires like the Incas and the Aztecs had forms of writing, many indigenous societies were suspicious of writing itself. Even the highly literate Laguna Pueblo writer Leslie Marmon Silko notes that "amongst the Pueblo people, a written speech or statement is highly suspect because the feelings and the interlocutors remain hidden."[133] Gordon Brotherston in *Book of the Fourth World* approaches the question differently—through a deeply informed dive into the many forms of phonetic and iconic "script" that existed in many parts of the pre-Conquest Americas. Literacy, in this sense, did not arrive with Columbus. "Writing" in the expansive Derridean diacritical sense, took myriad iconic forms: the knitted strings (*quipu*) of the Inca, the dry painting of the Navajo (Dine), the hieroglyphs of the Maya, the petroglyphs of the Pueblo peoples, the incised birchback scrolls of the Midewiwin, the scrolls and wampum belts of the Haudenosaunee, the screenful books of Meso-America, and the totem poles of the indigenes of the Pacific coast.[134] Scott Richard Lyons, in *X-Marks: Native Signatures of Assent*, finally, offers an ironic comment on literacy and the "scene of writing" by noting that many of the Treaties that defrauded Indians were signed by the non-literate Indians with "x"s. He speaks of his great-great-great-grandfather, the first in his lineage to write in the English language, adding: "What he wrote was the letter X."[135]

In an interview featured in the 1994 French edition of Jean de Léry's *Voyage*, Lévi-Strauss had said that the France Antartique episode had all the ingredients of a cinematic epic: "dramatic turnabouts, grandiose landscapes, and fascinating characters." Asked if he would write the scenario of such a film, Lévi-Strauss replied that he "would joyfully collaborate in such a film." (He seemed unaware that Nelson Pereira dos Santos had already made such a film in 1971.) But a parallel opportunity arose in 2005, thanks to a proposal by Marcelo Fiorini (aka Marcelo Fortaleza Flores), a Brazilian anthropologist/filmmaker with an NYU degree who had lived with the Nambikwara for five years and who, unlike Lévi-Strauss, is fluent in two dialects of Nambikwara.[136]

The resulting film, entitled *Levi-Strauss: Aupres de l'Amazonie* (shown on French TV in November 2008 and later in Brazil), offers a hybrid generic form, combining literary adaptation (of the canonical text *Tristes Tropiques*), a biopic and an anthropological essay film. The film fits perfectly into our themes because it concerns a French theorist, a Brazilian filmmaker, and indigenous characters from the three groups that Lévi-Strauss knew best—the Nambiquara, the Kadiwéu, and the Bororo. In his interviews in the film, Lévi-Strauss alludes to our familiar cast of historical characters and expresses a strong sense of identification with Léry:

> I had the impression of a complicity, a parallelism, between my existence and Léry's. I felt it from the beginning, and that feeling has only increased with the years. Léry went to Brazil at twenty-two or twenty-three years of age; I was twenty-six when I made the same voyage. Léry waited eighteen years before writing his *Voyage*; I waited fifteen years before writing *Tristes Tropiques*. In the interval, during those eighteen years for Léry, and fifteen years for me, [we have] the wars of religion ... the siege of Sancerre—all of which Léry lived and about which he wrote. And for me: the Second World War, and the flight from persecution.[137]

Such was Lévi-Strauss's devotion that the only book that he brought to Brazil was a paperback version of De Léry's *Voyage*. Given his insider-outside perspective on a Europe about to slaughter its "internal others," including his coreligionists, Lévi-Strauss perhaps found in the relatively gentle ways of the "external others" of Europe an alternative to what John Murray Cuddihy calls the "ordeals" of European "civility."[138]

To tell its story, the Fiorini film mingles interviews with Lévi-Strauss himself (in 2007); the voice-over narration of Jean-Claude Carrière reading passages from *Tristes*

Tropiques; interviews with indigenous leaders who remember Lévi-Strauss; archival extracts from Brazilian documentaries from the 1910s and 1920s; 1930s sketches, photographs, and films by Claude and Dina Lévi-Strauss; and scenes of contemporary indigenous life. The interviews with Lévi-Strauss reveal an element of ironic self-deprecation concerning his own naive assumptions: "I was looking for humanity reduced to its most simple expression," he tells us, "but what I found was human beings." He speaks of his own disorientation when encountering an unknown society full of signs and practices that he, the structuralist so at ease with the codes of abstruse French poetry, found hard to decipher. Rather than present himself as mastering the obscurities of an alien civilization, Lévi-Strauss confesses his bewilderment before a disconcerting maze of colors, customs, stratifications, and interlaced traditions, without knowing which "thread" to follow. Without a shared language, he and his Nambikwara interlocutors had to invent a "jargon," an improvised patois based on a few shared expressions, yet sufficient to enable a kind of friendship. In the film, Lévi-Strauss's discourse often performs sly reversals of Eurocentric assumption. Rather than assert the often-assumed "objectivity" of western social scientists, Lévi-Strauss claims to have received from the Kadiwéu "a lesson in objectivity." Rather than see indigenous societies as "primitive," he sees them as "*societies savantes*." Rather than speak of "fierce" tribes, he speaks of "kindness, open-mindedness, and a desire to help." When he finally meets the Indians that he had longed to meet in the flesh, he relates an anti-climactic encounter: "They were ready to teach me, but I didn't know their language. I received my reward and my punishment at the same time. They were as close enough to touch, as close as my own image in a mirror, but I couldn't reach them."

Lévi-Strauss, perhaps having in mind the intertextual memory of Montaigne's admired *cacique*, describes Chief Alberto Nambikwara as an intelligent and responsible leader. The voice-over reads Lévi-Strauss's famous comments on the "scene of writing," where the chief did not understand the written words but understood very well the function and power of writing, to the point that he would mimic written approval of a list of items through a mimicry of the act of writing as a gesture of potent leadership. The story then segues to another "scene of writing," this time showing a Nambikwara teacher explaining the vital importance of writing for his Nambikwara pupils, maintaining that "if we only speak their language we will become like them," which is why, he explains, that "I am teaching you to write in our own language." The teacher also explains the necessity of a certain bi-culturality: "We Indians have to continue our customs but also live in the other world."

Many filmic homages to famous intellectuals are hagiographic; they center on the anthropologist, not on their indigenous interlocutors. But in the Fiorini film indigenous voices—of elders, teachers, shamans—structure and permeate the film. A teacher, Mane Manduca, explains the ecological devastation brought by the Agrobusiness that poisons the rivers with mercury, and by the soy plantations—now 80 percent of Nambikwara territory—which deprive the local fauna of their alimentation and thus deprive the people of food. After calling himself a "teacher/researcher like Lévi-Strauss," Mane explains that the word "*asi'yautausu*" in Nambikwara is roughly equivalent to the word "structure" for Lévi-Strauss. Skillful editing shuttles us between the past of Lévi-Strauss's photographs and the present of indigenous life. A clip from a 1915 Tomaz Reis film shows officials measuring indigenous skulls and dressing the Indians in European clothing in a gesture of forced assimilation, exactly the attitude rejected both by Lévi-Strauss and by the filmmaker. In another note of protest, an older Nambikwara reminds us that the Coronel Rondon, one of the "good guys" of official Brazilian historiography, actually brought disease into the indigenous communities, and that Pareci Indians built the telegraph line that made the Rondon Commission famous. We learn that Jesuit missionaries, like their Protestant and Catholic colleagues in North America, weaponized schools to destroy indigenous culture by forbidding the use of the native language and proscribing prayer, hunting, and fishing, in a situation where "everything was forbidden."

Far from purveying the Indian-as-perpetual-victim syndrome, Fiorini, himself a tireless activist in the indigenous cause, reveals an indigenous culture of laughter, where the giddy cheer of children pervades the soundtrack. It also portrays a haptic, tactile world, where the Nambikwara are constantly, literally, "in touch" with each other, caressing and painting each other's faces. Delicately, the film cites Lévi-Strauss's comments about Nambikwara sexuality, where he speaks of couples that embrace (in an echo of Platonic androgyny) "as if in nostalgia for a lost oneness." He notes, as a scientist of course, a general lack of male erections, in a world where daily life is permeated by an erotic atmosphere, yet where "the pleasure seems less physical than playful and sentimental." The Nambikwara are not embarrassed to touch; "the caresses don't stop just because a foreigner passes nearby." The common formula: "making love is good." The films shows, through photos and live action scenes, what Lévi-Strauss describes—a caressing world where father and mother both take care of children, and where one never sees a child beaten, where kids play constantly with animals as quasi-friends, and young children take care of even younger children. We witness in sounds and images the world of indigenous conviviality described by Lévi-Strauss.

One can often tell where a film's heart is through its musical choices. A European orchestral symphonic score for a film set in the indigenous Americas, for example, makes clear that the film's affective allegiances are far from native peoples. In this case, there is no music in the Fiorini film that is not indigenous or highly indigenized; the music channels our feelings even when superimposed on archival clips. The film's music track, created by Caito Marcondes and Marlui Miranda, singer and scholar and well-known performer of indigenous music, consists of indigenous music or of stylizations of that music, replete with shimmering flutes and what might be called the ecological forest sounds of instruments made from wood and other natural materials. The film's final shots superimpose indigenized music on images of São Paulo at dusk, with voice-over commentary drawn from *Tristes Tropiques*, commenting on the long-standing Western gaze on the Indian: Other societies are not necessarily better than ours, and in any case there would be no method for proving such a thing, but knowing other societies gives us a way of detaching ourselves from our own society. Not because our society is absolutely bad, or the only bad society, but because it is the only one from which we must free ourselves.

His final words in the film sound a note of freedom: "with indigenous America … I recognized an era when the human species was at the measure of the universe and where there persisted an adequate relationship to the exercise of freedom." The underscoring of the image of the urban metropolis by indigenous sounds and music asserts a kind of acoustic sovereignty over an urban space that had always been and will remain at its base indigenous.[139]

The Fiorini film is not the only Brazilian film about Lévi-Strauss. Edson Matarezio's *What Levi-Strauss Owes to the Amerindians* (2013) gathers a bevy of anthropologists, some Brazilian (Renato Sztutman, Carlos Fausto, Manuela Carneiro da Cunha) and some linked to the French academe (Philippe Descola, Carlo Severi). The scholars assemble to discuss the impact of Brazil on Lévi-Strauss's thought, and especially on *La Pensée Sauvage*, where the emphasis is on the noun—indigenous *thought*—and not on the in some ways unfortunate adjective—*sauvage*. Yet even that archaic word can be seen as a declaration of affiliation with earlier writers like Jean de Léry, Montaigne, and Rousseau in opposition, as always, to the harsher line that goes back to Hobbes. The overall drift is to suggest that Lévi-Strauss saw himself not as original but as merely a medium for indigenous thought, which corresponds to his maxim that myths think themselves among themselves. In other words, the credit for his work goes to the indigenous people themselves and not to him as an individual. For Lévi-Strauss, the credit for whatever emerges from the encounter between his thought and that of his indigenous interlocutors belongs to them alone.

What also emerges from the collective discussion is that Lévi-Strauss sees native thought as simply another way of thinking, neither superior nor inferior to Western ways of thinking, but one which works less from the individual and from abstract principles—*cogito ergo sum*—than through reflection on the surrounding life forms, persons, objects, and spirits. In this encounter between European academics and the indigenous cultural world, the participants suggest that Lévi-Strauss "mimics" indigenous thought, that he ends up thinking like an indigenous person, but of course in a different idiom. Lévi-Strauss elucidates a science of the concrete, of thinking through things, in order to move beyond the precarious bounded ego as supreme subject. Thus, he starts from things and moves to abstraction rather than the reverse, taking elements from the indigenous environment and theorizes on that basis. Sztutman speaks of an "elective affinity" between indigenous thought and Lévi-Strauss, but which does not transform his work into mere imitation. His own books are bricolages, starting from a simple everyday contrast like the raw and the cooked, in order to discern larger patterns.

Lévi-Strauss also sees indigenous people as what the West would call "artists" in that they are constantly thinking through masks and design and performance, through dancing, singing, painting, designing, weaving, in relation to other human beings and fellow inhabitants of the earth. Lévi-Strauss also thinks in hemispheric terms of native peoples in all the Americas. His four-volume magnum opus *Mythologiques* traces the intertextual variations of indigenous myths, as they move from group to group, from South America to Central America and to North America, always having in mind not their specific content but rather their undergirding structures of "all their relations."

Pierre Clastres, the Anarchist Indigene, and the Wari

French anthropologist Pierre Clastres, a junior affiliate of both Lévi-Strauss and Deleuze, offers a particularly suggestive example of Franco-indigenous cross-cultural intellectual and political stimulation. Four decades after Lévi-Strauss's research in Matto Grosso, Clastres, basing his judgments both on the Huguenot corpus and his own fieldwork with the Guaraní, the Guayaki, and the Yanomami, spoke in terms reminiscent at once of Montaigne, Rousseau, the *Modernistas*, Lévi-Strauss, and the western anarchist left. In *Arqueologia da Violência* (The Archeology of Violence, 2004), Clastres argued that indigenous societies did not eschew the nation-state because they were *incapable* of developing state structures, but rather because they had a passionate desire *not* to have them.[140] Echoing Montaigne, Clastres claimed that the function of indigenous *caciques* or leaders was not to wield power or gain wealth, but rather to represent the social will toward equality and cohesion by *refusing* to acquire power. The chief's role was not to make decisions and then impose them but rather to represent the people's view of itself as a single people without social division. While one colonialist intellectual current infantilized these societies as embodying the "childhood" of humanity—concretized in policy terms by a tutelage regime—Clastres saw the indigenous peoples as politically mature in their conscious refusal of social division. Within a collective intentionality, their purpose was to conjure away social inequality in any form.[141] Much as Marx inverted Hegel, one can see Clastres as inverting Marxism: rather than the gaining of economic power being determinative of the state, here the "chief" of the non-state does not accumulate wealth but rather gives it away.

The West, for Clastres, could not "forgive" native societies for their refusal to exploit their resources in ways that Europeans found normal. A society without coercion and without the profit principle was for Europeans literally "unthinkable," an epistemological impossibility. A society without police had itself to be policed, for its own good of course. Even for many "progressive" Marxists, for whom the kernel of history was the development of forces of production, Indian societies were seen as the victims of the rosy dawn of primitive accumulation, or as historically condemned examples of "primitive communism," but not as an alternative social model with contemporary relevance.[142] But from a native perspective, accumulation was absurd in a society that had everything it needed, where any individual who tried to "hoard" goods would soon discover that those goods were instantly going to be devoured in equality by the community.

At the same time, Clastres does not offer an unblemished "positive image" of "noble savages." Some indigenous societies, such as the Kadiwéu, were hierarchical, and in many women were subordinated to men. For Clastres, they are less pacifist than anarchist, in both the positive and negative senses of the word. Wars with others form a constant and even necessary presence in some indigenous cultures, even if not aimed at territorial aggrandizement or ethnic extermination and actually killed very few people. Anticipating recent feminist revalorizations of a "subsistence perspective," Clastres combats the dominant portrait of native societies as suffering a meager life of "subsistence" in an economy of shared immiseration.[143] The picture, as Clastres puts it, is "of the savage crushed by his environment, constantly haunted by hunger, besieged by a permanent anxiety about obtaining for his group a way to keep from perishing."[144] In the conventional view, subsistence societies merely manage to survive, but not to thrive, because they do not accumulate goods to guarantee their future. In sum, the "primitives" are not good Weberian Protestants who "save for a rainy day." But Clastres, in the wake of Oswald de Andrade and alongside Marshall Sahlins, argues that so-called "primitive" societies are societies of abundance, where all needs are usually satisfied, and people do not have to work frantically to survive. In short, "Indians do not live in order to produce but rather produce in order to live."[145] Farther North, Robin Wall Kimmerer (Potawatomi), similarly, argues for "recognizing abundance rather than scarcity" as part of a culture of gratitude and reciprocity, which holds that "the gifts of the earth are all in one bowl, all to be shared from a single spoon."[146]

Ailton Krenak, in "The Eternal Return of the Encounter," affirms and elaborates Clastres's views concerning the native refusal of the state:

> Pierre Clastres, after living with our relatives the Nhandeva and M'bia, concluded that we are societies that organize ourselves in a manner against the state. There is no ideology here, we go naturally against the state, the way the wind follows its path, or the river follows its path, we naturally follow a path which does not affirm state institutions as necessary for our health, education, or happiness.[147]

Clastres's ongoing dialogue and shared life with indigenous peoples, including with shamans, had immense impact on his thought. Transformed by his experience, Clastres did not remain exactly the Frenchman he was when he arrived; rather, he became intellectually indigenized.

Migrating back to France itself in the period of Clastres's writing in Brazil, we find another French reference to indigenous thought in the films of arch-Auteur Jean-Luc Godard. It is now possible to trace the changing role of the "Indian" figure in Godard's oeuvre thanks to Eyal Sivan's online interactive website "Montage Interdit."[148] The site arranges digitized clips drawn from virtually all of Godard's films, catalogued under rubrics such as "Blacks," "Jews," "Indians," "Arabs," and "Third World." By scrutinizing the chronologically ordered clips, we can discern Godard's overall trajectory from apolitical right-wing anarchist, fond of Nouvelle Vague *clins d'oeil* in the early 1960s on to the theoretical practitioner of radical politics in the 1970s. Godard's approach to the filmic Indian is highly reflexive, focusing not on stories but rather on reflections on the status and interpretation of the Indian character. The trajectory of indigenous representation begins with Ana Karina playing a cabaret performer costumed in Sioux Indian headdress in *Une Femme est une Femme* (1961), in short as a "comic" stereotype. Later, in *Bande a Part* (1964), an off-screen voice places Indians, alongside Jews and Blacks, within a paradigm of similarly oppressed peoples. The satirical intellectual road-movie *Weekend* (1968), meanwhile, fits into our tale of intellectual history of French affection for radical Indigeneity, here in the form of a long voice-over citation of Engels' "The Origin of the Family, Private Property and the State" praising the egalitarian society of the Iroquois as examples of communalism, gender equality, and "primitive socialism."

In Godard's "Dziga-Vertov" period (1968–1972), the Indian of the Western becomes a synecdoche for Hollywood racism, which produces an "Indian" who is *"juste une image"* (just an image) rather than an *"image juste"* (an accurate image). The trajectory culminates in *Notre Musique* (2004) where Godard links two occupied peoples by creating a filmic relationship between two unnamed Native American elders/activists and the late Palestinian poet Mahmoud Darwish, the author of "The Speech of the Red Indian." The poem spins an extended analogy between the situations and sensibilities of Palestinians and of Native Americans as those who "lived and flourished before the onslaught of English guns, French wine and influenza, living in harmony side by side" who "refuse to sign a bill of sale/that takes possession/of so much as one inch of my weed patch." Thus, Godard moves over the decades from displaying Ana Karina as a stereotypically sexy "squaw" in a nightclub, to an implied categorization of Indians as paradigmatically oppressed people, to a homage to Marx and Engels on the Iroquois, to an indictment of Hollywood's racist iconography, culminating in a poetic evocation of a symbolic alliance between two "settled" and "unsettling" peoples besieged by settler-style colonialism, with the difference, in the Jewish/Israeli case, of an anomalous colonialism, one without a metropole and with a long cultural memory of a sacred land.[149]

An allegorical use of the "Indian," albeit a less reflexive one, also informs French popular music in the same period. A music video of Gilbert Becaud's song *"L'Indien"* (1973), with lyrics by Maurice Vidalin, features indigenous-style drumming and a motley of images of indigenous leaders and famous American statesmen and politicians. In a Frenchified revisionist version of the "White Indian" tradition, the singer/persona "becomes Indian" by assuming the identity of the son of Black Eagle, the first great chief of his tribe, who could kill a bison with one blow to the rib cage. The period of the song, the early 1970s, coincided with the Native American protests at Alcatraz, Wounded Knee, and American Indian Movement (AIM) but preceded the "Oka crisis" two decades later. The song becomes a *cri de Coeur* of identification with the Indian cause. Gilbert Becaud, renamed "Black Eagle," personifies freedom, hope, and action:

> And sometimes I feel a bow in the hand
> And I aim at the top of a building
> And arrow Mr. Rockefeller,
> And Monsieur Rockefeller falls from the heights of his empire
> With my arrow penetrating his eye
> The murdered eye of Mr. Rockefeller
> Who falls and falls again.

The final lines echo James Baldwin's "Nobody Knows my Name" and Ralph Ellison's *Invisible Man*.

> Noone looks at me
> Noone sees me
> I'm an Indian; I don't exist.
> They don't respect an Indian without feathers.

Yet they are on our land, *chez nous* my brothers
In Yacutapa.

This case of ethnic ventriloquism, or ethnic masquerade, invents a persona in some ways reminiscent of the Enlightenment French ally of the rebel Indian. We are reminded of Diderot's fantasy of taking up arms alongside the colonized against his own colonizing nation and of Sartre's incendiary preface to Fanon's *Wretched of the Earth*. But an element of postwar French communist and even Gaullist anti-Americanism pervades the song. Becaud chooses New York City as his villain, as the center of world capitalism, but in terms of indigenous sovereignty. The stories of the great Canadian cities like Quebec City, Montreal, and Toronto are not fundamentally different. It is not as if the Wendat and the Mohawk and the Haudenosaunee were now in power in those cities. In that sense, one detects a soupcon of "intercolonial narcissism," the implication that we French were more kindly to the Indians than those the French stubbornly persist in calling the "Anglo-Saxons," a term which whitens a multicolored nation.[150]

A very different kind of "French Connection," again with a link to anarchism, informs a short film directed by a French anarchist named Noe Vitoux. Filmed in Guajará-Mirim in the state of Rondonia, the film, a kind of satiric Mockumentary, is entitled *O Homen que Matou Deus* (*The Man Who Killed God*, 2013). In a sociohistorical inversion, the film's prologue sets up a provocative premise aimed at "whites." The Wari protagonist (Xidut Arowa) addresses the audience directly:

Since you whites have been killing us for centuries, since you've been destroying the game in our forests which guarantee our survival, and since it is apparently legal for you to kill us, since no one is ever punished, and since in effect you are hunting us down, we believe that it is only fair that it should be legal to hunt whites.

In sum, what is good for the Red gander is good for the White goose. Screened at the FICA Environmental Festival in Goias, Brazil, in 2013, the film pleased many in the audience with its pro-indigenous audacity, ecological relevance, and anarchist irreverence, while shocking others with its graphic scenes of murder and cannibalization of whites, including children.

A pro-indigenous revenge tale, the film hybridizes fiction and documentary, mixing the adventure film with verite-style reflexivity—a film about filming—with direct address to the audience both by the director and by the main Wari character. In so far as it is a fiction film, as Sandro de Oliveira points out, the direct address is Brechtian, a form of distanciation, a way of saying, "this is not real"; yet in so far as it is a documentary, the direct address implies the opposite: "what you are seeing is indeed real."[151] This strategy creates a zone of representational and ethical indeterminacy and thus a division within the audience, reflected, perhaps, in the film's split reception. The film's aggressive pro-indigenous stance, premised on a hypothetical indigenous right to murder whites as a response to white massacres, might have also disturbed the non-native public in its *bonne conscience*, provoking a "narcissistic wound " since the film shows whites as historically murderous and suffering its just deserts—being murdered *as* whites.

According to the credits, the film was made with the collaboration of the Wari community. The director Vitoux, inscribed as himself in the film, also takes part in the fiction. The film combines what Roger Odin calls "documentary effects"—i.e. the calculated technical imperfections that evoke documentary such as handheld camera, synchronous sound, direct-to-camera interviews, for an "authenticity effect," together with fictionalizing effects—Steadicam chases, rapidly edited action sequences—all within a story that we assume can only be fiction: the gleeful murder and cannibalization of the *Wayam* (whites) by the Wari. The film ends with a mock invitation to the spectator to contribute to Survival International in support of the "legalization of the hunting of white men."[152] Despite indigenous participation in the film, one suspects that this particular concept of a politically supportive film came more from the French anarchist than from the Wari themselves, for whom it might not have seemed the ideal supportive gesture. At the same time, through the staging of highly improbable forms of extreme violence, the film indirectly makes the crucial point that western audiences have calmly watched hundreds if not thousands of massacres of indigenous peoples in Hollywood films. Audiences all over the world have seen indigenous people massacred without protesting, so in this sense the film administers what comic Charlie Hill in a different context has called a "well-deserved spanking" to the white audience. Such massacres are featured even in "family entertainments" like the Disney version of *Swiss Family Robinson* (1960), with its cheery familial massacres of hosts of native Asians. Thus, massive killing of indigenous people characterizes not only history itself but also the cinematic translations of that history.[153] In Vitoux's pro-indigenous tweaking of the "Most Dangerous Game," it is the natives who hunt the whites. The *Man Who Killed God* thus reverses western expectations about fiction films, i.e. that in a film fight between Indians and Whites, only the Indians are bound to die, usually en masse, in conformity with the morbid disproportionalities of colonial death.

The film ends with the filmmaker fleeing through the forest, rendered through a mobile steadicam subjective shot from the Wari character's point of view. As one of the lecturers at the FICA Festival in Goias, Brazil, I witnessed the audience reaction and heard Celso Oro Eu, Wari spokesman for the film, defend the film against the objections of a white European who called it a "hymn to violence." Celso Ora's Oro Eu's answer was brusque: "Violence is killing Indians and find[ing] it lawful. Violence is the law of the whites."[154] A well-researched book by anthropologist Alice Conklin, meanwhile, suggests that the practice of Wari cannibalism had little to do with the satirical situation portrayed in *The Man Who Killed God*. Conklin, who spent two years among the Wari, found that cannibalism was practiced up through the 1960s, but that rather than being a form of aggression, it was an attempt—to offer a crude and inadequate summary of her argument—to deal with mourning and the loss of loved ones. In short, the Wari disposed of their own dead by consuming their corpses. Cannibalism thus had a socially integrative dimension as the most respectful way to treat a human body.[155]

Huron (Wendat) scholar Georges E. Sioui, meanwhile, also suggests that cannibalism existed among some indigenous peoples of North America, offering an explanation that parallels similar explanations of Tupi ritual cannibalism:

Amerindians did sometimes consume one or several parts (for example, the heart) of the body of a prisoner who died a particularly courageous death ... The Amerindian gesture of consuming human flesh was as consistent with their conception of the great circle as was their proverbial generosity. When they had to defend themselves against their fellow humans, they did not like to kill instantaneously or massively as is done with mechanical weapons.[156]

Sioui continues: "They preferred to glorify their enemies in death by giving them the chance to die courageously. The remains of a life thus ennobled until death and in death could not be simply thrown away as garbage; they deserved to be eaten."[157] Sioui's account runs in partial parallel to some analyses of Tupinambá cannibalism, which stresses that the enemy was honored as courageous and allowed a final speech promising vengeance.

Indigenous writers in North America (Turtle Island) have deployed the cannibal trope for their own purposes. In *Columbus and Other Cannibals*, Native American historian Jack D. Forbes (Powhatan-Renape and Lenape) uses the Cree term "*wetico*"— roughly "cannibal" or more broadly the evil spirit which terrorizes other creatures— to designate the "unimaginable death, destruction, exploitation and greed" brought by Europeans to the Americas.[158] While Oswald de Andrade was a Euro-Brazilian who deployed the literary trope of the Cannibal Indian, Forbes is a Native American activist invoking the same trope. But while Oswald roots the trope in a putative Indian (Tupinambá) cannibalism, Forbes's title suggests that the real Cannibals were not the natives but the Europeans.

The Franco-Brazilian Dialogue and the Politics of *The Falling Sky*

Returning to the Franco-Brazilian connection, subsequent to Lévi-Strauss's work in the 1930s and 1950s, and to Pierre Clastres's work in the 1970s and 1980s, the Franco-Brazilian-Indigenous philosophical dialogue has been picked up again by Michel de Certeau's writings about Jean de Léry, by Philippe Descola's work with the Achuar in the Amazon, by René Girard's use of Tupinambá cannibalism as the key to the scapegoat rituals informing all religions, and by Deleuze and Guattari, with their innumerable references to anthropology and indigenous peoples. A remarkable efflorescence, in twenty-first-century Brazil, of scholarship, novels, films, and TV mini-series, features the familiar cast of characters from France Antartique: Cunhambebe, Thévet, Villegagnon, Hans Staden, and Jean de Léry. In France, apart from the academic work of Ilda Mendes and Frank Lestringant, we find Serge Elmalan's dramatized account of the French colony in *Nicolas Durand de Villeganon ou L'Utopie Tropciale* (2002), and Jean-Marie Touratier's *Bois Rouge* (1993), which fictionalizes the stories of Hans Staden and Jean de Léry. Gilbert Pastor's novel *Le Valet d'Aventure* (1990) is also set in the time of France Antartique but its presentation of the Tupinambá is relentlessly negative, as if the author rewrote Jean de Léry's *histoire* in an upside-down manner, reversing that book's sympathetic treatment of the natives in order to portray them as cruel, libidinous, and prone to drunkenness, almost portraying them, in the manner of some Portuguese commentators of the time, as "animals with human faces."

The most notable success was Jean-Christophe Rufin's historical novel *Rouge Brésil* (Red Brazil, 2001), which brought the long-forgotten French colony into wide public consciousness. Winner of the Goncourt Prize and a bestseller, *Rouge Brésil* offers a romanticized and in some ways stereotypical version of the France Antartique story, recounted against the background of the European Wars of Religion. The novel recounts a rite-of-passage discovery by two young orphan siblings (Colombe and Just), drafted as *truchements*, who make their personal discovery of the New World while searching for their father. All the major figures, Villegagnon, Andre Thévet, Jean de Léry, appear under their own names or with aliases. The attitudes of the two siblings, as a kind of primordial couple from a tropical fable, replay the divisions in the colony itself: "Just" follows the racist autocrat Villegagnon, while Colombe joins the Tupinambá where she meets an indigenized older Frenchman (Pay-Lo) possibly modeled on Jean de Léry, the writer who supplied much of the proto-ethnographic information that informs the novel. The novel's epigraph comes from Montaigne, and the novel itself includes a Montaigne-style defense of cannibalism—"when they devour their enemies … it is to assimilate their power. They begin by having their prisoners live among them."[159] The novel re-asks Montaigne's question—who are the real savages? The novel becomes a humanist anti-racist allegory, but without ever exploring the socially radical implications of the indigenization of French thought.[160]

In 2013, *Bresil Rouge* was adapted as a telefilm directed by Sylvain Archambault. The Franco-Brazilian-Canadian production personnel was as transnational as the rivalries for domination in the period of the French colony: with a French-Canadian director, scripted by three screenwriters, one French (Daniel Tonachella), one American (Tom Richardson), and one Canadian (Christian Duguay), with actors from Brazil, Portugal, France, and Canada, but with no indigenous players or even extras. One highly questionable scene, doubtless informed by western sexual fantasies about the indigene, features a native woman (played by an actress in red face) aggressively seducing the reluctant French adolescent protagonist. Ill-prepared for the realities of the New World and torn apart by theological controversies and power struggles, French pioneers see their dreams of colonization gradually dissipate.

In Brazil, meanwhile, stimulated by the 2000 Quincentenary (and the protests against it) numerous publications and media productions have addressed the sixteenth-century Franco-Brazilian-indigenous relationship, whether in the Globo miniseries such as *Caramuru: The Invention of Brazil*, discussed in the next chapter, or major scholarly publications such as *A Outra Margem do Ocidente*, a collection of essays edited by Adauto Novaes featuring a brilliant array of Brazilian, French, and indigenous writers.[161] But perhaps most striking for our purposes are the revisionist versions of Cunhambebe as the hero of the France Antartique story. A chapter in Camil Capaz's *Memorias de Angra dos Reis* (1996), for example, bears the subversive title "The Creation of the World according to Cunhambebe," while the title of a Rio de Janeiro musical "The Incredible Encounter of Tupinambá Nobles and European Barbarians" proclaims its pro-native sympathies.[162] And in *Meu Querido Cannibal* (My Beloved

Cannibal, 2000), Antonio Torres, an author of mixed European and native ancestry, also returns to the topic of France Antartiqe in order to laud Cunhambebe as a "military genius" and inventor of "water-borne guerilla warfare." For Torres, Cumhambebe displayed immense political skills as the head of the "Superior Council" of the Tamoio Confederation, an alliance which fused a common resistance to the Portuguese with respect for the diverse social arrangements of the collaborating groups. In sum, Torres reenvisions Cunhambebe through an indigenist and revolutionary prism, as a fighter against slavery and an anti-colonialist *avant la lettre*. At the same time, the Torres novel provokes thoughts about the missed opportunities of comparative scholarship. What if we took Cunhambebe out of a narrow "Indian" paradigm and placed him in the ranks of anti-colonial and anti-slavery fighters like Nat Turner, Ho Chi Minh, and Frantz Fanon?

Unlike Brazil, North America has a multi-century tradition of native writers, often equipped with Western educations, going back to the seventeenth-century religious texts of Samson Occom (Mohegan) and including a canon that includes hundreds of essayists, novelists, poets, storytellers, and artist. In 1828, Pequot author, minister, and social organizer William Apes (1798–1839) published his autobiography *Son of the Forest*. Although he took on an English name, as a Methodist minister and a generally assimilated person, he also participated in a minor Mashpee uprising and was briefly sent to jail. He also performed his own brand of indigenous critique by asking provocative questions to a hypocritical Anglo-dominant society:

> If black or red skins of any other skin of color is disgraceful to God, it appears that he has disgraced himself a good deal—for he has made fifteen colored people to one white and placed them here on this earth … Now supposed these skins were put together, and each skin had its national crimes written on it—which skin do you think would have the greatest? I will ask one question more. Can you charge the Indians with robbing a nation almost of their whole continent, and murdering their women and children, and then depriving them of the remainder of their lawful rights, that nature and God require them to have?[163]

Although Brazil has a tradition of writers of mixed and partial indigenous ancestry, it does not have a long tradition of writers self-identified as indigenous and writing on indigenous themes in Portuguese, partially because contact for many groups came relatively late. But recent decades have seen the emergence of scores if not hundreds of indigenous writers and poets, to mention just a few: Ailton Krenak, Edson Krenak, Eliane Potiguara, Daniel Munduruku, Kaka Wera Jecupe, Angelo Kreta, Renata Machado Tupinambá, Marcia Wayna Kambeba, Olivio Jakupe, Rosi Waikhon, Tiago Hakiy, Zelia Puri, not to mention those who write poetry in the form of hip-hop and popular music.

We find a latter-day instance of the Franco-indigenous dialogue that goes back to Jean de Léry and Montaigne in the twenty-first-century collaboration between Yanomami shaman Davi Kopenawa Yanomami (henceforth Kopenawa) and French ethnologist Bruce Albert, whose collaboration resulted in a book—*The Falling Sky*. Unlike most of the other writers, Davi Kopenawa Yanomami—henceforth Kopenawa—

does not write fluently in Portuguese or in any language. In fact, he finds committing words to paper a melancholy necessity. (His attitude finds an echo in the Northern Hemisphere in the words of Russell Means, for whom the writing process "epitomizes the European concept of 'legitimate' thinking, the imposition of abstraction on the speaking relationships of people".)[164] Yet Kopenawa's spoken words form the creative force behind a paradigm-shattering book, *The Falling Sky: Words of a Yanomami Shaman,* published in the United States by Harvard University Press and by similarly prestigious presses in France (Terre Humaine) and Brazil (Companhia das Letras).

The book's status is hard to define. Unlike best sellers like *Don Juan: A Yaqui Way of Knowledge* (1968), first written by Carlos Castaneda as an MA thesis, which purports to document the author's apprenticeship with a Yaqui shaman, *The Falling Sky* consists of the actual words of an actual shaman offering a first-person account of his life and his cosmo-ecological thought, with minimal mediation. At the same time, *The Falling Sky* only exists as a book thanks to the collaboration with Bruce Albert, who functioned as more than a translator (from Yanomami into French), yet less than a co-author. The book is not really a translation, in that there was no pre-existing text; rather, the book emerged from Albert's long conversations with Davi Yanomami, with a constant back-and-forth to capture the nuances. Viveiros de Castro calls it a "collaboration situated at the unpredictable and fragile intersection of two cultural universes."[165] (The Portuguese version is brilliantly translated from the French by Beatriz Perrone-Moises, a leading scholar on Franco-Brazilian cultural relations and on sixteenth-century indigeneity.)

Davi Kopenawa Yanamomi is a profound thinker, but not an "intellectual." Dale Turner distinguishes between indigenous philosophy as articulated orally in indigenous languages by those regarded by the community as the keepers of distinct ways of knowing—the case of Kopenawa—and indigenous intellectuals educated in the Western academic tradition and who contest it in its own terms, the case of many indigenous intellectuals in North America and of some in Brazil.[166] *The Falling Sky* is also not an "as told to" book where the translator/collaborator "improves" and even invents a style and language that the nominal author would never have had the skill to create. Rather, in a hybrid *écriture*, Albert serves as a cultural mediator—a latter-day *truchement*—for a person, Davi Yanomami, who speaks very eloquently in his own language, to which the collaborator tries to be adequate. Being adequate, in this case, meant spending decades of close contact with the Yanomami, and two decades of direct collaboration with Davi Yanomami, in order to familiarize himself with the complex language and metaphorics of a culture vastly different from his own.

It is on one level a surprise that the book came to exist at all, in that Kopenawa has often expressed a Socratic-style skepticism about the capacity of written language to capture truth. In the case of colonial contracts, whites told lies on "image skins." In his rather disenchanted image of western intellectuals, sadly dependent on printed words, —Kopenawa complains that Western laws about protecting the forest are designed on paper made out of destroyed trees. Confirming speculations about the heightened memory powers of non-literate people, Yanomami claims that shamans hold the words of the forest spirits (*xapiri*) in the depths of their minds. But the *xapiris'* words are also his words because they are renewable, both by the shaman and even by the *xapiri* themselves. When he dies, he claims, the words will be as new and strong as they are now. Thus, the book claims an unusual intertext—that of orature (Walter Ong), but of a special kind—the words of the forest spirits called *xapiri*.

The Falling Sky has two epigraphs, one from Lévi-Strauss and the other from Kopenawa himself, both having to do with native prophecies. In a 1993 text, Lévi-Strauss points out that indigenous prophecies foresaw peoples arriving from afar, and that both indigene and nonindigene are threatened by epidemics and by the lust for profit, and that catastrophe can only be averted by mutual respect as the key to survival for everyone. Davi Kopenawa's prophecy is more uncompromising:

> The forest is alive. The only people who will die are the non-Indians who insisted on destroying it. If they manage to destroy the forest, rivers will disappear under the earth, the ground will be undone, and trees will wilt ... the dried up earth will be empty and silent ... They will not be able to scare away the smoke of the epidemics that devour us.[167]

Such indigenous prophecies are not unique to South America. Lakota activist Russel Means made a similar prophecy in the 1980s, foretelling a worldwide apocalypse which would leave only an indigenous remnant somewhere in the Americas, which would survive and repopulate the planet, allowing "harmony to be re-established."[168]

On a certain level, Kopenawa's book has points in common with Fanon's *Black Skin, White Masks*, in that it tells a story of alienation giving way to disalienation, with the difference that, unlike Fanon, Kopenawa did not begin from alienation but rather from the plenitude of being Yanomami. Nor was he an intellectual and psychoanalyst familiar with the white world like Fanon. Kopenawa found the first contacts with whites terrifying and understood almost nothing of what they said to him. Later, however, he goes through a phrase of wanting to become white, as in the following passage where he verbally reenacts the processes of colonial mimicry:

> I only wished for one thing now: to be like them! So I constantly observed them in silence, paying tremendous attention. I wanted to assimilate everything they said and did. I was already used to wearing shorts. The people of Teosi had distributed them to us since they lived among us so we would hide our penises. I also knew flip-flops.[169]

He learns to put on pants, for Kopenawa, "hiding one's legs," and putting on shoes "shutting one's feet," and even to "love merchandise the way white people do."[170] But in the end, Kopenawa warns young people that imitating white people "will not lead to anything good" and that if they "continue on this dark path ... [they will] become as ignorant as the white people can be."[171] Kopenawa decides that "I do not to be one of them. I think that we will only be able to become white people the day white people transform themselves into Yanomami."[172]

At one point in his life, Kopenawa makes a heroic effort to become Christian. He closes his eyes to pray, but his prayers are met with a deafening silence. In an inversion of the Christian story, where the Christian is tempted by Satan, here the temptation is Christianity itself. For Kopenawa, Christianity evokes fear, guilt, and the puritanism of the missionaries who "frighten us with *Teosi*'s [God's] words, and to constantly speak to us in anger. 'Davi, you are in sin. That is bad, Do not chew Tobacco! Do not desire married women. Do not drink the Yakoana. Satanas is deceiving you!'"[173] (Vine Deloria, Jr., in a similar but even more irreverent vein, attributes to the Judeo-Christian deity a personality that "has the egotism of Henry Kissinger, the stability of Donald Trump, and the military mind of George Bush.")[174] Unlike *Teosi*, "Omama always has friendship for us, no matter what we do! ... His image does not constantly tell us 'You are evil! If you refuse my words, I will make you burn!'"[175] The image of a vengeful deity is not so far from James Joyce's Irish-Catholic "pull out his eyes, Apologize." In his spiritually grounded materialism (or materially grounded spiritualism), Kopenawa bewails the Christian God's lack of visible and audible attributes: "What appearance does he have? What is the sound of his voice?"[176] For Kopenawa, the divine lack of attributes is not, paradoxically, a positive attribute. Ultimately, Kopenawa sees the Christian God as allied with the invaders who destroy the forest. Speaking in very pragmatic terms, Kopenawa prefers Omama over Jesus, yet his discourse implies that the Christian God really exists as a human being:

> Maybe Teosi will take revenge on me and make me die. I don't care. I'm not a white man! I don't want to know anything more about him. He has no friendship for the inhabitants of the forest. He does not heal our children. Nor does he defend our land against the gold prospectors and cattle ranchers. It is not he who makes us happy.[177]

Kopenawa ultimately finds Christianity ineffective and unable to fulfill its promises. The missionaries' "unceasing reproaches" never had their promised effect, never "succeeded in washing our chest like the missionaries said they would ... no one stopped lying or having desire for women,"[178] thus demonstrating what the Jesuits calls the "inconstancy" of the indigenous soul. The special vision of the *xapiri*, accessible to the shamans, in contrast, has concrete therapeutic medical effects, enabling the shamans to understand the pathogenic agents of disease. Although exactly how this process works might not be clear, the apparently excellent good health of the Yanomami prior to Western intervention suggests that they understood something about the nature of disease. (The shamans say they can cure the familiar forest diseases, but not the diseases brought by white people.) The case of Kopenawa brings us back to questions asked earlier. What constitutes philosophy? Must a philosopher be an excellent writer or is it enough to be verbally eloquent? Socrates, we know, had his doubts about publication, and we know that many canonical texts, such as *The Odyssey*, began as oral epic, an assemblage of formulae like "craftly Ulysses" and "the wine red sea." Non-literacy does not preclude brilliance or eloquence or even a vast vocabulary. In relation to Montaigne and his Tupinambá interlocutors, we asked whether philosophy has to be written or can it simply be eloquent. And what form must philosophy take? Can a shamanic vision constitute philosophy? Can a hallucinogenic vision generate concepts?

The Kopenawa book mingles multiple genres—autobiography, history, poetry, an anthology of legends, a work of shamanic philosophy, and a political pamphlet defending native rights and protection of the rainforest. It is also a novel of development (*bildungsroman*), a kind of "Portrait of the Shaman as a Young Man." It comprises the kernels of all these genres even though Kopenawa was not familiar with them. The book is divided into three parts. The first part ("Becoming Other") relates his discovery of the shamanic vocation and its processes of initiation. The second part ("The Smoke of Metal") relates his vexed relation with missionaries, prospectors, and government bureaucrats. The third part ("Fall of the Sky") relates his peregrinations in defense of his people and the forest in Brazil, Europe, and the United States.

Kopenawa paints an unforgettable picture of past and present Yanomami culture, living in the heart of a rainforest teeming with sounds and images, where ancient shamanic traditions confront the predations of landowners and prospectors. Here, millennial traditions meet contemporary crises generated by insatiable resource extractionism. In richly evocative language, Kopenawa recounts his initiation and experience as a shaman, as well as his first encounters with those he calls "whites"—i.e. not literally people of pale complexion but non-Indians of any color who harm the indigenous cause, whether government officials, missionaries, construction workers, gold prospectors, or cattle ranchers, in short anyone who adheres to the values of the non-indigenous world he describes so critically.

Kopenawa performs a kind of psycho-social analysis of white obsessions. He calls whites the "merchandise people," ready to sacrifice anything for profit and accumulation. The Yanomami associated the diseases that were killing them with the gold lusted after by the prospectors.[179] According to legend, the creator spirit Omama buried the *xawara* (lethal pestilence) deep in the forest, warning the Yanomami that horrific consequences would follow if it were ever to be dug out and brought back to the surface. "*Xawara*" is also the word for gold and the minerals extracted by prospectors and corporations, thus suggesting a causal link between white men's greed and white-induced epidemics.[180] (In North America, Robin Wall Kimmerer speaks of the "Windigo," the legendary monster of the Anishinaabe and of ecological devastation as the "footprints of the Windigo," and the "tracks of insatiable consumption.")

Although Kopenawa would clearly never see himself as a Marxist, his words resonate with Marx's account of the early days of colonial Conquest. Here is Marx: "The discovery of gold and silver in America, the extirpation, enslavement and entombment in mines of the aboriginal population, the beginning of the conquest and looting of the East Indies, the turning of Africa into a warren for the commercial hunting of black-skins, signalised the rosy dawn of the era of capitalist production."[181] Although unfamiliar with Marxism, Kopenawa is experientially familiar with colonialism, which he summarizes as a case of whites' bellicose traveling "great distances to plunder the land of people who had done them no harm."[182] Unequipped even to read Portuguese Kopenawa nonetheless offers his own vision of the history of the world. He ridicules the arrogant notion of European Discovery:

> The white people say that a Portuguese man said that he discovered Brazil long ago … I was born in the forest and I have always lived there.. Yet I do not say that I discovered it or that I want to own it because I discovered it. Just as I do not say that I discovered the sky or game.[183]

Interestingly, he portrays Europe as having had forest wisdom and dancing spirits and then losing that wisdom, forgetting a past when they too knew how to make the forest spirits dance. But then they cut down all their forests and discovered the "euphoria of merchandise" and of "killing each other for money in their cities and fighting other people for minerals and oil they take from the ground."[184] Kopenawa alludes to European enclosures of land as follows: "the ancient white people once drew their land to cut it up ... [and] covered it in crisscrossing lines." The whites "claim these land drawings have a price and this is why they trade them for money. Yet Omama refused for the same thing to happen to our forest."[185] At the same time, he laments that "these white people only think about covering over the land with their drawings so they can carve it into sections and only give us a few pieces encircled by their mines and plantations."[186] To compensate for the loss of the forest, the dominant society offers money and merchandise, but "the paper skins of their money will never be numerous enough to compensate for the value of the burned trees, its dessicated ground, and its dirty waters."[187] And whites, in his view, are short-sighted since "it never crosses their mind that the same epidemic smoke poison devours their own children."[188]

Kopenawa's text writes resonates with Marxist critiques of "reification," "wage slavery," and "false consciousness," but the thoughts are conveyed in metaphoric yet also down-to-earth human terms: "These white people who have created merchandise think they are clever and brave. Yet they are greedy and do not take care of those among them who have nothing. How can they think they are great men and find themselves so smart?"[189] Kopenawa discerns an erotic dimension of the white fetishization of merchandise:

> This merchandise is truly like a fiancée to them! Their thought is so attached to it that if they damage it while it is still shiny, they get so enraged that they cry! They really are in love with it! They go to sleep thinking about it like you doze off with the nostalgia of a beautiful woman. It occupies their thoughts even after they fall asleep.[190]

Kopenawa fears that this euphoria of merchandise will have no end and worsen and lead to chaos, since "they are already constantly killing each other for money in their cities and fighting other people for minerals and oil they take from the ground."[191]

Without having read Freud or any of the literature on fetishism so common in political economy and anthropology, Kopenawa at times comes close to the idea of "commodity fetishism." The word derives from Portuguese *feitiço*, used to refer to witchcraft, macumba, shamanism, and so forth. The word "fetish" is historically linked to the abrasive cross-cultural "encounter" between West African and European Christian cultures in the sixteenth and seventeenth centuries, in the context of radically different cultures. To the Europeans in Africa, the natives' attribution of talismanic and prophylactic powers to inanimate objects was the basis for their false economic valuation to material objects, whence the occasional exchanges of gold for worthless trinkets. At the same time, the *feitiço* became deeply imbricated in commercial relations. It was the practice to guarantee transactions by getting Africans to take "fetish oaths," which, while ensuring the efficacy of the transactions, also confirmed the innately superstitious nature of the indigenous people. The concept and discourse of fetishism has itself played an important part in justifying the colonization, exploitation, and oppression. It was this discourse of fetishism that Marx turned back onto his own society and that Freud used to define the furthest limits of the psyche's primitive (in)credulity. In this sense, Kopenawa intuitively reverse-engineers the concept of fetishism, which demonized the native, turning it instead into a critique of the western fetishization of merchandise.[192]

Kopenawa's reaction on his visit to the United States undercuts the "better or worse" debates, typical of intercolonial narcissism, which argues for one country's superior treatment of the Indian. Kopenawa points to similarities between the execrable treatment of native peoples in both countries:

> It tormented me to think of all those people similar to us who had died in that country. in the U.S. I thought that many of them must have lived in the land of New York before their forests were replaced by stone houses, destroyed to give way all those buildings made of stone. The white people in this place must have hated them as much as the gold prospectors and cattle ranchers in Brazil hate us. They probably told themselves 'We're going to do away with these dirty lazy Indians. We're going to take their place on this land. We will be the real Americans because we're white!' ... the gold prospectors and cattle ranchers want to get rid of us in Brazil with the same words.[193]

After visiting New York City, where he was shocked by the sad faces of the poor and the homeless, Kopenawa goes North to visit the Iroquois (specifically the Onondaga)—examples for Hobbes of a lawless "state of nature," and for Marx examples of primitive socialism—where he recognizes his distant brothers and sisters, as people "who look like us" and who were "created in the beginning of time on this land of the United States, like us in the forest of Brazil."[194] Delighted to see magnificent feathered headdresses in Onandaga homes, he compares Iroquois eagles to Yanomami hawks and Onandaga maple syrup to Yanomami honey. He pays what for him is the ultimate compliment—that the Onandaga "shamans make the images of these animal ancestors dance."[195] Saddened that the Onandaga, who lost most of their land, have retained only a "little enclosed plot," Kopenawa has a terrifying epiphany of a possible Yanomami future: "this is what the white people also want to do with us! ... they will kill all the game, the fish, and the trees ... they won't leave anything alive. They think we're not human and they all hate us."[196]

Finally, he utters words that echo Shakespeare, despite probably never having read the Bard, asserting the basic commonality of all of us "bare, forked animals." Even though "we are other people than they are, we have a mouth and eyes, blood and bones, just like white people ... we are all hungry and thirsty."[197] It is hard not to hear the echo of Shakespeare in *The Merchant of Venice*:

> I am a Jew. Hath not a Jew eyes? hath not a Jew hands, organs, dimensions, senses, affections, passions? fed with the same food, hurt with the same weapons, subject

to the same diseases, healed by the same means, warmed and cooled by the same winter and summer, as a Christian is? If you prick us, do we not bleed?[198]

Kopenawa's thoughts, at least by implication, extend Shylock's questions to the ancestral animal realm, as if he were asking:

Hath not the jaguar and the monkey eyes? Are they not fed with the same food, hurt with the same weapons, subject to the same diseases, healed by the same means, warmed and cooled by the same winter and summer? If we prick them, do they not bleed?

In his introduction to the Portuguese version, Viveiros de Castro compares *The Falling Sky* to *Tristes Tropiques* as a "canonical transformation" and a "self-ethnographic narrative at once poetic, philosophical, critical, and reflexive." For de Castro, Kopenawa is a representative of the "extra-national minorities of the planet that still resist total dissolution by the modernizing blender of the West." Playing on Roberto Schwarz's influential notion of "out-of-place ideas" to describe culturally alienated elite Brazilians' adoption of intellectual fashions from Europe, Viveiros de Castro argues that Kopenawa embodies the opposite trend of "in place" ideas, within a global theory of place itself, that of Indians who literally "know their place," not in the negative sense of social subordination, but rather in the sense of having a grounded knowledge of the place from which they come and where they still live, in keeping with the meaning of "indigenous" as persons natural to a place, born from their own place. But "own" for Kopenawa does not mean possess as property, since many indigenous peoples see the land as owning them. The implicit contrast is with those who come from abroad, who literally "do not know their place" in the sense of understanding the land in which they have come to dwell. Viveiros de Castro speaks of the end of a certain world and history, that of the Occident as a world imperially appropriated by European powers, by Europe's former colonies, and its emulators in Asia. That world is now thoroughly transnational since for the invisible spirits of the forest, the metallic fundaments of the earth, and the diabolical smoke of epidemics that degenerate the sky have no nation-state appurtenance.

The counterpart to the Enlightenment trope of Indian happiness is the indigenous observation of Western *un*happiness. Kopenawa is as unimpressed by western cities as the "Indians" seeing European palaces were in Montaigne's time. Visiting the Bronx in 1991, Kopenawa notes "houses in ruins" and a general melancholy: "The people who live in those places have no food, and their clothes are dirty and torn … they looked at me with sad eyes. It made me feel upset."[199] Just as the Tupinambá in France noted the ravages of the class system in the bodies of the starving, Kopenawa calls attention to the class-based cruelty of "whites" to its internal others:

They do not want to know anything about these needy people, though they too are their fellows. They reject them and let them suffer alone. They do not even look at them and are satisfied to keep their distance and call them "the poor." They even take their crumbling houses from them. They force them to camp outside in the rain with their children. They must tell themselves: "They live on our land, but they are other people. Let them stay far away."[200]

Perhaps Kopenawa is more shocked at the sight of such misery than we are because he has not been exposed to western media throughout his life; misery has not yet become normal for him, including the misery of the well-fed, who only "talk about working and the money they lack [who] live without joy."[201] It is precisely this exotopic distance from Western norms that lends such estranging power to his words. The indigenous indictment of the colonizing capitalist West, in sum, is for him not only what we in the West have done to the "Indian," but also with what we have done to ourselves. (We will return to Davi Kopenawa in other chapters.)

Notes

1. For informed speculation about Indians traveling to Europe before Columbus, see Jack D. Forbes, *The American Discovery of Europe* (Urbana: University of Illinois Press, 2007) and Jace Weaver, *The Red Atlantic: American Indigenes and the Making of the Modern World, 1000–1927* (Durham: North Carolina Press, 2014).
2. I would point out that, until recently, with the exception of a few scholars or individuals personally connected to this history, there was little consciousness of France Antartique in France itself, yet over the last few decades, as we shall see, there has emerged an intense interest inspired by films, novels, biographies, and the like.
3. Frank Lestringant, *Jean de Léry ou l'invention du sauvage: Essai sur l'Histoire d'un voyage faict en la terre du Bresil* (Paris: Honoré Champion, 1991).
4. "Guanabara" is also a favored vocable in Bossa Nova songs such as "Corcovado"
5. A colloquium on these events, featuring twelve historians, was held at Rennes on October 20–21, 2005, and published as *Les Aventures des Bretons au Brésil l a L'Epoque Coloniale* (Rennes: Portes duLarge, 2007).
6. For a multiauthor study of the role of Bretons in these exchanges, with participation by specialists from France, Brazil, Portugal, Switzerland, and Germany, see Jean-Yves Nerian, *Les Aventures des Bretons au Bresil a L'Epoque Coloniale* (Rennes: Les Portes du Large, 2007).
7. See Binot Paulmier de Gonneville, *Le Voyage e Gonneville (1503–1505): et la decouvere de la Normandie par les Indiens du Bresil*, with commentary by Leyla Perrone-Moises, trans. Ariane Witkowski (Paris: Chandeigne, 1995).
8. Ella Shohat and I began to refer to "Tupi Theory" in our public lectures for the Summer Programs of the Theory and Criticism Seminar at Cornell University in 2006.
9. Leite Goncalves and Sergio Costa, *Um Porto no Capitalism Global* (São Paulo: Boitempo, 2020), p. 3.
10. Rosa Luxembourg, Quoted in G. Leite Goncalves and Sergio Costa, op. cit., p. 15.
11. Goncalves and Costa, op. cit., p. 4.
12. Montaigne, "Of Cannibals" [1590], in *The Complete Essays of Montaigne*, trans. Donald Frame (Stanford, CA: Stanford University Press, 1957).
13. See Janet Whatley's introduction to her translation of Jean de Léry's *History of a Voyage to the Land of Brazil* (Berkeley: University of California Press, 1992), p. xxiv.

14. See Jack D. Forbes, *The American Discovery of Europe* (Illinois: University of Illinois Press, 2007).
15. For a fascinating study, see Leyla Perrone-Moises, *Vinte Luas: Viagem de Paulmier de Gonneville ao Brasil: 1503–1505* (São Paulo: Companhai das Letras, 1992), p. 155 and also "Essmoricq: O Venturoso Carijo," in Adauto Novaes, eds., *A Outra Margem do Ocidente* (São Paulo: Companhia das Letras, 1999), pp. 335–50.
16. Attempting to explain the apparent ease of this integration, Perrone-Moises speculates that (1) the physical and technical culture of Normandy at that time was not so different from that in indigenous Brazil—the cold climate was probably the greatest shock and (2) Carijo culture was oriented around travel and the search for a mythical "land without evil."
17. See Lestringant, *Le Huguenot et le Sauvage: L'Amérique et la controverse coloniale, en France, au temps des guerres de Religion (1555–1589)* (Geneva: Librarie Droz, 2004), p. 29.
18. See Gilles Havard, *L'Amerique Fantome: Aventuriers Francophones en Amerique* (Paris: Flamarion, 2019).
19. Beatriz Perrone-Moises, "Relacoes Preciosas: Franceses e Ameríndios no Seculo xvii" (doctoral thesis, University of São Paulo, 1996) and Leila Perrone-Moises, *Relacoes Preciosas: Franceses e Amerindios no Seculo xvii* (PhD thesis for University of São Paulo), cited by Renato Sztutman, op. cit., p. 327.
20. See Florestan Fernandes, *A Organizacao Social dos Tupinambá* (São Paulo: EDUSP, 1952).
21. See Alan Gallay, *The Indian Slave Trade* (New Haven: Yale University Press, 2002), pp. 308–10.
22. See Frank Lestringant's wittily titled "Tristes tropistes: Du Brésil à la France, une controverse à l'aube des guerres de religion," *Revue de l'histoire des religions*, Vol. 202, No. 3 (1985), pp. 267–94. Accessed from https://www.persee.fr/doc/rhr_0035-1423_1985_num_202_3_2710.
23. In a Jewish context, the theological disputations had a practical side already familiar from the Jewish diaspora: in the absence of grapes and wheat flower, could Mandioca and Cauim (the fermented native drink) serve as substitutes for the traditional foods?
24. Since the Eucharist constitutes a Christianization of the Passover Seder, it embeds Jewish history as well.
25. Andre Thévet, *Cosmographie Universelle*, cited in Sztutman, op. cit., p. 350.
26. The Portuguese priest José de Anchieta supposedly met Cunhambebe's son in Ubatuba to negotiate what became known as the Armistice of Yperoig, supposedly the first Peace Treaty agreed upon in the Americas.
27. See Frank Lestringant, "The Myth of the Indian Monarchy: An Aspect of the Controversy between Thévet and Léry (1575–1585)," in Christian F. Feest, ed., *Indians and Europe: An Interdisciplinary Collection of Essays* (Lincoln and London: University of Nebraska Press), pp. 37–60.
28. Jean de Léry also notes that the Tupinambá, like the iconoclastic Protestants, have no idols or graphic or visual depictions of the spirits.
29. All this has been endlessly analyzed, beginning with the innumerable interviews given by the director already in the 1970s, many of them cited in Helena Salem's *Nelson Pereira dos Santos: O Sonho Possivel do Cinema Brasileiro* (Rio de Janeiro: Nova Fronteira, 1987). For some of the literature in English, see Richard Pena, *How Tasty Was My Little Frenchman*, in Randal Johnson and Robert Stam, *Brazilian Cinema* (first published by Associated University Presses in 1982 and republished

by Columbia University Press in 1995). (Pena's commentaries are also included as "extras" in the DVD version). See also Robert Stam, *Tropical Multiculturalism: A Comparative History of Race in Brazilian Cinema* (Durham and London: Duke University Press, 1997). For a very thorough discussion that refers to France Antartique, see Darlene J. Sadler's *Nelson Pereira dos Santos* (Urbana: University of Illinois Press, 2003), pp. 58–74, along with work by Guiomar Ramos, Ismail Xavier, Joao Luiz Vieira. For full disclosure, I have often translated for the director and he has frequently addressed my classes at New York University.

30 See Randal Johnson and Robert Stam, eds., *Brazilian Cinema* (2nd edition) (New York: Columbia University Press, 1997).
31 Indeed, the film was rejected by the Cannes Film Festival, land of bikinis and semi-nude starlets, precisely because of its non-voyeuristic normalization of nudity.
32 One of the best-known cases, that of journalist Vladimir Herzog, murdered in prison in 1975, was denounced in the pages of *The New York Review of Books*.
33 The original script, written in 1962–3, focused on a largely exterminated indigenous group—the Caetes—hailed by the modernistas for having devoured the Portuguese Bishop Sardinha.
34 If I may be indulged with a personal anecdote, I served as dos Santos's interpreter when the film was screened at the PFA in Berkeley, California. A member of the audience, a rather paranoid figure well known for systematically harassing guest filmmakers (many representing the various New Waves of the period) with accusations of fascism, asked the first question. "Mr. Dos Santos," she said, "after 500 years of genocide, you have the audacity to give us a film where the villains are the Indians and the hero is the man with blue eyes and blonde hair." Nelson's response was devastating. "Madame," he said, "if you think the actor with blond hair and blue eyes was the hero of my film, that is perhaps because you believe real heroes can only appear in the guise of actors with blond hair and blue eyes."
35 Peter Hulme, *Colonial Encounters: Europe and the Native Caribbean, 1492 to 1797* (London: Metheun, 1986), p. 236.
36 See Mario Carelli, *Culturas Cruzadas* (Campinas, São Paulo: Papirus, 1994), p. 187.
37 Two of the most important scholars linked to Franco-Brazilian relations are Mario Carelli and Leila Perrone de Moises. See Mario Carelli, *Brasil-França: cinco séculos de sedução* (Rio de Janeiro: Espaço em Tempo, 1989) and *Culturas Cruzadas: Intercâmbios culturais entre França e Brasil* (Campinas, São Paulo: Papirus, 1994). For Leila Perrone Moises, see, for example, *Vinte Luas*, op. cit., her book about Essomericq.
38 Manoel de Nobrega, cited in Afonso Arinos de Melo Franco, *L'Indien Bresilien et la Revolution Francaise*, trans. Monique de Moing (Paris: La Table Ronde, 2005), p. 94.
39 The "white Indians" have been the subject of films from all around the Americas, for example *Little Big Man* in the United States (Cinema Center Films, 1970), *Jericó* in Venezuela (Foncine, 1990), *How Tasty Was My Little Frenchman* in Brazil (Condor Films, 1971), and so forth.
40 See Georges E. Sioui, *For an American Auto-History*, trans. Sheila Fischman (Montreal: McGill-Queen's University Press, 1992). Leanne Simpson notes that Lagitau congratulated missionaries for suppressing indigenous queer relationships. See Leanne Betasamoksake Simpson, *As We Have Always Done* (Minneapolis: University of Minnesota Press, 2017), p. 124.
41 See Benoit de L'estoile, *Le Gout des Autres: De L'exposition coloniale aux Arts Premiers* (Paris: Flammarion, 2007), pp. 357–8.

42 This fact is referenced in the "Arizona Jim" character of Renoir's 1936 film *Le Crime de Monsieur Lange* (Oberon).
43 See Olivier Maligne's fascinating ethnography of Indianist clubs in France and Quebec, *Les Nouveaux Indiens: Une Ethnographie du Mouvement Indianophile* (L'Universite Laval: CELAT, 2006).
44 See Marier-Claude Strigier, "Andre Breton et les Hopis: La Fascination de l'Autre" in Gilles Havard and Mickaël Augeron, eds., *Un continent en partage: Cinq siècles de rencontres entre Amérindiens et Français* (Paris: Les Indes Savantes, 2013), p. 489.
45 Cited in Mary del Priore, "Dans le Apaguer des Lumières: Francophilia e Lusofobia na Capital do Brasil Oitocentista," in Carlos Lessa, ed., *Enciclopedia da Brasilidade: Auto-Estima em Verde e Amarelo* (Rio de Janeiro: Casa da Palavra, 2005), p. 158.
46 A possibly fruitful comparison would be between this literary homage to an indigenous confederacy in Brazil and the parallel (uninformed) tribute by Oliver Wendell Holmes to the Iroquois Confederacy in "Hiawatha."
47 Ferdinand Denis, Resumo da História Literária do Brasil, cited in David Brookshaw, *Paradise Betrayed: Brazilian Literature of the Indian* (Amsterdam: CEDLA, 1988), pp. 35–6.
48 Ibid.
49 Ibid.
50 Jose de Alencar, "Introduction to Ubirajara," quoted in Brookshaw, op. cit., p. 80.
51 See Vicent Grégoire, "Jean de Léry: Un Monde non Cannibale est-il possible?," *Sens-Dessous*, Vol. 12, No. 2 (2013), pp. 75–94. Accessed from https://www.cairn.info/revue-sens-dessous-2013-2-page-75.html.
52 Here we find a clear contrast with Robinson Crusoe, who, after many years on his tropical island, is obsessed with remaining clothed, even though he is alone. Crusoe's wealth, incidentally, is generated by a sugar mill (*engenho*) in Bahia, Brazil.
53 Jean de Léry's *Histoire* cited in Rogerio Budasz, "Of Cannibals and the Recycling of Otherness," *Music & Letters*, Vol. 87, No. 1 (January 2006), p. 3.
54 Michel de Certeau, *The Writing of History*, trans. Tom Conley (New York: Columbia University Press, 1988), p. 211.
55 Marcio Souza, "Teatro sem Palavras," in Adauto Novaes, op. cit., p. 106.
56 Montaigne, "Of Coaches" [1590], in *The Complete Essays of Montaigne*, op. cit., pp. 131–2.
57 "Tive por muito tempo comigo um homem que permanecera dez a doze anos neste outro mundo que foi descoberto em nosso século, no local em que Villegagnon aportou ao qual chamou de França Antártica" Montaigne, *Ensaios I*, Chapter XXXI, Tradução de Sérgio Milliet (São Paulo: Editora Nova Cultural, 1996).
58 Montaigne, "Of Cannibals" [1590], in *The Complete Essays of Montaigne*, trans. Donald Frame (Stanford, CA: Stanford University Press, 1957), pp. 155–6.
59 Ibid.
60 See Claude Lévi-Strauss, *Tristes Tropiques* (São Paulo: Companhia das Letras, 1996), p. 292.
61 For an English version of the "Cannibalist Manifesto," see Leslie Bary's excellent introduction to and translation of the poem in *Latin American Literary Review* XIX, No. 38 (July–December 1991).
62 The more timid US American version took the form of Walt Whitman's "barbaric yawp" and Marcus Cunliffe's literary contrast of rebellious "redskins" versus shame-faced "palefaces."

63 Novelist/scholar Marcio Souza suggests that Oswald was also conscious of a perceived cultural contrast within the Tupi-Guaraní, between the smiling, almost "theatrical" Tupi, with their permanent search for the joy of life, and the "grey gloom of the Guaraní." In "Teatro sem Palvras" in Adauto Novaes, op. cit., p. 105.
64 See Renato Sztutman, "The Return of the Anthropophagites: Reconnecting Oswald de Andrade's Proposal to Amerindian Art-Thought" in *Cultural Anthropophagy: The 24th Bienal de São Paulo 1998*, ed. Lisette Lagnado (London: Afterall Books in association with the Center for Curatorial Studies, Bard College, 2015).
65 René Girard, *Violence and the Sacred* (Baltimore: Johns Hopkins, 1972), p. 8.
66 Eduardo Viveiros de Castro, *Cannibal Metaphysics*, ed. and trans. Peter Skafish (Minnesota University Press, 2014), pp. 142–3.
67 See Carlos Fausto, "A Inimizade: Forma e Simbolismo da Guerra Indígena," in Adauto Novais, op. cit., p. 268.
68 Castro Rocha, who studied with Girard at Stanford, had occasion to explain the relevance of Oswald to his work and said that Girard was very generous in his response.
69 Quoted in Joao Cezar de Castro Rocha, *Culturas Shakespearianas: Teoria Mimética e os Desafios da Mímesis Em Circunstâncias Não Hegemônicas* (São Paulo: É Realizações, 2017). The English version of the book is João Cezar de Castro Rocha, *Shakespearean Cultures: Latin America and the Challenges of Mimesis in Non-Hegemonic Circumstances* (East Lansing: Michigan State University Press, 2019).
70 Jose de Alencar, *Ubirajara* (Rio de Janeiro: Jose Olympio, 1965), p. 355.
71 See Peggy Sanday, *Divine Hunger: Cannibalism as a Cultural System* (Cambridge: Cambridge University Press, 1986) [translation mine from the Spanish].
72 João Cezar de Castro Rocha, "Mimetic Theory and Cannibalism," *Arcade*. Accessed from https://arcade.stanford.edu/blogs/mimetic-theory-and-cannibalism
73 Ibid.
74 Ibid.
75 Castro Rocha, op. cit., p. 350.
76 From Oswald de Andrade, "Marcha das Utopias," cited in Beatriz Azevedo, *Antropofagia—Palimpsesto Selvagem* (São Paulo: CosacNaify, 2016), p. 63.
77 Quoted in Benedito Nunes, *Oswald Cannibal* (São Paulo: Perspectiva, 1979), p. 73.
78 See Oswald de Andrade, "A crise da filosofia messiânica," in *A Utopia Antropofágica* (São Paulo: Globo, 2011), pp. 138–215.
79 "A Crise da Filosofia Messianica" is included in Oswald de Andrade, *A Utopia Antropofagica* (São Paulo: Globo, 2010).
80 See Ward Churchill, ed., *Marxism and Native Americans* (Boston: Bacon Press, 1983)
81 See Herbert Marcuse, *Eros and Civilization: A Philosophical Inquiry into Freud* (Boston: Beacon Press, 1955).
82 Oswald de Andrade, "Manifesto Antropófágica," in *A Utopia Antropofágica* (São Paulo: Globo, 2010), p. 48.
83 In the era of mass shootings, to say, for example, that "[t]he simplest Surrealist act consists of dashing down into the street, pistol in hand, and firing blindly, as fast as you can pull the trigger, into the crowd." no longer sounds as daring and provocative as it once might have. See Andre Breton, "Second Manifesto of Surrealism (1930)," in *Manifestoes of Surrealism*, trans. Richard Seaver and Helen R. Lane (Ann Arbor: University of Michigan Press, 1972), p. 125.
84 This evocative phrase is also the title of a short film on Maia Nuku and the mural work of Tongan artist Benjamin Work that she commissioned for a Harlem school,

the subject of the short film *Walking Backwards into the Future* (2018, 12 min) by NYU doctoral student in anthropology Anna Weinreich (Meier 2018). The phrase has also been used by Tongan academic Hūfanga Okusitino Māhina in his 1994 article *Our Sea of Islands* published in The Contemporary Pacific, where he writes that "[p]eople are thought to walk forward into the past and walk backward into the future, both taking place in the present, where the past and the future are constantly mediated in the ever-transforming present," quoted in Nan O'Sullivan, "Walking backwards into the Future: Indigenous Wisdom within Design Education," *Educational Philosophy and Theory*, Vol. 51, No. 4 (2019).

85 It is difficult to characterize Melo Franco's political position in any simple way. In 1937, he was clearly anti-left and even anti-Republican, yet he was instrumental in passing the famous 1951 anti-discrimination law—inspired by discrimination against African-American choreographer Katherine Dunham—that bears his name (the "Lei Afonso Arinos"). He subsequently became Minister of Foreign Affairs under Janio Quadros, with his unaligned foreign policy. After initially supporting the 1964 military coup, he became a Constitutionalist in the 1980s.

86 Afonso Arinos de Melo Franco, *O Indio Brasileiro e a Revolucao Francesa: As Origens Brasileiras da Teoria da Bondade Natural* (Rio de Janeiro: Topbooks, 2002).

87 Rouanet points out that Melo Franco, like all those of the aristocratic bent, was fascinated by his own ancestors, one of whom, a certain Francisco de Melo Franco, an eighteenth-century Brazilian doctor, wrote a treatise on education directly inspired by Rousseau's *Emile*.

88 Quoted in Graeber and Wengrow, op. cit., p. 52.

89 See Sankar Muthu, *Enlightenment against Empire* (Princeton: Princeton University Press, 2003), p. 31.

90 See Florent Guenard, "Rousseau, l'homme sauvage et les Indiens d'Amérique," in Gilles Havard and Mickaël Augeron, eds., op. cit.

91 See Georges E. Sioui Wendayete, "1992: The Discovery of Americity," in Gerald McMaster and Lee-Ann Martin, eds., op. cit., 81, as well as the same author's, *Pour Une Auto-Histoire Amerindienne* (Quebec City: Presse de l'Universite Laval, 1989).

92 Graeber and Wengrow, op. cit., p. 51.

93 Robert Nichols, op. cit., p. 157.

94 Mikhail Bakhtin, *Problems of Dostoevsky's Poetics* (Minneapolis: University of Minnesota Press, 1984), pp. 122–3.

95 Jack Weatherford, *Indian Givers: How the Indians of the Americas Transformed the World* (New York: Ballantine Books, 1989), p. 121.

96 Gerald Vizenor has pointed out that the American Revolution was not necessarily the first revolution in North America since the actual first took the form of the successful Pueblo revolt against the Spanish kingdom of New Mexico on August 10, 1680.Gerald Vizenor, "Transethnic Anthropologism: Comparative Ethnic Studies at Berkeley," *Studies in American Indian Literatures*, Vol. 7, No. 4 (University of Nebraska Press, 1995), p. 3, http://www.jstor.org/stable/20736879.

97 Nichols, op. cit., p. 24.

98 Quoted in Donald Grinde, Jr. and Bruce E. Johansen, *Exemplar of Liberty: Native America and the Evolution of Democracy* (Los Angeles: American Indian Study Center, 1991), p. 155.

99 John P. Foley, ed., *The Jefferson Encyclopedia* (New York: Harper and Row, 1900), p. 422.

100 Robin Wall Kimmerer, *Braiding Sweetgrass: Indigenous Wisdom, Scientific Knowledge and the Teachings of Plants* (Minneapolis, MN: Milkweed Editions, 2013), p. 319.
101 Bruce E. Johansen, *Forgotten Founders: Benjamin Franklin, the Iroquois, and the Rationale for the American Revolution* (Ipswich, MA: Gambit Incorporated Publishers, 1982), p. 14.
102 Quoted in Nichols, op. cit., p. 23.
103 Ibid.
104 See preface to *The American Heritage of Indians* (New York: Del, 1961). One wonders if JFK's "Irishness" played a role in his sympathies for another native people victimized by Great Britain.
105 In the early twenty-first century, the European Union tried to construct an American-style Federation—the United States of Europe. Had they succeeded, they too would have been indirectly indebted to the Iroquois.
106 I am indebted in this section to an important essay on Cohen, by Stephen Haycox, "Felix S. Cohen and the Legacy of the Indian New Deal," *The Yale University Library Gazette*, Vol. 68, No. 3/4 (April 1994), pp. 135–56. Yale University Library Stable URL: http://www.jstor.com/stable/40859096
107 Félix S. Cohen, *Handbook of Federal Indian Law* (Washington, DC: Department of the Interior, 1942, reissue of the original: Albuquerque: University of New Mexico Press, 1968). Cohen headed an extraordinary legal and research staff which compiled forty-six volumes of detailed information on tribes, treaties, and law in just a year. A reissue by the Interior Department in 1958, prepared by Frank B. Home and Margaret F. Hurley, eliminated much commentary originally included by Cohen. An expanded, scholarly version of the work appeared in 1982 from Michie Bobbs Merrill, edited by Rennard Struckland.
108 Cited in Stephen Haycox, op. cit., p. 148.
109 Félix S. Cohen, "Americanizing the White Man," *The American Scholar*, Vol. 21, No. 2 (1952), pp. 183–4.
110 See Luther Standing Bear, *Land of the Spotted Eagle* (Lincoln and London: University of Nebraska Press, 1933).
111 Cited in Grinde and Johansen, *Exemplar of Liberty*, p. 94.
112 Johansen, *Forgotten Founders*, p. 56.
113 Ibid., p. 16.
114 Grinde and Johansen, *Exemplar of Liberty*, p. 112.
115 Ibid., p. 21.
116 Thomas King, *The Inconvenient Indian* (Minneapolis: University of Minnesota Press, 2012), p. 224.
117 See James Tully, *Strange Multiplicity: Constitutionalism in an Age of Diversity* (Cambridge: Cambridge University Press, 1995), p. 4.
118 Ibid., p. 78.
119 See Patrick Petitjean, "As Missoes Universitarias Francesas na Criacao da Universidade de São Paulo" (1934–1940), in Amelia Imperio Hamburger et al., eds., *A Ciencia nas Relacoes Brasill-Franca (1850–1950)* (São Paulo: EDUSP, 1986), passim.
120 Claude Lévi-Strauss "New York Post et Prefiguratif," in Michel Izard, ed., *Le regard éloigné* (Paris: Plon, 1955, new edition 1993), p. 356. One wonders what form of social *pudeur* prevented the French ethnologist from introducing himself and conversing with the man; they possibly would have had a lot to talk about.
121 Page 260 of Portuguese version of *Tristes Tropiques*, quoted in Adauto Novaes op. cit., p. 432. Translation mine.

122 Claude Lévi-Strauss, *Tristes Tropiques* (New York: Penguin, 1973), p. 335.
123 Claude Lévi-Strauss, *Loin de Bresil* (Paris: Chandeigne, 2005), p. 18.
124 Claude Lévi-Strauss, *The View from Afar*, trans. Joachim Neugroschel and Phoebe Hoss (New York: Basic Books, 1984), p. 23.
125 Todorov argues that Lévi-Strauss, who claims to be a cultural relativist—since he speaks in *Structural Anthropology* of "the absurdity of declaring one culture superior to another"—ultimately "finds Indian culture superior"—thus still falling into the trap of ranking and mere binary reversal. Tzvetan Todorov, *On Human Diversity: Nationalism, Racism, and Exoticism in French Thought*, trans. Catherine Porter (Cambridge: Harvard University Press, 1993), pp. 60–89.
126 Vine Deloria Jr., *God Is Red: A Native View of Religion* (Golden, CO: Fulcrum Publication 1994), p. 90.
127 Claude Lévi-Strauss, *Tristes Tropiques* (New York: Penguin, 1973), p. 77.
128 Frank Lestringant, "La mémoire de la France Antarctique," in História (São Paulo), Vol. 27, No.1, Franca (2008), Online version ISSN 1980–4369, http://dx.doi.org/10.1590/S0101-90742008000100007.
129 Lévi-Strauss, *Tristes Tropiques* (Paris: Librairie Plon, 1955), p. 365.
130 Ibid. See pp. 296–300.
131 Ibid., pp. 341–2.
132 Jacques Derrida, "The Violence of the Letter," *Of Grammatology*, trans. Gayatri Spivak (Baltimore and London: The Johns Hopkins University Press, 1974), pp. 101–40, based on the original *De la Grammatologie* (Les Editions de Minuit, 1967).
133 Leslie Marmon Silko, "Language and Literature from a Pueblo Indian Perspective" in John L. Purdy and James Ruuppert, eds., *Nothing but the Truth: An Anthology of Native American Literature* (Upper Saddle River, NJ: Prentice Hall, 1998), p. 159.
134 Gordon Brotherston, *Book of the Fourth World: Reading the Native Americas through Their Literature* (Cambridge: Cambridge University Press, 1992).
135 Scott Richard Lyons, *X-Marks: Native Signatures of Assent* (Minneapolis: University of Minnesota Press, 2010), p. 7.
136 According to Fiorini, Lévi-Strauss agreed to collaborate only in order to call public attention to the necessity of protecting Indian land and culture. Conversation with Marcelo Fiorini in Paris in 2007.
137 Jean de Léry, *l'Histoire d'un voyage faict en la terre du Brésil* (Bibliothèque Classique, 1994), pp. 6–14.
138 See John Murray Cuddihy, *The Ordeals of Civility: Freud, Marx, Levi-Strauss and the Jewish Struggle with Modernity* (Boston: Beacon, 1974).
139 Before his death, Lévi-Strauss responded enthusiastically to the work of some of the indigenous filmmakers from the Amazon, praising *The Agouti's Peanut*, by Komoi and Paturi Panara as "far and away the best film that I have ever seen about the South American Indians … One has the sensation of seeing indigenous life from the inside." I would like to thank Ernesto Ignacio de Carvalho for a copy of this Lévi-Strauss communication. Carvalo is a filmmaker who works with the indigenous filmmakers and is currently a PhD candidate in anthropology at NYU. Ernesto points out that Lévi-Strauss, while praising the indigenous films, still sees them as somehow fulfilling an old anthropological project—of seeing native life from the native point of view, since he praises one sequence as "*un morceau d'anthropologie*."
140 Pierre Clastres, *Arqueologie da Violencia: Pesquisas de Antopologia Politica*, trans. Paulo Neves (São Paulo: Cosac and Naify, 2004), p. 86.
141 See Ward Churchill, *Marxism and Native Americans* (Boston: South End Press, 1983).

142 See Ward Churchill's critique of this aspect of Marxism in Churchill, ed., *Marxism and Native Americans* (Boston: South End Press, 1983).
143 See Veronika Bennholdt-Thomsen and Maria Mies, *The Subsistence Perspective: Beyond the Globalized Economy* (London: Zed, 1999).
144 Pierre Clastre, *Arqueologia da Violencia*, p. 177.
145 Ibid., p. 17.
146 Robin Wall Kimmerer, *Braiding Sweetgrass*, op. cit., p. 376.
147 Ailton Krenak, in Adauto Novaes, ed. op. cit., p. 30.
148 https://montageinterdit.net/
149 Shohat argues that while the relation between Israel and the Palestinians is a colonial relation, the situation is anomalous in the sense that Zionism claimed to be a liberation movement analogous to other liberation movements, and also constituted a colonialism, unlike French and British colonialism, for example, without a metropole. See Ella Shohat, *Israeli Cinema* (Austin: University of Texas Press, first published in 1989 and reprinted with a new Afterword in 2010).
150 In *Race in Translation: Culture Wars around the Postcolonial Atlantic* (New York: New York University Press, 2012), Ella Shohat and I try to deconstruct the pernicious "Anglo-Saxons" versus the Latins dichotomy, arguing that both terms are misnomers which hide the racial multiplicity of both Brazil and the United States. In demographic and cultural terms "Brazil" is not Latin but Indigeno-Afro-Asian-European, and the same could be said of the United States.
151 Sandro de Oliveira, "A Alegoria da Barbárie no filme O Homem que Matou Deus (2013)"DE JESUS, S. (Org). Anais do VIII Seminário Nacional de Pesquisa em Arte e Cultura Visual: arquivos, memorias, afetos. Goiânia, GO: UFG/ Núcleo Editorial FAV, 2015, https://files.cercomp.ufg.br/weby/up/778/o/2015.GT1_sandrooliveira.pdfManuela Penafria, "O ponto de vista no filme documentário" (Universidade da Beira Interior, 2001) http://www.bocc.ubi.pt/pag/penafria-manuela-ponto-vista-doc.pdf
152 Perhaps Vitoux was aware of another "French Connection," i.e. the use of the trope of cannibalism by the 1920s French avant-garde, for example, in the title of the Picabia journal *Le Cannibal*.
153 A YouTube "Wholelottabubblegum" video offers a montage of the massacres in the film, with the vast majority of the victims being indigenous.
154 My translation of the comments I heard at the festival.
155 See Beth A. Conklin, *Consuming Grief: Compassionate Cannibalism in an Amazonian Society* (Austin: University of Texas, 2001). See also Aparecida Vilaca, "Fazendo corpos: reflexões sobre morte e canibalismoentre os Wari' à luz do perspectivismo," *Revista de Antropologia*, Print version ISSN 0034-7701, *Rev. Antropol.* Vol. 41, No. 1 (São Paulo, 1998).
156 Georges E. Sioui, *Amerindian Autohistory* (Montreal: McGill-Queens University Press, 1992), p. 56.
157 Ibid.
158 See Jack D. Forbes, *Columbus and Other Cannibals* (New York: Autonomedia, 1992).
159 Jean-Christophe Rufin, *Rouge Brésil* (Paris: Gallimard, 2001), p. 431.
160 That the old quarrels about the meaning of France Antartique are still alive and well becomes evident in the debates that emerged about the book. In a reprise of the Catholic versus Protestant quarrels of the sixteenth century, Frank Lestringant, for example, found the book full of anti-Protestant clichés. Frank Lestringant, "La mémoire de la France Antarctique," op. cit.

161 See Adauto Novaes, *A Outra Margem do Ocidente* (São Paulo: Companhia das Letras, 1999). This remarkable collection features essays by historians like Frank Lestringant, Serge Gruzinski, and Ronaldo Vainfas, philosophers like Sergio Paulo Rouanet and Marilena Chaui, and native activist/intellectuals like Ailton Krenak and Davi Kopenawa Yanomami.
162 Here we can also mention a Brazilian novel from an earlier period, Antonio Callado's *The Montaigne Expedition* (1982). The novel is only very indirectly about Montaigne. It concerns, rather, the contradictory discourses and movements revolving around the Indians in Brazil. In a quixotic adventure, the journalist Vicentinho Beirão wants to gather an indigenous army from the Xingu to fight against white power and restore power to the Indians. But to advance this mission he solicits the collaboration of Kamaiurá Ipavu, a self-hating Indian and former collaborator with the SPI (Service of Protection of the Indian) who aspires to whiteness. The book orchestrates a polyphony of voices and discourses. Beirao's goal is to reverse 500 years of colonialism to install indigenous hegemony. The plan is to gather an Amazonian army—the Montaigne Expedition—to invade Rio de Janeiro. The army includes assimilated Indians like Ipavu but also the shaman Ierope who wants to use indigenous ritual cures to guarantee the purity of the customs of the tribe. In the end, the book is less about Indians than about the competing discourses about the Indian.
163 Quoted in Robert Nichols, op. cit., p. 104.
164 Speech given by Russell Means in July 1980 for the Black Hills International Survival Meeting.
165 From Viveiros de Castro's preface to the Portuguese version of *The Falling Sky*, p. 51.
166 Dale Turner, op. cit., p. 9.
167 The epigraph to Davi Kopenawa Yanomami, *The Falling Sky: Words of a Yanomami Shaman* (Cambridge: Harvard University Press, 2013).
168 Quoted in the preface to the Portuguese edition of *The Falling Sky*, p. 28.
169 Yanomami, *The Falling Sky*, p. 213.
170 Ibid., p. 213.
171 Ibid., p. 160.
172 Ibid., p. 22.
173 Ibid., p. 18.
174 Vine Deloria, Jr. op cit., p. 151.
175 *The Falling Sky*, p. 208.
176 Ibid., pp. 192–3.
177 Ibid., p. 206.
178 Ibid., p. 209.
179 John Hemming, op. cit., p. 542.
180 Yanomami, *The Falling Sky*, p. 307.
181 Karl Marx, *Capital, Volume I*, trans. Ben Fowkes (London: Penguin Books, 1990, First published 1867).
182 Yanomami, *The Falling Sky*, p. 145.
183 Ibid., p. 184.
184 Ibid., p. 338.
185 Ibid., pp. 254–55.
186 Ibid.
187 Ibid., p. 280.
188 Ibid., p. 295.
189 Ibid., p. 349.

190 Ibid., p. 333.
191 Ibid., p. 338.
192 For more on fetishism and colonialism, see Laura Mulvey, *Xala*, Ousmane Sembene (1974): The Carapace That Failed, *Camera Obscura* (1993), Vol. 11, No. (1 (31)): 48–70.
193 Ibid., p. 352.
194 Ibid.
195 Ibid., p. 353.
196 Ibid.
197 Ibid.
198 William Shakespeare, *The Merchant of Venice* (London, New York, and Bombay: Longmans, Green, and Company, 1899), p. 40.
199 Yanomami, *The Falling Sky*, p. 349.
200 Ibid.
201 Ibid., pp. 354–55.

2

The Indigenous *Cunhã*
The Metamorphosis of a Gendered Trope

A song by Brazilian composer and pop star-intellectual Caetano Veloso offers an entry point into the cultural circuitries swirling around the indigenous cultures of the Red Atlantic. The song sets to music such themes as the transnational flow of ideas around the "Indian" and the multifaceted encounter between various linguistic/cultural zones (Anglophone, Lusophone, Francophone, and Tupiphone). Although my close reading of the poem might be dismissed as a delirious attempt to turn a "pop star" into a minstrel-philosopher, Caetano's intellectualism has long been evident in his writing, his songs, and his interviews, which makes him a kind of public intellectual or, as I have put it elsewhere, playing on Gramsci, an "Orphic-Orphoganic" intellectual pop star, one who often turns to the theme of the "Indian."[1]

The Tupinization of Manhattan

Caetano's song "Manyata," from the 1997 CD "Livros," could be called transhistorical, not in the sense of moving beyond history through a flight into the musical sublime, but rather in the sense of "transiting between" and "counterpointing" various cultural spaces and historical periods. The song directly references the multidirectional movements of ideas between Brazil, Portugal, the United States, and indirectly, France. Here are the lyrics:

> A canoe canoes / Sweeping the morning from North to South
> The Goddess of Legend on the prow / Lifting a torch in her hand
> Everyone in the world / Turns their eyes in her direction / As one feels the taste of the wind
> Singing in the glass panes / The sweet name of the "*cunhã*"
> Manyatan, Manyatan, Manyatan
> A whirlwind of money / Sweeps the entire world, a light leviathan
> And here wars dance amidst / The peace of the dwellings of love
> Where is it all heading, when it goes / This immense joy, this exaltation
> Ah. Solitude, Multitude / And that beautiful girl

Biting the pulp of the apple.
Manyatan, Manyatan, Manyatan

Although the scene of the poem often goes unrecognized by Brazilian, American, and international students, the lyrics clearly refer to the Hudson River Bay and environs, depicted in an indeterminate time/space that mingles pre-Columbian time and the globalized present.[2] The "Manyata" of the title constitutes a nasalized Brazilianized version of "Manhattan," pronounced so as to sound like a word from Tupi, and therefore unrecognizable to many listeners as "Manhattan." The New York location is further stressed, however, by the North/South rowing of the canoe—the Lenape called the Hudson River *Shatemuc* ("the river that flows both ways")—and by thinly veiled references to the Statue of Liberty and Wall Street.[3]

Caetano was partially inspired by the nineteenth-century Brazilian poet Sousândrade, who wrote his thirteen-canto poem "*O Guesa*" while spending fourteen years in New York City. In the poem, Sousândrade laments the calamitous impact of the "gentle shadow of the cross" on Brazilian Indians. Joaquim de Sousa Andrade was a second-generation romantic, a contemporary of Baudelaire, whose ironic epic poem was first published in fragments in 1867. Inspired by the legends of the Muyscas Indians of Columbia, the poem's *Guesa* reference is to a legendary child stolen away from his parents, who was destined to fulfill a mystical destiny related to the Inca sun god. The climactic moment, set in 1870, arrives in Canto X, where the poem contrasts Orpheus, Dante, and Aeneas, who descended into Hell, with the Brazilian-Inca-*Guesa* poet, who descends into "the inferno of Wall Street," where he witnesses the corruption of a "young vanguard people" living in a "new world of candor and laughter [but where] the heart is saddened by evil."[4]

Caetano is rendering homage, then, to another Brazilian poet in New York who also touched on pan-indigenous themes. In his 1997 memoir *Verdade Tropical* (translated into English in 2002 as *Tropical Truth*), Caetano notes that "an indigenous word names the island where canyons of skyscrapers rise." "Manhattan" is an indigenous word, said to be derived from an Algonquin expression meaning "hilly island." The song's indigenous vocabulary and imagery remind us that what became New Amsterdam/New York was earlier a constellation of native communities encamped around a river. A subgroup of the Lenape (or Delaware), the Wappinger, are said to have "migrated to Manhattan each summer, assembled seasonal camps in the northern area of the island, cultivated maize on communal land and fished in the waters nearby."[5] Archeologists have found evidence of many habitation sites and planting fields and noted the intricate paths that later morphed into city streets like Broadway, whose winding ways differentiate it from the imperial rectilinearity of the Manhattan street grid.

While the music and lyrics evoke the calm cadence of rowing, the imagery of canoes on the Hudson evokes a time of indigenous sovereignty, while also conjuring up European amazement at the time of First Contact. The Dutch and the English in the Hudson Valley, like the Portuguese in Brazil, spoke of a "new Eden" and a "terrestrial Canaan" where the land flowed "with milk and honey." But the "whirlpool of money" reminds us that Manhattan soon got sucked into the maelstrom of competition between European empires and commercial companies. Ever since the days of the

Chartered West India Company (*Geoctroyeerde Westindische Compagnie*), the city has constituted a key node within what would later be called globalized networks.[6]

Caetano's legendary torch-holding goddess reminds us of another moment in New York history, when France gifted the Statue of Liberty as a token of the alliance between two "Sister Republics" emerging from Enlightenment political thinking. As a typical illuminist symbol—Enlightenment, "*Des Lumieres*," "*Iluminismo*," "*Auflkarung*"— Lady Liberty's torch metaphorizes the bright beams of freedom generated by the two revolutions. The young woman in the canoe, whose name echoes throughout the city, is thus multiply symbolic; she is at the same time Lady Liberty, the city of Manhattan, and a Native Eve in a pre-Columbian paradise. By depicting a contemporary woman eating an apple, Caetano plays both on the Edenic fruit and on "the Big Apple." The woman is also a native Brazilian, more precisely a Tupi woman, since Caetano calls her a "*cunhã*," Tupi for "young woman." Through the audacious fusion of a Native American woman with a Tupi woman, Caetano promotes a threshold encounter between the indigenous cultures of North and South America, against the implied backdrop of the illuminated culture of Europe incarnated in the Statue of Liberty, within a transhistorical chronotope that comingles leisurely pre-Conquest time with the frenetic pace of Wall Street in the late 1990s.

A shift in perspective accompanies the collective "eyes of the world" gazing toward Lady Liberty, evoking both Emma Lazarus's invitation to the "huddled masses yearning to breathe free" and the United States as a self-defined beacon of freedom. At the same time, Caetano's transnational, and in some ways subalternized gaze, assumes Manhattan as a magnet for capital and, for Caetano, a radiating center of popular culture. The vantage point is from the POV of a Global South obliged to turn its often unreciprocated gaze toward Global North cities like New York, London, and Paris. The music, meanwhile, evokes the African and African-American side of Manhattan through Afro-Bahian rhythms, Marvin Gaye-style talking interludes, and an orchestration reminiscent of the cool jazz of the Gil Evans/Miles Davis collaborations of the 1950s and 1960s, with their muted trumpets and suave French-impressionist harmonies. Just as Caetano poetically links native North America to native South America, his music evokes the felicitous marriage of Brazilian and American music, infused with a shared African influence.

Caetano deploys an oxymoron to name the force that sweeps the world. He calls it a "light Leviathan." The term simultaneously evokes the whale that swallowed the prophet Jonah, and Melville's Ishmael, narrator of another whale story, sitting in Battery Park and noting that "meditation and water are wedded forever."[7] The more crucial reference, however, is to Hobbes's *Leviathan*. For Hobbes, Leviathan refers to that awe-provoking entity, incarnated in the State or in a monarch, which prevents people from regressing into a barbarous "state of nature" and a life that is "solitary, poor, nasty, brutal and short."[8] The "whirlpool of money," meanwhile, conjures up a Manhattan buffeted, already in Hobbes's time, by the trade winds and oceanic currents of the slave trade and competing commercial empires. Caetano moves quickly, moreover, from Leviathan to war. In lines evocative both of native war dances and of Hobbes's "war of each against each,"[9] the lyrics tells us that "here wars dance amidst the peace of the dwellings of love." Caetano's choice of the cozy word *moradas* (dwellings) instead of the more impersonal *edificios* (buildings) meanwhile is more redolent of Native American longhouses or Tupi *malocas* than of Manhattan skyscrapers, thus reminding us, once again, of an indigenous presence.

Hobbes's *Leviathan* was published in 1651, at a time of tension not only between different factions in England but also between the Native Americans, the Dutch, and the British in New Amsterdam. American school children learn that the Dutch leader Peter Minuit "purchased" Manhattan from the Lenape in 1626, clearly an absurdity since the Lenape likely viewed the "sale" of Manhattan merely as a deal to share the land, but never to sell it, since the Lenape did not see land as alienable property. The "purchase" had less to do with indigenous appraisals of value than with rival land claims of competing Europeans. The Dutch, viewing the sale as legitimate, demanded that the Indians vacate what the Dutch considered to be "Dutch land." The transaction, enforced by the eventual building of a wall around New Amsterdam, marked the very beginning of the Lenape's forced migration out of their homeland. The wall eventually became Wall Street, and *Manahatta* became Manhattan, where part of the Lenape trade route, known as *Wickquasgeck*, became *Brede weg*, later Broadway. Much as the Tupi peoples traded with one another, the Lenape cultivated trade relationships with the Haudenosaunee, the Mohicans, and the Shinnecock. (We will return to the Lenape at the end of this chapter.)

What then do we make of this whale, this *monstrum horrendum*, swimming in the icy waters of financial calculation in South Manhattan?[10] Hobbes's greatest fear was of the anarchy inherent in a "state of nature," a putatively "repellant" condition which he imagined to characterize the indigenous peoples of North America. Hobbes cites the "savage people in many places of America [i.e. indigenous Americans] [who] have no government at all, and live at this day in that brutish manner."[11] Indians thus provide Hobbes with his sole non-hypothetical example of the "state of nature," in reference to a savage state of nature to the North of Manhattan, in what he did not know to be Haudenosaunee territory. Yet native and non-native historians inform us that the Hudson Valley, in Hobbes's own time, was the cradle of various native nations, some of which, the Iroquois (Haudenosaunee) being the most celebrated example, had long-lasting viable consensus governments.[12] The new Leviathan that inspires awe, meanwhile, is no longer the state but rather the "whirlpool of money" sweeping the world. The new sovereign monster is a "light" one operating, in the age of transnational capital flows, neither through the heavy hand of monarchy nor even through the modern nation-state monopoly on violence, but rather through the unbearable lightness of electronic currency transfers and plastic market transactions, i.e. the liquidities of financial capitalism. These overtones are not surprising, given that the poem was written in the mid-1990s, the apotheosis of euphoric globalization and neoliberal ideology, the Washington Consensus, and Fukayama's "End of History."

In his memoir *Verdade Tropical*, Caetano speaks of his feelings about New York, where he has his own *morada* and where he has performed innumerable times:

> I think I wrote this book … because of New York. … Coming for the first time in the eighties, I felt surprisingly at ease there, as I had never felt in England or even in continental Europe, even in the Italian or Iberian parts. I soon understood

why: I was—as I am in Rio or São Paulo, in Salvador or Santo Amaro [Caetano's home city in Brazil]—on American territory. [Obviously, Caetano means "American" in the Latin American sense of "all the Americas"].[13]

Keywords in the poem are of indigenous origin, beginning with the title and the very first word of the poem, "canoe," borrowed from Arawak by Columbus on his first voyage. Caetano then underlines the indigenous echoes in key words: "The word 'Manhattan' which I found in the amazing 'Inferno de Wall Street' ... by the Brazilian romantic poet Sousandrade, by dint of its metric and rhyme, would sound in Portuguese like 'Manyata.' So it comes back to mind like some Tupi word each time I walk through those canyons dotted with golden portals. I hum to myself fondly and smile at the instant understanding I am able to have of the North American adventure [and] of its inevitably mestiza reality."[14] This last line echoes a hidden polemic revolving around a Brazilian cliché about the United States, specifically the idea that "unlike the 'Anglo-Saxon Americans,' we Brazilians are racially mixed," since for Caetano the United States is also "inevitably mixed" (*fatalmente mestizo*) even though racism prevents the nation from acknowledging its own mixedness. By Tupifying Manhattan—and we cannot exclude the possibility that people of Tupi ancestry might actually have come to New Amsterdam from Brazil—Caetano, from the point of hearing of a sound-sensitive singer, renders audible the Tupi-Portuguese overtones of "Manhattan." The poem weaves together allusions to the song "Autumn in New York," with its "canyons of steel ... making [him] feel [he's] home." (Caetano was probably unaware that Haudenosaunee ironworkers raised and riveted the beams of the iconic skyscrapers that formed those "canyons of steel.")

Caetano's lyrics resonate with the multilayered history of New York City. After the period of indigenous sovereignty, seventeenth-century New Amsterdam ultimately became a multilingual and multiethnic city, and present-day New York City constitutes home for thousands of Native Americans, who celebrate their living culture and exercise symbolic power in cultural institutions such as the Native American Music Association, the various Native American Community Houses, and the New York-based Lenape Museum. Some 100,000 Native American people are estimated to live in New York City, a number which presumably does not include the immigrants and migrants of indigenous origin from Latin America, who might even speak indigenous languages like Zapotec or Guaraní, the second official language of Paraguay and the country of origin of thousands of New Yorkers, many concentrated in Queens. The September 11, 2001, terrorist attacks targeted a center of global financial power, but that center was located on the same few acres that included the Smithsonian National Museum of the American Indian, once a venue for indigenous media-makers, including some, as we shall see, who speak languages from the Tupi-Guaraní family. By opting to place a native Tupi "*cunhã*" in a Lenape canoe, in sum, Caetano transnationalizes and feminizes indigeneity.[15]

The Manhattan topography has more recently been the site of a different kind of storm. In a *New York Times* op-ed, Eric W. Sanderson, creator of a book and digital installation, called "Mannahatta," which depicts Manhattan island before European occupation, and which I have remixed with a YouTube clip of the Caetano song, explains that the damage caused by Hurricane Sandy in 2012, and by Hurricane Ida in 2021, had to do with the predictable flooding of what had been long-standing marshlands, disguised by landfill and topped with buildings. The Lenape people, he points out, knew better than to dig caves in stream beds, noticing that salt marshes and barrier beaches "worked together to protect the coastline and restore it after storms." They understood, he adds, "that we need to live on the land with humility and compassion" and that "water will go where water has always gone." In conclusion, he writes, "Let the streams run free."[16]

The "*Cunhã*" as Filmmaker

A contemporary incarnation of the *cunhã* figure comes to us in the person of Guaraní filmmaker Patricia Ferreira (Para Yxapi), who came to Manhattan in 2018 to show her film at the Margaret Mead Film Festival at the Museum of Natural History. Ferreira's 2009 film, *Nós e a Cidade* (The City and Us), stresses the importance of land, handicraft, and the fraught relationship with the white world for the Indigenous Mbya-Guaraní in the state of Rio Grande do Sul. A film about Ferreira's visit, *New York: Just Another City*, by Brazilian filmmakers Joana Brandão and André Lopes, accompanies Patricia as she walks through the museum on the occasion of the screening of her film. The Brandão/Lopes film consists of material about the Ferreira visit, clips from Ferreira's films, and footage of Times Square filmed by Ferreira herself. The filmmakers interweave Patricia's voice and point of view with their own images and sounds. In the film, we see Patricia admiring the immense 63-foot canoe constructed by the Haida nation of the Pacific Northwest, reminiscent of the capacious Tupi canoes. She notices the beautiful objects in the Amazonian Rain Forest exhibit and wonders aloud about their provenance and what they might have meant for the people who created them. In the Guaraní tradition, she notes, objects that people made were usually buried with the deceased, not made available for museums. The collected objects are beautiful, she says, but the sacred flutes should not have been separated from their community. If the people who created these objects tried to recover those objects, she speculates with an ironic smile, it would probably provoke a "tremendous fight."

Ferreira watches the visitors admiring the photos of Amazonian natives but suspects that very little real respect is involved. She finds the static figures and frozen poses of the exhibitions frustrating and expresses her preference for the film medium, with its capacity to show people in movement, and use dialogue and voice-over to comment on the images on the screen. The scene recalls another museum film—Alain Resnais/Chris Marker's *Les Statues Meurent Aussi* (1953), a long-censored avant-garde denunciation of the colonial museum and the theft of African Art. A sequence in that film accompanies a woman of color contemplating the exhibits of African artifacts, as the voice-over speculates about her thoughts. As was common even in leftist avant-garde films, the voice-over speaks for the woman; she never gets to express her own thoughts. In *A City Like Another*, in contrast, the "*cunhã*" speaks for herself, without mediation, as an honored producer of culture and participant in the museum's events.

During the Q&A after the screening, the Brandão/Lopes film shows Ferreira criticizing the Bolsonaro government's anti-indigenous policies. A Bolsonarista in the audience rudely objects that he did not come to see a "political film." She answers calmly, as if accustomed to such attacks, reminding him that indigenous peoples have been suffering for over 500 years and have every right to protest. The following sequence shows clips from her film screened at the Festival, which shows the Guaraní mastery of handicraft. The weavers explain that the elders had foreseen that the forest would become exhausted, obliging them to find other ways to support themselves. Not unlike Davi Kopenawa, Patricia is not terribly impressed by the "greatest city in the world." Riding the subway, she remarks that for her New York is "just another city" like São Paulo, with the same structures and atmosphere. Another section shows her filming Times Square with her cell phone as a favor for her mother, but she adds that in personal terms it leaves her cold. In an aesthetic commentary, she observes that Americans see great size as a value—the bigger the better—while the Guaraní prize small things. She worries about the energy wasted in maintaining the lights of the proliferating advertising screens in Times Square. Interestingly, Ferreira discerns the presence of nature even amidst the concrete—birds, stones, and plants peeping out from the cracks of the pavement, avatars of what she calls "the diversity of spirits existing in the world."

The *Cunhã* as Myth: Paraguaçu

In the long view, understanding the genealogy of the *cunhã* in the Brazilian context requires going back to the gendered tropes of Conquest and Discovery. The famous engravings of Johann Theodor de Bry figure the Americas as a woman. The metaphor of the "Virgin Land," similarly, must be seen in diacritical relation to the metaphor of the European "motherland." A "virgin" land is presumably available for defloration and fecundation; ownerless, it becomes the property of its "discoverers" and cultivators. The virginal "purity" that the term implies masks the dispossession of an already cultivated land and its resources. Throughout the Americas we find historical and literary figures, especially female figures who have become the foci of symbolic struggles over the politics of gender, nation, and sexuality. Many countries have "figured" the relation between Europeans and the indigenous peoples through tales of heterosexual romance with prestigious native women: Cortez and Malinche in Mexico, Martim and Iracema in Brazil, Captain John Smith and Pocahantas in the United States—but in each country the story is interpreted differently. In Mexico, the story of Cortez and Malinche (personal name Malinalli) was transformed by nationalists into a tale of *la chingada*, of female betrayal and violation, a story, which, according to Octavio Paz, makes the Mexicans metaphorically the offspring of the white European rape of the indigene, a view ardently contested by Mexican feminists and by films like *La Otra Conquista* (1998).

Understanding the long-term origins of the *cunhã* figure in Brazil requires a return to the very beginnings of post-Cabralian Brazilian history. The earliest example of the *cunhã* figure comes from the story of the relationship between the shipwrecked Portuguese cartographer Diogo Álvares and the Tupi Princess Paraguassu, daughter of chief Itaparica. A hybrid of fact and legend, the narrative has Diogo Álvares arrive in Brazil at the dawn of the sixteenth century, where he falls in love with Paraguaçu. Diogo, who the Tupi renamed "Caramuru," learned the Tupi language and participated in Tupi wars. In some versions, the Tupi were impressed with the explosions of his musket and renamed him "Magical Fire," but the more prosaic understanding is that they named him in Tupi "*Morae*," eel or Sea Dragon, because they scooped him up on the beach as a shipwrecked sailor on the verge of death.

Paraguaçu first became famous through the 1781 epic poem by José de Santa Rita Durão—entitled simply *Caramuru*—where Paraguaçu is described in Eurocentric terms as having "a color white as snow." The Brazilian story relates a tale of racial chiasmus of criss-crossed assimilations within uneven power relations. All the accounts celebrate the marriage of Diogo and Paraguaçu as a symbol of social harmony, conciliation, and racial diversity. The hero Diogo is both the conqueror of Paraguaçu and of her society, and is at the same time rescued and accepted by them, in a double role that conforms to Paulo Emilio Salles Gomes's formula that Brazilians are both the "occupier and occupied."[17]

The Paraguaçu story has obvious similarities with the story of Pocahantas. Just as Paraguaçu was the daughter of powerful Chief Itaparica, so Pocahantas was the daughter of an Algonquin chief from the Powhatan Confederacy. Both Diogo Álvares and John Smith were cartographers, and in fact John Smith was the first English explorer to map the Chesapeake Bay area and later the coast of New England. Both Pocahantas and Paraguaçu went to Europe and met royalty there. Diogo Álvares and Paraguaçu married in France on July 30, 1528, and met Catherine de Medici. Pocahontas and John Rolfe married near Jamestown on April 5, 1614, but traveled to London in 1617, where Pocahontas attended a Ben Jonson masque and a Shakespeare play. Presented to the King, she took the name Lady Rebecca, much as Paraguaçu took the name Catherine, in homage to Catherine of Medici. Both women were translators and mediators between European and indigenous civilizations, and both enjoyed high status in their respective groups.

A number of native American writers, such as Paula Gunn Allen and Gerald Vizenor, have reconfigured the Pocahontas story in versions that, to quote Heike Paul, "range from the deconstruction of popular stereotypes of Native Americans in general and of Pocahontas in particular to various new interpretations of the historical moment of cultural contact between Pocahontas and the English settlers/invaders and its consequences."[18] Laguna Pueblo-Metis-Scottish-Lebanese writer Paula Gunn Allen, one of the pioneers of native literary criticism, develops an indigenous approach to biography. Allen's "gynocritical" book *The Sacred Hoop* analyzes native concepts of gender and sexuality and the prominent role of female figures such as Spider Woman and Sky Woman in indigenous creation stories. In *Pocahontas: Medicine Woman, Spy, Entrepreneur, Diplomat*, Gunn Allen treats *Pocahontas* not only as a story about an indigenous woman, but as a story ideally told in an indigenous way, rooted in indigenous thought and life ways as a set of relations. In "Native traditional life stories," she writes:

[T]he subject of the biography—or, often, autobiography—is situated within the entire life system: that community of living things, geography, climate, spirit people, and supernaturals. ... Thus, I am basing my narrative on several assumptions: that *manito*—a complicated word that relates to paranormal, supernatural and transcendent conditions of consciousness, existence, and event—is reality. I am also assuming the reality of the *manito aki*, the spirit world or realm where supernatural live and where the laws of physics are distinct from ours.[19]

Gunn Allen writes explicitly from the standpoint of a Laguna Pueblo woman, a culture which she describes as holding women in high respect, where descent is matrilineal and the primary deities are female. Pocahontas's multiple names—Pocahontas (her childhood name), Matoaka (her adult name), Amonute (her medicine woman name), and Rebecca (her Christian name) reflect the layered complexity of her story.

The societies of the Powhatan Alliance (the Dream-Vision People), the loosely allied group of Algonquin-speaking tribes which settled in what we now call Chesapeake Bay, were matrilocal and matrilineal. For Gunn Allen, Pocahontas was a priestess and a medicine woman whose birth had been foretold. She learned from the *manito* (spirits) that the end of the Powhatan Confederacy had been prophesied in 1500. Gunn Allen notes that the English world and the Algonquin worlds were not as far apart as some self-aggrandizing narratives might suggest. Both groups lived in dwellings constructed out of large logs and roofed with thick branches. Both believed in the spirit world, whether in the form of shamans and forest spirits among the Algonquin, or the devils, witches, and faeries among the English. Both cultures enjoyed pageantry and masque-like festivities. Speaking of the long-term progeny of Pocahontas and John Rolfe, Gunn Allen writes: "The mixed-blood descendants of Powhatan-English stock number around three-million at the present time. They reside in the United States, England, and it is likely, all over the world. It is hoped that some of them dream."[20] Interestingly, Gunn Allen in effect "Brazilianizes" the story by making Pocahontas a kind of mother of the American nation.

The legends about Paraguaçu and Pocahontas both represent them as saviors of white men.[21] Within the standard North American version of the legend, the young daughter of the Indian chief saves John Smith from execution by offering her own head to receive the death blow in his place. But the notion that Pocahontas saved Captain Smith from beheading, for Gunn Allen, was a paranoid projection based on his traumatic memories of a Tower of London bedecked with the heads of the executed. What Smith thought was an imminent execution was in reality a diplomatic ritual preparing him for incorporation into the tribe; he did not understand that he was meant to be an adoptive Indian with the name Nantaquod.[22] Part of the Paraguaçu legend, similarly, is that she saved Diogo Álvares from drowning. Pocahontas helps Smith preserve a white colony from starvation and later marries into the English elite. Paraguaçu, meanwhile, formed part of a mixed power couple linked to the elite of Bahia. In ideological terms, both stories offer a reassuring benediction to Europe's dominating presence in the so-called New World, thus assuaging European guilt concerning the dispossession of indigenous peoples. All the accounts of Caramuru and Paraguaçu speak of their vast progeny, making them the forebears of a mestizo Brazil.

Doris Sommer, in the context of Latin American literature, speaks of such romances as "foundational fictions," usually involving a relationship between an indigenous woman and a European man. There was a brief period where a connection to Pocahontas was a source of pride for members of the Virginia colonial aristocracy—and although Thomas Jefferson expressed satisfaction that both of his daughters married descendants of Pocahontas,[23] later and more generally North American ideology promoted myths of separation, and the doomed nature of love between white and Indian (for example in the novels of James Fenimore Cooper), Brazilian ideology promoted myths of fusion. Whereas US tradition venerates the Euro-American founding fathers, the Brazilian literary tradition pays homage to an indigenous mother. While Brazilian literature lauded cross-racial heterosexual romance as the generative matrix of a mestizo nation, American literature stressed male bonding between white frontiersmen and Native American men. In the United States and Germany, characters like Leatherstocking in Cooper, and Shatterhand in Karl May, as we shall see, exemplified a different sexual dynamic, a subliminal attraction between White men and Red men.[24]

The romantic poets and novelists of the Indianist movement saw Brazil as the product of a fusion figured in the marriage of the Indian Iracema with the European Martins in Alencar's *Iracema* (1865), or in the love of the indigenous Peri and the European Ceci in the same novelist's *O Guarani* (1857). As Doris Sommer wittily puts it, "this putative mutuality of affection makes it hard to choose between *O Guaraní* and *Iracema* as *the* national romance; that is between Indian men loving white women and Indian women loving white men."[25] The Indianist romance story ignores some key actors in Brazilian history—the indigenous man, the non-assimilated indigenous woman, gays and lesbians, and especially enslaved Africans, then and for most of Brazilian history the majority population. Indianism, in this sense, promoted a double obfuscation of the two original sins of the Americas: slavery and genocide. The exaltation of the "Indian" thus involved an element of bad faith toward both the Indian and the Black. By celebrating the fusion of an idealized noble Indian with an equally idealized noble European, Indianist novels neglected the Black, seen at that time purely as a source of labor, shorn of all rights of citizenship, and an iconic reminder of the brutality of slavery, hardly an image the elite wanted to project. To valorize Blacks within a slave-holding society would be to cast whites as villains. At the same time, the exaltation of the Indian was dedicated to the very group afflicted by a process of literal and cultural genocide. The Indians of Ceará celebrated in *Iracema* were confronting a process of attempted extermination when Alencar published his novel. While the actually existing Indian was killed, marginalized, or "dissolved" through miscegenation, the remote, literary Indian was exalted. Tracy Devine Guzman sums up the situation: "operatic and literary Indianism hastened the destruction of Native lives and livelihoods by bolstering fables of benevolent colonialism and cordial miscegenation during extended periods of anti-indigenous violence."[26]

The cinemas of both the United States and Brazil return obsessively to the theme of European-indigene romance, but the gender and race politics are distinct. Hollywood films like *Call Her Savage* (1932) and *The Oklahoman* (1957) display a fear of blood-tainting which bars the "half breed" (Native American or mestiza) female protagonists from mixed marriages, even though the roles are usually played by white actresses. In these films, the female protagonists usually return to their tribe, people, or country; in others *(Broken Arrow*, 1950; *Across the Wide Missouri*, 1951) they are sacrificed for attempting to form a bridge between the races. The love affair between Pocahontas and John Smith, in the Disney version, ends with his return to England, even though the real-life Pocahontas did marry the Englishman John Rolfe, with whom she had a child who grew up in England. Yet neither that relationship nor the imagined romance with John Smith generated a national mythology of mixing: in the United States miscegenation remained taboo. The Indianist novelist James Fenimore Cooper has his character Leatherstocking state the taboo explicitly to his Indian friend Chingachgook: "I am white—have a white heart, and can't, in reason, love a redskin maiden, who must have a redskin heart and feelin's."[27] In silent films like *The Chief's Daughter* (1911) and *Comata The Sioux* (1909), as Joanna Hearne points out, the native woman's love for the white man leads her to breaking her bonds with her people. Why, Joanna Hearne asks, do films like *The Squaw Man* (1931) and other films like it "link Native women's marriage to white men with the women's suicide?"[28]

In Brazil, meanwhile, romantic Indianism remains alive and well even in the 1990s, as becomes evident with Norma Bengell's adaptation of *O Guaraní* in 1996. Peri, the Guaraní of the title, is pure, in harmony with nature, and loyal to his white masters. The film's score features the strains of the Italianate opera *Il Guarani* by the "Brazilian Verdi" Carlos Gomes, the "savage of the opera" in Europe, who happened to be of partial indigenous descent.[29] The actor who plays Peri, Marcio Garcia, looks more like a sun-bronzed Adonis from Ipanema than a member of any actual indigenous group. The character, the novel's "unvanquished warrior, the first in his tribe," works for Dom Antonio and his daughter Cecilia because of a debt—his mother was saved by the Dom. In love with Cecilia, this "good Indian" fights with the Portuguese against the "bad Indians," the Aimore cannibals. In the usual colonial splitting, the "Good" Indian is defined by service to the Colonialists, and the "Bad" Indian by his "savage" fight against them. Oswald de Andrade later switched the valence through his explicit hostility to "the Indian son of Mary, godson of Catherine de Medici"[30]—a reference to Paraguacu, while being enthusiastic about the rebel Indian, and in his manifestoes, Oswald cites Peri as an exemplum of servility to colonial power.

In both the United States and Brazil, indigenous women played a crucial symbolic role in the construction of national identity. In the United States, the native princess, sometimes in love with and willing to die for the white man, became a non-threatening symbol of white Americas's "right" to indigenous land. In the prevailing view, the princess was gentle, noble, unthreateningly sensuous, virtually a white Christian, and yet tied to native soil. The mid-nineteenth-century Indianism of Jose de Alencar or Gonçalves Dias in Brazil, for its part, exalted a mythic indigenous figure known for bravery, beauty, and honesty, without clothing, ambition, or vanity, a kind of ideal ancestor figure. The story served strategically to explain away the darker color of the majority of Brazilians in comparison with their Portuguese ancestors, eliding any awkward mention of the majoritarian black presence that actually typified most of Brazil's history. Romanticism was largely an invention of urban intellectuals elegizing an idealized group that was supposedly vanishing. Meanwhile, on the "frontier," as usually occurs with settler colonialism, things were more frankly brutal, lacking the veil of what Joseph Conrad called the "redeeming idea" of civilization. In those regions, the dominant group had an interest in painting the indigenous peoples as nomadic primitives, unworthy of retaining their own land. Within the dominant ideology, it was acceptable, even chic, to have indigenous ancestors as long as they had been "whitened," cleansed of any strong affiliation with an indigenous community.

The Brazilian accounts of mixed ancestry are highly gendered. It was no accident that the preferred ancestor was usually a grandmother and not a grandfather—Vine Deloria in the North American context speaks of the "Indian grandmother syndrome." The converse romance, a fecund heterosexual couple composed of an Indian Man and a European woman, rarely occurs in fiction. This taboo on gender equality and reciprocity is not merely literary; it has social ramifications in real life even today. The indigenous *Video in the Villages* film *Antonio and Pitti*, for example, concerns a socially momentous marriage between Antonio, an Ashininka leader, and a non-indigenous woman, Pitti. The match triggered widespread resentment and social opprobrium in the non-indigenous community, but not in an Ashininka community accustomed to adopting outsiders. Pitti herself comments in the film that the reverse situation—a non-indigenous marrying an indigenous woman—was common and not at all controversial.

Caramuru: The Invention of Brazil

It was within the context of the Quincentennial of Pedro Cabral's "Discovery" that TV Globo conceived of a multi-platform production based on the Diogo/Álvares-Paraguaçu story, entitled *Caramuru: The Invention of Brazil*, directed by the innovative directors Guel Arraes and Jorge Furtado. The project took the form first of a TV miniseries, then of a feature film, followed by a DVD. As the subtitle suggests, the miniseries exploits the Caramuru/Paraguaçu romance as the trampoline for a reflection on the "invention" of Brazilian identity. Just as Hayden White argues in *Metahistory* that the distinction between myth and history is a relatively recent invention, in that both involve writing and emplotment, the subtitle of the series—"The Invention of Brazil"—suggests a sophisticated "post" conception of the nation not as an essence, but rather as something narrated, figured, constructed, and invented, thus allying itself with notions of "imagined communities" (Anderson), "invented traditions," (Hobsbawm), and nations as "narrative constructs" (Homi Bhabha).

Like the Iracema/Martim romance in Alencar's novel *Iracema*, the romance between Paraguaçu and Diogo Álvares perfectly exemplifies Doris Sommers's concept of "foundational fictions," whereby a tentative Brazilian identity crystallized around an idealized erotic encounter. That fiction saw the heterosexual and fecund relation between Portuguese man and indigenous women as providing the cultural matrix from which arose the Brazilian nation. The TV series begins with the well-known Globo actor Marco Nanini relating a literally star-crossed romance. Like poet John Keats, the narrator reads the "night's starred face" to discern the "cloudy symbols of a high romance." As the CGI-generated imagery transports us magically back and forth across the Atlantic sky, the narrator tells us:

The Indigenous Cunhã   127

January first, 1500. A young Portuguese man looks out at the first night of the 16th century. The polar star, the guide for navigators, shines at a 25 degree angle to the horizon. The Orion Constellation is almost drowning in the Atlantic Ocean. He does not know it, but the stars are determining a remarkable destiny for him. At this very moment, seven thousand kilometers away, on the other side of the Atlantic, in a place called Pindorama, is shining the constellation of the Southern Cross in Tupi called *Paui-Podole*. A young Indian woman is looking at this other sky. She knows that the stars represent the souls of dead indigenous heroes. What she does not know is that she too will become a heroine. And that she will become a star in the sky. His name is Diogo, which in Latin means "educated person;" her name is Paraguassu, which in Tupi means "the great sea." She is a princess, but he will mistake her for a savage. A social outcast, he will become the "King of Brazil." And their story will become a legend.

The story is presented cinematically as a fast-edited shuttle back and forth across the Atlantic between Portugal and Brazil. The film gestures toward cultural reciprocity by having each side interpret the encounter through the cultural grid furnished by their own language and mythologies, for example by providing the Portuguese and indigenous names for the Southern Cross constellation.

Extraordinarily sophisticated in technical and aesthetic terms, *Caramuru*, in its various formats, audaciously mixes fiction and documentary, underscored by the indigenized pop music of Lenine. In aesthetic terms, the series performs what might be called the "vanguardization" of Brazilian television. The DVD version of the miniseries comes with an "interactive documentary" narrated by Marco Nanini, whose segments can be cued by clicking on the figure of a green parrot. In some ways, the documentary forms the most critical and least Eurocentric part of the series, offering a post-modernist didactic collage reminiscent of Jorge Furtado's brilliant short *Isle of Flowers* (1989), but now updated through the latest CGI effects. The multi-platform presentation allows for an open-ended and diversified reception, where spectators can enjoy the fiction and the documentary through their various remediations. An aesthetic of provocative transhistorical anachronism—e.g. a witty sketch comparing Vasco de Gama's *caravelas* to NASA space ships—enlivens the didactic material. "Historical representation, and their evaluations by viewers," as Richard A. Gordon puts it, are shown as "in flux and negotiable."[31] Mingling chromakey, hyperlink, animation, and all sorts of CGI effects, the documentary segments include such topics as "The Road to India," "Maps in 1500," "Cabral's First Mass," "From the Caravelas to TransAtlantic cruisers," "The Indigenous Habitants of Brazil," and "the Image of the Indian," much of it treated in pro-indigenous terms, at least insofar as the past is concerned.

The interactive documentary pays homage to indigenous culture by stressing the variety of indigenous languages, which contributed 4,000 Tupi words to Portuguese vocabulary, and by reminding us that Brazil "might easily have been bilingual." The documentary reflexively exposes its own dense and multifaceted intertext. Apart from the classic texts recounting the Paraguaçu story, the referenced intertexts includes Indianist novels like Alencar's *Iracema*, modernist novels like Mário de Andrade's *Macunaíma*, the 1940s musical comedies called *chanchadas*, the self-referential films of Godard, and alternative *Cine-Olho*-style alternative television. In a postmodern gesture, the series treats the very possibility of historicist verism with a keen self-reflexive skepticism. As for their first meeting, the documentary presents the alternative representations: "Did our couple meet on the beach? In the forest? We don't really know. Perhaps they looked just like our actors!" The series mocks "noble savage" stereotypes, along with Hollywood Indian-speak consisting of para-linguistic grunts. In a neo-futurist gesture, the series "Tupinambizes" the high-art canon by digitally painting Mona Lisa's face with indigenous colors and patterns. Influenced by modernist anthropophagy, one episode features a parodic TV cooking show in which Marco Nanini, in a cook's outfit, explains the recipe for "cooking a Portuguese." "If well-prepared and spiced," he gleefully assures the spectators, "the body of an average Portuguese man can feed seventy people." The interactive documentary portion of the fictional miniseries begins by declaring an intention to adopt a bifocal indigenous and European perspective, counterpointing the view "from the shore" where the Indians await, and the view "from the ships," where the Portuguese watch, all in order to discover "who we Brazilians are." While the Portuguese are amazed at the painted bodies and the beauty of the women, the narrator tells us, the Tupiniquim are amazed by the Portuguese men's hairy chests, their offensive smell, and the huge sails of the ships that they compare to birds with gigantic wings. Each side interprets the encounter through their own myths—the Garden of Eden for the Portuguese and the "Land without Evil" for the Tupiniquims.

Although the more critical documentary portion of *Caramuru: The Invention of Brazil* mocks a series of Indian stereotypes—the "noble savage," the "brave warrior," the "romanticized princess"—the fiction fails to deconstruct basic colonial axioms, while resuscitating other hoary stereotypes such as the disqualified infantile Indian man. Despite the sheen of CGI and postmodern sophistication, however, the miniseries relays some of the classic vices of literary and filmic representations of the "Indian" in Brazil: (1) a Eurocentric perspective which privileges the European side of the relationship; (2) a Euro-Brazilian narrator (TV star Nanini) who addresses the issue of "who we Brazilians are," thus embedding the assumption that indigenous people are "Brazilians," while in fact indigenous people, especially recently contacted indigenous people, do not speak Portuguese and are more likely to name themselves not as "Brazilians" but rather by their self-chosen names; (3) a male focalization of the story through the character Diogo/Caramuru rather than through the "*cunhã*" Paragassu, even if the latter is revealed in the end as the putative author of the story; (4) the projection of a harem fantasy, reminiscent of Gilberto Freyre's eroticized version of Brazil's colonial formation as a case of gleeful hanky-panky between over-sexed Portuguese men and lubricious native women. In a gesture of putative Tupi sexual hospitality, Paraguaçu encourages Diogo to sleep with her sister Moema, thus turning the Foundational Romance into a Foundational *Menage a Trois*, revolving around the European man. The series celebrates one (putative) aspect of the indigenous notion of communal property, but only in relation to sexuality; the idea does not extend to more crucial areas such as common ownership of the land; (5) a gendered binary allegorizes "America" as an alluring woman, available like the land for occupation, while indigenous men are represented as simultaneously inept and ridiculous, yet also threatening and bellicose. The film inadvertently conveys a gendered trope defined by Vine Deloria Jr.

in a North American context: "A male [indigenous] ancestor has too much of the aura of the savage warrior, the unknown primitive, the instinctive animal, to make him a respectable member of the family tree";[32] (6) the usual assimilationist narrative has Paraguaçu cheerfully abandon her culture and assimilate into the dominant western culture, including French culture since she marries in France and pays homage to the Empress; (7) a politics of casting whereby Afro-descended, mixed-race, or white actors play Indian roles instead of indigenous performers. Camilla Pitanga, the daughter of black actor Antonio Pitanga, is a very talented actress. The problem arises when the series not only bypasses indigenous performers in the fiction, but also never features any actual indigenous people even in the documentary portion, which includes vox populi street interviews, for example with Portuguese visitors to carnival but none with actually existing native people. (8) In the end, the series offers an allochronic denial of any sign of contemporary native life and culture, thus leaving the impression that Indians are vanished, and banished, to a remote past.

Just as disastrous however, is the (9) overdetermining choice of a generic emplotment—romantic/erotic comedy—which privileges the classical fiction of heterosexual European-indigene romance as foundational for the nation, thus foreclosing other possible genres, narratives, and critiques. It is difficult to imagine indigenous people in Brazil ever seeing their history under settler-colonialism as a romantic comedy, which is perhaps why Ailton Krenak dismisses the film as a "porno-chanchada."[33] The actual films and writings by indigenous people suggest that the relation to whites would more logically be seen through other generic grids, such as Tragedy, Satire, Dramatic Realism, or a myth-based Trans-realism.

Although the miniseries pays homage to Oswald de Andrade and modernism, it picks up largely on the movement's more co-optable trope of cannibalism, with its erotic and consumerist overtones, without carrying out Oswald's more radical call for the "DeCabralization" of Brazil.[34] The whole *Caramuru* project, after all, was conceived not as an homage to indigenous people but rather as a tribute to the Luso-Brazilian friendship. The concept of Anthropophagy, meanwhile, is treated in *Caramuru* as a kind of joke linked more to sexuality and fashion than to the creative incorporation of alterity that Oswald envisioned. Nor would Oswald have applauded what amounts to an exaltation of the nation-state and Brazilian "national identity." One of the aphorisms in Oswald's 1928 Manifesto calls for histories "without dates, without rubrics. Without Napoleon. Without Caeser" and, obviously, without Columbus and Cabral. Furthermore, since the series develops a systematic aesthetic of comic anachronism, constantly mingling past and present, one wonders why it would not show a modern-day indigenous woman, an activist for example, or a contemporary "high tech Indian" wielding a camera, given that indigenous people had been working with video decades before the release of *Caramuru* in 2000.[35] Such a gesture would have communicated the contemporary "view from the shore," or from the forest, or from the urban metropolis. Instead, the series simply "vanishes" contemporary indigenous people. Only the lyrics of the Lenine song ("*Tubi Tupy*") open up a space for indigenous cultural agency, as the song's narrator calls up a host of indigenous hero figures: "a Tupi astronaut, the grandson of Caramuru, Juruna [the first indigenous member of congress] and Raoni," the Kayapo leader whom we will meet elsewhere in this text.

The Filmic and Televisual *Cunhã*

In what follows, I will not offer an exhaustive overview of the thousands of representations of the "Indian" woman in Brazilian cinema and media—that would require a separate book—but rather an overview of privileged moments and texts. In the silent period, indigenous women appear mainly in adaptations of the nineteenth-century Indianist novels. The various silent versions of *Iracema* have largely been lost, but the idealized iconography of the posters and the drift of the reviews suggest that the films were faithful to the Indianist doxa in the two gendered versions of assimilation—the beautiful virgin with honey lips enamored of the Portuguese soldier, or the romantic Indian man worshipping at the altar of white femininity, in variant cases of gendered self-alienation into the dominant society. During the silent period, a thoroughgoing indigenous self-representation was out of the question; both male and female "Indians" were played by white and black actors. An early Indian role, of Peri in the film *O Guaraní* in 1911, cast a white actor, named Miguel Russomano, with painted face. Black actors also performed native roles, going back to black circus performer and play director Benjamin de Oliveira playing Peri in *O Guaraní* in 1908.

Given legal prohibitions on casting indigenous players, it is hardly surprising that female Indian roles in the silent period were played by white actresses. In the sound period, we find a "comic" example in the Alfredo Palacios's *I Married a Xavante* (1957), a musical comedy which revolves around a wealthy woman whose husband had disappeared for 15 years after his plane fell into the Amazon forest. But the "widow" is surprised to see a TV report about a "white cacique" who lives with five Xavante women. (Here we find a comic variation on the "White Indian" theme where the white man becomes the "natural leader" of an indigenous tribe, a theme that goes back to imperial safari tales and Tarzan and American film comedies like "The King of the Cannibals" in 1905.) In the Amazon, the husband, surrounded by beautiful "indigenous" women, lives a kind of Orientalist harem fantasy. Although on a lighter more romantic note, the film anticipated the later soft porn films in the 1970s with "Indian" women played by white actresses. The trope of the naked beauty of indigenous women goes all the way back to the famous 1500 letter to the King from Pero Vaz de Caminha, whose scribe described the women as "dark in color, all nude, and with nothing at all to cover their shameful parts"; their beauty, he added, would put some of the ladies of Lisbon to shame.

On Brazilian television, continuing a long tradition within Brazilian cinema, female Indian roles have almost invariably been played by white actresses. Although this monochromatic option might be explained by the fact that casting non-Portuguese-speaking indigenous peoples from the reserves was still illegal, it does not explain why the many actresses of partial indigenous ancestry were also not hired for such roles. The 1970 Globo series "*Irmãos Coragem*" cast the white actress Lucia Alves as the indigenous character Potrina. The already-discussed 2,000 *Caramuru* cast a series of non-indigenous actors and actresses to play Indians, including the two leading female characters, with Deborah Secco as Moema and the Afro-descended Camilla Pitanga as Paraguaçu. The 2005 Globo telenovela "*Alma Gemea*" cast Priscila Fantin as a "white

Indian" named "Serena." The 2007 Globo "*Desejo Proibido*" cast the white actress Leticia Sabatella as the indigenous protagonist Ana. In a way, such casting protocols literalize the imaginary inner whiteness of the fictive character.

In terms of the casting of male actors, the first telenovela to show an indigenous character was TV Tupi's "*O Mestiço*" (1965), where the white lead Hélio Souto played the role of the indigenous protagonist "Renato." As the son of a white man and an indigenous woman, despite the official celebration of *mestiçagem*, he suffers from the prejudice against mixed race people. In the Globo novela "*A Rainha Louca*" (1967) the white actor Claudio Marzo played the Indian character "Robledo," and a year later the white actor Stenio Garcia played the native character "Aimbe." A decade later, Carlos Alberto Ricelli had to darken his face and body to play Aritana in the 1978 novela of the same name. More recently, white actor Claudio Heinrich was cast as the blond Indian protagonist of the Telenovela "*Uga Uga*" (2000).

There is much to say in favor of ethnically non-literal casting, as when Orson Welles staged his all-black "Voodoo Macbeth" in 1936, or when the Public Theater in New York moved to multiracial casting for Shakespeare's plays. (After all, Shakespeare and the Globe theater were not literal in terms of literal identity, since men played women's roles.) These revisionist casting strategies, variously dubbed color-blind, multiracial, multiethnic, non-traditional, or experimental, have become very common in Anglo-American theater, cinema, and television since the 1960s, constituting a kind of affirmative action in casting, an attempt to remedy past inequalities. The problem arises when a marginalized group, as occurred both in the United States and Brazil, is invariably enacted by players from the dominant group, and when the roles are performed in stereotypical ways, within an aesthetics of normative whiteness. This asymmetry in agential and performative power constitutes a triple insult to the indigenous community, implying (1) that indigenous people are unworthy of self-presentation; (2) that no one from the indigenous community is capable of representing that community; (3) that the producers do not care about any possible offense to that community; and (4) that the community is powerless to change the situation.

A more explicit yet equally allegorical "*cunhã*" came with the already discussed 1971 film *How Tasty Was My Little Frenchman*, which, as we saw earlier, subverted the conventional identification with the European male protagonist of the captivity narrative. In this sense, the film, three decades before the Globo series *Caramuru*, inverted in advance the series' assimilationist perspective. The indigenous woman, Sebiopepe, marries the Frenchman, not out of love (or hatred) but as a communal responsibility to integrate him into the community. The nameless indigenous leader, a version of the historical Cunhambebe, is a warrior, but always portrayed as the dignified protector of his people. As we saw earlier, the title's first-person pronoun asserts identification with the *cunhã*'s point of view. When the Frenchman tries to escape, Sebiopepe arrows his buttocks while filling his canoe with sand to prevent escape. In this sense, the film offers an anti-foundational fiction, where the "*cunhã*" absolutely refuses assimilation, while it is the Frenchman who assimilates to his new tribe. He learns Tupi; she does not learn French. He dresses (or undresses) in the Tupinamba manner; she does not dress *a la Francaise* like Paraguaçu, nor does she convert, assimilate, or go with him to France to marry or adopt a European name.

A few years before *How Tasty Was My Little Frenchman*, the film *Macunaíma* featured a similarly subversive allegorical "*cunhã*" character. The author of the source novel, Mário de Andrade, published his *Macunaíma: The Hero without Character* in 1928. *Macunaíma* could be rightly called "the Mother of all Magic Realist novels" (and of all postcolonial-hybridity novels as well) in the sense that it was written decades before the Latin American "Boom," yet it anticipates all the vibrant syncretism of that movement. Himself a person of mixed ancestry like his protagonist, de Andrade compiled European, Amerindian, and African legends to create the novel. The "*Hero without Character*" of the title lacks character both in the ethical and in the ethnic sense, as a hybrid of indigenous, African, and European origin, like the book's author and like the country for which he constitutes the "hero." The novel proliferates in Tupi words and euphonious river names like "Uraricoeira." The very language of the novel is syncretic, weaving indigenous, African, and Portuguese words; its imagined speech carries the linguistic genes, as it were, of the peoples in Brazil. Within de Andrade's paradoxically archaic modernism, a trans-realist aesthetics, and where animals mate with human beings and characters are in constant transformation, mixes easily with the parallel trans-realisms of modernism and of indigenous fables.[36]

Mário de Andrade was partially inspired by the native legends collected by German anthropologist Theodor Koch-Grunberg in the headwaters of the Orinoco between 1911 and 1913 and published in his two-volume *Vom Roroima zum Orinoco: Ergebnisse einer Reise in Nord Bresilien und Venezuela in den Jahren 1911–1913* in 1923.[37] According to Koch-Grunberg, the Macunaíma of the legends was a mythic figure of the Taulipang (Taurepang) people, a mischievous figure beyond Good and Evil, whose name means "Great Evil." The natives found it amusing that the missionaries had translated their amoral trickster hero as "God." Unlike many ethnologists of his time, Koch-Grunberg's goal was not to measure the people with calipers but rather to celebrate the creativity of their stories and legends. On a human level, Koch-Grunberg speaks of indigenous generosity and openness, their "idyllic life," their "deep love of humor and mockery," and their "penchant for nicknames based on physical appearance or bizarre behavior."[38] In 1911, Koch-Grunberg also made a film, available on YouTube, entitled *Aus Dem Leben der Taulipang*, which portrays what seems to be a healthy, contented, and self-sufficient community. The film especially emphasizes women's incessant yet cheerful labor: preparing mandioca, fabricating hammocks, and creating string toys for their children. Unlike the Indians seen in other films from the same period, e.g. those of Thomaz Reis, the relatively self-determining Taulipang appear very relaxed and unself-conscious. (Koch-Grunberg was the prototype for the first of the ethnographer-characters in Ciro Guerra's *Embrace of the Serpent* in 2015.)

Drawn from what might be called the indigenous mythological commons, the legends gathered by Koch-Grunberg were more than just "raw material" for Mário de Andrade. Much of the humor of the novel comes directly from the legends, for example, the idea that the sun became yellow because Macunaíma threw an egg at it, or that Macunaíma lacks ethics because he "left his conscience on the island of Maroja." Both Koch-Grunberg and Mário de Andrade admired the tribally authored and collectively fashioned craft of the tales. At the same time, the novel, in a surreal and seemingly whimsical way, conveys real sadness at indigenous cultural losses. Its concluding lines are on one level comic but on another register a sad acknowledgment of the disappearance of a language and a tribe, in short, of a world: "No one on earth could speak the language of the tribe, or recount those juicy episodes [leaving] an immense silence [slumbering] on the banks of the Uraricoera. That's all folks." In a letter to fellow poet Carlos Drummond de Andrade, Mário spoke of his "artistic interest" in the "stupendous" tales of the Indians. Rejecting any primitivist attitude, and perhaps reflecting on his own ancestry, Mário adds: "I believe this propensity of mine [for indigenous legends] is not just of the moment or the result of fashion. I always had it and for me these great traditional legends of the tribal peoples are the finest histories, tales, and novels there can be."[39] In a sense, Mário, by studying the multiple identities within the Brazilian makeup and personality, was studying his own identity as a gay mixed-race man as well. Like two other gay international poets—Walt Whitman and Fernando Pessoa—Mário contained multitudes.

Long seen as an "unfilmable" novel, the film adaptation of *Macunaíma* came 40 years later, in the form of Joaquim Pedro de Andrade's adaptation in 1968. In both the novel and in the film, Ci is the Mother of the forest, with whom Macunaíma falls in love. Unlike the foundational romances, however, both members of the couple are indigenous. They have a son, but he dies as a baby. In the novel, Ci is also a warrior woman. When Macunaíma courts her, she first beats him up. But Macunaíma takes her by force and becomes her husband and the new Emperor of the Forest. When their child dies, he becomes a guaraná plant, part of the multidirectional becomings of the "forest literature" of the Amazon. After the baby's death, Ci ascends to the skies and becomes a constellation, as typically occurs with heroes and heroines in indigenous legends. Desolate, Macunaíma has only a lucky amulet or Muiraquita (stone-carved talisman) to remember her by. After losing the amulet, he discovers that it is now in the possession of a cannibal giant and capitalist, Pietro Pietra, an industrialist and people-eater, and in the film a typical figure for the peripheral literally fat-assed capitalist who is "proud of his American equipment," all "second hand." In the film, the national black-bean and meat dish *feijoada* is featured in a cannibalistic sequence in a swimming pool. On the one level, Pietro Pietra, who speaks with an Italian accent, evokes the Italian immigrants, like the Matarazos, who became wealthy in São Paulo in the 1920s, but the foreign name might also be a reference to the notorious Peruvian rubber baron Julio Cesar Arana, who was accused of exploiting and even enslaving the indigenous and mixed populations of the Amazon as part of what some have called another "Victorian Massacre" like that committed by King Leopold in the Congo in the same period.

Much as Mário de Andrade updated and remediated the legends which served as source for the novel, so the director updated and remediated the events and characters of the novel in function of the political events of the late 1960s. The actualization reinterprets the events and characters of the novel in function of contemporaneous events, especially in relation to the military dictatorship installed in 1964 and which became even more brutal in 1968, when the "*ditamole*" (soft dictatorship) gave way to the "*ditadura*" (hard dictatorship). In reaction to the closing down of democratic government and the arrest and murder of left militants and progressives, the left developed an urban guerrilla movement which robbed banks to finance the movement and on a few occasions kidnapped ambassadors in exchange for the freeing of their imprisoned comrades.

Although the film is much more concerned with the political issues of the 1960s than with indigenous issues per se, it devotes serious attention to the film's principal female "*cunhã*" figure—Ci. Although in other respects not at all feminist, the film does turn the novel's "Queen of the Forest" into a contemporary urban guerilla associated with sexual freedom, armed struggle, and direct action, much as the novel had linked Ci to the Icamiabas tribe—in Tupi a combination of *kama* and *iaba* ("split chest," i.e. single breasted)—i.e. the tribe associated with the legendary Amazons who defeated many male warriors. In this sense, the film connects "Ci" the urban guerilla to radical resistance to dictatorship. In *Macunaíma*, Ci's home is equipped with all the accoutrements of 1960s resistance movements: targets for shooting practice, stencil machines for pamphlets, and posters for the revolutionary eye. A song on the sound track, Roberto Carlos's "*E Papo Firme*," exalts a fearless mini-skirted modern woman. In one scene, she successfully attacks a secret police van with a rifle, throwing down the bloody severed arm of one of the policemen.

In an inversion of gender stereotypes, it is Ci who is not only the warrior but also the sexually aggressive partner. She goes off to war while her lazy husband rests in his hammock in a kind of post-partem *couvade*. When he compliments her, post-coitus, on her perfume, she answers, "It's gunpowder, darling." In interviews, Joaquim Pedro de Andrade repeatedly called Ci "the most positive character in the film," because, unlike Macunaíma and his brothers, she takes action, and in this sense she enacts, in shrewdly oblique terms, the voice and body language of resistance. The film does not show awareness of actual indigenous struggles per se, but it does take the figure of the novel's legendary indigenous woman as a model of political action. (As we shall see at the end of this chapter, in the present-day Amazon and urban Brazil, activist *cunhãs* like Gliceria Tupinambá, Sônia Guajajara, and countless others appear at protest rallies and on internet videos.)

As *Macunaíma* suggests, everyday Brazilian culture is deeply imbued with indigenous motifs and legends, not only in the high arts like painting and literature but also in everyday life in the form of names of plants, places, customs, and commonplaces, such as the idea that the frequent bathing of Brazilians, or the fondness for herbal remedies, is an indigenous inheritance. Ci is not the only indigenous legendary figure in the novel and the film. Macunaíma, at the finale, dives into a pond where he is dazzled by a beautiful mermaid named Iara, drawn from a legend about another woman warrior admired both for her beauty and for her military skills. The source legend offers a negative picture of men. Iara's brothers, envious of her skills, try to kill her, but as a strong fighter, she kills them. Her father throws her into a river to die but the fishes save her and transform her into a mermaid dwelling in the Amazon River. As occurs with *Macunaíma* she attracts men to the river where she drowns them. In another reference to strong indigenous legendary figures, a chapter in the novel is entitled "Letter to the Icamiabas," a reference to the women from São Paulo, but in the legend, the warrior women known as the Amazons. (A series of animation films on TV Culture in Pará treats the Icamiabas as contemporary feminist heroines; here the Amazons display their warrior powers to resolve present-day conflicts between various enchanted spirits and human beings.)

A number of films revisit the film and the novel *Macunaíma*. Paulo Verissimo's *Exu-Pia: Heart of Macunaíma* (1986) stages an encounter between the various remediations of the novel, the film, and the performative avatars of the character: the theatrical incarnations of Macunaíma in the form of Caca Carvalho, who played the main role, and the filmic incarnation, in the form of Grande Otelo, the star of the film version. Two more recent films root the novel and the film even more deeply in indigenous soil. Thiago Briglia's *Nas Trilhas de Macunaíma* (2019) visits the Roraima region that gave birth to *Macunaíma*, where local indigenous people talk about Macunaíma as a present-day culture hero and demiurge, blessed with the power to transform animals, trees, persons—into something other. In the novel and the film *Macunaíma*, the hero is linked to a kind of tutti-frutti tree, literally bearing every kind of fruit, a sign of abundance and survival for the Taulipeng. The Briglia film visits the enormous granite mesa (table mountain) Mount Roraima, which overlooks the territory of three nations—Brazil, Venezuela, and Guiana—and where the surrounding indigenous peoples celebrate Macunaíma as a creative force, beyond Good and Evil, the figure who transformed and petrified the tree-of-all-fruits into Mount Roraima. Rodrigo Sellos's *Por Onde vai Macunaíma* (Where Is Macunaíma Going? 2021), meanwhile, reflects on the meaning of Macunaíma for people in the region of Roraima. Most interesting for our purposes are two indigenous women, "Palpina" and "America," who express their love for Macunaíma as a culture hero vital to the literal and cultural sustenance of their lives. The indigenous interviewees see Macunaíma as a protean cultural force—as someone who constantly reinvents himself and the world. Since "America" happens to be an Evangelical, she interprets Macunaíma through a Christianized grid, turning the hero into a different figure of multiplicity—the three-in-One of the Trinity of God the Father, the Son, and the Holy Spirit.

The *Cunhã* Degraded

The Jorge Bodansky, Orlando Senna, and Wolf Bauer docu-fiction *Iracema: Uma Transa Amazônica* (made in 1975, but released only in 1980 due to censorship) is not, despite its title, an adaptation of the novel. The title explicitly references the Indianist classic by Alencar but only in order to turn its idealized portraiture inside out, through a subtitle where "*transa*" is used both in a sexual and in a business sense. The novel's Pocahontas-like story of romance between the virginal Indian and the Portuguese soldier here becomes a brutal tryst on the Trans-Amazonian Highway between a chauvinistic white trucker and a native adolescent forced into prostitution, whose short pants carry the Coca Cola logo, an index of a general commercialization of the Amazon. The princess and the nobleman of the novel, to put it crudely, become the prostitute and the john. The casting of a famous actor (Paulo Cesar Pereio) as the truck driver (and symbolic and literal "driver of the narrative") playing opposite a beginning indigenous actress (Edna de Cassia) homologizes on a thespian register the power dynamics in the story and in contemporaneous Brazilian society.

Paulo Cesar Pereio pretends to be a real-life truck driver around everyday people who do not recognize him as a celebrity, thus allowing for more honest and uncensored communication. Although Pereio was well known as a film and TV celebrity in the

South of Brazil—often playing amoral and rakish bohemian characters that triggered comparison with Jean-Paul Belmondo—he was largely unknown in the Amazon region. Playing more or less incognito allowed him to improvise dialogue with interlocutors unaware of his fame, thus generating a remarkable sense of authenticity. Iracema, meanwhile, is played, brilliantly and unpretentiously, by the non-professional Edna de Cassia. In the place of the "Virgin of Honey Lips" of the Alencar novel, we find a desperately poor indigenous adolescent, blessed with a sweet personality but forced to turn tricks to survive. This disenchanted version of the "*cunhã*" is steeped in the contemporaneous situation of governmental racism, rapacious development, and the hegemonic "ideology of whitening." Far from a proud Indian woman who gives birth to a race, this Iracema is ashamed of her origins and pathetically claims to be white, to which the truck driver mockingly replies: "Yeah, sure, no doubt you're the daughter of an English Lord!" Yet the quiet dignity of Iracema as played by de Cassia wins the audience's sympathy vis-à-vis the obnoxious Tiao Grande, who is further distanced from the audience by his parroting of the military regime's slogans such as "Brazil: Love it or Leave It!" and "Noone Can Hold Back Brazil!"

In the novel, Iracema dies but her child with Martim survives. The child Moacir becomes the founder of the state of Ceará, an emblem for the Brazilian nation as a whole. The film, in contrast, offers only rampant lust and naked exploitation. The trucker and the sex worker do not generate the "seed" of the Brazilian nation; they just exemplify the perverse effects of the Trans-Amazonian highway in terms of prostitution and the abuses of military-led "development." Ultimately, it is not the impoverished "*cunhã*" who is degraded, but rather the racist trucker, the frontier-like chaos, and the oppressive settler-colonial structures. But just as important is the film's revelation of the horrors taking place in the Amazon of the 1970s. The film, censured on the pretext of its status as a co-production with Germany, triggered outrage around the world about the social, ecological, and racial abuses in the Amazon, including the situations of virtual slavery shown in the film. Given the centrality of documentation to the film's project, the filmmakers carefully authenticate images and sounds registered in situ. A seemingly interminable shot, subsequently picked up by many environmental protest films, registers the forest ablaze, where the literal time-space of the tracking shot makes clear that the fire's dimension on the screen did not depend on manipulative editing. The filmed materials profile an enormous natural space defiled by "progress." Ecological disaster and social exploitation configure a social hell. The highway project provides a privileged setting for the "free" investment of capital from the Brazilian South and from corporations to carry out contraband in precious hardwoods and illegal seizures of indigenous land. (Subsequent to *Iracema*, Bodanzky has been developing virtual resource libraries, and multi-media projects launched from a boat in the Amazon region.)

The dominant media often give the impression that the Indians simply disappeared or lost their indigenous identity and transmuted painlessly into ordinary Brazilians through the social death of categorical-statistical annihilation. Thus, indigenous people transmute into peasants, *caboclos*, workers, homeless persons, and so forth. This "unbecoming" masks the violence involved in their involuntary social transformation. Colonial conquest was not only a series of military victories against indigenous peoples like those that occurred in the United States. Such wars also occurred in Brazil, but conquest also took place on a different level. During the rubber boom in the Amazon, for example, as Michael Taussig explains in *Shamanism, Colonialism, and the Wild Man*, the rubber baron Arana relied on "the Columbian traders who had been the first to 'conquer' … the Indians."⁴⁰ Thus, individual traders could be deputized, as it were, to be micro-agents of colonial expansion subjecting indigenous people to forced labor and debt peonage. Just as impoverished whites during slavery in the American South, within Master Race ideology, could be micro-masters vis-à-vis any black person, any armed "white" could take power over indigenous persons and reduce them to unpaid workers, i.e. to virtual slaves. In the present, slavery continues, intimately linked to deforestation and the stealing of indigenous land. Researcher Leonardo Sakamoto reports that virtual slave labor has been used systematically to deforest the Amazon in order to sell timber but also to create new farms and pastures. Products from slave labor are sold in the country and abroad. According to Sakamoto, "[f]rom 1995 to October 2019, over 54,000 people were rescued from modern slavery on cattle, soy, cotton, coffee, orange, potato, and sugarcane farms; and from charcoal kilns, construction sites, sewing workshops, and brothels in Brazil."⁴¹

Shifting mood and genre to the realm of popular music, poet/novelist/singer Chico Buarque de Holanda offers still another revisionist version of the romantic *cunha* in his song "Iracema." Her name forms an anagram of "America," but this time she actually goes to America, i.e. to the United States, not as a heroine but as just another undocumented immigrant seeking a better life. Here are some of the lyrics:

Iracema flew to America
Bringing woolen clothing
She goes around, full of enthusiasm,
From time to time, she goes to the movies
She hasn't mastered English yet, and she mops the floor in a chic cafe.
She goes out at night with a mime. And she plans to study lyrical singing,
She takes no chances with the cops
And if possible, she'll stay over there [in the United States]
Of course she misses Ceará. But not that much
And every once in a while, animated,
She calls me on the phone collect.

The song indirectly critiques the myth of historically generative miscegenation, not only through the exquisitely melancholy tones of Chico's music but also by suggesting that the contemporary Iracemas, given the difficult socioeconomic situation in Brazil, have had to go alone to the United States as economic refugees or migrant laborers. While Alencar's Iracema was the daughter of a prestigious cacique and the progenitor of a mixed race, this Iracema seems to be poor and more or less alone. Whereas Iracema's tribe lived in a "society of abundance," this Iracema leaves post-contact precarity in the Global South for a different kind of precarity in the Global North. And of course, Chico makes sure that this new Iracema comes from Ceará, the "country" (literally the state), in allegorical terms "Brazil," which was created, as the myth would have it, thanks to the novel's fecund romance between Iracema and the Portuguese soldier.

The *Cunhã* as Warrior

Missing in the conventional picture of inevitable decline and disappearance of the "vanishing" Indian is indigenous agency, including political, social, and even military agency in the form of armed resistance. In the long epic of anti-colonial struggle, indigenous people have not always been on the defensive. Peoples like the Puri and the Botocudo often initiated preemptive attacks, including even in territories assumed to be under colonial control. Indigenous groups, in sum, were not only the victims of violence; they were also, at times, the perpetrators. In the quincentennial year 2000, the same year as *Caramuru: The Invention of Brazil*, another film, this time by a woman filmmaker, offered a very different approach to a story about a relationship between a Portuguese man and an indigenous woman. Instead of an erotic comedy with faux Indians, we find a historical film with tragic overtones, with indigenous actors, and instead of a painless assimilation into whiteness we see assimilation as an illusion rife with dangers. The film, Lucia Murat's *Brava Gente Brasileira* (2000), offers a *"cunhã"* at the opposite extreme both from the compliant Paraguaçu of the TV film/series and from the exploited prostitute of the 1975 Iracema. Murat's well-documented film treats an eighteenth-century historical episode which took place at the Forte de Coimbra in Mato Grosso do Sul. The female protagonist is not technically a *"cunhã,"* since she belongs to a different linguistic-cultural group—the Kadiwéu, descendants of the Guaicuru. Among the few survivors of what have generally been seen as the "warrior nations" of South America, in the eighteenth century their ancestors adopted horses, became expert riders, and defeated Spanish and Portuguese colonists along the Paraguay River.

Before Murat's film, the Kadiwéu had featured largely in the accounts of anthropologists. When Lévi-Strauss visited the Kadiwéu in 1935, he noticed that, despite acculturation, they maintained key features of their ancient civilization. They also display a strong love of what the West autonomizes as "Art" in the form of asymmetrical arabesque-like face designs, along with ceramics, pottery, and toys for children, fashioned by women as well as men.[42] In a kind of hybrid authorship, the Kadiwéu in the Murat film are the protagonists and on some levels the authors of the story; they play themselves, speak in their own language, and re-enact their own history, in this case a quasi-military victory in which women played a key role.[43]

To recreate the tale, Murat delved deep into the historical and anthropological literature, perusing, for example, the account of Francisco Rodrigues do Prado, the Commander at the Portuguese Fort. She also consulted the work of Guido Boggiani, who visited the Kadiwéu in 1982, and who reproduced the same complex body paintings and designs that impressed Lévi-Strauss with their dazzling asymmetricality. Murat also built on work by Brazilian anthropologist/writer and public intellectual Darcy Ribeiro, the author of a celebrated 1940s study of the Kadiwéu.[44] Ribeiro describes the group as having a hierarchical ethos and a proud and lordly demeanor, far from that of the egalitarian Tupi-Guaraní and Yanomami. Known as Cavaliers, the Kadiwéu were famous for their warrior spirit. According to Ribeiro, Kadiwéu mythology reveals a belief in Kadaweu superiority, showing that ethnocentrism is not a western monopoly.

Their dualistic quasi-Manichean mythology speaks of two Creators, one generous and solar, bringing abundance and eternal Life, the other malicious and destructive.[45] In *Tristes Tropqiues*, Lévi-Strauss noted that the Kadiwéu, despite now largely living the situation of the Brazilian peasant, preserved a "haughty attitude" rooted in their noble and warrior past. An interesting character in the film is a young blond boy who speaks Kadiwéu, who seems completely integrated into the tribe and resists attempts to have him join the whites. Part of the tribe and loyal to it in the fiction, we learn from the DVD extras that he is the son of a mixed couple who form part of the tribe. Like many Amazonian societies, the Kadiwéu (formerly the Guaicuru), as Graeber and Wengrow put it, "took pride in their ability to adopt children or captives …. and, through care and education, turn them into what they considered to be proper human beings."[46]

The male protagonist of the film is a Portuguese soldier, Dom Diogo de Castro e Albuquerue, a sophisticated, well-intentioned child of the Enlightenment. A devotee of Jean-Jacques Rousseau, he entertains a Rousseauist vision of indigenous people as noble exempla of "natural goodness." In a thinly veiled allusion to the Genevan philosopher, he tells a racist fellow soldier, Captain Pedro, that "a certain Frenchman" claims that "the New World savage lives closer to nature and has more moral fiber than Europeans." This same Frenchman, he adds, "opposes white western education, because it might turn them into evil people like us, who kill out of greed." Unimpressed by Don Diego's favorite *philosophe,* the captain replies: "This French guy sounds crazy. I doubt if he ever lived in the colonies. The Indians I meet only know how to drink, eat, fuck, steal, and kill. They aren't sons of God or of the Devil; they're sons of whores." Then Pedro grabs a nearby Indian by the neck and forces him to repeat the insults addressed to him and his group. As his Enlightenment formation is challenged by the brutal reality of the colonial contact zone, a close-up reveals the acute discomfort of the colonizer who has doubts about his own role. The Diego character is thus a product of the same French Enlightenment of which we spoke in the previous chapter, and specifically of the pro-indigenous theories of Rousseau, the philosopher who comes closest to the caricature of "Noble Savage Discourse." Rousseau transformed the information he took from Jean de Léry and Montaigne to create a Manichean schema which revolved not around social arrangements but rather around comparative morality, pitting the "naturally good" Indian against the decadent and over-civilized European. Rousseau's root idea of "natural goodness" has two problems—the "natural" and the "goodness." No group of people is naturally good, and every society exhibits a variety of individual ethical practices.

At first glance, the film seems to offer another iteration of Sommers's foundational romance—a European soldier, like Diogo in the Paraguacu story and the soldier Martim in *Iracema*, falls passionately in love with a beautiful indigenous woman, named Adote, reminiscent at first of other romantic Indianist heroines. The scene of their first encounter seems bucolic; it shows a group of naked Kadiwéu women, laughing and cavorting in a paradisal stream. The scene evokes a feeling of pleasurable sensuality and indigenous comfort with nature. When the soldiers burst upon this idyllic scene, they rape and kill the women, transforming conviviality into terror. Diogo takes a woman, Adote, as his captive, and they become man and wife, but their relationship is marked by the ambiguity of a captive love object. At one point, Dom Diogo returns to the Fort with Adote, his face painted with graphic motifs similar to Adote's. Although they both appear contented, the racist Fort Commander ridicules Diogo for "going native," thus supposedly lowering himself in a way disturbing to established social norms. But subsequent events reveal the limits of Diogo's simulacral reverse acculturation. Away on a trip, Diogo writes to Adote about his feeling of having gained a fuller understanding of the newly encountered culture. While we hear his voice-over reading the letter, his pregnant wife watches the rain through her window. With a sad look, she rips up his letter. In the next scene, Don Diogo and Captain Pedro converse while a baby cries in the neighboring room, followed by silence. Diogo discovers that Adote has killed their baby. Furious, he expels her from the Fort. The foundational romance has been aborted, his noble savage vision has collapsed, and the enlightened free-thinker has witnessed the demise of his illusions.

A truce in the war between the Portuguese and the Kadiwéu ensues. To trick the Portuguese, the Kadiwéu simulate a gesture of peace by offering presents, including Kadiwéu women, to demonstrate their benevolent intentions. But just as the Portuguese men begin to flirt with the "gifted" women, the Kadiwéu, in a brutal form of poetic justice, ambush them.[47] This historical strategy, a sexualized version of the Grecian Trojan Horse story, forms an active part of Kadiwéu memory and identity. For the spectator, the experience is one of estrangement, of a battle between mismatched worlds. The film makes the spectators feel the opaque depths of a culture they do not completely comprehend. Reinforcing the sense of distance, indigenous exchanges go untranslated, confronting the spectator with the effects of linguistic opacity, immersed in a world whose signs are difficult to decipher. As a result, the film creates the feeling that something complex is happening but we don't know exactly what it is, as if a plot were being hatched, an uneasy affect that replicates the experience of the Portuguese protagonist. Replete with a meaning that escapes us, the scenes administer a lesson in cognitive humility. It is only at the end that the filmmaker opts to translate the dialogue, when an elderly Kadiwéu woman hints at historical continuities in the present: "Thus ends our ancient war chant. I could tell other stories, good and bad, about the Guaicurus. But they would be stories about today's wars."

The film shows Kadiwéu culture in its difference, neither exalting nor debasing it, as if to say "here it is," warts and all, while reminding us that western ways are equally strange to the Kadiwéu as well. After all, the kind of "encounter" that began in 1492 consists of a meeting of in some ways incommensurable worlds and modes of life, within a history overdetermined by colonial potencies. A colonizer devastated by the collapse of his own illusions, Diogo never becomes a white savior figure. In a way, the film indirectly exposes the brutality covered over by the foundational romance plots. Murat does not hide her sympathies for the Kadiwéu, including by highlighting, as a gesture of aesthetic respect, the complex Kawideu aesthetic in the form of striking facial designs and ceramics. The film suggests that the question is not one of individual character or goodness—given that the Kadiwéu commit what would normally be considered crimes—but rather one of undergirding social values and historical norms. *Brava Gente Brasileira* avoids the Manichean trap. While the film is "savage," in its critique of the colonizer, it treats the Kadiwéu not as savages but as a proud nation of fighters from a society marked by hierarchical and even cruel elements. The film implies the right to self-defense, even of a society which is (like all societies) imperfect, respecting the alterity of the tribe within a courageously feminist and decolonial posture.[48]

The *Cunhã* as Forest Princess

The next *cunhã* comes from the Amazon, a region shrouded in the mists of myriad legends and stories. The Americas generally, and the Amazon in particular, have been the magnet for European fantasies about the "New World," replete with imaginary paradises (Eldorado), cities paved with gold, fountains of youth, and other tropes, many with gendered overtones. One of the early legends to emerge from the Amazon had to do with the legendary "tribe"—the Icamiabas—composed of women warriors who defeated the Spanish and the Portuguese in battle. (The magical *Muiriquita* amulet in *Macunaíma* was found by the "Icamiabas.")[49] The Amazon region has variously been seen both as a terrestrial paradise blessed with exuberant nature and tremendous economic opportunities, a la filmmaker Silvino Santos, and as a green Hell where human beings descend into a barbarous heart of darkness, as suggested by some of the sensationalist titles of non-Brazilian fiction film—*Monster from the Black Lagoon* (1954), *Anaconda* (1997), *The Green Inferno* (2013)—that portray the Amazon as the scene of "the Horror." But the real horror is the ongoing devastation of the forest, murders of indigenous *caciques*, and the quiet criminality of "intellectual property rights."

An adventure film for children directed by Tania Lamarca and Sergio Bloch, *Tainá: An Adventure in the Amazon*, released in 2000, again in the quincentennial year of Cabral's "discovery," was the first in a trilogy of children's films about the Amazon. The film is by Brazilian commercial standards a financial blockbuster, featuring scores of technicians, an array of locations, auditions for hundreds of aspiring actresses, and a musical score performed by the Orchestra of Prague, with an Afro-Brazilian touch provided by Carlinhos Brown as the singer of the musical theme. Although not expensive by Hollywood standards, the Trilogy films are extremely expensive by Brazilian standards when compared to non-Globo Films fiction features, and even more so when compared to indigenous media. The Amazon, its fauna and flora, and to a minor extent, its indigenous peoples, are at the center not only of *Tainá: An Adventure in the Amazon*, but also of the two other films in the trilogy—*Tainá: The Adventure Continues* (2004) and *Tainá: The Origin* (2013)—all of which target a young audience and explore the same topic of native and non-native resistance to bio-piracy. *Tainá* tells the story of an eight-year-old indigenous orphan girl named Tainá (Eunice Baia) who lives in the Amazon region with her beloved and wise old grandfather Tige, a *pajé* from whom she learns the legends, wisdom, and knowledge of the tribe, who tells her about the crucial importance of the Amazon for the planet and the intimate relation between indigenous people, animals, and the environment.

Protected by an amulet bequeathed by her grandfather, Tainá becomes a guardian of the forest, where she lives intimately with the local flora and fauna, protecting them from the predations of bio-pirates trafficking in threatened animal species. In Tupi-Guaraní, her name signifies "morning star," associated with the Karajá (or Carijó) legend of "*Tainá-can*," a prized star and a god who visits the earth once every year. Pursued by the traffickers, she ends up in a small village where she meets a female biologist and her son Joninho (Caio Romei), who has reluctantly accompanied his mother to the Amazon as she pursues her research. When Tainá decides to leave the village, Joninho, who had already been on the verge of running away, follows Tainá and learns from her how to survive in the forest. Her gesture of teaching Joninho how to live with the forest recalls a historical reality in most of the Americas, i.e. that indigenous peoples protected the arriving European strangers and taught them how to survive, only to be subsequently dispossessed by these very same strangers.

The film is also a *bildungsroman*—a novel/film of education—less for Tainá than for her white companion. Toninho begins as an unpromising student; while she speaks to animals in their own language, he plays with electronic games. While she eats the fruits proffered by an abundant nature, he chews Chicklets. But he ultimately learns to treat animals with respect and joins the struggle. Toninho is not the white Indian pedagogue/savior; Tainá is the real teacher. A box office hit, *Tainá* orchestrates a medley of genres—suspense, nature film, action movie, melodrama, ecology film, and comedy. At its center is the struggle of a single indigenous girl and her white friend against bio-piracy, such as when Tainá outwits the traffickers to save a gallery of named animals such as "Catu" the monkey. On the one level, the film prolongs the romanticist tendency within Brazilian Indianism, with the difference that here the Iracema figure is not a woman but a pre-pubescent girl, thus narrowly avoiding the "foundational fiction" of the masculinist "foundational fiction." Significantly, Tainá is an orphan, a way of avoiding any idea of a competent agential indigenous Father and Mother. Thus, the trilogy constitutes an apparently "positive" image of a *cunhã* in a problematic frame—a kind of camu-camu-in-the-rice reminiscent of Sidney Poitier as the raisin-in-the-rice—where the only competing indigenous adult is a wizened grandfather. Moreover, despite its thematization of bio-piracy, the film elides the ecological tragedy that had long been assailing the region. As a commercially driven film, *Tainá* is more concerned with entertainment than with weighty social issues. The portrayals are Manichean, pitting adorable children against repulsive bio-pirates. The film sidesteps the role of Brazilian governmental complicity and of global capitalism in the destruction of the forest. It shies away from the key issue of land protection and the massive repression, and even assassinations, of indigenous leaders, a long-standing phenomenon that has become truly apocalyptic with Bolsonaro's direct attacks on the Amazonian peoples who for him do not merit "one millimeter of Brazilian land." Ultimately, the film sugarcoats some of the themes of indigenous social thought and media into a Disneyesque entertainment, full of articulate and witty parrots, frisky monkeys, and threatening crocodiles reminiscent of the fauna of safari films. In the end, it sweetens and prettifies a horrific situation, even while disseminating a "positive" image of a prodigiously talented indigenous girl played by the first indigenous female star in the history of Brazilian film.

The *Cunhã* as Hyper-Woman

Again changing tone and genre, the prize-winning film *Itai Kuegu: As Hiper Mulheres* (The Hyperwomen, 2011), the product of a partnership between VNA and the Kuikuro Cinema Collective founded in 2002, was directed and conceived by Kuikuro filmmaker Takuma Kuikuro, together with two non-indigenous anthropologists (Carlos Fausto and Leonardo Sette), along with mostly Kuikuro technicians. The film revolves around a song-cycle dealing with issues of romance and sexuality from a female perspective, demonstrating a subversive love of gendered laughter. Despite the Kuikuros's narrow escape from annihilation, the film is cheerful and the culture is rich and deep. Based on in-depth research by the anthropologist Bruna Franchetto in partnership with the indigenous anthropologist Mutuá Kuikuro, and with the collaboration of the village, the film documents a gynocentric Kuikuro festival—the *Jamunkumalu* or "super-women" festival. Although the title is reminiscent of a Whitney Houston song, it comes from one of the ritual songs that proclaims, "I am an extraordinary woman," collectively and anonymously created centuries ago. Writing from North America, from Turtle Island, Robin Wall Kimmerer speaks of collective ceremonies as ways to "remember to remember." In words that echo Bakhtin on carnival but also resonate with Kuikuro culture, she writes that "[a]nd then we dance. The drum begins the giveaway song … [and] the ground resonates with the fall of moccasined feet … [a]mid the laughter and the singing, everyone belongs."[50] According to Jack Weatherford, the Dakota, similarly, have danced in "one continuous dance for a thousand years into the past and a thousand years into the future."[51]

As a "process film" (Claudia Mesquita), *Itai Kuegu* "remembers to remember" by tracing the process of recovering a song-cycle and festival which had been in eclipse for 20 years, as part of a project of actually performing the festival as a way of passing on the songs to a younger generation.[52] The initial crisis is triggered by the fact that an older woman, Kanu, the only person deeply familiar with the songs, seems to be on the brink of death, in a situation where Kuikuro have forgotten the songs. Fearing the worst, Kanu's village elder husband asks his nephew to arrange a reenactment, so the songs can be passed on. In a collective collaboration, not unlike that which engendered the film, the village women painstakingly reconstruct the songs. One woman finds an old cassette tape with the songs, another remembers a few fragments, and they pool their knowledge to prepare the festival. At one point the women remember the songs through *quipu*-like mnemonic tools made out of a rope and knots.[53] A bond forms between Kanu, who hums the melody for a young adolescent girl who listens closely and then sings the same melody. The songs become contagious, passing like a virus from one "carrier" to another.[54]

The DVD edition explains the origins of the *Jamurikumalu* as told by Kanu and Kamangü, a story set in a time when the Kuikuro were still living in the spirit world, characterized by Ovidian metamorphoses from the human to the animal and back, but always in function of recognizably human motivations like jealousy and revenge. Some of the songs criticize male jealousy and even suggest the women leave their husbands. Offended, the men go fishing and plot revenge. A young boy sees his father and uncles transformed into spirit animals ready to devour the mother and the aunts. When the boy relays the men's plans, the women begin to mock the men. They go deep into the forest, the men follow them, and the women leave a "super-bat" at the entrance of a tunnel to devour any men who follow them.

As Carlos Fausto explains, the coded battle of the sexes in the film turns around women's critique of the men's laziness and reluctance to go fishing and thus end the seclusion of a boy who underwent the ear-piercing ceremony, while the men's resentment has to do with anger over women's supposed lack of respect for the *kagutu* flutes.[55] The central focus is on the strength of women in the community and on their traditional music and ancestral heritage. The film could not have been made without very knowledgeable directors and the total cooperation of the community. The guiding maxim, valid for much of Indigenous Media, might have been "it takes a village to make a film." The non-indigenous members of the production team spent eight years in preparation. Eschewing didacticism, the film never explains the meaning of the festival, instead conveying the information through the story and the dialogue. The background information is delivered only in the DVD "making of," where the participants like Kanu, some of the principal singers and dancers, and Kamangagü, a male village elder, explain the meaning of the festival and the songs. The film conveys a transgenerational legacy; the women learn to sing as their grandmothers did. The musical accompaniment consists only of singing and the rhythmic sound of shuffling feet and shaking bracelets. The film is a tribute to the power of women, although as Sara Shamash points out, the actual "transmission of filmmaking and technical knowledge appears to be reserved for indigenous and non-indigenous men."[56] Interestingly, male domination of the filmic medium in most indigenous societies contrasts, as we shall see in the next chapter, with the powerful agency and presence of women in almost every other cultural activity such as music, arts, pedagogy, and political activism. That said, many indigenous societies in both North and South America see men and women as having distinct roles, without that distinction necessarily involving domination or subordination.

The events play out in the village "round" and in the intimacy of the long-house *malocas* and the hammocks. In the tradition of archaic modernism, the film uses digital technologies to celebrate traditional legends. Nor does the film hide reminders of the globalized present such as Darth Vader T-shirts and digital watches. Shamash discerns references to literal and figurative cannibalism: "the twenty-first-century Kuikuro cannibalize digital technology to document and revive an ancient ritual rooted in cannibal mythology wherein the women assert their power by being the metaphorical devourers of men, rebuffing the men's own devouring."[57] (As occurs with many languages and cultures, eating often serves as a metaphor for sex.)

For Gregory Bateson, rituals have constitutive rules, which are announced in the festivity itself by a meta-communicative declaration that "this is a ritual."[58] *Hyper-Women*, in this sense, offers a metacommentary on a ritual. It becomes a film of rehearsals, as more and more women participate, learn the lyrics, rehearse the songs, make mistakes, and improve the performance. At times, parallel montage juxtaposes different characters practicing the lines, forest flaneuses "walking along, singing a song," as the dittie says, "side by side." The songs match the action, a song about bathing, for example, accompanies movement toward a favorite bathing spot. Within a structuring principle of accumulation, melioration, and growing excitement, more and more women, and their children, and sometimes their children carrying even younger children, dance together and, in a kind of apotheosis, perform the songs in the circular village patio. In a sense, Kuikuro rituals constitute a forest correlative to a kind of *Gesamtkunstwerk*, engaging multiple arts such as singing, dancing, percussion, wind instruments, costume, performance, and the like but obviously without the cushioned and well-funded grandiosity of a Wagnerian opera. By valorizing the immaterial patrimony of the Kuikuro, the film gained the support of the Institute of the National Historical and Artistic Patrimony (IPHAN) for creating an archive of songs of Kuikuro women, finally registering 130 hours of recorded music, with no repetition of melodies.[59]

The songs celebrate women through their singing, dancing, wrestling, and witty conversation. In line with other cultural rituals of gender reversal (e.g. Sadie Hawkins Day) or the carnival trope of the "woman on top," the women dress up and display sexually explicit humor. They poke fun at the men's penises and stage mock-sexual attacks on the Kuikuro men. They mention a "provocation songs" genre and, among themselves, use expressions like "he spilled some milk" (i.e. ejaculated). The women jump into the men's hammocks and make mischievous advances as the men laugh and feign resistance, within a ritual agreed to by the entire tribe. When one woman "attacks" an old man, he holds her off with a promise that "we'll do it tomorrow." The whole village, from the youngest to the oldest, participates in the festival and the film, without the kind of racialized aestheticism that led Busby Berkeley to line up impeccably white female bodies, "like pearls," for his big-budget musicals. In an aesthetic of the imperfect, the film includes people coughing and does not hide the fact that the dancers are sometimes out of breath. There is no hierarchical aesthetic requiring that everyone be conventionally beautiful. Men show no shame about their flabby buttocks; women show no embarrassment about sagging breasts. Laughter and the presence of children are constant.

While Brazilian analysts have rightly linked this film to some of the practices of Jean Rouch, the film reminded me of something very different—Hollywood musicals. First of all, it is quite likely that some of the collaborators were familiar both with Hollywood musicals and their Brazilian counterpart the *chanchadas*, also dubbed, as if in homage to Bakhtin, *filmes carnavalescos* or "carnivalesque films." As Alice Fátima Martins points out, the Kuikuro and the non-indigenous producers offer complementary forms of knowledge; "if the non-indigenous directors have as their inheritance a familiarity with filmic narratives ... and more access to the technologies of image and sound, the indigenous filmmakers have access to events, situations, and different ambient environments that the others do not have."[60] Whether some of the directors actually had musicals in mind is irrelevant. My point is that it is methodologically productive to discern common structural patterns. I am thinking especially of the "backstage musicals" (in theater) and the "studio backlot musicals" popular in Hollywood from the 1930s through the 1950s, with *Singin' in the Rain* (1952) as the most famous example. Like *Itai Kuegu*, the backstage musicals were about responding to a crisis by "getting a show on the road." During the depression, according to Andrew Berman in *We're in the Money: Depression America and Its Films* (1992), musicals came to allegorize the urgency of getting the economic show on the Road, i.e. to recover from the Depression. Both *Singin' in the Rain* and *Itai Kuegu* begin with crises of production: the technological challenge of the sound in *Singin' in the Rain*, and in *Itai Kuegu*, the human challenge of the possible death of Kanu, and with her the death of a whole tradition. The collective protagonists of both films confront a crisis of production, of a film in one case and of a festival in the other, a collective act of recuperating popular memory, and where the film depends on the performance of the ritual, and the ritual depends on collective performance and collaboration.

Some of the canonical analyses of pleasurable affect in the musical, such as Richard Dyer's classic "Entertainment and Utopia" essay, point to the transfiguration of the negatives of everyday existence into the positives of utopian performance, whereby calculating and hypocritical human relations become transparent, where scarcity becomes abundance, fatigue energy, boredom excitement, and loneliness community. Dyer's analysis, apt as it is for the Hollywood musical, and even for many TV soft-drink commercials, does not quite work for this film. Dyer's utopia is premised on a general social alienation, and an implicit whiteness, where the musical represents an escape from ennui, alienation, and a transcendence of everyday social life. In the Kuikuro case, however, the gap between the dominant social codes and the artistic utopia is much less stark.[61] The film, like the festival, is an exemplum of community but in a situation where community-belonging and celebration are a taken-for-granted part of life. *Itai Kuegu* is utopian but not in the sense of redeeming the tedium of everyday life; it is rather a joyful remediation of an ancient festival. But, as in many musicals, the movement is from the individual to the community, in that scenes of a few people, or of one person walking and singing, flow into the larger stream of the final collective performance in the village "round."

Apart from the structural parallels and the singing, what else could *Itai Kuegu* possibly have in common with a spectacular big-budget musical like *Singin' in the Rain*—and the answer is, more than one might suspect. Both films are reflexive; they show the actual process of producing collective spectacles. Both involve humor, laughter, and romance, although the Kuikuro sense of romance is less ethereal and less couple-oriented than the balletic *pas de deux* of Gene Kelly and Debbie Reynolds. Both involve rehearsals and the assembling of the requisite elements—the songs, the dancing, and the like. And both films have happy endings, in the Kuikuro case not only in the film but also in real life, since the film resuscitated the festival and the song cycle and thus gained the protection of the "cultural heritage" rubric. Another cultural difference is that virtually all Kuikuro seem to be quite accustomed to collective dancing and coordinated singing and dancing bodies—in fact, such tribal dance scenes, rather like the "dance presentations" of the *xapiri* for the Yanomami, are a standard feature of the Video in the Village films. There is no *Chorus-Line*-style competition; none are professionally trained yet they perform their roles beautifully, within what might be called an aesthetic of communal imperfection. So could one imagine a revisionist *Singin' in the Rain* remake that would incorporate Kuikuro codes and lifeways, without professional actors and without prior selection of beautiful actresses and handsome actors? This revisionist adaptation would not involve aesthetic censorship of human bodies. The men and women would be dressed in the equivalent of Kuikuro norms. Their painted bodies would wear headdresses, bodily designs, arm necklaces, bracelets, and the like, but the dress items would not hide what the official Western mind has declared "obscene" (etymologically off-stage)—i.e. the signs of sexual difference, what Bakhtin called the "orifices and protuberances" of the carnivalesque body—the "shames" mentioned by Pero Vaz de Caminha in his famous letter, fleshly appearances usually associated only with high art painting, sculpture, and pornography,

The film leads one to revisit film theoretical questions about male voyeurism and the fetishization of the female body. First, what constitutes nudity varies from culture to culture. The overdressed-ness of the Portuguese was as strange to the Tupinamba as their relative undress was strange to the Portuguese. For the Kuikuro, body painting, arm and leg bands, headdresses and bracelets, as marks of culture, constitute being dressed. Nudity per se is not erotic; only specific cultural conventions make it so. Desire can fixate on an ankle, or the glimpse of a face or a body behind a veil or suit. The "characters" in the film seem totally at ease with their own bodies, in an atmosphere devoid of any air of taboo or titillation. There is no gender-based selectivity that dictates differential treatment of men and women. After all the men are naked as well, and many of the women are cradling small children as they walk and dance, which western audiences might see as de-eroticizing. Nor does the camera or editing convey a fetishistic concern with the masculinist partialism of body parts; there are no zoom-ins to women's derrieres like those that typify Globo Network reportage on Rio's carnival. Commercial film industries have made billions of dollars through the slow, gradual unveiling of ever more parts of the female body, but how does one analyze scopophilia and voyeurism in a case where what might be voyeuristic and exploitative for some cultures are not seen as such by another culture, for example, by the confident and willing participants in *Hyper-woman*? Should the film not be shown to audiences unaccustomed to such customs? Does the film need "trigger warnings" for the culturally unprepared?

In a hypothetical indigenized remake of *Singin' in the Rain*, the recombinant Debbie Reynolds would not be a star but just a woman among others. She and the other women, and the men as well, would carry infants in their arms as they dance and the soundtrack would be crowded with the giggles of children. The actresses might make fun of the wilted penises of the aging male stars. In the Kuikuro film, the dancing women complain that the gravelly ground hurts their feet, so the revisionist Debbie Reynold character might complain about the bleeding of her feet, as actually happened with Debbie Reynolds, caused by Gene Kelly's real-life demands for endless dance rehearsals. One can easily imagine the *succes de scandale* of such an "avant-garde" spectacle on Off-Broadway or in Art Film theaters. Furthermore, none of the actors would be stars; in short, a cinema without stars for a society without chiefs.

Given films like *Itai Kuegu*, media theorists are more and more finding the documentary/fiction distinction problematic. The ancient trope of *theatrum mundi*—the "theater of the world," the Shakespearean "All the world's a stage," and Brecht's "everyday street theater" all imply that everyday life is imbued with art, creativity, and performativity. Hayden White, in a parallel move, collapsed the generic distinction between History and Myth, seeing both as emplotted within generic conventions.

Christian Metz famously argued that all films, insofar as they involve arrangement, editing, and mediation, are fiction films. Yet the converse is also true; all films are documentaries in that they document something, even if only the changing modes of production, reproduction, performance, and costume at a given point in time. The proliferation of syncretizing coinages such as "documenteur" ("docu-liar," the title of an Agnes Varda film), "fiction documentaire" (Jacques Ranciere), and "reality fictions" (Frederick Wiseman) also testifies to the burgeoning hybridization of the two modes.[62] In a generic aporia, just as space is inevitably conceived as both finite and infinite, so all films are inevitably analyzable both as fictions and as documentaries.

Itai Kuegu brings the oxymoronic nature of the docu-fiction into sharp focus. Rather than see documentary and fiction as distinct generic essences, we might better distinguish, with Roger Odin, between fictionalizing and documentarizing modes and operations.[63] In the case of *Itai Kuegu*, the documentarizing and the fictionalizing operations coincide. The staging of the preparations for the festival constitutes the film; the rehearsals *are* the performance. Bernard Belisário deploys certain Jean-Louis Comolli concepts about documentary to analyze the film, especially Comolli's idea that mise-en-scène can potentially become a joint project, where the filming subject (the director) exercises agency by filming, framing, editing, lighting, and so forth, but the filmed subject can also exercise agency, thus catalyzing "auto-mise-en-scene," where the desire of the filming and the filmed subjects play a transformative role in the construction of the film. In this case, the documentary becomes a co-production, where the desire of the filmed subjects and the community makes itself felt. By showing the process of preparing the spectacle, the film becomes, in a kind of gynocentric form of reflexivity, the spectacle itself.[64] Like Bakhtin's carnival, it offers a theater without footlights, a "participatory spectacle" characterized by "free and familiar contact."

The Ecological *Cunhã*

Although the Amazon is often treated as pure unsoiled nature, as virgin forest, it has always been molded by human hands. Indigenous thinkers mock the idea of natural "reserves" protected from the abuses of human presence; the point is for human beings to grow up and take care of nature, not to avoid it or fence it in to protect its picturesqueness. To understand the next version of the "*cunhã*"—the ecological/mediatic *cunhã*—it is important to reintroduce Mari Corrêa, a key member in the indigenous media movement in Brazil. After living for 20 years in Paris, studying filmmaking with the Jean-Rouch-inspired Atelier Varan, Corrêa returned to her native Brazil to make her own films, side by side with indigenous and non-indigenous collaborators, while also teaching filmmaking, first as part of the NGO *Video in the Villages* and later as part of her own organization *Catitu*. Fascinated by the Amazon beginning in 1991, Corrêa started filmmaking with Indians in 1998, at a time when equipment was still heavy and many indigenous people, given negative experiences with outsiders' abuse of their hospitality, were sometimes skeptical about possibilities of collaboration. Her films often concern the rituals, the feasts, the legends, and the daily life of indigenous peoples, always yielding authority to the people themselves, who are shown as imaginative, humorous, and very aware of what's happening in their world and beyond. The ancestral homelands of the Ashaninka, one of the largest indigenous groups in South America, range across Brazil and Peru. At one point drafted to work on rubber plantations, the group lost much of their land, and in the late twentieth century got caught up in the bloody conflicts between Sendero Luminoso and the Peruvian army. A large communal reserve set aside for the Ashaninka came under threat by the proposed Pakitzapango dam on the Ene River, part of a series of hydroelectric projects planned by the Brazilian Construction giants Odebrecht and Eletrobras, as usual without any consultation with the Ashaninka themselves. The project would displace thousands of Ashaninka who depend on the fertile soils of the Ene floodplains for their fish and other products from the surrounding forests. As experts on what in the West would be called agronomy, the Ashininka cultivate small plots of land on which they grow manioc, yams, peanuts, bananas, and pineapples. The forest provides edible and medicinal roots, honey, and materials for baskets and mats. Dressed in their elegant tunics, the Ashininka display a strong aesthetic sense, as men and women face-paint themselves with the seeds of the Urucum plant, in ways that reflect their feelings of the moment.

In a North American context, Leanne Betasamosake Simpson speaks of "land as pedagogy," land not as the object of "rights," but rather the subject of duties and responsibilities, whereby indigenous children learn by observing animals and finding the plants that nurture them.[65] Botanist/Nature writer Robin Wall Kimmerer (Potawatomi) speaks of the land as "a renewable source of knowledge and ecological insight" and an indigenous "Skywoman's Gardens" (aka global ecosystems) and of "rhizomes," which she describes as "underground stems … Brown and fibrous on the outside, they are white and starchy on the inside, almost like a potato … Soak cut rhizomes in clean water and you'll soon have a bowl of pasty white starch that can become flower or porridge."[66] We see a similar telluric form of joyful learning in the Ashininka documentary *A gente luta mas come fruta* (We Fight, but We Eat Fruit, 2006), directed by Isaac Pinhanta and Wewito Piyãko. Here young Ashininka learn the sheer joy of discovery, learning both from and with the land. Mari Corrêa, who worked with Ashininka indigenous trainees, had suggested they make "films about nothing"—much as Flaubert spoke of *Madame Bovary* as a "novel about nothing"—using the apparently innocuous and banal as an artistic resource. Instead of focusing on privileged moments of collective life, the goal becomes to uncover the quiet excitement of the everyday.

The "nothing" in *A Gente Luta* concerns a topic both ordinary and profound, in that it revolves around a basic question for indigenous peoples (and ultimately for all peoples): how to sustain life and people and how to educate children for this self-sustaining, especially in a situation where the natural elements necessary to the tribe's survival are endangered by "development"? In the film, Wewito Piyako teaches children about the interactive relations between the land, the fauna, the flora, and the human beings. Within the dense rhizomatics of forest sustainability, the fauna depend on the flora to survive so that the Ashininka can hunt; deforestation harms the animals, on whom the group depends; global warming reduces water supplies, which affects all sentient beings. The children point proudly to the fruits they planted and answer questions about the plant's potential uses. Since certain species of turtle are disappearing, they encourage their mating, leading to an exuberant scene where a swarm of newborn turtles breaks free from their basket, to the delight of the children. In sum, the adults teach children the pleasure of participatory learning. (Wewito's brother Benki is in the forefront of attempts to reconcile shamanic knowledge of the forest with western science.)

Correa, who has long been conducting filmmaking workshops for indigenous women, in her short film *Mulheres Cineastas Indigenas* (Indigenous Women Filmmakers, 2014) shows women from diverse groups, including the Yanomami, expressing their enthusiasm about video-making. Another of her shorts, *Encontro das Mulheres Yanomami* (A Meeting with Yanomami Women, 2014) shows Yanomami women, babies in arms, laughing and singing on their way to a festive encounter, also characterized by singing and dancing. Various women report on their activities, such as elders teaching the young ancient skills like cures and weaving. Davi Yanomami comes to warn them away from thinking that a new highway project will mean progress, since highways have always brought alcoholism, disease, and prostitution. The sounds of the film form a wonderfully chaotic continuum of conversation, laughter, children crying, and bird cries.[67]

Corrêa's documentary *Quentura* (2018) treats the experience and reflections of indigenous women farmers concerned about the challenges of climate change and its impact on their fields, their alimentation, and their way of life. The film travels to three different Amazonian regions, lending an ear to indigenous women concerned about marked changes in the forest, in the water, and in the production of food. Although they belong to different ethnic groups, they share the view that climate change is real and is threatening to indigenous ways of life. As "readers" of the land and vegetation, the women point out that the normal rhythms of the seasons have been disrupted, that pineapples and bananas rot before harvest time, that fish are becoming more scarce, and that fires lasting for months destroy areas rich in biodiversity. The "societies of abundance" to which indigenous people had been accustomed for millennia risk lying fallow, devastated, as it were, by "progress."

For Corrêa, the deep knowledge about natural resources of indigenous women has been underappreciated. With their intimate knowledge of the plants they cultivate, the women are the ones who manage the fields, plant the seeds, collect the fruits, and nourish the vines, some of which serve medicinal purposes. Here the practical knowledge of the women meets the self-reproductive wisdom of what Eduardo Kohn calls "the thinking forest."[68] The Rio Negro area hosts 280 varieties of *maniva*, thanks to long-standing human care and an extensive network of exchanges between women, in a continuous process of experimentation and innovation, but these elements, and these social processes, are at risk. The women lament the overheated "strange summers" that harm the plantations and literally weep when they see the plantations burned to make way for cattle pasture and the beef that ends up in McDonalds's hamburgers. The Bolsonaro government's favoritism toward Agrobusiness and its hostility to the indigene have only accelerated these catastrophic processes.

The "*Cunhã*" as Activist/Artist

Finally, I turn to another kind of *cunhã* figure—the contemporary indigenous woman activist. The chapter began with Patricia Ferreira, the *cunhã* as Guaraní filmmaker, an incarnation of audiovisual activism as a form of what native people in North America like Jolene Ricard have called artistic forms of "sovereignty." The present calamitous situation in Brazil is characterized by unending murders of indigenous leaders and elders (called "living libraries"), the rampant burning of forests, and most recently the ravages of the Coronavirus, all inflicting irreparable damage on tribal history, culture, medicine, and most of all people.[69]

While women directors are relatively rare in indigenous media, women activists are in the forefront of social activism. In 2015, indigenous Tukano lawyer/activist Naiara Tukano was spreading the word about the police killings of indigenous leaders. During one of these incidents, Naiara recorded her protest in a moving video clip (available on YouTube) captured on her cell phone and posted on Facebook.[70] Out of breath and barely controlling her sobs but soldiering through to the end, Naiara speaks in the language of mediatic sophistication and intersectional solidarity, while drawing on Agamben's ideas about "states of exception."

> I am Naiara Tukano, from the Tukano people. I live in Brasilia and I'm an indigenous activist. I'm sending this message to many movements on social media. I've participated in the landless movement, the feminist movement, the black movement, the indigenous movement. We need your help in a difficult moment. In Matto Grosso they've created a state of exception, in the manner of the former dictatorship. They are committing a genocide in the name of agribusiness and the big landowners.

With the historical consciousness typical of indigenous leaders, Tukano then calls for all her interlocutors to spread the news through social media:

> If you embrace our cause, you will be worthy of your slogans and banners, because the genocide of the Indian is the worst genocide in the history of humanity. Use any means to help us reach the international media, which is the only way we've managed to pressure the government. Spread the word through images, texts, videos. Do anything possible to tell Brazilians about what's happening with the Guaraní-Caiowá. They've killed many people. Even shooting at little children with rubber bullets. So many atrocities ... such inhumanity. We ask for your help, you who are our brothers. Tell social media that there will be a massacre, a war. Our people are organizing, everybody is doing what they can, but we are so few.

She ends with an appeal to those Brazilians who make a sentimental claim indigenous ancestry, but show little concrete commitment to the cause of indigenous people: "And for those Brazilians so eager to proudly claim their Indian blood and yet do nothing, where are you? Join us. Do not stand silent."

In 2019, Naiara Tukano gave a "Ted Talk" in Portuguese in São Paulo, and on January 9, 2020, offered a Webinar as part of the "Listen as the Earth Speaks" series. There she spoke about protecting and defending Mother Earth and her community's efforts to protect sacred natural places in the Amazon. She also relates the creation story of the Tukano people, their origins in *Opekõó Dehetaraâ* (Breast Milk Lake), their passage through various transformation sites until arrival at Iapnoré Waterfall (Tohõó Pahaâ Duri), the first recognized sacred site in Brazil and the place where their transformational trip ended. She describes a life collectively lived in the middle of the largest basin of black water on the planet, where food, bathing, transportation, and the economy are all water-dependent. The recognition of the strategic importance of the Amazon region for the planet's water resources, she argues, has to go hand in hand with a recognition of the centrality of indigenous knowledge and of the indigenous people who enact that knowledge.

Another *cunhã*, Zahy Guajajara—quite literally a *cunhã* since her mother tongue is Tupi-Guaraní—is an indigenous activist, photographer, actress, and poet. She was "discovered" when Globo TV interviewed her on the evening news as a speaker at a Rio de Janeiro pro-indigenous rally. In a clip (available on YouTube) she addresses the demonstrators, speaking first in Guaraní.[71] Despite not understanding the words, the crowd is obviously moved by a powerful speaker. She then asks the crowd in Portuguese: "did you understand what I said?" Few did. She then explains: "But you did understand, because I was not only speaking in words, I was speaking in emotion, and I know that you feel exactly what I feel, which is an immense feeling of indignation at what is happening to indigenous people … we are the originary peoples of this land and we are ready to die for it."

Zahy Guajajara describes her younger self as so naive that she believed that she belonged to the only indigenous group in Brazil, and only gradually became aware of the hundreds of other groups. Impressed by her beauty and charisma, Globo cast Zahy as an actress in the Globo Miniseries *Dois Irmãos*, based on a book by Arab-Brazilian novelist Milton Hatoom and directed by noted TV auteur Luis Fernando Carvalho in 2017. In *Dois Irmão,* Zahy plays a maid of indigenous origin, the mother of one of the narrators of the film. She came to conceive her role as one of representing not only her Guaraní people but all indigenous people, a choice consistent with her activism where she fights not for her group alone, but for all indigenous peoples and their land. With Globo, she would help actors immerse themselves in indigenous knowledge in order to understand the context of the stories presented in Brazilian novelas and series. At the same time, Zahy, given the ubiquitous role of art, craft, dance, song, and ritual in indigenous life, sees indigenous people as "natural performers" who lack only opportunity. An ability to culturally code-switch, frequently a historically shaped capacity on the part of oppressed multiple-identity persons, I would add, can be a major resource for performers.

Zahy also co-authored and acted in an experimental web-based short film with Felipe Bragança, entitled *Zahy: A Tale of Maracanã* (2012). The film relates the creation of the symbolic yet also concrete "indigenous village" as a site of protest, constructed next to the former site of the Museum of the Indian and strategically placed next to the famous Maracanã soccer stadium. The site was forcibly removed by the government in 2013 to make way for the World Cup. The remaining fifty or so Indians wanted to transform the decayed building into a vital hub of indigenous creativity. As one representative puts it, "we don't want to be objects but rather the creators of research." Zahy also appears in Felipe Bragança's *Don't Swallow My Heart, Alligator Girl!* (2017), and she played the protagonist of the medium-length short *The Society of Nature*. For her, art and activism are naturally interlaced with each other.

Zahy Guajajara and Daiara Tukano are hardly alone in their activism; many of their peers are active in the arts and media. Eliane Lima dos Santos Potiguara is a pioneer of indigenous literature in Brazil, nominated as one of ten "Women of the Year" in 1988, the year of the new, more indigenous-friendly Constitution. Jovita Maria de Oliveira is a "vice-cacique," a shaman (*pajé*) and practitioner of "ethno-medicine" from the Kai Village, and one of the leaders in the retaking of the Pataxó lands in the state of Bahia. Putanny Yawanawa is an expert in the culture of *ayahuasca* and traditional medicine, music, and song. Watatakalu Yawalapiti defends human rights and the "immaterial patrimonies" of indigenous peoples, including the right to the image in relation to sacred ceremonies. Márcia Wayna Kambeba is a composer, writer, and professor of Cultural Geography. Ana Terra Yawalapiti had a role in gender-desegregating indigenous villages, where the "Men's Houses" had become centers of exclusionary power. She and her sister Watatakalu therefore constructed a "Women's House" as a site of training in leadership as well as in lapsed crafts like ceramics and basket weaving, thus connecting elder grandmothers who wanted to teach the old ways and the grandchildren who wanted to learn. Graciela Guarani was one of the founders of the online platform "Índios Online." Many indigenous women are tribal leaders (*cacicas*) and, as a consequence, are being threatened by prospectors and vigilantes working for Agrobusiness or ranchers.

Native women artists have also become an insurgent force in popular music. Djuena Tikuna, a singer and journalist from Amazonas, in 2017, became the first indigenous artist to perform at the sumptuous Teatro Amazonas concert hall in Manaus, ironically a high-art relic of the arriviste pretensions of the turn-of-the-century rubber boom era. The legendary theater, inaugurated in 1896, where Enrico Caruso and Sarah Bernhardt were rumored to have performed (but never actually did), makes an appearance in Herzog's *Fitzcarraldo* (1982). Djuena appeared in the wake not of opera stars but rather of French pop stars like Mireille Mathieu and Sacha Distel. The songs and music videos in Djuena's album *Tchautchiüãne*in, in the Tikuna language, constitute for her a "decolonizing weapon, a call for respect for Indigenous peoples."[72] As she tours her music throughout Brazil, she emphasizes the centrality of music to indigenous culture, with genres ranging from sleepy time lullabies for children to sacred ceremonial chants. Every note, as she put it in a 2019 interview for *El País*, has a spiritual signification, "as if one were writing with one's soul."[73] In 2019 she participated in the first festival of indigenous music in Brazil, the YBY Festival in São Paulo. (Villa-Lobos, Milton Nascimento, Egberto Gismonti, and Lenine are among the popular musicians influenced by indigenous music.)

Tikuna singer and composer Weë'ena Tikuna, meanwhile, blends traditional instruments, such as the shaker *pau-de-chuva*, with violin and guitar, in music that speaks of love for people and nature. Besides being a musician, she is a visual artist, public speaker, nutritionist, fashion designer, and activist. Her designs draw on the multifaceted indigenous traditions of graphic design. In her words:

> ever since white people first came to Brazil, our Indigenous graphics have attracted the attention of historians, writers, and travelers. Apart from the beauty of the drawings, what surprised most whites was that we Indigenous people not only paint our bodies but also decorate our utilitarian pieces, such as bows, arrows, ceramics, and other handicraft … most of our body paintings represent fauna, flora, rivers, the forest, or everyday objects. A specific design matches each aspect of life we celebrate: one symbolizes our continuing fight for our rights; another, marriage; a third, death; and so on. All our rituals are portrayed in body painting.

She continues:

> Tikuna graphics represent our clans through face paintings that symbolize clan animals of the sky and the earth. During certain rituals (for instance, the one marking a girl's rite of passage into womanhood), paintings depicting animals and spirits also appear as graphics on the clothes of masked men. Our paints are made from plants like *achiote*, *genipapo*, or *babassu*, most of the time mixed with yellow clay and juices from palm trees.[74]

We'e'ena Tikuna's attitude toward the arts echoes a theme stressed throughout this text, i.e. the idea that indigenous arts, like indigenous social thought, are historically minded and triple-tensed, weaving together past, present, and future. In her own words, "I create my designs with an eye to our ancestry, but also with an eye to our future."[75] A composer as well as singer, her first album is entitled *We'e'ena: Indigenous Enchantment*. Her lyrics speak of cultural resistance, indigenous identity, and the preservation of nature.

Katu Mirim, for her part, is a Bororo lesbian rapper whose songs denounce the stereotypes and violent attacks against LBGTQ+ people and indigenous people generally. Singer and composer Kaê Guajajara, as her name implies, meanwhile, is a Guajajara from an un-demarcated part of Maranhao state in northeastern Brazil. Kaê left Maranhão when she was seven because of the slavery-like conditions in which her mother was forced to work, ultimately moving to the favela complex of Mare in Rio de Janeiro, where her fondness for indigenous face-paint made it difficult to get jobs. Using words from her Ze'egete mother tongue, Kaê portrays the reality of urbanized Indians and the danger of erasure of Indigenous identities. As what in the United States would be a seen as an "urban Indian," Kaê's work combines hip-hop with traditional instruments. Her "*Essa Rua e Minha*" (This Street in Mine) fuses Carioca funk with Indigenous flute. Her second EP "*Wiramiri*" (Birdie, in Ze'egete) revolves around self-care, self-love, resistance, and the Covid pandemic. She sees her mission as aiming to "infiltrate power structures that say indigenous peoples no longer exist."[76] Her songs, already used by school teachers as part of indigenous pedagogy, connect with a movement known as "Indigenous Futurism," a term coined by Anishinaabe professor Dr. Grace Dillon. Her specific goal is to use the new technologies to envision an indigenous future and "enhance Indigenous visibility."[77]

Although often forgotten both in the debates about gender and in the debates about indigeneity, indigenous women are gaining a place in the academe and in the public sphere, defending land rights, protecting the environment, and promoting health and citizenship. In a both/and attitude, many want to simultaneously maintain their culture, spiritual traditions, and land base, and occupy the gamut of positions in the dominant society. Naine Terena, an artist and expert on "ethnomedia," for example, advocates for the increased appropriation by indigenous people of all the means of communication available for constructing their own narratives, "whether through books, stories, films, and radio programs so that no one can distort our speech."[78] In 2014 Terena created "Indigenous News" on Facebook and the "Creative Indigenous Territories Project: Art and Sustainability" in Mato Grosso. Graciela Guarani, from the Guaraní Kaiowa territory in Mato Grosso do Sul, with NGO help, promoted media workshops for indigenous youth. Moving to Bahia, she co-created "Olhar da Alma" (Gaze of the Soul) and directed a number of short films like *Terra Nua* (2014) and *Mão de barro* (2016), and *Tempo circular* (2018)—a film which contrasts what she sees as western linear time with Guaraní circular time, where the past is embedded in a present which envisions the future, respecting the natural cycle within an ethos of peace and ancestrality.

As reported in the digital journal *Diario de Pernambuco*, activist/academic/filmmaker Joana Brandão, co-director of the already discussed *Just Another City*, organized, together with the Institute of Humanities, Arts and Sciences from the *Campus* Paulo Freire (IHAC/CPF), an event called "The Indigenous Women's Gaze" ("Olhares das Mulheres Indígenas") whose objective was to focus on the audiovisual productions of indigenous women, as often as possible with the indigenous artists present.[79] While acknowledging that indigenous women have produced fewer films than indigenous men, Brandão quickly adds "just as in the non-indigenous world," making it "even more important to open up space for their voices."[80] Against the dominance of ethnocentric and monocultural representations, the Festival fosters the visibilization of indigenous images, stories, and narratives, making it possible to register traditions, interethnic dialogue, and political empowerment.

The various filmmakers/guests of the festival stress different aspects of the indigenous struggle. Activist/cineaste Olinda Muniz, a Pataxó Hãhãhãe, emphasizes counter-hegemonic deployment of the media as an antidote to a mainstream media whose ethnocentric perspective almost always ignores or disqualifies indigenous struggles. Premised on a feminist project of "valorizing the lives of subalternized subjects,"[81] the Festival featured a cornucopia of indigenous films by women: Olinda Muniz's *Retomar Para Existir* (2015), Graciela Guarani and Alexandre Pankararu's *Mão de Barro* (2016), and Isael Maxacali and Suely Maxacali's *Yiax Kaax* (2010); Charles Bichalho and Isael Maxacali's *Konãgxeka: o dilúvio Maxacali* (2016), and Patrícia Ferreira Keretxu and Sophia Pinheiro's *Teko Haxy* (2018), just to name a few of the productions. A Facebook post of Radio Yande, the first indigenous web media, listed 100 indigenous women as present or potential leaders. Their last names indicate their ethnic affiliation—Renata *Tupinambá,* Joenia *Wapichana,* Azelene *Kaingáng,* Silvia Nobre *Waiãpi,* and Tuirá *Kayapó.* The last named, an elder among the Kayapo, was already seen in the film *Kayapo out of the Forest,* blandishing the long blade of a machete against the face of the CEO of Eletronorte as an expression of righteous anger against the construction of the Kararaô Dam.

An 18-minute music video, a collaboration by film director Andre d'Elia and musical director Chico Cesar, entitled "Demarcation Now!" (2017) gathers many of the cultural figures, indigenous and non-indigenous, mentioned in this book in support of the demarcation of indigenous land. The video was created in response to attempts by Bolsonaro to evade the pro-indigenous land requirements of the 1988 Constitution. The gallery of cultural and political leaders includes indigenous activists like Ailton Krenak, Davi Kopenawa, Raoni, Cacique Babau, and Sônia Guajajara, indigenous musicians like Djuena Tikuna, actresses like Letícia Sabatella, black rappers like Crioulo, together with luminaries from the world of popular music: consecrated singer/composer/performers representing different generations like Chico Cesar, Elza Soares, Lenine, Margareth Menezes, Maria Bethânia, Zeca Baleiro, Zeca Pagodinho, and Ney Matagrosso. A number of the figures, like anthropologist and social theorist Viveiros de Castro and Tropicalia popstar Gilberto Gil, are strongly connected to the anthropophagic thought of Oswald de Andrade, forging a link between Brazilian modernism and indigenous activism in a very practical way—concrete support for the protection of indigenous land. The refrain is simple—"Demarcation Now!"—but the stanzas of the song/poem touch on many of the themes of this book: colonialism, genocide, the indigenous resurgences, military repression, the Trans Amazonian Highway, deforestation, agri-business, industrial pollution, assassinations, but also indigenous victories, intersectionalities with blacks, gays, and lesbians, as suggested in some of the lyrics; "just like the black man and the homosexual/the Indian is seen as useless, but who would want to strip the Indians of all they have left—their territory and ancestral heritage."[82]

The video is festive, musical, artistic. The lyrics also defend "the high-tech Indian": "the Indian can have an iPad, a freezer, a TV, a pick-up, a motor boat, without ceasing to be Indian." The words are illustrated, counterpointed, amplified through extremely diverse kinds of materials—news footage of protests and repression, scenes from plays touching on indigenous issues, citations of films and the like. The range of faces crosses the spectrum of racially mixed appearances, where the lines between black, white, and indigenous are often not at all clear. Some of the stanzas convey the common claim that "we Brazilians are all Indians," a concept that would be seen as problematic by many indigenous people in North America by seeing colonization only as a metaphor, since "we" are not all colonized in the same way. It is hard to imagine anything like this video, involving celebrated musicians, activists, scholars, and artists, emerging from the United States, which certainly has its own creative forms of protest, but not often such dramatic and comprehensive forms of supporting native land claims. This contrast can be explained by the distinct cultural and political configurations. In Brazil, the indigenous peoples referenced in the video still control vast swaths of land, and the groups protesting are not "urban Indians" but Amazonians living in their land and trying to keep it. In the United States, indigenous groups want to regain or strengthen sovereignty over the land, while in Brazil indigenous groups do not want to lose the measure of sovereignty and the land base that they already have, but which is now dramatically threatened. In North America, most native people can communicate in English, which is not true of many of the groups in Brazil in terms of Portuguese. The video ends with citations of Kopenawa's prophecies about the *Fall of the Sky*, in a kind of collective celebration dance which simultaneously evokes an indigenous ritual and Brazil's carnival.

Indigenous issues have finally reached the media entertainment mainstream through Globo, with all the ambiguities that mainstreaming might bring. A series called "Falas da Terra" features 21 indigenous artists and leaders, caciques and pajes, activists and artists, rappers and surgeons, all arguing for protection of the forest. Many members of the production team were indigenous, produced by the Rede Amazonica branch of Globo, part of a larger series under the "Falas" rubric, such as "Falas Negras" and "Falas Femininas." The series opened on April 16, 2021, the National Day of Indigenous Peoples. The series features major indigenous activists like the inevitable Ailton Krenak and David Kopenawa, but also musicians like Narubia Werreria (Karaja), Edivan Fulni-O scientists (Fulni-O), all with a very strong feminist and feminine presence. Indigenous women are also appearing in what might seem a surprising venue—gaming. In a scene from *Araní*, a Brazilian game from Diorama Digital currently in development, the indigenous lead character Arani, a female warrior of the Sun Tribe, strives to save her people from a mysterious, mythological one-legged creature. Thus, beyond the "Indio Tecnizado" we find the "India Digitalizada."[83]

Another indigenous leader who has deftly used the media to spread the indigenous message is Sônia Guajajara, the 2018 vice-presidential candidate with the *Socialism and Freedom* party and chief representative of the pan-indigenous movement in Brazil. At a Senate public hearing on indigenous health, she debated a ruralist senator linked to the large landowners (Soraia Thronicke), who promulgated the hackneyed formulae of Indians-as-obstacles-to-Progress-occupying-land-needed-for-development. Their quarrel continues the 500-year-old debate about the meaning and definition of land. What is land? Can it be owned? Who deserves its fruits? After the senator exposes her position, which is basically to deny Indians land in the name of "development," Sônia Guajajara responds:

> I cannot sit idly by and listen to this racist discourse. You and I have a very different view of land. For you, land is statistics, ownership. This is the racist discourse linked to the corporations that want to exploit the Amazon. Ultimately it is about capitalist greed. We have a different view; for us land is a sacred trust, we need it to survive. But you see it as property, profit, exploitation. Now that the entire world is worried about climate change, reducing fossil fuels, you want to go backward![84]

Like many indigenous leaders, and like Raoni with his relationship with Sting, Guajajara is keenly aware of the potential of the media to disseminate indigenous perspective, including through alliances with international celebrities. Thus, in 2017 she appeared alongside a warmly supportive Alicia Keys at the *Rock in Rio* Festival, where she defended the indigenous cause before an audience of over a 100,000 people.[85]

Coming full circle, Sônia became another *cunhã* in New York when she appeared on a show linked to the other kind of "Indian," Hasan Minhaj and his "Patriot Act" show on Netflix.[86] Together the two agreed that globalized capitalism is destroying the Amazon and that the indigenous peoples are a major bulwark against its destruction. Throughout, Sônia held her own in terms of witty repartee. When Minhaj admits, in his usual self-mocking manner, that "[w]e Americans destroyed our own forests and killed the Indians, yet now we're lecturing you Brazilians. So we're assholes, right?" Sônia's response is diplomatic: "I'm not saying that you are assholes. You said it, I'm just affirming it." Together they support the "Guardians of the Forest," while the episode ends with Minhaj announcing a website supporting the project, called, in reference to a scandalous Brazilian video that went viral, "Presidente Golden Showers."

Most recently, on October 3, 2020, Sônia published an essay on the Amazon for the *New York Times* entitled "Can our Culture Survive Climate Change?" There she describes the evolution of the Guajajara from living in natural abundance to surviving poverty and scarcity within a cash economy:

> My memories of childhood are of abundance. In the old days it used to be easy enough to find monkeys, *pacas* and *tinamou* to eat, but now our government has opened our lands to mine for gold and iron, and to produce timber for paper and soy and cattle. They call our peoples and our traditions primitive and show disdain for our ceremonies. Prioritizing development at any cost is not just poisoning Brazil—it is threatening our way of life … Our lives are inextricable from the natural world. The creatures of the rainforest protect us, and in turn we protect them. We are the only buffers protecting our thinning forests. Our battle is not just for the future. It's for the present.[87]

Artemisa Xakriabá, for her part, is a nineteen-year-old activist from the Xakriabá tribe from southeastern Brazilian state of Minas Gerais, a group currently threatened by land loss and government-led deforestation meant to make way for farming and mining. Her aim is to stop environmental destruction, and especially, to take action against the thousands of forest fires deliberately spread across the Amazon rainforest. A representative of the *Global Alliance of Territorial Communities* for indigenous communities, she became another *cunhã* in the United States when on September 20, 2019, she addressed the U.S. House of Representatives and leader Nancy Pelosi, urging senators "to lead the community of nations in caring for our common home." On September 27, 2019, she was a featured speaker at the Climate March in New York, where crowd estimates ranged from 60,000 to 250,000. She explained:

> The Amazon is on fire. The Amazon agonizes year after year for the responsibility of the government and its destructive policies that intensify deforestation and drought, not only in the Amazon, but in the other five Brazilian biomes [plants and animal communities sharing common characteristics] … The governments of Brazil and the United States are not helping. They promote … a development model that attacks nature and indigenous peoples.

She went on to say that "[w]e, the indigenous peoples, are the children of nature, so we fight for our Mother Earth, because the fight for Mother Earth is the mother of all other fights."

Myths of Extinction: The Return of the Vanished Indigene

In this final section, we return to the *cunhã* in Caetano's canoe and to the Lenape in Manhattan, as well as to the Tupinamba whom we first encountered as the interlocutors of the French in France Antartique. Many of the declarations of indigenous extinction have turned out to be premature; their descendants are alive and speaking out. Completely annihilating a people is not easy; there are always human "remainders." Even the famous "last of the Mohicans" was not the last; more than a thousand Mohicans live on a reservation in Wisconsin.

In this text, we have witnessed multiple "first contacts": between Columbus and the Taínos in 1492; Cabral and the Tupi in 1500; the Italians (Verrazzano in 1524) and the English (Henry Hudson in 1609) and the Dutch in the 1620s. Prior to the European presence, the Lenape occupied an area known as *Lenapehoking*, which covered roughly the area between New York City and Philadelphia, including New Jersey, eastern Pennsylvania, and part of the state of Delaware. As discussed earlier, with the 1626 "sale" of Manhattan, and the building of a wall around New Amsterdam, the Lenape were forced to migrate out of their homeland. After a succession of what Lenape scholar Joanne Barker calls "defraudings," the Lenape, a group which Barker describes as adhering to "matrilineal values of shared governance," were dispersed around the country and now live in different parts of the United States including Pennsylvania, Ohio, Indiana, Missouri, Kansas, Oklahoma, and even Ontario in Canada.[88] Three Lenape tribes—the Delaware Nation in Oklahoma, the Delaware Tribes of Indians in Oklahoma, and the Stockbridge-Munsee Community in Wisconsin—are federally recognized in the United States. More than four centuries after the alleged "sale" of Manhattan, some Lenape-descended people are trying to reanimate the cultural heritage, for example, by hosting summer camps for children to learn Lenape spiritual practices, dances, and songs. They have also secured grants to help revitalize the endangered Lenape language. Historian Jack Forbes is part Lenape, as is one of the leading indigenous activists/theorists already cited (Joanne Barker). Meanwhile, the word "American" in the "American Wing" of the Metropolitan Museum of Art has been restored to one of its first meanings, to refer to Native Americans, thanks to its first indigenous curator Patricia Marroquin Norby (Purepecha), and the Museum's land acknowledgment plaque honors indigenous peoples in general and the Lenape in particular.[89]

In Brazil, meanwhile, the Tupinamba too were long thought to be "extinct." While Oswald de Andrade lauded the resistance and gregarious lifestyle of the sixteenth-century Tupinamba, and while he was obviously aware that many indigenous peoples existed in Brazil, he never addressed actually existing Tupinamba, presumably under the assumption that they no longer existed as such. Yet thanks to social media and the internet, we now know something Oswald, and for that matter Nelson Pereira dos Santos, could not know. The Tupinamba, since the days of Cunhambebe and France Antarique, have been massacred—a fact referenced in the final intertitle of *How Tasty Was My Little Frenchman*—and they have been enslaved, Jesuitized, evangelized, criminalized, and physically dispersed. But they are now very vocal, fighting for their land and rights in the south of the state of Bahia and in Para, in movements often led by women. Today, the internet proliferates in YouTube videos dedicated to the Tupinamba of Olivenca. The supposedly "extinct" group now has their public intellectuals, publishes essays, and produces animated videos, explaining their history and demanding their cultural and territorial rights.

Yakuy Tupinambá, for example, is an educator and activist with the Tupinamba of Olivenca, and author of texts on the Tupinamba and other indigenous topics. In 2008, she traveled to Europe to denounce Brazilian violations of indigenous rights. In "The Order of Disorder," she offers some very pessimistic observations:

> I had always heard that we human beings have been evolving and that the 21st century would be the apex of progress. It was understood that ignorance would disappear and that subservience and slavery would come to an end, along with hunger and misery and the division between oppressors and oppressed. A big mistake. Human evolution seems to be moving in reverse, and what has really evolved is the destruction of everything and everyone. With greed overcoming the jargon of development, what we increasingly see is the imposition of ideologies of verticality, where some command and others obey. Many people do not see the obvious, that [all this] is leading to the end of the human species, bringing with it the destruction of other species who lack the right even to defend their own lives, without respect for the diversity which maintains the equilibrium of nature and thus of life itself.[90]

Yakuy laments the fact that health professionals do not respect the ancient knowledge and traditions, and that religious figures in authority are making the same mistakes that they made in colonial times.

> We want to participate in the construction of a more just society, live with dignity, with our rights respected … we want our territories demarcated, without intruders, and even augmented … The syntheses produced by the pharmacetutical compananies come from us, our foods are distributed around the world. We, the peoples of the forest, are the ones who cared for the environment that the invaders encountered.[91]

At other times, Yakuy Tupinamba expresses more optimism. In "A Proposal for Life," she writes:

> We indigenous people know transcendence, we know the importance of being connected to other elements essential to life. Despite our particularities, we are part of a whole. In our vocabulary, there is no "me" only "us." This world can still

be transformed into a village, we can together reverse this destructive situation. Let us prepare an environment worthy of future generations, a world full of real people. Let's continue planting, the earth is still fertile.[92]

Much of the current activism and artistic activity takes place online through media organizations such as "Indios-Online" and "Indio-educa" (Indians Educate), although some indigenous media leaders note that countries like Mexico, Columbia, and Bolivia are more advanced in treating indigenous communications as human rights like health and education. Some of the Tupinamba *caciques* and shamans, like Cacique Babau, are male, but many are female, such as the Cacicas Jesuina, Paje Jandira, and Gliceria Jesus da Silva. Much of the contemporary Tupinamba resistance takes the form of taking back their land on the basis of their rights as originary peoples, according to the provisions laid out in the 1988 Constitution, in the name of which they have taken back scores of Cacau plantations that had been carved out of their land. Activism also takes the form of videos, for example a film by Celia Tupinamba and Leo Mendez entitled *Cipo Tupi* (2021) in which Tupinamba elders explore the forest looking for *cipo* vines in order to fabricate baskets, brooms, brushes, and the like: the film ends with a saying: "sweeping our homes equals sweeping the world."

The story of Tupinamba struggle is also told in a 2015 documentary film, *Tupinamba: The Return of the Land,* which uses interviews and archival materials to relate the struggle to demarcate part of the ancestral Tupinamba land in the South of Bahia, territory that was stolen by the landowners called "coroneis" in order to farm cocoa. Guided by their faith in the ancestral spirits ("Encantados")—for them the real guardians of the forest—the Tupinamba managed to recuperate some of their land, despite the hostility and repression of the Brazilian state and ambitious landowners in the form of death threats, murder, torture, and incarceration. Using archival footage and interviews with the principals, the film relates the imprisonment in 2010, of Cacique Babau in a maximum-security penitentiary for five months. During that same year, a woman leader, along with her baby, was imprisoned for two months. In 2014, a military base was installed in Tupinambá territory. About 500 soldiers were moved to the area. Since then, the Tupinambá people have reported being subjected to threats and acts of violence carried out by law enforcement officials. Despite the horrendous abuse, the Tupinambá remain committed to pressuring the Brazilian state to fulfill its constitutional duty by recognizing their right to land.

The Tupinamba story is told as well in a book in Portuguese by Daniela Fernandes Alarcon, whose title translated in English reads *The Return of the Earth: The Land Recuperation in the village Tupinamba da Serra do Padeiro, in the South of Bahia, 2019.*[93] One of the women leaders from Serra do Padeiro, Gliceria Jesus da Silva, wrote the following in the preface to the book: "As she listens to the laments, the tragedies, the expulsions, the violations of our rights, the violence against the land, the author shows how our people organized the recovery of our lands, attempting to reverse the negative impacts suffered by nature, and how through this process, the forests, the rivers and the animals came to feel more protected and secure."[94] The Tupinamba story reminds us of other oppressed cultural groups temporarily driven underground—sometimes for decades or even centuries—in order to survive. Such was the case of the covert

Jews (*Marranos*) and hidden Muslims (*Moriscos*) in Spain at the time of the Inquisition and the Muslim expulsion. In indigenous terms, we are reminded of James Clifford's account of the efforts of the North American Indian people of Mashpee, a town on Cape Cod, to establish, in court, their status as an Indian tribe. The opposition argued that acculturation and assimilation had turned them into just one more ethnic group like the Irish-Americans and the Italian-Americans, who had no more claim to Indian culture and a privileged legal status than any other.

Alarcon's book explains how the Tupinamba collective project created conditions for the reemergence of buried memories, for the return of the Tupinamba in the intranational diaspora—some of whom had been forced to work in slavery-like conditions as "*negros da terra*"—and for the strengthening of the traditional productive activities of the tribe, all of which improve both the individual lives of the group but also serve to protect the Atlantic forest surrounding the village. At the same time, *O Retorna da Terra* reveals the profound cosmological dimension of these struggles. The Tupinamba believe that the territory belongs not to individuals but to the enchanted nonhuman entities who rule diverse dominions within the physical world and who, like the Tupinamba themselves, were impacted by the advance of the capitalist frontier and by the degradation of their earthly place of dwelling. In sum, given the choice between "Tupi or not Tupi," the Tupi themselves have opted to be Tupi, and above all, simply "to be."

Notes

1. I elaborate on this play with Gramsci's concept of the "organic intellectual" in my (co-authored with Ella Shohat) book *Race in Translation: Culture Wars in the Postcolonial Atlantic* (New York: New York University Press, 2012).
2. When I teach the poem, I also show a remix I made of the song superimposed on digital images, borrowed from the book *Manahatta: A Natural History of New York* by Eric Sanderson, showing a simulacrum of the island of Manhattan before the arrival of Europeans.
3. David Hajdu writes that the Indians called the Hudson "the river that runs both ways." *New York Times* (March 22, 2009).
4. Sousândrade, "O Guesa" (Sao Luiz: Edicoes SIOGE, 1979), pp. 22–3 (translation mine).
5. From the entry on the "Delaware" by Ives Goddard, in *Handbook of North American Indians: Northeast*, Vol. 15, edited by William Sturtevant, cited in Thelma Wills Foote, *Black and White in Manhattan: The History of Racial Formation in Colonial New York City* (Oxford: Oxford University Press, 2004), p. 15.
6. See Edwin G. Burrows and Mike Wallace, *Gotham: A History of New York City to 1898* (New York: Oxford, 1999), p. 3.
7. Herman Melville, *Moby Dick* (New York: Penguin Classics, 2002), p. 4.
8. Thomas Hobbes, *Leviathan*, ed. A. P. Martinich (Peterborough: Broadview Literary Texts, 2002), p. 96.
9. Ibid., p. 95.
10. On two occasions, once around the time of the 2008 financial crisis, and on December 10, 2020, whales were sighted in the Hudson Bay.

11 Hobbes, *Leviathan*, op. cit., p. 96.
12 When Henry Hudson arrived, by one account, the "island-peninsula had supported the self-sufficient life of the Wappinger for at least 500 years." See Foote, *Black and White in Manhattan*, p. 23.
13 From Caetano Veloso, *Tropical Truth: A Story of Music and Revolution in Brazil* (New York: Da Capo Press, 2003), originally published in Brazil as *Verdade Tropical* by Companhia das Letras, São Paulo in 1997. This quotation is from *Verdade Tropical*, p. 270, my translation.
14 Ibid.
15 Long after writing this, I learned that my colleague Barbara Browning was writing along similar lines, in her wonderful book Caetano Veloso's *A Foreign Sound* (London: Bloomsbury, 2017).
16 See Eric W. Sanderson, "Let the Streams Run Free," *New York Times* (February 10, 2021).
17 Paulo Emilio Salles Gomes, *Uma Situação Colonial?* (Companhia das Letras 1st edition: 2016).
18 Heike Paul, *The Myths That Made America: An Introduction to American Studies* (Transcript Verlag, 2014), pp. 115–16 JSTOR, Accessed December 13, 2020, www.jstor.org/stable/j.ctv1wxsdq.
19 Paula Gunn Allen, *Pocahontas: Medicine Woman, Spy, Entrepreneus, Diplomat* (New Yorker: HarperCollins, 2004), pp. 2–4.
20 Ibid., p. 305.
21 Vianna Moog in *Bandeirantes and Bandeirantes* (New York: George Braziller, 1956), p. 102, elaborates on the Pocahontas/Paraguacu parallels.
22 It is worth noting that Captain Smith reportedly claimed to have been rescued by beautiful women in other "exotic" spaces as well.
23 See Robert S. Tilton, *Pocahontas: The Evolution of an American Narrative* (Cambridge: Cambridge University Press, 1994), p. 11.
24 Leslie Fiedler made this suggestion in his 1948 classic essay "Come Back to the Raft Ag'in, Huck Honey." Later incorporated into *Love and Death in the American Novel* (New York: Criterion, 1960).
25 Doris Sommer, *Foundational Fictions: The National Romances of Latin America* (Berkeley: University of California Press, 1993), p. 154.
26 Tracy Devine Guzman, *Native and National in Brazil: Indigeneity after Independence* (Durham: University of North Carolina Press, 2013), p. 67.
27 From Cooper's *The Deerslayer*, cited in Renata R. Maautner Wasserman, *Exotic Nations: Literature and Cultural Identity in the United States and Brazil, 1830–1930* (Ithaca: Cornell University Press, 1994), p. 174.
28 Joanna Hearne, *Native Recognition: Indigenous Cinema and the Western* (Albany: SUNY Press, 2012), pp. 56–7.
29 Cited in Tracy Devine Guzman, *Native and National in Brazil*, op. cit., p. 67.
30 Ibid., p. 95.
31 See Richard A. Gordon, *Cannibalizing the Colony: Cinematic Adaptations of Colonial Literature in Mexico and Brazil* (West Lafayette: Purdue University Press, 2009), p. 161.
32 Vine Deloria Jr. (1988), op. cit., pp. 2–4.
33 In conversation with the author at the Hemispheric Institute of Politics and Performance at Belo Horizonte in March, 2005.
34 Beatriz Nascimento criticizes interpretations of anthropophagi that reduce it to capitalist consumption or to postmodern cultural syncretism typical of the Market,

a conception which for her is the opposite of Oswald's radical conception. See *Palimpsesto Selvagem*, and the essay co-authored with Laura Francis, "Could this be the Future of the 21st Century" ile:///Users/robertstam/Downloads/Sera_esse_o_futuro_do_seculo_XXI%20(2).pdf S Ainda hoje é necessário aprofundar o tema, delineando as imensas diferenças teóricas entre "antropofagia" e "canibalismo," que acabam por gerar associações equivocadas da antropofagia com a globalização, consumismo capitalista, "misturas" indiscriminadas e "geleia geral" das massificações culturais do mercado—quando na realidade a utopia oswaldiana propôs exatamente o oposto.

35   We find a rare French homage to Paraguaçu in a 1950s novel by Olga Obry, entitled *Catherine du Bresil: Filleule de Saint Malo* (Catherine of Brasil: God-daughter of Saint Malo, 1953), which explores the significance of Paraguaçu's voyage to France. Using the various texts about Paraguaçu as her point of departure, Obry tries to reconstruct the events of her life from within what she imagines to be Paraguaçu's perspective and culture. Much of the narrative is devoted to the experience of the sea voyage and the shock of European culture for an Indian.

36   The director Joaquim Pedro de Andrade was extremely knowledgeable not only about Brazilian modernism and Mário de Andrade but also about Oswald de Andrade. His film *The Brazil-wood Man*, 1982, splits the Oswald figure into a man and a woman, thus tying the modernist utopia of the matriarchal Tupi homeland Pindorama to the role of women in the urban insurgency then taking place in Brazil.

37   Koch-Grunberg was the inspiration for the first ethnologist character in the Columbian film *The Embrace of the Serpent* (2015).

38   See Theodor Koch-Grunberg, *Do Roraima ao Orinoco*, Vol. 1, trans. Cristina Alberts-Franco (São Paulo: EUSP, 2005), p. 62.

39   See Tele Porto Ancona Lopez, ed. Mário de Andrade, *Macunaíma: O Heroi sem Nenhum Carater*, cited in Lucia Sa, "Part II: Macunaíma and the Native Trickster," Woodrow Wilson International Center for Scholars, Special Report (November 2008), p. 3.

40   Michael Taussig, *Shamanism, Colonialism, and the Wild Man: A Study in Terror and Healing* (Chicago: University of Chicago Press, 1987), p. 22.

41   See Leonardo Sakamoto, "Modern-Day Slavery in the Amazon," *News International* (January 20, 2020). Accessed from https://newint.org/features/2020/01/20/modern-day-slavery-amazon.

42   See John Hemming, *Die If You Must* (London: Macmillan, 2004), p. 444.

43   Among the Kadiwéu, one of the boy performers stands out because he is blond yet fluent in Kadiwéu and plays a role as a Kadiwéu. It turns out that he is simply the son of a mixed marriage who stayed with his native parent.

44   See Darcy Ribeiro, *Kadiwéu: Ensaios Etnológicos sobre o Saber, o Azar e a Beleza* (Rio de Janeiro: Global Editora, 2019).

45   One finds a similar pairing of moral opposites in the Yamomami divinities Omama and his mischievous son Yoasi.

46   See Graeber and Wengrow, op. cit., p. 191.

47   Although Lucia Murat is not indigenous, she suffered a very bitter experience as part of a guerilla movement against the dictatorship who was captured and tortured by the regime. So in this sense, she perhaps had a point of identification with the indigenous heroine.

48   O estranhamento como matriz estética em *Brava Gente Brasileira*, de Lúcia Murat 1201 Cássio dos Santos Tomaim** Valquiria Rodrigues Reis Tomaim*** Diálogos

49 A TV Cultura animated series called "Icamiabas" features contemporary feminist Icamiabas.
50 Robin Wall Kimmerer, *Braiding Sweetgrass*, op. cit., pp. 380–4.
51 Jack Weatherford, *Native Roots*, p. 165.
52 For an extremely sophisticated analysis of the music in the film, see Bernard Belisario, "Resonancias entre cinema, cantos e corpos no filme: *As Hipermulheres*," Galáxia (São Paulo) (32), May–August 2016, https://doi.org/10.1590/1982-2554201622345
53 Freya Schiwy claims that "indigenous video revives technologies of knowledge grounded in storytelling, *khipus*, and weaving." See Freya Schiwy, *Indianizing Film: Decolonization, the Andes, and the Question of Technology* (New Brunswick: Rutgers University Press, 2009), p. 173.
54 There is a good deal of excellent analysis of the film, beside Sarah Shamash, see Alessandra Santos, "Review of *Itão Kuêgü—As Hiper Mulheres—The Hyperwomen*. Directed by Takumã Kuikuro, Carlos Fausto, and Leonardo Sette." *E-misférica*, Vol. 11, No. 1 (2014), http://hemisphericinstitute.org/hemi/en/emisferica-111-decolonial-gesture/santos. Accessed September 15, 2015, and Bernard Belisario, "As Hipermulheres: cinema e ritual entre mulheres, homens e espíritos" (MA thesis for Belo Horizonte: Universidade Federal de Minas Gerais, Faculdade de Filosofia e Ciências Humanas, 2014).
55 Carlos Fausto, *Art Effects: Image, Agency, and Ritual in Amazonia* (Lincoln: University of Nebraska Press, 2020), p. 114.
56 See Sarah Shamash, "Utopic Cannibalism in Carlos Fausto, Leonardo Sette, and Takumã Kuikuro's *As Hiper Mulheres*," in Kim Beauchesne and Alessandra Santos, eds., *Performing Utopias in the Contemporary Americas* (New York: Palgrave Macmillan US, 2017), p. 143. The VNA website reflects the gender imbalance, with thirty-five indigenous male directors and only three female directors.
57 Sarah Shamash, op. cit., p. 140.
58 See Gregory Bateson, *Steps to an Ecology of Mind* (New York: Ballantine, 1972).
59 For an extensive analysis, see Alice Fátima Martins, "As *hiper mulheres* kuikuro: apontamentos sobre cinema, corpo e performance," *Sociedade e Estado*, Vol. 29, No. 3 (Brasília set./dez. 2014).
60 Ibid.
61 For an elaborate discussion of the submerged whiteness of the musical utopia, see Ella Shohat, "Ethnicities-in-Relation: Toward a Multi-Cultural Reading of American Cinema," in Lester Friedman (ed.), *Unspeakable Images: Ethnicity and the American Cinema*, University of Illinois Press, 1991, pp. 215–50; and Shohat/Stam, *Unthinking Eurocentrism* (Routledge, 1994).
62 The phrase "*fiction documentaire*" is in Ranciere, *La Fable Cinematographique* (Paris: Le Seuil, 2001), p. 201.
63 See Roger Odin, *De la Fiction* (Brussels: De Boeck, 2000).
64 Bernard Belisário, "Ressonâncias entre cinema, cantos e corpos no filme As Hipermulheres," *Galáxia*, No. 32 (São Paulo [online], 2016), pp. 65–79.
65 Leanne Betasamosake Simpson, *As We Have Always Done: Indigenous Freedom through Radical Resistance* (Minneapolis: University of Minnesota Press, 2017), p. 150.
66 Robin Wall Kimmerer, op. cit., 227.

67 https://amotara.org/portfolio/cipo-tupi/ https://vimeo.com/163166513 http://www.hutukara.org/index.php/galeria/videos/791-video-encontro-das-mulheres-yanomami-2014.
68 See Eduardo Kohn, *How Forests Think: Toward an Anthropology beyond the Human* (Berkeley: University of California Press, 2013).
69 See Don Philips, "We Are Facing Extermination: Brazil Losing a Generation of Indigenous Leaders to Covid-19," *New York Times* (June 21, 2020).
70 "Denúncia de Naiara Tukano!" uploaded by Star Dust (November 17, 2016), https://www.youtube.com/watch?v=kIotdf8XmtU
71 "zahy," *Youtube*, uploaded by Paula Kossatz (November 2, 2012), https://www.youtube.com/watch?v=LwcqfKLeZHg
72 Beatriz Miranda, "'The way I am is an outrage': The Indigenous Brazilian Musicians Taking Back a Burning Country," *The Guardian* (October 26, 2020). Accessed from https://www.theguardian.com/music/2020/oct/26/brazil-music-indigenous-tribes-environment-bolsonaro
73 Joana Oliveira, "O canto tikuna é muito espiritual, você escreve com a alma," *El País* (May 16, 2019), Accessed from https://brasil.elpais.com/brasil/2019/05/13/cultura/1557783452_873253.html.
74 We'e'ena Tikuna, "Overcoming the Odds to Reach My Dreams: An Indigenous Artist's Story," *Langscape Magazine*, Vol. 8 (September 2, 2019). Accessed from https://medium.com/langscape-magazine/overcoming-the-odds-to-reach-my-dreams-an-indigenous-artists-story-9a25050b9b31.
75 Ibid.
76 Beatriz Miranda, op. cit.
77 Ibid.
78 See Cibele Tenório, "Indígenas inspiradoras: conheça a história de cinco mulheres," *EBC* (April 19, 2016), Accessed from https://memoria.ebc.com.br/cidadania/2016/04/dia-do-indio-cinco-historias-de-mulheres-inspiradoras
79 See Emannuel Bento, "Coletivo de cinema indígena de Pernambuco faz campanha para contar histórias sem estereótipos," *Diario de Pernambuco* (Published April 27, 2019, and updated August 6, 2020). Accessed from https://www.diariodepernambuco.com.br/noticia/viver/2019/04/coletivo-de-cinema-indigena-de-pernambuco-faz-campanha-para-contar-his.html.
80 "Mostra audiovisual com produções de mulheres indígenas promove debates sobre arte, interculturalidade e gênero," *Universidade Federal do Sul da Bahia* (July 30, 2018). Accessed from https://ufsb.edu.br/ultimas-noticias/1016-mostra-audiovisual-com-producoes-de-mulheres-indigenas-promove-debates-sobre-arte-interculturalidade-e-genero.
81 Ibid.
82 For all of the lyrics in English, see Carlos Rennó—Letra de Demarcação já! + traducción al Ingléshttps://lyricstranslate.com › demarcação-já-demarcation ...
83 See article by Gabriel Leao, "Brazil's Indigenous Gaming Scene Is On," in *Culture* (December 3, 2022) https://www.wired.com/story/brazil-indigenous-gaming-arani/
84 "Sônia Guajajara desmonta discurso de senadora do PSL no Senado," *Redação RBA* (April 4, 2019) https://www.redebrasilatual.com.br/politica/2019/04/sonia-guajajara-desmonta-discurso-de-senadora-do-psl-no-senado/
85 Inspired by the indigenous movement Keys had penned a song in 2016 about "Mother Earth" entitled *Kill Your Mama*. Some of the lyrics: "Shame on us, on your sons and your daughters / Thieve all your gold and we poisoned all your waters /

Every piece of our soul is for sale ... All that you have given and we only disrespected / The rate that we're going, premature Armageddon / That's what gonna happen if we let it ... Is there any saving us? / We've become so dangerous/Is there any change in us? / Even for the sake of love/How you gonna kill your mama?"

86 "Brazil, Corruption and the Rainforest," *Patriot Act*, Vol. 3, *Netflix* (May 12, 2019).
87 "Can Our Culture Survive Climate Change?" in a special section "The Amazon Has Seen Our Future," *New York Times* (October 3, 2020), Accessed from https://www.nytimes.com/2020/10/02/opinion/amazon-indigenous-people-brazil.html.
88 See Joanne Barker, Territory as Analytic: The Dispossession of Lenapehoking and the Subprime Crisis, *Social Text* 135, Vol. 36, No. 2 (June 2018). See also Colleen Connolly, "The True Native New Yorkers Can Never Truly Reclaim Their Homeland," *Smithsonian Magazine* (October 5, 2018). Accessed from https://www.smithsonianmag.com/history/true-native-new-yorkers-can-never-truly-reclaim-their-homeland-180970472/.See also *Exiles in the Land of the Free: Democracy, the Iroquois* Nation *and* the US Constitution (Santa Fe: Clearlight Publishers, 1992).
89 See *NYT*, "A Native Perspective at the Met" (July 11, 2021).
90 Yakuy Tupinamb, "A Ordem da Desordem," June 13, 2018 https://racismoambiental.net.br/2018/06/13/a-ordem-da-desordem-por-yakuy-tupinamba/
91 An open letter from Yakuy Tupinamba to President Djilma Roussef titled "CARTA ABERTA PARA DILMA ROUSSEFF (Yakuy Tupinambá)" (November 1, 2010) Accessed from https://groups.google.com/g/populacao_indigena_abep/c/Cx0mttUl_oI?pli=1
92 Yakuy Tupinambá, "Proposta de vida," *Indios online* (December 1, 2006), http://www.indiosonline.net/proposta_de_vida
93 Daniela Fernandes Alarcon, *O retorno da terra: as retomadas na aldeia Tupinambá da Serra do Padeiro, sul da Bahia* (São Paulo: Elefante Editora, 2019).
94 Ibid.

3

The Transnational "Indian"

Although "Indians" have been endlessly featured first in Western philosophy and literature and subsequently in the cinemas of the world, the Hollywood Western, especially, has shaped their international image. Hollywood had inherited the stereotypes established in nineteenth-century theater and literature, for example, the "dime novels" in the aptly named genre of "Conquest fiction," through which figures like William Frederick Cody, known as Buffalo Bill, achieved national fame. Cody's Wild West Show featured indigenous warriors in photogenic costumes as showground attractions, creating the idealized image of the "prairie Indian." In this vein, the frontier western forms part of what Chickasaw scholar Jodi Byrd calls "the foundational paradigmatic Indianness that circulates within the narratives U.S. empire tells itself."[1]

Although North American exceptionalist discourse sacralizes the conquest of the West as "Manifest Destiny," that conquest clearly formed part of a broader pattern of violent European occupation of extra-European spaces and peoples in Asia, Africa, and the Americas. The word "frontier" euphemized colonial domination by obscuring the fact that the frontier was merely the leading edge of empire. As a key terrain of colonial conquest, the frontier forms the provisional "outside" destined to become the "inside"; it was the "not yet" of full nation-state domination, the "wild" and unruly territory on the verge of incorporation into the tamed and "respectable" Center. The central place of the myth of the frontier in the American imaginary has become a well-ploughed territory in scholarship, eloquently discussed by Francis Jennings, Richard Slotkin, Richard Drinnon, Michael Rogin, John Cawelti, R. F. Berkhofer, Paul Chaat Smith (Comanche), Vine Deloria Jr. (Standing Rock Sioux), Jacquelyn Kilpatrick (Choctaw and Cherokee), Beverly Singer (Tewa and Diné), S. M. Leuthold, Michelle Raheja (Seneca), Joanna Ahearne, Shari Huhndorf (Yup'ik), and many others.

Arguably one of the longest-lived of American myths, Manifest Destiny has its ideological roots not only in Conquest and Discovery Doctrine but also in a specific interpretation of the Biblical Exodus Story, the conquest of Canaan and the Puritan vision of America as the "New Israel." It was rooted as well in the competitive "laws" of Social Darwinism, in the hierarchy of races and genders, and in the redeeming idea of western-led "progress." What Slotkin calls the "American-History-As-Indian-War" trope has given a fantastical self-aggrandizing shape to "United Statesian" self-narration, with reverberations that echo throughout popular culture even today.[2] For

Jodi Byrd, Indians form "past tense presences" who are "typically spectral, implied, and felt, but remain as lamentable casualties of national progress who haunt the United States on the cusp of empire and are destined to disappear with the frontier itself."[3, 4]

Land and the Frontier Western

Central to the western is the struggle over land. If Hollywood films were to capture "the emotional center of Western history," writes historian Patricia Limerick, "its movies would be about real estate."[5] The reverent attitude toward the landscapes themselves—Monument Valley, Yellowstone, the Colorado River—occludes those to whom the land belonged. For Joanna Hearne, John Ford's films attempt to "deed" Monument Valley to a settler-nation audience.[6] In *The Lay of the Land: Metaphor as Experience and History in American Life and Letters* (1975), Annette Kolodny examines the exploration narratives in terms of the troping of the land as female, the explorer as male, and conquest as rape.[7] At the same time, the land is super-inscribed with biblical symbolism—"Promised Land," "New Canaan," "God's Earth." A binary division pits the sinister devil-filled wilderness against the beautiful well-ordered garden, with the former "inevitably" giving way to the latter through the machinations of "progress." The dry, desert terrain furnishes a stage for the play of expansionist fantasies. Nor do the films clarify that many of the native populations portrayed as an intrinsic part of the landscape had been driven there through "removal," the Trail of Tears and the White expropriation of lands back East.

A Manichean allegory also papers over two diametrically opposed views of the land and the soil: for most Native American cultures, as we have seen, the land is not real estate for sale but is sacred both as historically consecrated and as the "mother" that gives (and needs) nurture.[8] Many indigenous languages render the concept of "selling land" literally unspeakable, since the language lacks the vocabulary to convey it. For the settler, on the other hand, the land was seen as a soulless aggregate of exploitable resources, and the Indians a wandering horde lacking a recognizable concept of property, law, or government. "Civilization," as one Secretary of War put it, "entails a love for exclusive property."[9] Progress was seen as depending on *not* holding land in common, since, as Senator Henry Dawes, in a nineteenth-century forerunner of the Thatcherite "there is no alternative" doctrine, put it, "selfishness is the basis of civilization."[10] For settlers, land existed to be transformed, monogrammed, branded, as it were, by a human, societal presence. Hence, while for the Europeans land was a commodity that had to produce quickly or else be abandoned for greener pastures (or more golden mines), for the Native Americans land was a sacred trust. The forced privatization of the land, as occurred with the Dawes Act of 1887, constituted a cultural death sentence.

In the United States, the very titles of westerns stress a mobile, and mobilizing, European claim on the land, asserted in panoramas and aerial views. A disproportionate number stress European-designed state borders—*Oklahoma Kid* (1939), *Colorado*

Territory (1949), *California Conquest* (1952)—the irony of course being that a high proportion of American states (Alabama, Arizona), rivers (the Ohio, Potomac), Great Lakes (Huron, Ontario, Michigan), and mountain ranges (the Adirondacks) carry native names.[11] The titles themselves exhibit the Adamic/Promethean power to name: *El Dorado* (1967), *Northwest Passage* (1940). A kind of "Go West Young Man!" occidento-tropism informs the films, conveying a thrusting, trailblazing purposiveness, a divinely sanctioned crepuscular teleology evoked in *Red Sundown* (1956), *The Last Outpost* (1935, 1951), and *Heaven's Gate* (1980). Other titles resonate even more blatantly with westward-driving zeal—*Westbound* (1959), *Westward the Women* (1951), *The Way West* (1967). Such titles relay the settler "becoming" of the American nation, a boundless over-reaching, which reached its telos with the general transformation of nature into commercial culture all the way to the Pacific. The frontier western encapsulated Hegel's theory that the movement of world-historical thought moves from East to West. The West was thus less a place than a movement, a going west, a "vaguely realizing westward" in Robert Frost's phrase, a tropism in both senses of the word—a movement toward and a figure of speech. The western, in its various forms, thus served as an ideal medium for expressing both the genocidal thrust as well as the ethical dilemmas of a colonial settler-state.

The hybrid Hollywood western musical, meanwhile, cheerily choreographed this legitimation of conquest, as when the lyrics of the theme song of *Oklahoma!*—a state ripped out of native territory, with an indigenous name—tell us, apparently without irony, that "[w]e [whites] know we belong to the land/and the land we belong to is grand." Thus, even the native axiom of "we belong to the land" is appropriated by what Chadwick Allen has called "settler indigeneity."[12] For the conquering settler, Indian land is supposedly uncultivated ("unseeded"), while for the indigene it is "unceded." The hybrid western-musical *Calamity Jane*, where natives are called "painted varmits," has white settlers sing the glories of the sacred Black Hills of the Sioux. Ironically, even these acts of lyrical appropriation borrow from Indian conceptions of the land. But while Indians could be portrayed positively or negatively, they were always seen as obstacles to the forward momentum of progress. Even Pete Seeger's "progressive" song, "This land is my land," seems to ignore indigenous ownership. In his stand-up performances, comic Charlie Hill would change the song's meaning through a gesture—while singing "this land is *my* land," he would point to himself, and with the line "this land's not *your* land!" point at the largely white audience.

The elimination of the Indian allows for elegiac nostalgia as a way to treat Indians only in the past tense and thus dismiss present-day claims, while posthumously expressing thanatological tenderness for their memory. Renato Rosaldo calls this phenomenon "imperial nostalgia" when a dominating power laments the loss of what it has itself destroyed.[13] Here too the titles—*The Vanishing Race* (1912), *The Last of the Mohicans* (1920, 1932, 1936, 1992), *The Last of the Redmen* (1947)—embed the allochronic idea that Indians live in historically condemned time. An ambivalently repressive mechanism dispels the anxiety in the face of the morally "inconvenient" Indian, whose very presence is a reminder of the precarious grounding of the American nation-state itself. For Native Americans, meanwhile, the memories were vivid and painful. In the filming of *The Indian Wars* (1914), traumatized Sioux were obliged to reenact their own historical defeat and humiliation at Wounded Knee:

> The plan called for the battle to take place right over the Indian graves, which seemed to the Sioux a horrible desecration ... the Indians were resentful, remembering how the white soldiers had massacred their tribesmen and the women and children ... The greatest difficulty in getting these men together was to convince them that the purpose of this mobilization was merely to reproduce the wars and not to annihilate them, for when they saw the Hotchkiss guns, the rifles, revolvers and cases of ammunition, there was a feeling of unrest, as though the time had come when they were to be gathered in by the Great Spirit through the agency of the white men.[14]

Living Indians were induced to "play dead," as it were, in order to perform a narrative in which their role, ultimately, was to disappear. Over six decades later, the Mexican-indigenous-American rock band "Redbone" commemorated two "Wounded Knees" (1890 and 1973) in a hit song:

> We were all wounded at wounded knee
> You and me
> In the name of manifest destiny
> You and me you and me you and me.
> They made us many promises
> But always broke their word
> They penned us in like Buffalo
> Drove us like a herd.

Not all westerns were made in a single mold, of course, and I am not suggesting that there were never sympathetic portrayals of Indians or that westerns were free of ideological tensions and contradictions.

Going Native

Countless films from the Americas (and some from Europe) display the process whereby white characters "go native," even if usually superficially and without benefit to indigenous people themselves. As noted earlier, this "going native" was not just a fantasy; to some participants, it was a historical reality. The "real epic of America," Felix Cohen wrote, "is the yet unfinished story of the Americanization [i.e. the Indigenization] of the white man."[15] Already in the seventeenth century, at the heights of the puritanical regime in New England, the rebellious Thomas Morton, who danced and traded arms with indigenous people, argued in *The New English Canaan* that the native way of life was more satisfying and less frantic. "According to human reason, guided only by the light of nature, these people lead the more happy and freer life, being void of care, which torments the minds of so many Christians. They are not delighted in baubles, only in useful things."[16] The very title, *New Canaan*, betokens a Canaanite alternative to the "New Israel" grid of the Puritans. Anticipating Oswald de Andrade's praise of *sacer-docio* (sacred leisure), Pierre Biard, a Jesuit in "New France" in Canada, pointed out that "[u]nlike Europeans, [the Indians] are never in a hurry. Quite different from us, who can never do anything without hurry and worry ... our desire tyrannizes us and banishes peace from our action."[17]

The "going native" character appears in many Latin American films. This crossing over was a common occurrence during the first centuries of conquest: in Mexico, for example, Gonzalo Guerrero, a Spaniard kidnapped by Indians in the Yucatan, became a *cacique* with tattooed face and pierced ears.[18] The Mexican film *Cabeza de Vaca* (1989), in the same vein, tells the story of Alvar Nunez Cabeza de Vaca, the shipwrecked Spaniard who traveled by foot from Florida to Texas. The film's source text, Alvar Nunez's *Relacion de los Naufragios* (Story of the Shipwrecked), is an early recounting of the Conquest as a story of failure. Inverting the usual roles, Nunez portrays the Spaniards as vulnerable, as losing control, weeping, and supplicating. And while a phantasmatic cannibalism usually serves to justify European exploitation, here it is the Spanish who cannibalize one another and the natives who watch in horror. Although the film portrays the Indians as menacing, even freakish, it does expose the underside of European religious proselytizing and dares to suggest that the conquistadors, not the natives, might have been the real cannibals.

The Venezuelan film *Jerico* (Jericho, 1990), meanwhile, treats another case of a European who "goes native." The film concerns a Franciscan priest, Santiago, the lone survivor of a sixteenth-century expedition led by the conquistador Gascuiia in search of the mythic Mar del Sur. Although Santiago hopes to conquer the Indians spiritually, he is in fact spiritually conquered by them: as their captive, he comes to question his ethnocentric attitudes toward religion, the body, the earth, and social life, and finally renounces his evangelical mission. In the end, he falls back into the hands of Spaniards, who regard his indigenization as a form of madness and heresy. What makes this revisionist captivity narrative so subversive is that it transforms the indigenous culture that official Europe regarded with fear and loathing into a seductive pole of attraction for Europeans. The real purpose of Conquest, in this case, was not to force the indigenes to become Europeans but to keep the Europeans from becoming indigenes. The film largely adopts the indigenous perspective and shows extensive knowledge of the languages, histories, and cultural styles of the indigenous groups portrayed. While most Hollywood films have the "Indians" speak a laughable pidgin English, here the natives laugh at a European's garbled attempt to speak *their* language.

Hollywood films like *Little Big Man* (1970), *A Man Called Horse* (1970), and *Dances with Wolves* (1990), similarly, give expression to the white desire to "become Indian" through idealized stories of whites who assimilate to native ways. Arthur Penn's *Little Big Man* (1970), based on the Thomas Berger novel, portrays the Cheyenne as the good guys and the US Army soldiers as the villains. The narration contrasts the largely symbolic indigenous style of warfare with the massive violence of western-style warfare, asking the question: where is the courage when one side has all of the weapons? The film stages the paradigmatic recognition scene found in many of the White Indian films, the scene where the indigenized white is at first misrecognized as Indian by fellow whites and then exposed. In the spirit of the anti-war movement, the film draws subliminal allegorical parallels between the US cavalry invading Indian country with the US military invading Vietnam, an equation made almost explicit in real life through soldierly colloquialisms describing Vietnam as "Injun Country." Just as the Dustin Hoffman character was siding with the indigenous enemy in the movie theaters, anti-war protestors were chanting "Ho, ho, ho Chi Minh, the NLF is gonna win" in the streets, and hundreds of US towns and cities were signing Peace Treaties with the indigenous Vietnamese.

Kevin Costner's *Dances with Wolves* offers another "White Indian" in the form of US Army Lieutenant John Dunbar. He begins by respecting the Lakota "enemy" and ends up taking their side. The white lead "carries" the film; he "becomes Indian," but only in order to rediscover his implicitly white "true self." In the "misrecognition" scene where he is captured by his own people, the military first think he's an Indian, and when they discover he is not, the Indian they assumed him to be, remark: "turned Injun, didn't you ... I don't know whether to salute him or shoot him!" The film's final intertitles inform the spectator of the historical outcome, the closing of the frontier in 1893. The net effect is a past-tense compliment, an elegy for a vanished civilization. The film also falls into the old Manichean trap of binaristic oppositions, not only the good Dunbar versus the bad whites, but also the good Sioux versus the bad Pawnee. With all its innovations, its positive portrayals and tributes to indigenous dignity, the film is ultimately all about the white "us" and only secondarily about the indigenous "them." Dunbar is in some ways, if not better, at least as good as the indigenous warriors, who are relegated to supporting roles. The racial transformations are asymmetrical: the white men can become Indians and thus ennobled, but Indians cannot become White without losing their dignity, their authenticity, and their souls.

The related tropes of "going native," the White Indian, and "playing Indian" have a constant presence in the cultural history of the Americas. In 1997, Vine Deloria, Jr., noted a kind of inversion. Just as Native Americans "were looking increasingly like middle-class Americans," middle-class Americans were trying more and more to look like Indians, "convinced they are Oglala Sioux Pipe carriers and on a holy mission to protect 'Mother Earth.'"[19] In *Playing Indian*, historian Philip J. Deloria suggests that the tropes reflect the anxieties and aspirations of non-indigenous Americans in relation to an Indian figure at once admired and feared.[20] The Boston Tea Party, where American rebels dressed up as Mohawks to protest British rule, is for Deloria "a catalytic moment, the first drumbeat in the long cadence of rebellion through which Americans redefined themselves as something other than British colonists."[21] Indian masquerade allowed white Americans to be simultaneously insiders and outsiders, citizens and traitors, rebels and conformists. In this same vein, Deloria refers to a metaphorical "White Indian Treaty" in 1794, a collection of speeches by the heads of the "Six United Nations of *White* Indians" (emphasis mine), linking the American revolution to "the political strategy of actual Indian People."[22]

Deloria gives myriad examples of the constantly morphing identities and identifications of whites "playing Indian": the white Hobbyists, the powwow tourists, the countercultural leftists whose headbands evoked both Geronimo and Che Guevara, part of a long tradition of Americans "imagining and claiming an Indianness that was ultimately about being free, white, and male."[23] The American counterculture of the 1960s fused oppositional politics with Indianness as a latter-day iteration of the redface Mohawks of the Boston Tea Party. Playing Indian, he writes, "replicated the contradictory tensions established by the Revolution. An interior Indianness that's signified national identity clashed with an exterior Indianness linked with the armed struggle to control the continent."[24] Since the social circles of anti-war activists, the hippie counterculture, and coalitionary racialized resistance (Black Panthers, American Indian Movement, the Young Lords) at times came physically and ideologically close together, including in protest allies with their frequent assemblage of activists of color, it was almost inevitable that indigenous symbolism would enter the discursive and performative arena. These convergences of intensities reached a zenith in "The Gathering of all Tribes for a Human Be-In" in San Francisco in 1967, featuring Allen Ginsburg and LSD guru Timothy Leary.

Modern formulations of "going native," according to Shari Huhndorf (Yup'ik), reveal ambivalence about modernity as well as anxieties about the terrible violence marking the nation's origins, demonstrating the "changing relationship of the dominant, colonizing culture to Native America."[25] In this highly gendered account, the "White Indian" films give expression both to a historical reality—many whites did join the Indians or at least sympathized with them—and to a white desire to "become Indian" through idealized stories of white men—always men—adopting to native ways. Many critics, and internet parodists and remixers, have noted the parallels between commercial productions like *Dances with Wolves*, *Pocahontas* (1995), and *Avatar* (2009). The three films share a number of features: apart from the "going native" leitmotif, the militaristic context, the idea of "joining the enemy," the romanticized portrayals, and so forth. Both Dunbar and Sully are wounded soldiers, both develop a special relationship with animals (one dances with wolves, the other rides flying horses), both are appreciated by their adopted tribe. In the white-Indian (or more accurately blue-Indian) film *Avatar*, the familiar figure reaches a kind of apotheosis. Jake Sully becomes a hybrid creature fabricated from a cross between his own "Blood Quantum" and the DNA of the Na'vi. His amorous relation to Neytiri recalls Pocahantas but in a way Brazilianizes the story, wherein Neytiri forms the Iracema or the Paraguacu. Sully's process of "becoming" passes through the liminal stages of a *rite de passage*, which moves from initiation, to leadership, to permanent embodiment as a digitally enhanced cyborgian native leader, when, thanks to the spiritual power of the nature goddess Eywal, his consciousness fuses with his avatar Na'vi body. Sully literally becomes Na'vi.

The *Avatar* story is set in the year 2156 on Pandora, one of the moons of the Polyphemus planet, in a region covered by bio-luminescent foliage and literally "peopled," not unlike the *xipari*-peopled forests of the Yanomami, with mythologically inflected fauna and flora. In *Avatar*, the avatars of Hindu mythology meet the avatars of "Second Life" who meet the White Indian heroes of the revisionist western. In its palimpsest of genres—romance, animation, western, bildungsroman, colonial adventure film, anti-colonial film, sci-fi, and internet game—each genre brings its ambiguous ideological and aesthetic baggage in relation to indigenous peoples. In political terms, the film forms a kind of Rorschack screen, on to which diverse spectators project their own ideologies and discourses; indeed, the film has been read in different ways by every possible ideological current. The film instantiates Hollywood populist marketing, premised on appealing to an assemblage of disparate constituencies: a White Messiah figure for ethnocentric conservatives; ecology for the environmentalists; a critique of the military-industrial-complex for leftists; critical allusions to US imperialist wars for pacifists; cyber technologies for the techno-nerds; multi-chromatic casting for the multiculturalists; and spectacular militaristic violence, simultaneously denounced and fetishized, for the devotees of blockbuster action films.

Critics of *Avatar*, such as Shari Huhndorf, rightly argue that the film "reinforces the racial hierarchies it claims to destabilize, and thus serves another primary function of [the] going native" genre.[26] For Slavoj Žižek, "the film enables us to practice a typical ideological division: sympathizing with the idealized aborigines while rejecting their actual struggle."[27] As an ideologically contradictory film, *Avatar* is clearly anti-imperialist on one level, yet the production also incarnates an efficient, hierarchical, and domineering Hollywood production style not unlike that of an industrial army. In a mismatch of production and representation, the anti-ecological Hollywood style of the production is out of synch with the pro-ecological message of the film. The kind of society that *produced* the film—competitive, greedy, arrogant—is nothing like the harmonious and nature-loving Na'vi society portrayed *in* the film. It is also worth pondering the social implications of such huge budgets: how many thousands of indigenous or critical films could have been made with those 237 million dollars? The film also promotes new media technologies and an array of products made to the taste of those that Davi Yoanomami calls "the merchandise people."

While not an indigenous film—in fact as a Hollywood cyber-blockbuster it in most ways constitutes indigenous media's polar opposite—*Avatar* is nonetheless related to our themes, not only in its relation to the transtextual lineage of the "White Indian" films, but also in relation to (1) contemporaneous events involving indigenous peoples; (2) the incorporation of indigenous images, themes, and social critiques; (3) the critique of imperialist wars against native peoples; and (4) the post-release intersection with indigenous activism. M. Elise Marubbio links *Avatar* to roughly contemporaneous key victories for indigenous people such as the Second International Decade of the World's Indigenous People (2005–15), the election of an indigenous president (Evo Morales) in Bolivia, the United Nations' adoption of the Declaration on the Rights of Indigenous Peoples, and the 2010 Universal Declaration on the Rights of Mother Earth.[28] For Marubbio, *Avatar* highlights the "process of global recognition of Indigenous rights, sovereignty, decolonization movements and environmental justice [which] represent centuries of Indigenous resistance to ongoing systems of subjugation, racism and colonialism."[29] Cameron's Pandora reflects real-world struggles by foregrounding indigenous resistance to genocide and ecocide. Relying on revisionist and neo-Western formulae, Cameron, for Marrubbio, weaves together anti-militarism and anti-imperialism, environmentalism, pro-Nativism, and indigenous sovereignty into an allegorical critique of Manifest Destiny and settler nations' relationships with indigenous people.

The portrayal of the Na'vi people condenses myriad allusions to mythologies and spiritualities linked to indigenous peoples. The Na'vi practice customs, beliefs, and traditions that are closely tied to the land as the source of sustenance and inspiration.

Among the indigenous tropes: the typical self-naming of the Na'vi as "the people"; the idea of nature as alive; the concept of native people as the custodians of the land; the rejection of an instrumental, mechanical, and extractivist approach to nature; the leveling and mixing of the animal and the human in a kind of all-embracing personhood. For Brazilian cultural critic Ivana Bentes, *Avatar* can be read as a conversion of instrumental reason and the body/mind dualism to a "thought of the body," in which the "bodily point of view radically changes our identity and subjectivity," and where "lifestyles are totally subject to the holistic laws of nature."[30] For Bentes, *Avatar* is inspired by the indigenous cosmologies in the mold of Amerindian perspectivism proposed by Viveiros de Castro (1996), a concept that emerges from Lévi-Straussian-inspired concepts such as "savage thinking"[31] and has gained another meaning with the "ontological turn" in Anthropology defined as a "way of thinking that rejects dualisms typical of Western-modern thought."[32] Thus, perspectivism is the conception common to many peoples in the Americas, according to which "the world is inhabited by different kinds of subjects or persons, human and non-human, who apprehend it from different points of view."[33] These ideas have been criticized by some for indirectly re-establishing the nature/culture binary, privileging vision over the other senses, and hierarchizing animals over plants.[34]

Avatar proliferates in references to American imperialist wars, first against the Indian then against the neo-Indians like the Vietnamese (raided with "Apache" helicopters) and the Iraqis (targeted with "Tomahawk" Missiles). The film is anti-imperialist in its portrayal of a colonial situation-style war led by racists whose pejorative idiom of "pagan" and "voodoo" betrays their retrograde attitudes. The Sully character obviously represents a younger generation's version of the White Indian figures from *Little Big Man* and *Dances with Wolves*. Like the other Hollywood "going native" films, *Avatar* pits the hyper-violent American military against an admirably courageous Indigenous society. While the Na'vi have elements of the noble savage, this time their concerns are ecological and their capacities trans-human. Cameron was quite explicit about the film's anti-colonialist character: "*Avatar* is a science fiction retelling of the history of North and South America in the early colonial period. *Avatar* very pointedly made reference to the colonial period in the Americas, with all its conflict and bloodshed between the military aggressors from Europe and the indigenous peoples, the native Americans are the Na'vi. It's not meant to be subtle."[35]

Like a shape-shifting anthropologist, Jake spends three months of field research learning the ways of the Na'vi and undergoing the rites of initiation; he learns to ride, hunt, respect, and love, and in turn wins their respect. Native land, meanwhile, becomes a stage for the enactment of the redemption of the tired imperial warrior. Like many white Indians from philosophy, literature, and cinema, he begins to question his own Western values, learning to "see" and "feel" through the eyes of another culture. Despite all the well-considered critiques of the film as an aggregation of clichés criticized in the reviews and the remix parodies—White Savior Film, *Pocahontas*-style romance, *Dances with Wolves* in Space, Noble Savage, a corporate film that denounces corporations, and so forth—many indigenous people, especially in South America, have recognized an idealized version of themselves in the Na'vi and a lucid if hyperbolic account of the extractivist machinations of colonialism and its impact on indigenous people.³⁶ Evo Morales, the first indigenous president of Bolivia, praised *Avatar* for its "profound show of resistance to capitalism and the struggle for the defense of nature."³⁷ Native activists and supporters were less moved by the White Savior, one suspects, than by the depiction of the high-tech aggressions mobilized against them in the name of such substances as Obtanium—a shifter-word made to suit any extractable mineral or element. The scenes of powerful machines tearing up the earth remind us of Davi Kopenawa's denunciation of the "earth eaters" wrenching minerals out of the earth, thus provoking the fall of the sky.

While *Avatar* exemplifies the outlandish potency of Hollywood in production and distribution, such power can also be resisted, refunctioned, appropriated, and transformed at the point of reception through what Ella Shohat and I and others call "media jiujitsu,"³⁸ i.e. the deployment of the power of the hegemonic imagery produced by the dominant but this time against corporate domination, i.e. assuming the strength of the dominant discourse but redeploying that strength in the interests of oppositional praxis. Meanwhile, Henry Jenkins speaks of "Avatar activism,"³⁹ or the convergence of established media such as Hollywood film with new media activism through the language of participatory culture. After the film's release, as Emma Mitchell has pointed out, many activists, from Canada to Australia to Palestine to Peru, deployed the imagery of the film as part of their own struggles, donning Na'vi costumes in an effort to attract media attention and enliven their demonstrations.⁴⁰ In 2010, Aboriginal rights protestors against uranium mining in South Australia painted themselves blue in honor of the Na'vi. In India, the non-government organization *Survival* appealed to Cameron to help the Dongria Kondh tribe in their struggle against the threat of mining. A similar tactic was repeated by a coalition of fifty First Nations and environmentalist groups campaigning against the Alberta oil sands in Canada. The groups placed a punning full-page notice in *Variety*, headlined "Canada's AvaTar Sands," to support *Avatar*'s Best Picture nomination.

In the Amazon, indigenous groups prodded Cameron to marshal his status as a Hollywood super-Auteur to assist Indigenous peoples,⁴¹ to the point of Cameron campaigning to stop the construction of the Belo Monte dam on the Xingu River. As a by-product of his three tours of the Amazon, Cameron produced a twenty-minute documentary short, *A Message from Pandora*, about the plight of the Amazonian peoples, subsequently released in full on the collectors' edition DVD rerelease of *Avatar* and uploaded as a shorter segment to YouTube by *Amazon Watch*. Cameron even directly asked Brazilian president Lula to abandon the Belo Monte project. At the same time, the fact that indigenous struggles do not receive media attention unless framed in terms of the white, male hero reflects, as K. J. Madison points out, the contradictory relationship to media that activists must negotiate.⁴² For Emma Mitchell, Cameron became the diplomatic equivalent of the Jake Sully-style savior-mediating figure in real life.⁴³ The ethnocentric gaffes of the film did not prevent Amazonian indigenous activists from identifying with the fiction or from bonding with Cameron in opposition to the Belo Monte dam. A YouTube clip shows Cameron becoming an honorary Indian, with orange paint streaked across his cheeks, wearing a native headdress and dancing alongside indigenous leaders. The Amazonians embrace and thank him, shrewdly but also sincerely, seeing him as a potential ally in their struggle.

Europe's "White Indians"

The global appeal of the Hollywood Western has made it fodder for infinite adaptations, remediations, and transmutations. Within this context, many countries seem to have fantasized their own Indian, whether as a kind of imaginary friend, or symbol of a fantasy ally or a romanticized *ailleurs*. The "Indian" first became a major figure in international cinema, already in the silent period, through adaptations of Indianist literary classics. Multitudinous films adapted the hugely popular nineteenth-century Indianist novelists in various countries—James Fenimore Cooper in the United States, Jose de Alencar in Brazil, Karl May in Germany, and so forth. In the United States alone, the adaptations of *The Last of the Mohicans* go at least as far back as the 1912 silent version by James Cruze, on to a 1920s version, two 1930s versions, one 1940s version (*Last of the Redmen*, 1947), to a 1950s version (*The Iroquois Trail*, 1950), two 1960s versions, on to the 1992 version by Michael Mann starring Daniel Day-Lewis.

Europeans, as Christopher Frayling points out, have had a long-standing love affair with the Western genre. Prior to the advent of the cinema in France, between 1850 and 1870, Novelist Gustave Aimard published some fifty stories for children, with titles like *Les Outlaws du Missouri* and *Les Trappeurs de l'Arkansas*. The stories, revolving around French heroes and their Indian friends, inspired many silent films a few decades later. Some of the earliest American westerns made more money in France than in the home market. European Westerns (aka Euro-westerns) are as old as filmmaking itself. Just one year after the first public screenings of films in 1895, Gabriel Veyre shot *Repas d'Indien* ("Indian Banquet") for the Lumiere Brothers. In France, Gaston Melies himself filmed a series of French Westerns featuring Indians between 1907 and 1913. In 1918–19, the Winnebago director James Young Deer made short Westerns for the Pathe Brothers in France.

In Germany, meanwhile, *Der Letzte de Mohikanes* featuring Bela Lugosi as Cooper's Chingachgook formed the second part of the two-part *Lederstrumpf* film released in 1920. Over four decades later, the 1965 West German/Italian/Spanish co-production *Der Letzte Mohikaner* directed by Harald Reini set its story in the post–American Civil War era. The East German film *Chingachgook die Grosse Schlange* (Chingachgook the Great Serpent, 1967), starring Gojko Mitic as Chingachgook, meanwhile, became popular throughout the Socialist Bloc. Various European countries developed their own competing allegorical Indians. In Italy, for example, well-established stereotypes such as those of the ecological Indian, the victim Indian, and the warrior Indian surfaced in cultural discourse, remediated and reaccentuated for the purposes of local politics.[44] In the 1970s, the *Indiani Metropolitani* (the Urban Indians of Milan) appropriated the Native American for anarchist purposes. Updated avatars of Rousseau's invocation of *"lessauvages faits pour les villes"* ("city-ready savages"), their manifestos mingled the savage howls of Allen Ginsberg's poetry with homages to the rebel Indian. In a manifesto entitled "We shall never bury the hatchet again!," the *Indiani* denounced the forked-tongued oppressors of the new Italian "urban Indians." As Giorgio Mariani puts it, "[t]he 1876 Little Big Horn battle came to replace the Paris Commune or the Russian Revolution as an early example of revolutionary struggle, while General Custer was regarded as a prototype of American imperialism."[45]

Germans, especially, have claimed a special relationship to the Indian as cultural alter-ego.⁴⁶ Germans have been writing about the natives of the Americas ever since the time of Hans Staden, the German soldier taken captive at the time of France Antartique, whose story formed the basis for the plot of *How Tasty Was My Little Frenchman*. Thanks to their advanced post-Gutenberg publishing networks, the Germans began publishing books on the Brazilian Indian already in the first decades after Columbus and have never stopped doing so. Indeed, a number of German writers and ethnologists became deeply involved with indigenous people in Brazil. In the nineteenth century, Botanist Carl Friedrich Phillip von Martius published a three-volume account of his travels in Brazil between 1823 and 1831. In the twentieth century, ethnologist Theodor Koch-Grunberg published his two-volume study of the legends of the peoples of the Orinoco. The writing of German-Brazilian ethnologist Curt Unckel Nimuendajú, meanwhile, became an indispensable source of scholarship on the religion and the cosmology of indigenous groups such as the Guaraní. He became nominally Indian in the sense of being gifted, by the Apapocuva subgroup of the Guaraní people, with the surname Nimuendaju, meaning "the one who made himself a home." Upon taking Brazilian citizenship in 1922, he officially added his indigenous name as one of his surnames. More typically, the German fascination was with the Indians of North America and especially with the Plains Indians. Many Germans have seen the Indian as a benevolent doppelgänger. Frantz Kafka famously wrote a one-sentence story on the "Wish to become an Indian" (*Wunsch, Indianer zu werden*), published in 1913:

> If one were only an Indian, instantly alert, and on a racing horse, leaning against the wind, kept on quivering jerkily over the quivering ground, until one shed one's spurs, for there needed no spurs, threw away the reins, for there needed no reins, and hardly saw that the land before one was smoothly shorn heath when horse's neck and head would be already gone.⁴⁷

The flirtation with the Indian as secret sharer of the German soul reached a paroxysm with the Indianophile novels of Karl May (1842–1912), whose more than thirty novels recounted the adventures of Old Shatterhand and his Apache blood brother chief Winnetou the Warrior. May's hero came to incarnate the German reader's desire to re-enchant the world through a vicarious "Native" experience. Translated into over thirty languages, the May novels have sold hundreds of millions of copies worldwide. May's sources included the novels of writers like James Fenimore Coper, encyclopedias, and books on Apache culture. Indeed, May based some of Winnetou's traits on the Apache chief Cochise.

May's "Western novels" chronicled the adventures of two paired *Ubermenschen*— Old Shatterhand, the white Teutonic hero, and Winnetou the red Apache chief. Scholars like Frank Usbeck, Susanne Zantop, Colin Calloway, Hartmut Lutz, H. Glenn Penny, Christian Feest, and others have unpacked the historically layered complexities of this German form of cross-cultural identification. Rather than revisit issues already thoroughly examined by these scholars, I would like to place figures like Shatterhand within a broader spectrum of representations. To schematize shamelessly, if a certain French Indian is philosophical, abstract, and egalitarian, the German Indian is romantic and full-bodied. In sexual terms, while the US American films find miscegenation taboo and Brazilian films celebrate it, Anglo-American and German treatments of the Indian tend toward the homosocial and even the homoerotic, centered around blood-bonding between indigenous and Western men.

The Karl May novels, in this sense, offer latter-day iterations of a theme introduced by Defoe's *Robinson Crusoe*, with its romanticized relationship between Crusoe and Friday, who himself could be seen as a model for Rousseau's "noble savage." As Leslie Fiedler famously noted, a number of classic nineteenth-century American novels feature an unacknowledged homoeroticism between white men and men of color—Huck and Jim in *Huckleberry Finn*, Ishmael and Queequeeg in *Moby Dick*, Natty Bumpo and Chingachgook in the Cooper novels—all of whom can be traced back to Defoe's Friday, clearly described as indigenous. In the Defoe novel, Crusoe offers a long, affectionate, even caressing account of Friday's appearance: "He was a comely, handsome fellow, perfectly well made, with straight strong limbs, not too large, tall and well-shaped [with] a very good countenance ... he had all the sweetness and softness of an European."[48] Defoe goes out of his way to suggest that Friday is not black—a color too closely associated with slavery—but rather indigenous, with hair, *not* kinky but long and flowing, a nose, *not* flat and wide but fine, and so forth. At one point, Crusoe even suggests that their bonding was so complete that they were happier than the happiest couple.

We find a similar kind of non-explicit homosocial desire in Germany in the relation between Shatterhand and Winnetou. Here is May's presentation of their first encounter:

> His hair was so long and heavy that it cascaded down his back. Certainly many a woman would have envied him this magnificent bluish-black adornment. ... We scrutinized each other with long, searching glances, and then, I believe, I noticed that that his solemn dark gaze with its velvety sheen was briefly illuminated by a friendly light, as if the sun were sending a message to earth through an opening in the clouds.[49]

And later: "I admired his courage and strength. His face seemed sincere. I thought I could love him." Such barely sublimated homoeroticism fits well into the atmosphere of homosocial institutions like the army, which perhaps also explains Hitler's fascination with Karl May's heroes. Thus, we can see a broad contrast between the foundational heterosexual romances in Brazil (and Latin America generally) versus the homosocial and sometimes homoerotic non-foundational romances in the United States, England, and to some extent, Germany. The cultural fascination with the Indian, in sum, is not exempt from the mysterious workings of Eros.[50]

Winnetou teaches Shatterhand the Apache language and the Apache way of life. Reciprocally, Karl May subjects Winnetou to the civilizing process, making him literate to the point of being familiar with Longfellow's 1855 epic poem "The Song of Hiawatha," which features the fictional adventures of an Ojibwe warrior and his tragic love for a Dakota woman. Karl May writes of Winetoo: "the Indian, this son of people many call 'wilde,' could, apparently, not only read but possess a mind and taste for culture."[51] It goes without saying that the German Indian films follow the redface convention. Apart from the racialized casting norms of the time, it stands to reason that if Winnetou is in effect a red man with a white soul, the directors would logically cast white actors to play him. And like many of the "Good Indians" from Red Atlantic fictions, Winnetou abandons indigenous spirituality for Christianity. (Karl May is the subject of Hans-Jurgen Syberberg's fiction feature bio-pic *Karl May* (1974), which portrays May as a mystic and mythomane whose fantasies feed into the cult of the hero and of Adolf Hitler, who himself admired May's books as ideal didactic fare for children and German soldiers.)

The Indian Hobbyists

Karl May is cited as part of a Nazi parlor game in Tarantino's *Inglorious Basterds* (2009), a reference that reminds us of the intriguing case of the "Indian hobbyist clubs" dotting the German landscape, where Germans reenact their conception of an "Indian life style" in teepees on weekends. The "Indian clubs" trace their genesis to the cultural frisson engendered by Karl May's novels as well as by carnivals, Wild West shows, and Hollywood films. The movement excites hundreds of thousands of adherents, continuing today in the form of festivals, museums, powwows, plays, rodeos, sweat lodges, and clubs. In this context, Germans can become pretend-Indians by impersonating Lakota, Blackfeet, or Pawneee.

In political terms, the shape-shifting German Indian could be enlisted in virtually any cause, nationalist or anti-nationalist, Communist or anti-Communist, pro-American or anti-American. May's novels triggered the affection of an ideologically varied group that included Albert Schweitzer, Herman Hesse, Ernst Bloch, and Adolph Hitler. Sometimes the love for the "Indian" was accompanied by scorn for other ethnic groups, as when Hans Rudolf Rieder asserted that only the Indian, unlike the Black, had the requisite qualities to merit German friendship.[52] In the postwar period, the communist East and the capitalist West Germany film industries fabricated distinct images of the Indian. The East German Indian films bypassed the Karl May novels, seen by the Communist regime as symptomatic of a reactionary blood-and-soil romanticism. Films such as *Die Sohne der Grossen Barin* (1966), meanwhile, fused the "Red" of Communism with the "Red" of Native American by having the Indians outwit greedy white settlers.[53] While films from both East and West Germany heroicized the Indians and demonized the Whites, they did so from distinct national/ideological perspectives.[54]

This felt affinity between Germany and their imaginary Indians was a discursive palimpsest combining numerous elements: a common tribal feeling of a nation that became a nation-state relatively late, in 1871; a shared heritage of folklore and legend; the transcendental mystique of Nature; the German love of hiking and the outdoors; the desire of the disillusioned western citizen to revel in a bucolic premodern past; the appeal of masculinist notions of military courage; homoerotic attraction to handsome "Indian men" in films played by handsome white men; a sense of inferiority stemming from military defeat; and a feeling of victimization by other Europeans and therefore identification with putative fellow victims. At the same time, Indian enthusiasm betrays a longing to be a colonizer like the other Europeans, the desire, as Hartmut Lutz put it, to be "both superior tribespeople and superior colonizers."[55] Finally, the films offer the narcissistic pleasure of a genocide committed by another country, the idea of a colonizer loved by the colonized; "Indianthusiasm" suggested that Germans would be better and more kinder imperialists than the "Anglo-Saxons," because they genuinely cared about and identified with native culture. (An irony here is that the Angles and the Saxons were originally German tribes.)

According to the history laid out in H. Glenn Penny's *Kindred by Choice*, many Germans identify their deep roots as independent tribes subsequently colonized by Romans and forced to become Christian.[56] In fact, this pre-Christian tribal memory is embedded in the names in English of the days of the week, derived from "pagan" German gods—Wednesday from "Woden" (the Hermes-like God of eloquence) and Thursday from "Thor" (god of Iron and lightning and thunder, rather like the indigenous "Tupa" of the Guaraní, the Iansa of the Yoruba, and the Santa Barbara of Latin American Catholicism). Because of this distant tribal background—and presumably all ancient Europeans, and all peoples, lived tribally at some point—some Germans identified more with Native Americans than with any European nation.[57] This belief in a kindred lifestyle is detailed in Penny's in-depth study of German fascination with historical Native American peoples. If alienated Native Americans who want to be white are derided as "apples"—red on the outside, white on the inside—the Hobbyists feel that on the outside they are white German; on their affective inside they feel red and Indian.

Native Americans who meet hobbyists in Germany come back with varied reports. In 1982, a Canadian Ojibwe painter Ahmoo Allen Angeconeb discovered that most German hobbyists were only interested in the Plains Indian peoples and had no interest in the Eastern Woodlands peoples such as the Ojibwe or in modern First Nations peoples in general.[58] In short, he was "too real an Indian for them." Native American artists and filmmakers have responded to German Indianthusiasm through artistic productions. One response came from the aesthetically and politically radical native women's theater troupe known as Spiderwoman. Founded in 1976, the group consisted of three sisters of Kuna and Rappahannock ancestry, led by two-spirit woman Muriel Miguel. Known as the grandmothers of post-1970s indigenous performance, the group, named after the Hopi goddess who taught the people to weave, had authored their mischievously autobiographical play/film *Sun, Moon, and Feathers* before traveling to Germany and Europe in 1999. Deploying their usual mix of parody, satire, and feminist outrageousness, they performed a satire of the European and particularly the German fascination with Native Americans. By their own account, the women saw the show, titled *Winnetou's Snake Oil Show from Wigwam City*, as an act of resistance making fun of Karl May's characters and of New Age ethnic masquerade.[59] The show featured a fake shaman who monetized Indianphilia by promising to transform people into Indians for the modest fee of $3,000.

The documentary *Forget Winnetou! Loving in the Wrong Way* (2017) directed by Red Haircrow, meanwhile, offers native perspectives on cultural appropriation. The film argues that a philo-indigenist "Wrong-Way Loving" has reinforced the attitude that Europeans and neo-Europeans can unilaterally appropriate whatever and whoever they want for their own solipsistic self-gratification. In the US context, the

Elders' councils of the many indigenous groups like the Cheyenne, Hopi, Lakota have denounced New Age misappropriation of their immaterial legacies, rejecting "the expropriation of [their] ceremonial ways by non-Indians."[60] Many see the New Age movement as either not fully understanding, or trivializing, or deliberately distorting indigenous ways of life. A parallel critique is addressed to those individuals from within the indigenous communities who become "white man's shamans," or "plastic shamans," and they who "are prostituting our spiritual ways for gain without regard for the spiritual well-being of the people as a whole."[61]

Although "Winnetoo" is a Haudenosonae word for "spirit," May's Winettou is an Apache, as are the characters in the DEFA (Deutsche Film Aktiengesellschaft) production *Apachen* by Gottfriend Kolditz in 1973. Apaches are featured not only in German films, and in Hollywood films like the 1950 *Broken Arrow*, but they also appear in some surprising places. In the wake of the American film *Fort Apache the Bronx* (1981), Franco-Maghrebian director Nassim Amaouche, in his film *Des Apaches* (The Apaches, 2009), analogizes the native American group to the racialized and discriminated immigrant inhabitants of the Parisian *banlieue*, neighborhoods roughly equivalent to the US "projects." Significantly, the *banlieue* rebels and their radical allies in France gave their movement a boomeranged indigenous name—"*les Indigenes* de la Republique,"—thus reverse-engineering the colonialist *code indigene*. Meanwhile, in Brazil, black *Afro-bloco* carnival groups in Salvador, Bahia, call themselves "Apaches" and "Comanches," in homage both to the "braves" of Hollywood and the *bravos guerreiros* of Brazil, as well as to the feathered, peace-pipe-smoking *caboclos* of the Afro-Brazilian religion *Umbanda*. A difference from other kinds of appropriation here is that black Brazilians are often part indigenous themselves, just as many indigenous people in Brazil, conversely, are partially black, as becomes obvious in the physiognomies of the activists seen in the videos by the present-day Tupinamba.

An October 2008 event in Toronto, entitled "Culture Shock," sponsored by the Goethe Institute and the National Gallery of Canada, foregrounded these East/West contradictions. The yearly imagineNATIVE Film + Media Arts Festival, the world's largest indigenous film and media arts festival, focused on the film, video, radio, and new media work of indigenous, Aboriginal, and First Peoples from around the world. The event featured a festival of films drawn from two collections of postwar German "Westerns" prominently featuring Indian characters. Four indigenous artists from Canada (Bonnie Devine, Keesic Douglas, Darryl Nepinak, and Ehren Bear Witness) were then invited to respond to the films with short films reflecting upon the German stories and modes of representation. According to the festival participants, the West German films, such as *Winnetou und das Halbblut Apananatschi* (1966), spun variations on the Hollywood Western, emphasizing the close native contact with nature.

Germans have become characters in Native American novels by writers like Louise Erdrich (herself of German-Indian descent), Emma Lee Warrior, and Tomson Highway. A hallmark of some Aboriginal Peoples Television Network (APTN) productions in Canada, meanwhile, is irreverent humor. An APTN "Threes Company" becomes "Crees Company." Drew Hayden Taylor, as half Ojibwe and half Caucasian, calls himself "Special Occasion." One episode of "Mixed Blessings" lampoons German Indianphiles. A Cree waitress and her Ukranian husband, in a gesture of hospitality, invite a German-accented Indianist to dinner, where he berates his hosts for not having teepees and sweat lodges and not cooking caribou in the culturally correct manner. As the meal becomes a competition in authenticity as imagined by a German wannabee, he finally explodes in disgust: "In Germany, we have names for people like you. We call you 'Coca Cola Indians.'" Locking them into an allochronic prison of his own making, he declares: "You have been corrupted by the twentieth and the twenty-first century. I think, no, I actually know, I am more Indian than all of you!" After he leaves, the whole family reacts to his pretensions with uproarious laughter.[62]

It is almost too easy to make fun of German Indian Hobbyists because of the literal and figurative distance between indigenous and German cultures. But the Germans are hardly alone in their Indianphilia. As Christian Feest points out, Indian hobbyism exists not only in the United States but also everywhere in western, northern, central, and eastern Europe.[63] These issues become more layered and fraught with North American Indian hobbyists, whose behavior, as Philip J. Deloria suggests, ranges from sheer mindless appropriation to sincere respect and collaboration. US American "Wannabees" have been the butt of many Native American jokes, parodies, and satires. Unlike earlier groups safely distant from actual native people, the "people Hobbyists," for Deloria, "had to reconcile their cultural imaginations with the real Indian people they wanted to see dancing next to them in the powwow circle."[64] The hobbyists longed for Indian approval, but despite a degree of mutuality, Deloria argues, "differences over such social interactions lay just beneath the surface."[65]

While the box office success of film adaptations of Karl May's characters in the 1960s may have saved the West German film industry—much as Winnetou saves Shatterhand's life in his fictions[66]—other European countries proposed their own revisionist takes on the Western genre. In the Soviet Union, the Western was adapted into the *Ostern* ("Eastern") genre of Soviet films with the Wild West setting replaced by the steppes of the Caucasus, while Western stock Cowboys and Indians were replaced by Caucasian stock characters such as bandits and prostitutes. The spectacular success of the German Indian films partially inspired the spaghetti—westerns cooked in Italy, which in turn inspired other trends with culinary labels—Paella Westerns (co-productions shot in Spain); Camambert Westerns (produced in France); "curry westerns" and sometimes "masala westerns" (made in India), and Chop Suey Westerns (made in Hong Kong). The Japanese film *Tampopo* (1985) was promoted as a "ramen Western."

The Western genre provided a substratal generic paradigm for Hollywood films about what used to be called the "Third World." Just as the Hollywood Western turned history on its head by having "Indians" besiege innocent settlers, films set in the Third World turned American soldiers in imperial wars into besieged victims.[67] But the Western has even more obvious relevance to other Anglo-colonial settler states such as Australia. In "The Australian Western, or a Settler Colonial Cinema par excellence," Peter Limbrick addresses three Ealing Studios' Australian films—*The Overlanders* (1946), *Eureka Stockade* (1949), and *Bitter Springs* (1950)—through a settler-colonial grid, pointing out that they all shared Australian locations and a number of western conventions and images.[68] The western, he argues, provides a template for a settler colonial mode of cinema that turns to "certain narrative and representational strategies as part of a larger cultural project of grounding white settler cultures within colonized landscapes."[69] Limbrick sees in these Australian Westerns many of the traits signaled earlier in this text—the privileging of whiteness and heterosexual masculinity, discourses of regenerative violence, and the Terra Nullius disavowal of prior presence.

At times the Frontier Western forms a submerged, almost subliminal, presence in other national cinemas. Early Israeli Cinema, both pre-state and post-state, as Ella Shohat points out, constructs stories that are structured in a manner parallel to those of American pioneers in the Wild West, but this time about Jewish pioneers in the Wild Middle East, more specifically in a Promised Land (Canaan, the American West), who create "settlements," which are under siege (by Arabs or Indians). What Shohat calls the "frontier analogy" opposes courageous pioneers, whether American or Israelis, to demonized others (Indians/Arabs), the former being the agents of Manifest Destiny and the latter being historically doomed. Images of the Hebrew pioneer, the masculinized new Jew, the desert redeemer Sabra, mimicked the American Adam and his creation of order out of a wilderness chaos.[70] Tropes such as the "Promised Land," "Virgin Land," and "civilization-versus-savagery" in early Israeli Cinema clearly resonated with the American pioneer imaginary of settling the empty land and taming the frontier, with the difference that Israel has behaved like a colonial-style state, but it lacks a metropole and has some cultural roots in the Middle East.

Transmedial Indigeneity

In contrast to the superficial stereotypes promoted by the Hollywood frontier western, and the romanticized images of the European Indians, we will now highlight indigenous art that audaciously confronts settler-colonialism in its various dimensions, axioms, topoi, stereotypes, and even its falsely positive images and does so in very diverse modes. Indigenous art is trans-mediatic in ways that goes beyond the reduction of media to film. Rather than privilege feature films as the ontological quintessence of the "real film," we can regard all audiovisual moving-image materials as legitimate platforms for indigenous art. In the digital age, the feature fiction film has become a "bit" in a larger mediatic stream. "Political film" today might mean not a feature fiction or a documentary—projects that require considerable money and time—but rather a quickly produced music video, or a stand-up performance, or a YouTube channel, or an open-access user-generated database. And, now that virtually everything ends up being filmed, almost any text can be reconfigured and remediated to become an indigenous film. The internet brings tremendous advantages for both creation and dissemination. While 20 years ago most of the kinds of audiovisual materials mentioned in this book could have been seen only at art cinemas, or film festivals, or in media studies courses, much is now available at the click of a mouse granting access to the grand cinemateque called the internet.

Multiform, indigenous media can take any audiovisual-digital form, ranging from feature fictions to feature documentaries to small-scale YouTube video series (e.g., "Natives React"), internet websites, cable-TV programs, network series, stand-up comedy, music videos, online websites, and so forth. We find an example of this kind of audacity in Thomas King's poem (later video) "Not the Indian you had in mind." The incident that triggered the title literally involved a "transnational gaze." Traveling to Europe as the only non-German on a German ship, King answered the ship cook's question about his identity by saying that he was "an American Indian, a Cherokee." With a look of intense suspicion, the cook told him that he did not look like an Indian—that King was not "the Indian [he] had in mind." For the cook, the "Indian" had to conform to the image purveyed by the novels of Karl May; King simply did not meet his literature-derived standard.

The poem addresses the reader/spectator—the non-indigenous "you" of the title—as a trampoline for directly exposing the feelings of indigenous people about being on the receiving end of the ill-informed projections and doxa of whites. As an exotopic anatomy of the assumptions and imagery haunting the white psyche, the poem evokes the twinned and complementary negations inherent in racism—the denial of difference, in the sense of very different experiences and points of view—and the denial of sameness, in terms of radical equality in rights and a shared desire for freedom. In the extremely well-edited staging of the poem, Canadian First Nations actors Tara Beagan and Lome Cardinal, and writer Thomas King as themselves, perform the poem. Dressed not in buckskin and feathers but in jeans and business suits, they recite the poem, in a bare room with a TV monitor, a projector, and a cigar-store Indian, at times walking past movie posters. The words of the poem are superimposed on stock imagery drawn from a wide spectrum of media—animated cartoons, corporate commercials, frontier westerns, and the like—conveying the "Indian you had in mind" generated by "the clichés that we can't rewind." Other images in the video portray the world created by white "progress"—polluted, accelerated, war-obsessed, fossil-fuel dominated, and "Monsanto-mad," in short the material world produced by "the appetites that consumed the earth." Still other images bear on actual indigenous life—news footage of Indian protests, shots of everyday Indians, and the like. Set against these more critical materials, the poem-video deconstructs mass-media "India hating," the sheer mass of caricatural images makes them fall off their own weight. The props and the archival footage that flesh out, amplify and complicate the words in the poem weave together stereotypical footage of war-whooping tomahawk-wielding Indians with shots that convey the long-term consequences of capitalist modernity in the form of high-tech wars, fossil-fuel dependency, and a corporate system that has left the world "warm and dead." This ironic deployment of mediatic imagery forms another exemplum of "media jiujitsu" and of what the Birmingham Cultural Studies school called "resistant readings." The poem makes many allusions to the frontier western, moving through the various sense faculties aroused by such films, beginning with sight. (The italics are mine.)

> I'm not the Indian you had in mind
> I've *seen* him
> Oh, I've seen him ride,
> a rush of wind, a darkening tide
> with Wolf and Eagle by his side
> his buttocks firm and well defined
> my god, he looks good from behind.

The words conjure up the charms of the western genre, with its horses and cavalcades and tempestuous excitement. The poem also stresses the erotic attraction, both heterosexual and homoerotic, through the enthusiastic evocation of the well-defined buttocks of the Indian on horseback, while underscoring the camera setup ("from behind"). This eroticization of the indigenous body goes very far back. The early settlers both in North and South Americas spoke of the pleasing features of indigenous bodies, both male and female. Even when the cultures portrayed wore modest clothing, the painters preferred them nude. Describing sixteenth-century engravings, R. F. Berkhofer (1979) wrote that such pictures "established the muscular handsomeness and athletic virility of the Noble American Savage."[71] R. A. Billington mentions the description of an Apache "so perfectly formed that he would make Apollo envious."[72] King's exotopic vision makes us see white vision, as if objectifying it in distanced terms, as if a certain kind of sight were being itself scrutinized. Then, from sight, the poem moves to another sense faculty, to the ears and hearing:

> I'm not the Indian you had in mind
> I've *heard* him
> Oh, I've heard him roar
> the warrior wild, the video store
> the movies that we all adore
> the clichés that we can't rewind

The poem here evokes the soundtrack of the western, the war whoops, and the violent screams of the movies as disseminated through video stores and screens. Then, from sight and hearing and acoustemology, the poem moves to cognition and epistemology:

> I'm not the Indian you had in mind
> I've *known* him
> Oh, I've known him well,
> the bear-greased hair, the pungent smell
> the piercing eye, the startling yell
> thank God that he's the friendly kind.

The "knowing" here is less factual and cerebral than sensorial, having to do with smell (pungent), sound (the yell), and appearance (bear-greased hair). At the same time the "Indian" figure comes surrounded by an atmosphere of danger, and the fear that he might not be a "friendly." Racism here is less a matter of superiority than of fear: the "Indian" as always the object, and not the subject, of fear.

Then King undercuts this ambivalent romanticization of the "Indian" through a portrayal of the spectrum of everyday quotidian un-exotic indigeneity: the Indian who "lives just down the street," that you're "disinclined to meet," or the one who runs a bar or drives a bus. And then there's the "inconvenient" protesting Indian, the radical protester from Oka or Wounded Knee. King pluralizes the Indian figure to include the "urban Indians" who occupy a full spectrum of social positions, from the bartender, alongside the prestigious Indian, the CEO and the movie star, and the activist, like Leonard Peltier, languishing in jail, in short—Indians in all their dappled humanity and heterogenous variability. Nor does the poem shy away from the social ills of post-removal indigenous life, reflected in the missing father and Fetal Alcohol Syndrome (FAS). There is no flight into "positive image" idealizations, just the indicia of settler-colonialism inscribed on indigenous bodies. Thus, the poem acknowledges the possibility of disenchantment and demystification, warning us not to idealize the Rez, with its well-known social ills. The poem asserts a kind of tribal unity, an affirmation of all the indigenous personae, along with a mildly ironic self-critique, and nod to Walt Whitman of *Leaves of Grass*: "I'm all of these and they are us."

A scene set in an upscale restaurant with a war-painted waiter, the poem offers a sarcastic ode to assimilation and the indigenous apprenticeship in the language of financial capitalism: "I've learned your lessons well / what to buy, what to sell / what's commodity, what's trash." Implied here is a largely vanished utopia of a pre-Columbian non-capitalist communitas, leading to the pondering of some of the counter-factual "what ifs" of history. What if we indigenous had led? What if we had had the power? Would there have been a genocide, the trail of tears, alienation, land theft, residential schools, indigenous dispossession? Would we have destroyed the land? He leaves the question open, while implying a negative answer. At the same time the poem looks both backward and forward, "of generations still to be, seven forward, seven back." In a rebuff to the wannabees, King mocks their love of the "brave that you adore, the Indian you idolize," and pointing to a cigar-store Indian, sarcastically suggests that "he may well have a secret song, a dance he'll share, a long-lost chant." Then the poet warns the aspiring secret-sharer that he will not carry the burden of representation: "Don't look at me. I'm not the Indian you had in mind. I can't." The final "I can't" is polysemic, referring back to everything that came before: "I can't save you. I can't save the world. I can't play act the Indian you had in mind. You guys have made this mess. Don't look to me now to save you. I can't do it. It's up to you."

The Strategic Uses of Humor

Native American scholar Vine Deloria, Jr. (Standing Rock Sioux) wrote in *Custer Died for Your Sins* of his disappointment "that the humorous side of Indian life has not been mentioned by professed experts on Indian affairs."[73] For some reason, native humor sometimes provokes disbelief, in a form of "the racism of surprise," i.e. a racialized denial of shared humanity: "Oh, Indians get PhDs!" "Indians make films!" "Indians laugh!" "Indians write books!" "Indians have sex!" Young German pupils who showed weakness or tears would be reprimanded by teachers with the phrase "*Ein Indianer kennt keinen Schmerz!*"; literally translated as: "An Indian knows no pain!" and "*ein Indianer weint nicht*," "an Indian doesn't complain." Despite supposedly "good intentions," such adages nullify a common humanity. Since the German Indian of film and literature also rarely laughs, one wonders about this transcultural affective bond. Why would indigenous people be strangely devoid of the general human inheritance of humor, especially when many oppressed peoples such as Jews and Blacks are known for the bitter humor of the "laughing-to-keep-from-crying" genre? How can one really love para-human creatures who neither laugh nor cry? Thus, racism orchestrates two converse forms of inferiorization: the denial of sameness in humanity and the denial of difference in experience.

The social valence and drift of humor depends on who is the butt of the joke—the powerful or the powerless. Indigenous people have never stopped ridiculing the colonizer's perspective through what Bakhtin called "the culture of laughter."[74] Bakhtin famously argued that Rabelais was at his most profound when he was laughing the most heartily. Sherman Alexie made a similar point in different words: "comedy is simply a funny way of being serious."[75] The constructed image of the perpetually long-suffering "Indian," in this sense, obscures the indigenous tradition of sly humor. The arbitrary association of indigenous people with an ancient Greek philosophical movement called Stoicism is a poisoned compliment. Reassuring to whites, the epithet "Stoic" means that Indians can take abuse without anger or blame and that they would never blame or discomfort ontologically innocent white people; thus, indigenous people fall into the bottomless pit of Euro-narcissism.

Native writers have critiqued this supposedly "positive" trope of Stoicism. The preface to the film *The Business of Fancy Dancing* (2002), written by Sherman Alexie, explains "how to write the Great American novel": "All of the Indians must have tragic features: tragic noses, eyes, and arms. Their hands and fingers must be tragic and must reach for tragic food. The hero must be a half-breed, half white and half Indian, preferably from a horse culture. He should often weep alone." In line with this mocking attitude, Native Americans have made endless jokes about colonialism, many having to do with land. The tourist asks an Indian: "What did you call this country before whites came?" The answer: "Ours!" In his essay on "Indian humor," Vine Deloria points to a common bond in the native mockery addressed to the historical figure whose malign magic transformed indigenous people into "Indians." For Deloria, Columbus jokes, "[Give] a solid feeling of unity and purpose to the tribes."[76] He cites the rumor that "Columbus began his journey with four ships. But one went over the edge so he arrived in the new world with only three."[77] Colonialism itself has been the perennial butt of the joke of native humor. A perennial trans-indigenous adage points to the role of Christianity in the historical chiasmus of indigenous dispossession: "When the missionaries arrived, they had the Bible and we had the land; now we have the Bible and they have the land." Another hardy perennial has to do with indigenous responses to missionary explanations of the nature of Heaven and Hell, with indigenous leaders opting to join their relatives in Hell, since the Christian heaven sounded boring, alien, and overcrowded with Christians.

One of the key inspirational figures for what might be called Native American Counter-Cinema was Creek/Seminole activist, dramaturg, and filmmaker Bob Hicks, an underappreciated creator who was for many years a leading voice for Native Americans in Hollywood. Hicks's plays usually focused on indigenous themes, with native actors cast for native parts, even before he made a student film for his AFI Masters. The film was *Return of the Country* (1974), a 25-minute satire on what Indians would do if they got the country back. This theatricalized mockumentary performs a perspectival reversal by examining conquest from a native point of view.

The film opens with an extract from a parodically faux racist film—*The Magnificent Savages*—but then performs a millenarian overturning through a dream-fantasy of reversal. Now it is the Indians who discover America and promptly establish a Bureau of White Affairs, headed, logically enough, by Black Elk. This time the Indians mouth "some of my best friends" clichés, but now the "best friends" are white. Under the guise of a Brechtian farce, the film stages an indictment of the cultural massacre performed by the boarding schools, which enforced Master-Race education, and the suppression of native languages and cultures. But in Hicks's bottom-up utopia, Christianity and the English language are outlawed, while the courts, the Congress, and the presidency are now in indigenous hands, while the "rez" is reserved for whites.

Self-reflexivity and irony are frequent features of many indigenous films, programs, and internet interventions. The "White Earth Nation Constitution," after all, mentions "humor" and "irony" as inalienable rights. Kent Monkman's artworks offer revisionist interpretations of racist pictorial conventions, just as his reflexive film *Shooting Geronimo* (2007) riffs on the genre of the silent Western. The film forms part of a tradition of mocku-ficto-mentaries like Woody Allen's *Zelig* (1983), Kenneth Wilmott's *C.S.A.: The Confederate States of America* (2004), and Cheryl Dunye's *Watermelon Woman* (1996), films that mimic the technical and stylistic protocols of the silent films of the past—the use of intertitles, piano accompaniment, hyperbolic thespianism, irregular rhythms, and archaic devices like matte-shots and the iris-in—to make a point about the present. The Monkman film queers the frontier western by showcasing two sexy buff indigenous male stars. The enamored white director licks his lips while he cranks the camera, as close shots center on his aroused crotch. The director coaches the actors to be more "fierce" and trains them to dance and strut, as their fancy dancing and ghost dances morph into break dance. The insertion of Monkman's gender-bending alter-ego "Miss Chief Eagle Testickle" into a frontier western context radically disturbs the settler-colonial assumptions of the genre. By showing what is usually hidden, closeted, and off-screen, Monkman critiques the limits of onscreen representations. A number of Native American films, similarly, transfigure Hollywood stereotypes. Chris Eyre's *Smoke Signals* (1998) has the more mature Victor character instructs the naive Thomas on how to "look Indian" by being solemn, silent, and stoic, similar to "a movie Indian" who looks as if he just walked off the set of *Dances with Wolves* (1990). When Thomas objects that his group only caught salmon, Victor suggests adopting a more powerful animal as the tribal symbol, reminding him that the title was *Dances with Wolves* and not *Dances with Salmon*! In another scene, when a white racist allegorically "occupies" their seats on the bus, they reluctantly accept the occupation but respond a few minutes later by seeing a satirical John Trudell song about John Wayne.

The most famous line in *Smoke Signals* occurs when actor Evan Adams (Coast Salish) says, "You know, the only thing more pathetic than Indians on TV, is Indians watching Indians on TV!" Much less pathetic than "Indians watching Indians on TV," however, is the Indian who *analyzes* Indians on TV watching Indians on TV in order to make a critical film about the role of Indians on TV. In *Tonto Plays Himself* (2010), Native American filmmaker Jacob Floyd (Muscogee [Creek] Cherokee) combines a personal search for his indigenous identity with a historical analysis of the role of actual Indians in Hollywood films. With irresistible humor, Floyd neighbors iconic moments from films like *Poltergeist* with archival materials from Hollywood films. We learn that the Indian extras who worked with Cecil B. De Mille invented their own tribe—the "Cecil B. De Mille Indians." In the process of his search, Floyd discovers that Creek actor Victor Daniels, aka "Chief Thunderbird," is his cousin. Floyd contrasts Daniel's obligatory use of an idiotic "Indian speak" with the intelligent manner in which Daniels actually spoke. Relentlessly reflexive, the film's credits mischievously note that "Westerns *were* harmed in the making of this film."[78]

A trans-mediatic approach to humor includes stand-up and sketch comedy, often mediated by network TV, cable TV, YouTube, and so forth. One sterling example comes from the late Oneida/Mohawk/Cree stand-up comedian/activist Charlie Hill, who appeared on the Richard Pryor Show in 1977 and subsequently on the Johnny Carson, Jay Leno, and David Letterman shows as well as in films and TV shows. In fact, Hill was inspired by Vine Deloria Jr.'s "biting and funny" humour which "crystallized for [Hill] what [he] wanted to do."[79] On the Moesha episode "Road Trip," for example, Charlie Hill plays the Hopi owner of a convenience store in Flagstaff, Arizona, where he sells T-shirts with fake sports team names like the "Cleveland Caucasions" and the "Washington Rednecks." Charlie Hill would usually begin his stand-up performance by acknowledging white disorientation at seeing native Americans doing stand-up since they were schooled by Hollywood and the media to assume that "Indians didn't have a sense of humor." Then, shifting to a different tone and meaning of humor, Hill would add: "We didn't think *you* were too funny either!" Charlie Hill used various strategies such as analogy, understatement, and double entendres to disarm the audience and make non-Indians laugh at their own blind spots and stereotypical assumptions.

Under the aphorism (attributed to filmmaker Billy Wilder) that "you can get away with murder if you just make people laugh," Hill's martial art–style use of humor accomplishes a number of goals: (1) it defuses and sublimates the comic's own historically informed grief and rage through indirection, thus alchemizing anger into acceptably humorous form; (2) it creates a "likability" or humanization effect through the universality of laughter, while (3) offering emotional sustenance to a native audience. Hill's jokes convey a *longue-durée* historical perspective, assuring whites in the audience that he is not "white-bashing," just "administering a spiritual spanking you should have had 400 years ago." As a form of consciousness-raising, Hill's ludic didacticism produces insights about complex histories of settler colonialism through easily understandable analogies to everyday experience. Condensing centuries of history, Hill compares the initial indigenous welcome of the Europeans, followed by the loss of land, to settler-colonial situations where house guests overstay their welcome. "Doesn't it burn you up," he asks, "when people ask to stay at your house for just one night, and then stay until Thanksgiving?" Many of his jokes revolve around land. "We Indians," he reminds us, "possess the owner's manual for the continent." Invoking the race-baiters' standard outburst—"Go back to where you came from!"— Hill responds, "So I went to live in his backyard." Hill's comic routines distill centuries of pain into telling anecdotes and lethal wordplay. Using a rhetoric of litotes, or strategic understatement, he compares the Oneida's forced removal from New York to Wisconsin to a "little real estate problem"; here the miniscule serves to allegorize the momentous. Or he practices comic reversals, claiming "we Indians also celebrate

Halloween—by dressing up like white people," or calling Columbus an "illegal alien," or dubbing European immigrants "whitebacks." Or he plays on the word "our" to assert native land possession. In a sketch titled "Indian Press Conference," he answers a reporter's question "How do you like our city, he responds: "Fine, how do you like our country?" [80]

Like stand-up comedy, films too can practice tricksterism, and Charlie Hill actually played a trickster in the fiction film *Harold of Orange* (1984). The film was scripted by Gerald Vizenor, whose own work proliferates in tricksterish touches, and who wrote of indigenous artists that "we are tricksters in the blood, natural mixedblood tricksters."[81] Hill plays tribal trickster Harold Sinseer who leads his posse "the Warriors of Orange." The group embarks on a special type of raid, not a violent raid on a colonial settler fort, but rather a nonviolent "word-warrior" (Vizenor) raid on the coffers of a corporate foundation. To meet the challenges of ethnic grantsmanship, the Warriors of Orange appeal to liberal sympathies by stressing "safe" issues like land conservation, expressed in warm and fuzzy language. In this spirit, they request funding to produce rez-grown miniature oranges—actually outsourced from California—and promote pinch beans as a cure for native alcoholism. Fluent in the buzzwords that release Foundation funds, they speak of a "sober revolution" and of "socio-acupuncture." Issuing the hyperbolic promises typical of the grant-application genre, Harold vows to fight alcoholism, spark political debate, and open coffee shops on the reservation, in short, to "revolutionize the reservation way of life." The film forms what David James calls an "allegory of cinema," in that the fiction *in* the film mirrors the production *of* the film itself; a film mocking the paternalism of the cultural gatekeepers inhabiting liberal foundations was largely funded by those same liberal foundations (namely the Northwest Area Foundation, the National Endowment for the Arts and the like). The basic thrust of the film, like Hill's stand-up, is to make white people laugh at their own ethnocentric blind spots, in this case their paternalistic gullibility. The soundtrack, meanwhile, features songs like "Trickster" and "Fast Bucks," written and performed by the iconic native singer/activist Buffy Sainte-Marie and other songs by "elder" Floyd Red Crow Westerman, thus inserting the film into a longer tradition of indigenous pop-cultural critique.

In a circular structure, the film begins and ends in the native coffee house, while the story at its center revolves around a long bus trip in some ways reminiscent of Ken Kesey's *Merry Pranksters*, but this time carrying actual indigenous people rather than war-painted hippies imitating Indians. The film's caustic humor begins with the title's ironic reference to European royalty and continues with a series of historical reversals and surprising changes of (literal) direction. The jokes combine a structure of comic aggression combined with a pedagogic thrust. When a foundation dignitary asks "Sun Bear" how many Indians were in the Americas when Columbus landed, the answer is "none," since Columbus invented the term. When another dignitary endorses the "Bering Strait" theory of native origin, a Warrior agrees but asks for specification—in what direction—"East or West?," a comment that echoes Vine Deloria's ahead-of-the-scientific-curve questioning of the unidirectional Bering Strait narrative.

Rather than attack the safe, conventional, and classist scapegoat of liberal anti-racist films—toothless "rednecks"—the film "arrows" the putative "friends of the Indians"—well-meaning but patronizing white liberals. The film is full of self-demystifying allegories, as when a baseball game features competition between Whites and Reds, but where each team wears T-shirts for the opposing (racial) team; here a sports victory comes to carry allegorical weight. For Indians, as one Warrior explains, "stealing a base is like recovering land," regaining the "land base" as it were. The film portrays Foundation support for indigenous peoples as a kind of whitewashing or better "redwashing." Without sentimental obfuscation, Harold stipulates the real deal, the social contract: "We get a little money, they get a good name." The film shows a brazen lack of concern with the mystique of the "positive image." In superficial terms Harold is not a "good person"—he lies, tricks, flatters, and cheats. Harold slyly "kills" his own "traditional grandmother" just to avoid an annoying engagement. When the well-meaning liberal asks if he can attend the funeral, Harold solemnly claims that the (nonexistent) ceremonies are a "tribal secret." But "badassness" is in the eye of the beholder, as in the black slang sense of "bad" for bold gestures aimed at the oppressor. The question is "positive for whom?"[82] After all, Columbus had a "positive image" of the Tainos as servile and easy to convert; the image became negative when they rebelled, at which point they metamorphosed into fierce cannibals. Oswald de Andrade, in his effort to De-Columbusize discourse, preferred the "bad Indian," the mischievous Indian, the unconverted Indian, the cannibal Indian.

A "positive image" approach also ignores the perspective and the social positioning both of the filmmakers and the audience. We cannot equate the stereotyping performed "from above" with stereotyping "from below," as occurs in *Harold of Orange* or in the work of the Chicano group Culture Clash or in the paintings and films of Kent Monkman, whose work inverts sexual and power relationships between "Cowboys" and "Indians." In such cases, the stereotype operates, as it were "in quotes," recognized as a stereotype and reinvented for subversive ends. Indigenous people have lampooned most of the major institutions of settler colonialism: the inadvertently obscene missionary translations of the Bible; the erroneous speculations of some anthropologists; and the not always laughable ineptitudes of the Bureau of Indian Affairs (BIA). Deloria advises native people to call the BIA in case of fire, since they excel at "putting wet blankets on everything."[83] In a similar spirit, the brochure for an exhibition on "Laughter and Resilience: Humor in Native American Art" at the Wheelwright Museum of the American Indian, Santa Fe (November 10, 2019—October 4, 2020), offered the following statement about the vital role of indigenous humor:

> Clowns, Koshare, and Heyoka not only provide comedic performances during ceremonials; these contrarians serve an important cultural function by pointing out behavior that falls outside of community standards. Many Indigenous stories feature a trickster who often finds himself in situations related to folly, humor, and mortality. Following in the footsteps of these cultural icons, Native American artists featured in this exhibition use humor, parody, and satire to not only make the viewer laugh, but also combat stereotypes, comment on tribal politics, and critique the National scene.

The leveling of the hierarchy that pits the "high arts" like painting, endowed with millennial auratic prestige, against merely "folkloric" bead work, pottery, weaving, basketry, and animal effigies, undermines the conventional positioning of "Art" above "craft," a hierarchy in synch with other artistic hierarchies. Within Euro-dominant aesthetics, the canonical decorum going back to classical Greece has favored tragedy, associated with noble elite and well-spoken characters, over comedy, with its "vulgar" subaltern servant characters with their malapropisms. Both genres are historically linked respectively to correspondingly "high" and "low" styles. Film awards follow the same logic; Oscars usually go to prestigious literary adaptations or historical films, rarely to comic or satiric films.

Native artists have performed a historically conscious form of humor. One popular native Canadian comedy group is called "the 1491s," in a nod to indigenous hegemony in the world before Columbus. The group writes, produces, performs, and uploads videos on their 1491s website and YouTube channel. The website self-introduction reads: "The 1491s is a sketch comedy group, based in the wooded ghettoes of Minnesota and buffalo grass of Oklahoma. They are a gaggle of Indians chock full of cynicism and splashed with a good dose of indigenous satire … They were at Custer's Last Stand. They mooned Chris Columbus when he landed."[84] This "mooning" of Columbus recalls the Brazilian Modernist symbolic "mooning" of the same figure more than half a century earlier by dating their manifestos October 11, 1492, the last happy day on earth before the Colonial Fall from indigenous grace. The 1491s form an integral part of the trans-nation production, *Reservation Dogs*, co-directed by Taika Waititi (Maori and Jewish) and Sterlin Harjo (Muscogee/Seminole), notably in the presence of 1491s veteran Dallas Goldtooth playing the "Unknown Warrior," a bare-chested spirit guide who serves as a self-mocking yet profound wise man. In this indigenization of the Tarantino style, the series simultaneously points to the time-tested native norms and to the difficulty of respecting them in a commercialized capitalist world. A cameo by Gary Farmer, for example, has him claim to "live off the land, mainly," but where fast-food wrappers reveal the difficulty of realizing that idea.

Painterly Tricksterism

As many native writers have pointed out, the trickster figure forms a significant element in some native cultures of North America (and arguably, as we shall see, of South America). Cree-Metis writer Emma LaRocque speaks of the "cultural teaser," the psycho-prophetic *Wehsehkeha* now reduced to the "Western understanding of 'Trickster.'"[85] Indigenous painters like Kent Monkman, in this vein, have used their brushes and easels and laptops to become trickster-pedagogues while avoiding "positive image" sentimentality.

Monkman's work is simultaneously traditionally indigenous and aggressively avant-garde. His work alludes to the consecrated artists of the European canon—Titian, Delacroix, Rubens, Carvaggio—and to the American canon (e.g. the Hudson River School)—but his anti-canonical approach remediates, recontextualizes, and indigenizes the source paintings. First trained as an abstract painter, Monkman was deeply impacted by his family's history in Canadian government-sponsored religious schools, which forced indigenous children, in a kind of soul-murder, to assimilate into Euro-Canadian culture. As an artist, Monkman uses his "mastery" of painting in the canonical tradition to "unmaster" the colonial master narrative. The generative mechanism is to look at the classical tradition through (at least) three grids—settler colonialism, gay and two-spirit sexuality, and personal experience. Thus, he injects indigenous characters and themes into "noble" artistic spaces and genres such as historical frescoes and landscape painting, where such themes had not previously been welcomed or even acknowledged. Thus, he subtly critiques the power structures undergirding landscape painting, which in Europe translated the aristocratic pride of the nobles who had enclosed European land to form the country estates decorating the Heritage Films based on Jane Austen novels, and which in North America celebrated the sublime beauty of appropriated native land. Not only does Monkman reinsert First Peoples' histories and experiences into the master narratives of Western culture, he also demonstrates that indigenous people had always formed a submerged and formative presence in those same narratives. By appropriating images, motifs, and techniques from the canon, particularly those favored by the authoritarian and often nation-state-oriented genre of historical painting, he performs painterly jiujitsu, deploying the social power of the upscale art world against colonial domination.

A key agent in this process is his sexually transgressive two-spirited alter ego blessed with a multiply punning name: "Miss Chief Eagle Testickle." This ticklish subject, this flamboyantly polymorphous and polyandrous figure, occupies a third space of sexual negotiation. S/he/they tickle the canon and make it giggle. Miss Chief, as ancient as an Amazonian warrior, as traditional as the *berdache*, and as contemporary as an underground trans-performer, crashes the party not only of the classical museum but even of the *salon des refuses*. Their provocative agency forms a bold riposte to portrayals of native peoples as stoic and passive. The mere penetration of this mischievous *cacica* within the auratic space of canonical painting dramatically alters its valence and affect. While recombinatory allusive art has become a kind of norm in the contemporary art world, the "inconvenient" indigenous presence makes the gesture infinitely more radical. Monkman's painting *The Scream* (2017), with its echo of Edward Munch, shows indigenous children being violently wrenched from their families by police and Catholic priests and forced to attend the innocuously named "residential schools." Monkman's strategy here could be compared to that of the eighteenth-century caricaturist Hogarth, who would portray moments where a criminal, for example, a pickpocket, would be caught *in flagrante* in a kind of freeze frame, the difference here being that the criminal act in question was not a petty crime but rather an epoch-making historical catastrophe.

A YouTube video shows Monkman touring the Great Hall of Metropolitan Museum of Art—one of the Holy of Holies of the art world—literally returning the gaze of the figures in a museum deeply impacted by colonial appropriation. (Monkmon had been commissioned by the MET to create a piece for the Great Hall, which would create a dialogue with the existing artworks from the museum.) The title of the exposition performs an act of indigenous naming, in that *mistikôsiwak* derives from a Cree word meaning "wooden boat people," a term first applied to the French settlers of Quebec. Monkman produced two monumental paintings, *Welcoming the Newcomers* and *Resurgence of the People*, both of which involve boats in endangered shipwreck-like situations. *Welcoming the Newcomers* (2019) remixes two famous French Romantic art works, Géricault's *The Raft of the Medusa* (1818–19) and Delacroix's *Christ on the Sea of Galilee* (1854). Reconceiving First Contact as an aquatic conflict zone characterized by both hospitality and violence, it shows Miss Chief Eagle Testickle extending her hand to help various stranded figures, reminding us of a time when Europeans depended on indigenous generosity for their very survival. The figures on the raft—Queen Victoria, Marie Antoinette, a Conquistador, a Puritan, and Christ on the Cross—encapsulate western culture, religion, history, and power. The bedraggled swimmers represent a wide gamut of types—an English Puritan, a shackled black man, a missionary wielding a crucifix. Some wear the iron helmets of the Conquistadores; others don the black hats of the Puritans. The human figures form a motley intersectional crew: Africans mingle with Indians and many-hued migrants. Rather than the "white savior" figure of Hollywood fiction, Monkman's gender-bending protagonist now incarnates the mixed-race savior who drags the motley crew to safety from the angry waters.

The second canvas, *Resurgence of the People* (2019), references Leutze's *Washington Crossing the Delaware* (1851) but in such a way as to evoke contemporary aquatic disasters like the drowning of desperate migrants in the Mediterranean. Radically transtextual and transtemporal in its counterpointing of times, places, and art pieces, Monkman's work links them all through the common thread of coloniality. The art is variously drawn from the Bible, Greek mythology, Renaissance and Modern Art history, all layered over one another in a multi-stratum approach. These layered temporalities are then filtered through the present of the painting, which replaces the "Father of the Nation" with a transsexual mother/father hero/ine, naked except for high heels and transparent wrap. The rowers, significantly, are largely indigenous and mostly female. The resurgent nation, meanwhile, is not the American nation-state but rather the indigenous nation-people. Monkman expresses a spirit of what Bakhtin called "gay relativity" or the free play of thought, manifested again in the "Rendezvous" series; in *Wildflowers of North America*, 2017, where trappers, traders, mountain men, and Indigenous nations enjoy a transhistorical celebration of the arrival of spring. The scene evokes the English anti-Puritan rebel Thomas Morton dancing around a New England maypole with the Indians. With her shape-shifting spirit, Miss Chief plays *magister ludi*, the MC of libido and liberation.[86]

In 2016, Monkman was inspired to pay artistic homage to the resistance at the Standing Rock Indian Reservation in North and South Dakota, where masses of indigenous people and their allies had been protesting the Dakota Access Pipeline project. Incorporating this contemporary reference into art history, Monkman discerned a visual-emotional relationality, an isomorphic structure of feeling, between the tortured iconography of news photos and video reportage, on the one hand, and the iconography of pathos in classical painting on the other. This artistic serendipity generated a series of paintings dedicated to the protests, told from the point of view of the "water protectors." Monkman and his collaborators mounted a collage of iconic images juxtaposing Standing Rock with historically similar confrontations from historical paintings of battle scenes, drawn for example from American Revolutionary art and from French Romantic paintings. Monkman's professed goal, in the spirit of people making their own history, was "to make the contemporary feel historic and the historic feel contemporary."[87]

Indigeneity and Music

Indigenous media arts are open to many fields and genres, such as music video, stand-up comedy, and painting. In the vibrant tradition of indigenous protest music going back to Buffy Sainte-Marie, Floyd Red Crow Westerman, John Trudell, Redbone, Robbie Robertson, Sadie Buck, Joy Harjo, Pura Fe, Soni Moreno, Alanis Obomsawin, Jani Lauzon, Mishi Donovan, Lucie Idlout, Mary Youngblood, Joanne Shenandoah, and JB the First Lady, many of the groups are full-throatedly anti-colonialist. Aztlan Underground, a band from Los Angeles that combines hip-hop, punk rock, jazz, and electronic music with Chicano and Native American themes and indigenous instrumentation, for example, performs a song entitled simply "Decolonize!" Some of the lyrics include: "Now learn the word called colonization / Stranger in your own land under exploitation / This is the state of the indigena today." Continuing, "Till a Hopi and a Mexica can really understand / That invaders divided indigenous people / Under English, French, or Spanish it made us all feeble / Unable to recognize each other / From Xicano to Lakota all sisters and brothers / In the spirit of Pontiac, all the red keepers of the earth mother / From the top of Alaska to the tip of South America / Abya Yala, Anahuak, Turtle Island / 506 years of indigenous resistance / … The 7th fire has arrived / Cihuatl is reclaiming / We have returned to Aztlan!!!!"[88]

Changing register, scores if not hundreds of fiction films, documentaries, and music videos have explored the topic of the residential schools, whose horror was recently confirmed by the discovery of indigenous children buried anonymously in Canadian graves. Kevin Willmott's *The Only Good Indian* (2009) tells the story, set in the early 1900s, of a Kickapoo youth forced to leave his family and attend a resident school but who escapes and resists assimilation. The rap music video "Indigenous Holocaust," (2008) by native (Anishinaabe) hip-hop artist Wahwahay Benais, and directed by Missy Whiteman (Arapaho/Kickapoo), revisits the same oppressive history of the schools where native children were separated from their parents and shorn of their hair, their language, and their culture, in a form of what historian David Wallace Adams calls "education for extinction."[89]

The "Indigenous Holocaust" music video accomplishes its goal in a few minutes and in an especially trenchant manner. By having the ghost-like artist emerge from wintry haze into focus and clarity, as Michelle Raheja points out, the video's opening "de-vanishes" the Native American presence.[90] The artist's literal coming into focus metaphorizes the crystallization of the image of a formerly marginalized cultural identity. The video is a kind of hybrid docu-fiction in that the visual track draws extensively on archival photos of indigenous children, taken by the institutions themselves. The photos show rigidly regimented children, all conveying a facial and postural affect of a desperate and precocious sadness that one would normally assume to be completely alien to young children, without a trace of a smile or mischief, with nothing but unrelenting pain etched across their faces. The photos offer irrefutable evidence that the ordeal of a colonial schooling has severely damaged the youthful spirits. We are reminded again that the trope of indigenous happiness advanced by French philosophers and the American Founding Fathers, and by many indigenous commentators themselves, had as its counterpart the reality of post-Conquest indigenous *un*happiness. The refrain of Benais's rap, probes and cures, as it were, the wounds of that deep sadness:

> They took his son from his home.
> Yeah, they pulled 'em apart
> They took her daughter from her home
> They were forced to depart ...
> Another native fell victim to the holocaust.

As Benais raps direct to camera, first against a forest background and then against a starry nighttime sky, the lyrics tell us of "priests stealing children," "girls raped," and "women sterilized," where the Bible served to "teach 'em and bleach em" and where native mouths were washed with soap if they dared to speak in their native tongue.

Musically modeling a symbolic red/black/white coalition, the video conjoins a largely black performance style—hip-hop—with its percussive thrust and typical corporeal expressions and gestures, with "red" percussive chants, in counterpoint with a largely white-presenting musical genre—country music—in the form of a sample from the song "Not Ready to Make Nice" by the Dixie Chicks:

> Forgive, sounds good
> Forget, I'm not sure I could
> They say time heals everything
> But I'm still waiting.

The cited lyrics, from the 2006 *Taking the Long Way* album—the Dixie Chicks's response to right-wing demonization and boycotts for having criticized George Bush and the Gulf War—on one level offer an homage to fellow musicians combating the same enemy. But on another level they constitute a native appropriation of Dixie Chicks's lyrics, here refunctioned for the collective purposes of indigenous peoples, who are also "still waiting" for justice and sovereignty. "Indigenous Holocaust" gives audiovisual-musical form to what Lakota scholar Maria Yellow Horse Brave Heart calls "historically unresolved grief"—the "cumulative emotional wounding ... across generations, emanating from massive group trauma."[91] Contemporary indigenous youth in North America have felt drawn to rap and reggae and video-jockeying as forms of cultural protest. "A Tribe Called Red," a play on "A Tribe called Quest," excites crowds into collective frenzy with their video-jockey collages and mixed media techno-dance events. Different genres enjoy a capacity to relate what they see as historical truth, but they relate the truth that they see differently, through a generically differentiated gaze.

Irreverent humor, even in the face of horror, has always been part of indigenous culture in all of the Americas since the beginning. Native filmmakers are also making trans-indigenous internet features such as Loretta Todd's female buddy film *Fierce Girls* (2018), the world's first superhero interactive web series created with indigenous girls in mind, starring two teens with warrior spirits—Kisik, a Cree-Métis girl in Canada, and Anika, a Maori girl in Aotearoa (New Zealand)—who develop a long-distance relationship through social media and "use their newly acquired superpowers to create a series of comics to empower young women and celebrate the strength and beauty of being Indigenous in a challenging world."[92] The transmedia innovative cross-platform project artfully explores a hybrid form of digital media storytelling that includes live action, social media, comics, and indigenous hip-hop.

First Peoples, First Features[93]

The swelling productions of indigenous film and media in Canada and in other parts of the world over the last four decades have been well covered by many excellent indigenous and non-indigenous critics, and I will not try for an impossible coverage here. Rather, I will focus on a miniscule sampling of some recent films from Quebec related to our themes—the sequels of colonialism, residential schools, resilient culture, the use of humor, healing, forward vision, archaic revisionism, and alternative aesthetics. Shelley Niro (born 1954), for example, is an accomplished multidisciplinary artist skilled in photography, painting, sculpting, bead work, multimedia, and independent film. A member of the Kanienkehaka (Mohawk Nation), Turtle Clan, from Six Nations of the Grand River Territory, she explores the oral history of the Iroquois in general and the Mohawk diaspora in particular. Her photography combines portraits of contemporary native women with traditional Mohawk imagery. Her work also proliferates in puns and pop culture references as evidenced in her 1992 photographic series, *This Land Is Mime Land*, and *500 Year Itch*, whose punning title links five centuries of colonialism to Marilyn Monroe's adulterous wordplay in *The Seven Year Itch*. Niro's work is at once highly conceptual, socially engaged, culturally layered, and richly sensuous. It touches on serious themes of gender inequity and cultural appropriation, treated in tones of parody, satire, masquerade, and remediation.

Kissed by Lightning (2009) treats a theme at once personal and historical—grief and mourning. The film revolves around Mavis Dogblood (Kateri Walker), a Mohawk painter devoted to the memory of her deceased husband Jessie Lightning, a virtuoso violinist whose compositions still haunt her imagination. Mavis keeps his memory alive through her own artwork, which often refers, like his art, to Iroquois history and society. While she struggles with her painting, she has to put up with the distractions triggered by the presence in her house of Jesse's first wife and children. Meanwhile, an infinitely patient suitor, Solomon King (nicknamed "Bug"), waits in the wings as she tries to exorcise her individual and collective demons. On the way to participating in a New York art exhibition, she visits Jessie's grandmother Josephine, who lives in the ancestral territories of the Mohawk in New York State. The encounter gives her permission to love her friend and lover Bug while always honoring the memory of Jesse and the Iroquois heritage.

But this is to speak merely in terms of plot, when what is most intriguing in the film for our purposes is its dense and multilayered intertext. *Kissed by Lightning* is revisionist in two very different senses. First, in its choice of a source text not drawn from the Western canon, but rather from the Iroquoian cultural archive—the story of the founding of the Haudensaunee Law of Peace. The Niro film offers a present-day love story symbolically grounded in the Iroquois legend of Peacemaker and Hiawatha. In a perceptive essay, Penelope Myrtle Kelsey analyzes the film as "a tribal feminist recuperation" of the Iroquois narrative and explains some of the feminist resonances between the personal and the historical dimension of the film. As Niro herself points out, the film envisions the three characters as reincarnations of their legendary forebears: Mavis the Mother of Nations, Jesse the Peace Maker, her patient suitor Solomon, the Hiawatha.

Second, the "text" in question, from a classical Eurocentric perspective, would not usually even qualify as a text. The source is not a novel, or play, or poem, or biography, or history, or even a text in any conventional sense. Indeed, much of the history of the Iroquois-Euro-American relationship has revolved around precisely this issue of what qualifies as a text, and therefore what would qualify as a legitimate treaty, a definition heavy with implication. The Canadian state refused to accept the legitimacy of a series of treaties between the Iroquois and European settlers, first with the Dutch and then with the British, because the treaties had not been articulated in the medium of alphabetic letters and script but rather in the medium of Two Row Wampun, i.e. "a wide belt of white shells divided horizontally by two parallel rows of purple shells."[94]

The official refusal was based, as Daniel Coleman puts it, on "Eurocentric assumptions of what constitutes literacy and therefore what kinds of texts can be read (recognized and respected) as authoritative historical and legal documents."[95] Huron Miller, an Onondaga interpreter of the treaty, has translated its meaning as a metaphorical evocation of principles of equality, reciprocity, and respect for difference:

> This [belt] symbolizes the agreement under which the Iroquois/Haudenosaunee welcomed the white peoples to their lands. We will not be like father and son, but like brothers. These two rows will symbolize vessels travelling down the same river together. One will be for the original people, their laws, their customs, and the other for the European people and their laws and customs. We will travel the river together but each in our own boat. And neither of us will try to steer the other's vessel.[96]

The visuality of the two-row wampum depicts the Haudenosaunee in a canoe, and the Dutch in a ship, sailing side by side down the river, in equality, with each group keeping their language and culture. The belts "translate" various diplomatic agreements, both among indigenous nations and between the Iroquois and settler governments. Like the cinema and like philosophy according to Deleuze, the Two Row Wampum "generate concepts" by conveying meaning visually. The Canandaigua Treaty Belt (1794), for example, records a crucial treaty made between the Six Nations and the then fledgling United States; its iconography shows the thirteen colonies as figures holding hands with the Haudensaunee alongside a longhouse, hardly a surprising connection since the US dollar itself is overlaid with Iroquois symbolism.[97]

The film preps the spectator through a set of hermeneutic cues in the form of a series of intertitles conveying crucial information.

> The combined confederacy of the Six Nations is known as the Haudenosaunee.
> The word "Haudenosaunee" means "Peoples of the Long House."
> The term is said to have been introduced by the Great Peacemaker at the time of the formation of the Iroquois Confederacy.
> It implies that the nations shall live together as families in the same Long House.

As the final sentence of the historical/textual preamble lingers through a dissolve, the opening shot reveals a contemporary version of a longhouse—a modest, elongated trailer-home redolent of post-Contact relative poverty. The first words we hear are "Good Morning, Six Nations!" like the Samuel L. Jackson DJ program in *Do the Right Thing* (1989). The film centers not only on the protagonist, or even the couple, but rather on a wider web of relations between various empowered mothers, in remembrance of the central role of the Mother of Nations, of the clan mothers, the powers behind the throne, who were supposed to install and "fire" the chiefs.

The *Kissed by Lightning* story recapitulates on a domestic and personal level the social history of the Haudenosaunee Confederacy and the Consolation Ceremony. In this sense, *Kissed by Lightning* resembles literary classics like James Joyce's *Ulysses*, where the daily lives of contemporary characters like Leopold and Molly Bloom are made to resonate with the lives of their classical prototypes. Thus, the heroic epic events of the past hover over the mundane domesticity of the present, much as the momentous episodes of The *Odyssey* lurk in the background of Leopold Bloom's quotidian existence in present-day Dublin. In *Kissed by Lightning*, the intra-familial domestic and amorous tensions in the present story "rhyme," on a lesser scale, with the cycle of violence that tormented the Seneca, Onandaga, Cayuga, Oneida, and Mohawk peoples prior to the installation of the Law of Peace. The past is made to resonate with the present; the micro-story in the present homologizes the macro-story from the past, in ways that each reinforces the other. The Jesse character speaks of the Iroquois going back to "time immemorial," suggesting that while the discourse time of the film is the conventional hour and a half, the deep diegetic *longue durée* is millennial.

In an allegory relevant to many indigenous nations suffering from historically repressed grief, Josephine herself affirms the need to come to peace with what has been lost in order to survive. On the level of the narrative, the final grief ceremony and gift exchange led by Josephine, with a pregnant Mavis, Bug, Kateri, and Zeus all in attendance, reveals Mavis's newfound serenity in her relationship with Bug. While the film on one level would seem to have a conventional Sundance-style happy ending, the historical overtones of the Iroquois Confederacy bring an added sense of volume and depth. "Double voiced" (Bakhtin) the film can be taken in dramatic realist terms as the moving story of a widowed woman who rediscovers her love of life and art. On the other, it can be taken as an actualization and rereading of an earlier formative text of the Iroquois and more broadly of indigenous people. The film proliferates in the signs and symptoms of indigeneity—native chants on the soundtrack, six nations flags, colorful corn husks, moccasins, canoes, dream catchers, turtles, beaded baskets, beaded purses, beaded everything—a leveling of the old arbitrary arts versus crafts hierarchy. Art, in sum, is integrally connected to the craft. The main character, a surrogate and alter ego of the author, creates art that is inseparable from the cultural riches of her community. In fact, the arts are omnipresent in the film: Jesse plays the viola, his son plays the piano, and Mavis paints. Through a reflexive mise en abyme, Mavis's paintings, inspired by her husband's stories about the Iroquois heritage, actualize the ancient stories, telling analogous versions of the same tale as the film itself. In a transartistic fusion, the visual track shows her paintings while the soundtrack plays his music. The past erupts into the present through dreams, through art, through phantasies, just as the paintings in Mavis' New York exhibit portray the Peacemaker's journey and the human lives touched by that journey, and Josephine's wall of photos and paintings exhibits the highlights of indigenous history.

Indigenization of Horror

Seventeenth-century French commentators like Father Pierre Biard claimed that the Mi'kmaq people of Quebec saw themselves as superior to the French since "you are always fighting and quarreling among yourselves; [while] we live peaceably … you are covetous, and are neither generous nor kind [while]as for us, if we have a morsel of bread we share it with our neighbor."[98] Most irritatingly for the settlers, they claimed that they as Mi'kmaq were richer than the French, since they had ease, comfort, time, and general well-being, thus anticipating the "societies of abundance" theories of Marshall Sahlins. Centuries later, Mi'kmaq Canadian director Jeff Barnaby demonstrates a different kind of confidence. Barnaby is a "generically incorrect" or "generically challenging" director, first, in favoring a genre rarely associated with an indigenous point of view—horror—second, in choosing a genre often dismissed by the cine-literate as overly commercial, apolitical, and even reactionary. But Barnaby refunctions horror, and indigenizes it, as it were, flipping the script to portray his vision of the existential horrors lived by indigenous people. (While indigenous comics like Charlie Hill disarm the audience through humor, Barnaby educates them through terror.) Horror films have an abstract, trans-realist side that lends itself to social allegory, as when George Romero's pods in *Night of the Living Dead* hint at racism. Barnaby makes horror work for what he sees as the social and cinematic purposes of indigenous people. In this sense, Barnaby's films stage a reterritorialization, an indigenous occupation of generic terrain.

Barnaby goes against the grain not only of dominant cinema but also against any "positive image" approach. In an interview with Susan Dunne, he is forthright about his purposes:

> I flat-out didn't want to make a drum-and-feather movie … I didn't want my Indian crying over a pile of buffalo skulls or holding a feather up to the sky. In a lot of ways, I inadvertently made an anti-Indian movie. Instead of hugging trees, he'd be cutting them down … Instead of being in commune with nature, he'd be saturated in concrete and industrial skank; he'd speak his language and be unapologetic

about his downfall and in complete ignorance of what he was doing to his spirit ... No romance, no buckskin, just judicious reflection of reality.[99]

Or again, in reflecting on his artistic choices: "My entire life, I've wanted to tell a story about this kind of Indian. To have them encounter all the things that make living Indian ugly, and to represent all the things that make surviving it beautiful. I wanted to take all the violence, drunkenness, sadness and death and make a human hero."[100] If these images are so negative, one might ask, what makes Barnaby an indigenous filmmaker? The short answer is, virtually everything! He casts indigenous actors, he presents indigenous themes, he creates often disturbed or enraged indigenous characters, places them in indigenous locales, while referencing indigenous colonial history, often in a bitterly humorous manner. Although he does not portray his characters as impeccable heroes, he does portray them as complexly human subjects.

Colonialism haunts all of Barnaby's films. Unlike anti-colonialist films set in the distant past, Barnaby's films remind us the today and tomorrow "nowness" of colonialism. The attitude is that truth itself, even unpleasant, is revolutionary, and "positive image" be damned. From a deeper perspective, the films are, if not positive, at least truthful. Barnaby excoriates what he calls "positivity porn" i.e. calls for idealized images, including from his own community: "How do you go through these atrocities [against Indians]," he asks, "and pretend that we are all well-adjusted?"[101] For Michelle Raheja, Jeff Barnaby's dystopian fictions offer counter-narratives that reveal the often dismal and depressing aspect of inhabiting homelands that are still colonized in an otherwise seemingly postcolonial world.[102]

Barnaby's films are very "sanguine" in the double sense of displaying a kind of oblique optimism and courage, and of having a high "quantum of blood," that is, his films gush with Tarrantino-esque rivers of blood (frankly not my "cup of tea"). The idea of "blood quantum," i.e. the portion of one's blood that indicates indigenous ancestry, is at the center of the story, just as that same issue has been at the very kernel of indigenous life and history in North America. Ever since 1492, Blood and Power flowed together, beginning with Spain and the early empires, which formed the cutting edge of a bloody history, until the colonial baton was passed to the English, the French, the Dutch, and the North Americans. Colonialist discourse racialized what had been a religious blood trope favored by the Inquisition, to wit the "*limpieza de sangre*," that is the multi-generational cleansing of Jewish blood through conversion to Christianity. The same blood trope was weaponized in the Americas to justify and reinforce racial supremacy. Forked-tongued, the blood quantum is worked in opposite ways for African Americans as opposed to indigenous people. In a disastrous form of demographic alchemy, a mythically potent single drop of black "blood"—the "one drop rule"—turned persons of partial African ancestry "black," while a similarly miniscule yet equally mythical quantum of European "blood" had an opposite effect, magically turning indigenous people partially "white." The common purpose was exploitation, to multiply slaves in the Black case, and to sabotage land rights in the Indian case. According to Gerald Vizenor, "the notion of arithmetic blood quantum was concocted as a measure to determine federal services, tribal membership, and identity," which would lead to natives, through intermarriage, becoming "extinct over time."[103]

(Mohawk director Tracey Deer's *Club Native* (2008) partially addresses the issue of blood quantum laws in relation to Deer's home community of Kahnawake and women who risk losing their right to live on the reserve after marrying non-natives.)

Barnaby wrote, directed, edited, co-produced, and composed the score of *Blood Quantum*. Set in 1981 and shot on the Mi'kmaq Red Crow reserve in Quebec—Barnaby's own community—the film tells the story of a troubled-but-trying-to-do-his-best local sheriff Traylor (Michael Greyeyes), his wife Joss (Elle-Máijá Tailfeathers), their son Joseph (Forrest Goodluck) and Joseph's half-brother, the very violent Lysol (Kiowa Gordon), who struggle to protect their community from outsiders seeking refuge from zombies and the rising undead. One problem with the positive image norm is that it places a taboo on historically generated and vindictive rage of the kind a "postcolonial Indian" (Barnaby's term) like Lysol might display, when in fact such rage is an inevitable by-product of a gendered and sexualized colonialism. The film opens during the early stages of a mysterious contagion that ends up turning white folks into violent monsters intent on infiltrating protected lands. The first images show degutted salmon flopping back to life—and we recall that many indigenous protests in Canada have concerned fishing rights—followed by a dog who has been subjected to canine euthanasia, administered by bullet, who also comes back to life.[104] As a virulent zombie-virus spreads, it turns out that the members of the Red Crow reserve are immune. They debate whether they should risk their lives by allowing outsiders into the reserve. With the "Zs" coming for them, the immune Red Crow must fight the enemy outside while dealing with tensions within their own walls: Are native people duty-bound to help the white survivors, or do past misdeeds and exploitation give them license to lock their gates and leave the outside world to its fate, just as the world left indigenous people to their fate? Do they let the outsiders in—thus risking not only the extinction of their tribe but also the end of humanity? The oppressed and neglected "rez," the product of colonial oppression, has now become, ironically, a *terre d'asile* for the newly oppressed victims of the white zombies.

Blood Quantum transforms the blood quantum, a classic divide-and-conquer mechanism, into an aesthetic and narrative resource, for in this case that usual racial quantification operates in reverse, rendering indigenous peoples immune to various forms of zombification. An allegorical reading through a political grid might point to oppressed peoples being immune to ideological zombification by the pale-faced zombies. That the zombies eat brains also suggests an allegory about assimilationist brain-washing, a metaphor for the eternal return of colonial dispossession. We are reminded of the eugenic movement lurking in the forest shadows of Jordan Peele's *Get Out*. Like that film, *Blood Quantum* is "infectious," infecting the audience, including the white audience, with a fear of white people, a boomerang against all the films that made white people afraid of Blacks and Indians. In a historical reversal, this time "blood" works for the native.

Barnaby's chameleonic style goes from action-movie brutality to efficient dramatic realism to animated fable, largely told in a neo-expressionist style reminiscent of directors like fellow Canadians George Romero and David Cronenberg, along with Guillermo del Toro, Jordan Peele, and French "extreme horror" films. Barnaby's choice of the horror genre authorizes virtuoso flights of fancy and imagination in a morbid kind of "magical realism." What distinguishes the film from the standard slash-and-splash gore film is its serious social and historical preoccupations. The film is rich in historical inversions: the reservation, in the public imagination often seen as a kind of degraded non-place, as the remainder of severe land loss, becomes an object of desire. The irony recalls that of federal policy removing native peoples to land deemed worthless, only to discover that the land harbored precious minerals—some version of an "unobtanium"-like mineral—coveted by the same people who had generated the exile.

Departing from the positive image model, Barnaby deploys media jiujitsu by exploiting the popularity of splatter cinema—and the arch stylization of violence recalls Tarantino's (faux-Fanonian) *Django*—to create a conversation about settler colonialism. A spray-painted sign reads: "If they're red, they're dead, and if they're white, they bite." A mention of infected blankets, meanwhile, makes transparent allusion to the historical smallpox infections of indigenous people. The allegorically named "Lysol" character incarnates generations of historically repressed rage, embodying the dilemmas of those who have to restrain their anger in order not to be destroyed by it. As Barnaby puts it, "[The postcolonial Indian like Lysol] is going to be angry and self-destructive, and the worst thing about it is, he's going to be righteous in the sense that he knows he's right. So anything he feels like he does afterward is justified, including destroying himself or anybody else around them. And that's Lysol. There you have your postcolonial Indian."[105] Needless to say, the story of immunization takes on new relevance with the emergence of the Covid-19 virus, where biological horror has become the worldwide "new normal," turning all of us into potentially infected and infecting zombies. Since Barnaby had conceived the idea of the film years before the Covid pandemic, he was inadvertently taking on the traditional shamanic role of prophecy. Indigenous thinkers and shamans, after all, have been prophesying catastrophe for centuries. One scene shows the natives building barricades to keep the zombies out, much as the present-day Navajo and the Oglala Sioux in North America, and the Kraho in Brazil have been obliged to set up checkpoints to keep outsiders away for the group's own self-protection.

Despite its polished sheen of sensational entertainment, the Barnaby film is very much in tune with intersectional theory and some of the native writers mentioned in this text. Kester Dyer argues that "*Blood Quantum*, underscores longstanding Indigenous viewpoints which anticipate the tensions magnified by this crisis ... [and] partly through intertextual allusions to earlier anti-racist horror cinema, highlights the convergence of Indigenous responses to colonialism with interventions that oppose anti-Black racism."[106] *Blood Quantum*'s implied alignment with other non-white victims of colonialism is a move consistent with Leanne Betasamosake Simpson's call for indigenous activists to form "constellations of co-resistance with other movements," especially radical communities of color.[107] Dyer sees an affinity between the deeper logic of *Blood Quantum* and Glen Coulthard's concept of "grounded normativity," which emphasizes connections between land, knowledge, and ethical relationships. For Coulthard, indigenous struggles are "not only *for* land in a material sense, but also deeply *informed* by what the land *as a system of reciprocal relations and obligations* can teach us about living our lives in relation to one another and the natural world in non-dominating and non-exploitative terms."[108]

The film is almost too painfully a propos of a present when so many spectators have themselves been in lockdown, imbibing acid snippets of news from miniaturized filmlets on their laptops and smart phones. Barnaby's films proliferate in instances of poetic justice in the form of filmic redress of minority victimization. With indigenous people long hemmed in and cut off from humanity in general, now non-indigenous humanity is eager to stay on the reservation. As we see in the contemporary United States, the literal pandemic goes hand in hand with a political pandemic of viral mendacity. For Barnaby, "Capitalists are asking people to die for the dollar the same way the colonists expected natives to do the same thing. Hey, welcome to the club everybody."[109] Within a system of historical reversals, non-native people experience what native peoples have been experiencing for a long time. Up until the 1980s, native people needed written permission to leave the reservations. In 2020 almost everyone was under a quarantine, and many employees need to have an app that proves their sanitary innocence. Now non-indigenous people have an inkling of what it means to be penned in to a reserve, even if opened into our apartments.

With climate change and the pandemic, everyone has come to be threatened with the indigenous situation of marginalization and bio-terror, while some still remain privileged by staying in the digital realm. As Deborah Danowski and Eduardo Viveiros de Castro put it: "In the case of the Anthropocene, the countries which most contributed to global warming are the same countries which now enjoy greater security, even if only temporarily, due to their greater capacity to mitigate the disastrous economic effects of climate change on their own territories."[110] The angry hounds of the apocalypse already lived by indigenous people are now snarling at the doorstep of rich white people, as capitalist globalization nibbles on the derriere of the privileged. In this sense, indigenous people have always been the canaries in the mineshaft, those who have proleptically lived disasters that others were destined to live later, such as apocalyptic ruptures in cultural continuity, shortage of food for the planet and the like, figured through situations often prefigured in horror and disaster films. So many indigenous shamanic prophecies have come true—the arrival of people from elsewhere, apocalyptic climate change, and the like. At the same time, another, more hopeful, indigenous prophecy is also coming true, a prophecy of indigenous unity across the Americas, metaphorized by the friendly avian encounter of the Eagle of the North with the Condor of the South.

Notes

1 Jodi Byrd, op. cit., p. 11.
2 See Richard Slotkin, *Regeneration through Violence: The Mythology of the American Frontier* (Durham: Duke University Press, 1973).
3 Jodi A. Byrd, *The Transit of Empire: Indigenous Critique on Colonialism* (Minneapolis: University of Minnesota, 2011), p. xx.
4 Ibid.

5   Patricia Limerick, *The Legacy of Conquest: The Unbroken Past of the American West* (New York: Norton, 1987), p. 55.
6   Joanna Hearne, *Native Recognition: Indigenous Cinema and the Western* (Albany: State University of New York Press, 2012), p. 203.
7   See Annette Kolodny, *The Lay of the Land: Metaphor as Experience and History in American Life and Letters* (Chapel Hill: University of North Carolina Press, 1975).
8   In a pro-indigenous documentary entitled *To Protect Mother Earth* (1987), Native American women repeatedly lament what they call "the rape of Mother Earth."
9   Henry Knox in a letter to George Washington, July 7, 1789. U.S. National Archives and Records Administration, Washington, DC: RG 46, First Congress, President's Messages.
10 Quoted in Noam Chomsky, *Year 501: The Conquest Continues* (Boston: South End Press, 1993), p. 232.
11 On Indian names, see Jack Weatherford, *Native Roots: How the Indians Enriched America* (New York: Ballantine, 1991). On Native American names in New York City, see Robert Steven Gromet, *Native American Place Names in New York City* (New York: Museum of the City of New York, 1981).
12 See Chadwick Allen, *Blood Narrative: Indigenous Identity in American Indian and Maori Literary and Activist Texts* (Durham: Duke University Press, 2000).
13 See Renato Rosaldo, "Imperialist Nostalgia," *Representations*, No. 26, Special Issue: Memory and Counter-Memory (Spring, 1989), pp. 107–22.
14 Passage from Henry Blackman Sell and Victor Weybright's *Buffalo Bill and the Wild West*, cited in Friar and Friar, op. cit., p. 74.
15 Felix S. Cohen, "Americanizing the White Man," *The American Scholar*, Vol. 21, No. 2 (Spring 1952), p. 180.
16 Thomas Morton, *New English Canaan* (Stoneham, MA: Digital Scanning, 2000). First published in Amsterdam, in 1637.
17 James Tully, *Strange Multiplicity: Constitutionalism in an Age of Diversity* (Cambridge: Cambridge University Press, 1995), p. 76.
18 See Stephen Greenblatt, *Marvelous Possessions* (Chicago: University of Chicago Press, 1991), p. 141.
19 Vine Deloria Jr., *Red Earth: White Lies* (Golden Colorado: Fulcrum, 1997), p. 1.
20 Philip J. Deloria, *Playing Indian* (New Haven and London: Yale University Press, 1998).
21 Ibid., p. 2.
22 Ibid., p. 42.
23 Ibid., p. 146.
24 Philip J. Deloria, op. cit., p. 162.
25 See S. M. Huhndorf, *Going Native: Indians in the American Cultural Imagination* (Ithaca and London: Cornell University Press, 2001), p. 14.
26 Huhndorf, op. cit., p. 3.
27 Slavoj Žižek, "Avatar: Return of the Natives," *New Statesman* (March 4, 2010). Accessed November 23, 2020, https://www.newstatesman.com/film/2010/03/avatar-reality-love-couple-sex
28 M. Elise Marubbio, "Decolonizing the Western: A Revisionist Analysis of *Avatar* with a Twist," in M. Paryz, J. R. Leo, eds., *The Post-2000 Film Western* (London: Palgrave Macmillan, 2015).
29 Ibid., p. 167.

30 Ivana Bentes, "Eu vejo você: antropologia reversa em *Avatar*, ciber-índios, pós-cinema ou como arrancar um pensamento complexo dos clichés," Erick Felinto and Ivana Bentes, eds., *Avatar: o futuro do cinema e a ecologia das imagens digitais* (Porto Alegre: Sulina, 2010), p. 73.
31 Lévi-Strauss, *La Pensée sauvage* (Paris: Librairie Plon, 1962).
32 Aristóteles Barcelos Neto, Danilo Ramos, Maíra Santi Buhler, Renato Sztutman, Stelia Marras, Valeria Macedo, "Abaeté, rede de antropologia simétrica: entrevista com Marcio Goldman e Eduardo Viveiros de Castro," *Cadernos de Campo*, Vol. 15, No. 14–15 (2006), p. 177.
33 Eduardo Viveiros de Castro, "Os pronomes cosmológicos e o perspectivismo ameríndio," *Mana*, Vol. 2, No. 2 (1996), p. 115.
34 Curator Glenn Shephard pointed to these criticisms in his informal remarks at the "Image, Memory, and Museums in the Amazon" Conference held April 14–15, 2022 under the aegis of the Amazon Lab at Duke University, organized by Gustavo Furtado.
35 Kirsten Acuna, "James Cameron Swears He Didn't Rip Off the Idea for 'Avatar,'" *Business Insider* (April 28, 2010). Accessed December 27, 2020, http://www.businessinsider.com/james-camerons-45-page-declaration-proving-avatar-was-his-idea-2012-12?page=1
36 For one of an infinity of examples of very legitimate critiques, see M. Elise Marubbio op. cit.
37 "Evo Morales Praises Avatar," *Huffington Post* (January 12, 2010).
38 See Ella Shohat and Robert Stam, *Unthinking Eurocentrism* (London: Routledge: 1994), p. 31.
39 Henry Jenkins, "Avatar Activism: Pick Your Protest," *The Globe and Mail* (September 18, 2010). Accessed November 23, 2020, https://www.theglobeandmail.com/opinion/avatar-activism-pick-your-protest/article4190179/
40 See Emma Mitchell, "Seeing Blue: Negotiating the Politics of Avatar Media Activism," originally a thesis submitted in partial fulfillment of the requirement for an Honors degree in the Department of Gender and Cultural Studies, University of Sydney, October 2011. Accessed from https://core.ac.uk/download/pdf/41235981.pdf.

See also Matt Wade, "Indian Hill Tribe Scores 'Avatar' Victory," *The Sydney Morning Herald* (August 28, 2010). Accessed November 23, 2020, https://www.smh.com.au/environment/conservation/indian-hill-tribe-scores-avatar-victory-20100827-13vym.html.
41 Jessica Lee, "'Avatar' Activism: James Cameron Joins Indigenous Struggles Worldwide," *The Indypendent* (April 26, 2010). Accessed November 23, 2020, https://indypendent.org/2010/04/avatar-activism-james-cameron-joins-indigenous-struggles-worldwide/#:~:text="AVATAR"%20ACTIVISM%3A%20James%20Cameron%20Joins%20Indigenous%20Struggles%20Worldwide,-Jessica%20Lee%20Apr&text=While%20he%20said%20that%20he,helping%20illuminate%20these%20struggles%20worldwide.
42 Kelly J. Madison, "Legitimation, Crisis and Containment: The 'Anti-racist-white-hero' Film," *Critical Studies in Mass Communication*, Vol. 16, No. 4 (1999), pp. 399–416.
43 See Emma Mitchell, op. cit.
44 Giorgio Mariani, "The Red and the Black: Images of American Indians in the Italian Political Landscape," *Studia Anglica Posnaniensia*, Vol. 53, No. S1 (December 2018), pp. 327–45, DOI: 10.2478/stap-2018-0016.

45 Giorgio Mariani, "Was Anybody More of an Indian than Karl Marx?: The 'Indiani Metropolitani' and the 1977 Movement" in Christian F. Feest, ed., op. cit., pp. 585–98.
46 Some have even argued that the ancient Germans had been the symbolic "Indians" of the Romans. See Christian F. Feest, ed., *Indians and Europe: An Interdisciplinary Collection of Essays* (Lincoln and London: University of Nebraska Press), p. 612.
47 In Franz Kafka, "The Wish to Be a Red Indian," in *Betrachtung* (Leipzig: Rowohlt, 1913).
48 Daniel Defoe, *Robinson Crusoe* (London & Cambridge: Macmillan & Co., 1866), p. 208.
49 Cited in Susanne Zantof, "Close Encounters: Deutsche and Indianer," in Colin G. Calloway et al., eds., *Germans and Indians: Fantasies, Encounters, Projections* (Lincoln: University of Nebaskra Press, 2000), p. 1.
50 For an excellent study of gender politics in films about Indians see Elizabeth Bird, "Gendered Construction of the American Indian in Popular Media," *Journal of Communication*, Vol. 49, No. 3 (September 1999).
51 Quoted in Christopher Frayling, *Spaghetti Westerns: Cowboys and Europeans from Karl May to Sergio Leone (Revised paperback edition)* (London and New York: I.B. Tauris, 2006).
52 Cited in Feest, op. cit., p. 459.
53 Information drawn from the VTape publication about the Conference/Festival.
54 In *Playing Indian*, Philip J. Deloria stipulates two types of Hobbyism: "people Hobbyism" and "item Hobbyism." See Philip J. Deloria, op. cit. Indian item hobbyism goes back to Montaigne who collected Tupinamba memorabilia. Some "item hobbyists" in other countries occupy the upper strata of the cultural and political sphere; French president Jacques Chirac, for example, was the proud collector of "primitive" indigenous artifacts. See Sally Price, *Paris Primitive: Jacques Chirac's Museum on the Quai Branly* (Chicago: University of Chicago Press, 2007).
55 See Hartmut Lutz, "German Indianthusiasm: A Socially Constructed German National(ist) Myth," in Calloway et al., op. cit., p. 167.
56 H. Glenn Penny, *Kindred by Choice* (Durham: The University of North Carolina Press, 2013).
57 See Adam Gilders, "Ich Bin Ein Indianer: Germany's Obsession with a Past It Never Had," *The Walrus* (October 12, 2003). Accessed December 27, 2020, https://thewalrus.ca/ich-bin-ein-indianer/.
58 See Renae Watchman et al., op. cit., p. 25.
59 Spiderwoman Theater, "Winnetou's Snake Oil Show from Wigwam City," *Hemispheric Institute Digital Video Library* (1999). Accessed December 27, 2020, http://hdl.handle.net/2333.1/q2bvq8dh.
60 *Declaration of War against Exploiters of Lakota Spirituality*, June 10, 1993.
61 Ibid.
62 For more on Karl May and the Hobbyiata, see Jace Weaver, *The Red Atlantic* and Philip J. Deloria, *Playing Indian*.
63 See Philip J. Deloria, op. cit.
64 Ibid., p. 135.
65 Ibid., p. 146.
66 See Rivka Galchen, "Wild West Germany: Why Do Cowboys and Indians So Captivate the Country?" *The New Yorker* (2012). Accessed December 27, 2020, https://www.newyorker.com/magazine/2012/04/09/wild-west-germany.
67 Ella Shohat and I expand on this point in *Unthinking Eurocentrism*, op. cit.

68 See Peter Limbrick, "The Australian Western, or a Settler Colonial Cinema Par Excellence," *Cinema Journal*, Vol. 46, No. 4 (Summer, 2007), pp. 68–95. Accessed December 27, 2020, https://www.jstor.org/stable/30137720
69 Ibid., p. 69.
70 See Ella Shohat, *Israeli Cinema: East/West, and the Politics of Representation* (Austin: University of Texas Press, first published in 1989 and reprinted with a new Afterword in 2010).
71 See R. F. Berkhofer, *The White Man's Indian* (New York: Vintage Books, 1979).
72 R. A. Billington, *Land of Savagery, Land of Promise* (Norman: University of Oklahoma Press, 1981), p. 110.
73 Vine Deloria Jr., *Custer Died for Your Sins: An Indian Manifesto* (Norman: University of Oklahoma Press, 1988), p. 146.
74 Mikhail Bakhtin, *Rabelais and His World* (Bloomington, IN: Indiana University Press, 1984).
75 Cited in Dustin Tahmahkera, *Tribal Television: Viewing Native People in Sitcoms* (Chapel Hill: University of North Carolina Press, 2014), p. 14.
76 Ibid., p. 147.
77 Ibid., p. 148.
78 On a personal note, Jacob studied at NYU with me and Faye Ginsburg and was kind to thank us in the credits.
79 Cited in Dustin Tahmahkera, op. cit., p. 182, Note 82.
80 On the career of Charlie Hill and other native comics, see Kliph Besteroof, *We Had a Little Real Estate Problem: The Unheralded Story of Native Americans & Comedy* (New York: Simon & Shuster, 2021).
81 Cited in Dale Turner, op. cit., p. 71.
82 Ella Shohat and I explore this question in depth in *Unthinking Eurocentrism*.
83 Vine Deloria Jr., *Custer Died for Your Sins: An Indian Manifesto* (Norman: University of Oklahoma Press, 1988), p. 148.
84 See http://www.1491s.com/
85 See Emma LaRocke, *When the Other Is Me: Native Resistance Discourse, 1850–1990* (Winnipeg, MB: University of Manitoba Press, 2010), p. 154.
86 Through a happy coincidence, the 1636 edition of Morton's book *The New Canaan* was published in Amsterdam by Jacob Stam, which happens to be the name of my father.
87 Dakshana Bascaramurty, "The Modern Touch of an Old Master," *The Globe and the Mail* (December 1, 2017). Accessed December 29, 2020, https://www.theglobeandmail.com/arts/inside-the-process-behind-kent-monkmans-art/article37126241/
88 Source for lyrics, "Decolonize Lyrics," *Lyrics on Demand*. Accessed from https://www.lyricsondemand.com/a/aztlanundergroundlyrics/decolonizelyrics.html
89 See David Wallace Adams, *Education for Extinction: American Indians and the Boarding School Experience, 1875–1928* (Lawrence: University Press of Kansas, 1997).
90 Michelle H. Raheja, op. cit., p. 238.
91 Quoted in Amy Lonetree, *Decolonizing Museums: Representing Native America in National and Tribal Museums* (Chapel Hill: University of North Carolina Press, 2012), p. 5.
92 From the show's press release as cited in Sabrina Furminger, "Fierce Girls Web Series Empowers Indigenous Girls," *Vancouver Is Awesome*, published June 12, 2018. Accessed from https://www.vancouverisawesome.com/courier-archive/general-archive/fierce-girls-web-series-empowers-indigenous-girls-3077317

93 The title "First Nations, First Features" is taken from the title of a 2005 indigenous film festival at the Museum of Modern Art in New York. To my knowledge, my friend Faye Ginsburg came up with the title.
94 See Daniel Coleman, "Canadian White Civility and the Two Row Wampum of the Six Nations," in Aloys N. M. Fleischmann et al., eds., *Narratives of Citizenship: Indigenous and Diasporic Peoples Unsettle the Nation State* (Edmonton: University of Alberta Press, 2011), p. 186.
95 Ibid.
96 Ibid., p. 187.
97 See Penelope Myrtle Helsey, *Reading the Wampum: Essays on Hodinöhsö: ni'Visual Code and Epistemological Recovery* (Syracuse: Syracuse University Press, 2014), pp. xix–xx.
98 Quoted in Graeber and Wengrow, op. cit., p. 38.
99 See Susan Dunne, "Film Director Crystallizes Mi'gMaq Perspective," in the *Hartford Courant* (October 24, 2010). Accessed December 29, 2020, https://www.courant.com/hc-xpm-2010-10-24-hc-jeff-barnaby-1024-20101024-story.html
100 Jeff Barnaby, "Director's Statement," *Press Kit* (Montreal: Prospector Films, 2013).
101 Interview with Jamaias DaCosta, "Interview with Filmmaker Jeff Barnaby on Rhymes for Young Ghouls," *Muskrat Magazine* (February 1, 2014). Accessed December 29, 2020, http://muskratmagazine.com/interview-with-filmmaker-jeff-barnaby-on-rhymes-for-young-ghouls/
102 See Michelle H. Raheja, op. cit., pp. 153–5.
103 Gerald Vizenor in Gerald Vizenor and Jill Doerfler, *The White Earth Nation* (Lincoln: University of Nebraska Press, 2012), p. 43.
104 On June 11 and 20, 1981, the Quebec Provincial Police (QPP) raided Restigouche Reserve, Quebec. At issue were the salmon-fishing rights of the Mi'kmaq. Because salmon has traditionally been a source of food and income for the Mi'kmaq, the Quebec government's decision to restrict fishing aroused consternation and anger. Released in 1984, *Incident at Restigouche*, a groundbreaking and impassioned account of the police raids, brought Alanis Obomsawin to international attention. Decades later, Jeff Barnaby cited her film as an inspiration.
105 See Jordan Crucchiola, "Jeff Barnaby Made an Apocalypse Movie to Watch the System Fall. Then a Pandemic Hit," *The Vulture* (May 6, 2020). Accessed December 29, 2020, https://www.vulture.com/2020/05/jeff-barnaby-is-worried-white-people-wont-get-blood-quantum.html.
106 As I was writing a late draft of this text, I happened to come across Kester Dyer's excellent essay on *Blood Quantum*, "Anticipating the Colonial Apocalypse: Jeff Barnaby's *Blood Quantum*." I realized that we were very much of like mind about the film. I cite him here and heartily recommend his essay. https://pandemicmedia.meson.press/chapters/activism-sociability/anticipating-the-colonial-apocalypse-jeff-barnabys-blood-quantum/
107 See Leanne Betasamosake Simpson, op. cit.
108 See Glen Sean Coulthard, *Red Skin, White Masks: Rejecting the Colonial Politics of Recognition* (Minneapolis: University of Minnesota Press, 2014).
109 "Interview: Jeff Barnaby Talks Blood Quantum," *Scream Horror Mag* (May 12, 2020). Accessed December 29, 2020, https://www.screamhorrormag.com/interview-jeff-barnaby-talks-blood-quantum/
110 Deborah Danowski and Eduardo Viveiros de Castro, *Ha Mundo por Vir? Ensaio sobre os Medos e os Fins* (Is there a World to Come? Essay on Fears and Ends) (São Paulo and Florianopolis, Cultura e Barbarie and ISA, 2017), p. 16.

4

Cross-national Comparabilities

The Indigenization of Brazilian Media

The most obvious comparison of national representations of the "Indian" involves the only continent-size multiracial countries of the Americas—Brazil and the United States—two countries where indigenous people have a history and a presence that goes far beyond demographic statistics.¹ Literally hundreds of books and essays in English and Portuguese have addressed the salient comparabilities between Brazil and the United States.² The sheer volume of this corpus, which swells with every passing year, is itself remarkable. The comparisons are asymmetrical and power laden, of course, since Brazilians have historically made the comparisons from a position of relative geopolitical weakness, while North Americans have made them from a privileged position of taken-for-granted hegemony. Brazil-US comparisons also take place against the larger ideological frame of the widely disseminated Hegelian and Weberian tendentious comparisons of South America and North America. In *The Philosophy of History*, Hegel not only derided the indigenous peoples but also Eurocentrized the North/South comparison by contrasting a prosperous, orderly, unified, and successful Protestant North America with a militarized, disorderly, and disunited Catholic South America.³

Although countless studies have treated such cross-national topics as comparative colonization, comparative political institutions, slavery, discrimination, literary culture, mass media, and so forth, very few studies have addressed comparative indigeneity, comparative genocide, comparative indigenous struggles, comparative image studies, and so forth. Yet Brazil is the country that has the most in common with the United States—and more broadly North America—in terms of the historical indigenous presence, the frequency of artistic thematizations of the indigenous theme, and the symbolic/allegorical and even political-discursive role of the figure of the Indian. The projections cast on the relatively small indigenous population—small because of genocide—in both Brazil and the United States have profoundly shaped the ways each country has come to imagine itself as uniquely American or as uniquely Brazilian. Despite constituting less than 1 percent of the population, the Indian has been at the center of debates about Brazilian identity. As Tracy Devine Guzman puts it, "popular notions of Indianness and Brazilianness continue to feed off one another in 'anthopophagous' symbiosis."⁴

In the case of Brazilian thinkers—from Gilberto Freyre and Sérgio Buarque de Holanda to Vianna Moog and Roberto DaMatta—comparisons between Brazil and the United States have sometimes come close to the very heart of debates about *Brazilian* identity, at times forming an integral part of a specular process of national self-definition. Sociologist Jessé Souza discerns a stubborn pride behind the obsessive comparisons: "Explicit or implicit comparison with the United States is the central thread in practically all of the 20th-century interpretations of Brazilian singularity—because we perceive that only the United States is as great and influential as we are in the Americas."[5] As Caetano Veloso put it, "Brazil is the other giant of the Americas, the other melting pot of races and cultures, the other paradise promised to European and Asian immigrants, the other. The double, the shadow, the negative of the great adventure of the New World."[6] Within the fraught dialectics of attraction and repulsion, even strong and reiterated statements of difference—"we are not at all like you!"—are still addressed to a privileged interlocutor. For many Brazilian intellectuals (and for many American Brazilianists), then, the inevitable historical comparison has not been with the mother country Portugal or with an admired cultural mentor country such as France or even with a Spanish-speaking neighbor such as Argentina but rather with the United States. Because of the predominance of this Americano-centric model, some have called either for South-South comparisons or have questioned the Eurocentric premises of the comparative paradigm itself.

The histories of Brazil and the United States run on parallel tracks. Prior to Conquest, both countries were inhabited by many millions of indigenous peoples, in Brazil, Tupí, Bororo, Nambiquara, and so forth, and in the United States, Cree, Mohawk, Seminole, Dene, and so forth. In a primordial act of racialization, 1492 and the Conquest reconfigured and homogenized an extremely variegated ensemble as "Indians." Neither territory hosted the grand empires like the Mayan, the Aztec, and the Inca, characterized by monumental cultural artifacts. Both nations conducted an implacable ethnocide of indigenous peoples—reduced from an estimated 7 million in Brazil in 1500 to almost a million in the present, and in the United States from many millions before the Conquest to about 3 to 5 million, depending on the degree of inclusion of people of mixed ancestry. The histories of both countries feature endless massacres of Indians. Mem de Sá, governor general of the Portuguese colony of Brazil from 1557 to 1572, who defeated the French of France Antartique, littered a beach with their supposed allies the Tupiniquim in 1559, seventy-eight years before the Pequot (Mystic) massacre on May 26, 1637, which left 700 dead, including women and children. In both countries, religious leaders sanctified the massacres of indigenous people seen as "pagans" and "wild beasts."[7] The priest José de Anchieta, around the time of the Mem de Sá operation, speaks of sending massacred Indians to Hell and of "sixty villages burned down, a thousand houses ruined by the devouring flames, fields and their wealth devastated."[7] The Jesuit Priest João Daniel cites another critical priest, Padre Vieira, to the effect that the Portuguese had violently put to death more than "two million Indians, not counting those that they killed secretly."[8]

Nothing signals the era of pre-Columbian indigenous sovereignty more powerfully than the manifest pronominal agency of first peoples everywhere in the Americas, as those who had already named and mapped the continent and described it through language long before Columbus. At the time of contact, according to scholars such as Aryon Rodrigues, over a thousand indigenous languages were spoken in what is now the United States, of which only 15 percent have survived.[9] According to Jack Weatherford, English contains 2,200 words taken from native languages.[10] In North America, settlers came to speak of "wigwams" (Algonquin) and "tepees" (Dakota). Europeans used native names to term "surprising" animals such as "moose," "caribou," "racoon," and "skunk." In Brazil, "tapir" and "jaguar" came from Tupi. Native names designate Brazilian and US American states (Ceara, Piaui, in Brazil; Massachusetts, Idaho, in the United States), cities (Curitiba in Brazil; Chicago in the United States), rivers (Tiete and Orinoco in Brazil; the Mississippi, Wabash, Potomac in the United States), and lakes (Ontario, Michigan, Huron). The presence of indigenous names, on both continents, are reminders (and remainders) of the massive presence and sovereignty of millions of indigenous people in both territories at the time of invasion. (A striking sequence in Raoul Peck's *Exterminate all the Brutes* shows a map of the United States, at first crowded with indigenous names, then slowly "washed" away in blood and replaced by European names.)

In both Brazil and the United States, early religious figures learned Indian languages in order to proselytize. Just as John Eliot translated the Bible into native tongues, Father José Anchieta in Brazil devised a Tupí grammar. Some of the American Founding Fathers such as Jefferson studied Native American languages, and words such as "caucus" (from Algonquin) came to enrich the English political vocabulary. In Brazil, the Tupí-Guaraní language was even more deeply woven into the fabric of ordinary social life. As the language of communication between the Portuguese and the indigenous peoples, Tupí, colloquially called "*nheengatu*," formed the lingua franca up through the eighteenth century, including among non-Tupí Indians and among non-Indians.[11] Tupí was proposed as the country's official language in the 1824 Constituent Assembly. The Emperor Pedro II learned Tupí, and in the twentieth century, the titular character of a famous Brazilian novel by black writer Lima Barreto, *The Sad End of Policarpo Quaresma* (1911), argued passionately for restoring Tupí-Guaraní as the official language of Brazil. A decade later, the Brazilian modernists lauded the riches of the Tupí language. Today, Tupí is currently undergoing a revival to the extent of producing sophisticated rap music in Tupí or Guaraní.

The look through the comparative mirror is often marred by narcissistic provinciality and the fetishization of minor differences. The dominant group in both the United States and Brazil justified indigenous dispossession through Discovery and Conquest Doctrine, in both cases with a Christian Benediction, but one with a Catholic, the other with a Protestant, accent and inflection. By framing the Tordesillas Treaty in 1494, the Pope and the Spanish Monarchy gave to the Spanish and the Portuguese what was not theirs to give—the South American continent. In what amounts to a US-Americanization of the Conquest and Discovery Doctrine, the Euro-descended dominant strata that founded the United States, meanwhile, expanded into the continental space, later declaring the conquest the country's "manifest destiny," sometimes rooted in the putative racial superiority of the "Anglo-Saxons." Like other *herrenvolk* (master-race) discourses, Anglo-Saxonism fueled exterminationist attitudes toward the indigenous peoples who "happened" to live where the dominating group had territorial, military, and commercial ambitions. Indeed, anti-colonial writers like Patrick Wolfe have argued that genocide is always a temptation for settler-colonial states, which are inherently "eliminatory but not invariably genocidal."[12]

Both countries "began" their official histories as European colonies, one of Portugal, the other of Great Britain. In the United States, the occupiers were called soldiers, pilgrims, pioneers, settlers, and later immigrants; in Brazil they were called *soldados, bandeirantes,* and *mamelucos* and later immigrants. Both butted up against the territorial claims of other European nations, namely the Spanish, the French, and the Dutch, who ruled for a time both in Brazil and in what became the United States, before being defeated by the Portuguese, in the first case, and by the British in the second. The conquest of the US American West, meanwhile, did not first take place on an East/West Axis, but rather on a South/North axis, as the Spanish conquistadores moved north-by-northwest from the Caribbean into Florida and from Mexico into Texas and California. The Spanish were firmly implanted in what was later seen as the American "West" at a time when English and Dutch and French settlers were only beginning to build cities like Boston, Philadelphia, New Amsterdam (New York), Montreal, and Quebec. The Spanish established a Jesuit mission in Chesapeake Bay thirty-seven years before Jamestown. The Spanish were the first to reach the Appalachians, the Mississippi, the Grand Canyon, the Great Plains, and even Alaska, whence the absurdity of "English Only" protests in states with Spanish names like Florida and California and cities like Los Angeles, San Francisco, and Santa Barbara. The United States created "Chicanos" by conquering half of Mexico, and yet Mexicans are treated by the media as "recent" immigrants. As the Mexican-Americans put it: "We didn't cross the border; the border crossed us."

Brazilian and US American cinemas have represented and refracted diverse yet comparable historical realities, exhibiting variant forms of indigenous dispossession. In the case of some issues such as race, a long tradition of comparison has itself shaped national self-understanding on both sides. The concern with comparison is absolutely asymmetrical, however; Brazilians, both intellectuals and ordinary citizens, are very aware of the comparison, while in the United States only intellectuals and specialists are aware of it. Similar historical elements exist in both countries, but with reshuffled cards. Brazil became thoroughly mixed in terms of indigenous peoples, enslaved Africans, and white Europeans early in its history and to a greater degree than in the United States. The United States is also miscegenated with a very high proportion of the population not only mixed but multiply mixed, first across indigenous nations and then with Africans and Europeans of all shades. Many American celebrities, such as Johnny Cash, Robbie Robertson, Cher, Angelina Jolie, Rosario Dawson, Jessica Biel, and Jimi Hendrix, claim partial indigenous ancestry, along with native writers like Thomas King, who is Greek, German, and Cherokee. In the case of the Metis, the name itself signals the mixing of indigenous and European (Scottish and French). John Rolfe and Pocahontas had a son, Thomas Rolfe, but his birth, and the fact of widespread mixing in the United States, never generated a mythology of mixing as in Brazil. The official discourse, until recently, tended not to acknowledge the broad, mixed spectrum of appearances and histories. Brazil, on the other hand, despite a countervailing "ideology of whitening," became proud over time of its essentially mixed character, resulting in a kind of Mestizo essentialism and the common claim "that we Brazilians are all mixed." The real difference has been less factual than discursive—the grid through which the difference has been seen, the lessons drawn from it.

Unlike the United States, Brazil did not make treaties with the indigenous people and then violate them, since it was assumed by officialdom that all the land "belonged" to the Portuguese already. Unlike the United States, Brazil did not leave a trail of broken treaties, because the historical process did not involve treaties. Instead, the trail of betrayal consisted of constantly changing settler-dictated laws, often just pious wishes whose idealizations did not correspond to the violent facts "on the ground." Both Brazil and the United States infantilized indigenous people. For most of Brazilian history, indigenous peoples were forced into a regime of tutelage and "protection" assigned the status of children. In the United States, similarly, indigenous peoples were declared "wards of the state" and "dependent domestic nations." In Brazil, indigenous people living more or less autonomously were not allowed to act in films until 1988, when a progressive new Constitution made it possible for indigenous filmmakers to travel with passports and meet other indigenous filmmakers at film festivals in Europe and North America. In the United States, official policy revolved around "blood quantum" as a criterion for status as "Indian." In Brazil, while millions of Brazilians had partial indigenous ancestry, there was no legal question of "blood quantum"; instead, there was a wide spectrum of terms registering nuances in appearance and ancestry ("*mameluco*" for white indigenous mixture, "*caboclo*" for Black and Indian, "*mestizo*" for mixed ancestry of any form, and so forth).

While indigenous peoples in Brazil, like those in the United States and Canada, form a relatively small demographic minority, institutions and businesses in both nations brand themselves with indigenous names, or that contemporary Brazilian slang uses "Tupiniquim" as a synonym for "Brazilian." Perhaps as a sign of Brazilian ambivalence, one early TV network was called "Tupi" in homage to the first native people encountered, while another was named "Bandeirantes," in homage to the explorers/conquerors who killed and dispossessed the same indigenous people. While Brazilian TV began with an indigenous name, American TV began with an often unnoticed Indian symbol—the commonly used 1938 Indian Test Pattern featuring a flamboyantly feathered chief. As signs of both homage and appropriation, the words "Tupi" and "Tupinquim" have become synecdoches for Brazil itself, the given names of many products and even of oil reserves off the coast of Rio de Janeiro.

The occupation of the two countries took distinct forms. In the initial period, the Portuguese exploited an abundant supply of subjugated labor in the form of two peoples both defined as "blacks," at first indigenous (called "negros da Terra," Blacks from the Land) and later Africans (called "negros de Guinee"). In Brazil, the official end of indigenous enslavement came only in 1758. In North America too, native peoples were sometimes enslaved both by the English and the French. The Pawnee became known as the "Negros of America."[13] The "Database of Indigenous Slavery in the Americas (DISA)" documents the many instances of indigenous enslavement in the Americas between 1492 and 1900 (and beyond, where relevant). Scholars now estimate that between 2.5 and 5 million natives were enslaved in the Americas between 1492 and the late nineteenth century.[14]

Centennial Commemorations and First Contact Films

For many Native Americans, celebrating Columbus and the "Discovery" is the equivalent of asking Jews to celebrate Hitler or Goebbels.[15] Not only did Columbus inaugurate the transatlantic slave trade (in reverse) by taking six shackled Taínos back to Spain on his second voyage, but his brief rule over "Hispianola" accounted for the deaths of thousands of people. Although Columbus's early diaries describe the natives as "the best people in the world and the most peaceable" (December 16, 1492) and as "gentle and ignorant of evil ... [not knowing] even how to kill one another" (November 12, 1492), yet Columbus nonetheless proceeded to enslave and dispossess these "peaceable" people. Columbus's split attitude toward the indigenous peoples made them simultaneously the best and the worst of humans, at once noble and savage. His radical dichotomizing of the Carib and the Arawak, of the fierce cannibal and noble savage, marks a perennial bifurcation within European perception of the indigene. "The old story of ferocious Caribs chasing timid Arawaks up the island chains from Venezuela, eating the men, possessing the women," as Peter Hulme and Neil Whitehead put it, "is endlessly repeated, even though fewer and fewer scholars accept it."[16]

In both Brazil and the United States, the Columbus/Cabral debates were played out in the realms of official and popular culture. For the official celebrations of the Columbus quincentennial of 1992, millions of US dollars were poured into spectacular events, climaxing in a grand international regatta of tall ships that sailed from Spain and arrived in New York Harbor for the Fourth of July. At the same time, widespread activism subverted the official celebration; Columbus "got mugged," as it were, on the way to his own *fiesta*. Countless demonstrations, conferences, pedagogical projects, media events, exhibitions, and publications forged a powerful counternarrative.[17] An anti-colonial narrative was also performed via the "view-from-the-shore" projects and through didactic films and videos whose titles clearly reveal their anti-colonial thrust: *Surviving Columbus* (1990), *Columbus on Trial* (1992), *The Columbus Invasion: Colonialism and the Indian Resistance* (1992), *1492 Revisited* (1993), *Columbus Didn't Discover Us* (1992), *Falsas Historias* (False Histories, 1992), and *Outros Quinhentos* (Another Five Hundred Years, 1993).

The quincentennial celebration in Brazil was also a colossal failure. Two years before the quincentennial, the Brazilian Council of Indian Peoples and Organizations (Capoib) sent a letter to Pope John Paul II denouncing the "triumphalist festivity" planned by the Brazilian government. Mauricio Guaraní, a member of the council, reminded the Pope that forty-two indigenous leaders had been assassinated during the previous year.[18] Six indigenous nations from Mato Grosso do Sul signed a "Letter Repudiating the 500 Years of the Discovery," reminding everyone that it was impossible to "discover" a territory where some 5 million people were already living. The reaction to the protests was harsh. Senator Antônio Carlos Magalhães, a powerful figure in the state of Bahia, symbolically expelled the natives from the Brazilian nation with an ontological denial of their existence, declaring, in a kind of rhetorical *gens nullius*, that "[w]hoever demonstrates against the celebration of the 500 years is obviously not Brazilian."[19] Later, an indigenous leader symbolically brandished an arrow and brushed it against Magalhaes' face.

The Brazilian government decided to celebrate the quincentennial with a ceremony at Porto Seguro (Safe Haven), the site where the Portuguese flotilla had first arrived on Easter 1500. A replica of the original *caravela* was to carry the Presidents of Brazil and Portugal, but the *caravela*'s engine failed and it had to be towed to its "porto Seguro." But for indigenous people there was nothing to celebrate; Cabral's arrival had led to the loss of their land and the shattering of their cultures. Three thousand indigenous protestors converged on Porto Seguro, some traveling thousands of miles. Monte Paschoal also happened to be the homeland of the Pataxó, the territory that they had lost and which they symbolically reoccupied in 1999. An Indian delegation presented a petition, a video, a book, and a CD to President Henrique Fernando Cardoso, explaining the horrific situation of indigenous peoples in Brazil. "Although we come without bitterness or anger," the petition elaborated, "we protest that Indian land is still threatened by development projects which do not take into consideration our thinking and our lives."[20] The protestors were met by hundreds of police firing tear gas and rubber bullets. But rather than denounce the police, some government officials denounced the protestors. The "leftist" Minister of Culture, Francisco Weffort, compared the protests to "someone invited to a wedding ceremony and then spitting on the floor of the ceremony," as if the protests were a violation of proper etiquette.[21]

Indigenous movements usually have an acute historical consciousness of Columbus, Cabral, and colonial conquest. The protest movement, within this logic, came to be called "Brasil: Outros 500," a Brazilian expression meaning "500 years; that's a whole other story." An early sign that the government would adopt a repressive stance came when 200 military police destroyed a monument bearing a plaque denouncing "the genocide of the Indian race," a plaque constructed by the Indians on the very Monte Paschoal site where Cabral had celebrated the famous "first mass."[22] The final declaration of the "Conference of the Indigenous Peoples and Organizations of Brazil," featuring the representatives of more than 140 indigenous peoples, included comments such as the following: "We observe with great emotion the regions where Indians died defending their land from *bandeirantes*, from prospectors, and later from highways, plantations, and entrepreneurs hungry for land, profit, and power." The statement included twenty demands concerning the demarcation of native lands, the end of "all forms of discrimination, expulsions, threats to Indian leaders, and violence," along with the "punishment of those guilty of sterilizing Indian women, recognition of the true history of Brazil in schools, and the construction of Indian schools up to the highest level." The declaration concluded:

Despite the weight of the old history, written by the dominant classes ... we have issued our war cry and founded a new history—the history of a 'different 500 years.' Our struggle is a homage to the innumerable Indian heroes who fell in war over the past five centuries. It is for our children and grand-children, free peoples in a free land.

The protests and the repression are registered in the film "*O Relogio e a Bomba*" (The Quincentennial Countdown Clock and the Tear Gas, 2000.)

Over the history of the cinema and media, thousands of visual and filmic representations have portrayed the "first contact" between Europeans and the indigenous peoples of the Americas. The real-life contacts must have been extremely varied in experiential and ideological terms, depending on the European group involved, the indigenous group involved, and the power relations between them. Such first contacts were perhaps the most momentous human encounters in history in that they brought together two halves of the world, separated by what Clarisse Alvarenga calls "historical and cosmological incommensurability."[23] First contact was a complex multilayered experience. In the context of recent contacts in the Amazon, Alcida Rita Ramos speaks of three dimensions: mythic, historic, and political. Each side has its myths, symbolisms, discourses, genres, practices, and ways of seeing.[24] Yet what is most striking is that the mainstream cinematic representations of such a humanly complex and momentous event have been so shallow, and one-dimensional, reduced to a few self-flattering clichés about heroic discoverers and naked savages within a narrative of native acquiescence in European domination.

The quincentennial of Cabral's "Discovery" in Brazil generated feature films, TV series, animations, parodies, documentaries, samba school pageants, and parades. One way to grasp the differences between colonial domination in Brazil and in the United States is to examine two comparable filmic versions of "first contact," a kind of "primal scene" for settler colonialism in the New World and more specifically of Columbus's arrival in Hispianola in 1492, and Pedro Alvarez Cabral's arrival in Brazil in 1500. The films crystallize slightly different visions of Conquest and Discovery and two attitudes toward the Indian. The British/American production, David Macdonald's 1949 film *Christopher Columbus*, portrays Columbus as a man whose fundamental motivations were not mercantile but religious ("converting the heathen") and scientific (to prove a thesis about the shape of the globe). Millions of benighted heathens, the dialogue informs us, are simply "waiting to be converted." Commentative music translates the film's Manichean channeling of spectatorial affect: the music linked to Columbus is choral, religious, triumphant, while that associated with the natives is ominously Orientalist, provoking an acoustic sense of menace and encirclement. As the Indians, armed with bows and arrows, observe the arrival of the strangers, the feeling of triumph is interrupted by a moment of possible resistance. As the music tenses the spectatorial pulse, a single native raises his bow and prepares to shoot, but another nudges him to stop, as the music regains its composure. Any potential rebellion is alluded to but contained. In a case of colonial mimicry, the natives imitate the possession rituals of European power by performing obeisance in European feudal style, genuflecting before the invaders to mark their fealty, spontaneously applauding their own dispossession.

The film translates into veristic sounds and images the Spanish style of Conquest, embodied in a historical document—the *requerimiento* (requisition)—that Spanish conquerors were supposed to read to the natives as a form of legitimation. The film's Columbus quotes the document literally, declaring that the Indians will become subjects of the Spanish King, that they will become Christian, and that they will speak Spanish (a mandate stated, paradoxically, in English). The Columbus character of Iciar Bollain's more critical Spanish film *Tambien la Lluvia* (Even the Rain, 2010) also cites the *requerimiento*, but with the crucial addition of the excised final part, in which the Spanish conquerors warn native peoples of massive retaliation for any refusal to collaborate: "with God's help we will make war against you by every means available to us, and will ... take all your goods and do all kinds of ill to you and cause all the damage which a sovereign can commit against disobedient vassals." In this theater of the absurd, the natives were scripted as devoid of language yet forced to agree to rules articulated in a language they did not know, in a legal code whose assumptions about land and sovereignty they did not share and whose diktats they never would have accepted. Astonishingly, the film critics of the time, and presumably the audiences as well, seemed to take the film as a reasonably factual account of what first contact must have been like.

Although the credits of the Macdonald film assure us that the "Indians" are played by native people from Dominica, they form an expressionless mass, oddly shorn of voice, language, and dialogue, exercising no apparent agency beyond a blithe acquiescence in European designs. In a manifestation of the muteness of subaltern speech, the members of this tribe, their admiring gaze riveted on the invaders, do not even speak to one other. (Columbus's parrots have more dialogue lines than the natives, since they get to squawk "Long live the King! Long live the Queen!") The film simply "vanishes" native agency in a cinematic correlative to an attitude consecrated by Enlightenment philosophers like Hegel in *The Philosophy of History*, who claimed that the "physical and psychical powerlessness" of the indigenous peoples of the Americas was clearly demonstrated by the fact that they "vanished at the breath of European activity."[25] Hegel's chillingly matter-of-fact account of colonial dispossession naturalizes the primal scene of native genocide. The indigenous peoples simply evaporate, not because of guns, massacres, enslavement, and maltreatment, but through mere contact with a preternaturally powerful European "*geist.*"[26] Contemporary indigenous media proclaims the opposite: "We're not vanishing, We're still here! We're alive! And now we have digital cameras and laptops!"

A logical Brazilian counterpart for comparison to the Hollywood Columbus would be Humberto Mauro's similarly heroic *O Descobrimento do Brasil* (The Discovery of Brazil, 1937). If the Anglo-American version shows the Spanish style of conquest, but in English and within a US American style, the Brazilian portrayal of first contact differs in that it does not present the Indians, even momentarily, as a threat. *The Discovery of Brasil* is in a sense an adaptation in that it is based on the letter—sometimes called the "Birth Certificate of Brazil"—sent by Pero Vaz de Caminha, the official scribe of the Portuguese fleet, to the Portuguese monarch. Not unlike Columbus in his diaries, Caminha's letter describes the natives as healthy, innocent, devoid of all religion and thus available for conversion. Sponsored by the Cocoa Institute, an organization of large landowners—quite literally the heirs of the *capitanias*, or land grants, distributed by the *conquista*—*O Descobrimento do Brasil* idealizes the European role.

The film's staging of the European-indigenous encounter was partially inspired by a 1861 painting by Victor Meirelles, entitled "The First Mass," a work that was in turn itself inspired by a French painting by Horace Vernet entitled "Messe em Kabylie" (Catholic Mass in Kabylie), which shows Algerians attending a Catholic mass. In the Brazilian painting as well as in the film, the Portuguese "discoverer" is center frame, with the Indians in the background. A priest advances the civilizing process by wrapping a native woman in a kind of shawl to hide her breasts. Both films infantilize the Indians, thus figuring the official status of Indians as children in need of care and "tutelage." Taking its cue from the Caminha letter, one scene shows the Portuguese on their *caravela* using blankets to literally "tuck in" two grown Tupi for sleep, as if they were children in need of adult care, in a literalization of the infantilization trope. The performance style reinforces an impression of child-likeness. The "Indian" extras, not actually indigenous but just everyday mixed-race Cariocas, were obviously directed to be in constant frenetic movement, as if they lacked adult control of their bodies. At once infantile and servile, they easily obey white commands, chopping down the trees to make a cross and carrying it to the appropriate site.

As in the Hollywood film, the triumphal choral music of the Mauro film sacralizes European conquest, "blessing" it with a religious aura. At the same time, notable cultural differences separate the two films. In various ways, the Mauro film "softens," *a la Bresilienne*, the racism of the Hollywood film while retaining its Eurocentric drift. Rather than racist demonization a la Hollywood, the film offers affectionate paternalism. Unlike the Hollywood Indians who either do not speak or speak in Hollywood "Injun" talk, here the natives not only speak but also speak in their native Tupí. The Villa-Lobos musical score, meanwhile, harmonizes European-style orchestration with indigenous songs and chants, thus illustrating another signal feature of Brazilian culture—the emphasis on musical hybridity and cultural syncretism. The film also exemplifies a specific scientific angle on Conquest Doctrine. While the Spanish weaponized the *requerimiento*, and while the English occupied, farmed, and fenced the land, the Portuguese claimed a scientific dimension stressed by Patrician Seed in her book. Given that Portuguese navigators and astronomers, largely Jewish and Muslim, perfected the Astrolabe and the compass, in her view, the Portuguese could claim to have "discovered" the land not only through physical occupation but also by establishing precise latitudes and longitudes. As a result, *O Descobrimento do Brasil* foregrounds maps, compasses, astrolabes, and other technical devices, to the point of their becoming what Sheila Schvartzman calls "veritable characters."[27]

For many indigenous groups in the Amazon, "first contact" came only at the end of the twentieth century. Some indigenous-made films bring an opportunity to witness twentieth-century "first contacts" as experienced, remembered, and reenacted from an indigenous point of view. (It is as if the Taínos had filmed a reenactment of Columbus's arrival.) In *Prinop: My First Contact*, the group, called by outsiders Txicao ("waspsting"), but which calls itself the Ikpeng (the people), was first contacted in 1964 by the Villas-Boas brothers. The villagers reenact their first experience of seeing planes flying above their village, imagined as "big birds defecating packages." An Ikpeng elder reminisces about the group's life before contact with whites, giving his own version of the happiness trope: "in the past, there were no white people ... life was good without them. They didn't think about us and we didn't think about them. They were the ones who came looking for us." The elders give human meaning to Oswald's aphorism: "Before Cabral discovered the Indian, Brazil had discovered happiness."

The elder's mimicry of the movement and humming sound of the planes cues a shift to the archival footage of the first contact as seen from the air. The film establishes what Gustavo Furtado calls "a rich dialogue between embodied and archival forms of remembering, interweaving the two into a crescendo that appears to involve the entire community."[28] Instead of the counterpoint of the "view from the ships and the view from the shore" seen earlier in *Caramuru: The Invention of Brazil*, the film counterpoints the view from the (native) ground and the reverse view from the (national Brazilian) air. The Ikpeng see what the whites in the air could see from above, and the whites see what the Ikpeng could see from below. As a cinematic example of Bakhtin's "excess seeing," the film orchestrates a rack-focus dialogue between indigenous self-telling and the documentary's narration by non-Indians, in this case the voice-over of the Villas-Boas brothers film, with their profoundly sympathetic yet in some ways paternalistic approach. The scene then segues into what has become an obligatory topos within indigenous media—the scene where native people watch and react to films about themselves. The filming becomes a catalyst for transgenerational memory, whereby an older generation explains to the younger the story of first contact, followed by a whites-led removal to another territory for their protection. It offers what Amalia Cordova calls a "corrective form of telling stories previously told solely from the dominant point of view, for which there are often no written records."[29]

Brazilian films, unlike Hollywood Westerns, rarely portray the Indian as a violent enemy. The silent period of Brazilian Cinema does not feature arrows raining down on white stage-coaches, or war-whooping attacks, or "Injuns" or "half-breeds," or pejorative names for Indians. The problem is not explicit racism but rather a paternalistic "positive" stereotyping, and the relegation of the Indian to the remote past. Despite the high proportion of indigenous, black, and mixed-race people, the elites saw Brazil as a symbolically "white" tropical appendage of Europe where indigenous people could only have a minor role. The silent period coincided with the heights of colonialism-derived racist ideologies such as eugenics and other forms of the "scientific racism" that infected fields such as history, geography, law, and criminology. Some turn-of-the-century intellectuals called for the "Aryanization of Brazil," expressed as well in immigration policies that favored Germans and Italians over Asians and Africans. Blacks and Indians were seen as obstacles to progress and the development of Brazil as a modern white-dominant society.

Another difference between Hollywood films and Brazilian films has to do with the relation between discourse and actual practice. Classical Hollywood films generally mirrored the largely anti-Indian ambient ideologies of dominant American society itself; discourse and practice were "in synch." Brazilian films, in contrast, display a disjuncture between the cinema and actual practice. In a Brazil that forged itself out of armed conquest and the forced removal of indigenous people, the numerous film adaptations of Indianist novels advanced a sentimental positivity. Discourse and reality, theory and practice, were in contradiction. What was later called the "ideology of whitening" relayed a patronizing view, which simply assumed that Indians would disappear, not massacred en masse with bullets as in Hollywood westerns, but rather disappeared through miscegenation and assimilation. Through this schema, Indians ultimately "vanish" into the general population, thus conforming to a Gilberto Freire style ideal of a Brazil neither white not black but *moreno* ("brunette, or brownish.")

Although no Brazilian film of the first few decades advances an explicitly racist perspective—there is no Brazilian equivalent to Griffith's virulently racist *Birth of a*

Nation (1914–15)—the films are inferentially racist. One is struck by the almost total absence of blacks in contrast with the frequent presence of "Indians" thanks to the many adaptations of Indianist novels such as *O Guarani* (four versions in the silent period), *Iracema* (three versions), and *Ubirajara* (one version), in contrast with the general slighting of indigenous and Afro Brazilian themes. Here too, the cinema simply played out the chosen themes of the dominant ideology. Within the nineteenth-century Indianist movement, the Indian was celebrated as "brave warrior"—usually against other Indians rather than against whites—and as the naively good and deeply spiritual source and symbol of Brazil's nationhood. In a mix of what Doris Sommer calls "Mariolatry and white supremacy,"[30] the servant Peri, the "good Indian" from *O Guaraní*, is amorously enslaved to the white Cecilia and more loyal to her family than to his own tribe.

Indeed, it is significant that black actors often performed Indian roles. The black circus performer Benjamin de Oliveira, the first black to act in Brazilian films, played the role of Peri in an adaptation of *O Guarani* in 1908. Thus, the largely absent Blacks occasionally appear, but as faux Indians. Female Indian roles, meanwhile, were played by white actresses like Ilka Soares. Whites and occasionally Blacks played Indians from literature in a situation where neither black nor Indian had substantive power over self-representation. Indeed, at the time it was illegal to hire Indians as actors because they had the legal status of children, a status that changed only with the 1988 Constitution.

The bipolar dichotomy between the good Indian who helps the white and the bad Indian who does not, as Doris Sommer points out, was not unique to Brazil: "there was nothing especially Brazilian about the fight between good Indian allies of good whites against bad Indians helping bad whites: that conflict between civilization and barbarism ... was the common history of the Americas."[31] Imagistic positivity, in this case, went hand in hand with self-negation. As a result of "positive" stereotyping, both blacks and whites rushed to claim partial Indian ancestry, whether via an actual or an imagined grandmother. Vine Deloria, Jr., addressed what he called the "Indian-grandmother Complex," whereby whites proudly claim Indian blood, and always on the grandmother's side, and usually a Cherokee.[32] The phenomenon is well known in Brazil as well, but with the difference that the grandmother—and in Brazil too it is usually a grandmother but usually a more plausible Tupí grandmother. Since colonial times, genealogist-bricoleurs created fictions of an ancestral "Indian Princess"—daughters of chiefs who married the first colonists—as legitimate forebears, a tendency that even today takes the form of naming non-indigenous Brazilian children after the native heroes and heroines of romantic novels, with "Iracema" as a popular favorite.

A number of historical factors and morphing ideological strains contributed to this ambiguously "positive" image of the Indian: the Jesuit tradition of formally recognizing indigenous humanity; the informal abolition of Indian slavery by the middle of the eighteenth century; the Portuguese custom of conferring nobility on collaborationist *caciques*; the international vogue of the "noble savage"; and the need for an autochthonous figure to betoken cultural difference from the colonial fatherland. The ambiguous "compliment" toward the Indian helped elites evade the vexed question of slavery. The proud history of the rebellious *quilombos* was ignored; the brave Indian, it was subtly insinuated, resisted slavery while blacks did not. Praise for Indians became a disguised insult to Blacks. The white filmmakers of the silent period, taking their cue from their literary antecedents, chose the safely distant and mythically connoted Indian over the more problematically present majority black population, victim of a slavery abolished just 10 years before Affonso Segreto filmed the first Brazilian "views" in 1898.

Despite the idealizations of the fictions, in real life the actually existing indigenous peoples were both the object of slow-motion genocidal policies and the symbolic beneficiaries not only of the romantic Indianist movement but also of a positivist philosophy that preached a "progressive" tolerance of the not-yet-"civilized indigene." The positivist current within Brazilian intellectual history, officially founded in Rio in 1876, was inspired by the work of Auguste Comte (1798–1857). This post-Hegelian current of thought saw social evolution as marked by "the law of three stages"—moving from the theological (itself moving from the fetishistic, to the polytheistic, to the monotheistic), followed by the metaphysical, and finally the positive phase. Each stage correlated with a specific social regime—the theological with slavery, the metaphysical with feudalism, and the positive with an enlightened capitalism. The symptomatically religious idiom of "positivist catechisms" in which this supposedly secular movement was "spoken" revealed the ways in which Enlightenment notions of progress could constitute a secularized version of Christian Providentialism.

The silent period brings a contrast between the "Indianist" fiction films and the documentary films of Luis Thomaz Reis, which recorded the work of Coronel Rondon and the SPI (Service of the Protection of the Indian). Coronel Rondon, the mixed-race positivist head of SPI, for his part, rejected violence against the Indian, famously declaring "To Die, perhaps, to kill, never," a slogan often contrasted with the frankly exterminationist North American "the only good Indian is a dead Indian." (Cree activist Harold Cardinal's summary of the assimilationist ideal as "The Only Good Indian is a non-Indian," meanwhile, applies to the dominant ideology in both countries.)[33] Yet the very word "protection" in the SPI's title implied an infantilizing regime of "tutelage" for the members of formerly self-ruling nations. The assimilationist policies of the SPI were also quietly lethal in their way, meant to gradually "civilize," pacify, de-Indianize, and literally "phase out" the native peoples. The point was to cleanse them of their "primitive" myths and legends and inconvenient practice of common land ownership, moving them, as the cliché went, "from the Stone Age to Modernity." Meanwhile, the mass of settlers, less well-read in Auguste Comte, were taking matters into their own hands by violently invading indigenous land.[34]

The cinematic activities of the Rondon Commission gave birth to numerous films about the indigenous peoples of the interior, many of them directed by Major Luiz Thomas Reis. In films like *Rituas e Festas Borôro* (Bororo Rituals and Feasts, 1916) and *Os Sertões de Mato Grosso* (The Backlands of Mato Grosso, 1916), Euro-Brazilian officials use anthropometric tools to measure the skulls and bodies of Amazonian Indians and dressing them with European clothes. The films also highlight the installation of telegraph lines in the interior of Brazil, while the intertitles inform us of "the pacification of numerous Indian tribes encountered in a primitive, Stone Age state."[35] César Guimarães notes that the first photographic and cinematic images of the contact between whites and Indians, in films like Thomas Reiz's *Ao Redor do Brasi*l

(1932), "materialize" through their framing and execution, which depict the advance of conquest through the filmmakers' desire to capture, and classify the indigenous peoples, and to project (colonial) unity on the indigenous multiplicity. The Indians, for their part, cast their gaze directly at us, interpellate us, and question the mode through which we construct the relation between the person looking and the person looked at, between the person filming and the person filmed.[36]

Since the very beginnings of cinema, the Amazon region has attracted the attention of filmmakers and distributors. Films were already being screened in Manaus in the 1890s, shortly after the first screenings of the Lumière films in Paris, at a time when the Rubber boom was bringing fantastic wealth—and mass enslavement and death—to the region. The exploitation and killing of rubber workers—most indigenous or partially indigenous—has been compared to other Victorian Massacres like the King Leopold genocide in the Belgian Congo. In the 1910s and 1920s some of the films of Silvino Santos were financed by Peruvian rubber magnate Julio César Arana, who had been accused of committing massacres against the indigenous populations. Yet Santos portrayed the Amazon as a paradisal land of opportunity, full of sympathetic natives eager to work, and a golden opportunity for entrepreneurs.[37] His films enthusiastically document the work of rubber extraction alongside intimations of the exuberance of Amazonian nature, creating a sense of a marvelous forest paradise, conveyed through magical superimpositions, with little or no intimations of the labor and indigenous dispossession then taking place.

A century later, Aurélio Michiles's docu-fiction feature *The Secrets of Putumayo* (2020) offers a more critical view of the rubber boom. The film deploys archival material and reenactment to relate the story of gay Irish nationalist Roger Casement (1864–1916), a pioneer in the investigative reports of massive violations of human rights both in the Congo by King Leopold and by the horrors of the rubber boom in Brazil and Peru. The film is based on Casement's *Amazon Diary* (1910), a Jeremiad denouncing exploitation along the Putumayo River, where 30,000 Indians died because of the slave labor conditions created by Julio Cesar Arana, the rubber baron who dominated an empire larger than England along the borders of Brazil, Peru, and Colombia. In a bifurcated performance, the Casement character is played by two actors, one for the sound of his voice—recorded by Irish actor Stephen Rea, Oscar nominee for *The Crying Game* (1993)—and the other for the physical performance by Brazilian actor Dori Carvalho. The film is structured around the intersection of three mutually impacting forms of oppression—the racist exploitation that created an indigenous holocaust in the Amazon, the British imperialism that turned Ireland into a colony, and the homophobia that demonized Casement and led to his execution as an Irish nationalist.

Variations on a Westward Theme

Like US history, Brazilian history also entails Westward movement, but of a less explicitly teleological kind. Although ideologists spoke of a country blessed by God, no one spoke of "Manifest Destiny" as a form of a nation coming into its fullness by reaching the Pacific, partly because a religiously mandated Destiny shared with Spain had already been decreed by the Pope with the Tordesillas Line in 1493. Although the line legally precluded both the Portuguese and the Spanish from moving all the way to either the Atlantic or the Pacific coast, Brazil pushed the line farther West at certain points, thus creating the country's irregular shape. The domination of a vast territory was carried out by military formations of variable size called *Bandeirantes* (flag-bearers). Descendants of the first generations of the Portuguese, they were mixed with a motley of indigenous women, covert Jews ("new Christians"), *caboclos* (mixed white and Portuguese), and "Indians." Starting out from the huge state of São Paulo, the *bandeirantes* fanned out across the interior of Brazil in a project of mineral extraction and indigenous dispossession. They opened up the forests and later mines throughout the seventeenth and up through the nineteenth century. The verb used to describe their work—"*desbravar*"—means to tame or domesticate the forest, but has overtones of "de-braving" or "de-barbarizing," as it is linked to the Latin *bravus*, for which a synonym was "barbarian." In the colonial period, the *Bandeirantes* did not work for the Portuguese government, even if their deeds ultimately served government interests. They spoke a mix of Portuguese and Tupí called "Paulista" and were responsible for the enslavement and massacres of hundreds of thousands of indigenous people. At the end of the nineteenth century, and especially in the 1920s, their image was cleaned up in the service of Paulista regionalism. (A huge monument dedicated to their colonizing feats graces the Ibarapoeira Park in São Paulo.)

Two films by Humberto Mauro, the already discussed *Discovery of Brazil* (1937) and *Bandeirantes* (1940), purvey separate but related foundational myths. The former film, as we have seen, relays the myth of the "discovery" and the putative warm indigenous welcome of Conquest and Christianization. The latter film relays the story of the Bandeirante conquest and domestication of the interior of Brazil. As Eduardo Morettin points out, films like *O Descobrimento do Brasil* (1937) and *Bandeirantes* (1940) advance the patriotic discourse and nationalist ideology of Getulio Vargas's New State. *Descobrimento* celebrates the Discovery and First Mass as part of a cordial relationship between European and indigene, simply assuming the right of the Portuguese to occupy land and convert Indians to Christianity. *Bandeirantes*, made just a few years later, celebrates the settlers as the "tamers" of the Brazilian interior and by implication of the Brazilian indigene. Behind the statist ideologies of the films were prestigious nationalist intellectuals like the historian Affonso D'Escaglione Taunay and the anthropologist Edgard Roquette-Pinto.[38]

Scenes of the massive destruction of the forest, which in the era of climate change bring a very negative charge, were celebrated at the time as a glorious victory over nature. The film monumentalizes and heroicizes the *bandeirantes* and indirectly supports the expansionism of Vargas's New State. That state ended in 1954 with the introduction of democracy, but the frontier conquest was revived again by the military junta that took power in 1964. The TransAmazonian Highway, initiated in 1973, which cut through many indigenous territories, furthered that same goal of Westward conquest. Filmic efforts to exalt the *bandeirantes* have a long history. Especially linked to São Paulo, they became part of a conscious attempt to create another origin myth, that of the brave patriots who civilized vast swaths of Brazil. The *bandeirantes* were especially idealized in the city of São Paulo in the wake of the prosperity generated by the coffee plantations. The *bandeirantes* were reenvisioned as a superior race of heroes, as the Paulistas who engineered the proverbial economic "locomotive" pulling the heavy load of the more inert and sluggish rural states along the train tracks of progress.

Brazilian cinema and media give voice to these historical differences and rival political-ideological projects. A quincentennial TV event tied to Globo's commemoration of 500 years of Brazilian history was the mini-series *A Muralha* (The Wall, 2000). Inspired by a 1954 book by Dinah Silveira de Queiroz, the miniseries was designed to commemorate 400 years of the history of São Paulo. With forty-nine chapters between January and March of 2000 and a 13-hour DVD version launched in 2002, both novel and series laud the courage of the *bandeirantes*. The series opens with the soldiers encountering Indians cheerfully chatting and bathing. One *bandeirante* suggests trading a mirror for ten native slaves, another disagrees and fires on the Indians, as if to say, "no need to bargain." In a 5-minute sequence, the slaughter begins, the village is burned, and prisoners are taken.

Against the record of indigenous rebellion going back to the Tupinamba, the series portrays a remarkable indigenous passivity in the face of aggression. The "Indian" characters include the *cacique* Apingorá (André Gonçalves), the enslaved Moatira (Maria Maya), and the "healer" (Stênio Garcia). The rest are extras speaking a language incomprehensible for the spectators. The portrayal is a study in victimology. Moatira, for example, sees her companion shot in the head, has her son torn from her arms, and is subsequently raped, yet she barely reacts. The cacique Apingora, a faithful servant to the Master Dom Braz (Mauro Mendonca), meanwhile, is killed, suspected of impregnating the niece of a *bandeirante*. The priest Padre Miguel, meanwhile, literally describes the Indians as "blank pages" on which Christianity can be written. "Look at them. So innocent ... soon they'll be singing the Lord's praises!" The telenovela portrays the Indians as Stoic, a view disputed by the many historians who insist on the variegated forms of indigenous resistance.[39] Overall, the series gives the impression that indigenous dispossession was a necessary evil within the larger cause of progress.[40]

The differences between the filmic "Indian" in the two countries partially derive from the fact that the Hollywood and the Brazilian films have very different literary antecedents. Hollywood westerns often adapted the genre of "Conquest Fiction," the "dime novels" of writers like Zane Grey, O'Henry, and Stephen Crane. This largely racist body of popular fiction stereotyped two partially overlapping groups—Mexican "greasers" and Indian "half-breeds"—in pigmentocratic representations that correlated nobility and virtue with whiteness, and vulgarity and degradation with darker pigments. As befits a literature dedicated to justifying the colonization of the Americas and the conquest of Mexico, the imagery of anyone mixed with "Indians" in the dime novels was overwhelmingly negative. Brazilian cinematic portrayals of indigenous people, in contrast, were more likely to adapt the novels of the more high-brow tradition of literary romanticism, with its beautifully remote honey-lipped virgin princesses like Iracema, and its Christianized "Indian men with white souls" like Peri.

Brazilian Cinema has no constituted genre that resembles the Hollywood frontier western. On the other hand, Brazilian cinema does have a long tradition of films, going back to the silent period, about the *cangaceiros*, the rebel bandits, sometimes seen as violent thugs, and sometimes as valiant defenders of the poor and oppressed, who wreaked havoc and justice around the backlands from the late nineteenth century up through the late 1930s. The *cangaceiros* rode horses, wore leather clothing and star-studded hats, and armed themselves with shotguns, pistols, and long, narrow knives. As part-time Robin Hoods, they often received considerable support from the common people. One infers from their physiognomies in photos and archival footage that many of them had partial African and indigenous ancestry, but they are never seen within the "Indian" paradigm.

The most famous *cangaceiro* film—Lima Barreto's *O Cangaceiro* (1952)—a product of the ersatz Hollywood-style studio Vera Cruz, was imitative to the point of having six sound stages modeled on MGM. Vera Cruz's colonized approach left little room for indigenous or mestizo faces. The title of an early feature, *Caiçara* (1950), portrays the legends of a coastal people, doubtless remnants of the decimated Guaraní population, but they are never referred to as "Indians." *O Cangaceiro* features one scene where an "Indian" makes a tokenistic cameo. Approaching in a canoe, he exchanges some friendly words in Tupí with the male lead. The obvious point is to show the white hero's fluency in the language, an ability assumed to reinforce his sympathetic character and show his friendly respect for the equally friendly native. Impressed by the beauty of the man's collar, the female lead asks the hero to ask the man to give it to her; the hero gladly accords with the request. Does such an image offer a "positive" portrayal of indigenous generosity, or merely of naivete, a display of cordial relations between whites and "Indians," or simply an exhibition of asymmetrical knowledge— the white man has mastered the Indian's language but the Indian has not learned the white man's. The indigenous man is portrayed as a supplier of trinkets to satisfy the *caprices* of the heroine. The actors and extras playing *cangaceiros* in the film are what in the United States would be called "people of color," most probably a mixture of European, African, and indigenous, but the villainous lead Cangaceiro "happens" to be black. In the finale, the male hero (who according to the chromatic norms of the period "happens" to be lighter-skinned than all the other characters) is shot dead by the *cangaceiro* leader. As the hero lies dying, he clutches the soil, a token of his profound love for the *sertão*; there is no indication, however, that the soil he is grasping so lovingly is in fact indigenous land; settler domination and proprietorship, in sum, is simply a given.

An overview of the representation of indigenous peoples prior to Cinema Novo in the 1960s reveals: (1) a privileging of the clichés developed by nineteenth-century Indianist romanticism; (2) a binaristic portrayal pitting good Christianized Indians, variously called "pacific," or "domesticated," against demonized barbarians called *bravos* (both "brave" and "angry"), reflecting exactly the binary upended by Brazilian modernists like Oswald de Andrade; (3) the backgrounding of Indian characters in favor of white protagonists; and (4) a generalizing portrayal of an undifferentiated generic Indian, without recognition of the wide gamut of indigenous social systems, languages, cultures, and histories. During much of the century of cinema, the "Indian" served as a decorative ornament, usually linked to nature and separated from "civilization," in films that gave no inkling of the everyday life and struggles of actually existing Indians.

Brazil does have "Northeasterns," i.e. films about the arid and impoverished Northeast, with *vaqueros* (cow men), landowners, and local thugs for hire called *jagunços*. The films set in the Northeast, which go back to the silent period, display a Western-like iconography—horses, cavalcades, leather clothing, desert landscapes, and the like. The hot arid climates and jagged topographies, with cactus and tumbleweeds and sage brush, recall those of the Hollywood western Indians, but no "Indians" lurk behind the sage brush waiting to attack. Native people have always lived in these regions during this period, although they were slowly being driven out or turned into impoverished peasants. The small towns were wild-West like, with fragile law and order, cut off from state intervention, places where individuals, gangs and milennarian cults run free, for example, the mixed-race revolt led by Antonio Conselheiro, the charismatic mestizo leader who a kind of guerrilla war *avant la lettre*, against the Brazilian government, brilliantly registered in Euclides da Cunha's classic "novel" *Rebellion in the Backlands*. The adherents to the movement were mestizo, the result of centuries of post-contact miscegenation, beginning with the Portuguese and indigenous people, but they were "disappeared" as "Indians."

The revisionist Cinema Novo "Northeasterns" of the early 1960s, meanwhile, were influenced not by sentimental romantic literatures but rather by the high-prestige modernist and social realist novels of figures like João Guimarães Rosa, Graciliano Ramos, José Lins do Rego, and Raquel de Queiroz. Unlike the sensationalist and racist novels of Conquest Fiction, these novels were socially progressive and harshly critical of *latifundistas*, corrupt politicians, and even of Brazilian presidents. Although largely written in the 1930s and 1940s, many of these novels, like Graciliano Ramos's *Vidas Secas* (Barren Lives, 1939), were adapted only in the 1960s. While American frontier Westerns set their tales of conflict and domination in the past, the Brazilian Northeasterns from the 1960s are set in the present or the recent past. The Cinema Novo films, like the famous "Northeast trilogy" consisting of dos Santos *Vidas Secas* (1963), Rui Guerra's *Os Fuzis* (1964), and Glauber Rocha's *Deus e Diabo na Terra do Sol* (1964), have to do with hunger, poverty, class oppression, and sporadic rebellions. The relevant categories are not racial but social aggregates like peasants, cowmen, landowners, *jaguncos*, and priests. In the films of Glauber Rocha, whose first film reviews were of Hollywood Westerns, and who actually met *cangaceiros* from his native region in the state of Bahia, the *cangaceiros* are treated, a la Eric Hobsbawm, as pre-political bandits; they rebel against the *latifundistas* but lack political consciousness. The emphasis is not on individuals but on collectivities or individuals who encapsulate collectivities—such as the mass followers Antonio Conselheiro referenced in Rocha's *Deus e Diabo na Terrra do Sol* (God and the Devil in the Land of the Sun, 1964, mistranslated as *Black God, White Devil*) and *Antonio das Mortes* (The Dragon of Evil against the Holy Warrior, 1969). The loner character in Rocha's *cangaceiro* films, Antonio das Mortes himself, winks at the Western by personifying the "hired gun" type from the Western.

Although some of the actors who portray the bandits might have partial indigenous ancestry, moreover, the films are not interested in that fact. The more political Northeasterns like Glauber Rocha's also emphasize the from-below rebellions typical of Brazilian history such as Canudos. Despite an inferential indigenous presence, Brazilian films rarely pit non-indigenous Brazilians against "Indians," even though historically Palmares, portrayed in films like *Ganga Zumba* (1963) and *Quilombo* (1984), included indigenous people. There is an assumed comfort with the idea of a partial indigenous ancestry, but not in a way that actually foregrounds a never-ending slow-motion genocide. To be fair, the details of that genocide were not always available to a larger public. I am not suggesting that Cinema Novo was colonialist, only that its anti-colonialism focused on American imperialism, slavery, and racism rather than on indigenous dispossession, with "Indian" characters appearing only at the end of the 1960s, in the form of the "proto-indigenist films" to be discussed later in this text.[41] Half a century later, Kleber Medonza Filho's revolution-inflected film *Bacurau* (2019) alludes critically to the conventional characters and structures of the Hollywood Western, like the trouble-making stranger and the climactic stand-off, while also referencing famous popular rebellions in Brazil, from the seventeenth-century maroon Republic of Palmares to fin de siècle Canudos—the mixed-race millennial movement rebellion led by the mestizo leader Antonio Conselheiro.

Long stretches of Brazilian Television, meanwhile, offer a rather bleak picture. Brazilian television has largely seen the Indian in terms of romance—the televisual adaptation of the same Indianist novels already adapted by the cinema—or as objects of comedy in sitcoms. Until recently, almost all the Indian roles were played by whites or by non-indigenous people of color. An early novela to feature an indigenous character was the 1965 TV Tupi Channel novela *O Mestico*, where white actor Helio Souto played the indigenous character "Renato," a man who suffered prejudice as the son of a white father and indigenous mother. In the 1967 Globo novela "The Crazy Queen," white actor Claudio Marzo played the indigenous character Robledo. In the 1978 novela *Aritana*, white male star Carlos Alberto Ricelli plays the role of son of a white father and an Indian mother. In a mild form of political critique, the novela has the protagonist become an activist in the defense of Indian land demarcation against prospective American buyers. In a dramatic exchange with his uncle, he makes the following declarations: "every person, every people needs land ... I don't want profit, I want land. Indians don't need money. They don't buy, they don't sell, they don't like money. All they want is to stay on the land."

The 1995 novela *The Courage Brothers*, meanwhile, cast Dira Paes, an actress of white, black, and indigenous ancestry, for the role of the Indian Potira. The Globo novela *Alma Gêmea* (Soul Twin, 2005) features white actress Priscila Fantin as Serena, daughter of an Indian woman and a white prospector, who grows up in an indigenous village before moving to the city. The Globo novela *Desejo Proibido* (2007) cast white actress Leticia Sabatella in dark makeup to play an indigenous role. Overall, only a small proportion of novelas include indigenous characters and those that do employ white players and rarely treat indigenous issues in any depth. In 2005, the miniseries *Mad Maria*, based on a novel by Amazonian novelist Márcio de Souza, created a character, Joe Caripuna, who suffered the twentieth-century violence visited by whites against the Indian: he has his hands amputated because he dared to expose white crimes.

Proto-indigenist Cinema in Brazil

This situation of a mainstream Brazilian cinema with little contemporaneous "Indian" presence changes dramatically in the late 1960s. After the idealized Indian of silent-era romanticism, and the objectified positivist about-to-be-civilized Indian of the 1920s documentaries, and the allegorical cannibal of the Modernists and Tropicalists of the 1960s, 1970s, and the 1980s, the 1990s bring new, more critical, versions of the resistant Indian and, as we shall see, the beginnings of the activist Indian of "indigenous media." It was only in the late 1960s and early1970s that indigenous characters become protagonists of feature films, even if their "protagonism" was sometimes compromised both by non-indigenous casting and by the instrumentalization of characters for political purposes.

Since to speak of indigenous people is necessarily to speak of occupation and oppression, the "Indian" theme became an indirect way of sending subversive messages that could escape the notice of the military government and its censors. The 1970s and 1980s bring a turn to Indian-related themes. Gustavo Dahl's *Uirà: Um Índio a Procura de Deus* (Uirà: An Indian in Search of God, 1973), Andre Luis de Oliveira's *Ubirajara: O Senhor da lança* (Ubirajara: Lord of the Spear, 1975), Oswaldo Caldeira's *Aukê* (1976) and *Ajuricaba: O Rebelde da Amazônia* (1977)—critically recycled and politicized the Indianist theme by having Indian characters metaphorize the general national struggle against dictatorship. This politicization partially derives from a growing awareness of the abuses by the military government and a growing awareness that corrupt officials, land speculators, prospectors, and squatters were busy killing indigenous people, using everything from bacteriological warfare to aerial bombardment. Although there was little conscious articulation between the leftist filmmakers and indigenous activists, it is in all probability not an accident that the two, as if in synch on some semi-conscious level, emerged at the same time, and simultaneous with the activism of the American Indian movement in the United States.

Gustavo Dahl's *Uirà: An Indian in Search of God* was inspired by anthropologist Darcy Ribeiro's true story about an extended Urubu family impacted by diseases brought by the white settlers who inadvertently triggered the death of two-thirds of the Urubu population. Afflicted by extreme melancholy, a chief named Uirà, after losing his child to disease, sets out to the city of São Luís, Maranhão, to find his God Maíra and the legendary Guaraní "Land without Evil." The film begins with a documentary-inflected section concerning Urubu funerary rites and strategies for dealing with loss and then relates Uirà's disastrous encounters with urban whites. After the traditionally attired Uira is arrested for "nudity," he is jailed and beaten until he is freed by the SPI. His liberation is followed by communal celebrations of his courage as a warrior, yet he ultimately decides to reach his personal Promised Land through suicide. Undergirding the film is an implied, and in many ways problematic, analogy of two incommensurable forms of suffering—that of the cultural and physical massacre of the Urubu people and the personal torment of leftists, like the filmmaker persecuted by the military regime. As if to confirm the film's thesis of government repression, the regime's censors demanded major cuts in the sequences treating police abuse, cuts that would have made the film virtually incomprehensible. The censors' objections had everything to do with the ideological-discursive conjuncture described earlier. The key complaint was that the film portrayed the white population as hostile to the Indians—in short, it undercut the "cordial racism" of Brazilian mythologies about the Indian.[42] (We will return to indigenous Guaraní Cinema in later sections.)[43]

Oswald Caldeira's *Ajuricaba: The Rebel of the Amazon*, meanwhile, stresses historical continuities by counterpointing indigenous resistance in the eighteenth century with resistance to multinational companies in the twentieth. It tells the story of an eighteenth-century Manau chief named Ajuricaba, who organized a guerrilla movement that inspired many other native rebellions against Portuguese domination. After fighting against his people's enslavement, he leaped to his death rather than be captured. In keeping with local indigenous legends of human-animal metamorphosis, he was variously said to have transformed himself into a fish, a jaguar, and other forest entities.

In the 1990s, a different kind of critique emerges within dramatic-realist conventions of fiction feature films. Hector Babenco's *At Play in the Fields of the Lord* (1991), based on Peter Mattheissen's 1965 novel, changes the novel's setting from the Madre de Dios region of Peru to the interior of Brazil. Cowritten with Bunuel's favored screenwriter Jean-Claude Carrière, the plot revolves around diverse social contingents—opportunistic adventure pilots/mercenaries, assorted missionaries, a few Indians, and the government functionary Commander Guzman who desires indigenous land for economic reasons. The Brazilian Commander tells the two aviators to bomb the Niaruna village "just to scare them." The mixed-race Lewis Moon (Tom Berenger) is ethically and ethnically split in his loyalties, while his partner Wolf (Tom Waits) wants to simply finish the bombing and move on. The gallery also includes uptight Protestant missionaries (John Lithgow, Daryl Hanna) portrayed as neurotic, puritanical, prejudiced, and ultimately dangerous to the general welfare and to the environment. The Quarriers (Aiden Quinn and Kathy Bates) are more ambivalent—they preach the gospel to the Indians but they also admire indigenous language and culture. The missionaries never really succeed, furthermore, in their goal of converting Indians, thus instantiating what the Jesuits lamented as "the inconstancy of the savage soul."[44] The pilots and the missionaries are symbolically linked in their mission; as the mercenaries fly over the Amazon, the plane casts its shadow on the water in the form of a cross.

All the characters are implicated in the fate of the Niaruna, a fictitious group reminiscent of the Yanomami. The group's invented language is an amalgam of words from various indigenous language families such as Karaja, Ge, and Tupí. In the film, even well-intentioned decent characters can provoke calamities. Lewis Moon, the half-Cherokee character played by Berenger, feels an affinity with the Niaruna; he learns bits of the language, is accepted to a certain extent by the tribe—and in this sense he belongs to the White-but-not-quite-Indian paradigm—and then tries to lead them in a crusade to drive out the missionaries. He ultimately refuses to follow the corrupt politician's request to dynamite the Niaruna and even defects to the "enemy" side. His actions seem to offer a glimpse of possible transnational indigenous solidarities, but he inadvertently provokes disaster by becoming sexually intimate both with Andy (Daryl Hannah) and with his native wife, thus spreading a disease fatal for the Indians. The film suggests that Western culture, in its two forms of evangelization and extractive capitalism, has brought only devastation. Contact with the literal or spiritual "blood quantum" of whites, the film suggests, means death for the indigene. The American identity politics of self-realization, it turns out, cannot be exported to the Amazon. Martin Quarrier tells Lewis Moon that "as an American he would be proud to have Indian blood," to which Lewis responds sardonically, "And just how much Indian blood would an American be proud to have?" Despite the tensions among them, the missionaries, the pilots, and the gold-seeker mutually reinforce one another; all harm the indigenous people.

The various characters project their own historically shaped ethnocentric visions onto the Indians; the Jewish character Wolf, for examples, resurrects the old canard of "the lost tribe of Israel, Jewish just like me." At the same time, the film presents Indians not as noble savages, but rather as human beings faced by devastating challenges. Revealingly, the Babenco film was released in the same year as the Bruce Beresford film *Black Robe*, also concerned with missionaries and indigenous people, in that case the Jesuits in French Canada. That the Babenco film was widely panned, while the Beresford film was largely praised, had in my view a lot to do with spectatorial sensitivities and the portrayal of the missionaries—Protestant and negative in the first case; Catholic and relatively positive in the other. While the Babenco film offers little narcissistic satisfaction to the white spectator looking for a pale-faced hero, the Beresford film tries to persuade us that the Jesuits "did it all for love." If in politics it is a wise policy to "follow the money," in the analysis of spectatorship it can also be wise to "follow the narcissism."

Zelito Viana's *Avaeté: Semente de Vingança* (Avaeté: Seeds of Vengeance, 1985), for its part, memorializes the 1963 extermination of an Avaeté village by dynamite and machine gun, a decimation that left only two survivors. Viana uses the story, originally recounted in Darcy Ribeiro's *Os Índios e a Civilização* (Indians and Civilization), as the prologue to a story about how one of the survivors, Ava (played by indigenous actor Macsuara Kadiweu), seeks vengeance. Befriending the expedition's cook, Ramiro (Hugo Carvana), who is repentant about his role in the massacre, Ava discovers the rapacious landowner-businessman behind the massacre. In the climactic sequence, Ava, dressed and painted as an Indian warrior, invades the businessman's home and executes justice with his own hands.

Another 1980s film, Rui Guerra's *Kuarup* (1989), adopts the 1967 Antonio Callado novel of the same name. The title refers to a spectacular Xinguano gathering of neighboring tribes to celebrate life, death, marriage, and rebirth. Like the novel, the film portrays Brazilian history from the Getulio Vargas New State period (1937 to 1954) up through the 1964 coup d'état. The life of the protagonist—Jesuit priest Padre Nando (Taumaturgo Ferreira)—reflects the political and cultural twists and turns of the era. The story is focalized through the priest who, not unlike the poet of Glauber's *Terra em Transe*, careens from religious faith to idealism and orgy to armed struggle, in synch with the various ideologies circulating in the late 1960s of the novel. The protagonist becomes a walking allegory of political trends, an empty space, as

Lucia Nagib puts it, "to be occupied."[45] Encouraged by his politicized friends to work with indigenous people on the Xingu reservation, he ultimately realizes that his real vocation is to struggle against the military dictatorship.

André Klotzel's *Capitalismo Selvagem* (Savage Capitalism, 1993) also points to the issue of divided loyalties, where the fragmented and trans-genre aesthetic—part social-realism, part telenovela—mirrors the fragmented personality and situation of the protagonist. The film concerns the internal dilemmas of an industrialist character who turns out to be the survivor, not unlike Ava of *Avaeté*, of a massacre of an indigenous group. Throughout the film, he suffers from epilepsy-like trances, underscored by indigenous-sounding music, which derive from the irruptions of these repressed aspects of his past, emblematic in this sense of the parallel erasure of the Indian past from the official Brazilian history. He is unconsciously torn between his ancestry and the company's suspect economic activities in the Amazon, which threaten the indigenous peoples of the region. Indigenous Krahô appear in the film, but are called Caetes, perhaps in homage to the Brazilian Modernists who celebrated the Caetes for having devoured Bishop Sardinha.

Cao Hamburger's feature fiction *Xingu* (2011) traces the three-decade trajectory of the three indigenista Villas-Boas brothers: Claudio (João Miguel), Leonardo (Caio Blat), and Orlando (Felipe Camargo)—latter-day, more progressive, heirs of the spirit of Coronel Rondon—from the moment when they join the Roncador-Xingu expedition, part of Vargas's westward march in 1943, until the 1960s, and the foundation, in 1961, of the Xingu National Park, the equivalent in size of Belgium. Each brother has a specific character and role; Orlando is the mediator; Claudio the intellectual; Leonardo the passionate advocate who courageous to the point of risk. They make contact with the indigenous peoples, learn to live in the rainforest, and become successful advocates for the park as an indigenous reserve and an ecological haven. Along the way, the film raises topical issues such as epidemics and land demarcation. Unlike many earlier features, the film makes full use of indigenous actors. After a disastrous epidemic, Claudio sums up the role of the non-indigenous Brazilians, in words that recall Derrida's meditations on the *pharmakon*: "We are the poison, and we are the antidote."

Silvio Back's feature documentary *República Guarani* (1981) treats the same subject as Roland Joffe's *The Mission* (1986), the Jesuit missions between 1610 and 1767 among the Guaraní Indians. But instead of idealizing the Jesuits a la Joffe, Back shows that the priests did not ultimately renounce the Christian colonization of the native soul or the colonial enterprise in general; their denunciation was limited to physically genocidal practices. For Back, the Jesuits were the "first ideological multinationals, transmitting the Gospel to Africans, Asians, and Amerindians, superimposing over the mythical universes of each nation and tribe the spiritual imperialism of modernity."[46]

Over the last three or four decades, some documentaries have attempted to divest themselves of vestigial colonialist attitudes. The title of Zelito Viana's film *Terra dos Índios* (Indian Land, 1979) signals its indigenous-friendly posture. Whereas the old ethnographic films feature self-confident "scientific" voice-overs delivering the "truth" about subject peoples unable to answer back, sometimes prodding the "natives" to perform practices long abandoned, the new ethnographic films strive for "participatory filmmaking," "dialogical anthropology," "reflexive distance," and "interactive filmmaking." Documentary and experimental films thus began to discard the covert elitism of the pedagogical or ethnography model in favor of an acquiescence in the relative, the plural, and the contingent, as artists experience a salutary self-doubt about their own capacity to speak "for" the other. Some filmmakers, such as Andrea Tonacci, an early advocate for indigenous media already in the 1970s, handed over the camera to the indigenous people to facilitate a two-way "conversation" between urban Brazilians and indigenous groups. Seeing film less as a product than as a shared experience, Tonacci tried to incorporate an indigenous vision into the process of creating the films. Thus, the filmmaker assumes some of the risks of a real dialogue, of potential challenge from interlocutors. The question changes from how one represents the "other" to how one collaborates with the "other" in a shared space, while seeing that the Western filmmaker is just another other. After all, there is no other, only otherization, and no exotic, only exoticization.

Indigenous Media in Brazil

Some 300 indigenous peoples, speaking some 180 indigenous languages, live in Brazil or on its borders. Unlike the United States, where "first contacts" began in the seventeenth century and ended in the nineteenth century with the closing of the frontier, in Brazil "first contacts" began in the sixteenth century when some indigenous nations such as the Guaraní were contacted. But for many groups, substantive contact came only centuries later, in the interior of Brazil, in the 1970s. Although native resistance in Brazil has existed since the beginning of conquest, when the *Confederação dos Tamoios* led by Cunhambebe fought dispossession and enslavement by the Portuguese, and while resistance has never ceased since then, it was only in the 1970s that a pan-Indian movement took recognizable shape. This process culminated in 1988 with a new Constitution that abandoned the old language of native infantilization to embrace an idiom of land right, cultural rights, and indigenous sovereignty. The approval of the new Constitution on October 5, 1988, after 20 years of military dictatorship, ended the old "tutelage" and integrationist policies to begin a new chapter in the Euro-Brazilian-indigenous relationship. Article 231 recognized both the cultural and territorial rights of indigenous peoples based on their traditional heritage:

> Hereby are recognized Indian rights to their social organization, customs, languages, beliefs, and traditions, and the originary rights to the land which they have traditionally occupied, along with an obligation of the government to demarcate and protect the right to traditionally occupied lands, with the government required to zealously assure the fulfilment of these laws and respect the heritage of these peoples.

The new Constitution recognized indigenous customs, languages, beliefs, and collective rights, establishing indigenous rights to permanently live on their traditional territories, including the exclusive use of the natural resources necessary for securing their welfare and cultural integrity. Article 67 ordered the demarcation of all indigenous territories in Brazil within five years. While the old Civil Code (installed in 1916) spoke of the "relative incapacity" of the indigenous peoples, Article 232 of the New Civil Code in 2002 proclaimed that the indigenous communities and organizations had every right and capacity to defend their interests in court.

On the ground, however, every assertion of indigenous rights triggered backlash and sabotage, leading to innumerable confrontations, many violent, with local landowners, with the government, or with transnationally connected corporations. In response, the indigenous movement carried out occupations of government-linked public buildings and FUNAI headquarters. The movement became directly involved in political life through the elaboration of laws, the creation of NGOs, and pressure on key votes in the National Congress. The indigenous movement also promoted encampments of thousands of protestors in the Capital, under the banner of "Indigenous blood in the veins; the struggle for land and territory." In 2002 the Indigenous Peoples of Brazil Organization (APIB) was founded to foster direct pressure on the National Congress.

The prime issue has always been land, not simply in terms of technical ownership in "deeds" in the form of documents, but rather in terms of actual deeds, i.e. actions and attitudes. Land is connected to a host of other issues such as health (dependence on the land for plant remedies) and cultural recognition, both of the indigenous collectivity in general and of the right to cultural difference of particular groups. Under the Lula Presidency (2003–10), the Brazilian government, after many years of allowing Euro-Brazilian encroachments on indigenous land, declared vast territories "out of bounds," ceding territory the size of Switzerland, for example, to the Yanomami. Subsequently, however, various Brazilian governments failed to uphold the 1988 constitutional decisions. The gains were weakened in the name of "development," first during Dilma's presidency (2010–11) and then completely reversed by Bolsonaro (2019 on). From the moment he took office, Bolsonaro and his allies have tried to paralyze all work being carried out in benefit of indigenous nations and the environment, dismantling the recognition of the rights of indigenous peoples expressed in the 1988 constitution drafted after centuries of struggles to this effect. With the assassination of indigenous leaders, the devastating forest fires, and the coronavirus, the situation has become absolutely calamitous.

Despite the widespread prediction of the inevitable disappearance of the indigenous peoples of Brazil, indigenous activism and the dynamism of indigenous media over the last few decades clearly demonstrate that far from becoming "extinct" or liquified into a de-ethnicized cultural smoothie, thanks to the racial democratic blender, indigenous people have managed to assert their cultural diversity and their pan-indigenous unity. In 1983, Mário Juruna, son of a Xavánte cacique, famous for always carrying a tape recorder to register the unkept promises of Brazilian politicians, became the first indigenous leader to be elected to the Brazilian Chamber of Deputies and the first native leader to use new technologies to demand rights, spread demands, and pressure the authorities. And in 1987, while the Constituent Assembly was drafting early versions of the new Brazilian Constitution, indigenous activist Ailton Krenak captured the attention of the mass media through an efficacious coup de theater. In a presentation to the Assembly, he slowly blackened his photogenic face with *jenipapo* paste—a traditional form of mourning for the Krenak—while eloquently skewering official government policies toward indigenous people, in a performance widely disseminated by the media.

Oswald de Andrade's prophecy of a coming "*indio tecnizado*" in the 1920s came to life in the 1980s in the form of "indigenous media." Indigenous contacts with film, however, actually go at least as far back as the mid-1970s with a documentary about a Kayapo cacique named Raoni Metuktire, also known as Chief Raoni or Ropni. The Kayapo, a Jê-speaking people of central Brazil, were admired by American anthropologist Darrell Posey for their deep knowledge of their natural environment and their creation of ecological zones linked to specific plants and animals.[47] An active leader of his people for over a half century, Raoni became world-famous, thanks to a 1977 film entitled *Raoni*, by two filmmakers, one Brazilian (Luiz Carlos Saldanha) and the other Belgian (Jean-Pierre Dutilleux). The narration in the English version was by Marlon Brando, a huge Hollywood star and a radical supporter of the indigenous cause.

A few years earlier, on the night of March 27, 1973, Marlon Brando had asked Sacheen Littlefeather (White Mountain Apache and Yaqui elder) to take the stage at the 45th Academy Awards and refuse the Best Actor Oscar for his performance in *The Godfather*. The sorrowful face of 26-year-old Littlefeather, in buckskin dress, moccasins, and long, straight black hair, clashed with the lily whiteness of the usual Oscar crowd. Brando could not accept the award, Littlefeather explained, because of "the treatment of American Indians today by the film industry." As half the crowd booed and the other half applauded, she reminded them of the protests at Wounded Knee, the site of a month-long standoff, sparked by the murder of a Lakota man, between Native American activists and US authorities. The event had special impact because it coincided with the first Oscar to be broadcast internationally via satellite. Reportedly, self-proclaimed white supremacist and on-screen assassin of Native Americans John Wayne had to be restrained by security guards from physically removing Littlefeather from the stage. She was the first woman of color, and the first indigenous woman, to use the Academy Awards platform to make a political statement.

Raoni makes a trans-hemispheric connection by having Marlon Brando interview Native American activists participating in "the Longest March" protest by 2,000 Native Americans, representing seventy native tribes, who had marched from San Francisco to Washington. Thus, the film linked indigenous activism in Brazil and the United States. Made in the wake of the formation of American Indian Movement (AIM) and the protests at Alcatraz and Wounded Knee, the film begins with Brando interviewing native activists, showcasing their eloquence as well as Brando's well-informed support for the native cause. Brando does not speak of "inclusion," for example, but rather of a more radical "sovereignty." Many of the statements both by the activists and by Brando echo concepts encountered throughout this text—indigenous society as more democratic, native gender roles as more progressive, and the native way of life as generally happier and less destructive of people and nature. Brando also speaks of a different political model, which corresponds roughly to Clastres's definition of chiefdom as "discourse without coercion," where the chief is eloquent but does not give orders or have power to decide or repress.

One remarkable sequence, filmed immediately after a murderous invasion of Kayapo territory by non-indigenous "whites," shows furious Kayapo calling for the death of all the invaders they could find, including the two filmmakers. The Brazilian cameraman captured the extremely apprehensive look on the Belgian collaborator's face as he hears a Kayapo leader call for their death. In a highly dramatic yet completely unstaged moment, the then young Raoni persuades the Kayapo to spare the filmmakers, arguing that "their film can take our message to the world." And the film did indeed spread the Kayapo message to the world when it was nominated for the Oscar for Best Documentary in 1978, generating a significant buzz in Hollywood and major fundraising for the Rainforest Foundation.

A decade later, the Granada TV documentary *Kayapo: Out of the Forest* (1989) shows Raoni appearing with fellow Kayapo alongside representatives of forty other native peoples, leading a mass ritual performance to protest the planned construction of a hydroelectric dam by the Eletronorte Corporation. The project would have diverted the flow of the Xingu River and flooded dozens of communities, crippling local fishing, destroying flora and fauna, and devastating the environment. In the film, one of the Kayapo leaders explains that the dam's name (*Karararo*) is taken, ironically, from a Kayapo war cry. Another leader shows samples of the herbal medicines threatened by the potential flooding. Within the globalized contact zone, indigenous leaders and the Eletronorte spokesman engage in a profound debate about the nature of progress, energy, and ownership. At one point a native woman brushes a machete against the corporate spokesman's cheeks as she scolds him in Kayapo. In a reversal of colonialist *ecriture*, she demands that the corporate spokesman write down her name, reminding him that her family will suffer the consequences of the construction of the dam. "Since you also love your children, you should understand us." Corporate arrogance meets articulate indigeneity. Here the spectator, enamored of "development," might begin to question the axiomatic equation of hydroelectric dams with "progress." Chief Raoni, meanwhile, in a veritable coup de theater, appears with the rock star Sting in a successful attempt to capture international media attention. The outpouring of indigenous, national, and international protest captured international media attention, leading to the cancelation of the World Bank loan financing the dam.

The Kayapo have shown themselves to be among the most media-savvy of the indigenous groups. A pioneer project founded in 1985, *Mekaron Opoi D'joi* ("He Who Creates Images") led by Monica Frotta, Renato Pereira, and Luiz Henrique Rios, in collaboration with the Kayapo, resulted in the film *Taking Aim* (1993).[48] When the documentary crew from Granada Television first went to film the Kayapo in 1987, the Kayapo demanded video cameras, a VCR, a monitor, and videotapes as the quid pro quo for their cooperation. They subsequently used video to record their ceremonies, demonstrations, and encounters with white officials (so as to have the equivalent of a legal transcript). They documented their traditional knowledge of the forest environment and recorded the transmission of myths and oral history. In 1987, the Kayapo not only sent a delegation to the Brazilian Constitutional Convention to lobby delegates debating indigenous rights but also videotaped themselves in the process, thus winning international attention for their cause. Widely disseminated images of the Kayapo wielding video cameras, appearing in *Time* and *The New York Times Magazine*, at that point in history, derived their power to shock from the premise that "real" Indians don't carry camcorders. Decades later, Raoni demonstrated against still another iteration of the same hydroelectric project for the Xingu River—the Belo Monte Dam. As a practitioner of "forest diplomacy," Raoni has relentlessly defended the indigenous cause internationally, including directly to a series of French presidents, accompanying Sting to speak with Francois Mitterand in 1983, and later communicating in person with Jacques Chirac and Francois Hollande. As a living symbol of the fight to protect the environment, in September 2011, Chief Raoni was made an honorary citizen of Paris by Paris mayor Bertrand Delanoë, and in 2014, he received an honorary Medal of Freedom from the French National Assembly.

For anthropologist Terence Turner, Kayapo camcorder activism does not try to retrieve an idealized pre-contact past; it focuses instead on identity construction in the present. As agile strategists in the realm of the politics of the image, the Kayapo filmed their events to disseminate their cause in a "synergy between video media, Kayapo self-representation, and Kayapo ethnic self-consciousness."[49] Just as people all over the world have turned to cultural identity as a means of defending their social, political, and economic interests, according to Turner, media activism and pedagogy serve to protect threatened identities or even to forge new identities, a catalyst not only for the public-sphere assertion of particular cultures but also for fostering the "collective human potential for self-production and transformation."[50]

Video nas Aldeias

As Amalia Cordóva points out, "the documentary has proven to be the weapon of choice for recording subaltern histories, contesting multinational extraction, and denouncing human rights violations on Native lands and bodies."[51] It would be a Herculean task to "cover" the hundreds if not thousands of indigenous and pro-indigenous hybrid documentaries coming out of the indigenous communities in Brazil, so I will focus here only on a small sample. The earliest and most prolific of these movements was the Video nas Aldeias project (Video in the Villages, henceforth, VNA), created in 1987 as an NGO and film training school for indigenous people, and closely linked to pro-indigenous social activism. VNA's founder Vincent Carelli came with his parents from France to Brazil at age 5. At 16, in 1969, he made his first visit to an indigenous (Ikpeng) village, where he learned to hunt and clear paths and glimpsed another kind of existence. Enamored of this alternative way of life, he returned four years later to live in the village, now adopted by the father of the Akruantury family. Adoption meant full and equal participation in the activities of the group. Thus, he entered indigenous society, as he has often said, not as a colonial father, but rather as an adoptive son, not as a teacher but as a learner, not as an "expert" but as an apprentice, still enjoying the settler advantage of course, but slowly learning to use his privilege to empower rather than exploit. It is important to say that Carelli always had many non-indigenous collaborators such as Dominique Galois in the Waiãpi's and Zo'ë's films, Gilberto Azanha and Maria Elisa Ladeira for the Krahô films, Carlos Fausto for the Kuikuro films.

A striking trait of Carelli's films—a result of his long *convivencia* with indigenous groups—has to do with the corporeal semiotics of interlocution, evident in the extremely relaxed postures and attitudes of the indigenous people in his films. Their comfort level bespeaks the intimacy of a family or a group of friends. Filmed in wide shots, they relax in their hammocks, shoo away insects, and scratch their bites; here, Jean-Louis Comolli's "anxiety of the filmed subject" is minimized. Rarely do they appear in the talking-head close-ups typical of conventional documentaries; rather, the films usually place their subjects in a wide-frame socio-relational space. Partially inspired by Andrea Tonacci's earlier efforts to create "intertribal communication through video," Carelli saw his photographs, and later his films, as a way to help indigenous people get in touch with their own past and with each other, deploying media as a means of coping with historical change. VNA worked with an enormous variety of indigenous groups with different languages, cosmologies, and histories. The group initially had three declared ambitions: (1) to give visibility to indigenous struggles; (2) to transfer authority for filmmaking to the Indians themselves; and (3) to serve the communities more generally. The Indians themselves would propose the genres and subjects of the films but with VNA help and community participation. The normal procedure was to show the footage to the community for their approval and gather suggestions in a collaborative process. Subsequently, the films would be shared with other indigenous communities so as to compare different strategies of mediatic empowerment and cultural self-determination.

Although indigenous cultures in Brazil are extremely varied, they share common concerns such as a need for land demarcation, cultural expression, and a historical awareness of momentous challenges. In its affirmation of indigenous cultural identity and indigenous struggles to protect territorial and cultural patrimonies, VNA has trained scores of native filmmakers representing diverse peoples such as the Kayapo, Xavánte, Ashaninka, Ikpeng, Guaraní, Waiãpi, and the Kuikuro. The VNA project shows, as Ivana Bentes points out, that a socius can pass from an oral-communal culture to an audiovisual-digital one, without necessarily passing through literate culture as the privileged domain of knowledge.[52]

Projects like VNA provoke many questions from skeptics: Who actually makes the films? Who actually sees them? Is it dangerous to integrate Indians into the capitalist world of the media? Or, conversely, why push young indigenous people back into the old world of their elders by reviving outdate traditions? If the film teachers are not indigenous, how do they avoid imposing their own ideas? Does VNA dictate a Western aesthetic? How do film teachers avoid bringing in their cultural baggage and introjecting alien assumptions or grids? What is the role of film and cultural theory? Are the usual *maitres a penser* an aid in the interpretation of their films? (In Brazil, the most frequently invoked names are Lévi-Strauss, Deleuze-Guattari, Agamben, Foucault, and Jean-Louis Commoli.) Is there such a thing as an *ecriture indigene* analogous to the *ecriture feminine* of the 1970s?

VNA films form a heterogenous corpus—ritual films, historical films, mythical films, reflexive films, activist films, re-enactment films, archival films, daily-life films, and the like. Some focus on privileged moments of tribal life such as ceremonies and initiation rites, while others stage myths and legends. In a first phase, the images produced were meant for the internal consumption by the community itself. Seeing themselves in videos would theoretically enable community self-examination about their own self-image, about the image they would like to present to the world, and about the relation between that self-image and what the existentialists would call "le regard d'autrui." *O Espirito da TV* (The Spirit of Television, 1990), a collaboration between Carelli and anthropologist Dominique Gallois, for example, offers a cross-cultural dialogue about the role of the image. Waiãpi elders, encountering the medium for the first time, articulate the benefits of seeing themselves on the screen through video self-production, for example, by recording the image of the elders for posterity, or teaching the songs to young people, or by encountering the language and image of their close relatives in other communities. *Como Irmaos* (Like Brothers, 1993), in a similar vein, recounts the cultural exchange between the Parakatêjê of Para and their relatives, the Krahô of Tocantins. The two groups compare strategies for maintaining their language and identity. In these films, the "outside" spectator is no longer the privileged interlocutor; rather, video primarily facilitates exchange between indigenous groups themselves.

Many VNA films feature young filmmakers interviewing elders about the loss of cultural heritage. In Carelli's documentary *Eu já fui seu irmão* (I Was Already Your Brother, 1993), the elders lament the fact that some young indigenous people "no longer want to be Indian, no longer speak the language, and no longer know their festivals and rituals." In this spirit, many VNA films practice a kind of "revolutionary nostalgia" (Walter Benjamin) through cultural reimmersion and the reenacting of stories from the narrative commons. Dominique Gallois and Carelli's *Segredos da Mata* (Secrets of the Forest, 1988), for example, adopts four indigenous tales about cannibal monsters—"The Secret of the Invisible," "Lord of the Hunt," "The Magic Arrow of the Cannibal," and the "Cannibal Bat"—narrated and performed by native actors. Karané, Kumaré, and Natuyu Ikpeng's docu-fiction, *Moyngo, o sonho de Maragareum* (Moyngo, the Dream of Maragareum, 2003), recreates the myth of the origin of the tattooing ceremony among the Ikpeng. The shaman Maragareum dreams that everyone in the neighboring village has died, and then, arriving in this village, finds that the dream has become a reality.

A Arca dos Zo'ë (Zo'ë's Ark, or Meeting Ancestors, 1993) treats a different kind of "first contact," this time not between "whites" and "Indians" but between distantly related indigenous peoples, here in the form of an unprecedented encounter between two recently contacted groups—the Waiãpi and the Zo'ë—who had known each other only through videos.[53] Both groups are recently contacted, and both had suffered from colonialist incursions. After contact with outsiders in 1973, the Waiãpi had tried to demarcate their land to protect it for generations to come. Although they were granted 1.5 million acres of rainforest in 1996, copper interests threatened to remove them anyway. The Waiãpi responded that they would fight to the death for their land. The Zo'ë, meanwhile, had come into sustained contact with outsiders in 1987, when the New Tribes Mission built a base of spiritual operations on their land. Subsequent to contact, epidemics devastated the tribe, leading to the death of about one quarter of the Zo'ë population between 1982 and 1988. Reacting to the catastrophe, FUNAI expelled the missionaries in 1991 and tried to persuade the Zo'ë to return to their old villages. In the film, the two groups, who lived 200 miles apart but shared a linguistic variant of Tupí, exchange gifts, examine body ornaments, and articulate their cultural differences. While one group finds nudity normal, the other finds it shocking but then moves rather easily from shock to acceptance. The Zo'é explain their way of life and their ancestral knowledge while the Waiãpi inform the Zo'é about the dangers of the modern white world slouching their way. The nuances between indigenous tribes, in the end, pale in importance compared to their cultural commonalities and to the threat posed by the invaders.

The VNA films of the late 1980s usually revolve around filmed cultural exchanges between groups becoming aware of each other through the film medium. The films are short, usually less than a half hour, rapidly paced and conventionally edited in function of a need to construct a comprehensible narrative for a broader public.[54] Frequently, a scene shows the indigenous public watching themselves on TV monitors and commenting on the videos. Ruben Caixeta de Queiroz cites as examples such films as *A festa da moça* (Nambiquara, 1987), *O espírito da TV* (Waiãpi, 1990), *Boca livre no Sararé* (Nambiquara, 1992), *A arca dos Zo'é* (Zo'é/Waiãpi, 1993), and *Eu já fui seu irmão* (Gavião- Parakatejê/Krahô, 1993). The films of this early phase, as Debora Herszenhut sums it up, are socially engaged and reflexive by showing the impact of video on the self-perception of indigenous people, the video-mediation between different tribes, and the distinctive cultural traits and rituals of the groups.[55]

VNA has gone through many changes: technological (from film to video to digital), personal (with the entry in 1998 of Mari Corrêa into the group), and financial (in sources of support). In production terms, VNA is deeply "glocal," first local in being connected to minimal tribal social units and global in terms of transnational audience and funding by NGOs and foundations (MacArthur, Rockefeller, Guggenheim, Ford, and the Norwegian Agency for Development Cooperation). After Lula's election in 2003, the group received, for the first time, some official Brazilian government support. The Lula government generally nurtured existing popular cultural movements promoting social inclusion and full citizenship, leading to a kind of peaceful revolution in the politics of public culture. As Minister of Culture, pop star intellectual-musician Gilberto Gil encouraged the decentralization and democratization of culture, moving cultural power away from the wealthy south of Rio de Janeiro and São Paulo toward the urban peripheries and the impoverished Northeast. A correlative of his "points of culture" strategy was support for the vital cultures of the marginalized, whether those of indigenous filmmakers or of Afro-Brazilian rappers. The VNA films were very much in tune with the generally progressive thrust of the Lula period. At the same time, the production values of the films kept on improving, as the filmmakers also gained a clearer sense of what appealed to a larger public.

The films of the second phase of VNA are the result of the workshops, which bring in the collaboration of Mari Corrêa, trained in the Rouch-inspired Ateliers Varan based in Paris, and films by the indigenous directors themselves in collaboration with Carelli and Corrêa.[56] This wave of films, according to Ruben Caixeta de Queiroz, gain a more intimate feeling generated by longer takes, a more relaxed and intimate style, and a timing more in synch with an indigenous sense of temporality. Some examples of this phase would be *No tempo das chuvas* (In the Rainy Season, 2000), *Dançando com cachorro* (Dancing with the Dog, 2001), *Shomōtsi* (2001), and *Um dia na aldeia* (A Day in the Village, 2003). Many of the films blur the lines between the indigenous and non-indigenous collaboration, but the overall movement is toward the indigenous side of the equation. In a kind of self-anthropology, a director like Divino Tserewahú explores his own culture, as in *Wapté Munhōnō: iniciação do jovem xavante* (Initiation of a Young Xavante, 1999), which examines an initiation ritual for young Xavánte men, but where the multi-dimensional portrayal includes all the intra-cultural and inter-generational negotiations that go into the filming itself. As Queiroz puts it, "the elders think about their world and its contradictions, and their doubts about the tradition, and thus invent their culture, under the watchful eyes of the young people who also observe, film, and participate in a culture which is being both practiced and invented."[57]

Many of the VNA films feature interviews with elders who relate their first contacts with whites, lamenting the losses of traditional culture among young people, but who appreciate the role of cinema in re-indigenizing their people. Divino's *Wai'a Rini* (The Power of Dream, 2015) treats a ritual whereby Xavánte boys confronted series of exacting ritual challenges in order to enter an exhausted state in which they are ready to receive the reanimating power of shamanic dream. Thus, directors like Divino become translators and mediators both within their own culture and between their cultures and the world. His films are characterized by processual reflexivity, interviews with the elders, close collaboration with the community, the careful restaging of rituals and skillful orchestration of the movement of large groups of people, and always, a sly humor. The films have a didactic quality, but here it is the Xavánte who explain their own social codes and practices; they themselves are *les sujets supposes savoir* (those presumed to know).

The Archival Turn

Divino's process-oriented films frequently use archival footage and reenactment to portray "resurrectable" rituals. In a reflexive touch, the films reveal the processes of pre-production by showing Divino and his collaborators commenting on archival footage related to the project at hand. In the documentary *Piõnhitsi, mulheres xavante sem nome* (Xavante Women without Names, 2009), co-directors Divino Tserewahú and Tiago Campos Torres encourage the community to reenact the "Festa da Onca" (Jaguar Festival), a nearly abandoned festival linked to the women's naming ceremonies. The filmmakers discuss clips from earlier films on the same topic—those made by Vincent Carelli and by Tserewahú himself in 1995 the last time the ritual took place in the village, along with Divino's own footage from 2003 and the films of the Salesian priest Adelberto Heide in 1967.[58] While many films hide their own intertext to generate a sense of "originality," here the directors reveal it as partially the product of the editing table. As a film about a failure—in this case the failure to persuade the village to reenact the ceremony—the film resembles, on a smaller scale, other films about incompletion, such as Terry Gilliam's *Lost in La Mancha*, an essay-film about his unfinished *Don Quixote* (or Fellini's *8 ½*) where the story of failure becomes the film itself. In his analysis, André Brasil delineates the film's reflexive procedures, the discussion of the aesthetic and political choices made in the film itself, and the complications provoked by the different expectations of the various constituencies (the Xavánte themselves, other Indians, non-indigenous Brazilians, the wider world, and so forth).[59] The filmmakers constantly explain themselves and their purposes, for each other, for the children, for the community, and for the non-indigenous audience.

Brazilian analysts such as Claudia Mesquita, Ismail Xavier, Clarisse Alvarenga, Bernard Belisário, and others employ the category of "process films" to emphasize the complex dialogic negotiations in indigenous media between the diverse participants, between the community and the film, and where this process of negotiation comes to form part of the film itself.[60] For film scholar Claudia Mesquita, a "process film" is at once about its own subject and about its own making, where the cinema, in her words,

> exists in relation to and intermingles with lived experience in such a way as to be limited, stimulated, transformed, "conformed," expanded and potentialized by that experience ... [where] filming and life flow together, where the dividing lines are porous, where control over the scene is not always possible, where the film, in a very corporeal exchange within an experience that it cannot completely dominate, serves, or invents, its singular movement.[61]

Process films are marked by the scars of history and themselves seek to impact history. Form, as Claudia Mesquita points out, becomes indissociable from the process of realization and its intersection with lived experience.[62]

As Divino's films attest, IM in Brazil has also experienced its own "archival turn" by repurposing the archive for its own ends. *Ma Ê Dami Xina - Já me Transformei em Imagem* (I've Already Become Transformed into an Image, 2008), directed by Huni Kuin filmmaker Zezinho Yube in collaboration with Mari Corrêa and Vincent Carelli, exemplifies this tendency. The film concerns the history of the Huni Kuin (true people, people with traditions), also known by the originally pejorative name the Kaxinawa (bat people, night people). Contact for the Huni Kuin meant enslavement, corporeal branding, debt slavery, and disease. At the same time, the Huni Kuin/Kaxinawa and other indigenous nations have demonstrated impressive resilience and creativity in their efforts to preserve their lands against rubber bosses, cattle ranchers, and land speculators.

The 1980s were the time of the *seringueiros* (rubber tappers) movement led by Chico Mendes, which carried out direct-action *empates* (stalemates) whereby rubber laborers and their families would form human walls to block bulldozers and chainsaw gangs about to fell forests. The rubber tappers, including the Huni Kuin, became widely known during this period, when their struggle to protect their forest against cattle ranchers became an environmental *cause celebre*. Having lost their land base, and without outside help, they opened up trails, created new villages, supplied food to their peoples, and even sold rubber on their own. In August 1984, exasperated by FUNAI's false promises, Huni Kuin and Kulina peoples decided to take direct action. Rather than work within a debt-slavery regime, they decided to work for themselves. Chief Pambo told his people that they could now hunt, fish, farm, and raise their children in peace, proudly proclaiming that "[w]hen Indians undertake something, we are serious, and we do it ourselves. We were born in the forest, so we understand it and know how to work. Now we are going to secure our area."[63]

In *Ma Ê Dami Xina - Já me Transformei em Imagem* (2008), the elders answer questions from the young people about the past, accompanied by archival footage, as tribal leaders offer their version of Contact and their subsequent struggles. Their voiced version of their own history is interspersed with illustrative photos, archival materials, and ethnographic films showing their own villages in the past. They depict their own history as a forced ejection from communal well-being, followed by a series of traumatic shocks, leading finally to glimpses of liberation. What we have called "the trope of Indian Happiness," the film suggests, is more than a trope. Indeed, the film begins with an elder making the point explicit: "We lived happily before contact. Despite hardship, we had a good life, living peacefully." Film after film, community after community tells the same story of a descent from contented self-sufficiency into dependent precarity within capitalist modernity, but with a small measure of recovery at the end.

In the background of the film is the virtual enslavement of the Huni Kuin as workers during the Rubber Boom, a story also told in the already mentioned Aurelio Michiles film *The Secrets of Putumayo* (2020). The elders tell their history in five stages: (1) the felicitous communal pre-contact "time of the malocas" (thatched-roof longhouses) when they lived in peace, unperturbed by the outsiders; (2) the time of rupture or "first contact"; (3) the "time of massacres" and white occupation; (4) "the time of captivity" as semi-enslaved workforce engaged in rubber extraction. The spoken words about each phase "anchor," in Barthian terms, the polysemic imagery of the archival footage, whether drawn from the 1920s promotional films of Silvino Santos or from the more native-friendly documentaries of Harold Schultz. Western "progress," for the Huni Kuin, has meant only dispossession, solitude, exploitation, debt peonage, and the loss of collective festivity. The only relatively happy note comes with (5) the final period of the "time of rights," beginning in the 1970s, characterized by the struggle to reclaim land and natural resources. This section features footage of activist Chico Mendes, the assassinated labor leader who had forged an alliance between indigenous peoples and the rubber workers. This final phase embraces a movement toward cultural self-production—the film shows the Huni Kuin filming and teaching filmmaking—and in writing (with books written in Huin Kuin). The film concludes with the elder's words that inspired the title: "Now I've become an image, When I die you will see me," and it is implied, "learn from me."

Against the canonical hierarchy that elevates a disinterested (Kantean) Art over a merely practical Craft, some cultural anthropologists and art critics have disputed that hierarchy in favor of a more equal dialogue between Western and non-Western art. Els Lagrou claims that the artistic practices of body painting and designs of the Kaxinawá people, for example, produce a certain kind of body, one with both individual and cosmological overtones; artistic spirituality is inscribed on the body itself.[64] A Huni Kuin film, *Kene yuxi: As voltas do Kene* (The Return of Kene, 2010), directed by Zezinho Yube, explores weaving as a trampoline to question the status and role of art in indigenous life. More specifically, the film treats the Huni Kuin struggle to maintain the complex designs of their weaving traditions. As connoisseurs, the older women have a veritable passion and aesthetic pleasure in weaving. Thanks to their deep knowledge of what Henry James in a different context called "the figure in the carpet," they recognize the weavers by the patterns. Along the way, the film also exposes the culturally corrosive effects of evangelization. The "good news of the gospel," ironically, leads to the "bad news" of Indian inferiorization. Evangelized Indians sadly note the lack of prestige of their old faith: "Our religion is not mentioned in the Bible, so it must not exist" or "White religions are everywhere, but ours are nowhere." While weaving used to be for "gifting," now it's all about money. Meanwhile, a spiral of decline dictates that every generation knows less about weaving than the previous generation; the mothers know less about weaving than their mothers, their daughters know even less, and so on.

The TV series *Indians on TV* (2000), produced in conjunction with the Federal University of Mato Grosso, constituted an early indigenous production for Brazilian television. Carelli served as general director, with Ailton Krenak as presenter and moderator, assisted by well-prepared collaborators with a long experience of indigenous cultures such as Bruna Franchetto, Carlos Fausto, Dominique Gallois, Luis Donisete, Benzi Grupioni, and Virgínia Valadão. In the series, Indians mock the stereotypes polluting mainstream Brazilian TV. The Globo telenovela *Uga Uga* (2000–01), for example, has scientists lead an expedition in the Amazon forest where they are attacked by an indigenous tribe. The melodramatic novela features a "white Indian" raised in the Amazon by the "good" Indians, whose parents were murdered by the "bad" Indians. In an open letter to Rio's *Jornal do Brasil*, members of the National Indigenous Conference protested the telenovela in the name of their collective memory: "we are peoples with living memory. We have not forgotten what has happened over the last five-hundred years."[65]

The charm of indigenous children, a secret resource in some VNA films, pervades *Das Criancas Ikpeng para o Mundo* (From the Ikpeng Children to the World, 2002). The film offers still another kind of "first contact," here in the form of video-letter exchanges between two villages, one in Brazil and the other in Cuba. Ikpeng children explain their everyday life, their family relations, their games, and their encounters with white technologies. Young friends kid and fake-punch each other as children might do anywhere in the world. A mischievous young boy jokes that his tiny sister is not a human being but rather a battery-operated alien; laughingly, he points to her little butt as the hiding place for the battery. Later he demonstrates a key technological innovation—an outdoor toilet. Mimicking a bowel movement, he explains: "This is how the white man taught us how to take a shit." The many scenes in these films of children splashing gleefully in rivers, even swimming while mounted on wild boars, not only remind us of the ordinary happiness of children playing everywhere but also serve as a token of the kind of communal well-being that indigenous people have too often lost.

A number of indigenous videos emphasize a trait stressed by the first Europeans to arrive in Brazil such as Jean de Léry, and later by Lévi-Strauss, Pierre Clastres, and Viveiros de Castro—i.e. the role of humor and laughter both in everyday life and in indigenous myths and legends.[66] The VNA film *Video Cannibalism* (1995), whose title echoes the themes of modernist anthropophagy, introduces the Enauené, an isolated yet extroverted group that skipped the pen-and-pencil literacy stage to join the age of electronic media. Like the 1920 modernists, the filmmakers emphasize the group's playfulness, where men play act at making love together while their compatriots laugh. One man gleefully exposes his anus to the lens, communicating a clear sense of violation of a taboo, the kind of transgressive gesture one sometimes sees applauded as an avant-garde provocation in the New York art world. The Enauené also reenact a meeting between themselves and gold prospectors, resulting in a film-within-the-film—"The Invaders"—which the tribe enjoys on a VCR. Here video becomes a catalyst for cultural identity, potentially dynamizing what Afro-Brazilians call in Yoruba "axé" or the spiritual force of communal realization.

In the face of dispossession and even massacres, the Krahô people, for their part, have maintained their culture through partial accommodation to the dominant society. The Krahô practice a kind of diplomatic policy with non-indigenous religions. According to anthropologist Delvair Montagnet Melatti, the informal Krahô sociology of comparative religion sees the Christianized among them as divided between Catholics and Protestants, where the differences are less doctrinal than behavioral, with the former "drinking cachaca, carrying guns, swearing, smoking and cheating on their wives, with the latter committing none of these sins."[67] The Krahô also enjoy, alongside the traditional festivals, "Brazilian style parties, night-long affairs with national dances and food ... and the Indians wearing [western] clothes."[68]

The Krahô also celebrate a sequence of festivals commemorating every stage of their people's life cycles. Some of the festivals feature sacred clowns, a tradition well-known in native American communities, whether the *nanabozho* of the Ojibwe, the *wesakaycha*k of the Cree, or the *heyoka* of the Lakota. A documentary by two non-Indians (Leticia Sabatella and Gringo Cardia), entitled *Hotxua* (2009), a product of the aptly named "Caliban Productions," calls attention to Krahô festivities and the group's well-known penchant for mischievous play. (By prior agreement, all the profits from the film went to the Krahô themselves.) The Krahô invited the filmmakers to film the "Festa da Batata," a kind of harvest and fecundity celebration linked to the consecration of marriages. The title refers to a sacred clown trickster figure—Apraki, linked to shamanism and curing—the star of the Festa who entertains and educates the community. If some Amazonian tribes have been described (by Viveiros de Castro) as culturally "Deleuzian," the Krahô might be said to be "Bakhtinian" in their faith in the healing power of laughter and of the "grotesque body" as a way of sustaining their culture in the face of external and internal challenges.

In Ana Gabriela Morim de Lima's analysis, Krahô myths and ceremonial clowns revolve around the dialectic of the open and closed body—a concept reminiscent of Bakhtin's references in *Rabelais and His World* of the "self-transforming body" with its "orifices and protuberances," and the active, creative body that defecates, urinates, secretes, farts, spits, menstruates, and so forth. One episode in the film stages a version of what Bakhtin saw as the paradigmatically carnivalesque image—the improbably old hag giving birth to new life—by having an even more improbable parent, as elderly man, give birth, not to new life, but to a grown boy, to the laughter of the crowd. The scene recalls the opening scene of *Macunaima* (1969), where a white male actor in drag gives birth to a 50-year-old black man, combining Bakhtin's pregnant hag with the carnivalesque penchant for transvestitism and the bodily lower stratum. (Not to be outdone, avant-garde "anthropophagic" dramaturg Ze Celso staged a similar scenelet where he, as a proud and very gay pregnant father, "gives birth" to one of his actors.)

Corumbiara: On the Trail of Massacres

On a more somber register, Vincent Carelli's archival documentary *Corumbiara: They Shoot Indians, Don't They?* (2009)—whose title alludes to the American film *They Shoot Horses Don't They?*—ranges across different time periods, specifically 1986, 1995, 1996, 1998, 2000, and 2006.[69] The dramatic story is told in Carelli's usual understated way, without commentative music, manipulative montage, or overheated rhetoric. Over a period of 20 years, Carelli and his indigenist friend Marcelo Santos had hoped to film specific events and materials, in hopes of proving the existence of the remnants of a massacre by landowners of Kanoê and Akuntsu natives. More specifically, the filmmakers sought to contact isolated indigenous massacre survivors, without any kind of official protection from the Brazilian state, a non-status that would leave them vulnerable to further violence.

Corumbiara is a quest film where the filmmaking protagonists confront tremendous obstacles. The search for indigenous "remainders" ran into an obstacle course of hurdles and frustrations. Aspiring landowners and corrupt politicians were eager to efface any evidence of an indigenous presence and would do everything in their power to prevent allies like Carelli to make the case for land demarcation. Finding the *indigenes*, in this case, went hand in hand with finding evidence of attempts to eradicate them, since the cover-up, as the adage has it, is often as serious as the crime. While difficult to prove that a massacre took place, it was less difficult to detect attempts to hide the evidence. As Clarisse Alvarenga points out in her illuminating study of "first contact" films, what makes *Corumbiara* a "process film" is the long 20-year trajectory of its realization, where that trajectory becomes part of the story, evidenced by the stigmata of changing formats, technologies, and attitudes. The vicissitudes of filmmaking and the "risks of the real" (Comolli)—interruptions, accidents, postponements, reshooting, the drying up of funds—inflect the narrative itself through incidents, which are simultaneously historical and filmic.[70] History leaves its mark not only on Carelli's changing ways of making films but also on his aging body. Instead of a Linklater-style longue-durée registry of a boyhood, we get Carelli's registry of decades of struggle during his adulthood.

At one point, the filmmakers encounter two figures wending their way down a jungle path; their appearance and behavior suggest a lack of any previous direct contact with outsiders.[71] As witness to something rarely seen in the cinema, the film powerfully conveys the sublime gravitas of actual first contact. Upon seeing the pair, Marcelo panics, less out of fear *of* them than of fear *for* them, given the possible horrific consequences of an unsought-after contact. He anxiously suggests: "Let's leave the initiative up to them. If they want to come closer, we'll make contact. But it depends on them." The cameraman's labored breathing relays a visceral sense of how threatening, but also how exhilarating, such first contacts must always have been, with anxiety and nervous uncertainty on both sides. The weight and pressure of history has a visceral impact on the cameraman; in a kind of cine-vertigo, the image becomes decentered and unstable. As César Guimarães points out, the contact itself "provokes a discontinuity in filmic *ecriture* in the form of a loss of focus and equilibrium."[72]

Alvarenga mobilizes Viveiros de Castro's concept of "equivocation" to refer not to a mistake or error but rather to a profound cognitive gap between indigenous and non-indigenous interlocutors at the moment of first contact, where any common understanding is extremely difficult. For Viveiros de Castro, "first contact" is always equivocal and dense with misunderstandings, even with the best of intentions. The question is not one of lack of knowledge or competence, but rather of the fraught underpinnings of European/indigenous interlocution. Nor is it only a question of asymmetrical power and uneven historical experience; it is also a question of incommensurate perspectives on a common world or even of people dwelling in very different worlds. As Alvarenga and Belisario, drawing on Viveiros de Castro, put it in another context, "The world which the indigenous people describe within its understanding is different from the world described by the landowners, which is different from the world of the indigenistas and government functionaries."[73]

During the encounter, both sides essay verbal communication in a futile attempt to get to know each other. In a tactile negotiation, a haptic attempt at corporeal understanding, the indigenous pair initiate physical contact by holding hands and touching their interlocutors, trying to feel the vibe, as it were, without the mediation of language. Carelli is disappointed: after years of waiting he thought everything would be clarified, but without language the encounter is unsatisfying. (The anti-climactic breakdown in communication recapitulates that of Lévi-Strauss in *Tristes Tropiques* when he finally met the "sauvages" but could not communicate with them.) The filmmakers later discover the language family, thanks to an indigenous translator, but in the final edit Carelli deliberately maintains this first moment of reciprocal opacity, obviously a deliberate choice since a translation could easily have been provided in the post-production.

The pair turn out to be siblings, named Tiramantu and Pura. We meet them again later, this time with subtitle translation. While the earlier scene reproduces the initial situation of mutual incomprehension, the later scene offers retrospective comprehension. After a multisensory tactile negotiation, the filmmakers accept to be led to the pair's village. In another scene, Tiramantu and another indigenous woman, Umoro, encounter the anthropologist Virginia Valadao, probably the first white woman they have met. In a literally "touching" encounter, they cautiously and curiously undress her to see and feel and discover if she has the same female body that they have. (The character playing Amazon filmmaker Silvino Santos in Michille's *Cineasta da Selva* recounts a similar incident of corporeal examination in relation to his wife Sara.)

At one point, Carelli and his collaborators find evidence of a lone Indian recluse, in all probability the survivor of a massacre. They find several stick huts, presumably abandoned in an attempt to avoid contact. They eventually discover his actual hut, slowly approaching as the camera reveals an opening from which protrudes the tip of an arrow, aimed straight at the camera. The scene constitutes a hyperbolic and literally dangerous version of Jean-Louis Comolli's theme of the "anxiety-of-the-filming-subject" of documentary meeting the reciprocal "anxiety-of-the-filmed-subject."⁷⁴ Here the severe trauma of one group meets the ponderous sense of responsibility of another group; a case where the cumulative suffering of centuries of painful historical contacts impinges on the present. For this traumatized "Indian who is not yet Indian," the result is an apparently desperate desire to be opaque, to *not* be filmed. Viveiros de Castro writes of the present-day isolated Indian: "[He] does not know he is an Indian; he is an Indian only for FUNAI, not for himself. The isolated Indian has the courage to say he is not an Indian, especially because he is not yet an Indian … In other words, you have to first become Indian in order to stop being Indian later."⁷⁵

Along with the physical danger lurks an ethical danger. The filmmakers are intensely aware of the long-term consequences of contact, aware, as Gustavo Furtado puts it, that "the yearning to produce archives of primal contacts has led to the production of another kind of archive, an archive of fevers, records not of contact but of disease and devastation."⁷⁶ The scene triggers a crisis of conscience for Carelli, provoking worries over the ethics of forcing contact, while also knowing that contact might actually be the only way to protect the person refusing contact. Carelli starts to doubt his own motives: how badly do I want this image? What right do I have to initiate contact? Am I a hunter with my *fusil cinematographique*? Am I a predator grabbing filmic loot?⁷⁷

Corumbiara goes beyond the subjectivity of the filmmakers and the dramatics of the encounter, however, to hint at an analysis of the social forces arrayed against indigenous people. Police, press, and the judiciary are revealed to be at the service of agro-business and corrupt politicians. Carelli uses the common device of the hidden camera—used by filmmakers as diverse as Claude Lanzmann and Michael Moore—to expose the exploitative synergies connecting large landowners and corrupt politicians. Carelli's hidden camera, as Alvarenga points out, exposes not only the literal face of the landowner but also the mise-en-scène of power itself, as exerted through the collaboration of landowners, politicians, the police, the judiciary, and the press.⁷⁸ The film embraces what has become an effective topos in many radical films—the efforts of the violent agents of the powerful to remain off-screen by breaking the camera, covering the lens, or beating up the cameraman.

The anti-indigenous interviewees display their own *mauvaise foi* by deploying the usual tired ontological disqualification—i.e. the Indians are not "real" Indians. The lawyer for one of the landowner even lauds the American Way of Extermination, of "killing all its Indians" in order to become the "largest grain producer in the world." The doctrine of terra nullius, to put it in the language of analytic philosophy, turns out not to be a constative, a description of fact, but rather a performative, a command. Terra Nullius does not mean that the land is empty of indigenous people; it means that the large landowners can declare the land empty de facto as an excuse to literally empty the land of indigenous people, or to justify having done so retroactively, thus confirming the original claim of terra nullius. But in this process film, as Mesquita puts it, "the cinema is not only touched and modified by historical experience; it intervenes and alters experience, participating in change."⁷⁹

The Guaraní and Contrapuntal Narration

Some of the later VNA films emerge from the Guaraní, a group that has been symbolically central to the Brazilian national imaginary—celebrated in romantic novels yet where contemporary reality has little to do with the novels' idealized images. Part of the larger group of Tupí peoples, the Guaraní inhabit various nation-states, including Argentina, Paraguay, Uruguay, and Brazil, with a present-day population estimated at 280,000 individuals, 85,000 of whom live in Brazil, 80,000 in Bolivia, 61,000 in Paraguay, and 54,000 in Argentina, usually described as belonging to four clusters: Kaiowá (the denomination used in Brazil, also known as Paĩ-Tavyterã in Paraguay), Nhandeva (also described as Ava-Guaraní), Mbya (in the south of Brazil, Paraguay and Argentina), and Chiriguanos (in the Andean foothills in Bolivia).

At the time of Cabral's arrival, the Tupí and the Guaraní numbered in the millions and dominated a huge territory, reduced over the course of history to scattered slivers of land. From the beginning, the Guaraní have been victims of colonial border-drawing, first by the Pope and the Treaty of Tordesillas in 1493, and then by the Treaty of Madrid in 1750, decisions made without consulting the Guaranís and since then leading to the slow-working dismemberment of their territory. The Jesuits tried to Christianize the Guaraní by learning Tupí and paying homage to those communal traditions deemed compatible with Christianity. The endless debates about the Jesuit "reductions" have variously seen them either as models of a Christian socialism cum liberation theology avant la lettre or as sanctified forms of enslavement and cultural destruction. Accused of founding an independent empire, the Jesuits were expelled in 1759 and the order dissolved in 1773, while the Guaraní were dispersed. The twentieth-century episodes in this trajectory trace their roots to the devastating aftereffects of the War of Paraguay, to the assimilationism of the Rondon Commission in the 1910s and 1920s, through the expansionist take-overs of the Vargas regime in the 1930s, then to the military dictatorship's attempt, in the 1960s and 1970s to "integrate the national territory" at the expense of indigenous peoples themselves.

Alberto Mussa describes the Tupí peoples, including the Guaraní, as measuring time and forecasting natural phenomena by observing the stars. As excellent fighters, they formed armadas of 200 canoes, each with 20 men. Although involved in constant vengeance wars, they did not take territory from the vanquished or seek economic advantage. They captured enemies only in order to integrate them as brothers-in-law, and then kill them, and devour them in elaborate rituals.[80] Their culture hero Maira ("transformer") taught the Tupí-Guaraní to make hammocks and culinary utensils, who prohibited marriage between father and daughter. According to Guaraní spirituality, the forest areas, including those lost to the colonizers, were populated by an array of invisible entities requiring spiritual nurturing. The invisible world of their ancestors and the dream of a "Land without Evil," it is thought, will restore the rightful relations between the dead, the gods, and everyday life. Marcelo Fiorini points out that the concept of land in the Land without Evil is the polar opposite of the Colonial Frontier Mentality, in that it is a movement away from the violence of the frontier, an exodus from the masculine warrior society and a return to the nourishing, feminine ethos of the Karaí, the prophet and the *cantador*, a practice of transhumance.[81] This spirit explains, perhaps, the readiness of the Guaraní to endure immense physical suffering through what might be called a Guaraní version of Ernst Bloch's "principle of hope." With the Guaraní, the supernatural world exercises agency in everyday life.[82] Already in the sixteenth century, French commentators like Andre Thevet admired the complexity of Tupí-Guaraní mythologies and cosmologies. The Tupí-Guaraní wondered if the arriving Europeans were gods, which the Europeans took as flattery, but in fact it meant something quite different, that the Guaraní thought of all selves as potential gods, having in mind their conception of humans who become gods through spiritual preparation. The parallel to Christianity is not that the Land without Evil is the same as heaven, but rather that both heaven and the *Terra sem Mal* have a similar function, to inspire people on earth and in life.

Non-indigenous knowledge of Guaraní spirituality is deeply indebted to Hélène Clastres's classic study of Tupí-Guaraní cosmology—*A terra sem Mal* (The Land without Evil, 1978). Basing herself both on the writings from the France Antartique era and on contemporary linguistic and anthropological research, she sees "The Land without Evil" as emblematic of an ethic of a perpetual search for a land wherefrom death is banned. Christians in Brazil, quite logically but inaccurately, linked it to the Christian Heaven. Unlike the Christian heaven, it could be sought after on earth through ritual prayer, song, and dance.[83] Guaraní spiritual nomadism, according to Hélène Clastres, constituted a journey toward self-improvement and divinity.[84] For Clastres, the search emerges from a culture of the sacred word, of discourse, and of the prophecy of the *karais* (healers, spiritual leaders) who mediate between the natural and the supernatural by bringing the divine words to human beings. Migration need not be literal and physical, as Renato Sztutman points out; it can take the form of prayers, songs, plays, performances, and obviously, films.[85] The role of the *karais* is both cultural and political, reminiscent perhaps of the role of Black preachers in North America who foster communal cohesion through prophetic charisma and wisdom.

Guaraní spirituality is worldly or, better, earthly, with room for doubts and dilemmas since the quest is infinite and constantly changing. As forest flaneurs, the Guaraní construct themselves over the course of the voyage. The titles of the Guaraní Collective films—*Two Villages, One Path, Bicycles of Nhanderu, On the Road with Mario*—all evoke what Bakhtin called the "Chronotope of the Road," a transgeneric trend with philosophical overtones of a search for truth furthered by roadside encounters. Conceived of in analogy to Einsteinian mathematics in the 1930s and 1940s, the chronotope refers to the "intrinsic connectedness of temporal and spatial relationships that are artistically expressed."[86] The road offers rich potential for encounter, where people separated by social and spatial distance can accidentally meet and "various fates may collide and interweave with one another."[87] The Guaraní films, in this sense, convey an ethics and aesthetics, if not of the road, at least of paths informed by mobile intersubjectivities. Within an aesthetic of movement, the Guaraní films give us "path movies" or "bicycle movies." The moving camera subjective shots in the Guaraní films, in this sense, convey this spiritualized idea of movement. As a historically nomadic people, the Guaraní on a practical level migrated because they hunted and gathered in different places, in obedience to seasonal rhythms. But for the Guaraní, movement forms part of an endless search where the search itself was as important as the result. A possible analogy would be to the Ojibwe in North America, also peoples "on the move," who saw nomadism as a primary value and envisioned life as a path and an endless search. Anishinaabe writer Gerald Vizenor's concept "transmotion" as a "sense of native motion and an active presence [that] is sui generis sovereignty. The idea of Native transmotion as survivance, a reciprocal use of nature, not a monotheistic, territorial sovereignty" would seem to be highly relevant to the Guaraní concept of mobile sovereignty.[88]

For the colonizer, nomadism was simply a real estate-disqualifier since the indigene had supposedly not settled the land and mixed it with their labor and made it productive. In fact, of course, migratory peoples like the Guaraní did actually mix labor with the land. The real difference was not the lack of labor but rather the lack of a bureaucratic imprimatur in the form of a "deed" and the "failure" to produce commodities. Édouart Glissant, for his part, makes a distinction very relevant to the case of the Guaraní. He distinguishes between "circular nomadism"—where the nomadism was over given areas and not related to territorial domination or conquest, clearly the case of the Guaraní, in contrast with the aggressive "straight-arrow" colonial-style nomadism of settler colonialism which dispossesses the indigene. For the Guaraní, circular nomadism was part of a collective self-cleansing, or self-purification, a *rite de passage* guided by the *karais,* rather like a utopia or a terrestrial carnival that would make sacrifice worthwhile.[89]

The Guaraní Mbyá Collective, in the wake of the other indigenous VNA film collectives (Xavánte, Kuikuro, Ashaninka, Panará, Kisêdjê, Huni Kuin), was one of the last groups to join, in 2007, the VNA video-training workshops. The films often bear the signatures of multiple directors within a flexible schema that allows various participants, in an indigenization of the strategies of early French New Wave short films, to take over diverse production functions (camera, sound, lighting). At times, multiple native directors (Ariel Ortega [Kuaray Poti], Patrícia Ferreira [Pará Xxapy]) collaborate with non-native directors (Vincent Carelli, Ernesto Carvalho). The Guaraní films convey a kind of modest and sad serenity. The films are quietly, not ostentatiously, reflexive, with "actors" nodding to the camera and even commenting on the shots, but without any aspiration to be "postmodern." The films are also inferentially decolonial in their treatment of the complex negotiations between the village world and that of the "whites."

The Guaraní Collective film *Mokoi Tekoá Petei Jeguatá* (Two Villages One Path, 2008) signed by Ariel Ortega, Jorge Ramos Morinico, and Germano Benites is divided into two parts. The first part shows the everyday life of the village of Anhetenguá, where the lack of land prevents the once-independent villagers from practicing their traditional activities of hunting and planting corn and manioc, thus necessitating the production of handicrafts as a means of survival. The second half takes place in a different village, Koenju, and also treats the production of handicrafts. The two villages are very much interconnected, however, because the products of both villages end up in the same place—the ruins of the Sao Miguel Jesuit Missions in the South of Brazil, the site of the Jesuit "Reduction" of the seventeenth and eighteenth centuries—where they now sell their handcrafts to tourists. The Missions, stony mementoes to colonial history, incorporated into the UNESCO World Patrimony in 1983, are heavy with meaning for the Guaraní, whose ancestors slaved to build them.

At one point, the Guaraní visit the quarry where their ancestors found, cut, and carried the stones that built the Missions. One is reminded of Brecht's poem "A Worker Reads History" about the role of invisible, literally buried labor, in constructing monuments:

Who built the seven gates of Thebes?
The books are filled with names of kings.
Was it the kings who hauled the craggy blocks of stone?
And Babylon, so many times destroyed.
Who built the city up each time? In which of Lima's houses,
That city glittering with gold, lived those who built it?

In the Guaraní collective films, the Missions ruins take on multiple roles—a movie set for a famous Hollywood film, a workplace for the Guaraní, a *lieu de memoire* for the Guaraní and the guides, and a picturesque site for the tourists. The film incarnates the "crossed gazes" of colonialism by counterpointing two versions of settler history, that of the guides, some of them grammar school and high school teachers, who mythify the Jesuit "protectors" of the Indians; versus another group, not usually recognized as legitimate narrators of history, to wit, the Guaraní handicraft vendors, who remember the Jesuits as those who enslaved and worked them to death. As one Guaraní explains, "the whites always look down on us, but they themselves were the ones who left us in this mess … they bordered our territory. They imposed boundaries. Put up a fence for us to obey." In their more disenchanted view: "The whites took everything from us [and] appropriated these ruins built by our kin who were forced to build it by the Jesuit priests."

The tourists, meanwhile, apparently unaware that the Guaraní are the originary inhabitants, naively ask, "Why did you choose to live here?" One Guaraní woman gets so tired of the charade that she refuses to let the tourists take her picture and even refuses to sell her handicrafts.[90] In an encounter haunted by the asymmetries of colonial history, the tendentious ignorance of the tourists meets the soft-spoken recalcitrance of the Guaraní. As Ruben Caixeta de Queiroz explains, the film casts a sharp look at the colonial gaze on the Indian, framing the white gaze in such a way as to reveal its historical potency and overbearing presence. Provincialized, the white gaze is made visible to whites themselves; the objects of the gaze become the subjects.[91]

The point of such films is not just to provide information but to disturb and change spectatorial subjectivity. While non-indigenous people cannot become Guaraní, they can begin to doubt their own apprehensions. Indigenous cinema presents a counterpoint of at least two gazes. One group looks at ruins of churches and sees the power and beneficence of the Christian West; the other sees forced labor and the agony of a culture. In this sense, the film offers a critical anatomy of colonial-inflected spectatorship. It is not a mere difference of opinion, but of conflictual grids, prisms, and affects. Other indigenous-related films reveal a similarly bifurcated vision, as in the already discussed *Claude Lévi-Strauss: Auprès de l'Amazonie*. In that film, a bus full of Nambiquara children passes an orderly sprawling soy plantation giving us soy as far as the eye can see. A non-indigenous person might think "progress," "order," and "export economy"; the Nambiquara, meanwhile, look at the same plantation and remember the disappeared forest that provided sustenance and that is no more.

Another Mbyá Guaraní Collective film *Bicicletas de Nhanderú* (The Divine Spirit's Bicycles, 2011), directed by Ariel Ortega and Patrícia Ferreira in collaboration with Tiago Torres and Amandine Goisbault, immerses us again in the world of Guaraní spirituality. Here the figure of Tupã, sometimes called the "God of Thunder," exerts his presence. Associated with the thunder and lightning literally heard and seen in the film, this divinity is figuratively linked to storms and storm-like events. The film is divided into Ariel's conversations with those older and those younger than himself: with the old spiritual shaman Solano at one extreme, and at the other extreme, two young brothers, Neneco and Palermo who "migrate" around the village and environs. Indigenizing the theories about off-screen space developed by film theorists, André Brasil sees the film as constantly playing between two worlds, the on-screen space of the natural world, and the off-screen space of the supernatural world as an inferential presence, hinted at through conversations and interactions among the Guaraní as they move through the world.[92]

Bicicletas de Nhanderú begins with the images and sounds of an imminent storm, provoking a comment by *karai* Solano: "The *tupans* not only bring rain and thunder, they also protect us. While we humans cannot see the spirits that wish us harm, the *tupans* can see them." Solano explains the meaning of the title—that the *pajes*, as spiritual leaders, are the "bicycles for the gods." The metaphor of spiritual "riding" recalls the parallel riding within Afro-Brazilian culture, the mediums, the "Divine Horsemen" of candomblé "ridden" by the *orixas* of West African religions. Only the vehicle of the metaphor—animal (horses) in the candomblé case, and mechanical (bicycles) in the Guaraní case—has changed. Collective dance, for Solano, can serve as a means of purification, part of the tireless search for the Land without Evil and the house of prayer as the place where the search is actualized through meditation. Festive multi-generational parties, mixing indigenous with non-indigenous music, also stimulate spiritual capacities.

Two effervescent young brothers, Neneco and Palermo, converse with their mother as she works, in typical child-mother exchanges that mix affection with gentle reprimands. At the same time, the film testifies to a tense "double-consciousness"-style relation with the "white" world. The Guaraní, at once Brazilian and Native, transit between two worlds, one where they are at home and welcome and another where they are resented or pitied, always under a cloud of suspicion. The white world remains present even when physically absent. The children number among those that Ranciere calls "those who don't count, those who have no part."[93] The two boys act like mischievous children everywhere, but mischievous middle-class white boys do not usually speak of "spirits dwelling in these trees" or complain about being shot at by landowners. Palermo expresses a kind of camera-conscious anger, a fury beyond his age—at once self-aware and earnest. His frantic gestures recall Fanon's analysis of the corporeal frenzies and transports of the oppressed in *The Wretched of the Earth*. In a kind of cultic rage, Palermo acts as if the landowners are killing him, but he is also killing them. Waving his machete, he shouts: "Landowners! Ugly landowners! Come here and kill me. I'm ready to die." Then, in the tone of one reporting a banal everyday occurrence, he casually mentions that the landowners had fired three rifle shots at them.

Bicicletas offers a thoroughgoing reflexivity, but not of the cute postmodern kind, which says "this is not real," but rather a reflexivity that says this is really a film with real cameras being really made about real people and real things. The film occasionally shows Ariel with his camera, but more often the reflexivity takes place through the dialogue of the child "characters" with the cameraman. "Did you film me saying those swear-words yesterday," Palermo asks. The two boys banter with the cameraman, something normally eliminated as annoying "noise" destined for the digital trashcan. As the childlike ID figures of the film and as youthful surrogates for the director, the two boys defy all kinds of borders—the fence, the fazenda, and the frame itself. Implicit is a different conception of both property and propriety and their inter-connections, conveying a suspicion of borders and private property as alien and oppressive, a hostility to all that encloses and limits their search and wandering on land formerly available for their peregrinations. At the same time, demarcation of land is not sufficient; it gives agency to the state, but for the Guaraní the land does not belong to the state or even to the indigenous population—it belongs to Nhanderu.

In another "path film" by the Collective, *No caminho com Mário* (On the Road with Mario, 2014), the young protagonist (Palermo again) promotes all kinds of interaction with the camera: he almost runs it over with his bicycle, destabilizing the frame, and throws corn at the lens. Like a precocious assistant director, he mocks the filmmaker for asking stupid questions: "Are you playing the fool, filmmaker?" At another point, he suggests what scholars call a subjective point-of-views shot, recommending that the movement of the camera follow the movement of his eyes. Later, the kids enter a neighboring fazenda to gather the wood the community needs to fabricate their handicrafts. On their return, they see a *sabiá* and kill it with a sling. They grab the bird, sheer its feathers, and remove the guts, and then in a pre-pubescent exercise in spectatorship theory, predict the probable white reaction to the sequence—"they are going to feel sorry for the bird."[94] One is reminded of those protests against filmic cruelty to animals that overlook the cruelty to human beings in the very same film, or of those lachrymose appeals for stray dogs, with saccharine music tugging at our heartstrings. Aware of the assumptions of the middle-class audience, the boys foresee a tendentious channeling of empathy in reaction to the sequence just filmed.

In another reflexive note, one of the boys retroactively criticizes the veracity of their own representation, acknowledging that while "our grandparents did actually hunt that way, at a time when they killed bigger animals; now we are reduced to killing little birds." Correcting a possible mis-impression and perhaps defending their honor, they explain that "[w]e are not starving, we just wanted to show how our ancestors acted in the past." They then eat the birds, find them delicious, and jokingly fight over who gets to eat the last piece. In a kind of juvenile double-voice discourse, they are acutely aware of outsiders' assumptions about them, so the boys justify killing the bird by explaining that they are hungry. The scene offers the reverse anthropology of a Guaraní child's critique of a hypothetical western spectator. (That hypothetical spectator might also remember that whites cage, fry, grill, and roast birds all the time—as Hitchcock himself reminded us in a witty trailer for *The Birds*, a film that ends with a moment of avian subjectivity, shot from the point of view of four crows observing the departing humans.)

The title of *Desterro Guarani* (2011), directed by Ariel Ortega and Patrícia Ferreira in partnership with Vincent Carelli and Ernesto de Carvalho, refers to exile, literally "de-landing" or "de-grounding," evoking the Guaraní historical experience as well as Deleuze's "deterritorialization" and "nomadology." The Guaraní, to paraphrase an Oren Lyons and John Mohawk title, are "exiles in the land of racial democracy." The Guaraní films constantly highlight migration as a positive value, reflecting a nostalgia for a time of borderless peregrination. The film deploys the classic film-within-the-film strategy by showing the villagers watching a sequence of Roland Joffé's *The Mission* (1986). Unlike the Jean Rouch films that show the participants watching the rushes, here the Guaraní watch the Hollywood portrayal of their own ancestors, in a film that ends with complete extermination. Guaraní wearing contemporary western clothes (with indigenous variations) watch actors representing Guaraní wearing Jesuit-mandated robes. As the Joffe film pans over a choir of Guaraní children, we hear Ariel's off-screen critical analysis: "But if they all died, then who are we!?"

Desterro conveys a sense of Guaraní territory as an open, expansive *tekoa*, without the need for settling down in a single place.[95] This displacement, this centrality of wondering and wandering within an expanded sense of territoriality, is incorporated into the very materiality of the film, which for André Brasil relays a mimesis of theme and technique in a "nomadic device."[96] In a different context, Kobena Mercer and Teshome Gabriel, in an earlier period of post-Third Worldist aesthetics, had spoken of a metaphorical "nomadic" aesthetics shaped by postcolonial sensibilities in the metropole. But here the nomadism is not a case of well-traveled cosmopolitans but rather of a very literal, concrete, ancestrally grounded spiritual exercise. In that spirit, the film has its characters literally move through fences and borders, recapitulating the Guaraní's calculated bypassing of official national borders. For the colonizer, meanwhile, nomadism—sometimes desired and imagined rather than real—served as an alibi for denying indigenous land rights. But could absentee plantation owners not also be seen as migrants whose land should be available for reappropriation? Given the mobility that results in the *Jeguatá* (sacred walk), in Ariel's reflection, the Guaraní became foreigners in a land where they have always lived. Ariel, as camera-carrying narrator, wonders what white people think when they see the sign "Guaraní Village," much as a present-day Haudenosaunee might wonder what white Americans imagine when they see the New York Throughway Exit for "Onandaga."

The Martyrdom of the Guaraní-Kaiowá

The inherent contradiction between Conquest and Discovery doctrine and a Brazilian legal system that supposedly guaranteed the rights of indigenous peoples and the protection of their cultural and material needs explodes when the issue becomes one of land. The history of dispossession of the various branches of the Tupí-Guaraní continues today under the reign of the new empires of cattle and soy. Between 1915 and 1928, SPI demarcated small reserves earmarked for the thousands of Guaraní-Kaiowá who had lived in their traditional territories in the South of Mato Grosso do Sul State. The Guaraní-Kaiowá have lived in this part of Mato Grosso do Sul for over 1,200 years and have a strong spiritual connection with the land. The official expectation was that after a provisional "containment" in small reserves, indigenous peoples would assimilate into the rest of national society, a policy goal similar to that implemented in the United States at the end of the nineteenth century, although articulated in deceptively "humane" language. Their sacred lands were gradually dismembered and expropriated by large landowners and commercialized by the federal government. The common practice was for *fazendeiros*, aided by soldiers, to seize the land whenever the Guaraní left for one of their pilgrimages. During their absence, their land would be deforested to make way for raising livestock and monocultural farming. The ensuing degradation of nature made it impossible to maintain their traditionally viable way of life. Without a land basis, the Guaraní often ended up desperately poor and penniless in encampments alongside the roads, near bus stations, vulnerable to the random aggressions of the cities.[97]

In 2013, when VNA lost the financial support of the Brazilian government that had been linked to the progressive policies of Gilberto Gil as Minister of Culture, Carelli, and co-director Tatiana Almeida resorted to crowdfunding to finance a lengthy epic-documentary entitled *Martírio* (2017). The film was meant to denounce the relentless dispossession of the Guaraní-Kaiowá of Mato Grosso do Sul. That state currently has a very high incidence of violent attacks on indigenous communities, with intense conflicts between the indigenous communities and influential landowners supported by powerful political lobbies. As indigenous ancestral lands are taken to make way for industrial farming of soy, corn, or sugarcane, the Guaraní-Kaiowá find themselves struggling with food shortages, evictions, and attacks. They live precariously with increasing reports of murder, torture, malnutrition, and the "disappearances" of indigenous leaders.

In the face of these threats, the Guaraní-Kaiowá articulate a form of resistance operating in the interstices of the state apparatus, showing a capacity to attract support from a heterogeneous array of organizations.[98] Displaced from their ancestral lands and confined to minuscule reserves, the Guaraní-Kaiowá have also experienced socio-ecological exploitation (ranging from underpaid work to deforestation of their reserves for timber extraction). Their lives, traditionally nurtured by the environing land, and cared for by large families moving around the region, were suffering from the impact of the commodification of labor, drug trafficking, and cross-border contraband. Encircled by the advance of soybean and sugarcane production, the situation of the Kaiowá-Guaraní fits into those definitions of genocide that go beyond mass murder to include issues such as cultural destruction and ecological devastation as genocidal practices.[99]

A veritable film event, *Martírio* (2017) offers a searing account of a century of massacres and dispossession of the Guaraní and attempts to re-indigenize a territory once theirs or at least hang on to what remains. The weapons in this unequal contest with landowners have been protests, bows and arrows (and sometimes guns), performances, films, and a combative form of spirituality. Embedding materials filmed over the course of four decades, *Martírio* mingles indigenous people speaking in their own voice with archival material narrating what amounts to the attempted destruction of a people. Striking footage in the film shows the first regiment of indigenous soldiers under General Medici—in some ways analogous to the thousands of native Americans who served in US wars against indigenous peoples—where the "Indians" march in military parades while demonstrating the torture techniques of the military. The Good Indian of romanticism was coerced into becoming the Indian torturer coerced into supporting the dictatorship against leftists and against his own people.

Reflecting again the archival turn within VNA, the film draws on various kinds of clips to dramatize the history of Guaraní-Kaiowá struggles. The film gives us a sense of an indigenous nation under perpetual siege, suturing us into a Guaraní point of view even as they are being targeted by random rifle shots. The film was a shock for those clinging to the myth of cordial co-existence—a myth cultivated not only by nineteenth-century literary Romanticism and assimilationist positivism, but also by the twentieth-century Freyrean Luso-Tropicalism embrace of a chimerical "racial democracy." Polyvocal, the film stages contrary views and gazes—both the "Indians" and their enemies speak for themselves—but leaves no doubt about its ultimate allegiances. With painful lucidity, an indigenous interviewee laments that "capitalism is killing us." Another interviewee puts it poetically: "The markets wake up in a bad mood, and decide to devour mountains." Archival TV reportage footage shows Brazilian parliamentarians displaying their tendentious ignorance about the indigenous peoples whose rights they are abusing, including the blatant racism of the "ruralistas"—the congressional allies of Agro-business and the latifundistas. One ruralist Senator, Katia Abreu, proudly reminds her admirers of their successes in getting rid successively of the landless movement and then of the *Codigo Florestal* (the ecology-friendly law protecting the vegetation of indigenous land). All that remains, she proclaims, is a last frontier or final solution—to get rid of the "Indian problem."

In a kind of paratactic stream-of-consciousness, the pro-ruralista interviewees in the film deploy the usual colonialist non-sequiturs to disqualify indigenous sovereignty and cover over their bad faith—"they're nomads and savages and they're really Bolivians anyway, and besides there aren't many Indians, and most of them aren't 'real Indians' since some wear jeans and have cameras, and after all there are 'too few Indians for too much land.'" This latter argument falsely suggests that the Amazon would provide a demographic escape valve for desperate migrants from the overcrowded cities of the littoral, when in reality the policy usually resulted less in new urban centers than in vast soy plantations and cattle pastures, and thanks to mechanization, with few actual people in sight. A Brazilian "state of exception" subjects indigenous people to the acts of not-so-random violence to which the film bears indisputable witness. In its soft-spoken understated way, *Martírio* demonstrates that anthropology and solidarity, emotion and reason, art and indignation, need not be mutually exclusive. At a time when indigenous peoples are protesting injustice from Belo Monte to Standing Rock, few films have more burning relevance.

Another documentary, this time not a VNA film, Dulce Queiroz's *Terras Brasileiras* (Brazilian Lands, 2017) also treats the struggles of the Guaraní-Kaiowá. Drawing on archival and historical footage, but without the personal angle or the life history of the Carelli film, the film counterpoints the indigenous perspective with that of the landowners, while showing clear sympathy for the former. The film documents the struggle of the Guaraní-Kaiowá communities against human rights violations, while simultaneously offering a brilliant image of their culture and history. The film shows how a cruel process was leading inexorably to a kind of mini-war in Mato Grosso do Sul. By ignoring the historical presence of traditional peoples and "entitling" aspiring landowners, the Brazilian state triggered the inevitable clashes between the communities. The film depicts the struggle for the demarcation of ancestral lands and for respect of their human and minority rights. On November 20, 2017, the Unrepresented Peoples' Organization (UNPO) organized a consciousness-raising screening for the European Parliament entitled "The Guaraní-Kaiowá and the Assault on Indigenous Rights in Brazil," which took place on May 30, 2017.

Andrea Tonacci, as we have seen, was one of the first filmmakers to promote the theory and practice of a hybrid form of indigenous media in Brazil in films like *The Arara* (1981), *Conversas de Maranhao* (1971–83), and *Serras da Desordem* (2006). This last film mixes fiction and documentary to tell the story of a lone survivor of a 1970s massacre, when a group of landowners set fire to a native village. The only survivor, Carapiru, a Guaja Indian from Maranhao, playing himself, retraces his 10-year-long journey in search of some kind of refuge and friendship despite his not speaking Portuguese. After ten years of wandering, he is discovered by FUNAI agents 2,000 miles from his homeland. The film counterpoints the personal reenactment of his 10-year odyssey with a swiftly paced collage of archival materials that form a concise summary of the same ten years of public Brazilian history—including the construction of the Trans-Amazonian Highway, the building of hydroelectric plants, military parades, and the like. The status of the images and of genre vacillates constantly, provoking a kind of generic and epistemological vertigo. Like Carelli in *Corumbiara*, Tonacci often withholds translation from indigenous languages. Reflexive as he had always been since his avant-garde days, Tonacci unpacks the challenges of a situation where his own integrity is at stake and where the events concerning Carapiru in some ways echo his own infinitely less-violent experience of marginalized wandering in the wild fields of the cinema. The film's aesthetic of fragmentation mirrors the zig-zagging trajectory of the indigenous protagonist with the unpredictable turns of history. (Since this film has been analyzed astutely by a number of critics such as Ismail Xavier, Ivone Margulies, Luis Alberto Rocha Melo, Clarice Cohn, Rodrigo de Oliveira, and Daniel Caetano, among others, I will not linger on it here.)

In focusing on the films of Video nas Aldeias, I have neglected the scores of indigenous-related collectives and filmmakers not affiliated with VNA. Renato Neiva Moreira's *Esses e outros bichos* (Assorted Animals, 1979) mingles interviews of the Villas-Boas Brothers, with footage of Xavánte dancing and staged episodes, to argue that the land belongs to the Indians. In Marcelo Felipe Sampaio and Paulo Alvarenga's *O guardado* (The Saved, 2010), a man from an urban center moves to Mato Grosso do Sul to live with the Kadiwéu, where through a mystical experience he discovers a 200-year-old legend that haunts the village. A number of other indigenous and indigenous-adjacent films draw inspiration from legends. Olinda Yawar Muniz Wanderley's experimental narrative film *Kaapora, O Chamado das Matas* (The Call of the Forest, 2020) revolves around a folkloric forest-dwelling spirit, variously male or female, called the Kaapora. By developing an environmental recovery project on the land of the Pataxó Hã-hã-hãe, the director explores her people's connection with Earth and spirituality. In *Txêjkhô Khãm Mby* (Mulheres Guerreiras, 2011), directed by Yaiku Suya, Kamikia P. T. Kisedje, Kokoyamaratxi Suya, Whinti Suya, and Kambriti Suya, two elders tell a mythical story, staged as fiction by the young Kisêdjê, in which a girl is secretly in love with her own brother; the consequences of forbidden passion lead to the "War Womens' uprising." Leandro Tadashi Duarte's *Naia e a lua* (Naia and the Moon, 2011) combines animation and live action to relate a tale about a young Indian woman who falls in love with the moon after hearing an elder woman tell the story of the origins of the stars in the sky. In *A história do monstro Khátpy* (The Story of the Khatpy Monster, 2009), a young Kĩsêdjê man outhunting monkeys encounters the legendary bear-like monster Khátpy. French director Joan Salvat's *Brasil, la guerre de l'or* (Brazil, the Gold War, 1986), finally, retells Yanomami cosmologies about the first man on earth. Tired of being alone, Omama creates the Yanomami people out of a dark foam and then divides up the earth, giving the best part to the Yanomami.

A number of indigenous films thematize play. Komoi Panara's *Priara Jo* (After the Egg, the War, 2008), for example, foregrounds Panará children at play. The non-indigenous documentary *Waapa* (Medicine, 2017), directed by David Reeks, Paula Mendonça, and Renata Meirelles, meanwhile, explores childhood as experienced by the Yudja people in Mato Grosso. The film forms part of a larger educational project called "The Territory of Play," dedicated to the educational role of play for indigenous children. In philosophical terms, one thinks of Rousseau's admiration for the educational practices of *les sauvages*, or of Nietzche's *frohliche wissenschaft* (joyful knowledge), or Huizinga's *Homo Ludens*, or Bakhtin's "culture of laughter," all writings that see life under the aspect of the ludic and play. The film could be seen as a Wordsworthian celebration of childhood as a site of wisdom, "trailing clouds of glory" and the agile physicality of "glad animal movements," a phrase that connects the human and the animal in a kind of nature worship. *Waapa* is an ode to childhood love of the forest like that expressed in Wordsworth's "Intimations of Immortality":

> There was a time when meadow, grove, and stream,
> The earth, and every common sight,
> To me did seem
> Apparelled in celestial light

In this film, children learn by imitating everyone and everything, humans, animals, and machines, as a kind of rehearsal for life. It is thanks to this imitative predilection that children learn to walk, run, and talk. *Waapa* explores an indigenous approach to education, which involves children in all aspects of life, where children can learn from any adult, and any adult can take care of a child.

Unlike the allegorical "Indians" of the 1970s, where white actors incarnated indigenous characters and advanced allegorical themes, the twenty-first-century fiction films feature indigenous players and consultation with indigenous people. A number of fiction films treat the dilemmas of the contemporary shaman in a world invaded by capitalism and evangelicalism, usually at the same time. Renée Nader Messora and João Salaviza's *The Dead and the Others* (2018) is inspired by the book *Mortos e os outros* (1978) by anthropologist Manuela Carneiro da Cunha, an expert on Krahô cosmologies. The film centers on a young Krahô father named Ihjac, who feels the call to become a shaman like his own deceased father, but who is frightened by the personal transformation it would require, and escapes to a nearby city to reflect. After a visit from the spirit of his father he decides to organize the traditional end of mourning festival that forms the climax of the film.[100]

Anthropologist-filmmaker Luiz Bolognesi's docu-fiction *Ex-pajé* (Ex-shaman, 2018) examines real situations in an intermittently documentary and fictional style. The film brings up an issue too often left unexamined—the role of evangelicals in the psychic destruction of indigenous peoples, often preparing the way for powerful interest groups who complete the process. The New Tribes Mission, for example, has been working in Brazil for decades, with nefarious consequences for the literal and spiritual health of indigenous people. The missionaries were expelled in the early 1990s, but some stayed and in 2015 were accused of forcing Zo'é people to collect Brazil nuts. Journalists speak of "an evangelical conquista" across Latin America, with Amazonia as a sought-after prize.[101]

Ex-pajé portrays religiously motivated assimilation as a form of cultural genocide for the Paiter Suruí people. The group made its first contact with Euro-Brazilians in 1969 and have been dealing with the consequences ever since. The fulcral character is Perpera Surui, a *pajé* living on the indigenous reserve in Amazônia. Surui's cultural tradition made him an intermediary between the people and the spirits, but he lost his position when the evangelicals denounced his magic flutes and natural medicines as the "work of the devil." While people used to seek out his cures, he complains, "[N]ow they just buy an aspirin." The traditional *pajé* has lost his charismatic and curative power because of the strategic power moves of what the film's director calls the "Evangelical Inquisition," a movement that has turned the loving words of Jesus into an epistle of indigenous self-rejection. The story begins with Perpera Suya's attempts to heal an indigenous family from the effects of snakebite. Home videos showing the traditional way of life segue to a present-day Indian on a motorbike wearing Western clothes and speaking in English. Perpera's painfully ironic job, after his spiritual "demotion," is as a janitor in a Church led by an old blue-eyed white priest. Calmly, Perpera still practices his vocation secretly but complains that the forest spirits are angry in the wake of Christianization. Since the pastor speaks only Portuguese, a fellow Indian translates his words for the benefit of the congregation. The Indian congregants seem sad and sleepy, and the choir indifferent even to the songs it is singing. Meanwhile, bored-looking young congregants play distractedly with their tablets and cell phones.

Maya Da-Rin's feature *A Febre* (*The Fever*, 2019) offers another example of close collaboration with indigenous people, where not only the theme but also the principal roles and players are indigenous, and where much of the dialogue is in an indigenous language (Tukano). The story revolves around an "urban Indian" (played by Regis Myrupu, the son of a Desana shaman) who has migrated from his village to join the masses of laborers in the larger cities in search of education, a salary, and health care. His character is a middle-aged native widower, who has spent half of his life in his native village, and the other half working as a security guard in the Port of Manaus, a populous industrial and shipping hub surrounded by Amazon forest. He lives with his daughter Vanessa (Rosa Peixoto), a nurse in a health clinic who has just learned that she can attend medical school in Brasília—perhaps as a beneficiary of the "quotas" destined for Black and indigenous students. Father and daughter treat each other with a quiet but intense tenderness; when he offers to send her money, she reminds him of her scholarship and promises to find a job so he will not need to help. The rest of the family, a brother, his wife, a nephew, and a grandson complete the picture, with each bringing more background on Justino's life and experience as well as on generational changes. The plot is structured around two departures—Justino's from his village to Manaus and the daughter's imminent departure from Manaus for Brasília. Each entails a moment of transition; she is about to master the kind of Western medicine that seems to be of no use to her father.

It is worth noting how rare this kind of character has been in Brazilian cinema—a "normal" native bilingual character at ease in Portuguese and in Tukana, and familiar with both indigenous and dominant culture. The language in the film is a lived-in language, not a made-up amalgam like the one in *Playing in the Fields of the Lord*, or the archaic-sounding Tupí of *How Tasty Was My Little Frenchman*. One of Vanessa's patients, meanwhile, speaks a different indigenous language—the intertitles translate her words for the spectator but not for Vanessa—reminding us that Brazil speaks scores of native languages rarely heard in films. Yet the patient's appreciative clasping of Vanessa's hand conveys all we need to know about natives and simply human solidarity across difference. One way to appreciate *The Fever* is to note all the traps it avoids—no photogenic images of the Amazon; no sensationalist treatment of the character's situation that would make him a victim or a hero; and no allegorical superstructure that would subordinate the character to a grand political message. All the social issues are present, but in the most understated and oblique way possible. The film subtly registers the racism of Justino's co-worker, who sees him as a "tamed Indian" unlike those dangerous "real Indians." The co-worker's expression and body language suggest a mixture of superiority and suspicion. Without any explicit denunciation, the film also calls attention to the world of the globalized capitalism, embodied in the cuboid containers—metallic incarnations of globalization—that bring merchandise to the Amazon from China, Brazil's second commercial partner. Manaus's Free Economic Zone forms a metonym for Brazilian contradiction, at once settler and indigenous, occupier and occupied, local and global.

As Justino suffers from his mysterious fever, a sequence reveals the faux-sympathetic intervention of the "Human Resources" Department representative who feigns concern with his mental and physical health, but only as a veiled threat of dismissal. When Justino reminds her that he has been working all his life, she replies dismissively that "it's what's on the books that matters, not how long you've been alive." In a marvel of understated acting and direction, Justino never openly reacts against corporate cynicism or casual racism, but miniscule changes in his body language, intonation, and facial expression hint at an anger that we feel as spectators and introject into the image. This aesthetics of constraint and understatement arguably makes the film even more moving.

The remarkable soundtrack is devoid of both diegetic and non-diegetic music—with the exception of a traditional indigenous song, heard during the final credits, consisting of the melodic variations called "Ahãbeaki" or "Hãde Hãde" created by Rosa Peixoto. Thus, the film refuses the kind of commentative music that manipulates emotion in the manner of an emotional traffic cop. The film's art of refusal and constraint mirrors, in a way, the subdued acting of the protagonist. Instead of music, the sound design of the film—more immersive sensorium than soundtrack per se—uses slight modulations to shape an amorphous yet stirring affect that spreads a feeling of febrile anxiety. It subtly conveys the feelings connected to two worlds—that of the metallic industrial sonorous port cityscape and that of a city near the forest—sounds that sometimes merge, as bird, insect, and industrial noise become indistinguishable, while also conveying an animal-human continuum.[102] Sound design becomes a form of the mini-plotting of affect. The deliberately paced flow of images and minimalist less-is-more aesthetics perfectly suits the characters and the milieu. Combining quotidian realism with an oneiric atmosphere, the style is at once realist and magical, just as Justino's home, penetrated by rain and wind, is part city and part forest, a kind of half-way house between the indigenous forest and the urban jungle.[103] The cinematography—beautiful without being "pretty"—imbues the poverty of Justino's home with a kind of austere grace, just as the brightly colored containers convey a cold abstract beauty reminiscent of the industrial scenes in Antonioni's *Red Desert*.

This contemplative film privileges the unsaid, the unseen, and the unanswered questions about the precise meaning, for example, of the "fever." Is Justino somehow connected to the animal carcass with a beating heart that he dreams about? The fever is less a symbol than a kind of art film MacGuffin, a suggestive signifier around which the film supposedly revolves. Even apart from the multileveled allusions in the title—with its corporeal, social, human, political, and tribal overtones—*The Fever* generates a number of "hauntings" that exceed the here and now of the locations in Manaus. Apart from the haunting of globalization, with Manaus as one of its epicenters, Justino is haunted by the legends, shamanic cures, and animal-human crossovers from his native culture, where wild boars, monkeys, and dogs co-exist as equals alongside human beings. Indigenous life is also haunted by an over-determining settler-colonial power—summed up in the word "white"—which increasingly penetrates indigenous life, especially in the case of the younger members of the family. This penetration is suggested in the frequent references to those who are "becoming like whites": the prediction that Vanessa, after her medical training, will "write out prescriptions like the whites" or that the nephew harms his body by consuming bad supermarket food "like the whites." When the younger people refuse collaboration for the good of the family, their selfish individualism is seen as "acting like whites." In an implied contrast with native shamans, Justino points to the inadequacy of the gaze of the white doctors, who "have big eyes, but can only see what is front of their eyes."

The Transmediatic Indigene of Popular Culture

In recent decades, indigenous artists are reaching out to Brazil at large and to the world, not only through films but also through installations, popular music videos, and internet activism. One popular indigenous musician is Guaraní rapper Kunumi (aka Werá Jeguaka Mirim), an "urban Indian" from São Paulo. Kunumi inherits his longue-durée historical consciousness from his father, Guaraní-mestizo writer Olívio Kaka Wera Jekupé whose autobiography is entitled *Whenever We Said Goodbye*.[104] In his poem "Twenty-First Century," the father had linked the annihilation of indigenous people to the devastation of the land, worrying that "no longer will we see the trees, or the birds, or the animals. The rivers all polluted." Son Kunumi is also a Michael Jackson fan who has been rapping since the age of 10 and making films since the age of 6. Kunumi's activism gained momentum after Brazil's 2014 World Cup, where he unfurled a "Land demarcation now!" banner in the middle of the soccer stadium.

Kunumi's music video "Xondaro Ka'aguy Reguá" (Forest Warrior) speaks of a legendary water-born forest warrior who will carry indigenous people into the future. The lyrics touch on many of the themes discussed in this book. By combining traditional culture with futurism, the song evokes what I call "archaic modernism."[105] The video references 1492/1500 and the Conquest by referring to 519 years of oppression by whites and the "colonial attitude" that "ignored our science and knowledge." The lyrics denounce the allochronic Indian "frozen in time" and laud the "high-tech Indian" at ease with Facebook and the internet. The final images show Kunumi wandering in the middle of São Paulo traffic wearing a VR headset and a feathered Guaraní headdress. Smoking a stylized peace pipe, he encapsulates an oxymoronic traditional futurism, as headlines about forest devastation float across the screen. The music combines Guaraní chants, indigenous chord instruments, and allusions to reggaeton, rap, and trap music. In interviews, Kunumi also touches on the long-term origins of racism in the Christian Crusades, and the "European expansion that oppressed the originary peoples spread around the world."[106] Kunumi defends his choice of rap music as a vehicle by saying that he uses rap to defend his culture, while defending Brazilian blacks as brothers in suffering. (The black-indigenous relationship has also taken the form of Kunumi's musical collaboration with black Brazilian composer/actor/rapper Criolo.)

Kunumi sings in Guaraní to tell the story of his ancestry, while his music videos show what Guaraní collective life has been reduced to—living in favela-like enclaves along the side of a super-highway. In interviews, he rejects the term "Indigenous futurism" in favor of less stagist expressions. "We, native Indigenous people don't think about the future," he says. "We don't have the white man's vision of progress. For us, progress is to preserve our culture … to live in the present and remember our past."[107] His favored "technologies" are not smartphones but "sacred food, rap, and medicine." He finds São Paulo frightening because of pollution and spiritual and physical diseases. (Many in his Krukutu subgroup—about 150 people—had been infected by coronavirus at the time of writing.)

Indigenous rap in Brazil is largely the creation of what in North America would be called "urban Indians." Another indigenous musician, Joao Nyn, son of a Potiguara father, was born in Rio Grande do Norte, the only Brazilian state with no demarcated indigenous land, despite being home to at least fourteen self-declared indigenous communities. An LGBTQ+ rights activist based in São Paulo, Nyn is the founder of the band "Peerless Android," a name reminiscent of Janelle Monae's rebellious Android figure in the United States. Calling the Brazilian State "more obsolete than the past itself," his project seeks to rescue the indigenous memory through music: "How can we demand land demarcation if we don't first claim and demarcate our imaginaries?"[108] The music blends pop and rock styles in Guaraní-inflected songs about love and ancestry. While Nyn shies away from the term "Indigenous Futurism," he thinks contemporary indigenous artists are making a change by "rescuing traditions to reinvent imposed cultures."[109] The term "indigenous futurism" has a North American connection, in that it was coined by Grace L. Dillon, Anishinaabe author and professor, for whom "indigenous futurism" is a movement consisting of art, literature, and other forms of media, which express indigenous perspectives on the past, present, and future in the context of science fiction and related subgenres.[110]

The music of Zandhio Huku, Krahô frontman of indigenous heavy-metal band Arandu Arakuaa, depicts indigenous "cosmovisions" where Nature provides a planetary raison d'être. "You only understand the Indigenous struggle if you get [our] worldview, which intertwines nature and the sacred."[111] The band's music video for *Am'mrã* (Falling Star) sings the connection between nature and indigenous culture.[112] Blending indigenous music with Afro-Brazilian percussion and folk guitar, the clip was released on the same day that eight European nations reprimanded Brazil for its failure to combat deforestation. São Paulo's first indigenous rap group, "Oz Guaranís," comprising Xondaro MC, Gizeli Para Mirim, and Mirindju Glowers, raps both in Portuguese and Guaraní about land demarcation and other forms of indigenous resistance, in music marked by Northeastern and indigenous musical traditions.

Apart from indigenous films, indigenous activists have enthusiastically taken to the internet, evidenced in proliferating websites like "Indios Online" and "Arte Eletronica Indigena" (Indigenous Electronic Art). VNA launched an online platform (videonasaldeias.org.br/loja) in 2018 as a way of allowing the rental or purchase of almost a hundred of its videos/films. At the beginning of the twenty-first century, indigenous communities started buying smartphones and built "strategic music partnerships" via WhatsApp and social media. With the web, with affordable digital cameras, and laptop filmmaking, indigenous media makers gained unprecedented access and adopted (and adapted) the new media with gusto and competence. The Tupinamba, whose resurgence we discussed in Chapter 2, have also gotten into the act with websites and "Radio Tupinamba." Journalist Renata Tupinambá, co-founder of the indigenous radio station Yande, which helped organize Brazil's first festival (YBY) devoted to contemporary indigenous music, favors an "Indigenous Futurism" (Grace Dillon) that uses technology to make "art, music and literature tools of cultural survival defying the racist mindset that confines Indigenous to a 16th-century colonial imaginary."[113]

Ashininka activist Benki Payako, meanwhile, produces videos to promote his project of reconciling Western science with indigenous knowledge to save the Amazon. He has also proposed a "collective cure" using the sacred plant *ayahuasca* to rid indigenous people of the spiritual malaise caused by Pentecostalist proselytizing, which for him has "devoured the brains" of some Indians. Indeed, it is not an accident that the non-indigenous world has become fascinated by the idea of "decriminalizing Nature," and endorsing the sacramental use of "plant medicines" such as *ayahuasca* and *peyote*, long used by indigenous peoples, not as a drug, but within well-defined spiritual and communal circumstances.

A self-description statement by the Digital Village Ecosystem collective gives a sense of the technical and theoretical sophistication of contemporary indigenous media in Brazil. Digital Village describes itself as a

> transmediatic participatory eco-system based on horizontal self-representation which connects the Xavante, Terena, Bororo, and Kraho peoples, as autonomous subjects of their own history and culture, to the digital world. Everyone inside and outside the village can communicate a content-producing digital presence using smartphones and computer interface linked to our territory via GPS, QR Code, computer vision and the like. Everyone can visually relate such contents, gather information and disseminate knowledges through the internet. Every perspective on the eco-system will be accessible to others, who can participate in trans-cultural experiments, interpreted and communicated in a dialogical manner and through the eyes of the others ... This ecosystem is interconnected with social networks and its cultural impulses are connected to the profiles on Twitter/Facebook/Linked. It favors porous communication allowing for relationality and reciprocal mutual contamination, dissemination, and relational distribution.[114]

The Digital Village Ecosystem was elaborated by Domingos Mãhoroë'ö together with Divino Tserewahú Tsereptsé, Rafael Franco Coelho, Natal Anhahö'a Tsere'ruremé, Massimo Canevacci, and Kleber Meritororeu.[115]

For indigenous young people, video and the internet offer a more accessible and direct medium for communication, including poetry and music and design, one that respects an oral authoritative regime while bypassing the necessity of literacy. Thanks to the internet, pan-Indian movements can operate across the Americas; Purepecha in Chicago communicate with Aymaras in Bolivia, the Yanomami in Venezuela, and the Guaraní in Paraguay. In the Amazon, "First Contact" is still occurring, but this time the "Indians" come armed not with bows and arrows but rather with books, computers, digital cameras, websites, blogs, and LISTSERVES. Unlike the peasantry for Marx, first peoples are now capable of representing and performing their individual and collective selves. The "high-tech Indians" and YouTube activists of Brazil's "indigenous media" have been deploying media to reinscribe and reinvigorate their collective life and to strategize against dispossession. For native peoples in Brazil (and elsewhere), the media become a recombinant means of cultural invention, a form of technological anthropophagy. While hardly a panacea, indigenous media at its best becomes an empowering vehicle for communities struggling against displacement and cultural annihilation.

Notes

1. Tuscarora artist Jolene Rickard, during a very brief visit to Brazil, made a very perceptive impromptu exercise in historical comparison, which went to the heart of the matter: "I get it. Just like the U.S.—few Indians, but huge symbolic importance." In personal conversation at a conference on indigeneity held by the Hemispheric Institute for Performance and Politics in Belo Horizonte, Brazil in March 11-19, 2005.
2. My contribution to this comparative corpus can be found in *Tropical Multiculturalism: A Comparative History of Race in Brazilian* Cinema *and* Culture (Durham: Duke University Press, 1997) and with Ella Shohat, *Race in Translation: Postcolonial Wars around the Postcolonial Atlantic* (New York: New York University Press, 2012).
3. G. W. F. Hegel, *The Philosophy of History* (New York: Dover, 1956).
4. Guzman, *Native and National in Brazil: Indigeneity after Independence*, op. cit., p. 131.
5. Jessé Souza, ed., *A Invisibilidade da Desigualdade Brasileira* (Belo Hirozonte: UFMG, 2006), p. 100.
6. See Caetano Veloso, *Verdade Tropical* (São Paulo: Companhia das Letras, 1997), p. 14.
7. Marcio Souza, "Teatro sem Palavras: Pindorama no Primeiro Seculo" in Adauto Novaes, op. cit., p. 97.
8. João Daniel, *Tesouro Descoberto no Rio Amazonas,* cited in Adauto Novaes, op. cit., p. 98.
9. See Bruno Franchetto, "O que se Sabe Sobre as Linguas Indigenas no Brasil" in Carlos Alberto Ricardo, ed., *Povos Indígenas no Brasil 1996/2000* (São Paulo: Instituto SocioAmbiental, 2000), p. 84.
10. Jack Weatherford, *Native Roots*, op. cit., p. 205.
11. *The New York Times* (August 28, 2005) reported that "língua geral" was making a comeback in the Amazon.
12. See Patrick Wolfe, "Settler Colonialism and the Elimination of the Native," *Journal of Genocide Research*, Vol. 8, No. 4 (2006), pp. 387-409.
13. David B. Davis, *The Problem of Slavery in Western Culture*, cited by Jack Weatherford in Native Roots (New York: Fawcett, 1991), p. 142.
14. DISA promises to support the slow centralization of biographical information related to enslaved indigenous people and to place them online where historians, researchers, students, tribal members, and families can use the information to reconstruct histories, chart networks, and make connections in ways that have never before been possible.
15. Ward Churchill compared Columbus to Hitler in "Deconstructing the Columbus Myth," in *Anarchy* (Summer 1992).
16. See Peter Hulme and Neil L. Whitehead, eds., *Wild Majesty: Encounters with Caribs from Columbus to the Present Day* (Oxford: Clarendon, 1992), p. 3.
17. My partner Ella Shohat and I participated in these events. Ella organized a "Goodbye Columbus" Conference at Cornel with Annette Jaimes, Ward Churchill, and Jose Barreiro, and I offered an anti-quincentennial course and film series. I promised my students that I would only teach the course once every 500 years.
18. *O Globo* (October 23, 1998).
19. *O Diario de Porto Seguro* (January 1, 2000).
20. *Folha de São Paulo* (April 24, 2000).

21 *Povos Indígenas no Brasil*: 1996–2000, op. cit., p. 70.
22 *Folha de São Paulo* (April 9, 2000).
23 Clarisse Alvarenga, *Da Cena do Contato ao Inacabamento da história* (From the Scene of Contact to the Unfinishedness of History, Salvador, Bahia: UDUFBA, 2017).
24 Alcida Rita Ramos, "Vozes indígenas: o contato vivido e contado," *Anuário Antropológico 87* (Brasília: Ed. UNB: Tempo Brasileiro, 1990), pp. 117–43.
25 Georg Wilhelm Friedrich Hegel, *Lectures on the Philosophy of World History* (translated from the German edition of Johannes Hoffmeister from Hegel papers assembled by H. B. Nisbet) (New York, 1975), p. 81.
26 Genocides, as Hitler learned, rarely completely fulfill their mission. The supposedly extinguished Taínos can be seen on websites participating in festivals and family gatherings. See Maximillian C. Forte, "Amerindian@Caribbean," in Kyra Landzelius, ed., *Native on the Net* (London: Routledge, 2006), pp. 132–51.
27 See Sheila Schwartzman, *Humberto Mauro e as imagens do Brasil* (São Paulo: UNESP, 2004).
28 See Gustavo Furtado, *Documentary Filmmaking in Contemporary Brazil* (New York: Oxford University Press, 2019), p. 78.
29 Amalia Cordova, "Reenact, Reimagine: Performative Indigenous Documentaries of Bolivia and Brazil," in Vinicius Novarro and Juan Carlos Rodrigues, eds., *New Documentaries in Latin America* (New York: Palgrave, 2014), pp. 123–44.
30 Doris Sommer, *Foundational Fictions: National Romances in Latin America* (Berkeley: University of California Pres, 1991), p. 141.
31 Ibid., p. 150.
32 See Vine Deloria Jr., *Custer Died for Your Sins* (New York: Macmillan, 1969).
33 Cited in Dale Turner, op. cit., p. 25.
34 The National Museum inaugurated its cinematheque in 1912 with films about the Nambiquara Indians that Roquette Pinto brought back from Rondonia along with the films of the Rondon Commission. Teddy Roosevelt also had contact with the Rondon Commission from 1913 to 1914, as a result of which he became an enthusiast of the "ideology of whitening." Seeing Brazilians as basically white people, Roosevelt praised the indigenous element as having a positive effect and believed European immigration would turn black blood into an "insignificant element." Surprisingly, given the extreme racism of Roosevelt's earlier writing, he recorded favorable impressions of Brazil's mulattoes and mestizos.
35 Quoted in Fernao Ramos, *Historia do Cinema Brasileiro* (Porto Alegre: Martins Livreiro, 1987), p. 74.
36 See César Guimarães "A cena do contato," proferida no II Colóquio Cinema, Estética e Política, promovido pelo Programa de Pós-Graduação em Comunicação Social da Universidade Federal de Minas Gerais (UFMG), between April 10 and 12, 2013.
37 For a portrait of Silvino Santos, with many clips from his films, see Aurélio Michilles's intriguing film *Cineasta da Selva* (1997).
38 For insightful historically grounded analyses of Humberto Mauro's films, including *Descobrimento do Brasil* and *Bandeirantes*, see Sheila Schvarzman, *Humberto Mauro e as imagens do Brasil* (São Paulo: Edusp, 2004), and, Eduardo Victorio Morettin, *Humberto Mauro, Cinema, História* (São Paulo: Alameda, 2013). Morettin emphasizes the role of The National Institute of Cinematic Education (INCE) in purveying the dominant modernizing capitalist ideologies of the Vargas government, which ultimately supported and controlled this kind of cultural production.

39 See John Manuel Monteiro, *Negros da terra: índios e bandeirantes nas origens de São Paulo* (São Paulo: Companhia das Letras, 1994).
40 For an insightful analysis of *A Muralha*, see Veronica Eloi de Almeida, "A Muralha e a representação indígena na televisão, na literatura e nas ciências sociais" in PROD Revista de antropologia e artes, No. 4 (2012), https://www.ifch.unicamp.br/ojs/index.php/proa/article/view/2359
41 To get a sense of the immense variety of representations of the Brazilian Indian, Silvio Back's *Indio do Brasil* (1995) offers a capacious anthology of Brazilian and foreign representations of indigenous peoples of Brazil, with scores of clips from documentaries and feature films, both Brazilian and international, featuring the Brazilian Indian—counterpointed with ironic, poetic commentary: including George Dyott's *The River of Doubt* (1913–27); Aloha Baker's *The Last of the Broros* (1930); Jorge Konchin's *Iracema* (1931); Vittorio Capellaro's *O Caçador de Diamantes* (The Diamond Hunter, 1933); Franz Eichorn's *Eine Brasilianische Rhapsodie* (A Brazilian Rhapsody, 1935); Genil Vasconcelos's *Frente a Frente com os Xavantes* (Face to Face with the Xavantes, 1948); Eichorn's *Mundo Estranho* (Strange World, 1948); Eurico Richer's *Tabu* (1949); Vladmir Kozak's *Xetá na Serra do Dourados* (Xetas in the Dourados Mountains, 1956); William Gerik's *O Segredo de Diacui* (Diacui's Secret, 1959); Marco Altberg's *Noel Nutels* (1975); Andre Luis Oliveira's *A Lenda de Ubirajara* (The Legend of Ubirajara, 1975); Plácido de Campos's *Curumim* (1978); and Luis Paulino dos Santos's *Ikatena* (1983).
42 See Frederick B. Pike, op. cit., pp. 202–3.
43 For a summary of the critical analyses of the film by prestigious Brazilian critics like Ismail Xavier, Jean-Claude Bernadet, José Carlos Avelar, and Maria Rita Galvão, see Margarida Maria Adamatti, "As Duas Faces de Gustavo Dahl em *Uira*: entre o realizador e o critico," *Revista Fronteiras: Estudos Midiaticos*, Vol. 21, No. 1 (January/April 2019), pp. 99–110.
44 The phrase became the title of a 2002 book by Eduardo Viveiros de Castro.
45 Review of *Quarup* originally published in *Revista USP*, 3 (September, October, November 1989), pp. 185–6.
46 See Silvio Back script of his film, *República Guaraní* (Rio de Janeiro: Paz e Terra, 1982), p. 37.
47 Cited in Hemming, op. cit., p. 111.
48 See Monica Frota, "Taking Aim: The Video Technology of Cultural Resistance," in Michael Renov and Erika Suderburg, eds., *Resolutions: Contemporary Video Practices* (Minneapolis: The University of Minnesota Press, 1996), pp. 258–82.
49 Terence Turner, "Defiant Images: The Kayapo Appropriation of Video," *Anthropology Today*, Vol. 8, No. 6 (1992), pp. 5–16.
50 See Terry Turner, "Anthropology and Multiculturalism: What Is Anthropology That Multiculturalists Should Be Mindful of It?" *Cultural Anthropology*, Vol. 8, No. 4 (1993), pp. 411–29. Accessed January 24, 2021, http://www.jstor.org/stable/656475.
51 Amalia Córdova, "Reenact, Reimagine: Performative Indigenous Documentaries of Bolivia and Brazil," *New Documentaries in Latin America* (New York: Palgrave Macmillan, 2014), p. 124.
52 See Ivana Bentes, *Midia-Multidao: Esteticas da Communicacao e Biopoliticas* (Rio de Janeiro: Mauad, 2015).
53 The Zoë are reportedly polygamous; both men and women may have more than one partner, and it is fairly common for a woman to marry several men, some of whom may later marry one of her daughters. The society is egalitarian, without chiefs per se.

54 Ruben C. Queiroz, op. cit., p. 8.
55 See Debora Herszenhut's master's dissertation at the Federal University of Rio de Janeiro, defended in 2014, and entitled "Militância, performance e devires imagéticos: ocinema indígena brasileiro através das três décadas do projeto vídeo nas aldeias."https://www.academia.edu/39198587/MILIT%C3%82NCIA_PERFORMANCE_E_DEVIRES_IMAG%C3%89TICOS_O_CINEMA_IND%C3%8DGENA_BRASILEIRO_ATRAV%C3%89S_DAS_TR%C3%8AS_D%C3%89CADAS_DO_PROJETO_V%C3%8DDEO_NAS_ALDEIAS
56 The Atelier Varan in Paris, launched by Jean Rouch to train international documentarians, in this sense, offers a counter-model in the form of a sustainable cinema, whereby each production leads to other productions, with equipment left for others to use, with ex-trainees becoming trainers who launch other ateliers. Zoe Graham speaks in this context of a "sustainable documentary ecosystem" to refer to films meant to be "passed on to future generations; as 'ecosystems' that thrive in different ways in different locations." (Zoe Graham, PhD thesis proposal at NYU Cinema Studies, provisionally entitled "Transnational Pedagogy: Film School without Borders.")
57 Ruben C. Queiroz, op. cit., p. 11.
58 On this film and others by Divino Tserewahú, see Bernard Belisario's doctoral thesis on Xavánte film: "Desmanchar o cinema: pesquisa com filmes Xavante no *Waia Rini*" (Universidade Federal de Minas Gerais, Faculdade de Filosofia e Ciências Humanas, 2018.
59 See André Brasil, "Mise-en-abyme da cultura: a exposição do 'antecampo' em Piõnhitsi e Mokoi Tekoá Petei Jeguatá," *Significação*, Vol. 40, No. 40 (December 2013), p. 254.
60 A number of theses have been written about the Xavánte involvement with the cinema, for example Caio de Salvi Lazaneo, "Produção Partilhada do Conhecimento: Uma experiência comas comunidades indígenas Xavante e Karajá," a master's dissertation with the School of Communications at University of São Paulo. See https://www.teses.usp.br/teses/disponiveis/27/27152/tde-21052013-120828/pt-br.php. See also Bernardo Belisario, "Desmanchar o cinema: pesquisa com filmes Xavante no *wai'a rini*, Universidade Federal de Minas Gerais Faculdade de Filosofia e Ciências Humanas Programa de Pós-Graduação em Comunicação Social, Belo Horizonte 2018," https://repositorio.ufmg.br/handle/1843/BUBD-AWFLDS. Both authors develop the idea of the process film in relation to the collaborative work of Divino Tserewahú. See also "Desmanchar o Cinema: pesquisa com filmes xavante no wai'a rini" Belo Horizonte 2018.
61 Cited in Clarisse Alvarenga and Bernard Belisario, "O cinema-processo de Vincent Carelli em *Corumbiara*," in Roberta Veiga et al. (orgs), *Limiar e partilha: uma experiência com filmes brasileiros* (Belo Horizonte: PPGCOM/UFMG, 2015), pp. 72–98. See also Claudia Mesquita, "Retratos em diálogo: notas sobre o documentário brasileiro recente," *Revista Novos estudos—Cebrap* (March 2010), pp. 105–18, and Claudia Mesquita, "Obra em processo ou processo como obra?" in Cleber Eduardo, Eduardo Valente and João Luiz Vieira, eds., *Cinema Brasileiro Anos 2000: 10 questões* (2011).
62 Cláudia Mesquita, op. cit.
63 See John Hemming, op. cit., p. 552.

64 See Els Lagrou, *A fluidez da forma: arte, alteridade e agência em uma sociedade amazônica* (Rio De Janeiro: Topbooks, 2007). Also relevant would be the work of Sally Price, *Primitive Art in Civilized Places* (2nd edition, 2001) and Peter Gow's *Aesthetics Is a Cross-cultural Category* (1993). Art began to be seen as autonomous during the Enlightenment with its delight in the separation and hierarchization of categories and taxonomies, but wherever people are creating and designing things with a sense of individuality and variation, you have art.
65 Cited in Tracy Devine Guzman, op. cit., p. 155.
66 See Pierre Clastres, *A Sociedade contra o Estado* (São Paulo: Cosas & Naify, 2003). Also, on indigenous humor see "Rir do poder e o poder do riso nas narrativas e performances Kaxinawa," *Revista da Antropologia*, Vol. 49. No. 1 (São Paulo, USP, 2006), pp. 55–90; and J. Overing et al., eds., *The Anthropology of Love and Anger: The Aesthetics of Conviviality in Native Amazonia* (London: Routledge, 2000).
67 Quoted in Hemming, op. cit., p. 180.
68 See Ana Gabriela Morim de Lima, *Hoxwa: Imagens do Corpo, do Riso e do Outro Uma Abordagem Etnografica dos Palhacos Ceremoniais Kraho* (Master's thesis for UFRJ, Rio de Janeiro, 2010).
69 The title draws on an intertext that goes back to Sydney Pollack's *They Shoot Horses, Don't They* (1969).
70 See Clarisse Alvarenga, *Da Cena do Contato ao Inacabamento da história*, op. cit.
71 Which is not to say that such individuals they did not have had mediated contact in the form of objects, pieces of clothing or even through smells, e.g. of the oily odor of an outboard motor.
72 César Guimaraes, "Apresentação," *Devires: Cinema e Humanidades*, op. cit., pp. 6–9.
73 Clarisse Alvarenga and Bernard Belisario, op. cit., p. 81.
74 See Jean-Louis Comolli, *Ver e Poder: A Innocencia Perdida: Cinema, Television, Ficcao, Documentario* (Belo Horizonte: UFMG, 2008) and *Corps et Cadre: Cinema, Ethique, Politique* (Paris: Editions Verdier, 2012).
75 Eduardo Viveiros de Castro, "No Brasil todo mundo é índio, exceto quem não é," *Povos indígenas no Brasil* (São Paulo: Instituto Socioambiental, 2006).
76 Gustavo Furtado, op. cit.
77 Ibid., p. 25.
78 Clarisse Alvarenga, op. cit.
79 See Claudia Mesquita, "Obra em processo ou processo como obra." Cited in Clarisse Alvarega and Bernard Belisario, op. cit., p. 98.
80 See Alberto Mussa, *Meu Destino e Ser Onca* (Rio: Editora Record, 2009), pp. 18–19.
81 Correspondence with the author in November 2021.
82 See Eduardo Viveiros de Castro, *Araweté: Os Deuses Canibais* (Rio de Janeiro: Jorge Zahar, 1986).
83 See Pierre Clastres, *Society against the State* (New York: Zone Books, 1978), p. 66.
84 See Hélène Clastres, *Terra sem Mal* (São Paulo: Brasiliense, 1978).
85 Renato Sztutman, *O Profeta e o Principal* (São Paulo: Edusp, 2012).
86 See M. M. Bakhtin, *The Dialogic Imagination*, trans. Caryl Emerson & Michael Holquist (Austin: University of Texas Press, 1981).
87 Ibid., p. 243.
88 Gerald Vizenor, *Fugitive Poses: Native American Scenes of Absence and Presence* (Lincoln: University of Nebraska Press, 1998), pp. 15–16.
89 See Édouart Glissant, *The Poetics of Relation* (Ann Arbor: University of Michigan, 1997).

90 On a panel at the literary FLIP conference in Parati in 2019, located near the center of Tupí-Guaraní power, Ailton Krenak offered an observation that resonates with this film. "You know, those Guaraní in the streets selling trinkets to tourists, you know that they know the land is theirs, right?"
91 Ruben C. Queiroz, op. cit., p. 116.
92 See André Brasil, "Bicicletas de Nhanderu: lascas do extracampo," *Devires: Cinema e Humanidades*, Vol. 9, No. 1 (2012), pp. 98–117.
93 See Jacques Ranciere, *Dissensus: On Politics and Aesthetics* (New York: Continuum, 2019).
94 I am reminded of the kind of sensibility that generated the film *A River Runs through It* (1992), an ode to fishing, which has a final note that "no animal was harmed in the making of this film."
95 For a thorough discussion of the path and movement motif in these films, see Moacir Francisco de Sant'ana Barros "Tava: Cenas da Caminhada e da Conversacao no Cinema Mbya-Guaraní," in Paulo Sergio Delgado and Naine Terena de Jesus, eds., *Povos Indígenas no Brasil* (Curitiba: Brazil Publishing, 2018).
96 André Brasil, "*Mise-en-abyme* da cultura," op. cit., p. 261.
97 See A. Brand, "'Quando Chegou esses que são Nossos Contrários': A Ocupação Espacial e o Processo de Confinamento dos Kaiowá/Guaraní no Mato Grosso do Sul," *Multitemas*, Vol. 12 (1998), pp. 21–51.
98 This can be described as "latent geographical agency." See Antonio A. R. Ioris, "Political Agency of Indigenous Peoples: The Guaraní-Kaiowá's fight for Survival and Recognition," in *Vibrant: Virtual Brazilian Anthropology*, Vol. 16 (Brasília, 2019) (Epub October 17, 2019).
99 D. Short defines genocide in these inclusive terms. See D. Short, *Redefining Genocide: Settler Colonialism, Social Death and Ecocide* (London: Zed Books, 2016).
100 As a film about a religiously sanctioned figure having doubts about his calling, it provokes comparisons with the very different Western art film approaches to the same theme, for example in Ingmar Bergman's *Winter Light* (1963).
101 See Manuela Lavinas Picq "Spreading Faith and Disease," *The New York Times* (October 2, 2020), https://www.nytimes.com/2020/10/02/opinion/amazon-missionaries-tribes-disease.html.
102 We are reminded of *Apocalypse Now*, in the scene where the sounds of American helicopters and the Vietnamese forest in Martin Sheen's transmute into the sounds of the hotel fans and the streets of Saigon.
103 The opening montage foregrounds the long trajectory home, by train, by bus, by foot, thus emphasizing the distance from the city itself, reminiscent of worker Antonio's long walk home in Rouch's *Chronique d'un Ete* (1961).
104 Kaka Werá Jecupé, *Oré Awé Roiru'a Ma: Todas as vezes que dissemos adeus, Whenever we said goodbye* (Triom, 2nd edition, 2002)
105 See Kumuni, "Futurismo Indigena," an interview with Fred de Giacomo, https://www.uol.com.br/ecoa/reportagens-especiais/kunumi-mc-quer-quebrar-estereotipos-e-mostrar-como-tecnologias-indigenas-sao-avancadas/#cover
106 See "We Belong to Nature; She Does Not Belong to Us," and interview of Kunumi by Lucass Gabriel Bosso (July 27, 2020), https://hitsperdidos.com/2020/07/27/kunumi-mc-entrevista-rapper-indigena/.
107 Ibid.
108 Ibid.
109 Ibid.

110 See Grace L. Dillon, "Imagining Indigenous Futurisms," in Grace L. Dillon, ed., *Walking the Clouds: An Anthology of Indigenous Science Fiction* (Phoenix: University of Arizona Press, 2012).
111 See Beatriz Miranda, "'The way I am is an outrage': The Indigenous Brazilian Musicians Taking Back a Burning Country," *The Guardian* (October 26, 2020), https://www.theguardian.com/music/2020/oct/26/brazil-music-indigenous-tribes-environment-bolsonaro.
112 "Arandu Arakuaa—Am'mrã (Estrela Cadente/Shooting Star/Estrella Fugaz—432 HZ & 528 HZ) HD," YouTube (premiered September 16, 2020), https://www.youtube.com/watch?v=FViBOdoNuVQ.
113 See the anthology by Grace L. Dillon, *Walking the Clouds: An Anthology of Indigenous Science Fiction* (Tucson: University of Arizona Press, 2012), where Dillon outlines how science fiction can advance decolonization through tools like slipstream, science fiction, and anthropological first contact scenarios, thus critiquing the exclusion of indigenous people from contemporaneity and advanced technology.
114 Sent to me by one of the participants in the group.
115 "Aldeia digital," *Wikipédia, a enciclopédia livre*. Accessed June 8, 2022, https://pt.wikipedia.org/wiki/Aldeia_digital.

5

Triumphs and the Travails of the Yanomami

The Yanomami consist of about 33,000 people living in over 600 communities on almost 200,000 square kilometers of rainforest straddling the borders of Northern Brazil and Southern Venezuela. One of the best-known constellation of forest-dwelling communities, they are the largest indigenous nation to have survived more or less isolated into the mid-twentieth century. The Yanomami have lived for centuries if not millennia in communal roundhouses called *shabonos*, which John Hemmings describes as "architectural masterpieces" consisting of a "great framework of pillars and beams that soars above the tree canopy like a proud circus tent."[1] The diversity of habitats in their territory has enabled the Yanomami to use hundreds of plants for medicinal purposes, all linked to elaborate etiological mythologies.[2] Botanists have been impressed by Yanomami knowledge and use of the forest, notably as discussed by Richard Schultes on hallucinogens, Ghillean Prance on edible fungi, Anthony Anderson on palms, and William Milliken on medicinal plants.[3] They have also long used hallucinogenic plants drawn from the forest for ceremonial and recreational purposes.

It was precisely Yanomami isolation that attracted the attention of outsiders. The dense forest had long made access to the territory difficult, and serious contact with whites began only in the 1940s. "Whites," in this case, meant prospectors for gold, and missionaries prospecting, as it were, for souls. The predictable result of these two forms of prospecting was death, disease, and spiritual ruination. As an isolated group that had never experienced epidemic disease, the Yanomami were seen by a 1968 expedition as a "control group" ideally suited for the study of genetic mutations. Led by Napoleon Chagnon and James V. Neel, the geneticist who headed the Atomic Bomb Casualty Commission, the expedition members collected samples of blood, saliva, and other bodily secretions. Yanomami territory was transformed into a laboratory for epidemiological and genetic research. The blood samples were used over the following decades and even came to form part of the Genome Project.

The expedition's methods raised an array of ethical issues. The Yanomami were not informed about the genetic research or about the comparative study with the Hiroshima victims, nor were they asked for their "informed consent." Many of the premises of the project were questionable; the lack of curiosity about how the Yanomami view of their own society; the failure to explain the project's real motives; the lack of precautions against disease; and the attempt to prove an a priori theory of a putative penchant for violence. The scientists saw the Yanomami as "objects of study," not as subjects endowed with intellectual agency and self-awareness, capable of explaining their own society. The Yanomami became world-famous due to a book—Napoleon Chagnon's *The Fierce People*. The end product of a 1964 scientific expedition, the book describes the Yanomami as extremely violent re-incarnations of Hobbes's bellicose savages. Just as Hobbes hypothesized that native tribes in seventeenth-century North America incarnated a hypothetically barbarous "state of nature" and the "war of each against each," Chagnon claimed to have discovered a society where the primum mobile was a penchant for war, motivated by male domination and competition over women, in sum, a toxic Darwinian struggle among men to dominate women and procreate. A best seller and a required text in many anthropology courses, the book was taken as the gospel truth. The book was published, ironically, in 1968, the year of anti-war, anti-colonialist, and anti-racist movements in many parts of the world, and a time when many in the United States were questioning the "fierce" war in Vietnam with its millions of casualties, most of them Vietnamese.

Chagnon's argument was angrily rebutted in Patrick Tierney's book *Darkness in El Dorado: How Scientists and Journalists Devastated the Amazon* (2006).[4] Tierney argued that warfare and violence among the Yanomami were largely induced by the scientists themselves, who offered steel trade goods (e.g. machetes, axes, fishhooks, and pots) in exchange for data for their biomedical investigations. The book enumerated a host of unethical practices perpetrated by Chagnon and his colleagues, while also focusing critical attention on the implications of the Atomic Energy Commission's long-term funding of the Yanomami project. Tierney was then in turn accused of his own inaccuracies. (A book by Robert Borofsky, in collaboration with experts like Bruce Albert and Terence Turner—*Yanomami: The Fierce Controversy and What We Can Learn from It*—provides a nuanced account of the opinion and memories of the principal figures involved in the debates.)

If there was ever a case of crossed and contradictory gazes on a people, it is the case of the Yanomami. The title of an essay by Eric Michaels—"How to Look at Us Looking at the Yanomami Looking at Us"[5]— conveys this sense of transcultural looking relations. The many outside observers who turned their gaze toward the Yanomami rarely saw the same thing. While Napoleon Chagnon saw the Yanomami as "fierce," fellow anthropologist Brian Ferguson argued that Yanomami culture was not particularly violent and that the violence that did exist was largely a result of sociopolitical reconfigurations due to colonization.[6] Anthropologist Marshall Sahlins claimed that Chagnon's trade of steel weaponry for blood samples and genealogical information amounted to "participant-instigation."[7] Other scientists argued that Yanomami violence was an adaptive response to a lack of protein in the local diet, while still other scholars blamed the introduction of metal instruments. Yanomami violence was often taken as a given; the question was about why the Yanomami were so violent, not about if they were actually violent. Rarely did the experts address their questions to the Yanomami themselves. In what anthropologist Kenneth Good called "the worst misnomer in the history of anthropology," the word that Chagnon translated as "fierce" (*waiteri*) actually meant "a subtle combination of valor, generosity, and good humor."[8] For Viveiros de Castro, Chagnon's book is a "festival of reactionary idiocy."[9]

The Yanomami were portrayed in ethnographic films by Tim Asch and Napoleon Chagnon—for example, *The Axe Fight* (1968) and *The Feast* (1970), made during the joint Neel-Chagnon study. Serious differences separated the two collaborators; whereas Chagnon was agenda driven, Asch preferred to emphasize everyday activities in films like *A Father Washes his Children* (1974) and *A Man and His Wife Weave a Hammock* (1974), scenes of harmony rather than conflict. The opening intertitle of *The Axe Fight* offers a slanted hermeneutic frame of understanding: "large Yanomamö villages are volatile, and the slightest provocation can start a violent outburst." The intertitles encourage the spectator to see the entire film as an evidential working out of the initial axiom of volatility. The ensuing film is divided into four segments: (1) the unedited film of a fight as observed and filmed by Asch and Chagnon; (2) the same footage replayed and slowed down to explain the kinship relationships of the participants in the fight; (3) kinship charts which explain the relationships of three lineages; and (4) the final cut integrates the original footage with more coherent explanations. The film clarifies the process of editing and reediting and even acknowledges mistakes of interpretation, for example, that the incident first thought to be about incest was actually about the beating of a woman.

A close look at the film reveals aspects of social behavior that do not really confirm Chagnon's view of fierce male domination. First, the film as a whole reveals that the fight was not an example of the promised "volatility" and "violent outbursts," but rather a result of a long and complicated history. The women as participants both encourage violence and restrain violence. They hurl pungent aesthetically based insults denouncing their rivals as "a people of pus and pimples" in which "ugly mothers produce ugly children." One is struck both by the violent atmosphere of shouting and agitation, and the presence of axes and machetes, in contrast with a striking lack of actual violence or real blood. Much of the appearance and the behavior, furthermore, was staged. A Yanomami informant said he was told by Chagnon "to dress up in my ritual paint, the way my ancestors did, and he asked me to get the whole village to dress up like that."[10]

According to accounts mentioned in the Tierney book, Chagnon clearly encouraged violent performances. The fact that Chagnon himself distributed machetes and axes leads to an obvious question: if the Yanomami were as fierce as he claimed, why did he arm them? Would not outsiders like scientists be especially vulnerable targets? And why were none of the filmmakers ever harmed? Chagnon never managed to film an actual death, or even evidence that a death had occurred. Chagnon was clearly staging his own theories in a tautological demonstration. Indeed, in his interview for Padilha's *Secrets of the Tribe*, Chagnon expresses a Hobbesian perspective in his explanation of Yanomami's violent behavior. Substituting the "nation-state" for Hobbes's Leviathan, or Sovereign, Chagnon claims the film shows what happens when people "live in the conditions that our ancestors lived in without a nation-state to constrain and interdict their political behavior." (Chagnon seems to have forgotten the violence of nation-states that engendered two World Wars).

Many native people have complained that they do not recognize themselves in the abstractions of a certain style of anthropological description. Made before the reflexive turn in Anthropology and the self-representational turn in documentary, the *Axe-Fight* deploys the conventional devices of didactic maps, Voice-of-God narration, and agenda-driven intertitles that cumulatively suggest an indictment. The film creates a sense of voyeuristic outsiderness, in the tone of observers proudly "cracking the code" of an alien society. In the case of the Yanomami, it is important to note, the anthropologists have been very diverse in ideology and behavior, with many of them being courageous defenders of the Yanomami. Apart from occasional skirmishes and revenge-killings, the critics argued, the Yanomami were not especially violent, indeed much less violent than most modern western societies. It was also ironic that scientists linked to the "The Atomic Bomb Casualty Commission" concerning the effects of radiation on the Japanese population should regard any group as "fierce." The Yanomami had become a specular object for alien projections and ideologies. While Chagnon was interested in abstract principles of social organization, the more relaxed and anecdotal French anthropologist Jacques Lizot told love and sex stories about gentle polyandrous horticulturalists living in a community that constituted, in line with the views of Oswald de Andrade, Marshall Sahlins, and Pierre Clastres, a "society of abundance," which maximized leisure rather than work, favoring *ocio* rather than *neg-ocio*. Indians, according to Lizot, needed to work only three or four hours a day to feed themselves.

Michael Taussig argues that the film's long shots hold the Indians "at arm's length, like lab specimens." For Taussig,

> *The Ax Fight* comes across as a confusing melee of irrational savages, saved at the last moment by, of all things, a classic anthropological kinship diagram shown while the narrator assures us that the causes, character, and resolution of the fight are to be found in some abracadabra logic within the diagram ... once again "science saves the day," and we leave the movie thankful for experts.[11]

Despite a simulacrum of objectivity, the film's clear agenda was to portray the Yanomami as a fractious and quarrelsome people, divided between hostile villages.[12] In light of the subsequent transformations both of documentary theory/practice and of anthropological theory, it retrospectively seems astonishingly arrogant to theorize a people without ever asking them how they see themselves and their society. The film's shallow reflexivity is merely procedural, since it ignores the asymmetries of power and the investments (financial and figurative) of the filmmakers themselves.[13]

With knowledge of the various accounts, and with information gleaned from the collectively authored Robert Borofsky book, it seems that Chagnon was obsessed with projecting his own Social Darwinist theories onto the Yanomami. Another collaborator in the project, Kenneth Good, wrote: "Chagnon made [the Yanomami] out to be warring, fighting, belligerent people ... That may be his image of the Yanomami; it's certainly not mine."[14] Jacques Lizot, who lived with the Yanomami for many years, in his book *Tales of the Yanomami*, meanwhile, rejects the exaggerated emphasis on Yanomami violence, writing that "they can be brutal and cruel, but they can also be delicate, sensitive, and loving."[15] His emphasis is both on taboos—for example, the taboo on making love with a woman who is nursing—and the lack of taboos, for example, the tolerance for polyandrous relations. He tells of an overheard conversation of a kind that might occur anywhere in the world: The man: "Let's Make

Love." The woman: "We don't value each other enough for that." The man: "We have always respected each other. Today I desire you."[16]

On gender relations, Lizot reports that "although women suffer under male dominance, they do have means of coping with it [through] mutual help groups ... and they are irreplaceable in the life of the community."[17] Confirming Oswald de Andrade's thesis about the lack of puritanism among the Tupi, Lizot reports that "adults speak openly of sexuality and reproductive functions; the role of copulation and the pleasure it gives are not hidden from children."[18] Asch, meanwhile, reports an amusing incident that reveals the culturally relative character of sexual modesty. When Asch decided to walk around naked like the Yanomami, their reaction of was one of shock; the men shouted angrily, "You're naked!" The scandal, it turned out, was that he had not tied up his foreskin in the cotton waist string, the item whose lack marked the border between acceptable and unacceptable nakedness for the Yanomami.[19]

Anthropologist Kenneth Good, who lived intimately with the Yanomami for many years, also portrayed the Yanomami as warm, loving, and gregarious. It was impossible for Good to be alone, since the Yanomami would seek him out, touch him, and want to know everything about him, full of tenderness and curiosity. Hundreds of families lived together more or less peacefully under the same thatched roof of the Shabono, in a world where work is collective and pleasurable: "The women go out together in groups [carrying] the babies and talk and laugh."[20] Good saw the collective life of the *shabono* as a "model of cooperative living."[21] Despite problems, fights, and insults "you've got 80 or a hundred people living in this rather close quarters without partitions or privacy. I don't think any Western society, group, or extended family could do it."[22]

Good's memoir *Into the Heart: One Man's Pursuit of Love and Knowledge among the Yanomama* (1991) offers an intimate version of life with the Yanomami. He recounts an evolution from friendship with a young girl named Yarima who matures into a woman, whom the Yanomami themselves encourage to take as a wife, since "every man needs a wife." (Apparently it was a common practice to assign girls to a husband at an early age, but the ensuing marriage was not necessarily permanent, and a woman could have several husbands and lovers.)[23] Good describes falling in love and being "flooded by happiness."[24] After a slow courtship, they become a couple, presumably a rare mixed couple in the community, and ultimately married and had three children.

Unlike those who arrived in Yanomami land with romantic ideas, Good arrived with very negative assumptions, but changed with close contact. He noticed that Yanomami women "simply did not spend time thinking about how they looked, nor did they watch to see who was looking at them. It didn't seem to be part of their sense of self."[25] (In feminist terms, they had not internalized the male gaze.) Good's positive experience conforms not only to that of many historical "white Indians," but also to the idea of "exemplars of liberty," in that he observed an all-embracing egalitarianism: "Though skills in hunting and shamanism were valued, still every person was on the same level as every other one. There were no traces of superiority, no status consciousness, no class consciousness,"[26] human relations were simple and down to earth. "You talked to men, you talked to women, there were no walls, no consciousness about how they were projecting themselves, how they were being perceived, and what that might mean for their future."[27] Good describes a spontaneous sense of freedom: "It took me a while to realize that what I was seeing was equality, a basic egalitarianism of life and other people—equality not as principle or belief, but wholly spontaneous. It was deeply ingrained in them, and it radiated through their culture."[28]

At the same time, Good describes Yanomami naivete about technology. Like the "scene of writing" in Lévi-Strauss's account, the non-acculturated Yanomami at first saw writing not as signifying meaning but only as a form of pictorial art or design. When he explains the operation of his tape recorder, they are at first shocked to hear their own voices, to the point of becoming pale and even angry. Despite the general egalitarianism, Yanomami society is clearly male-dominant, a fact that emerges in his account of rape, where women are seen as needing the "protection" of marriage. The memoir ends with their formal marriage in Rutherford, New Jersey, with their three children watching "Mister Rogers" and "Sesame Street." The final words are a tribute to Yanomami pride in their own society and "their conviction that despite the *nabuh*'s technology, despite his wealth, despite the comforts of his life, it is they and not he who defines what it means to be human."[29]

Another key figure in this story was Claudia Andujar, a Swiss-Jewish photographer who had been working with the Yanomami since the 1970s. On their first meeting in 1977, Davi Kopenawa found it unusual that any white woman not a missionary would live closely together with them. Andujar lived with the community in the *shabono*, the center of Yanomami communal life. Kopenawa thanked Andujar for using her photographs to reveal their lives and humanity to the wider world. Andujar totally rejected the idea that the Yanomami practiced chronic warfare. And as a child of Holocaust victims, she felt a "Never Again" affinity with the Yanomami as a people threatened with extinction. Andujar's collaborative work was deeply impacted by Yanomami culture and history. For example, the scientists from the 1960s expedition, in order to acquire medical records, violated the Yanomami taboo against revealing the names of dead relatives, paradoxically because they were so valued, when the scientists assigned a number, written on a wood necklace, to each Yanomami. Andujar registered these practices in her photographs, showing young Yanomami staring back at the camera, their numbers recalling for her the branded arms of the concentration camps.[30] The goal of Andujar's photography was to communicate a sense of the individuality and beauty she found in the Yanomami. As part of her apprenticeship in the culture, she participated in the *reahu*, a gigantesque multi-community festival involving the ingestion of hallucinogenic plants, dances, and trance. A decade of cultural involvement prepared her to use light to communicate the phototropic imaginary of Yanomami visual culture. After a long immersion in Yanomami culture, living close-up for periods of up to a year, and despite the anthropologists' conjectures about violent competition over women, Andujar said she never felt any fear of these supposedly "fierce" people, and even felt she had gained a family.

One courageous woman preceded Andujar as an outsider living with the Yanomami. A white Brazilian girl named Helena Valero, kidnapped at the age of 12, was adopted by indigenous people, became a woman among them, married two Yanomami men in succession, had four children over four decades, but returned to the "white" world in 1961. Valero related her discussions with the Yanomami about endo-cannibalism, which she opposed. The Yanomami would say, in effect, that "you bury your dead under the ground where they are eaten by worms, so clearly you do not love your parents. We eat the ashes of their bones in a banana paste and thus honor them." She said of her Yanomami husband, that "he was the only one who really loved me. His mother and his whole family loved me well too. But the Indians killed him and wanted to kill my children."³¹ Her story first reached the world in 1965 through a book by Italian anthropologist Ettore Biocca, subsequently translated into French, and into Spanish in 1984 as *Yo Soy Napëyoma - Relato de Una Mujer Raptada Por Los Indígenas Yanomami*. According to Tierney, Helena walked on foot alone for thousands of miles and was the first white person to explore many regions and mountain ranges. Fluent in Yanomami, she was admired by James Neel, an expert on genetics, for her knowledge of Yanomami genealogies. Tierney suggests that "every geographic discovery and anthropological first contact in Chagnon's career had really been already achieved by Helena Valero ... a remarkable fact and a remarkable theft. Every single place ... and every single village ... that Chagnon has cited as his discovery, was intimately known and visited by Helena Valero."³² Although Chagnon met Valero, he claimed that he never asked her about her life among the Yanomami, an improbable notion to say the least given his curiosity about all things Yanomami.

Juan Downey and "The Laughing Alligator"

As the most isolated indigenous people, the Yanomami, ironically, have been among the most filmed. The proliferation of such films made it possible for Jean Rouch to dedicate a festival to them in Paris in 1978. Apart from the Asch-Chagnon films, the festival included a French TV documentary; two films from a Yugoslavian TV series on the rain forest; a Canadian film from the TV series "Full Speed to Adventure"; a Japanese TV film; and, perhaps most significant in aesthetic and social terms, three videos by Chilean avant-gardist Juan Downey. A cosmopolitan maker of experimental films, Downey, who moved to the United States in 1965, combined a fascination with Jack Kerouac-style road trips with the indigenous obsessions of artists like French writer/actor/dramaturg Antonin Artaud, who had experimented with peyote with the Rarámuri in Mexico. Like Che Guevara, Downey embarked on a personal and political voyage of self-discovery across Latin America, and, equipped with a Sony Portapak, went to live with indigenous people in the Amazon. An unacknowledged early advocate of indigenous video, he helped members of his host tribes record themselves and their traditions, while also documenting them himself. A constant leitmotif in his work was an acid critique of Western racism and Eurocentric ontologies and epistemologies.

Prolonging the tradition of avant-gardists fascinated by indigenous cultures, Downey engaged with the Yanomami in three videos shot in southern Venezuela in 1976 and 1977—*The Abandoned Shabono* (1977), *Guahibos* (1978), and *The Laughing Alligator* (1979)—films that were then completed in New York between 1977 and 1979. *The Abandoned Shabono* chronicles Yanomani practices in forming alliances through inter-village feast—an opposite approach to that of Chagnon—and also, within a perspective close to that of Pierre Clastres, explains their rejection of central power so that the chief has more duties than actual power. Although nothing suggests that Downey was familiar with Brazilian modernism, he exhibited strong anthropophagic inclinations. Gazing into the camera, Downey explains that he had become bored with filming US American topics and that, as part of a search for transcendence, he would like to be eaten by some Indians of the Amazon rainforest. He was especially drawn to the Yanomami practice of tender, familial endo-cannibalism. One Yanomami friend almost fulfilled Downey's desire of being eaten. When Downey was ill with malaria, the friend told him, "I love you so much I want to eat your ashes if you die of malaria." Not only did Downey breathe in the powder of the sacred *yakoana* plant, he also participated with his Yanomami friends in the endo-cannibalistic act of devouring the ashes of deceased relatives in a banana paste.

As an avant-gardist invested in the improvisational and the aleatory, Downey was fascinated by the features of Yanomami life that coincided with his long-term artistic and philosophical concerns. In *The Abandoned Shabono*, Downey explains that when the physical structure of the communal *shabono* begins to decay because of ineluctable forest processes, the community takes it as a sign that resources have been exhausted and that it was time to move on. In avant-garde parlance, the *shabono* is a self-consuming artifact. These strategies for dealing with impermanence are isomorphic with the Yanomami approach to the universal challenge of burying the dead. In a migratory forest culture, according to Downey, there is no point in burying the dead in a specific place, since the place itself will disappear. Here lies a basic problem for an architect: how do nomadic societies deal with the deceased? In Yanomami society, this is dealt with at a corporeal level: the dead are cremated, not buried, and their bones are ground up and imbibed by family or friends in the form of plantain soup.

Downey went to live with the Yanomami together with his wife Marilys and her daughter Elizabeth (Titi), then a teenager. In the film, Titi tells personal anecdotes, while Marilys offers more "scientific" information. The story that gives the film its title—"The Laughing Alligator"—has to do with a Yanomami myth about the discovery of fire. The alligator had discovered fire, but selfishly kept it hidden in his mouth. The Yanomami ancestors tricked the alligator by making him laugh: when it opened its mouth, they snatched the fire, thus infuriating the alligator for having been tricked into giving up his wonderful secret. In some versions, according to Downey, the alligator's wife weaponized her urine to extinguish the fire. The film then segues to a postcard-like image of a young woman, in Michael Taussig mischievous words, "poking her splendid behind in orange shorts into all-too-close proximity to the alligator's tooth-lined mouth, as if she were about to pee into it."[33] Taussig wonders if this "sterling example of fetish-mixing … one of the highest forms of collage played out on the great stage of colonial history" is not "the secret—akin to the laughing alligator's fire—that works its way into every twist and turn of Downey's video, in its multi-channel form of storytelling."[34]

Downey's videos hint at a trait stressed by Pierre Clastres in his ethnographic essays on the Yanomami—their penchant for punning nicknames and obscene practical jokes, such as sadistic tickling and collective blasts of flatulence in the face of a sleeping friend. Asking the specific name of a plant, Clastres would get answers that turned out to be one of the many words for "penis." Clastres also speaks of Yanomami love of music, dance, festivity, and hallucinogens.[35] One moment in the Downey film briefly elicits horror. For a long trek through the forest, he joins two Yanomami guides, one armed with bow and arrow, the other with double-barrel shotgun. Midway, the two guides, with a serious demeanor, turn and aim their weapons at him. In response, Downey then aims his video camera, his *fusil cinematographique* at them, and films them as his voice-over underlines the irony of the situation. One of the hunters continues to threaten him with shotgun drawn, filling the frame, but then makes a noise signifying "bang" before lowering his weapon and smiling. The video then cuts to the *shabono*, where they tell the story to a young woman holding a child, who laughs uproariously while the subtitle translates the reasons for her laughter—"the foreigner was afraid."

As Amalia Cordova points out, Juan Downey "pushed the boundaries between ethnography and autobiography [immersing] himself in a quest to explore issues of identity in the Americas and in western culture, bridging indigenous worldviews from the Americas and cutting-edge, experimental western communication technologies."[36] Downey's interest in media technologies and his attempt to make visible the invisible systems of energy correlates with indigenous assumptions about the relation between the visible and the invisible, the natural and supernatural. For Cordova,

> Downey's body of video work maintains an uneasy relationship to visual anthropology; too aesthetic and self-reflexive for the classical study of the Other, he is often overlooked in the teaching of early visual anthropology and ethnography. However, he is highly regarded in the art world as an imaginative early media artist, as well as a precursor of indigenous media who produced thought-provoking, challenging, and profound visual commentaries on Western and indigenous culture, with unprecedented practices of collaborative video-making and what we could perhaps call experimental auto-ethnography.[37]

Another scene in the film shows two men blowing psychotropic powder into each other's nostrils, thus triggering hallucinatory, trance-like episodes. In a liminal state, as both Kopenawa and Deleuze would put it, they "become animal," as they are possessed by animal spirits and moving and roaring like jaguars. Juan Downey was very much in tune with this kind of shamanism. In fact, art historian Edward Shanken argues that Downey's "guerilla tactics deployed video as a shamanic device to expand consciousness and reveal alternative realities."[38]

Crossed Filmic Gazes

A number of Brazilian films treat the issues raised by Chagnon, the Scientific Expedition, and the Yanomami. In 2004, Nadja Marin, then a student at the University of São Paulo, made a documentary—*Napepe* (the Yanomami word for "whites" or "foreigners"), detailing the cultural clash between the Yanomami and the scientists. Marin interviews Kopenawa, along with a native teacher, and various Yanomami who remember the expedition, as well as Brazilian scholars and activists. The film emphasizes two related projects: the attempts by the Yanomami to recover the blood samples taken from their relatives, and the attempts to demarcate their own land as protection against prospectors, corporations, and the Brazilian government, all eager to exploit the vast resources of Yanomami territory.

Ethnologist Bruce Albert claims in the film that the rituals, interpreted by Chagnon as symptoms of an in-born penchant for violence, were actually social mechanisms for exorcizing violence. What the anthropologists saw as primitive ferocity—and the Yanomami did have a tradition of "revenge killings"—was actually a much more nuanced phenomenon. Albert further points to the indirect link between Chagnon's theories and the theft of Yanomami land, since the interested parties were using Chagnon's theories to justify the dismemberment of Yanomami territory. The Brazilian government and the foreign corporations desirous of land and raw materials weaponized Chagnon's arguments about a perpetually warring people as a pretext for dividing up the land, dressing it up as a supposedly humanitarian gesture to prevent tribal strife. In response, Bruce Albert and Claudia Andujar pushed for a continuous officially demarcated tract of land for the Yanomami. Together, the pair helped create the Commission for the Creation of the Yanomami Park, resulting in a 1992 land demarcation that stretched over 96,650 square kilometers. Despite legal protections, however, serious challenges remain, since thousands of illegal gold miners are operating in the Yanomami Park, with the tacit permission of a Bolsonaro government, the president who said publicly that he did not want to cede so much as a single millimeter of Brazilian land.

Jose Padilha's better-funded documentary *Secrets of the Tribe* (2010), meanwhile, focuses on the debates among the anthropologists about the 1968 expedition, treating the same issues in a more sensationalist manner reminiscent of the director's action movies. Just as Padilha's *Elite Squad* films leave us unsure about the director's sympathies, here too it is not clear whether Padilha identifies with Chagnon or with his critics. What is clear is that the anthropologists—nomadic hunters and gatherers of facts and theories—are his objects of study, rather like specimens under a filmic microscope. At the same time, the tone is one of bemused neutrality, signaled by a musical finale that signals a nonchalant relativism—the refrain "You say tomato, I say tomato … let's call the whole thing off"—as if the whole debate had been a waste of time.

In the Padilha film, the real "fierce tribe" is the anthropological tribe itself, with its fierce rivalries and toxic competition. Perhaps ventriloquizing Padilha's own feelings, the film begins with the angry words of a Yanomami: "You *Nabäs* (whites) are always such liars. I don't believe anything you say because you always lie. We don't want you here." The cast of characters is as wild as those in Padilha's police thrillers, although the violence is more subtle. Among the characters are the self-heroicizing Chagnon, with his self-image as a martyr for science; his gentler collaborator Tim Asch; and finally, French anthropologist and pedophile Jacques Lizot. (The film interviews one of his adolescent victims.) The title evokes many kinds of secrets—nuclear secrets, genetic secrets, the ritual secrets of the Yanomami, and the trade secrets of the anthropologists. The wars here are not so much the literal wars among the Yanomami, but rather the wars of discourse within the disciplines—biologically oriented social Darwinists versus humanists, cultural constructionists versus cultural essentialists, Right versus Left, and so forth. Importantly, Padilha includes many Yanomami witnesses of varying age who remember their direct contacts with Chagnon and Lizot; their memories and perspectives are interwoven with information about the political economy and social conflicts of the region.

Davi Kopenawa appears in almost all the films about the Yanomami. After reading Chagnon's description of the "fierce people," one is taken aback by Kopenawa's personality as it reveals itself in these films. Far from "fierce," he appears to be a gentle and dialogical person with a deep tenderness and love for his people. Aurelio Michilles's *David against Goliath* (1993) casts Kopenawa as the Biblical David of his people fighting against Goliath, now reincarnated in the form of prospectors, the Brazilian government, and allied corporations. (The Biblical trope was rather provocative at a time of the swelling power of evangelicals, the declared enemies of "heathen" and "pagan" indigenous religions.) More specifically, the film denounces the July 1993 massacre of twelve Yanomami from the Haxumi village by prospectors who invaded Yanomami territory. As the families of the victims explain what happened, the film punctuates their reports with poetic flourishes—superimpositions, baroque visual flights—to underscore the horror of the massacres, including emphatic shots of newspaper headlines, bones, skulls, and considerable gore, including a bloody hand beating on the camera lens.

Kopenawa is unyielding in his critiques of the outsiders, saying, in a submerged cannibal metaphor, that "whites do not only devour land, they also devour people." (It is important to know that Kopenawa does not mean "whites" in an ethnic sense or as a color: it refers to all those who form part of the colonizing project, no matter their color.) When all the Yanomami have died, he warns, their spirits will haunt white people. Kopenawa also throws the accusations about the "fierce people" back in the face of the accusers. He acknowledges occasional "mourning killings" motivated by sadness over the losses but totally rejects the idea of a general penchant for violence. In traditional Yanomami wars, Kopenawa points out, no one ever killed women and children, unlike the whites in the *haximu* massacre, did not hesitate to kill whole villages, including women and babies. Kopenawa explains: "We never killed each other without restraint, the way they do. We do not have bombs that burn houses and all their inhabitants … we do not kill … for merchandise, land, or oil, the way they do. We fight about human beings." Kopenawa argues, in effect, that the real "Fierce People" are those who "have done much violence against us Indians in order to kill us off."[39] While acknowledging mourning killings inspired by grief, Kopenawa insists that today the inter-village disputes barely exist: "Today we are all friends. Disputes are rare, and when someone is killed, it does not lead to fighting year after year. … They think the Yanomami are like them … The whites speak this way [about the Yanomami] because they want to use the minerals of our land."[40]

Kopenawa is also contemptuous of the claim that the cause of "war" was women: "Our Elders certainly did not arrow each other because of women, unlike what the white people claim [but only] when they wanted to take revenge."[41] In words that evoke deforestation by B-52s in Viet Nam and the War in Iraq, Kopenawa says that whites set fire to the earth and sky and even fight over oil: "I watched them on television, fighting each other for oil with their airplanes in a land with no trees … I told myself, these people are truly dangerous and warlike!"[42] We are reminded of Montaigne's bitter commentary on the behavior of the Spanish in Peru—"So many cities razed, so many nations exterminated, so many peoples cut down by the sword, and the richest and most beautiful part of the world overthrown for the sake of pearls and pepper"—a commentary that could be easily updated to apply to many indigenous peoples, but with gold, pasture land, and "intellectual copywrites" substituting for "pearls and pepper."[43]

Chagnon's portrayal of a ferociously masculinist people had an inordinate influence in the larger world, even to the point of influencing some feminist writing, which took the Chagnon theory as unvarnished truth. In their 1994 essay "Anthropology's 'Fierce' Yanomami: Narratives of Sexual Politics in the Amazon," feminist anthropologists Sharon W. Tiffany and Kathleen Adams unpack this unfortunate situation.[44] The essay begins with a pedagogical miscue, a Hitchcockian "red herring." The authors invite us to "imagine a society in which one woman of every three is raped, usually by a man she knows; consider the consequences of living in a society where one-third of all women are beaten during pregnancy and 35 percent of women using emergency medical facilities are battered." Cued by the title's reference to the "fierce" Yanomami, the reader assumes that the statistics refer to the Yanomami, only to learn that they actually describe the frequency of rape in the United States.

The Yanomami are considered especially important in the anthropological record as paradigmatic examples of the "mythic pristine" of a people unpolluted by Western contact. Thanks to Chagnon, the Yanomami are now the best-known ethnographic example of primordial primitives living in a "state of nature." Tiffany and Adams personally attest to the uncritical enthusiasm that greeted the Chagnon book in anthropology graduate programs in the late 1960s and early 1970s. The view of the Yanomami as violently misogynistic and given to ritualized male combat, incessant raids against neighbors, and the routine abuse of women, became popular common sense. The authors note that ethnographic and popular media images of the violent Yanomami had been widely disseminated not only in college-level anthropology texts but also in popular magazines like *Science*, *National Geographic*, *Newsweek*, and *Time*, despite the fact that Chagnon's conclusions had been challenged by many anthropologists.

The circulation of Chagnon's views was especially dangerous at a time when the Yanomami were threatened by policies of expropriation and genocide carried out by the federal and state government and military interests in Brazilian "national security," as well as by the international financial institutions that loaned billions of dollars for Brazilian "development" of the Amazon region. The authors point to the gendered tendentiousness of Chagnon's interpretation, where "the ethnographer's casual disregard for women intensifies his presentation of normative male violence toward women." Their "Hobbesian interpretation," the two authors suggest, is hypocritically accepted by members of a Western society where a "third of female homicide victims die at the hands of their husbands or male companions." For Tiffany and Adams, Chagnon and his followers, even feminist followers, inadvertently convey a pseudo-universal message that "male violence against women is expected in conjugal relations [and that] a woman is supposed to know that she is cared for by her husband through the punishment he inflicts upon her." A subliminal message was—how lucky you women are to be living in the relatively humane and woman-protecting West.

The two authors discern a rather sinister process at work in the demonization of the Yanomami:

> In the process of watching films, reading texts, and writing exams and papers, [the students] are permitted—indeed encouraged—to compare for themselves just how fortunate they are relative to their primitive sisters. The illusion is that American women escape physical abuse and rape because they are protected by civilized men and their social institutions. Thus Western women who abuse their bodies with cosmetic surgery and rigorous dieting-women who live with the daily reality of male violence can favorably compare their material lives with those of their less fortunate sisters who appear in anthropology books and in the popular media, whether half-naked or cloaked in veils and *burqas*, hauling babies and loads of wood on their backs.[45]

In other words, stated in Hobbesian terms, male power constitutes the new Sovereign, which prevents regression into a "state of nature." But for the Yanomami, one might argue, happiness itself is living *au naturel* in a state of *nature*, and nothing is more natural than to avoid a State.

Other anthropologists with fieldwork experience among Yanomami peoples provide a different perspective on the Yanomami. Anthropologist Alcida Ramos brought a different sensibility and set of concerns, both as a woman and a Brazilian. Basing herself on her research among different Yanomami subgroups between 1968 and 1985, she disputed the image of female passivity.[46] Ramos witnessed a number of "physical confrontations" between husbands and wives "One married couple was frequently involved in quarrels. During our 1968-1970 field trip we observed that sometimes verbal attacks escalated into physical fights, in which husband hit wife and wife hit husband, after which both spouses would display their wounded heads with a certain pride." One domestic dispute involved a couple "whose married life was normally harmonious" but where her husband's sexual interest in two unmarried women precipitated a quarrel: "She challenged the husband, and he hit her. She hit back with the flat side of the machete, as is common in some kinds of duels, according to the rule of 'be hit and hit back.' ... A few days later she and her husband had resumed their normal, peaceful domestic existence."[47]

While some 1970s feminists accepted Chagnon's view of Yanomami female victimization uncritically, feminist anthropologists during the 1970s and the 1980s began to "thicken" ethnographic discourse by including the lives and feelings of women. When asked, Chagnon condescendingly dismissed Kopenawa as having been deluded by occidental romanticism, as a well-intentioned but manipulated, mission-educated, Amerindian who ventriloquizes Western discourse: "Everything I know about Davi Kopenawa is positive, and I am confident that he is a sincere and honest man. When I read his proclamations, I am moved-but I am also sure that someone from our culture wrote them. They have too much the voice of Rousseau's idealism and sound very non-Yanomamo."[48] Chagnon here presents a new form of infantilization: Kopenawa does not know whereof he speaks; someone else, some kind of "outside agitator" perhaps, is speaking through him. Chagnon's tendentious judgment fits into the history of the conflict between two views, one that denies indigenous agency, and the other that affirms it. The Chagnon debate, in this sense, is a latter-day iteration of the post-contact debates going back to Sepulveda versus de las Casas, continuing with and Hobbes versus Rousseau, and prolonged with Chagnon versus Kopenawa.

The Poetics of *The Falling Sky*

Over four decades after the Scientific Expedition, Davi Kopenawa's *The Falling Sky* was published. Earlier we discussed the Kopenawa book largely in terms of social philosophy and its relation to the radical tradition in the West, here I turn to its literary and thematic qualities, before addressing the recent films related to the book and to the Yanomami. For a person schooled in both the canonical and anti-canonical literary tradition like myself, *The Falling Sky* inevitably elicits associations with a number of consecrated literary movements and styles. It is not a matter of dignifying the book by association with a more "noble" tradition but rather of placing both on the same plane of value. The Kopenawa book calls up memories, for example, of the proto-magic realism of Mario de Andrade, and the quasi canonical magic realism of Garcia-Marquez, even though it is certain that Davi Kopenawa never read those authors.[49] Just as Macunaima can turn himself into a telephone booth, Omama can turn himself into a metal bar. The following passage, for example, could have been taken from *100 Years of Solitude*: "In the beginning of time, the day never ended. The night did not exist. Our ancestors had to hide in the smoke from their wood fires to copulate without being seen. Finally, they arrowed the Titikiki birds of night, when they cried while naming our rivers, so that darkness would descend upon the forest." Kopenawa describes a world in constant transformation, not only of animals into human beings, and animals into other animals, but also of natural phenomena into animals: "Thunder was an animal then, a kind of big tapir who lived in a river, near a waterfall. At first our ancestors did not know him. They were merely exasperated by constantly hearing the powerful roar of his voice echoing through the forest. They grew weary and decided to make him shut up."[50] At other times, the *xapiri* act like characters in an animation film, designing, dismembering, and reassembling Kopenawa's body, putting his skull and torso in the lower part of his body, and then putting him "back together upside down, placing my rear where my face was, and my mouth where my anus was."[51] It is as if we are reading magical realism from an author who had never read a word from a magic realist novel.

In another sense, however, it is hardly surprising that Kopenawa's text reminds us of Marquez and Macondo, or that the Yanomami remind us of Mario de Andrade, Macunaima, and the Taulipang/Penom. Kopenawa and the magic realist writers form two branches—that of orature and literature respectively—of what Lucia Sa calls "Rain Forest Literatures."[52] Koch-Grünberg drew his account of the legends that inspired *Macunaima* from the folklore native to the same Roraima cultural area that gave birth to Davi Kopenawa. Alejo Carpentier's *"lo real maravilloso americano,"* similarly, was partially inspired by the grandeur of the Orinoco River that runs through Yanomami territory, as does the euphonious River Uraricuara cited in the first paragraph of de Andrade's novel. Both Mario de Andrade and Garcia Marquez draw on the same tropical taproot of what might be called forest trance-multinaturism. Thus, Marquez refers in *One Hundred Years of Solitude* to "an immediate reality that came to be more fantastic than the vast universe of ... imagination."[53] Instead of realistic inventories a la Defoe deployed as "reality effects," magic realism mingles fact and fancy to engender "irreality effects," as when Isabel Allende's *House of the Spirit*s creates a coastal town where it rains fish, or when, in Carpentier's *The Lost Steps*, the mere smell of mushrooms induces hallucinations, and swarms of butterflies darken the sky.

Yet this literary magic is not so distant from the quotidian surreal of the Amazon region, where sacred plants like *yakoana* and *ayahuasca* inspire powerful hallucinogenic visions, and where birds and butterflies in the Pantanal can suddenly darken the sky. The very title of the book—*"The Falling Sky"*—a phrase usually meant to dismiss a panicked warning as hysterical nonsense—comes to evoke an all-too-real climate apocalypse. Analogies to modernist and postmodernist techniques of collage and bricolage, similarly, form part of the multidirectional circulation whereby modernist artists themselves—Picasso, Antonin Artaud, Andre Breton, Maya Deren, Alejo Carpentier, Oswald de Andrade, Mario de Andrade, and countless others—were deeply impacted by indigenous cultures like that of the Yanomami. Marquez's Aracataca is literally and spiritually not so far from Kopenawa's Wakitori.

The Falling Sky represents an anomaly in relation to the mainstream tradition of narrative. We are accustomed to the literary device of the faux naif, for example, the character from Voltaire's philosophical fable *Candide*, whose titular character takes literally Leibniz's notion that "we live in the best of all possible worlds." Kopenawa, however, is not a faux naif but a true naif; that is a truly naive person, but only in relation to the West, just as we are equally naive in relation to the Yanomami and the forest. Kopenawa also creates, presumably without any explicit or conscious desire to do so, the Amazonian equivalent of still another subversive tradition within western literature, to wit, what the Russian Formalists called *ostrenanie*, the artistic procedure that renders our normal life strange and alien. Part of the sharp bite of the book is seeing Kopenawa's outraged reaction to our taken-for-granted modern realities of smog, noise pollution, poverty, and commercialism. With an acute eye for social contradiction, Kopenawa finds the dominant society's life choices absurd: why waste time destroying the forest, when in your "cities many of [your]sleep on the ground like dogs?"[54] In a salutary shock, his insights and impressions estrange or "make strange" conventional habits of thought through the alchemy of indigenous *ostrenanie*, thus giving us a glimpse of an "outside" to our assumptions and even our physical sensations.

In the context of theater, Brecht spoke of *verfremdungeffekt*, sometimes translated as "alienation effect," a technique that exposes the artifice both of artistic production and of dominant social structures. A related manner of making strange within the canonical western tradition is the literary device whereby perspicacious outsiders (often indigenous)—three Tupinamba for Montaigne, a Huron for Voltaire and

Lahontan—serve as springboards for the allegorical deconstruction of European social codes. The difference is that Kopenawa is not using a literary device, but simply seeing and describing western civilization through his Yanomami eyes, ears, noses, and minds. He even estranges our "normal" sensorium, relaying what he experiences as the shock of white peoples' smells, described by Yanomami as "intense and frightening ... like when a young hunter is overcome by a herd of wild pigs in the forest for the first time."[55]

The Estrangement Effect in Kopenawa's prose arises in part from a decision by the translator/collaborator to translate his words literally rather than adjust them to western understandings. Thus, money becomes "image paper"; minerals become "metal pestilence"; Europe becomes "white peoples ancestors' land"; Paris, because of its rumbling Metro, becomes "shaking land"; and the Eiffel Tower a "tall and pointy house" like an "antenna covered in vines of sparkling light." Some of the poetry emerges from the "buried metaphors" found in every language, such as the Yanomami "chest of the sky" and "the upstream of the sky" to refer to the West. Kopenawa's characterizations also estrange western bureaucratic normality, as when he says of a Border Commission official that "I did not think such beings could exist!"[56] It is museums, however, that Kopenawa finds most strange and even offensive. Like the disappointed Patricia Ferreira wandering through the Amazon wing of the Museum of Natural History, Kopenawa is saddened by museums that remind him of prisons where our "forest people ancestors" have been "confined in these distant houses."[57] The usually cool Kopenawa becomes truly irate at the sight of the glass cases in the *Musee de L'Homme* containing the "bodies of dead children, their skin hardened and dry."[58]

> Where do these dead come from? Aren't they ancestors from the beginning of time? Their dried out skin and bones are a sorry sight. The white people ... killed them with their epidemics and shotguns to take their land. Then they kept their bodies and now they exhibit them for all to see! What ignorant thought! ... The white people should not treat these dead ancestors so poorly by arranging them for all to see, surrounded by the objects they left behind when they died.[59]

Kopenawa's accounts of shamanic visions, meanwhile, remind us of still another literary tradition—the evocations of psychotropic experience, for example, Baudelaire's rendering of the hashish experience in *Les Paradis Artificiels* or Jean Cocteau's account of opium.

At one point in his life, Kopenawa makes a heroic effort to become Christian. He closes his eyes to pray, but his prayers are met with a deafening silence. In an inversion of the Christian story, where the Christian is tempted by Satan, here the temptation is Christianity itself. For Kopenawa, Christianity evokes fear, guilt, and the puritanism of the missionaries who "frighten us with *Teosi*'s [God's] words, and constantly speak to us in anger. 'Don't chew tobacco leaves! It's a sin, your mouth will be burned by it!, Don't laugh and copulate with others' wives. It's filthy.'"[60, 61] Unlike *Teosi*, "Omama, he always has friendship for us, no matter what we do! ... His image does not constantly tell us: 'You are evil! If you refuse my words, I will make you burn...!'"[62] The image of a vengeful deity is not so far from James Joyce's Irish-Catholic "pull out his eyes, Apologize." (Vine Deloria, Jr., in an even more irreverent vein, attributes to the Judeo-Christian deity a personality that "has the egotism of Henry Kissinger, the stability of Donald Trump, and the military mind of George Bush.") In his spiritually grounded materialism (or materially grounded spiritualism), Kopenawa bewails the Christian God's lack of visible and audible attributes: "What appearance does he have? What is the sound of his voice?"[63] (Vine Deloria, in a similar vein, asks, "What kind of a body did Jesus actually have?") For Kopenawa, the divine lack of attributes is not, paradoxically, a positive attribute.

Kopenawa frequently opposes Yanomami beliefs and practices as a performative spirituality to Christianity as a revealed religion of the book. For him, spirituality is not textual but experiential, based not on a sacred text but rather on the multi-temporal and trans-dimensional experience of trance and dream. Omama did not bequeath the Yanomami with any books inscribed with the words of *Teosi*'s (i.e. the Christian God). Kopenawa associates the written texts of Christianity with dogma, guilt, and rigidity, while he associates the *xapiri* with music, dance, visions, and change. The two brothers Omama and Yoasi were the only humans on the earth thousands of years ago. Yoasi is believed to have unleashed many evil spirits who were buried deep in the earth by Omama. Kopenawa and his tribe engage frequently in shamanic rituals to ward off the evil spirits believed to spread deadly diseases and poison the rivers with mercury.

The Yanomami Creation story in some ways resembles the patriarchal Biblical account, in that both see the first creation of humanity as being from the earth (*adama* in Hebrew) and beginning with the man rather than the woman. In the "Adam's Rib" story, Eve is "called Woman because she was taken out of man." In the Yanomami version, the world began with only Omama and his ill-behaved brother Yoasi, but when Omama copulated with Yoasi's knee, his sperm impregnated the calf of his brother's leg, whence the first son. The daughter, for her part, was fished out of the water. Such sacred origin stories seem normal to their adherents, but strange to outsiders, but then almost all origin stories seem strange to outsiders. The Jewish Bible stories of forbidden apples and seductive snakes and gendered ribs, of burning bushes and magical partings of the waters, as well as the Christian Bible's replicant fishes, virgin births, resurrections, and water turned into wine, might seem equally implausible to the Yanomami.

It is hard to know, in the end, whether to read *The Falling Sky* as poetry or science, or science spoken in mytho-poetic language, as when we speak metaphorically in English of the Amazon as the "lungs of the planet." People in or of the West are accustomed to imagining a hierarchy that places the human above the animal; the worst insult, for example, is to call someone an "animal." Yet common sense, evolutionary science, and indigenous wisdom tell us that animals are embedded in our body and in our very genes. According to some genomic studies, all current life evolved from a single organism that emerged roughly 4 billion years ago. Apparently human beings and the amoeba share DNA. Benjamin Oldroyd, an expert in behavioral genetics, claims that genomic imprinting is not limited to placental mammals and flowering plants but also extends to insects.[64] The fact of so much commonality between human beings and other creatures undercuts any rigid line between the animal and the human. The anthropomorphic treatment of animals, even in commercials with their talking bears and lizards, bespeak a recognition of shared qualities. Even the classical Aristotelian coinage of human beings as "political animals" suggests a shared inheritance. The danger comes when human beings weaponize the human/animal distinction to buttress social hierarchies so as to "animalize" some human beings, those supposedly not in control of their desires and thus "natural slaves," while angelizing or deifying other human beings as Masters.

Ultimately, Kopenawa sees the Christian God as allied with the invaders who destroy the forest. Speaking in pragmatic terms, Kopenawa prefers the Omama over Jesus, yet his discourse implies that the Christian God really exists as a human being:

> Maybe Teosi will take revenge on me and make me die. I don't care. I'm not a white man! I don't want to know anything more about him. He has no friendship for the inhabitants of the forest. He does not heal our children. Nor does he defend our land against the gold prospectors and cattle ranchers. It is not he who makes us happy.[65]

The special vision of the *xapiri*, accessible to the shamans, also has therapeutic medical effects, enabling the shamans to understand the pathogenic agents of disease. Although exactly how this process works might not be clear, the apparently excellent good health of the Yanomami prior to Western intervention suggests that they understood something about the nature of disease. (The shamans say they can cure the familiar forest diseases, but not the diseases brought by white people.) The case of Kopenawa brings us back to questions asked earlier. What constitutes philosophy? Must a philosopher be an excellent writer or is it enough to be verbally eloquent? Socrates, we know, had his doubts about publication, and that many canonical texts, such as *The Odyssey*, began as oral epics, assemblages of formulae like "craftly Ulysses" and "the wine red sea." Non-literacy does not preclude brilliance or eloquence or even a vast vocabulary. In relation to Montaigne and his Tupinambá interlocutors, we asked whether philosophy has to be written, or can it simply be eloquent? And what form must philosophy take? Can a shamanic vision constitute philosophy? Can a hallucinogenic vision generate concepts?

Indeed, a key part of Yanomami spirituality is the ingestion of the *yakoana*, a powerful hallucinogenic powder made from the resin of the nutmeg relative *Virola elongata*. The *yakoana* powder is inhaled in collective ceremonies, or taken individually by more experienced shamans. In Kopenawa's account, the power of the plant took him over and made him roll and thrash on the ground.[66] The body reacts with tears, runny nose, accelerated heartbeat, muscular spasms, convulsions, and a lack of bodily coordination, and most importantly, with visions. The *yakoana* experience is supposed to trigger the participants' symbolic "death" and transformation into "ghosts." In the participants' own words, "the spirits feed on the *yakoana* through us, who are their fathers." For Kopenawa, *yakoana* opens up the portals of wisdom whereby the words of the spirits reveal and broadcast themselves into the far distance. The experience as Kopenawa describes it sounds like something from the bio-luminescent and zoo-cyborgian world of *Avatar*. (Might we see the shamans as covert cinephages sitting in the front row of the *xapiri* spectacle, spellbound in psychotropic light?) In fact, since the growth of indigenous media coincided with the growth of the internet, indigenous peoples themselves also compare the experience of sacred plants to new media spectacles.[67]

By taking *yãkoana*, the shaman "dies" or "becomes other" and experiences the spirit world directly. Kopenawa tries to convey *yãkoana*-induced visions as a portal to perennial wisdom and fantastic perception, verbalized as images of haunting beauty:

> The *xapiri* float down through the air from their mirrors to come protect us ... Their mirrors arrive from the sky's chest, slowly preceding them. They suddenly stop in the air and remain suspended ... When they arrive, their songs name the distant lands they came from and travelled through. They evoke the places where they drank the waters of a sweet river, the disease-free forests where they ate unknown foods, the edges of the sky where, without night, one never sleeps.[68]

In Kopenawa's sharply imagined forest, one finds enormous trees that are "decorated with shiny down feathers of blinding white. Their trunks are covered in constantly moving lips, ranged one above the other. These innumerable mouths let out splendorous songs, which follow each other as countless as the stars in the sky's chest."[69] In this forest utopia peopled with singing sprites, it is not only evil that is lacking but also pollution and ugliness.

Miniscule yet magically powerful, the *xapiri* are very sociable, talkative, and performative, and here again we enter the world of the aesthetic. The *xapiri* are skillful dancers, and their "ways of dancing are as diverse as their songs are different."[70] At times, they become dance instructors: "their images take you by the arm and teach you to follow their steps with confidence. If you look awkward, with stiff legs, they get impatient and admonish you: 'Follow me! Look! This is how I dance! Pay Attention!'"[71] They come and dance together by the thousands, shining like stars and dancing on resplendent mirrors. The shamans hear and reproduce the *xapiri*'s songs, which funnel into their ears as if into microphones.[72] Usually friendly, *xapiri* at times play a helpful role similar to that of Catholicism's "guardian angels." But they are nauseated by any bad odor: "the spirits observe and smell us from afar before they come close. If they find us greasy and nauseating, they instantly run away."[73] As performative chaperons, they worry when young people start to make love too early and refuse to dance for them.

Kopenawa's account raises as many questions as answers. Is the Yanomami collective consciousness so unified that it allows for no individual variations? Do all the shamans, in their trance-state, see the same *xapiri*, with the same appearance, dancing in the same way? Are the hallucinations individual, collective, or both, in the manner of the collective dreams of the Surrealists? Since the *xapiri* have their homes in the forest, do they die with the fires and deforestation? In historical terms, do the *xapiri* change under the impact of the Anthropocene? How far down the ladder of animal existence do the human/animal spirits go? (Viveiros de Castro suggests that they concern only the larger animals, those that can be friends or prey.) When a species becomes extinct, do their animal spirits become extinct as well? What will happen if the forest no longer produces the plants necessary to create the *yãkoana*? Would it be as if the Eucharist depended on the availability of grapes for wine, or Rosh Hashana on the presence of pomegranates?

The shaman is a person who has access to the cosmos beyond ordinary perception. Although the term comes from Siberia, it was adopted by the scholarly community to designate practices that have existed since time immemorial. The *xapiri* spirits "people," as it were, the cultural universe of the Yanomami. Taking human form, their names signal their special powers, connected to the abilities of their corresponding animals—bird spirits with long beaks like the Tucano are gifted at picking at human sores containing a poison; the Jaguar spirit can attack a distant enemy, all within a comparative system of analogies between animals and humans. For Renato Sztutman, a thinker inflected both by Walter Benjamin and Viveiros de Castro, shamanic speech is a prophetic, even cosmopolitical discourse, a reading of historical events through mythology and cosmology. As a kind of diplomat, the shaman uses strategic language to negotiate the transit between worlds.[74] The shaman offers a new kind of spiritual "representative government," not of, for, and by the people, but a kind of indirect, mediated regime where the shamans act for the people and for the earth itself, which includes the people.

Meanwhile, in three-dimensional life, Davi Kopenawa is our mediator, our *truchement* in relation to the Yanomami. As Sztutman points out, Kopenawa is not only literally a diplomat as world representative of his people; he is also a diplomatic envoy of the *xapiri*. In her article "Xamanismo e tradução" (Xamanism and translation), Manuela Carneiro da Cunha compares shamans to creative translators who go beyond ordinary language through a deliberately twisted allegorical idiom.[75] Kopenawa, in this sense, performs translational diplomacy, tirelessly insisting that the shamans "work to prevent the forest from turning into chaos."[76] His vocation as a guardian of the forest is not tribal or particular but rather universal: "We shamans simply say that we are protecting 'nature' in its entirety. We defend the forest's trees, hills, mountains, and rivers; its fish, game, spirits, and human inhabitants. We even defend the land of the white people beyond it and all those who live there."[77] In the forest, various kinds of entities cohabit and enjoy a trans-species Convivencia, one existing in what Bruce Albert calls "inter-ontological tension," concepts also encountered in indigenous societies in North America.[78] The idea of a co-habitation of human and other kinds of beings finds an echo in the writings of Leanne Betasamosake Simpson about similar Anishnaabeg beliefs about animals: "There is an assumption on the part of the Nishnaabeg that the deer have language, thought, and spirits—intellect, and that intellect is different from the intellect of the Nishnaabeg because they live in the world in a different manner, and they therefore generate different meanings."[79]

The shaman's world is a deeply aesthetic universe of beauty, pleasure, storytelling, and blurred lines between truth and fiction. Preternaturally beautiful, the *xapiri* in Kopenawa's account, are multi-talented artists, described as perpetually dancing, singing, and poetizing. Both male and female, they have individual human characteristics and tastes. Kopenawa repeatedly analogizes the *xapiri* world to the everyday human social world. In their dance presentation, for example, "the female spirits always dance first, just like our women who dance to convince us to join the large celebrations like the *reahu*."[80] The tales are also full of humor, much of it sexual. Kopenawa's erotic visions of polyamorous "magic" help him mature into shamanhood. The psycho-sensorial altered state provoked by *yãkoana* is interpreted as a glimpse of the ontological superiority of the *xapiri*, at times reminiscent of the hybrid animal-human-machine creatures of *Avatar*, unencumbered by the physical limitations of ordinary human beings. At times, Kopenawa seems to be pulling the anthropologist's and the readers legs, as when he claims that the *xapiri* are so pure that "their farts give off a pleasant smell!"[81]

It would not be completely out of school to compare the Yanomami love of animals and plants to poet Gerard Manley Hopkins' animistic love of "finches' wings" and "dappled things [and] rose-moles all in stipple upon trout that swim." *The Falling Sky*, in this sense, corresponds to Lucio Paiva Flores's understanding of the role of the forest in indigenous culture as one of nurturing dreams and utopias: "it is in the forests, in rivers, alongside the animals" that indigenous peoples search for "harmony between humans and nature so that they can develop into one sole being."[82] The forest forms a creative festival of forms, including verbal forms. Although lacking in a sacred written text, shamanic language is nevertheless highly verbal. According to Bakhtin, every generation reaccentuates the cultural productions of the past in its own way, rendering every text susceptible to surprising "homecomings." The words of the ancestors, as Kopenawa puts it, are "ancient and numerous" and our "thoughts unfurl in every direction"[83] and the *xapiri*'s words "become new again each time they return to dance for a young shaman."[84] Thanks to the forest lyricism of the songs and poetry of the *xapiri*, their words come to dwell within the shamans' minds and bodies. According to Bakhtin, every generation reaccentuates the cultural productions of the past in its own way, whereby every text is susceptible to surprising "homecomings." Although lacking in a sacred written text, shamanic language is nevertheless highly verbal. Thanks to the forest lyricism of the songs and poetry of the *xapiri*, their words come to dwell within the shamans' minds and bodies. Myths, in this case the words and songs of the *xapiri*, are not dead texts from the past, but rather communicative utterances renewable in the urgent present, available to be re-invoiced by every generation. But apart from that, Kopenawa's thought reveals a vast reserve of ideas, like the forest itself, a kind of conceptual and imagistic commons. The words and songs of the *xapiri* are not dead texts from the past, but rather communicative utterances renewable in the urgent present, available to be re-invoiced by every generation. But apart from that, Kopenawa's thought reveals a vast reserve of ideas, like the forest itself, a kind of conceptual and imagistic commons.

For Viveiros de Castro, Amazonians like Kopenawa do not think of a generic Nature but of plural humanities cohabiting the forest. "Cosmological perspectivism" sees "the world as inhabited by different sorts of subjects or persons, human and non-human, which apprehend reality from distinct points of view and open up cinematic intensities and potentialities."[85] Darwin and acting coaches are right to see animals and humans as co-implicated and mutually embedded. Even the talking animals of animation films hint at trans-species kinship. For many indigenous societies, "our relatives" include four-legged and winged relatives. Many people think they once spoke the language of animals, but that now only shamans know its secrets. Thus many indigenous societies see people as learning from animals about how to do things, since many animals have physical abilities superior to our own and survive conditions that we could not survive.[86] For the Yanomami, as for many Amazonian peoples, human beings exist alongside animals and supernatural spirits, invisible to ordinary human beings but visible to shamans. According to Lévi-Strauss, the leveling of the animal and the human is common to indigenous thought in the Americas generally, since a myth can be defined as a story from the time when humans and animals did not distinguish themselves from one another.[87]

In the context of indigenous Amazonian philosophy, Viveiros de Castro speaks of the "reversible" gaze of the shamans, capable of seeing animals as human and humans as animals. Viveiros de Castro, it should be noted, is a person with a long involvement with photography and 1980s Underground Cinema in Brazil ("Udigrudi" in deliberately mispronounced English). Shamanism, in his view, entails the capacity of some individuals to cross the corporeal barriers between species to adopt "foreign" subjectivities in order to administer relations between them. In a kind of "figure and ground" switch, shamans can alternate their point of view by manipulating the vision of their two bodies, one human and one animal, alternating between seeing humans as animals from the point of view of his animal body, and seeing animals as human from the point of view of his human body.[88] We can only imagine how a film might "realize" or "translate" such a human/animalic "rack focus" between different ways of seeing. For the native peoples of the Amazon, according to Viveiros de Castro, each animal species instantiates a point of view. This concept has implications that go beyond the anthropocentric and masculinist POV shots of gendered Nature Documentaries—"in his enthusiastic pursuit of the female, the male aggressively courts his mate by proudly displaying"—to evoke a world where animals and humans share a more complex kind of humanity as an "ontological potentiality."

In a passage not without its dose of humor and self-mocking certitude, Viveiros de Castro speaks for the subaltern animal when he writes: "In seeing us as non-humans, animals and spirits regard themselves (their own species) as human … they perceive their food as human food—jaguars see blood as manioc beer, vultures see the worms in rotten meat as grilled fish."[89] Instead of the "hierarchical Great Chain of Being," a ladder that leads up to Human Beings as the master of the Chain, a horizontal network of beings. What Viveiros de Castro's describes as the strong perceptual relativism of Amazonian groups suggests that multiple visions of the world can cohabit within the same person or culture. The question is not only a question of different points of view, but differences about what constitutes a point of view. What people in the West call "presents," the Yanomami, for example, call "merchandise." What, then, would constitute an indigenous anthropology? Viveiros de Castro here cites Henry James, for de Castro the "consummate genius of perspectivism" as suggesting an "indigenous turn" that instead of "screwing the native" would be the ultimate indigenous "turn of the screw."[90] This kind of "altercognitivism" would help us avoid the "pathologies that threaten communication between anthropologists and native peoples, whether linguistic incompetence, ignorance of context, lack of empathy, literalist ingenuity, indiscretion, bad faith and sundry other deformations."[91] In Brazil, the cosmo-political approach has spawned many mediatic cognates and variants such as an indigenous "cosmocinepoliticas" (Rubem Caixeta de Queiroz and Renata Otto Dinis), "shamanic translation" (Andre Brasil), indigenous media as "bricolage" and an "art of the concrete," "salvational images" (Amaranta Cesar), and "cinema as an enchanting (or incantatory) cosmotechnology" (Catarina Amorim de Oliveira Andrade and Alvaro Renan Jose de Brito Alves). Marcelo Ribeiro defines "cosmopoetica" as an ensemble of "forms of invention (poiesis) of the world as a common world (cosmos), signifying a world constituted ... principally as a commons invested by regimes of intelligibility, visibility, and sensibility."[92]

Although Yanomami society is in most ways communal and egalitarian, certain hierarchies still operate in Kopenawa's text, first in terms of a kind of cognitive-spiritual elitism. While ordinary people are deaf and blind to the forest spirits, the shamans hear them clearly; the spirits dance and sing only for them. These superlative kinetic images are only visible to those equipped, so to speak, with an expanded cinema of the mind. The hierarchy of spiritual powers is apparently not translated or substantiated into social hierarchies, however, since Yanomami society practices a radical communal equality. The major exception to egalitarianism has to do with gender. Although Kopenawa mentions that some shamans are women, we do not see them in the filmed cross-community reunions of the shamans. Moreover, they can only become shamans if their fathers are shamans and they are "born of the sperm of his spirits."[93] I would add that on a practical daily level, internet videos such as "Encontro das Mulheres" (Meeting of Women) show festive meetings of Yanomami women leaders speaking about opposition to the prospectors and other invaders, along with practical issues of health, weaving, and the like.

The spiritual center of Yanomami life seems to be clearly male. But at times the quotidian intercedes to undercut the mystique of the shamans, for example, through the agency of Davi's wife who, perhaps like Socrates's wife Xanthippe, poses skeptical questions and complains that her husband inhales too much *yãkoana* and spends too much time in the Yanomami *agora* with the other shamans rather than with her.[94] Shamans are not Plato's "philosopher kings," although many indigenous societies share the Platonic idea that leaders should be precisely those who do not seek wealth or domination: discursive persuasion without coercive power, in Clastres's formula. Yanomami society is basically acephalous. Asked by strangers if he is a chief, Kopenawa's reply is always irritated: "We don't have chiefs!" *The Falling Sky*, in the words of Viveiros de Castro, "changes the level and terms of the usually poor, sporadic, and terribly unequal dialogue between the indigenous people and the non-indigenous majority of Brazil."[95] We must take absolutely seriously, Viveiros de Castro insists, that what indigenous people—"the extranational minorities of the planet who still resist total dissolution provoked by the modernizing blender of the West"—are saying through the voice of Davi Kopenawa.

The Visual Imaginary of the Yanomami

Although many Yanomami were initially hostile to the camera, Yanomami culture has always been oriented around the image, visionary dreams, and aesthetic preoccupations. The concept "the gaze" is a constant: a chapter is entitled "the Xapiri's Gaze:" the shaman, by incorporating the *xapiri*'s gaze, can see the same spirits that they see. "White" inadequacies are seen as a failure to see: "Even when they fly over [the forest] they don't see anything."[96] Body decorations and the painting of a friends' bodies are frequent activities. It would be a misnomer to call what Kopenawa describes as "artistic," since for the Yanomami art is not a separate "disinterested" realm. It is a normal quotidian affair, produced by virtually everyone through singing, dancing, adornments, and inter-personal body painting. The aesthetic sense of the Yanomami includes an appreciation for the spectacular beauty of the animals themselves, for the chromatic audacity of parrots for example, reproduced in Yanomami feathered headdresses. For the Yanomami, the word "*utupë*" is understood in a shamanic context as a vital principle or quintessence that animates all beings. The *utupë* images are even more beautiful than actual animals. The forest too is a world of images. The *xapiri*, he tells us, are not the actual animal ancestors but the improved images of animal ancestors. Every entity has its imagetic double, comparable to photographs, which the shamans, like mental puppeteers, can induce to move and dance. The sun and the moon have their images that dance only when animated by the shamans.

The spirituality of the Yanomami is strangely visual, iconophilic, and cinematic. The power of the cinematic apparatus—the control of color and light—refracts and mirrors the sensibility of the shamans. Against those who assume that the West alone privileges the sense of sight over the other senses, anthropologist Viveiros de Castro argues that many Amazonian societies also see vision as the model of perception and knowledge. In his analysis of the *xapiri*, anthropologist Viveiros de Castro, a person himself deeply involved with cinema and photography, identifies basic visual traits of the *xapiri* associated with intense light. The sacred plants are prized because of the visions they provoke and Shamanic language is highly visual.[97] Within a kind of forest Platonism, the concrete world forms the imperfect image of another world of imagistic doubles. But here the simulacra are not mere lure; they are more perfect than the real. In these attempts to capture the trance-natural, everything in the world has this detachable image; not only people, but also animals, and topographical formations (rivers, mountains) and ancestors.

Kopenawa describes the *xapiri* as "tiny, like luminous flecks of dust, invisible to ordinary people who have only ghost eyes. Only shamans can truly see them. The shiny mirrors they dance on are huge. Their songs are magnificent and powerful … they work forcefully to protect us."[98] Continuing with this highly cinematic account, Kopenawa describes *xapiri* heads as "covered in white down feathers, which cast a dazzling light, preceding them wherever they go. Only the *xapiri* are adorned this way. This is why they shine brightly, like stars moving through the forest."[99] Although the book includes Kopenawa's sketched attempts to design the *xapiri*—they look like spritely carnivalesque humanoids—only contemporary CGI effects could begin to do them justice. How, then, might one represent, or better recreate, a cinematic equivalent of Kopenawa's vision of the shamanic experience and the world of the *xapiri*? How might one translate these paradisal images/sounds and apocalyptic prophecies into film language? The options are endless, few of which have been tried. One might create the cinematic equivalent of a mystical experience through an immersive cinema of 360-degree virtual reality. Some more questionable options would take the form of a tabloid TV episode focusing on the more sensational aspects of trance, or of a Disneyesque Bambi-like idealization, or a didactic ethno-documentary with Voice-of-God commentary, talking heads, and maps, or a feature fiction CGI-enabled blockbuster like *Avatar*. Or perhaps a big-budget Hollywood action-film about Davi Kopenawa's heroism. One imagines the off-screen narration with a stentorian male voice and deafening Dolby sound: "In the depths of the treacherous Amazonian jungle [pause plus explosive sound], one man [pause plus explosive sound] dared to fight for his people! [deafening theater-shaking explosion]."

Yanomami director Morzaniel Iramari Yanomami provides one answer to these questions in his film *Urihi Haromatipë* or *Curadores da Terra-Floresta* (Healers of the Earth-Forest, 2014). Explicitly addressed to the *nape* (non-indigenous) audience, the film accompanies the entire process of an intercommunal meeting of Yanomami shamans, with explanations both by the director, whether through direct speech or voice-over, or through Davi Kopenawa's intermittent comments. Arguably "Bazinian" in its preference for long-takes, minimal interventions, synchronous sound, and general respect for the spatio-temporal integrity of the scene, the film begins with the warm greetings and embraces of the guest shamans arriving by small plane, followed by an explanation of the making of the *yãkoana*. Morzaniel Iramari shows us the plant itself—the physical catalyst for a spiritual experience—and the manner of its preparation. Within a pragmatic spirituality, the shamans and the *xapiris* are thirsty for the potent sap of the tree, which has to be mixed with chestnuts and be pure enough to serve as a cure, rather like a Catholic Mass, but where the transubstantiations of the wafer and wine into the blood and body of Christ would involve sacred roots and hallucinogenic visions.

The subsequent scenes privilege the ring-shaped *shabono*, where families live in a radial, thatched longhouse that faces a common open space, surrounded by the evergreen Amazonian rainforest. Each family has its own hearth where food is cooked during the day. At night, hammocks are slung near the fire, stoked to keep people warm. Like most Amazonian tribes, tasks are divided between the genders. Men hunt for meat like peccaries, alligators, tortoises, and monkeys. The shared space serves whatever purpose its dwellers propose—such as rituals, feasts, and games—and constitutes an architectural demonstration of balance, restraint, and collective existence. Unlike those filmmakers who cleanse the image of any reference to the present, the film does not hide the indicia of a globalized post-modernity in the form of flip flops, Bermudas, sports team T-shirts, and wristwatches. Much of the film is taken up by the "performances" of the shamans under the influence of the sacred plant, embroidered with Davi Kopenawa's explanations for outsiders. The relaxed audience of shamans talk among themselves, sometimes laughing, rather like the nightclub audiences in a backstage musical, our surrogates watching the same production numbers that we as spectators are seeing. The performances seem to be multi-genre, mixing tones of exaltation, anger, and animal sounds. At times, the shamans seem to be mimicking animal movements. If we have evolved from animals, as Darwin teaches and some acting coaches stress, and if humans and animal spirits are close human relatives from whom we have learned, and as the Yanomami believe, it makes sense that the potentialities of animal performance live deep within us.

In the background of the main action, everyday life goes on as relayed both by the image and by a sonic continuum that embraces the murmurs of the "audience," a mix of bird calls, children crying, people laughing, and talking. In his on-screen remarks, Kopenawa compares the shamans to doctors serving the people and the earth itself. Their role is to make contact with the *xapiri* who protect the forest, the Yanomami and the entire world, in order to keep the earth from "becoming sad and sobbing." As with Afro-Brazilian *candomblé,* only some people are mediums, or shamans, yet they act out the desire of the whole community. Although one might expect a kind of drugged frenzy, everything, despite the hallucinogenic trigger, is quite orderly; individual shamans appear and perform one at a time in an orderly sequence of dance and verbal performances. From the visible and phenomenological, the non-initiated infer the unreproducible visions of the shamans, while the director films the phenomenal manifestations of the effect of the spirit-images.

Cinematizing Shamanism: *Xapiri*

The film *Xapiri* (2012) offers a complex response to the questions of representation and performance posed earlier. Made with the collaboration of the indigenous organization Hutukara[100] Yanomami Association, the Brazilian Cinematica, and the Socio-Environmental Institute, *Xapiri* is not technically a work of "indigenous media" but rather a collaboration between the Yanomami and knowledgeable outsiders. But clearly the film would not have been made, or would not have been made in the way it was made, without the close collaboration of the Yanomami. *Xapiri* was produced by a quintet of non-indigenous intellectuals and artists—Leandro Lima, Gisela Motta, Laymert Garcia dos Santos, Stella Senra, along with the already mentioned Bruce Albert, who had worked with the Yanomami for decades. With five people credited as directors, the film is a polyphonic utterance rather than reflective of the particular sensibility of an auteur.

As for the collaborators, Laymert Garcia dos Santos is a philosopher deeply involved with a transmedial theatrical project related to the Amazon—"Transcultural Amazonas as Shamanism: Technoscience in the Opera"—sponsored by the Goethe Institute and presented for the first time in Munich on May 8, 2010. The concept recalls the premise of Manthia Diawara's *Opera of the World*, a dialogue between European and African opera, which reimagines the European operatic tradition through the prism of African culture, but this time the prism is Yanomami. Laymert Garcia dos Santos's project exhibits a salient feature of modernist and postmodernist Brazilian culture—the ceaseless interplay of the erudite and the popular, the national and the transnational, the mainstream and the indigenous.[101] The other collaborators include journalist, researcher, photographer and cinematic essayist Stella Senra, and plastic artists Leandro Lima and Gisela Motta, who had collaborated with the already mentioned Claudia Andujar.

Xapiri is not an adaptation of *The Falling Sky*, although Kopenawa briefly appears in the film (without speaking) and even though the filmmakers were well-informed about his concepts. Rather, *Xapiri* is an indirect visual homage to the poetic riches of Yanomami shamanism, insofar as they can be evoked through external manifestations. Informed by various genres and intertexts—ethnographic film, indigenous media, video art, psychedelic films, nature films, installations, and avant-garde experimentations, the film melds the traditional topic of millennial Yanomami rituals with cutting-edge digital and graphic effects. The film exists at the opposite end of the aesthetic spectrum from *Curadores da Floresta*. While that film was realistic, transparent, Bazinian, naturalist, and naturist, a self-effacing cinema with minimal filmic interventions, *Xapiri* is more Eisensteinian/Vertovian/Stan Brakhagian, with constant interventions and mediations. The film accompanies the work of the *xapiri* indirectly, by displaying the external signs of the different stages of the ritual, generating some sense of its evolving presentation, where shamans, according to Kopenawa, conjure up entities who help them cure ills and evils that impact the cosmo-ecological order of the world.

Xapiri is structured around footage of two annual meetings of 37 Yanomami shamans, called by Davi Kopenawa Yanomami in March 2011 and March 2012, taking place in the village of Watoriki in Roraima. Thus a shamanic voyage is anchored in the sights and sounds of a specific time and circumscribed place. While restricting itself to that space and time, it opens up the space-time continuum through oneiric effects as manifest in visual and multi-temporal distortions. Defiantly not an explicatory Anthropology 101 documentary with maps and talking heads, the film avoids the Voice-of-God narration of the traditional ethnographic or sociological documentary. Since film conventions have taught us to be vococentric—spectators tend to pay inordinate attention to the voice as the vehicle of truth and meaning—the lack of translation/subtitles leaves us confused, but also more likely to look and listen closely. No experts or insiders explain what is happening. Kopenawa is briefly glimpsed, but neither he nor any key character is made the organizing center of consciousness. We are on our own, attending a ceremony in a language we do not understand; words are omnipresent, but they are not made available to our understanding.

The film is organized by thematic episodes, separated by slow fades. A few force-ideas orient the construction: the first scenes present the spiritualized forest through altered colors, then a fade followed by a marvelous cacophony of forest sounds and images, then the inhalation of the sacred powder, followed by shots of faces that seem deformed and disfigured. Male bodies move into a frenzy of activity and wild gestures. Then the images slow down, the bodies lose their recognizable shape, reaching toward abstraction, as if the participants had experienced a dissolution of the self, a version of Rimbaud's "deregulation of all the senses."[102] The film ends with children playing in the trees, hanging from the branches like monkeys, with translucent bodies as if enchanted. Despite moments of veristic presentation, in general the images are disturbed, distorted, mediated in some way. The homage to Nature is treated, paradoxically, in an anti-naturalistic manner. Ancient practices meet the digitalized avant-garde, while the film exploits every possible cinematic resource (focus, color, editing, dissolves, lighting) not to communicate the architecture of a theology, but rather to create an outsider impression of the visceral feel of an immersion into shamanic culture. The originality of the film derives both from the riches of the culture portrayed, and from the aesthetic and cultural preparation of the filmmakers. The film partially takes its cues from Claudia Andujar's photography, which used double exposure, infrared filters, and the smearing of substances on the lens to communicate Yanomami spirituality. In a practice reminiscent of Jean Rouch's "cine-transe," Andujar would shake the camera to capture gyrating shamans, while her obscuring of the light source would convey a mystical uncanny dimension. The palimpsestic layering of digital strata or filmic tracks correlates, in this sense, with the Yanomami conception of the lived universe as consisting of superimposed times and spaces, where the past and the present, the natural and the spiritual, constantly merge and intersect.[103]

The film repeatedly seizes on privileged moments, especially those involving the *yãkoana* and the blowing of the *rappé* powder through a tube into the nostrils of the shaman. The sensorial and phenomenological distortions involved in the experience are suggested only indirectly. The camera registers a certain anxious expectation on the part of the receiver of the sacred powder, followed by the shock of the inhalation, like the kick-back of a rifle as the body suddenly shifts backward under the impact. But once the initial effects pass, disorientation and discomfort give way to a perspectival shift of vibrating multi-colored light—reminiscent of the vibrations of aboriginal painting in Australia—as voices of animal and forest sounds become magnified and corporeal movements become distorted, as if in an attempt to offer the sensory correlative of shamanic experience. The film never tries, however, to convey the speech or the words or the appearance of *xapiri*; we can only infer their attributes on the basis of the palpable gestures and visible movements of the celebrants. Here we find partial parallels with the dilemmas confronting those who film or photograph the phenomenon of trance in Afro-diasporic religions, whereby many artists and anthropologists claim that one can film the medium, the person possessed, but not the *orixas* themselves; one can register the effects of possession such as the contortions of the face but not the *orixa*, or for that matter, the feelings or visions of the medium in trance. Thus the features of the *xapiri* can only be inferential for the spectator. The technical procedures can only show the effects and affects of the sacred plant on actual bodies, creating spatial disorientation and temporal vertigo.

Parallel to the verbal and kinetic frenzy of the *xapiri*, the film offers a *frenesi* of filmic technique. In a mimicry of the oscillating impressions of psychotropic experience, the film disturbs our sense of iconic designation; the polysemy, in Barthian terms, is not "anchored" in the verbal or the discursive. A frequent technique in the film, in this sense, is to render iconic recognition difficult through shallow focus, shot superimposition, or the blurring produced by camera movement. The effect is to privilege percept over concept, experience over knowledge or better to see the sensorium as a basis for knowledge. Rather than a conventional documentary, *Xapiri* is a free-flying performance that takes off from the visual and conceptual universe of Yanomami shamanism, without trying to "represent" the shamanic experience.

The film proliferates in avant-garde-style interventions, reminiscent on some levels of Maya Deren's trance-modernist attempts to communicate the multi-chronotopic ritual trances of Haitian Vodun. Naturalistic shots neighbor with digitally enabled psychotropic perturbations. Superimpositions of distinct takes create a kaleidoscopic effect. The film resonates with some of the phenomenological insights of Vivian Sobchack in *The Address of the Eye*, and later in *Carnal Thoughts*, where she speaks, in language that itself mingles the conceptual with the corporeal, of "tactile foresight" and the "carnal foundations of cinematic intelligibility."[104] Her concept of the cinesthetic subject combines synaesthesia (the intermodal stimulation of the senses) and what she calls co-anaesthesia (the pre-logical unity of the sensorium and the perception of one's body as the sum of its perceptions).[105] The Yanomami shamans, for their part, do affect theory one better, seeming to experience some kind of communal, transindividual, even trans-species subjectivity.

The film also recalls the techniques of impressionist painters, for whom painting consisted in the close observation of nature, especially in the form of the ever-changing sunlight that sustains nature's vitality. Like the painters, the film pays close attention to dappled forest light.[106] Like impressionism in painting, the film is attentive to everything that intervenes between the object and the (camera) eye-subject, in consonance with the impressionist approach, which pays acute attention to *plein air* effects, to sense impressions, to what is seen and perceived rather than known. In Impressionism, the atmospheric mutations caused by haze and mist and vapor play a compositional and textural role. Visual phenomena in *Xapiri*, similarly, are intrinsically unstable, changing like the slightly altered exteriors of Monet's "Rouen cathedral" (1892–94), where Monet would take photographs at various times of the day to help shape his famous series of paintings. Like the Impressionist paintings, whose very titles speak of atmospheric effects such as the *"effet de pluie"* (rain effect) and *"effets de brouillard"* (mist effects), the film creates atmospheric and luminous "effects." In *Xapiri*, light becomes an active principle transforming everything it touches: we see the effects of rain, of haze, and of intense sunlight. Light has directionality, transformability, and energy; it quivers and breaks and shatters and spreads with camera movements and changing lenses. It scintillates with trembling luminous patches of forest; objects have no intrinsic color beyond what light has momentarily and provisionally granted them. The film, in this sense, shows the *shabono,* the vibrant center of Yanomami conviviality, through a wide variety of light conditions, from morning to harsh midday light to the dusk and to the evening. The film spots the oscillating light on leaves in the forest clearing, or the darkness of the interior of the thatch-roofed shabono. Digital cinema's capacity to play with and alter light rhymes with the Yanomami cosmological valorization of light, manifested, for example, in the flickering lights of the *xipiri*. Backlighting at times hides the details of the face and the human figure, reducing the human person to an outline. At other times, technical transformations create a sense of blinding light, the blur of disorientation, presented as somehow corresponding to the effect of the sacred plant.

The film combines shots of conventional beauty and normal proportions with disconcerting compositions, fragmentations, and temporal distortions. At the same time, this accelerated fragmentation co-exists with another, calmer rhythm, that of everyday life co-habiting with the world of trance. The Yanomami seem relaxed—at home in their own culture—with many embraces and signs of affection between the visiting shamans and the villagers, offering a dramatically different portrait of Yanomami life from that proposed by *The Axe Fight*. Women, the elderly and children, those not directly involved with shamanism, are spectators like us, manifesting a wide range of reactions. While respectful of the rituals, their body language and manner does not suggest any special reverence or servility to charismatic leaders. Some spectators might look bored or skeptical, as was Kopenawa himself when he was an uninitiated adolescent wondering if the shamans were spouting nonsense, lying about the effects of the *yãkoana*.

The sound in the film is intermittently synchronic. The voices are often incorporeal, like songs echoing from a distant valley. The sounds are stylized, used less for realism than for aesthetic effect. The atmospherics are at once somber, exhilarated, chaotic, and preternaturally calm. The music track consists largely in the songs of children, the cries of birds, and the chants of the shamans. Music is ubiquitous in the film, as it seems to be in the community itself. A group of women speaking in Yanomami communicate via a short wave radio, one of the rare items that invoke capitalist modernity, alongside with wrist watches and glasses. One imagines a metaphoric approximation between the shamans and the voices from beyond, the "acousmatic voices" of film theory, the voices whose origin is not revealed in the image.

The filmmakers, meanwhile, are generally self-effacing. Unlike the Davi Yanomami/Bruce Albert book, which shuttles back and forth between the white and the Indian world, here the white world is apparently absent, off-screen, present only in the mediating techniques from which we can infer the behind-the-camera presence of the camerapersons and other technicians. In this sense, the unseen presence of the film's creators emulates the transparency of the classical ethnographic film, prior to the reflexive move of the 1980s. But perhaps the real reflexivity takes the form of the film's self-flaunting artifice, which is not inappropriate or imposed because the shamanic rituals, given that the *xapiri* themselves with their "presentation dances," are also performative.

In his exhaustively researched thesis on *Xapiri*, entitled "Obfuscating Mirror," João Pedro Turri examines the film in both cultural and aesthetic terms.[107] In the essay, Turri relates his bewildered yet fascinated first reaction to the film. The cinematic techniques, Turri suggests, require that the spectator suspend Enlightenment-inspired notions of "objectivity." Both difficult and intoxicating, the film dissolves borders between the natural and the supernatural, the everyday and the sublime, the mundane and the spiritual. Disoriented by the supernatural character of the images, without understanding the webs of relations informing them, Turri decided to concentrate on the cinematic techniques used to convey a trance-like experience, resulting in an attempt to decipher *Xapiri* through a shot-by-shot analysis. Drawing on his knowledge of film history, ethnographic film, and the avant-garde-inflected styles of Vertov, Jean Rouch, Agnès Varda, Glauber Rocha, and of the Sensory Ethnography Lab in Harvard, Turri sees *Xapiri* as condensing high density and rapidly paced information, requiring intense concentration and thought on the part of the spectator. The world of shamanism is refracted through "an aberrant chromatism" with saturated blues and oranges, for me reminiscent simultaneously of fauve painting, Brazilian Tropicalism, and psychedelic art. The editing, as Turri points out, plays with techniques familiar from the Soviet avant-garde such as dilation (extension of time) and the *faux raccords*—deliberate mismatches between similar superimposed shots—typical of Alain Resnais films. The effect is to slow down and dilate time, expanding and compressing the duration of actions.

Xapiri, in this sense, represents an attempt, in a collaborative indigenous and non-indigenous text, to convey the Yanomami world of thought, practice, image, and performance. In this crossing of gazes, the various participants imagine each other through a grid or framework of references and understandings. All in all, *Xapiri* is a remarkable achievement, respectful in its cultural attitudes and agile in exploiting cinematographic and editing resources to engender a dense and complex sensorial experience, one that exceeds conventional expectations of transparency and clear exposition. The difficulty of the film and its techniques also serve to subvert voyeuristic spectatorship; ambiguity, disorientation, and opacity become part of the experience. To suggest that outsiders "get it" without translation or explanations, would be a self-flattering illusion. Most films assume a common culture and aim to be understood, this film seems to say that "we as an audience can share some aspects of the experience, but should not have the illusion of a full understanding."

The Last Forest

Our final Yanomami-related film, this time both about and in major ways by the Yanomami, is *A Ultimate Floresta* (The Last Forest, 2021), a collaboration between Davi Kopenawa—who furnished the basic story—and Luis Bolognesi, the director of *Ex-Pajé* and other films about indigenous peoples. First featured in the Panorama section of the Berlinale Film Festival and now available on Netflix, the film was produced in the village of Watoriki during five weeks, with a small six-person crew. The film has a shamanistic plotline, constructed out of Kopenawa's spoken stories about the creation myths, everyday lives, and present-day challenges for the Yanomami. All the participants are Yanomami. A kind of poetic docu-fiction, the film develops a free form, by turns informative and didactic, or magical and spiritual, often blurring the borders between dream, legend reenactment, and real life. The film conveys the physical presence, and the literal voice and vision of Kopenawa, mingling legends about human origins with a dramatic plot about a prospector invasion.

The Last Forest combines Kopenawa's concepts with the filmic artistry of Luis Bolognesi and his collaborators, many of them Yanomami. The director courageously relinquishes control over the narrative, basically turning it over to someone who not only had no experience in making films but also almost no experience in watching films. The film is really a mediated self-presentation by the Yanomami, with few interventions by the director to make the film more palatable or more exciting for western audiences. Bolognesi simply executes the shaman's vision, but translates it into the filmic idiom. The "translation" is facilitated by the fact that Kopenawa's way of thinking, as we have seen, is intensely visual, even visionary. The film relays the by-now familiar metaphorical voice from *The Falling Sky*, speaking both in mythopoetic and practical tones. The film relays the familiar themes—the Creation myths, the crimes of the "whites," the dis-alienation of Kopenawa, the struggles against prospectors and invaders, and above all the dangers that beset the forest and the planet.

According to Bolognesi, the nature of cinema became clear to Kopenawa when he realized—as many film theorists have argued—that film is like a dream, in this case the dream of a society, which cultivates and prizes dream and what elsewhere would be called magical thinking is a habit of mind. In a visit to Boa Vista, a major city, the director also learned that Kopenawa had been under death threats from the gold miners; threats that did not prevent Kopenawa from maintaining his preternatural calm. The only point where the director challenged Kopenawa's version was on the issue of female empowerment, with Bolognesi suggesting a heightened presence of strong women characters, and a reference to the women's association requests to which Kopenawa assented. Bolognesi's account of the production process gives us a sense of a people unaccustomed to taking orders, including from film directors. (Many native peoples in North and South America believe in a kind of parenting that involves not giving orders but rather modeling behavior.) When Bolognesi would confidently announce the schedule for the shoot the following day, the Barnaby-like response was a breezy and philosophical "perhaps, but who knows what tomorrow will bring?" On the other hand, Bolognesi could dispense with warning the actors not to look at the camera, because they had no desire to do so and would simply immerse themselves in the fictive performance. Thus we sense a deeply communal society, yet one that allows for considerable personal freedom, a society with deep respect for the individual—shown in a reluctance to commit the indecency of giving orders—but not individualistic.

Unlike arrogant code-crackers and self-proclaimed experts like Napoleon Chagnon, Bolognesi started from the Socratic premise of knowing nothing and having everything to learn. Like the author of the classic anthropological/autobiographical fiction, *Return to Laughter,* Bolognesi acknowledges the extreme ridiculousness of the anthropologist-stranger arriving in indigenous territory. The anthropologist presents the figure of a childlike person unable to speak the language (and where almost no one speaks European languages), the one who understands nothing, who has to ask about everything, and where children, less polite than adults, constantly laugh at the clueless outsider. Ordinary people constantly protected the filmmaker from his own ignorance, pointing out that he should not film in a specific spot in the morning because jaguars would be visiting that spot at that time, or should not film in a specific lake because contact with its electric fish might be fatal. Even children had a practical expertise denied to outsider adults, for example, in climbing tall trees or starting fires.

Portrayed not as a Chief but only as an elder emissary, a kind of diplomat, Kopenawa announces his mission to his community— to bring his message to the "whites." He tells them that he is not going to "bring festive food" or to display "traditional dances," but rather to teach the others about the Yanomami way of thinking. There are no Hollywood crowd scenes and eloquent speeches where Kopenawa excites the people to action. At the same time, the film plays out Kopenawa's own life dilemmas by portraying the dangerous attractions of "white" society through a young figure who meets in secret with the prospectors, who tempt him by showing the attractions of the big cities on their smart phones. Kopenawa addresses the youth in both practical and emotional terms. "I once thought like you, but now I see differently." He lauds the freedom of the Yanomami lifestyle: "Here you can hunt ... you can play ... you can do what you want." Kopenawa also explains the racism that will greet the Yanomami stranger: "You will be treated with suspicion ... they will not care about you, you will be lonely." Without money, Kopenawa explains "you won't be able to eat"—an idea absolutely shocking, almost incomprehensible, for any non-westernized Yanomami. The film also stages the Yanomami creation myths, magical realist like all creation myths, about the origin of men and women and the creation of the earth by Omama. The story involves male copulation, fraternal betrayal, misshapen penises, dangerous water spirits, and the first woman fished out of water. Creation stories are usually implausible for outsiders, but Kopenawa, and the film, recounts the legends in a matter-of-fact manner.

The film has both cosmological scope and the intimacy of life lived in the hammocks of the *shabono*. Kopenawa tells the story of Omama burying the pathogenic metal (*xawara*) and the mandate to never take minerals out of the earth. Through Kopenawa, we learn about the infinite value of the forest, the *yãkoana* ceremonies—whose effects we witness—and the grave menace posed by the mining companies with the complicity of the Brazilian government. Under Bolsonaro—who regretted in a 1988 speech that "the Brazilian cavalry had not been as efficient as the American soldiers who exterminated all its Indians"—land occupations and deforestation massively accelerated. The gold miners polluted the waters and brought diseases to the remote villages. The film informs us that the government did for a time protect Yanomami land and defend the 1988 constitution, but that everything changed in 2009 with Bolsonaro, facilitated forest fires and land occupations. The film talks about everything that books talks about, but with no attempt to visualize the supernatural. The film is a pleasure to look at, a composed and immersive homage to the exuberance of the Yanomami forest and the beauty of Yanomami people, made in hopes that non-indigenous spectators will become fond of the forest like the Yonamami, and become invested in conserving it.

The film conveys a strong sense of the reality of what for the West was a trope—indigenous well-being, in line with the thinking of Marshal Sahlins and Pierre Clastres, that societies like the Yanomami, perhaps because they remained uncontacted for so long and are still not easily accessible to outsiders, are societies of natural abundance. At the same time, the film foregrounds the practicalities of Yanomami life—the hunting, skinning, and cooking of an alligator, the preparation of mandioca, the weaving techniques bequeathed by a legendary ancestor. The film also portrays Yanomami society as physically healthy—the film was made before the outbreak of Covid—and as stress-free, as many outsiders had noted. The soundtrack consists largely of orchestrated forest sounds rather than music in the conventional sense. The film gives a sense of a sensorium unlike those that most spectators have known, a medley of animal sounds, insects and birds, percussion and wind instruments serving to structure the film and filter spectatorial feeling.

The film ends in a surprising yet quite logical place, with Kopenawa giving a guest lecture at Harvard, where he warns the elite audience that the western love of merchandise is destroying the planet. The film has come full circle, completing the journey announced at the beginning, as Kopenawa fulfills his promise to go to the white world to explain the challenges facing the Yanomami. Alone in his hotel room, we see Davi Yanomami's face in contemplative close-up as we hear the remembered singing of Yanomami children, from his point-of-hearing, followed by the heartbreaking photos by Claudia Andujar of the Yanomami victims of white-provoked maladies and violence.

The other, more personal story brings together many of our themes—the *cunha* in New York, transnational circularities, crossed gazes, the colonial museum, Indians with Cameras, and the native refusal to be impressed by Western grandeur. Here we return to a story that began in the last chapter about the anthropologists and the Yanomami. In 1990, Kenneth Good published his book about his life with the Yanomami and his marriage to a Yanomami woman named Yarima. Just a few years ago, Yarima re-entered the picture. Although she returned to Yanomami land and did not return to her husband, she left three children in New Jersey with their father. One of the children, David, was five years old when his mother left, leaving him extremely bitter about abandonment. At his tender age, Yarima was not a Yanomami woman but just a wonderful "Mom."

One day, as an adolescent, David wandered with his friends through the Museum of Natural History in New York, not unlike Patricia Ferreira in the same museum looking at the same objects. In a section on Amazonian Indians, David was taken aback to see a picture of his mother, in Yanomami attire. His father was credited with the picture. Shocked and ashamed, he hid from his friends. He became distraught and even started to drink in excess. But later he picked up his father's book and learned in detail about his father's relationship with his mother. (It is not clear why his father told him so little.) David says he made a 180-degree turn, and suddenly wanted to learn everything about his Yanomami heritage. As a graduate student doing an M.A.in biology, he became obsessed with finding his mother. As David has been unfolding the story in a series of YouTube videos, we see him, together with his father, reaching her by cell phone. David shows us pictures of Yarima and her children at a pool wearing sunglasses, looking like any other suburbanite of color. David researches everything about the Yanomami, and ultimately goes to Yanomami land, where he meets Yarima and his Yanomami half-brother, who he teaches how to use a camera. Later, he brings his mother back to New Jersey to meet her children again as well as David's own son, her grandchild.

In his YouTube videos, David explains not only his own experience, but also the Yanomami culture as a society without loneliness, a people who see human beings and nature as one and the same. He also imagines how she must have felt at first in New Jersey, that it must have been "like a time machine, a portal to an alien cosmos." When she left her Yanomami village, she thought that "New Jersey" was just another Amazonian village. But she ended up telling Kenneth that life in New Jersey was "no way to live," that "people were not made to live that way." David Good has started a project, logically enough called "The Good Project," which will hopefully become a feature documentary and a means to fundraise for the Yanomami cause. His project involves charting the Amazonian biome to protect it from predators of all kinds. The story departs dramatically from the canonical immigrant story, which begins with hardship but ends with assimilation, a green card, citizenship, a happy life in the suburbs or the acceptance of the immigrant son or daughter at an Ivy League University. The story brings together many of our themes. the native refusal to be impressed, the trope of communal happiness, the *cunha* in, if not Manhattan, at least in what was once Lenape territory, the high-tech Indian half-brother, Kenneth Good as the white Indian, the crossed transnational gazes, the foundational romance, and the anti-foundational romance. Summing up, David says it is not only a happy ending to a long family story, but a chance to promote what is now their common cause.

Notes

1. John Hemming, *Die if You Must* (London: Macmillan, 2003), p. 483.
2. Ibid.
3. See Hemming, op. cit., p. 484.
4. Patrick Tierney, *Darkness in El Dorado: How Scientists and Journalists Devastated the Amazon* (New York: Norton, 2002).
5. See Eric Michaels, "How to Look at Us Looking at the Yanomami Looking at Us," in Jay Ruby, ed., *A Crack in the Mirror: Reflexive Perspectives in Anthropology* (Philadelphia: University of Pennsylvania Press, 1982).
6. Brian R. Ferguson, *Yanomami Warfare: A Political History* (Santa Fe, NM: School of American Research Press, 1995).
7. Marshall Sahlins, "The National Academy of Sciences: Goodbye to All That," *Anthropology Today*, Vol. 29, No. 2 (2013), pp. 1–2.
8. John Hemming, op. cit., p. 487.
9. Portuguese translation of *The Falling Sky*, p. 26.
10. Cited in Patrick Tierney, *Darkness in El Dorado; How Scientists and Journalists Devastated the Amazon* (New York: Norton, 2001), p. 85.
11. Michael Taussig, "A Lesson in Looking and Laughter," in Valerie Smith, ed., *Juan Downey: The Invisible Architect* (New York: Bronx Museum of the Arts, MIT List Visual Arts Center, 2011).
12. A loud sound presented by the voice-over as the sound of an axe blow that left a man unconscious, it was revealed, was actually the post-synchronized sound of Asch striking a watermelon in the studio. Ibid., p. 44.
13. As Faye Ginsburg sometimes ask of unnecessarily opaque documentaries: "why don't they just talk to them?"
14. Kenneth Good, *Into the Heart: One Man's Pursuit of Knowledge among the Yanomama* (New York: Simon and Schuster, 199), p. 175.
15. See Jacques Lizot, *Tales of the Yanomami* (Cambridge: Cambridge University Press, 1985), p. xiv The book was first published in 1976 by Editions de Seuil as *Le Cercle des Feux*.
16. Ibid., p. 14.
17. Ibid., p. 71.
18. Ibid., p. 31.

19 From Timothy Asch, "Bias in Ethnographic Reporting," cited in Patrick Tierney's *Darkness in El Dorado*, p. 90.
20 Kenneth Good, op. cit., p. 81.
21 Patrick Tierney, *Darkness in El Dorado*, p. 251.
22 Ibid., p. 25.
23 Kenneth Good, op. cit.
24 Ibid., p. 184.
25 Ibid., p. 80.
26 Ibid.
27 Ibid., p. 81.
28 Ibid.
29 Ibid., p. 338.
30 On Andujar, see Oliver Basciano, "Shamans, Spirits, Survival; how Claudia Andujar Fought for the Yanomami Tribe," *The Guardian* (January 29, 2020), https://www.theguardian.com/artanddesign/2020/jan/29/claudia-andujar-photography-yanomami-brazil-jair-bolsonaro
31 1996 interview with Valero cited by Tierney, op. cit., p. 245.
32 Ibid., p. 246.
33 Michael Taussig, "A Lesson in Looking and Laughter: Juan Downey's Amazing Yanomami Video, *The Laughing Alligator*," in Valerie Smith, ed., op cit., p. 50.
34 Ibid.
35 On the sense of humor of the Yanomami, see Pierre Clastres, *Arqueologia da Violencia* (São Paulo: Cosac & Naficy, 2004), pp. 29–54.
36 From a term paper written for an NYU course (with Barbara Browning) sent to me by the author.
37 Amalia Cordova, "After-effects: Mapping the experimental ethnography of Juan Downey" in *The Invisible Architect, Brooklyn Rail* (June 2012).
38 Edward Shanken, "Broken Circle &/Spiral Hill?: Smithson's Spirals, Pataphysics, Syzygy and Survival," *Technoetic Arts: A Journal of Speculative Research*, Vol. 11, No. 1 (2013), pp. 3–14.
39 Davi Kopenawa, "A Yanomami Leader Speaks: A Message from Davi Kopenawa Yanomami." Transcribed by Bruce Albert and translated by Terry Turner. Anthropology Newsletter (September 1991), p. 52.
40 Ibid., p. 20.
41 Kopenawa, op. cit., p. 366.
42 Ibid., p. 360.
43 Davi Kopenawa makes very similar statements in interviews and in *The Falling Sky*.
44 Sharon W. Tiffany and Kathleen J. Adams, "Anthropology's 'Fierce' Yanomami: Narratives of Sexual Politics in the Amazon," *NWSA Journal*, Vol. 6, No. 2 (Summer, 1994), pp. 169–96.
45 Ibid., p. 182.
46 Alcida R., Ramos and Kenneth I. Taylor, "The Yanoama in Brazil," Document no. 37. Copenhagen: International Work Group for Indigenous Affairs, 1979, p. 186.
47 See Alcida R. Ramos, "Reflecting on the Yanomami: Ethnographic Images and the Pursuit of the Exotic." *Cultural Anthropology*, Vol. 2, No. 3 (1987), pp. 284–304.
48 Napoleon Chagnon, *Yanomamo: The Last Days of Eden* (San Diego: Harcourt Brace Jovanovich, 1992), p. 276.
49 See Lucia Sa's fascinating *Rain Forest Literatures: Amazonian Texts and Latin American Culture* (Minneapolis: University of Minnesota Press, 2004), p. 40.

50 Davi Yanomami, p. 135.
51 Ibid., p. 95.
52 Ibid., p. 22.
53 Gabriel Garcia Marquez, *One Hundred Years of Solitude* (New York: Avon, 1971), p. 44.
54 Davi Yanomami, op. cit., p. 252.
55 Ibid., 178. A sensitive reader might object to "reverse racism" at this point but we must remember that Kopenawa is relaying his own experience of those he calls whites, but which means anyone aligned with the colonial project.
56 Ibid., p. 174.
57 Ibid., p. 345.
58 Ibid., p. 346.
59 Ibid., p. 347.
60 Ibid., p. 188.
61 Vine Deloria, Jr. op. cit., p. 151.
62 Kopenawa, op. cit., p. 208.
63 Ibid., pp. 192–3.
64 Dr. Oldroyd presented this research at a seminar held at the Wissenschaftskolleg on January 12, 2021.
65 Ibid., p. 206.
66 Ibid., p. 43.
67 See Paula Morgado, "Cinéma amérindien brésilien et utilisation du cyberspace. Pour qui?" *Anthrovision*, Vol. 2, No. 2 (2014). Accessed from http://journals.openedition.org/anthrovision/1448.
68 Ibid., p. 115.
69 Davi Kopenawa, op. cit., p. 58.
70 Ibid., p. 93.
71 Ibid., p. 93.
72 Ibid., p. 59.
73 Ibid., p. 81.
74 Renato Sztutman. "*Cosmopolíticas transversais*: a proposta de Stengers e o mundo ameríndio." Lecture presented at the Museu Nacional, Rio de Janeiro, November 29, 2013. Unpublished.
75 Manuela Carneiro da Cunha, "Xamanismo e tradução," in Manuela Carneiro da Cunha, ed., *Cultura com aspas e outros ensaios* (São Paulo: Cosac Naify, 2009), pp. 101–13.
76 Davi Kopenawa, op. cit., p. 133.
77 Ibid., p. 398.
78 See Adrian Tanner, *Bringing Home Animals: Religious Ideology and Mode of Production of the Mistassini Cree Hunters* (New York: St. Martin Press, 1979).
79 Leanne Betasamosake Simpson, *As We Have Always Done: Indigenous Freedom through Radical Resistance* (Minneapolis: University of Minnesota Press, 2017), p. 61.
80 Davi Kopenawa, op. cit., p. 71.
81 Ibid.
82 Lucio Paiva Flores, *Adoradores do Sol* (Petropolis: Vozes, 2003), p. 15.
83 Davi Kopenawa Yanomami, op. cit., p. 22.
84 Ibid. p. 23.
85 Ibid., p. 45. https://haubooks.org/cosmological-perspectivism-in-amazonia/

86 See André Brasil and Bernard Belisario, "Desmanchar o Cinema: Variações do fora-de-campo em Filmes Indígenas," *Sociologia and Antropologia*, Vol. 6, No. 3 (Rio de Janeiro September/December 2016). Accessed from https://www.scielo.br/scielo.php?script=sci_arttext&pid=S2238-38752016000300601&lng=pt&tlng=pt.
87 See Claude Lévi-strauss and D. Eribon, *De près et de loin* (Paris: Odile Jacob, 1988)
88 Ibid.
89 Viveiros de Castro, *Cannibal Metaphysics*, p. 57.
90 Ibid., p. 88.
91 Ibid., p. 89.
92 Dale Turner, op. cit., p. 36.
93 Davi Kopenawa, op. cit., p. 67.
94 Davi Kopenawa, op. cit., p. 82.
95 Taken from the Portuguese version of *The Falling Sky, A Queda do Ceu* (São Paulo: Companhia das Letras), p. 13.
96 Davi Yanomami, p. cit. 65.
97 See Eduardo Viveiros de Castro "Cosmological Perspectivism in Amazonia and Elsewhere," op. cit.
98 Davi Kopenawa, op. cit., p. 56.
99 Ibid., p. 57.
100 Hutukara is the shamanic name for the sky that fell and created and defended the forest.
101 To select just a few from a cornucopia of examples: dramaturg Bia Lessa mingles Thomas Mann and popular pilgrimages in her *Crede-Mi*; Guimaraes Rosa re-envisions Faust in the Sertao backlands in his novels; and Glauber Rocha mingles Villa-Lobos with samba and Shakespeare.
102 *Rimbaud: The Works, A Season in Hell; Poems & Prose; Illuminations*, trans. Dennis Carlile (US: Xlibris, 2001), p. 403.
103 See Oliver Basciano, "Shamans, Spirits, Survival: How Claudia Andujar Fought for the Yanomami Tribe," *The Guardian* (January 29, 2020), https://www.theguardian.com/artanddesign/2020/jan/29/claudia-andujar-photography-yanomami-brazil-jair-bolsonaro
104 Vivian Sobchack, *Carnal Thoughts: Embodiment and the Moving Image* (Berkeley: University of California, 2004), p. 64 and p. 59.
105 Ibid.
106 In the cinema, the term "impressionism" tends to refer to an avant-garde tendency within the French silent cinema, one that invoked impressionism in painting, embodied by such figures as Epstein, Delluc, Gance, and Dulac, who tried to express feelings through mobile cameras, intense close-ups of faces, and subjectivized editing, rather than projecting feelings outward onto the decor in the expressionist manner. But in general, impressionism represents a "road not taken" by dominant cinema, where conventional lighting, at least in the classical cinema, conveyed an ontologically stable world.
107 João Pedro Turri, "Espelho Ofuscante: *Xapiri* e a etnografia digital," Bachelor's Thesis presented in the Dept. of Cinema, Radio and Television (ECA), at University of São Paulo, under guidance of Dr. Eduardo Victorio Morettin. http://www3.eca.usp.br/sites/default/files/form/biblioteca/acervo/textos/tc3683-turri.pdf.

Conclusion

The Theoretical Indigene: Becoming Indian and the Elsewhere of Capitalism

This concluding chapter gathers together some of the themes and threads pursued so far: "the philosophical centrality of the Indian," the "sacred land," "indigenous media," "becoming Indian," the "Carib revolution," "aboriginal matriarchy," and "radical traditionalism." It brings to the surface what had been implicit—the indigenous challenge to social theory and its relevance to a historical moment plagued by extremely grave crises. Completing the trajectory that began with Montaigne and the Tupinamba, the text moves to a present characterized by a disenchantment with liberal democracy, worldwide anxiety about pandemics, and the fire and brimstone of climate change, all simultaneous with a resurgence of indigenous creativity in writing, the arts, film, media activism, and social theory.

The present also brings, if not any thoroughgoing equality between indigenous and non-indigenous social thinkers—five centuries of colonialism are not easily erased—at least some intermittent glimpses of what a minimal reciprocity might look like in the era of revisionist anthropology, now redefined by Viveiros de Castro, as "the theory/practice of the permanent decolonization of thought."[1] In an era where it is often said that "we now find it easier to imagine the end of the planet than the end of capitalism," indigenous thinking is more necessary than ever.[2] It evokes the possibilities of thinking before and beyond alongside the savage neoliberalism that is corroding democracy and destroying the planet, at a time when saving the planet depends on the end of capitalism. Of course, on a practical level, indigenous people, like everyone else, have had to be entangled with capitalism—Indian reservations depend on infusions of capital, the Yanomami are surveilled by corporations, most people depend on a daily cash flow, and so forth. Yet indigenous thinkers have been thinking beyond capitalism and beyond republican Constitutionalism since a time before modern capitalism and republican Constitutionalism were sparkles in the eye of an embryonic colonialism.

Colonial Ambivalence and the Transnational Gaze

Tiago Torres-Campos's documentary *O Mestre e o Divino* (*The Master and the Divine*, 2013) condenses a number of our themes by orchestrating a constellation of interactive transnational gazes. The title refers to the two characters whose relationship structures the film—the "Master," a eccentric German-speaking Silesian monk named Adalbert Heide, who has been filming the Xavante for decades, and "Divine," a Xavante named "Divino," a former altar-boy with Father Heide, and now a well-known filmmaker. Multiply reflexive, *The Master and the Divine* is not only a film about filmmaking but also a film about the fraught yet friendly dialogue between three filmmakers—Torres-Campos, Divino, and Heide—representing distinct backgrounds and cultures. On one level, the film is a "process film" (Claudia Mesquita) in that the film involves negotiations between Torres-Campos, the actual director, together with Divino, director of some of the clips included in the film; and Adalberto, a prolific maker of films about the Xavante, some of which are included in the film. Reflexive on every level, the film discusses such issues as preproduction, research, negotiations, archival materials, aesthetic choices, and so forth.

After arriving in Mato Grosso in 1957, Heide spent 60 years filming the daily life of the Xavante, edited into short films where he portrays himself as a modernizing and Christianizing force. The key motive for making the new film was the discovery by Divino and Torres-Campos that Adalberto's numerous films about the Xavante were housed in a Silesian archive in Germany. Just as Divino and Torres-Campos needed access to Adalberto's films which Torres-Campos was willing to bring back to Brazil, Adalberto had needs of his own— (1) that Torres-Campos make digital copies of the films and (2) that Torres-Campos includes a 10-minute sequence showing Heide as a "white Indian" hunting with the Xavantes, dancing with the boars, as it were. The German Master is on one level a colonizer who Christianizes the natives and corrects their "pagan" beliefs and unproductive ways. Yet he is not your ordinary colonizer. He is fluent in Xavante defends some Xavante customs, and is on some levels accepted by them. The name gifted to him by the Xavante (*tsa amri*) means the "white man who became an Indian." Heide is, in short, the *colonisateur sympathique* who adores indigenous culture, but only in its ideal "primitive" and proselytizable *tabula rasa* form. At the same time, Divino has some respect for Heide as a person and one-time mentor. The relationship is one of affectionate kidding, tinged with colonial resentment and subtle competition. The film also shows a wrestling over the access to the archive, one that resonates with indigenous struggles to repatriate sacred objects and even the images made about them. Adalberto's entitled assumption of full rights to his images of the Xavante, as Kathryn Lehman points out, forms part of a colonial "eminent domain" logic that traces back, ultimately, to Conquest and Discovery Doctrine.[3]

Commenting on Heide's films, director Torres-Campos notes that Heide "constructs himself as a hero." Heide sees himself as a mini-God, the self-described *factotum* (etymologically, he who "does everything") who schools the Xavante in the love of God and Hard Work. In his own mind, he embodies a pantheon of western culture heroes—at once Prometheus and Prospero, pastor, pedagogue, and boss. Presented on a German TV program as a white adventurer in the tropics, Heide is a self-declared "white Indian," a European who has "gone native" to the point of sporting war paint and a Xavante head-dress. Heide's relation to the Xavante is strangely ambivalent; he loves them, but mainly as in their past incarnation. He is disappointed that present-day Xavante have not maintained their customs in a way he would have liked. At the same time, he senses a power shift. As the Xavante are taking over the institutions, he no longer wields the same charismatic power as before.

The dialogue between the Master and Divino stages a battle of two (or more) cultures and two (or more) aesthetics. But rather than a Manichean struggle, the battle reveals a number of paradoxes and ambivalences. Ironically, it is the filmmaker-priest who cultivates a "positive" image of the Xavante—one steeped in primitivist narratives and iconography—while Divino has no qualms about showing negative Xavante behavior such as drunkenness and tribal dissension. While Heide sweetens everything in an epic-romantic style, Divino prefers a self-reflexive critical realism which foregrounds the tensions not only between the Xavante and the whites, but also among the Xavante themselves. While the priest prefers pastoral shots of traditionally attired Indians rowing canoes on pristine creeks, underscored by Andean flutes, the supposedly nature-loving Indian prefers talking heads, especially those of elders like his father who can provide vital information about Xavante history.

In a kind of phantasmatic indigeneity, the older European filmmaker, who imagines himself as "protecting" the image of the Xavante seems threatened by the indigenous upstart who might end his imagistic and cognitive monopoly. When Heide needles Divino for having forgotten traditional skills such as head-dress making, Divino responds that although he has personally forgotten how to make them, any Xavante can learn how to make them by seeing his films. More high-tech than the "Master," Divino mocks Heide for his slow computer and lack of Final-Cut-Pro. The "Indians" are answering back, giving as good as they get, as they probably always have, even if that backtalk did not usually make its way into the official histories. Divino's father too has a slightly aggressive kidding relationship with Heide, reminding him of the co-construction of knowledge, saying of the priest in the third person that "I taught him everything he knows. I taught him how to speak Xavante." If Divino's desire to make a different kind of film represents an Oedipal break with the colonial father (*padre*), the same Oedipalism does not operate in relation to his own father, to whom Divino pays warm homage. The film does not pit an essential colonizer against an essential colonized but rather shows a constant process of redefinition and renegotiation of roles. Divino is at ease with indeterminacy and never decides whether the Christian God exists, nor does he choose between Christianity and indigenous spiritism, thus illustrating what the early missionaries lamented as the "inconstancy of the savage soul." At the same time, he disputes Heide's idea that the Xavante worship a Sun God, explaining that the Sun was not a god but rather an embodiment of energy.

Not only does the figure of Heide as a White Indian go far back into cultural history, so too does the Divino-Heide relationship. Overdetermined by a complex web of images and tropes, their relationship reincarnates the German Shatterhand's alliance with Winnetoo in the Karl May novels and their filmic adaptations. At one point Heide even jokingly calls Divino "Winnetoo," just as the German film about Heide features the "Winnetoo theme" harmonica music from the Karl May films. Their friendship recalls those already discussed cross-race homosocial "bromances" between European and indigenous men that have marked literary and filmic history: Crusoe and Friday in *Robinson Crusoe*, Ishmael and Queequeeg in *Moby Dick*, the Lone Ranger and Tonto in the TV Western. The Winnetoo character in the Karl May film (a white actor in redface) is decidedly the "good" Indian ready to die for the whites. Indeed, in the film that Heide projects for the Xavante, the Winnettoo character actually does sacrifice his life for his German blood brother.

On Brazilian television, even Indians get to "play Indian," as we see in a climactic sequence that shows Divino appearing on Globo TV as a child responding to the siren call of blonde TV pop star an indigenized Euro-Brazilian Xuxa—attired in a Sioux warrior headdress—singing, as if in homage to Philip J. Deloria, "Vamos brincar de Indio" (Let's Play Indian). To the accompaniment of putative "Indian war cries," Xuxa leads the children in a happy song featuring fake Indian-speak lyrics:

> Let's play Indian, but without anyone to capture me!
> Come, join my tribe? I'm chief and you're my partner.
> Indian make noise. Indian have pride.
> Come paint your skin so the dance can begin.

In a stagey show of *mauvaise foi*, Xuxa plays the putative "white Indian" defender of Indian rights, like Heide but with even less reason to make the claim. In Hollywood-style Injun-speak, she sings "Indian need land." Ironically, she is better at playing Indians on TV than the Indians themselves; she has to teach them to become themselves. As Xuxa drags the frightened-looking Xavante boys into her photogenic circle of fun, they look stiff and reluctant. With their body paint, they become Hollywood-style "spearchuckers" in a film where she plays the starring role and they play the "extras." The sexualized icon of eternally young white beauty tries to teach them to be good little Indians, but they are not really good at "becoming Indian," and in a kind of sullen opacity, refuse to perform her caricatural image of themselves.[4] At this point in the film, the non-indigenous co-director's voice over informs us that as a child he probably saw that Xuxa show, and that he probably sang along with "Let's Play Indian," blithely unaware of its racist implications, yet now he is a collaborator/ally/friend of Divino, an indigenized Euro-Brazilian culturally transformed by his personal knowledge of people like Divino.

Transformational Becomings

O Mestre e o Divino's crisscrossed "becomings" bring to mind the Deleuze/Guattari leitmotif of "becoming" (*le devenir*). In the tenth plateau of *A Thousand Plateaus*, Deleuze and Guattari theorize a multitude of "*becomings*"—"becoming animal," "becoming woman," "becoming Indian," "becoming minor," and so forth. Almost every chapter in this book could be a seen as a variation on the theme. Chapter 1 suggested that French philosophers have been "becoming Indian" for more than five centuries. Chapter 2 began with a Native American *cunha* paddling downstream in the middle of the Hudson River, and traced the metamorphoses of the *cunha* over a century of Brazilian film and media history. Chapter 3 discussed the faux "becomings" of the White Indians of Hollywood and its imitators, and the Indian Hobbyists described so well in Philip Deloria's *Playing Indian*, for whom "play was powerful, for it not only made meanings, it made them real. The donning of Indian clothes moved ideas from brains to bodies, from the realm of abstraction to the physical world of concrete experience. There, identity was not so much imagined as it was performed, materialized through one's body and through the witness and recognition of others."[5] Chapter 4 showcased the indigenization not only of Brazilian Cinema but also of Brazilian scholarship by and about indigenous peoples.

In a broader historical context, the most massively dramatic case of "becoming-other" came in the wake of the "long 1492s", as millions of indigenous people, Africans, Europeans, and Asians in the Americas were variously dispossessed, othered, advantaged, oppressed, and generally transformed by asymmetrical contact with people from elsewhere. These power-laden encounters left manifold traces in cultural life, generating a wide range of terms for the mixing that resulted in diverse etymological, historical, and disciplinary genealogies, whether religious (syncretism), biological (miscegenation), botanical (hybridity), linguistic (creolization), cultural (indigenization), political-cultural (assimilation, transculturation), and even culinary-musical (fusion). Each form of asymmetrical difference generates diverse, intersectional modalities, crudely summarized as top-down, bottom-up, lateral, and the like. These protean "becomings" form part of the afterlives (and afterdeaths) of Conquest, resulting in the millions of natives who "became Indians" because of Columbus's mistaken assignation; including the French *truchements* who become Tupinized in Brazil, or Ojibwe-ized in Canada; the indigenous people becoming Christian through coercive indoctrination; kidnapped and adopted Europeans taking on indigenous ways; Boston Tea Party rebels masquerading as Mohawks; Hollywood actors donning redface; characters in films like *Dances with Wolves* "becoming Indians" through reverse assimilation; the shape-shifting Brazilian Macunaima ("hero of his people") variously becoming Indian and Black and White; Woody Allen's Zelig, Black, Indian, and Jewish and thus a "triple threat" to the KKK; French popular singers assuming an Indian identity ("Je suis l'Indien"); Afro-Brazilians in trance possessed by an indigenous "*caboclo*" as part of *candomblé*; black "Apaches" and "Commanches" in Bahia's carnival; the Black Mardi Gras Indians in New Orleans, celebrating their historical alliance with the Seminole.

On rare occasions, indigenous people have invited their proven allies to become honorary tribal members as when radical lawyer William Kunstler, defender of Leonard Peltier and the AIM activists at Wounded Knee, was posthumously drummed into the Lakota tribe as an honorary member.[6] Finally, the text has addressed cases of Indians themselves "becoming Indians," whether in Massachusetts or the Amazon, by coming out officially as self-identified Indians,[7] or as Leanne Betasamosake Simpson puts it: "endlessly creating our indigenous selves."[8] Indeed, Indigenous activists speak about "re-nativization," and the "re-indigenization" of the peoples of the planet.[9] Davi Kopenawa's *The Falling Sky*, finally, offers a festival of polymorphous becomings: shamans becoming jaguars, jaguars becoming crocodiles; human beings becoming other under the influence of sacred plants like ayahuasca or yãkoana; indigenous shamans whose ancestors were humans who became animals and never stopped transforming themselves in a kind of Heraclitan stream, wherein no one can step into the same identity twice.

Individual and collective self-shaping is arguably at the very kernel of world history generally, but especially of the history of the Americas with its power-laden mixing of indigenous peoples and shape-shifting Europeans, Africans, and Asians. After 1492, indigenous peoples throughout the Americas were obliged to "become White" and "become Christian" and "become slaves" and "become workers." On the other side, some Europeans "went native," married native women, learned indigenous languages, and partially adopted indigenous ways. This nativizing trend was often condemned by officials, leading to laws forbidding "Indianizing." As a result of this jagged history, very diverse people, as performance artist Guillermo Gómez-Peña puts it, fantasize

> about wanting to escape their own race and ethnicity … whites wanting to be Black or Latino, Latinos wanting to be blonde or Spanish, blacks wanting to be white, everyone wanting to be Native American. The desire to become Indian is a quintessential American desire … as much as they hate "real" Indians, they'd love to become Indian warriors or shamans.[10]

The becoming-other formulations are appealing because they seem to move away from a paternalistic tolerance toward a warm embrace of the other, to the point of partially becoming the other. The utopian dream is to be whoever one wants to be, as occurs with a carnival *fantasia* or Halloween costume. At the same time, the concept has more than a whiff of the unilateral chameleonism of the privileged, where entitled white, male, straight, middle-class, western individuals play with identity in a way unavailable to their historically otherized counterparts. The question could be summed up as follows: when does Deleuze's "becoming Indian" turn into Deloria's "playing Indian"? The other question reveals the reverse side of the coin: what about all the indigenous people virtually forced to "become white," "become Christian," and "become English speakers," for example, in residential schools? Or to "become Americans," or "become Brazilian?" Within the quiet normativities of domination, the empowered enjoy the privilege of "occupying" and "settling into" subaltern identities. The dominant pole is silent but present; the empowered masquerade as the disempowered: whites become Indians, and so forth, in a one-way process that risks reproducing historical hierarchies and the *faits accomplis* of colonial domination. Historically, it is indigenous people and people of color who had to whiten their speech or straighten their hair to become worthy subjects, women who were prodded to internalize the male gaze, and LBGTQ+ people who had to cower in the closet and conform to a threatening hetero-normativity. Hybrid and syncretic becomings, as Deleuze was doubtless aware, are power-laden. Racially advantaged global elites can easily traverse borders without suffering the usual real-world consequences.

It is no surprise, then, that some feminists have criticized the notion of "becoming woman," while some native and non-native scholars have questioned the notion of "becoming Indian." Describing acts of passing, Sara Ahmed (2000) asserts the importance of being able to replace "the stranger," or take the place of the other, in the consolidation and (re)affirmation of white identity. To "become without becoming" is to reproduce "the other as 'not-I' *within* rather than *beyond* the structure of the 'I.'"[11] So the idea of non-indigenous people, especially those who inherited the advantages of European settlement "becoming Indian" has something of the obscene. It involves a claim that one has appropriated everything, except, as Greg Tate wrote in an African-American context, "the burden." And the debt to Native Americans, like the debt incurred by slavery, can never be paid in full, unless the dead were to be brought back to life, and indigenous land and well-being restored. But full restoration of indigenous life and culture is as impossible as totally restoring a damaged river; one can mitigate the damage but not really compensate for it. In her reading of *A Thousand Plateaus*, Sara Ahmed, in the persona of a self-declared "skeptical feminist," interrogates the Deleuze-Guattari invocations of "becoming." For her, the "fascination with woman as radically other to masculinity/femininity," and all the dualisms that this carries with it, can be seen as implicated in a long history of fascination with women as a figure of alterity within Western Philosophy, becoming "a phantasy of the very necessity and impossibility of philosophy itself through figuring of its other."[12] She compares the philosophers' "becoming Indian" to the "becoming Indian" of Dunbar in *Dances with Wolves*, noting the double process by which Dunbar distances himself from his own society and unlearns anti-Indian stereotypes and the colonialist perspective. Dunbar's "becoming Indian," she notes, is closely related to his "becoming animal" as manifested in his performative renaming as "dances with wolves." But as the blurb on the video proclaims, in the end he "found himself," and his "discoveries"—he is a Columbus to himself—"allow the reassertion of the agency of the dominant subject."[13]

Analysts like Amy Herzog, meanwhile, remind us that Deleuze/Guattari's purpose is to dismantle binary notions of gender, race, and so forth. For Deleuze, identity is always in a state of flux, always in motion, with a collective dimension of not simply representing preexisting groups but rather of shaping new subjectivities, solidarities, intensities, affiliations, and identifications. For Deleuze, it is not a question of representation of a pre-constituted group but rather a dynamic process of what Ranciere would call political subjectification. Indigenous media, in this sense, could be seen as a mediatic movement for political subjectification. For Deleuze, "becoming" (*devenir*) is not an imitation or reproduction of a preexisting group but rather an exit, a line of flight from the dominant, not an arrival but a "movement toward." (An ambiguity in the hyphen in *devenir-minoritaire* creates doubts as to whether it should be translated as "becoming-minoritarian" or "minoritarian becoming"; the first implying one-way role-playing from above while the latter suggests a collective dynamism from below.) At the same time, a radical thinker like Deleuze cannot be reduced to a conservative. In a wonderfully evocative phrase, Deleuze speaks (in his *ABCdaire*) of the "assemblage of all the minoritarian becomings," a phrase that intimates a rhizomatically multiple alliance of social becomings in an emancipatory direction. In this sense, one might speak of catalyzing new constituencies and intensities of affiliation and solidarity, reminiscent of Simpson's "constellations of co-resistance."[14]

The idea of "becoming Indian" has been received with a certain reticence by some indigenous intellectuals. In contemporary academic life indigenous intellectuals dialogue with, but also talk back to, non-indigenous intellectuals and even the consecrated *maitres a penser*. Chickasaw scholar Jodi A. Byrd, in *The Transit of*

Empire (2011), offers a rigorous, doubly "insider" critique of Deleuze-Guattari notions of "nomadism," "becoming Indian," and "Indians without ancestry." Inhabiting while questioning Deleuzian language, Byrd argues that within post-structuralist theories the Indian becomes a vessel or cipher for projection—one might say an "obscure object of desire"—which "functions as a dense presence that cannot be disrupted by deconstruction or Deleuzian lines of flight, because the Indian is the ontological prior through which deconstruction functions."[15] The Deleuzian version of a rhizomatic American wildernesss as a site of constant transformation is not so different, for Byrd, from that posited by Frederick Jackson Turner. "As a philosophical sign," she writes:

> [T]he Indian is the transit, the field through which pre-signifying polyvocality is re/introduced into the signifying regime, and signs begin to proliferate through a series of becomings—becoming-animal, becoming-woman, becoming-Indian, becoming-multiplicity—that serves all regimes of signs. And the Indian is a ghost in the system, an errant or virus that disrupts the virtual flows by stopping them, redirecting them, or revealing them to be what they are and will have been all along: colonialist.[16]

While Byrd acknowledges the generally progressive drift of the Deleuze/Guattari concepts, she finds their project compromised by the legacy of colonial *realpolitik*.[17] It is as if some "post"-theorists, however progressive and even radical in other respects, have baked colonial power arrangements into the historical and discursive cake, evading the foundational question of indigenous dispossession as profoundly shaping capitalism, modernity, postmodernity, and post-theory.

And what is the desire that speaks in such becomings? Many indigenous people reluctantly become "white but not quite" as a melancholy necessity and acknowledgment of real power situations. On the other hand, many indigenous writers, from Paul Chatt Smith to Davi Kopenawa, insist that they have no desire to become white, although they have no objections to using "white" technologies or theories at their own discretion. Here is Davi Kopenawa: "Whites think we should imitate them in all things ... But in no way do I want to be white. To my mind, we can only become white the day the whites become Indians."[18] And Ailton Krenak, at a conference on indigenous cosmologies in Brazil when someone used the phrase "becoming Indian," sarcastically pointed out: "OK, I get it. All you whites become Indians. That means, 'Voila: no more Indians.' If everyone is an Indian, no one is an Indian!"[19]

From Republican Constitutions to the Carib Revolution

As the rise of nativist right-wing chauvinism in the world attests, it has become quite obvious that we live in an era of disenchantment with liberal democracy and the legacy of the republican revolutions like the French and American revolutions. As what Bourdieu calls the "two imperialisms of the Universal," the French and American republics have historically proposed themselves as models for all peoples. (The Haitian revolution, arguably more revolutionary than the others, is usually ignored in the thousands of books about the Republican revolutions which also almost invariably ignore the indigenous revolution within, and outside of, the revolution—from the first indigenous rebellions of Alcatraz and Wounded Knee and Standing Rock.) The two "model revolutions" —for Bourdieu the two "imperialisms of the universal" —turned out to be quite compatible with empires and with unequal societies characterized by epidemic corruption, epidermic racism, political paralysis, toxic polarization, and the demonization of decolonial and critical race projects, now occurring both in contemporary France and in the United States.

In an attempt to remodel the republican revolutionary tradition through ecology, feminism, and critical race, Hardt and Negri propose a new credo:

> [O]nly a constituent principle based on the common can offer a real alternative. We hold these truths to be self-evident; that all persons are equal, that they acquire, through political struggle, certain inalienable rights, among them life, liberty, and the pursuit of happiness, along with free access to the Commons, equality in the distribution of wealth and in the sustainability of the Commons. It is also evident that to assure such rights democratic governance must be instituted. Finally, it is self-evident that in the case that any form of government which becomes destructive to these ends, it is the right of the people to abolish that government and institute another, which will base itself on these principles and organize its power in the form which will best guarantee the security and happiness of the people.[20]

These formulations obviously riff on the American Declaration of Independence and the French "*Droits de L'homme*" but with crucial amendments: In the tradition of revisionist feminist versions of the "Declaration of the Rights of Man [sic]," in the style of Olympe de Gouge's "Declaration of the Rights of Woman and the Female Citizen," penned in the wake of the French Revolution, Hardt and Negri remind us that all *persons*—not *men*—are created equal; that rights are achieved not through top-down *noblesse oblige* but through *struggle*; that these rights include not only political rights but also *economic* rights in the form of equal distribution of wealth; and ecological rights to a sustainable commons. In this sense, they go a long way—but not all the way because they do not define the role of the earlier indigenous common, nor take into account James Tully's demand that Constitutions should be rethought in terms of a negotiation with the lifeways and values of indigenous peoples.

In fact, indigenous peoples have been taking on that task themselves by writing hundreds of tribal Constitutions.[21] The White Earth Nation of Anishinaabeg Natives, to take just one example, ratified a new constitution in 2009. Like Hardt and Negri, the indigenous framers build on the US Constitution, hardly surprising, since that Constitution itself incorporated indigenous social thought. The Preamble reads as follows:

> We the Anishinaabeg of the White Earth Nation are the successors of a great tradition of continental liberty, a native constitution of families, totemic

associations. The Anishinaabeg create stories of natural reason, of courage, loyalty, humor, spiritual inspiration, survivance, reciprocal altruism, and native culture sovereignty.

> We the Anishinaabeg of the White Earth Nation in order to secure an inherent and essential sovereignty, to promote traditions of liberty, justice, and peace, and reserve common resources, and to ensure the inalienable rights of native governance for our posterity, do constitute, ordain, and establish this Constitution.[22]

In this document, the continuities are as important as the innovations, including Article 5 under "Rights and Duties," which states that it is not only "freedom of thought" that should not be denied but also "*artistic irony*"[23] (italics mine).

In the *Magna Carta Manifesto* (2008), Peter Linebaugh points to the fundamental flaw in Republican Constitutions—the refusal to take the forest and the economies of survival into account. Thus, virtually everyone learns about the 1215 Magna Carta, a primordial document in the history of political rights, but not about the other "Carta"—the "Charter of the Forest"—its counterpart in relation to economic rights.[24] Linebaugh briefly evokes the history of revolts around the world, for example, in Ireland, India, and the Amazon, that had to do with reclaiming the "commons," defined as "the theory that vests all property in the community and organizes labor for the benefit of all."[25] Linebaugh charts the struggle between the defenders of the forest common and those who would privatize and enclose it. Enclosure laws prevented peasants from supplying three primary needs: food, firewood, and building materials. Common rights were embedded in a "particular ecology" and practical needs. "The specter haunting Europe," Linebaugh writes, "was of having all things in common."[26] "Prophets and messiahs," Linebaugh writes, "preached the doctrine of having all things in common, which made sense to peasants who resolutely defended their customs and communal routines against the encroachments of feudal landlords and grasping clergy."[27] The slow shrinking of the commons and the decline of power of the Charter of The Forest in England, and in Europe generally coincided with the colonial conquest initiated in 1492: "[the Commons'] disappearance and the settlement of the Atlantic colonies (Ireland, Caribbean, mainland America) are inseparable."[28] With the Conquest, the political Magna Carta went to the Americas but the Charter of the Forest was left behind. Over centuries, even the Magna Carta was corrupted when its key notion, "the due process of law," was deployed on behalf of capitalist corporations, now redefined as "persons." As Linebaugh puts it, "the corporation, personified as a legal person, became the principal epiphenomenon of the capitalist class."[29] Political rights were undermined, and economic rights for common people were sabotaged.

The idea of common ownership of land did not have to be explained to indigenous people defending their customary law and communal practices against the encroachments of the nation-state and land-grabbing settlers. In a way, Oswald de Andrade's "Tupi Theory" anticipated, in poetic and aphoristic form, later ideas about the limits of Republican revolutions, but in a way that incorporated what he intuited to be indigenous thought.[30] Oswald called for a revolution infinitely "greater than the French Revolution," that is, the "Carib revolution," without which "Europe would not even have its meager declaration of the rights of man."³¹ Not only did Oswald assert, alongside Montaigne, Melo Franco, and Lévy-Strauss, the revolutionary impact of ideas generated by contact with the Indians, but he also proposed a new kind of revolution. Oswald's concept of an all-encompassing revolution, as Beatriz Azevedo points out, constituted a revolution within the very conceptualization of revolution itself, one thought and conceived from an indigenous imaginary, a revolution that does not pass through the state.³² In a way, Oswald's affirmations rhyme with what many indigenous thinkers in North America, coming from a very different subject position, have been saying about the limitation of American democracy, just as his poetic trope of indigenous matriarchy echoes across the decades with indigenous feminist claims about very different gender and sexual codes among some indigenous groups, all of course without needing to read Oswald de Andrade manifestoes!

Oswald's critique of the "meager" Rights of Man, I would suggest, has to do not only with the fact that those "rights" were never offered to native peoples, but also with the fact that the French *Droits de L'Homme*, like the U.S. Bill of Rights, however indispensable in a constitutional republic, are still socially insufficient because they are based on a competitive notion of individual rights, of *my* right to property, of *my* right to free speech. The classical legal theorist William Blackstone spells out this despotic and exclusivist aspect of possessive individualism in his 1765 "Commentaries on the Laws of England."

> There is nothing which so generally strikes the imagination, and engages the affections of mankind, as the right of property; or that sole and despotic dominion which one man claims and exercises over the external things of the world, in total exclusion of the right of any other individual in the universe.³³

Thus, the Western conception of rights according to Blackstone is explicitly premised on a "despotic" logic of inclusion/exclusion, not based on a more gregarious *communal* conception rooted in consensus and a notion of a commons linked to the radical indigeneity of native peoples. The rights are based on freedom *against* rather than with the others, freedom as *against* equality rather than based *on* equality. Thus the Divine Right of Monarchs became the quasi-divine right to private property, resulting in the false freedom of "stand my ground," of "private property-armed response" and "don't tread on me!" In a preface to *Serafim Ponto Grande*, Oswald anticipates the concept of the Creative Commons License by the readers' right to "read, translate, or deform the text in any language."³⁴ Even "equality under the law," as Graeber and Wengrow point out, was equality before some form of Sovereign, and thus "equality in common subjugation."³⁵ Oswald's provocative aphorisms rhyme across the decades with Lightfoot's interpretation of James Tully's precise and judicially informed remarks, which echo around global indigenous movements as aiming at long-term transformation in structures of domination, in that they "not only [seek] the inclusion of indigenous rights within the body of human rights, but, in addition, [seek]s a set of rights that, if implemented, would ultimately bring legal, political, social, and cultural change to the entire international system."³⁶ "Rather than simply engaging in shaming and pressure tactics to get states to conform to a body of rights, Lightfoot suggests, global indigenous politics is more revolutionary [in that they] ... push for a set of fundamental changes in the international order."[37]

In his later work, Oswald de Andrade elaborated on something latent in his 1920s manifestoes—the issue of aboriginal matriarchy, not as an add-on but as a fundamental rethinking of the genealogy of power. Here an important influence was his collaborator Patrícia Galvão, nicknamed "Pagu," who co-founded the journal *O Homem do Povo* together with Oswald, where she wrote articles about feminism and politics. As an adolescent, she scandalized the bourgeoisie by smoking in the street, sporting audacious clothes, swearing, and making love to whomever she liked. In her proletarian-feminist novel *Parque Industrial* (1933), she denounced the oppressive conditions for working-class women, along with the bourgeois feminists who had forgotten about them. Only middle-class women, she pointed out, got the vote, while working-class women lacked the required literacy. As a journalist, she interviewed Sigmund Freud, was arrested over twenty times, and was tortured during her five years in Vargas's prisons.[38]

Since Oswald de Andrade was linked through collaboration and at one point through marriage to Galvão, he was clearly familiar with her published feminist writings. In his own work, he develops a kind of theoretical feminism which contrasts patriarchal societies, seen as authoritarian, capitalistic, monogamous, and statist, with matriarchal societies, characterized by collective ownership of the land, open social relations, and the enjoyment of leisure. Linking these philo-indigenous ideas to a Hegelian-Marxist dialectic, de Andrade sees the thesis as "natural man" (Rousseau's vision of the Brazilian Indian), the antithesis as "civilized man," and the synthesis as the "technicized Indian." The technicized Indian would be dedicated, as we have seen, to *sacerdocio* (*sacer*, sacred and *ocio*, leisure or the "sacred ritual of leisure"), instead of *negocio* (business, or etymologically, "not-leisure"). Here de Andrade implicitly contrasts his imagined indigenous Brazil not only with the conservative values of the Brazilian bourgeoisie but also with the Weberian productive Protestantism of the "North" generally, and with what de Andrade saw as the mercenary and Messianic utilitarianism of the United States. In the posthumously published "A Marcha das Utopias," Oswald went beyond seeing Matriarchy as the past-tense utopia of Pindorama and its fabulously powerful Amazon warriors, moving to a present and future tense utopia. "At the bottom of every utopia," he writes, "there is also a protest" and adds "unlike ideologies which maintain the established order, every utopia becomes subversive, because it reflects a desire to break up the dominant order."[39]

De Andrade sees Messianism as the product of patriarchal societies, which generate paternalism and class domination. He cites Frobenius's argument that Matriarchy always preceded Patriarchy.[40] Graeber and Wengrow suggest that the idea of

> primitive matriarchy has become such a bugaboo that it amounts to a taboo: "even to suggest that women had unusually prominent positions in early farming communities is to invite academic censure."[41] The Amazon, meanwhile, was seen, a la Chagnon, as either the land of hostile Hobbesians or of affectionate Rousseauistes. In *A Crise da Filosofia Messianica* (The Crisis of Messianic Philosophy, 1950), another critical account of western intellectual history, de

Andrade denigrated patriarchy—the masculinist social organization based on dualism between human beings and nature, on the inheritance of the father and on the private property of land—in favor of matriarchy—the social organization that, according to him, existed in Brazil before the arrival of the Portuguese. In his manifestoes, this theme of pre-contact happiness was expressed in his past-perfect "we already had" formulations, the claims that "we" Indians "already had Matriarchy," already had Communism,

and "already had" freedom. Formulating what Glissant would call a "prophetic vision of the past," through a novel conjunction of grammatical and historical tenses, Oswald mobilized the "past perfect" as a critique of "the imperfect Present" in order to imagine a "Future Perfect." Matriarchy, for Oswald, is grounded in the common property of land and in the belonging of children not to the father but to the tribe; these double aspects of matriarchy meant that all social difference is progressively diluted within the tribe, to the extent that each new child is the heir not of an individual father but of a social whole or set of relations to which he or she belongs.[42] Within this social structure, the tribe is itself responsible for the administration of the entirety of the social relations, making the State superfluous. The conceptualization of the Law would no longer be derived from the arbitrary decisions of human beings but rather from ancestral customs. The lamentable transition from matriarchy to patriarchy, according to Oswald, entails the transference of power from the ancestral customs of the community to the domain of arbitrary law. Much of the Americas before Columbus was ruled by the customary law of the various indigenous groups—the "as we have always done" of Leanne Simpson—a law subsequently done away with by republican Constitutions that refused to recognize the self-government of the peoples they conquered.

Documents like *The White Earth Nation Constitution* basically inscribe the idea of customary law, as does Leanna Betasamosake Simpson in her affirmations of Anishinaabe social theory: "our theoretical understandings were different than western theory: they are woven into doing, they are layered in meaning, they can be communicated through story, action and embodied presence."[43] The idea of customary law is also confirmed by many close observers of Amazonian societies. The answer to the question asked by Hobbes—i.e. how a society without coercion or hierarchy can avoid chaos—ironically lies in the kind of society that Hobbes wrongly imagined to incarnate a brutal "state of nature"—i.e. a different kind of customary law developed over centuries or over millennia. In the Amazonian case, customary law might be composed of unspoken, taken-for-granted norms and customs never formally articulated as a code. In North America, the Baron de Lahontan has the Wendat figure Kundiaronk articulate an indigenous refusal of western-style laws: "we are determined not to have laws—because since the world was a world, our ancestors have been able to live contentedly without them."[44] The code, given long-standing group intimacy, consists of that which does not even need to be said.

Many Europeans who came to live with Amazonian Indians, even those who came to the experience with racist ideas, were impressed by a lived and taken-for-granted equality and freedom that they had never experienced. The French explorer

Henri Coudreau (1859–99), a member of a French expedition, disobeyed orders and struck out on his own for a 2-year journey in the Amazon. There his encounter with indigenous people changed his life dramatically. In Federico Ferretti's account, Coudreau's experience with the indigenous peoples led him to an alternative life with Amazonian tribes that contradicted the view of indigenous peoples as childlike and dependent on European care and tutelage.[45] In his favorable account of native societies, Coudreau both recalls Montaigne on the indigenous chief as servant of the people, and anticipates Clastres in his view of Amazonian chiefs as having "no authority other than their moral one [in a situation of] pure anarchy, realized by a simple people without needs."[46] Coudreau reiterates the trope of indigenous happiness, but this time on the basis of his own lived experience: "Indians are happy ... freer than every citizen of Europe or North America, without chiefs, without functionaries ... As they have no notion of progress, they do not struggle for progress—what else does one need to be happy?"[47] Furthermore, like some of the French philosophes, Coudreau links happiness to the French Revolution's "liberty and equality" with "liberty that knows not the tyranny of any law, and all the fraternity compatible with the human heart."[48] Coudreau also contrasts indigenous social equality with rigid European social hierarchies, while lamenting the strength of social caste in France, which "we are inculcated to consider as having always existed and having to exist always like a fatal necessity ... the caste of those who are born accursed and the caste of those who are born blessed."[49] Coudreau's experience with native peoples confirmed Proudhon's critique of the constraints of bourgeois democracies. "One is shocked not to find those hundreds of thousands of laws, decrees, regulations which in our land command, forbid, restrict, explain, constrain, warn, and punish, making man the material thing of that abstract thing called the state."[50] Like Jean de Léry earlier, and Clastres later, Coudreau described living in an indigenous society "without subordination and authority centers, where property does not exist."[51]

The already mentioned Villas-Boas brothers, all three knowledgeable about the Amazonian societies of the Xingu (the Xinguanos), encountered and lived with many of the recently contacted societies in the Amazon, and they were well aware of this kind of customary law. The brothers describe an indigenous world where people eschew the discursive violence of giving orders and parents rarely reprimand their children, in favor of simply modeling behavior. (One suspects that this only works in a non-authoritarian society.) The non-authoritarian native family forms a microcosm of the non-authoritarian society. The brothers describe chiefs without any authority except for the rhetorical powers of persuasion or the shamanic powers of vision. The chief, according to Orlando Villas Boas, "is just an intermediary, a link between daily life and the supernatural world [with] no executive power to command."[52] "Power as we understand it," for Orlando, "does not exist ... it is diluted for the community's benefit. No-one may profit from power nor exploit it, just as no one wants to command."[53]

Anthropologist/statesman/writer/popular singer Darcy Ribeiro, with the indigenous peoples of the interior in mind, speaks to the power of estrangement provoked by the first deep contact with indigenous societies in the Amazon: "no-one is unaffected by the experience of seeing the world through the eyes of an Indian.

You will never again be the same person."⁵⁴ Journalist Washington Novaes said he almost envied indigenous people because they are "happier ... sing more, dance more, wear plenty of decoration ... co-exist with spirits, work less [without being] preoccupied by property, or transport."⁵⁵ What then creates this easeful conviviality? For the Villas Boas brothers, the sense of cohesion derives from the shared code of tribal unity and the tacit customary law of a society "strictly bound by its conventions and unwritten rules ... with no place for non-conformists."⁵⁶ For many people from mixed, dissensual, and heteroglossic societies, without any universally shared code, of course, such an obligatory affirmation, would seem a "deal-breaker," but that may be the problem, the deep psychic investment in the "deal" that can't be broken, which is actually a "bad deal."

By Lockean logic, the land belonged to those who worked it, not to those who happened to live on it. The franchise in the freshly minted United States, we recall, was at first limited to landholding men, i.e. those men who had themselves taken and speculated on indigenous land. The Jeffersonian project asked Indians to accept a change from self-government to acquiescence in a government by those who had invaded their land and to conform to a Constitution that inscribed their own disempowerment. In words that apply to Brazil, Canada, and the United States, Viveiros de Castro contrasts the meanings of "native" and "citizen": "To be a native is to ... be part of a community tied to a specific place, that is, it is to integrate a 'people.' To be a citizen, by contrast, is to be part of a controlled 'population' (at the same time 'defended' and diminished) by a State."⁵⁷ Interestingly, de Castro envisions the difference as a change in looking relations, reflected in the directionality of the gaze: "The native looks down, to the land to which s/he is immanent; s/he takes strength from the ground. The citizen looks up to the Spirit incarnated in the form of a transcendent State; s/he receives her/his rights from on high."⁵⁸ These concepts are very relevant to the North American indigenous objections to a pseudo-democracy which "includes" native people as citizens, but only as an "honor" that is also a form of subjection, since subaltern citizenship is a poor substitute for self-rule. While citizenship for the immigrant is a goal devoutly to be wished, for the native it is a synonym for dispossession and the loss of one's world.

Oswald de Andrade's concept of the high-tech Indian, meanwhile, avoided the trap of an allochronic relegation of the indigene to a condemned temporality. As Alexandre Nodari and Maria Carolina de Almeida Amaral argue, de Andrade called for "an anthropophagic consumption of modern inventions," namely to use the new technologies for the sake of liberating men and women from the obligation of labor.⁵⁹ In their account, a Carib revolution would

> liberate those vital energies for other activities more closely related to the flourishing of the fundamental powers of humanity; indeed, free from those obligations, it is possible to develop "the innate laziness of human beings, [...] the mother of fantasy, invention and love", so as to allow the blossoming of a central feature of humanity, its "ludic instinct". Only then could the *Homo Ludens* (the Player) prevail over Man the *Faber*, (the Maker), the Viator (the Traveller) and the Sapiens (the Knower).⁶⁰

De Andrade's "Caraiba revolution" is an all-embracing revolution which "devours," i.e. inherits, all previous revolutions: "The anthropophagic descent is not a literary revolution. Nor a social revolution, Nor political revolution. Nor a religious revolution. Rather, it is all of these at the same time."[61] As Beatriz Azevedo points out, the Cannibal manifesto also cannibalizes other manifestos; thus "Proletarians of the World Unite" becomes "Only cannibalism unites us." Like so many others before and after him, de Andrade saw a link between indigenous social structures and socialism, with the difference that he did not see those structures as relics of a vanquished past but rather as promises for the future. Beatriz Azevedo notes that de Andrade was reading an anthropological work called "Communism among the Kayapo," a connection reminiscent of Marx and Engels's readings of Henry Morgan as a source for their praise of primitive socialism among the Iroquois.[62] In a spirit of revolutionary nostalgia, Chilean writer Fausto Reinega, in *La Revolución India* (1970), in a longer span of history, spoke of an "immortal pre-American socialism" as a "luminous concrete reality" that existed thousands of years before Marx, Engels, and Lenin had formulated their ideas.

North American feminism was also partly inspired by the model of the Iroquois/Haudenosaunee, whose creation myth revolves around Skywoman, and where women nominated (and could impeach) the male leaders. The clan mother's requirements for male leaders were that they (1) had no committed theft, (2) had not committed murder, and (3) had not sexually assaulted a woman. (Many currently powerful leaders and Supreme Court Justices would have been disqualified on at least two of the counts.)[63] Some of the white leaders of the women's rights movement, such as Elizabeth Cady Stanton and Mathilda Joslyn Cage, who lived in Haudenosaunee territory, cited the social power of Iroquois women as proof that the subordination of women was not natural, necessary, or divinely inspired. They also challenged the patriarchal ideas expressed in the Bible, which cursed women in their maternity, saw painful childbearing as a divine curse, and subjected the wife to her husband in marriage. At the 1888 International Council of Women, ethnographer Alice Fletcher quoted an indigenous woman, who said: "As an Indian woman I was free. I owned my home, my person, the work of my own hands … I was better as an Indian woman than under white law."[64] Much as de Andrade referred to the "meager French rights of Man," for indigenous women the idea of "women's rights" was a meager idea, lacking in meaning within a communal society where women enjoyed considerable power. As an unnamed Seneca woman put it: "You ought to hear and listen to what we women shall speak, as well as the sachems, for we are the owners of the land, and it is ours!"[65]

Along later indigenous-feminist lines, Paula Gunn Allen, in *The Sacred Hoop: Recovering the Feminine in American Indian Traditions*, meanwhile, points not only to long-standing gynocritic traditions within indigenous cultures but also to affinities between the feminist suffragettes and Iroquois women at Seneca Falls in New York, "just a stone's throw from the old council house where the Iroquois women had plotted their feminist rebellion."[66] Some of Gunn Allen's major points include: (1) traditional tribal lifestyles are more often gynocentric than not, and rarely patriarchal; (2) in many tribes, the nurturing male constitutes the ideal life-model for boys while the decisive self-directing female forms the model for girls; (3) the physical and cultural genocide of American Indian tribes is and was rooted in the patriarchal fear of gynocracy; and (4) despite colonial genocide, there remain gynocracies which are matrilocal, matrifocal, and matrilinear; (5) traditional tribal cosmology features female deities of the magnitude of the Christian God; and (6) the Iroquois Constitution codified women's decision making and economic power, as in article 44, which states: "The lineal descent of the people of the Five Fires shall run in the female line. Women shall be considered the progenitors of the nation. They shall own the land and the soil. Men and Women Shall follow the status of their mothers."[67] Speaking of her own Laguna Pueblo people, Gunn Allen claims that the Laguna do not equate womanhood exclusively with fertility and childbearing but rather associate the "essential nature of femininity with intellectual fecundity and the creative power of thought."[68] For the Kuna people, similarly, "the Earth Mother is said to have exerted her intellect in conjunction with a male companion and, together, they conceive the future 'from the very beginning'"[69]

The Theoretical Indigene

The Indian in Thomas King's words is "inconvenient." While obviously threatening to white supremacists and patriotic chauvinists, the Indian, and indigenous thinking, are also "inconvenient" for a complacent left in that they throw shade on some left heroes, heroines, movements, and theories. In North America, indigenous academics/intellectuals are challenging the settler-colonial premises of some supposedly progressive projects and movements. In her path-breaking book *Red Pedagogy*, Sandy Grande opens up an imaginative dialogue, from the indigenous left of the left, as it were, with radical advocates of "critical pedagogy," giving the movement considerable credit while also finding it wanting from an indigenous perspective. As a person of Quechua origin and a professor of pedagogy at the University of Connecticut, Grande's personal trajectory incarnates, as it were, the avian/aerial rendezvous of the Eagle of the North and the Condor of the South. Grande subjects a wide array of left-leaning projects to indigenous scrutiny.[70] For her, far-left thought is insufficient; Marx is anticapitalist, yet secretly shares many of capitalism's deep cultural and productivist assumptions. As Grande puts it: "Colonialism is not just a symptom of capitalism. Socialist and communist empires have also been settler empires"; both "view land and natural resources as commodities to be exploited, in the first instance, by capitalist for personal gain, and in the second by Marxists for the good of all."[71]

John Mohawk (Seneca), along the same lines, speaks of three approaches to a hypothetical tree in terms of three ideologies: the capitalist cuts down the tree in the name of profit and rational choice; the socialist cuts down the tree to share it with the proletariat; while the native nourishes the tree so that it can sustain life and reproduce itself for everyone.[72] (That is perhaps what Davi Kopenawa Yanomami means when he says that the Yanomami are protecting the forest for everyone, including Europeans.) Sandy Grande further points out that the left speaks of "democracy," but for indigenous peoples "democracy" has often been a "weapon of mass destruction." The Marxist left speaks of "revolution," but some Latin American nation-state revolutions have dispossessed Miskitus, Sumus, Ramas, and Quechua.

In the realm of education, according to Grande, critical pedagogy is transformational but ignores the value of intergenerational knowledge. It opposes the colonialist project yet remains informed by individualism, stagism, and anthropocentrism, epistemic axioms that worsen the ecological crisis. Students are encouraged to be "independent" and "anti-traditional," goals premised on a denial of transgenerational wisdom. Multicultural identity politics, for its part, sometimes obfuscates the real motors for oppression—colonialism and globalized capitalism. Pointing to the limits of "whitestream feminism," Grande insists that "[i]ndigenous women do not view themselves as the oppressed victims of a male patriarchy; rather, they perceive both men and women as subjects of an imperialist order, choosing to confront their struggles as indigenous people and not only as indigenous women."[73] The enemy is not Men but Settler Colonialism. Progressive politicians call the United States an "immigrant country" where "we are all immigrants," forgetting the crucial addendum "except for native Americans." Grande also points to the blind spots of "recognition liberalism," which ultimately serves to "sustain colonial systems of power and undermine indigenous sovereignty by keeping intact the asymmetric relations of power whereby the dominant agent (the settler state) retains the authority to 'recognize' the subjugated polity (indigenous peoples)."[74]

While the Occupy Movement wanted to liberate Zuccotti Park from private ownership, that "enclosure" by a single Euro-American was made possible, Grande reminds us, by an earlier "occupation"—the theft before the theft, as it were—the theft of indigenous land by Europeans. Despite the in some ways thoroughgoing radicalism of the Occupy movement, it forgot the indigeneity of the land being occupied. In "Accumulation of the Primitive: The Limits of Liberalism and the Politics of Occupy Wall Street," Grande examines the Occupy Wall Street (OWS) movement and its basic elision of indigenous peoples as the first and already "occupied" peoples of this land. While recognizing the achievement of inscribing the concept of the 1 percent on the public mind, Grande argues that "deploying the discursive trope and strategy of 'occupation' as its central organizing principle, OWS reconstitutes (territorial) appropriation as the democratic manifest and fails to propose something distinct from or counter to the settler state." In so doing, Grande argues, "the movement dissolves colonialism into capitalism by courting a limited and precarious equality predicated on (or more pointedly in exchange for) the 'elimination of the Native.'" Within days of the initial occupation of Zuccotti Park in lower Manhattan, the posts of indigenous scholar-activists (John Montano's [Nishnaabe], Jessica Yee [Mohawk], and Joanne Barker [Lenape]) called attention to the inconvenient truth that Wall Street, New York, and, for that matter, all of the Americas were/are already in the perennial state of occupation. Thus, in response to the question provocatively posed by the OWS poster: "What is our one demand?" Grande answers: "abandon 'occupy' and take up 'decolonization.'"[75]

Written in the wake of the "Occupy" Movement, the Eve Tuck/K. Wayne Yang's essay "Decolonization Is Not a Metaphor" offers a powerful analytic synthesis of this kind of critique, insisting again on the primordial importance of land, reminding readers of what is unsettling about decolonization, to wit that it "brings about the repatriation of Indigenous land and life; it is not a metaphor for other things we want to do to improve our societies and schools."[76] For the authors, truly decolonial thought "unsettles" everyone, including "white, non-white, immigrant, postcolonial, and oppressed people," who can be "entangled in resettlement, reoccupation, and reinhabitation that actually further settler colonialism."[77] Without dismissing the other liberation movements, the authors argue against any facile conflation of the various anti-oppression movements with decolonization in the indigenous sense, by insisting on the repatriation—rematriation?—of land. The "easy absorption, adoption, and transposing of decolonization is yet another form of settler appropriation [it is not] an approximation of other experiences of oppression."[78] In their thoroughgoing critique and close analysis, the authors warn against various forms of equivocation in "progressive" discourse in so far as it relates to indigenous peoples: the too easy hybridization of decolonial thought with Western critical traditions by "hawkeye" scholars who see—here we return to the question of the gaze—"from a loftier station."[79] What is striking in this remarkable essay is the synthesis of total radicality with indigenous traditionality in its return to the land as the central issue. Even the ideal of a socialist redistribution of wealth "camouflages how much of that wealth is land, Native land."[80] When the United States offered "40 acres and a mule" to newly freed blacks, the authors remind us, it was offering indigenous land, the very land that forms "the basis for U.S. wealth. If we took away land, there would be little wealth left to redistribute."[81]

In a related trope, the *nous sommes tous* (We are all ...) formulations, going back to the Paris 1968 slogan ("We are all German Jews"), led to other "we become others" coinages and conflations such as "We are all Charlie," "We are all Moors," and so forth are usually meant as laudable gestures of trans-communitarian solidarity. But they can also erase significant differences. The phrase "We are all colonized," for example, does not acknowledge that not all groups have been colonized in the same way; not all groups have lost their land and language for example. Indigenous thought might also throw "inconvenient" shade on a leftist aesthetics tethered to notions of modernism, postmodernism, and the avant-garde. Those movements have been premised on a Hegelian or Marxist historical trajectory, implicit in the pre-to-post trajectory of progress, as well as in the military metaphor of the "avant-garde," which cues a stagist mythos that indirectly led to a "cult of the new." At times such aesthetics become the artistic equivalent of corporate-planned obsolescence theory, whereby the fashionable new replaces the archaic old within an inexorable dialectic which equates change with progress. Gómez-Peña speaks of the "junkies of futurity," while Alexander Kluge mocks "the Assault of the Present on the Rest of Time." But in fact, the Old and the New are mutually embedded; the new usually reaccentuates and remediates the old. Leanne Betasamosake Simpson orchestrates these tenses in transgenerational terms in her call to indigenous peoples to "work alongside our Ancestors and those not yet born to continually give birth to an indigenous present that generates Indigenous freedom."[82] Oxymoronic figures of co-presence and multi-temporality such as "revolutionary nostalgia" (Walter Benjamin) or archaic modernism, strategic traditionalism, traditional radicalism and the like convey this complex temporality, none of which precludes indigenous art from being experimental, innovative, and so forth.

Indigeneity and the Postcolonial Left

Contemporary indigenous thought, both directly and indirectly, raises questions about many of the "posts." Indigenous social thinkers address some sharp questions to postcolonial theory, for example. First, indigenous lives and culture cannot be reduced to an epiphenomenon of colonialism. In "*Godzilla vs. Postcolonial*," Thomas King challenges the view that all Native literature is merely a reaction to colonialism, when in fact it is an extension of longer Native traditions. Glen Sean Coulthard, unknowingly identifying the corrective drift of this book, makes the further point that "indigenous contributions to anti-colonial thought have been generally underappreciated for their transformative value and insights."[83] The term "postcolonial," in King's opinion, sometimes serves, ironically, to reinforce the legacy of colonization. The debate recalls the arguments that swirled around Sartre's *Anti-Semite and Jew*, where critics pointed out that Sartre reduced Jews to being mere by-products of gentile anti-Semitism, a people without agency or any enduring culture worth saving.

Despite the postcolonial project's in many ways radically progressive character, many of its topoi seem questionable from the standpoint of indigenous critique. Cherokee scholar Jace Weaver notes that postcolonial studies seem "oddly detached" when it comes to indigenous issues,[84] while Jodi Byrd laments the surprising lack of conversation between the two fields, especially since postcolonialism is so concerned about forced diasporas and "colonial traces." For Eric Cheyfitz, the "scandal" (as of 2002 at least) of postcolonial studies was "that it has ignored the histories of indigenous peoples within what is now the United States."[85] Sheryl Lightfoot talks about "incomplete postcolonialism," while Youngblood Henderson speaks of the "unfinished business of decolonization."[86]

Some of the problems in some versions of early postcolonial theory include the following: (1) indigenous thinkers tend to see their situation as *colonial* rather than postcolonial, or as simultaneously colonial, postcolonial, or even paracolonial, depending on the time period, the location, and the axis of analysis. While postcolonial studies in its earlier incarnations emphasized the latter-day empires, it too often ignored the foundational dispossession which made the other empires possible. Patrick Wolfe distinguishes between "settler colonialism" and "franchise colonialism," which was briefer and more superficial in that it exploited the resources of an India or a Senegal, but never overpowered and displaced the indigenous peoples to become the dominant group.[87] Indigenous social thinkers, in contrast, see colonial domination as going all the way back to 1492 and Iberian imperialism as the *primum mobile* that set the colonial machine in motion, whence the constant references in writing and in activist speech to "500 years" and "Outros quinhentos" and T-shirt slogans like "Fighting terrorism since 1492."

(2) While postcolonial theory celebrates a cosmopolitan "travelling theory," indigenous discourse, whatever the cosmopolitanism of indigenous individuals, valorizes a *rooted* existence rather than a cosmopolitan one. Indigenous forest diplomats like Deskeha in the twentieth century—the representative of the Haudenosaunee to the League of Nations—along with Raoni Metuktire, and Davi Kopenawa Yanomami in the twenty-first century—in this sense can be seen as grounded cosmopolitans.

(3) While the post-structuralist theory that informs postcolonial theory uses the word "originary" as a negative—as part of a valid critique of hegemonic discourses—indigenous peoples rightly claim to be the "originary peoples" of the Americas. The emphasis is on rootedness in the land, in the local landscape, in the local fauna and flora and the earth that gives sustenance. Etiological legends, similarly, often trace an origin that does not begin with a voyage from elsewhere but is linked to the face and physiognomy of the environing territory.

(4) While a post-structuralist-inflected postcolonial critique questions any nostalgia for lost origins, native groups often seek to recover and restore customs, rituals, and language as a matter not only of sheer survival but as a recuperative anti-colonial practice, without which the group, in a kind of spiritual death, would disappear as members of a specific culture, whence cultural recuperation and revival as goals for indigenous media.

(5) While postcolonial theory revels in the "blurring of borders," indigenous communities often seek to literally *affirm* borders by demarcating land against encroaching squatters, miners, corporations, and nation-states. Rather than "deterritorialization," those who live on their own land speak of "homelands," or of being "guardians of the forest." Those who have been made strangers on their own land, meanwhile, literally seek "reterritorialization" in the form of the recovery of ancestral land. And land here is collective and communal, not individual. In one of the paradoxes of latter-day capitalism, indigenous peoples in the Americas sometimes buy back land in order to restore it to communality.[88] Some Native Americans say, in effect, that "you whites took our land, but at least pay the rent," which leads me to a fantasy: could Congress pass a law requiring that powerful realtors be replaced by native representatives, with all the profits from newly fair rents going to the native peoples so they can buy back indigenous land in order to communalize it?

(6) While the left, with the possible exception of some trends within Liberation Theology, is generally assumed to be secular or minimally religious, many indigenous movements embrace words like "spirituality," the "Great Spirit," the Creator, Nhanderu, Omama, and the like, insisting on the love of a land regarded as "sacred" and imbued with spirituality.

(7) The various "post" movements shape a theoretical context where the notions of a coherent subject identity, let alone a broader community identity, have come to seem epistemologically suspect. In the era of the "death of the subject" it became all too easy to dismiss as a lure and mystification the idea of indigenous peoples becoming the "subjects" of history. But the atomistic decentering of identities should not mean that one cannot draw boundaries between oppression and liberation, privilege and disempowerment. Sandy Grande speaks of "the paradox of having to prove 'authenticity' in order to gain legitimacy as a 'recognized' tribe, while simultaneously negotiating a postmodern environment where all claims to authenticity are dismissed as essentialist (if not racist)."[89] Social constructivist theories, as Arif Dirlik pointed out, do not compute very well with indigenous struggles, which stress an ongoing indigenous collective that has survived centuries of colonial aggression and degradation.[90] What Spivak calls "strategic essentialism" is crucial for any struggle that hopes to allow for communities of identification, even if those communities are multiple, discontinuous, and partly imaginary.

Before and After the Nation-State

The ancient radicalism of many social expressions of indigeneity of the kind we have discussed here, in both North and South America, goes against the grain of any social thought premised, even if surreptitiously, on the centrality of the nation-state form. For Dale Turner, "the idea that indigenous nations are nation 'states' represents a fundamental error in thinking about indigenous cultures."[91] The indigenous critique of the nation-state takes place both "below," "above," and "beyond" the default mode of the national. Indigenous critique of the nation-state is thus much deeper and more radical than other critiques, for a number of historical and philosophical reasons: (1) most self-governing indigenous communities came into existence long *before* the emergence of modern nation-states; (2) the dispossession of indigenous communities was largely the product of expansionism by settler nation-states; (3) the symbolic national identity of colonial-settler states in the Americas (and elsewhere) was constituted in relation to the "Indian" and the "aborigine" whether as the enemy to be eliminated and displaced, or as the co-opted symbol of national difference from Europe; (4) the present-day boundaries of many indigenous communities exceed the borders of nation-states (e.g. the Yanomami in Brazil and Venezuela; the Mohawks in the United States and Canada; the Guaraní in Brazil and Paraguay, etc.); (5) many indigenous peoples, due both to infra-national "removals"— the Guaraní-Kaiowá in Brazil and the Cherokees and Seminoles in the United States—and to transnational shifts, in the case of those displaced by globalization from their original land base and spread across the globe as migrant workers, like the Bolivian Quechua-speaking flute players or Mexican mariachi performers found in the urban centers of many parts of the world; (6) while Western Republics are founded on the Lockean triad of "life, liberty, and property," many indigenous communities are founded on a slightly different set of values: life, land, liberty, equality, reciprocity, respect, and happiness. Indigenous peoples are often less invested in "inclusion" within a settler-state national polity than in tribal and pan-indigenous sovereignty, although they sometimes argue for "both/and." The goal, for Taiaiake Alfred, is to build "appropriate postcolonial governing systems [that] disconnect the notion of sovereignty from its Western, legal roots and transform it."[92]

Sheryl Lightfoot (Anishinaabe, Lake Superior Band of Ojibwe), the first indigenous woman from Canada to represent North America on the "Expert Mechanism" Council meant to assist member states to achieve the goals of the UN Declaration of the Rights of Indigenous Peoples, asks for a thoroughgoing decolonization of culture and society that goes beyond rights and formal independence:

> Indigenous rights aim to eradicate the discursive, normative, and ultimately, material remnants of the colonial project and complete the unfinished business of decolonization. However, global Indigenous politics seeks a post-colonialism markedly different from that which has come before, because a world that accommodates Indigenous nationhood, Indigenous ontologies, and Indigenous political practices will be a world characterized by an entirely different set of values and power relations.[93]

Lightfoot points to a way to reconcile universal principles with cultural and social difference. And here she rejoins on another register and gives juridical flesh to de Andrade's poetic critique of the French Revolution's "meager rights of man." By individualizing human rights, the international system—and Republican revolutionary constitutions—"created a particular injustice for Indigenous peoples who also needed their collective rights (for instance to land, language, culture, political and social institutions) protected from the violence caused by dispossession and assimilation."[94] Indigenous rights, she continues, "problematize the exclusive individual rights construction of human rights that, in their effort to protect all persons equally, actually *cause* discrimination by overlooking or failing to recognize *all* of the sources of ongoing oppression."

For Lightfoot, "sovereignty" is compromised by its links to the global nation-state system. A global indigenous politics, she argues, "imagines and practices international relations differently, incorporating Indigenous culture, spirituality, world views, and decision making-processes into international politics."[95] It is worth remembering here that the word "international" can also mean "inter-indigenous-nation-al." For Lightfoot, indigenous rights push the meanings of decolonization and self-determination beyond purely statist conceptions, which is why nation-state-oriented thinkers find the indigenous movement both baffling and threatening. She explains the resistance even of rights-advocating, liberal, and democratic societies to indigenous proposals as based on fear of the indigenous questioning of the basic foundations of European-derived rule over indigenous peoples and lands. Some European nation-states, she points out, feel less threatened by indigenous rights because their empires have already been dismantled. I would add, however, that although the external empires have been largely dismantled, colonial remainders continue both in the former colonies through the inertia of colonial-based inequalities, and in the metropole through postcolonial patterns, like the resistance to anti-colonial critique and, the racialization of Islam in France, to the point that a major right-wing party calls for a "*reconquete*" a literal translation into French as we have seen, of the Reconquista that Christianized Spain and expelled Jews and Muslims.[96]

Global indigenous rights are the most threatening, in Lightfoot's view, to the Anglo-settler societies as those "with the most to lose by reallocating land, self-determination, and power."[97] Latin American governments, she points out, give rhetorical support to indigenous causes in order to placate and pacify not only the indigenous people but also to becalm foreign critics of their anti-indigenous policies. The relentless state assault on indigenous land, self-determination, and power in Brazil, under both left and right governments but especially under rightist policies, suggest that the dominant stratum in Brazil is very much invested, even lethally invested, in undermining indigenous self-determination, as seen in the innumerable assassinations of indigenous leaders. In Latin America, Lightfoot reminds us, Discovery Doctrine is "firmly intact, in both legal and discursive senses."[98]

Lightfoot also critiques liberal "recognition" discourses as preserving the colonial status quo. She cites Vine Deloria's 1974 *Behind the Trail of Broken Treaties*, which offers five proposals for a redesign of US-Indian relationships: (1) international protectorate status; (2) end of US right to extinguish Aboriginal land title; (3) end of claim to "first purchase" rights to tribal land; (4) prohibition on purchase of indigenous land; and (5) restoration of the treaty relationship. Lightfoot hails the advances made in Deloria's book but regrets that the framing still privileges or assumes existing structures, discourses, and institutions. She looks with more optimism to activist movements like "Idle no More" and the "Leap Manifesto," aimed at weaning Canada away from the dependency on fossil fuels. The Manifesto states, in part: "This leap must begin by respecting the inherent rights and title of the original caretakers of this land. Indigenous communities have been at the forefront of protecting rivers, coasts, forests, and lands from out-of-control industrial activity. We can bolster this role, and reset our relationship, by fully implementing the UN Declaration on the Rights of Indigenous Peoples."[99] She also cites Walter Echo-Hawks' view of the UN Declaration, as "planting the seeds of change." "This harbinger of change asks every nation to restore the native rights of Native peoples that fell by the wayside during the colonial era. If that call is answered, the Declaration will someday be seen as the Magna Carta for the world's indigenous peoples."[100]

Postcolonialism and the Nurture of Nature

The post-structuralist currents that undergird early postcolonial theory highlight the inventedness not only of nations but also "denaturalize the natural." Postcolonial discourse in this sense inherits the valid Marxist, Brechtian, and Roland Barthesian critiques of the doxa that naturalize oppressive institutions, whence the emphasis on the "denaturalization" and "estrangement" of social doxa. On one level, this strategy makes perfect sense in that Marx and Brecht and Barthes were interested in "denaturalizing" or "denormalizing" social oppression and bourgeois normativities, making them strange and therefore alterable, just as it made sense to denaturalize and de-biologize gender, to suggest that "women," a la Simone de Beavoir, "are made and not born." (Feminists have mocked the stereotype of the "earth mother," but if one reverses adjective and noun to maternalize not individuals but the earth itself— i.e. Mother Earth—the idea becomes more persuasive.) But within the various post-theories, as opposed to later ecological theory, words like "nature" and "naturalization" became synonymous with blind essentialism and the doxa of the unthought. Native social thought suggests a different conception of nature and the natural, which conveys reverence for Nature in a way that is simultaneously practical, political, spiritual, cognitive, and (para) scientific.

Rather than reject naturalism, Eduardo Viveiros de Castro, pluralizes it by calling for an "indigenous multinaturalism" that challenges not only the rhetorical anti-naturalism of the "posts," but also what might be called the primordial othering which separated nature from culture, and animals from human beings. Asked how he understood the pandemic attacking the world, Ailton Krenak reacted in a similar vein:

> We are very divorced from this living organism called the earth. This divorce from the integrations and interactions with our mother the earth has created orphans, not only those who are called Indians or Indigenous, but everyone. While

humanity is displaced, a hoard of too-smart-for-their-own good corporations take command and dominate the planet; they get rid of the forests, mountains, transforming everything into merchandise ... We began to think that the earth was one thing, and ourselves, another completely different thing, but in reality the two are inseparable.[101]

Rather than "denaturalize the natural," Krenak renaturalizes thought by thinking *through* the natural, even while performing a kind of Brechtian estrangement of neoliberal and scientistic doxa:

> I do not perceive anything which is not nature. All is nature. The cosmos is nature. Everything which I manage to imagine is nature. Some suggest that we humans are going to live in artificial environments created by the masters of money, those same corporations that destroyed the nature on which we depend. Has it occurred to people that nature might be tired of us and is "disengaging" by taking away our oxygen? ... Will we have to produce ventilators for 6 billion people? Mother Earth gave us oxygen for free, it let us sleep at night, lets us wake up in the morning with the sun, let the birds sing, the currents ripple, the breezes blow, creating this marvelous world for us to share, and what have we done with it? Perhaps Mother Nature is a loving mother who has decided to discipline her child, not because the mother doesn't love the child, but because she wants to teach him a lesson. "My son: shut up!"[102]

Although we often speak of genocide in the cold abstractions of statistics, Krenak speaks not of numbers of individual lives lost but rather of the loss of entire life-worlds and modes of being, accompanied by the total eclipse of languages, cosmologies, spiritualities, experiences, affects, practices, and knowledges. When Ophelia thinks that Hamlet has lost his mind, she laments that "a noble mind" has been "o'erthrown?" But what does it mean to overthrow an entire culture and to annihilate a language? Some Western literary liberals, who make a living thanks to the cultural capital of their knowledge of English, see the loss of an indigenous language, incoherently, as a "victimless crime."[103] Robin Wall Kimmerer, in words that echo Heidegger's "language is the house of Being," writes: "Language is the dwelling-place of ideas that do not exist anywhere else ... a prism through which to see the world ... [where even] numbers are imbued with meaning ... Every time the Haudenososaunee count to three in their own language, they reaffirm their bond to creation."[104] Without language we are but bare-forked animals uttering incomprehensible grunts. And what does it mean when complex cultures and worlds are "o'erthrown?" as occurred with millions of indigenous people. Viveiros de Castro puts it differently: "Since Europeans thought that the Americas were a world without men, the Indians became men without a world."[105] "We indigenous people," Krenak points out, "have become accustomed to losing our worlds; now we are concerned with you losing your world, and carrying everyone else away together with that loss."[106] Odile Joannette (Pessamit Innu), Executive Director of Wapikoni Mobile, makes a similar point: "In the conversation between indigenous people and whites, the dialogue is traumatic for both sides: the difference is that we are used to trauma."[107]

In his most recent book, *A Vida Não é Útil* (Life Is Not Useful, 2021), dictated by a physically exhausted Ailton Krenak to an interlocutor in a forty-hour stream of discourse, Krenak offers similar reflections.[108] Although Krenak, unlike Kopenawa, is a fluent Portuguese speaker and an educated person who cites Foucault, Donna Hathaway, and Oswald de Andrade, he nevertheless shares many assumptions with the Davi Kopenawa who does not literally write books but speaks them, as others write down his words. Krenak's title, which seems to claim that life is useless, actually means quite the opposite, i.e. that life is not about being productive; life itself is the point; in other words, it is about working to live rather than living to work, producing life rather than living for production.

Ailton Krenak's group was formerly known as the Botocudos because of their wooden lip plugs. Their image was popular enough in France Flaubert to have his pharmacist Homais complain that French mothers were dressing up their children to look like Botocudos. The Botocodos/Krenak were the victims of one of the most violent genocides of Brazilian history. Krenak himself spent much of his early years fleeing with his family from the invaders chasing them from their ancestral territory near the Rio Doce, their symbolic mother, to the point that for a while almost no Krenak lived on the original territory. If in the past it was indigenous people who were threatened with rupture and the extinction of the sense of their lives, the current situation is one of imminent failure of the earth to support the outlandish demands the privileged portion of the worldmake of it. Life after Covid, for Krenak, is a time of salutary withdrawal and deep reflection, where nature is giving humanity a lesson in humility, signaling an end to our "arrogant dream of self-sufficiency." He speaks of the dominant society as "viral"; like a virus, "our civilization imposes its codes on other civilizations, destroying its material support and its cultural base, forcing other peoples to become like us."[109] There is no point in returning to a toxic normalcy, which for him would mean that the thousands of deaths around the world would have meant nothing, "proving that humanity is a lie."[110]

Krenak mocks the "delirious dream" of those who think that humanity can move to another planet when this one becomes uninhabitable. He suggests that the "bosses of the Amazon" remove themselves to that other planet, and leave their address so we can send them supplies. "How many planets do these people have to destroy," he asks, "before they realize they are on the wrong path?"[111] The earth, for Krenak, has been devoured by giant corporations with enormous financial power. The Western colonizing and scientific imagination fancies a future humanity spending most of its time in artificial environments. This select elite obviously will continue to exclude all the "sub-humans" and socially marginalized who cling to a land linked to their identity and ancestry. Then, in a trans-indigenous reference, he repeats a sad prophecy from Lakota elder Wakya un Manee (aka Vernon Foster): "Only when the last fish dies in the water, and the last tree is removed, only then will human beings perceive that one does not survive by eating money."[112] Although people have survived by eating ants, grasshoppers, and even scorpions, Krenak adds in his own voice, "no one has survived by eating money."[113]

Krenak compares those who think we can save ourselves by colonizing Mars or through high-tech environments to children who fantasize that they can go on playing forever.[114] But we are now adults, at a time when the media normalizes a situation where corporations are devastating the planet and digging a giant ditch of inequalities between peoples and societies. The virus, a planetary organism, according to Krenak, responds to this human alienation with an attack against the unsustainable life that we imagine to have adopted of our own free will, in the name of a phantasmatic "freedom" that everyone praises without asking what it costs. Krenak laments the tragedy of Covid killing so many indigenous elders, those whose memories contained vast archives of history and legends. Making the comparison often made in relation to African *griots*, Krenak analogizes each death of an elder to the burning of a library, entailing the destruction of the elders' scientific knowledge about plants and animals, along with complex philosophies and narratives of histories of connectedness. Their knowledge, according to Krenak, is not abstract but embodied, indissociable from bodies, gestures, ways of speaking, walking, dancing, and narrating.[115]

Citizens who become consumers, according to Krenak, lose the capacity to live on an earth full of meaning, an earth as a platform for different cosmovisions. Echoing H. L. Mencken on Puritanism as the "awful fear that someone, somewhere, is enjoying themselves," Krenak, in a new twist on the happiness trope, claims that those formed by the capitalist productivist world begrudge the happiness of those who experience the simple pleasure of being alive, of dancing and singing together. Those he calls the "zombies" cannot bear the thought of so much pleasure, of so much fruition of life. We can learn, he suggests, from the poetry, the creativity, and the survival strategies of the originary peoples who survived colonization.

The Fear of a Red Academe: Indigenous Decoloniality

In Brazil, contemporary indigenous thinkers have maintained an intense dialogue with non-indigenous scholar-activists. Rather than see anthropologists as code-crackers exposing the secret mechanisms and kinship relations of indigenous societies, Viveiros de Castro reminds us of the intellectual debts of anthropologists to the peoples they study. The "most interesting concepts, problems, entities and agents introduced by anthropological theory," Castro suggests, "find their source in the imaginative power of the societies (or peoples, or collectives) that the anthropologists propose to explain."[116] As theory becomes a hybrid co-authored practice, the anthropologist is inspired by the theoretical imaginary of the indigene, who in turn responds to the anthropologist. The phenomenon of indigenous academics is relatively new in Brazil, largely because contact for most groups is very recent. North America, in contrast, has a very long history of indigenous writers and academics, going back to Caleb Cheeshahteamuck, the first "Indian" to graduate from Harvard's "Indian College" founded in the 1640s. Two centuries later, Pequot author, minister, and organizer published a book, *A Son of the Forest*, perhaps the first autobiography written by an indigenous person in North America. And in 1920, an Oneida woman author and activist, Laura Cornelius Kellog, published *Our Democracy and the Indian,* a passionate defense of Haudenosaunee democratic self-government and a proposal for a new political economy that she sometimes called "Indian Communism."[117] Elite "Indian Schools," for their part were always assimilationist, in contrast with the indigenous projects that began in the 1960s as part of the "seismic shift" that led not only to activism in the streets but also in the academe with forms of alternative "studies" and transdisciplines (Women's studies, Ethnic studies, Third World studies) and in the native case to what are variously called Native American studies, American Indian studies, First Peoples studies, Indigenous studies, whose goal was to decolonize knowledge, defend indigenous land and rights, study oral and written literature, and critique Eurocentric forms of anthropology and other social sciences.[118] Since that time there has been a tremendous resurgence of indigenous arts, writing, and political theory, which has begun to have an impact far beyond any indigenous demographic presence.

In his essay "Inside the Machine: Indigeneity, Subversion and the Academy," actor and choreographer Michael Greyeyes (Plains Cree, Muskeg Lake First Nation), offers a parodic portrayal of the University in the guise of an earnest "Caucasian anthropologist," from the Department of Caucasian Anthropology, with a research interest in "White Dance Forms through History."[119] He describes the defensive reaction when he dared to question the assumptions of a curriculum that was "all Western, all white, all the time."[120] Questioning of the standard curriculum by Native American thinkers go at least as far back as the early 1960s, when Jack D. Forbes was proposing the creation of an American Indian University, leading to the establishment of indigenous-controlled colleges and Native Studies Programs. Ironically, such a proposal was anticipated, although only half seriously, in Benjamin Franklin's unpublished "Remarks Concerning the Savages of North America," where he recounts an episode, meant to be humorous, where the white leaders were offering to educate Indians, but where the Native Americans politely refused the offer, saying that earlier experiments along that line had only turned the Indians into "bad Runners, ignorant of every means of living in the Woods, unable to bear either Cold or Hunger, [who] knew neither how to build a Cabin, take a Deer, or kill an Enemy, spoke our Language imperfectly; were therefore neither fit for Hunters, Warriors, or Counsellors; they were totally good for nothing." The "Indians" proposed instead an alternative reverse pedagogy, a kind of non-violent residential forest school for white people, whereby the "Gentlemen of Virginia will send us a dozen of their Sons, we will take great Care of their Education, instruct them in all we know, and make *Men* of them."[121]

Protests by native people and their allies against Eurocentric curricula are taking place all around the Americas. Although we tend to associate the Coloniality/Modernity movement of recent decades with the innovative work of established decolonial academics working in North American and Latin American universities, a "decolonial manifesto" written by indigenous Awaete *paje* Timeu Assurini, questions the normality of non-indigenous academics being regarded as the sole representatives of indigenous peoples in halls of learning. Assurini's ethnos, called the Assurini and sometimes the Awaete, was first contacted some 40 years ago. They have suffered the disastrous consequences not only of colonialism in general, but also of the "progress" supposed to emanate from development projects like the Transamazonian Highway, the Belo Monte Dam, and the Belo Sun Mining project. Assurini created the *marytykwawara* collective and the "Awaete Agenda for the exchange of knowledge." By his account, his grandfather, one of his people's last active shamans, asked him to go to the white [non-indigenous] world, to research their documents and archives, and find out what they had done with our culture.

Although the title "Decolonial Manifesto," echoes the decolonial language both of Brazilian Modernism and of the Coloniality/Modernity project, Assurini goes to places that we anti-colonial/decolonial academics do not usually go.[122] He challenges the academe itself as a kind of "contact zone," characterized by asymmetries in standards of admission and academic credentials vis-à-vis Indian students and scholars. Assurini calls not only for decolonization of curricula within the academe, but also for decolonization *of* the academe as an institution and for new modalities of reciprocity:

> We had long been hearing promises from the researchers who studied us that their research would help us in our struggle against all the damage wrought by the presence of non-indigenous Brazilians in our territory. But when I brought up the possibility of working together to present our joint research, I was informed that I would have to acquire an academic record, as the only way to secure funding for the project. But what kind of a deal is this? There is no way non-indigenous scholars could have performed their research had we not set up the structures to enable them to do it. And who are the real experts? We have our own kind of university of knowledge, significant enough to attract the attention of international scholars. Yet why is it whenever we apply for a grant we are seen as unqualified.[123]

Assurini points to the Catch 22s of the cross-cultural dialogue, saying, in effect: "We Indians taught you most of what you know about our language and culture—and we set up a situation where you could pursue your research. You make a lot of errors and gaffes, yet when we ask to teach our own culture, we are told we need advanced degrees. Yet, that very process of getting degrees is an exercise in de-indigenization."

Then, in a provocative reversal of positions, Assurini offers a witty "modest proposal":

> Perhaps we should invert the situation and require non-indigenous scholars to submit to *our* requirements in the form of tests of cultural competence in our rites of passage and rituals and dances and songs before we grant outsiders degrees in our culture? Yes, I think that's a great idea![124]

Assurini's ironic suggestion conjures up the hilarious specter of anthropologists in their 50s struggling to master the fine art of Xinguano wrestling or trying to perform strenuous Xavante rites of passage that amount to endurance tests with spiritual overtones.

More important, Assurini problematizes the "whole relation between researcher, native informant, and object of study."[125] After fighting successfully for the acceptance of indigenous students in the University, he argues, the protocols for the production of knowledge remain unchanged. He therefore pleads for indigenous participation in the production of knowledge about indigenous people:

> Theoretically the academe should be dedicated to the construction of knowledge. Wasn't that why we indigenous peoples struggled to have access to these institutions? Wasn't it to enroll indigenous students and hire indigenous faculty? But a right has been transformed into an obligation. What happened to transculturality? Respect for the other should be the norm, according to the constitutions and to human rights discourse, especially when the other is the object of research, yet this norm is constantly disrespected.[126]

Assurini formulates what amounts to an Indigenous Academic Bill of Rights. If the non-indigenous want to speak about us, he suggests, both groups have to enjoy the same conditions within which to construct a truly collaborative project, with ourselves not as "native informants" but as co-authors contributing mutually to the text and also certifying the validity of what is published. Anything else, he argues, would be unfair not only to the indigene but also to scholars, readers, and students.[127]

In words reminiscent of those of US Native American and indigenous parents lamenting the depersonalization of their children in white residential schools, losing not only their sense of identity but also their usefulness to the community, Assurini speaks in a similar vein of the alienating role of public schools in indigenous villages. In the Brazilian equivalent of residential schools in North America, students "learn to unlearn," forgetting their language, customs, and skills. Just as their parents were sent away to perform alienated labor for strangers, including doing virtual slave labor on rubber plantations, Assurini points out, now their children suffer from alienated learning. For Assurini, there are many paths to knowledge, wisdom, and science. "For indigenous people," he tells strangers, "life itself is a university." His conclusion is unsparing: "If my culture is the subject," he writes, "I already have my diploma."[128]

These kinds of assertions find some concrete support within the Brazilian University itself. The "Meeting of Knowledges" Project in Brazil and Columbia, for example, not only offers an incisive critique of the colonial university, but also actively incorporates knowledge of the kind Assurini invokes. In "The Meeting of Knowledges: A Project for the Decolonization of Universities in Latin America," Jose Jorge de Carvalho and Juliana Flórez-Flórez elaborate their transdisciplinary project of decolonizing the dominant academic model transplanted from Europe to Latin America.[129] Latin American universities, they point out, were conceived as Catholic institutions following the Iberian model. As a result, both public and private universities

> are predominantly white, segregated, and racist institutions that reproduce the Eurocentric model of knowledge developed in the West in the modern period [at a time when] the so-called West was at the height of its dominion over the rest of the world and European scholars had no doubt that their science was superior to any other tradition of knowledge in the world.[130]

The current university in Latin America, the authors argue— and the point applies to most universities in the Western world—"are neo-colonial institutions because they accepted the hierarchy of knowledge imposed by the settlers who validated European scholarly knowledge in order to disqualify, censor, and exclude Indigenous, African and other traditional peoples' ancestral knowledge."[131] In an analysis parallel to that developed by Ella Shohat and myself in *Race in Translation* in relation to the "seismic shift,"[132] the authors suggest that the various disciplines had all devalued non-Western knowledge: "The sciences and technologies of our traditional peoples were considered erroneous because they had not been modelled on mathematics; their History was unacceptable because it did not separate the mythological from the historiographic; their Geography was dismissed because supposedly lacked mathematical precision."[133] Native Medicine was considered untrustworthy because it lacked accurate instruments and procedures. "Thus, all the foundations of modern Western knowledge were marshalled against the Latin American continent (and the South in general) to justify domination and exploitation of the continent's resources."[134] Military power, meanwhile, formed a silent backup line of support "for the legitimation of the supposed epistemic superiority of Western nations over the rest of the peoples of the planet."[135]

The authors therefore argue for the "incorporation of the knowledges of Indigenous, Black and other marginalized peoples as part of the repertoire of valid knowledges to be taught and expanded, on an equal footing with modern Western knowledge."[136] Indigenous leaders and movements and arts are now included in their curriculum with the collaboration of indigenous and Afro-diasporic individuals and groups themselves. Decoloniality in the academe, they point out, usually takes the form of highly intellectualized critiques. While acknowledging their validity, the authors endorse the construction of "multi-epistemic" universities, open to the presence not only of *maitres a penser* but also of *maitres a connaissance indigene,* i.e. masters of traditional indigenous knowledge. After acknowledging the success of Affirmative Action policies in Brazil supporting the inclusion of black and indigenous communities, the authors ask the essential question that haunts all of the Americas—"why should young Indigenous and Black students be educated in an entirely Eurocentric academic system dominated by Whites with no respect for Afro-Brazilian and Indigenous traditional systems of knowledge?"[137]

As a response, the University of Brasilia developed an innovative project to invite shamans, *caciques,* artisans, traditional architects, performers, and specialists in the healing power of plants into the academe to teach courses and modify curricula. Summing up, the "Meeting of Knowledges" project proposes an epistemic renovation that welcomes all valid traditional knowledges present in the area where the university is located. Rather than a form of entertainment for the privileged, the renovated curriculum is conceived as a forum for interactive solidarity. In North America, Leanne Betasamosake Simpson has expressed some skepticism about attempts to "indigenize the academy by bringing Indigenous Knowledge into the academy ... on the terms of the academy itself,"[138] favoring instead the creation of "a generation of land-based, community-based intellectuals and cultural producers who are accountable to our nations" and not to what she calls the "Western academic industrial complex."[139]

Although one might see both arenas as legitimate terrains of struggle, her probing question is clearly relevant to all of the Americas.

The dialogue between indigene and non-indigene, as Viveiros de Castro has repeatedly stressed, is not just a question of a different point of view, but rather a difference about what constitutes a point of view. In a volume, ironically entitled *Pacificando o Branco: Cosmologias do contato no norte-Amazonico* (Pacifying the White Man: Cosmologies of Contact in the Northern Amazon, 2002), edited by Bruce Albert and Alcida Rita Ramos, the editors formulate an indigeno-centric view of the task of anthropology.[140] Going beyond Jean Rouch's *"anthropologie partagée,"* they define the task as a question not of seeking to understand the "others," but rather to understand their understanding of us, to comprehend their "cosmologies of contact, and their comprehension of the contemporary world. The idea is that indigenous peoples have also been analyzing us, trying to domesticate us, pacify us, anthropologize us."[141] The goal was to understand interethnic contact and the historical consciousness of these societies through a grid which privileged their symbolic and political agency and creativity. It is a matter, as they put it, "of reconciling analyses of cosmological systems with the social histories of contact situations, to re-articulate the mythic and the historical as instanced in oral expression, rituals and with ethno-politics, and classifications with mobilizations, structures with strategies and inventions with traditions."[142]

These syntheses reveal, according to the authors, the "dispositives not only of representation but also of the symbolic domestication and ... neutralization of the nefarious powers (pestilence and violence) of the whites."[143] Thus, the goal is not to define the identity of the other but rather, inversely, to practice and perform what Marc Auge calls "the anthropology of the anthropology of the others."[144] While laudable goals, such formulations might be seen by skeptics as a new version of "it's all about us," as in the joke: "Now let's talk about you; what do you think of me." But actually this rethinking of dialogue goes deeper, because to see how one is seen through the others' cosmology, in a kind of excess seeing, is to relativize oneself and combat the complacencies of Eurocentric arrogance. The project is especially valid in the case of someone like Bruce Albert who has "put in the time" to understand how someone like Davi Yanomami sees and thinks in order to serve as intermediary between the Yanomami's and the wider world.

The Power of Shamanic Critique

Indigenous critique takes expressive form against the backdrop of globalized exploitation. Over the centuries, natural resources thought to be an integral part of the natural "commons" have been "poached on" by corporations. Since corporations can package H_2O in fancy bottles, decorated with simulacra evoking the Wordsworthian sublime, and sell it at exorbitant prices and at great environmental cost, a number of multinational corporations are eager to privatize everything. The key profit-generating resources, as Peter Linebaugh suggests, have changed over time: one of the "Oils" of the seventeenth century was Wood (e.g. Brazil-wood or "pau Brasil"), the Oil of the twentieth century was oil itself, and the Oil of the twenty-first century might become water. "The 'commodification of water,' Sean Cubitt points out, has become a major biopolitical tool in enforcing the regime of the corporate cyborg."[145] In this realm too, aquatic metaphors bubble up to the surface. The "liquidation" of the indigenous commons was performed, as it were, in the name of "liquidity." Indigenous activists in Canada have taken advantage of the fact that Aboriginal and Treaty Rights were never abrogated and thus technically continue in force. Often struggles around oil extraction are inseparable from struggles around water, since oil extraction actually threatens water supplies. Indigenous groups in the Amazon, for example, defend their land rights and resist the oil interests determined to sacrifice the forests in the name of extracting carbon. The protestors at Standing Rock proclaim in response that "water is sacred," a slogan that all human beings, largely composed of water themselves, should readily understand. Robin Wall Kimmerer speaks of women especially as "Keepers of Water": "We carry our babies in internal ponds and they come forth into the world on a wave of water. It is our responsibility to safeguard the water for all our relations."[146]

While classical Marxism is anti-capitalist yet ultimately productivist, the indigenous movements are often more radically anti-capitalist in their assertion not only of their collective right to ancestral communal land but also in their universalizing claim that "mother earth" should never be commodified. Not only were indigenous societies the most likely to have communally owned land—for example, the *allyus* of Andean societies and the *ejidos* of Mexico—they were also the major targets of land confiscation or what in a Western context would be called "enclosure." This commodification of nature at times reaches absurd lengths. The Spanish film *Tambien la Lluvia* (Even the Rain, 2010) counterpoints Columbus's exploitation of the Taínos in the past with the exploitation of the Quechua people by multinational corporations in the present. While the conquistadores lusted after gold, the multinationals crave for water and want to privatize "even the rain"; only the material to be extracted has changed. While classical Marxism is anti-capitalist but ultimately productivist, the Andean "Water Rebellions" were more radically anti-capitalist in their assertion that the commons of "mother earth" should never be privatized. Activists in that struggle spoke of communal forms of politics and what Arturo Escobar calls "the political activation of relational ontologies." In Escobar's account, the activists call for (1) substantive rather than formal democracy, (2) "biocentric" sustainable development, and (3) interculturality in polyethnic societies. The goal is to move beyond capitalism, liberalism, statism, monoculturalism, productivism, Puritanism, and the ideology of growth.[147]

There seems to be no "bottom" to globalized capitalism's desire to monetize everything and thus plunge human relations into an unfeeling cash-nexus world. When a few corporations control the seeds of the planet, we have become hostages to global greed. A situation where the market defines value ends up impoverishing the multitude and enriching the profligate wealthy and corporations. After the rain, what is left for corporate enclosure? What could be more "common" and equally shared, for example, than the milk from a mother's breast, the "lactose commons," as it were. Yet the Trump administration, in league with the baby food corporations like Nestle, argued to World Health officials that breastfeeding in the Global South should be discouraged in favor of the marketing of breast milk substitutes.[148] What is left after breast milk and water are privatized? Only the air. One can imagine a day where the financial elites walk around inside elaborate portable habitats, their own private ecosystem, with supplies of oxygen—reminiscent of those satirical absurdly awkward Yes Men's "survivaballs"—while the rest of us desperately gasp for breath like defenseless wretches biding the pelting of a pitiless world.

In both North and South America, one hears the same devastating critiques of Western capitalist culture from indigenous thinkers. Davi Kopenawa's *The Falling Sky* demonstrates the profound political significance of the abuse of nature. The book takes its title from a creation myth of the Yanomami people. The original primordial world was destroyed by the collapse of the sky, throwing its inhabitants into the underworld. The exposed "back" of the previous sky became the forest canopy where the Yanomami have been sheltered from time immemorial. A new sky was erected on top of foundations set deep in the ground by the demiurge Omama. But chaos threatened and the shamans, with their spiritual allies from the forest, the *xapiri*, try to avert a new apocalypse. This creation story, like the Biblical creation story, or the story of the Flood, speaks in the idiom of myth. Kopenawa sees Europeans and neo-Europeans as having a distant indigenous past which they have forgotten, just as Peter Linebaugh speaks of the English "Charter of the Forest" whose thrust was undermined by the enclosure movement.[149] Naomi Klein also reminds us that many cultures prior to colonialism and capitalism have buried memories of a dimly remembered *communitas* of equality and communal lands.

Davi Kopenawa, unread in official occidental history, offers his own version of the "dialectic of Enlightenment," wherein Whites too began as "guardians of the forest."[150] In early times, he writes, "whites lived like us in the forest … but once they created tools, machines, cars and planes, they became euphoric and said: 'We are the only people to be so ingenious, only we know how to produce machines and merchandise.' That is when they lost all wisdom."[151] Building on his own experience and intuitions, Kopenawa stresses the ecological devastation created by Europeans, first in Europe itself and then in the colonized world: "First they damaged their own land, before going off to work in other lands in order to endlessly create their merchandise. And they never stopped to ask: 'If we destroy the earth, will we be able to create another one?'"[152] Kopenawa's remarks about damaging land evokes the short-lived boom-and-bust "prosperity" in the Americas—the poverty generated by the wealth of Potosi, the extracted gold and diamonds of Minas Gerais, the mined devastation of Appalachia—places where ephemeral prosperity in the long run gave way to immiseration.

For Kopenawa, the demiurge Omama was the source of what whites call "ecology": For Kopenawa, the forest is intelligent and thinks like the Yanomami. "The ecology words were our ancient words, those which Omama gave to our ancestors."[153] It was with the environmental movement, according to Kopenawa, that whites began to listen to indigenous peoples. But for him, words like "environment" and "ecology" are impoverished; they designate only the remainders, that which was left after the destruction of nature. Colonial extractivist modernity, for Kopenawa, constitutes a kind of curse: "We don't want factories, or [artificially created] holes in the ground, nor dirty rivers. We prefer a forest in permanent silence, a clear sky, and a night that really falls where we can really see the stars, unlike the land of the whites, contaminated by the smoky epidemic *xauwara* stretching high into the sky's chest."¹⁵⁴ Significantly, Kopenawa speaks not of "our land"—evocative of private ownership and nation-state boundaries—but rather of the forest, which ignores national borders.

Kopenawa insists that the forest does not belong to the Yanomami; they merely live in it and could never sell it. In fact, Kopenawa also radically rejects the idea of personal property in general. He distinguishes between the ludic practice of trade within what some scholars would call a "gift economy"—the non-commercial exchange of goods—and the hostility to actual long-term possession. Although the Yanomami enjoy trading useful objects, Kopenawa expresses a kind of rage against the very idea of permanent possession. The Yanomami even destroy the possessions of the dead, as if they would bring bad luck. As he explains:

> We don't have personal possessions. I'm an inhabitant of the forest. I don't want to keep merchandise like the whites ... We know that we will die, this is why we easily give our goods away. Since we are mortal, we think it is ugly to cling too firmly to the objects we happen to possess. We do not want to die greedily clutching them in our hands. So we never keep them for very long. We have barely acquired them before we give them to those who might in turn desire them.¹⁵⁵

Kopenawa performs a conceptual defamiliarization of capitalist assumptions. Kopenawa's views on inheritance and the transgenerational transmission of wealth echo those of the Tupinamba who ridiculed Europeans for worrying about legacies for the children since the same abundant nature that nourished the parents would nourish the children. For Kopenawa, "[w]hen a human being dies, his ghost does not carry any of his goods onto the sky's back, even if he is greedy." In an interview with Amy Goodman on "Democracy Now" (December 3, 2019), Kopenawa said that Bolsonaro "will not take any of his wealth beyond the grave, not even his underwear!" In a reference to the ways the laws of inheritance corrupt human relations, Kopenawa notes that whites sometimes rejoice at the death of a relative, in hopes of inheritance, with all human feeling, even familial solidarity, undermined by selfish calculation. The Yanomami, in contrast, destroy possessions precisely in order to avoid the kind of divisiveness that sets brother against sister. One is reminded of the right wing's privileging of inherited wealth by combatting "death taxes," thus catapulting already horrific inequalities into the future. Inheritance is a key factor in creating plutocracy and the huge wealth gap between the 1 percent and the rest, an aspect of the capitalist system that would doubtless strike the Yanomami as profoundly irrational. Nor do the Yanomami believe in divine recompense in the afterlife, a kind of God-given laying up of dividends for eternity, the religious equivalent of an inheritance.

For Kopenawa, whites are virtual slaves of possessions: "We exchange gifts among ourselves to strengthen friendship. If it were any other way, we would mistreat one another without cease because of merchandise."¹⁵⁶ Kopenawa even relates love of merchandise to museological appropriations and what Renato Rosaldo calls "imperial nostalgia"; "Whites love the objects of those people they themselves killed as if they were enemies. And since then, they keep them shut up behind glass in the museums, to show to their children what remains of those who their ancestors killed."¹⁵⁷ For

Kopenawa, the forest is infinitely valuable but not for sale: "All the merchandise of the whites will never be sufficient to compensate the loss of trees, fruits, animals and fishes. Your paper money will never make up for our burned trees, dried up soil, and contaminated waters."[158] In the end, he warns, whites will suffer a kind of poetic justice, to be destroyed by what they themselves had created: "Whites don't understand that when they rip minerals from the earth, they spread a poison that invades the world and from which they themselves will die."[159]

Capitalism versus the Planet

Naomi Klein's *This Changes Everything: Capitalism vs. the Climate* offers multiple examples of indigenous-non-indigenous collaboration.[160] In an epigraph, Klein quotes a very relevant passage from Arundhati Roy (2010), for whom any possible end to capitalism necessarily passes through the indigenous peoples: "The day capitalism is forced to tolerate non-capitalist societies in its midst and to acknowledge limits in its quest for domination, the day it is forced to recognize that its supply of raw materials will not be endless, is the day when change will come."[161] Roy too speaks of a potential "outside of capitalism." The first step toward reimaging our world, she writes, "would be to stop the annihilation of those who have a different imagination—an imagination that is outside of capitalism as well as communism," and also, I would add, outside of the narrow world of that oxymoron "neoliberal democracy."[162] Klein stresses two interrelated points: (1) the prominence of women in the climate change struggle and (2) the key role of indigenous people in these struggles. On the first point, she cites Mohawk midwife Katsi Coo: "At the breast of women, the generations are nourished. From the bodies of women flows the relationship of those generations both to society and to the natural world. In this way is the earth our mother ... in this way we women are earth."[163] On the second point, Klein attended a signing ceremony in December 2011 for the "Save the Fraser Declaration," i.e. the indigenous peoples' declaration to prevent the Northern Gateway Pipeline and other tar sands projects from getting access to British Columbia territory, a declaration signed by 130 First Nations representatives. Marilyn Baptiste, elected chief of Xeni Gwet'in, alluded to an aquatic commons in the form of interconnected bodies of water, calling for all its peoples to join together.[164]

Klein registers a historically novel awareness of the centrality of indigenous resistance to justice everywhere: "What is changing is that many non-Native people are starting to realize that indigenous rights—if aggressively backed by court challenges, direct action, and mass movements ...—may now represent the most powerful barriers protecting all of us from a future of climate chaos."[165] Klein cites journalist Martin Lukacs on the centrality of indigenous struggles: "implementing Indigenous rights on the ground, starting with the United Nations Declaration on the Rights of Indigenous Peoples, could tilt the balance of stewardship over a vast geography, giving Indigenous peoples much more control, and corporations much less."[166] (In this same spirit, rock legend Neil Young kicked off a cross-Canada tour called "Honor the Treaties.") Similar movements and victories have occurred farther South, as in 2005 when the Black Mesa Water Coalition, led by Navajo and Hopi youth, shut down the Mohave Generating

Station as well as the Black Mesa Mine.[167] Klein cites Leanne Betasamosake Simpson on the Anishinaabe systems as "a way of living designed to generate life, not just human life but the life of all living things."[168] What is emerging, according to Klein, is

> a new kind of reproductive rights movement, one fighting not only for the reproductive rights of women, but for the reproductive rights of the planet as a whole—for the decapitated mountains, the drowned valleys, the clear-cut forests, the fracked water tables, the strip-mined hillsides, the poisoned rivers ... All of life has a right to renew, regenerate, and heal itself.[169]

Contemporary *enclosure* forms a direct threat not only to indigenous people—threatened with the loss of their land, streams, biodiversity, and even knowledge—but also to the ecological sustenance of the planet. While indigenous theorists are rightly skeptical about a generic and insufficiently theorized commons and what Glen Sean Coulthard calls "a blanket return to the commons," he also lauds a commons that "belongs to somebody" i.e. entrusted to the care of "the First Peoples of this land." He adds that the Commons "deeply inform and sustain Indigenous modes of thought and behavior that harbor profound insights into the maintenance of relationships within and between human beings and the natural world built on principles of reciprocity, nonexploitation, and respectful coexistence."[170] At the same time, corporate *enclosure* sabotages artistic and political creativity by fencing in the *commons* of artistic ideas and human creativity. In Bolivia and Ecuador, indigenous populations have enshrined the "rights of Mother Earth" creating new legal tales that assert the right of ecosystems not only to exist but to "regenerate."[171] John Mohawk writes that the first principle of indigenous traditional organization is that "nobody owns anything—not the state, not the individual."[172] Robert Nichols, for his part, clears up the common critique of indigenous claims as contradictory, as at once claiming to be the originary owners of land that has been stolen, and that the earth is not something amenable to exclusive proprietary rights. He explains the confusion by appealing to the idea of recursive dispossession, the idea that colonialist discourse is characterized by a self-referential and self-reinforcing logic, whereby the recursive logic of dispossession "produces what it already presupposes." [173] The reign of proprietary logic is thus a product of the world that colonialism shaped. And the native demand for land sovereignty is not about control of the land but rather a different relation to the land, as Mohawk legal scholar Patricia Monture-Angus puts it, the "right to be responsible" to the land.[174] For Leanne Betasamosake Simpson (Michi Saagig Nishnaabeg): "The opposite of dispossession is not possession it is deep, reciprocal, consensual *attachment*... We relate to the land through connection – generative, affirmative, complex, overlapping, and nonlinear *relationship*...The opposite of dispossession within Indigenous thought is grounded normativity."[175]

Summing up, indigenous thinkers in North and South America have revealed to the world an alternative homeland of thought which rejects the doxa of settler-state hegemony and global capitalism. Living, or having lived, or remembering a situation where communal solidarity was the norm, and private property the exception, allows indigenous thinkers to "estrange our capitalist world," to reveal its fundamental self-destructive insanity. As Glenn Coulthard put it in an uncompromising title: "For Our Nations to Live, Capitalism Must Die."[176] Recently contacted indigenous people like the Yanomami, who find the idea of private ownership of land to be absurd, even laughable, offer a glimpse of a psychic and ideational "outside of capitalism." The West, meanwhile, needs to unthink the absurd normalcy of the inordinate privileges of private property and corporate enclosure in the era of climate catastrophe and a global capitalism now both at the zenith of its power and at the end of its rope.

That there exist peoples who find the idea of private ownership profoundly problematic pushes the ideological needle to the left of neoliberal social reformism and fossil-fueled pseudo-democracy. The macro-level claim that "there is no outside of capitalism" is matched on a micro-level with the Thatcherite diktat that "There is no Alternative." But indigenous thought, in its radical traditionalism, suggests the possibilities of critical distance or exotopy. Why should two rich brothers, the proprietary heirs of oil wealth pumped out of indigenous ground, oil which ultimately ends up polluting and heating up the planet, have a right to make our politics oleaginous to the point of dominating our politics through the misnamed "freedom caucus," whose very name "caucus" embeds an Algonquin political memory? Indigenous nature-oriented egalitarianism provides an injection of audacity. Rather than propose a mere tax on oil corporations, it questions the very idea of "owning" a public good such as oil and exploiting it for profit to the detriment of the populace and the planet.

Marx and Engels, Ronald Reagan, and the Bureau of Indian Affairs were not wrong to see many indigenous societies as "socialist"—even though the word has a different meaning for each of them—in assuming that everyone in the community deserves the same access to sustenance and the pleasures of life. Here is a sampling of Leanne Betasamosake Simpson's statements, at once radical and traditional, addressing the issue of an "outside of capitalism": In words that echo with Oswald's "we [Indians] already had communism," she writes:

> I see the dismantling of global capitalism as inseparable from the struggle for Indigenous sovereignty, self-determination, and nationhood ... Indigenous peoples have extremely rich anticapitalist practices in our histories and current realities ... Indigenous peoples in my mind have more experience in anti-capitalism and how that system works than any other group. We have thousands and thousands of years of experience building and living in societies outside of global capitalism. We have hundreds of years of direct experience with the absolute destruction of capitalism with its ... apocalyptic devastation.[177]

Or again: "There is an assumption that socialism and communism are white, and that indigenous peoples don't have this kind of thinking. To me, the opposite is true ... my Ancestors didn't accumulate capital, they accumulated networks of meaningful, deep, fluid, intimate and collective and individual relationships of trust."[178] And again: "'Capital' in our reality isn't capital. We have no such thing as capital. We have relatives. We have clans. We have treaty partners."[179]

An indigenous-based *commons* calls for a deep restructuring to restore the common good. Such utopian ideas, like indigenous social thought, are usually dismissed as utopian, but the function of utopia in social life is similar to that of the alien, the stranger, the *ailleurs*—something which prods us to look in a different direction and reinvent a capacity to imagine alternatives. The point is less the immediate realizability of the proposal than the directionality and potentialities of the critique. Placing the indigenous *commons* at the center of discussion has the capacity to haunt privatizing neoliberalism with the specter of communalizing egalitarianism. The term evokes resistance to "enclosure" in all its forms, from its early proto-capitalist form of fencing in shared European land and the criminalization of traditional uses of the forest, to its colonialist form of appropriating indigenous land, on to its contemporary global capitalist form of the "second enclosure"—that is, the marshaling of juridical "patent" and "intellectual property" to assert the corporate ownership of ideas. In the wake of the fall of communism and the crisis of capitalism, the "*commons*" calls up the planetary struggle to reclaim the "common wealth."

In a crucial intervention, Sheryl Lightfoot points to "the transformative potential of Indigenous rights" as a "subtle revolution" in the global order.[180] She cites Ondandaga Faith-keeper Oren Lyons's comment that the U.N. Indigenous Human Rights Declaration was significant because for the first time "we became human." It was as if he were saying that ever since Sepulveda in 1550 pondered whether "Indians" were animals or human, we have been waiting to be recognized as human, and thus deserving of human rights.[181] Lightfoot questions the binaristic assumption that a nation-state either commits to a deep human rights regime that would include indigenous thinking, or it does not, when in fact many negotiated compromises are possible. The Indigenous rights movement, she argues, is a unique force in global politics which is "reshaping how politics can be done at the U.N. and in other international fora ... practicing global politics that fundamentally differ from predominant state-centric practices."[182]

By drawing on Indigenous ontologies, values, and commitments, global indigenous politics offers a new (old) method of practice in international politics. Unlike a politics that depends on the election cycle, the Indigenous rights movement tends "toward long-term thinking that decisions should be made with the impact of multiple generations in mind."[183] The native concept of consensus implies not a merely numerical electoral victory nor a facile unanimity but rather a deeply negotiated agreement, with respect for all, where the actual vote is merely an afterthought. Among the lessons Lightfoot draws for global postcolonial relations of power are the following: (1) "marginal global actors can forge change in international systems by exposing structural injustice, and boldly, tenaciously demanding change"; (2) a different style of political relations made possible on the global level; and (3) "indigenous rights do not need to be zero-sum vis-à-vis states."[184] Global indigenous rights "[seek] a post-colonialism that is markedly different from that which has come before, because a world that accommodates Indigenous nationhood, Indigenous ontologies, will be a world that is characterized by an entirely different set of values and power relations."[185]

I have tried to suggest that Indigenous thought has always provoked western thinkers to imagine an "outside," not so much a utopia (no-where) but an "elsewhere," whether an elsewhere to monarchy, to capitalism, to Stalinism, or to neoliberal globalization. Indigenous social thought, since Jean de Léry, has prodded the non-indigenous to imagine the "outside" as a potential "inside." Indigenous critique incarnates a temporal paradox: it is very traditional and ancient and, at the same time, very radical and innovative.

Two failures of the imagination haunt our thought; the failure to imagine an end to capitalism, and the failure to imagine the end of the nation-state form. Many consensus native societies have actively rejected the very concept of the nation-state, not because they could not achieve it, but because they did not want it. They speak of sovereign nations and/or of autonomy—but not of nation-states with armies and police. For Georges Sioui, "the notion of people's freedom to arbitrarily divide the land into 'fatherlands' was absent in Aboriginal America."[186] Scott Richard Lyons speaks not of nation-states but of "nation-peoples." Luis Macas (Quechua) asserts boldly asserts that "we indigenous peoples are not 'states' as in 'nation-states.'" Macas claims he is Ecuadoran and Quechua, an ancient people "which existed thousands of years before Ecuador existed."[187] Taiaiake Alfred (Mohawk), like Oswald de Andrade and many others before him, transvalues and reverse-engineers colonialist dicta by asserting as a positive value to the indigenous refusals, of having "no absolute authority, no coercive enforcement of decisions, no hierarchy and no separate ruling entity."[188] Through a transvaluation of signs, what settler-colonial discourse saw as "lacks" becomes a tremendous asset. Indigenous leaders in Brazil utter similar sentiments. Ailton Krenack declares that "we indigenous people do not feel a need for nations-states, countries, armies, and flags."[189] The indigenous rights movement, for Sheryl Lightfoot, constitutes a call to "move beyond the state-centered, individual rights focus of human rights and the existing international system."[190]

Indigenous radicalism also questions the productivism of Marxism, the nomadism of postmodernism, and the constructivism of post-structuralism. Indeed, this process of indigenous questioning has never stopped, and has in fact reached new heights in the present, in the era of climate change and pandemics, when totemic Western keywords like "Progress" and "Civilization" and "Liberal Democracy" have more and more lost their allure, a moment when capitalist "progress" and "development" have been exposed as a kind of planetary death warrant. It is these superimposed crises that have made the non-indigenous world more open, even desperately eager, for indigenous thought.

While Eurocentric commentators see indigenous people as vanished and "behind the times," others see them as "ahead of the curve." Indigenous activists are more and more articulating their own political positions, thus relieving non-natives of the burden, as it were, of speaking for them. Indigenous people and their non-indigenous interlocutors, in sum, have never stopped posing profound questions about culture, nature, property, energy, wealth, and equality. Indigenous thought, in its theoretical and practical manifestations, has thrown up challenges to the nostrums of Marxist, modernist, and postmodernist thought. Trying to regard everything from an indigenous point of view—something the non-indigene can only try—operates a salutary estrangement from the dominant values that the West lives by. It makes us see how capitalist property relations and what DuBois called possessive individualism, so basic to Western culture, virtually guarantees loneliness, aggression, and distrust, turning everyone into a potential competitor within a Hobbesian world. And who could be more Hobbesian than the United States' forty-fifth president—the ultimate

Settler whose wealth is directly and indirectly based on land and the unreality of "real estate"— and for whom the "war of each against each" is to be carried out within the firm, within society, between the sexes, between races and countries, and even within the family. In contrast with the elaborate codes of politeness in many indigenous societies, in political talk shows or press conferences, even conversation becomes a form of war and verbal combat, where the purpose is not to communicate but to aggress, provoke, mislead, dodge, gaslight, and ultimately, to silence. The indigenous "talking stick," designed to allow everyone to speak and not be interrupted, is replaced by talking *as* a stick. The contemporary extreme right offers a hyperbolic version of the perpetual warring and endless acquisitiveness of a social Darwinian society. As usual, the outside of empire comes to infect the inside; the frontier corrupts the center. Indifference to mass-death of indigenous genocide, or to mass death of "others" in Vietnam and Iraq and Afghanistan, prepares the way for indifference to mass-death from Covid in the metropole.

The Transnational Trope of Indigenous Happiness

One of Oswald's innovations, and an indigenous insight, was to dare to see the question of happiness as a political question, linked to the collective effervescence of carnival, the idea that happiness is necessarily trans-individual and intersubjective. Is it an accident that the citizens of the most capitalist, supposedly most advanced society in the world, seem so deeply and irremediably unhappy? White middle-class Americans, surely among the most cushioned and privileged minorities of the planet, are burning with irrational fury, not at those who have power over them, but about the powerless below them on the ladder of advantage. While bemoaning the "discomfort" supposed triggered by "woke" education, they pursue policies that comfort the comfortable and create the physical and emotional discomfort of housing foreclosures, odious debt, and the denial of health care. Rightist media, meanwhile, actively fabricate unhappiness and resentment, fomenting rage for monetary and political gain. People who value property over life, who are obsessed with their "ownership" of a piece of merchandise called a gun, and even speak of "owning" the libs, believe they are entitled to destroy what remains of our already very much shredded and inadequate "democracy." The extreme rightists believe in "replacement theory" that the red, black, brown and Jewish hoards, those who do not "know their place," are trying to "re-place" them. But the haters are the heirs of the real "re-placers" of indigenous peoples in the Americas, those native people who have refused to be "dis-placed," but who do actually know their real place, and know it to be "home." In a historical first, spoiled and entitled people want to overturn a system that has always worked to their advantage. In such a time, taking into account the views of originary peoples like the Yanomami, who find buried metals a "pestilence" rather than a profit-source, who find the idea of private ownership of nature ridiculous, even unthinkable, offers a salutary provocation.

But the question of happiness had been posed long before Oswald de Andrade, during the emergence of the republican revolutions. What I have been calling the trope of Indigenous Happiness is common to various cultural traditions. In his "Remarks

Concerning the Savages of North America"—"savage" being the common term used in the period by both European and North American Enlightenment thinkers—Benjamin Franklin stresses not only his admiration for Indian culture but also Indian scorn for European culture: "Having few artificial Wants, they [Indians] have abundance of leisure for improvement by conversation. Our laborious manner of life, compared with theirs, they esteem slavish and base; and the learning, on which we value ourselves, they regard as frivolous and useless."[191] The Indians, Franklin added, "have never shown any inclination to change their manner of life for ours, or to learn any of our Arts."[192] Perhaps "happiness" is not the most appropriate word, since "happiness" evokes an individual psychic state, usually an ephemeral feeling and a delusion in a life-world necessarily characterized by suffering and death. A more precise approach would focus on collective well-being, a general at-easeness, and the capacity of different social systems to achieve it. "Indian societies," for Franklin, generated more happiness than European cultures. In elegiac tones reminiscent of Montaigne and Rousseau, but anticipating the reactions of many contemporary natives to Western poverty, in words that anticipate those of Kopenawa on observing Western poverty, Franklin writes, "… the sight of so many Rich wallowing in superfluous plenty, whereby so many are kept poor and distress'd for Want, the Insolence of Office … the restraints of custom, all contrive to disgust them with what we call civil Society."[193]

Related to the happiness trope is the idea of societal non-coercion. This motif animates both indigenous and non-indigenous writing. In 1749, administrator Cadwallader Colden, Mohawk adoptee, declared that the Indians had "such absolute Notions of Liberty, that they allow no kind of Superiority of one over another, and banish all Servitude from their territories."[194] Indigenous leaders in North and South America have stressed this motif, as when Taiaiake Alfred contrasts the Western understanding of power as coercion as the imposition of individual will upon others, with a broad indigenous understanding of power as flowing from respect for nature and the modeling of behavior. In "Notes on Virginia," Jefferson remarks, in a complimentary but also somewhat totalizing way, that the natives had never "submitted themselves to any laws, any coercive power and shadow of government."[195] There is a bitter irony in his praise, for in fact it was Jefferson and the American nation-state itself that subjected the Indians to its "laws, coercive power, and shadow of government." Jefferson's conception of freedom was problematic not only because it was not meant to apply to Blacks or Indians or women or non-propertied Whites, but also on its own terms, because of its potentially perverse extrapolations. On the one hand, it opened the way to an idea of permanent revolution, that any government that no longer represented its people should be overturned. The nostrum that "that government is best that governs least" suggests an anarchist endorsement of society without coercion. But the idea of "less-is-more" government has historically opened the way to anti-government paranoia, and even to denunciations of a putative "Deep State." Far from the "society without coercion" instantiated by some indigenous peoples, the idea can transmute into the frontier individualism of "Stand my Ground" and the suspicion of government, where Steve Bannon's "deconstruction of the administrative state" can lead only to the new tyranny of plutocrats, corporations, grift, and white supremacist mobs who think freedom consists in owning and wielding a gun.[196] If as Eric Foner suggests, American history is a debate about the meaning of freedom, it is also a debate about the meaning of "government," "property," and the "general welfare."

Marx and Engels picked up the theme of governments without coercion in their readings of Lewis Henry Morgan's *Ancient Society,* where Morgan (an adopted Iroquois) wrote about the profoundly democratic organization of the "League of the Haudenosaunee." For Marx, the Iroquois meshed a communal economic system with a democratic political organization, thus offering a model of economic equality achieved without state domination. For Engels,

> everything [among the Iroquois] runs smoothly without soldiers, gendarmes, or police, without nobles, kings, governors, prefects or judges, without prisons, without trials … the land is tribal property … there are no poor and needy. The communistic household and the gens know their responsibility toward the aged, the sick and the disabled in war. All are free and equal—including the women.[197]

Speaking more generally, indigenous consensus societies inspired both Marxists and anarchists. While Marxists prized the idea of communal ownership of land, anarchists valorized indigenous societies for their lack of hierarchy, coercion, and authoritarian power. Could it be that the Marxist idea of the "withering away of the state" was linked to such indigenous-linked conceptions? The problem, with Marx and Engels, was their stagist assumption that tribal community culture was a primitive precursor to the nation-state and therefore historically condemned to be "broken" in the name of the dialectics of "progress."[198] Glen Sean Coulthard asks for a more fecund dialogue with Marxism, pointing wisely to two negative trends in the dialogue between Marxists and indigenous theorists: "the premature rejection of Marxism by indigenous scholars on the one side, and the belligerent, often ignorant, and sometimes racist dismissal of Indigenous people's contributions to radical thought and politics by Marxists on the other."[199] Scholars like Maracena Gómez-Barris, meanwhile, speak of "anarcho-feminist indigenous critique" as a "queer decolonial approach" that leads us out of the "impasse that is extractive capitalism."[200]

Coda

Coming full circle, we return to the point where we began, with the "Shaman's Message" to the world, a dramatic instance of the returned gaze of the falsely accused "fierce people." Many of the words and tropes in this rapidly paced 2-minute video clip with flash images come directly from *The Falling Sky*. (The clip is so rapidly edited that it has to be slowed down to note the individual images.) The video offers a whirlwind history of conquest, colonialism, and capitalism. It begins with an interpellation via intertitles, framed as a direct address from a collective "we" of the Yanomami people and more broadly from all the indigenous peoples, to a collective "you," i.e. to the non-indigenous world and particularly Western elites. The interpellation "Hey!" is followed by a whirlwind history of the world and the Yanomami relayed through a quick succession of chronically arranged maps, examples of colonial cartography, beginning with the "capitanias" or land grants distributed by Cabral, moving toward more modern maps, conveying the advance of colonialist capitalism in Brazil. The cartography of domination segues to the words "Look at us!" followed by well-known woodcuts and paintings of indigenous people in Brazil (including a flash glimpse of Kopenawa). The words "We See You" are followed by images of the anti-indigenous Bandeirantes monument in Ibirapoeira Park in São Paulo, by paintings of Cabral and his *caravela*, and by various painted images of "first contact" and military domination, of Indians being hunted and killed, in short a capsule history of genocide. Then the words in segmented and percussive visual presentation: "We-tried-to-show-you" segue to images of the natural beauty and bounty of the Amazon region, with broad rivers and giant rock formations, and the rest of the clause in intertitles "-but-you-never-bothered-to-learn-our-language"—followed by images of indigenous artifacts and handcraft and longhouses.

The following lines literalize a visual leitmotif in the Kopenawa book, the idea that white people are always looking down at the sidewalk— here literalized by images of white people looking down at their cellphones—and not up to the sky. The words become more ominous: "We've been warning you since the beginning," followed by photos and moving images of Amazonian fires; that "the land is alive," shots of waterfalls, rivers, the Yanomami in their *shabono*; then: "This land can't be owned," more forest images. Then the common indigenous acclamation: "This land is us," images of the Yanomami at work and play, along with a graphic match of the circular *shabono* with the planet earth, and the various roots that the Yanomami cook and eat. To clarify that they do not mean that the land belongs to the Yanomami alone, the intertitle adds "[the land is] all of us," which could mean "all of us indigenous peoples" or all people. Successive shots show us the earth as seen from space, followed by "You wanted the stones," illustrated by images of gold and silver from sketches of prospectors plus color images of contemporary mining; followed by flash edits of various forms of gold and silver and the machines that extract them, summarized as "Your shining things," shots of neon lights of Times Square on New Year's Eve; brand names like TDK "your titles," gold bars; and "your flags" your "money," various currencies and "profits," stock market listings. The clause "you called that progress" give way to images of globalized commerce, freighters, and tankers.

The message "We tried to teach you," followed by images of proliferating trash, segues to the charge: "But you've always been too greedy," images of mass production of food, hamburgers, the insignia of Agro business, lumber; and "too primitive," images of garbage dumps, slaughterhouses; and "too savage," images of processed foods "to understand" and "now you still ring curses against the Yanomami," images of blood invading a map of the Yanomami territory, "bring illnesses" microbes and masks and "once again we are dying" and "indigenous land is being turned into ashes," images of forest fires and dead animals, "and mud," mudslides and aerial views of devastated land. The following words have to do with seeing and vision. "For Five centuries," images of Yanomami children with characteristic bird feather headdresses, "you never looked up to see what we were holding in place," images of shamans, Davi Kopenawa, "the sky itself." Images of flooded lands and other forms of devastation, but "your cities can see it," images of traffic and pollution, and "your crops can see it," images of desiccated land and dried up river beds, and, drawing a generational distinction, "your kids can see it," shots of young demonstrators with signs saying "there is only one planet earth." Then a reference to our common breath: "we can see it in your lungs," X-rays of the rib cage. Then an imperative: "Take a deep breath," images of forest fires, and "open your eyes," an exhibit of colorful world cultures, and then images of Oakland Bay Bridge rendered red/orange by the smoke from forest fires, and a final question: "Are you finally ready to see it?" The clip ends with the words: "Help the Yanomami hold up the sky." Sign the petition "Miners Out; Covid Out!"

My suggestion in this book has been that indigenous thinking has helped everyone not only imagine an alternative to capitalism but also try to imagine a way to avoid the destruction of the planet. Brazilian indigenous leader Ailton Krenak expressed this idea in the sad but lucid title of his book *Some Ideas for Postponing the End of the World*. While we cannot *become* indigenous—despite the Deleuzian mandate—we can at least follow the indigenous lead, indigenizing our thinking for their survival and our own. Eduardo Viveiros de Castro, the defender of the philosophical dimension of indigenous thought, reports on a symposium in Manchester, England, where an audience member (who turned out to be Stuart Hall) remarked somewhat skeptically about his talk of "Indian philosophy" that "your Indians seem to have studied in Paris." By his own account, Viveiros de Castro responded to Hall's *boutade* with a *boutade* of his own: "No, in fact exactly the opposite occurred: Parisians went to study with the Indians."[201] In any case, I have tried to show that the West has been "studying with the Indians," ever since French sailor/merchants landed as strangers on indigenous shores. That West, I would suggest, still has a lot to learn.

Notes

1   Eduardo Viveiros de Castro, *Cannibal Metaphysics* (Minneapolis: University of Minnesota Press, 2014), p. 40.
2   The expression is variously attributed to Fredric Jameson and Slavoj Žižek.
3   Kathryn Lehman, "Beyond Academia: Indigenous Media as an Intercultural Resource to Unlearn Nation-State History," *Revistas Tempos e Espacos em Educacao*, Vol. 10 (January–April 2017), pp. 2–40.
4   For an excellent analysis of the Xuxa show, and of the role of the Indian within the Brazilian imaginary generally, see Tracy Devine Guzman, *Native and National in Brazil: Indigeneity after Independence* (Durham: University of North Carolina Press, 2013).
5   Philip J. Deloria, op. cit., p. 184.
6   William Kunstler's memorial took place at The Cathedral of St. John the Divine on November 20, 1995.
7   Sociologist Joanne Nagel attests that between 1960 and 1990, the number of Americans identifying themselves as American Indian on the census tripled. Cited in Sandy Grande, op. cit., p. 153.
8   Leanne Betasamosake Simpson, op. cit., p. 83.
9   See Melissa K. Nelson, ed., *Original Instructions: Indigenous Teachings for a Sustainable Future* (Rochester Vermont: Bear & Company, 2008). Passim.

10   Guillermo Gómez-Peña, *Conversations across Borders* (London: Seagull, 2011), p. 43.
11   Sara Ahmed, *Strange encounters: Embodied others in Postcoloniality* (New York: Routledge, 2000), p. 132.
12   Sara Ahmed, "Phantasies of Becoming (the Other)," *European Journal of Cultural Studies*, Vol. 2, No. 1 (1999), p. 55.
13   Ibid., p. 60.
14   Leanne Betasamosake Simpson, op. cit.
15   Jodi A. Byrd, *The Transit of Empire* (Minneapolis: University of Minnesota Press, 2011), p. 35.
16   Ibid., p. 9.
17   Ibid.
18   Davi Kopenawa and Bruce Albert, *A queda do céu: palavras de um xamã yanomami* (São Paulo: Companhia das Letras, 2015), p. 75.
19   Krenak made the remark on a panel on "Indigenous Cosmologies," held June 10–14, 2020, at The International Literary Festival in Parati (FLIP).
20   Hardt and Negri, op. cit., p. 73.
21   See Melissa A Tatum et al., *Structuring Sovereignty: Constitutions of Native Nations* (Los Angeles, UCLA: American Indian Studies Center, 2014), which provides a kind of toolbox for structuring sovereignty in a nation-state like the United States, hosted and curated by the Native Nations Institute at the University of Arizona and the Harvard Project on American Indian Economic Development, and the Constitutions Resource Center, dedicated to Native nation-building, governance, and leadership. Among the groups that have formulated constitutions are the Haida, the Hopi, the Yaqui, the White Mountain Apache, the Shoshone, the Pequot, the Mohegan, the Standing Rock Sioux, the Cherokee, the Cheyenne-Arapaho, the Commanche, the Delaware, the Kiowa, the Pawnee, the Seminole, the Osage, the Kickapoo, the Spokane, and the Oneida and hundreds of others.
22   Cited in Gerald Vizenor and Jill Doerfler, *The White Earth Nation* (Lincoln: University of Nebraska Press, 2012), p. 63.
23   Ibid., p. 65.
24   Peter Linebaugh, *The Magna Carta Manifesto: Liberties and Commons for All* (Berkeley: University of California Press, 2008).
25   Ibid., p. 6.
26   Ibid., p. 55.
27   Ibid., p. 25.
28   Ibid., p. 72.
29   Ibid., p. 189.
30   Ella Shohat and I first spoke of "Tupi Theory" in a two-part lecture entitled "Tupi or not Tupi a Tupi Theorist" in conjunction with our co-taught seminar at the School of Criticism & Theory, Cornell University, July 17th and July 24th, 2006.
31   Oswald de Andrade, "Cannibalist Manifesto," trans. Leslie Bary, *Latin American Literary Review*, Vol. XIX, No. 38 (July–December 1991).
32   Beatriz Azevedo, *Antropofagia—Palimpsesto Selvagem* (São Paulo: CosacNaify, 2016).
33   Quoted in Robert Nichols, op. cit., p. 16.
34   See Oswald de Andrade, *A Utopia Antropofágica* (São Paulo: Globo, 2001), p. 54.
35   Graeber and Wengrow, op. cit., p. 45.
36   Cited in Lightfoot, op. cit., p. 12.
37   Ibid., p. 33.

38 For more on Patrícia Galvão, see Augusto de Campos, *Pagu—Vida e obra* (São Paulo: Companhia das Letras, 2014).
39 See Oswald de Andrade, "A Marcha das Utopias," in *A Utopia Antropofágico* (São Paulo: Editora Globo, 1990), pp. 161–210.
40 See Oswald de Andrade, "Variacoes sobre o Matriarcado" in *A Utopia Antropofágico* (São Paulo: Editora Globo, 1990), pp. 161–210.
41 Graeber and Wengrow, op. cit., p. 54.
42 Oswald de Andrade, *Poesia, antipoesia, antropofagia* (São Paulo: Cortez & Morães, 1978), p. 204.
43 Leanne B. Simpson, op. cit., pp. 56–7.
44 Cited in Graeber and Wengrow, op. cit., p. 54.
45 Ferretti speaks of Coudreau in his essay "Tropicality, the unruly Atlantic and social utopias: the French explorer Henri Coudreau (1859–1899)," *Singapore Journal of Tropical Geography*, Vol. 38, No. 3 (September 2017). The quotations of Coudreau here are all taken from Ferretti's essay.
46 Cited by Feretti, but from Henri Coudreau, *La France équinoxiale, Vol. I* (Paris: Challemel, 1886), p. 389.
47 Feretti, citing Henri Coudreau, *La France équinoxiale, Vol. II* (Paris: Challemel), p. 397.
48 Feretti, citing. Henri Coudreau, *Chez nos Indiens* [Visiting Our Indians] (Paris: Hachette, 1893).
49 Feretti, citing *Chez nos Indiens*.
50 Ibid.
51 Feretti, citing Henri Coudreau's *La France équinoxiale*.
52 As reported by John Hemming, *People of the Rainforest: the Villas Boas Brothers, Explorers and Humanitarians of the Amazon* (London: Hurst and Company, 2019), p. 111.
53 Ibid., p. 113.
54 Ibid., p. 113.
55 Ibid.
56 Ibid.
57 Viveiros de Castro, "Eduardo Viveiros de Castro: Landed Natives against State and Capital," *Autonomies* (May 8, 2017), https://autonomies.org/2017/05/eduardo-viveiros-de-castro-landed-natives-against-state-and-capital/ republished and translated from the published text on raiz.org 26/07/2016.
58 Ibid.
59 See Alexandre Nodari and Maria Carolina de Almeida Amaral, "A Revista Antropofago," *Direito e Práx*, Vol. 9, No. 4 (Rio de Janeiro, 2018), pp. 2461–502.
60 Oswald de Andrade, "Do Pau-Brasil à Antropofagia e às Utopias," *Obras Completas*, Vol 6. (Rio de Janeiro: Civilização Brasileira, 1978), p. 73.
61 Nodari and de Almeida Amaral, op. cit., https://monoskop.org/images/9/94/Oswald-de-andrade-Obras_Completas-vol6.pdf.
62 Oswald de Andrade, "Do Pau-Brasil à Antropofagia e às Utopias," p. 151.
63 See Sally Roesch Wagner, *The Untold Story of the Iroquois Influence on early Feminists* (New York: Sky Carrier Press, 1996).
64 Ibid.
65 Cited in Robert Nichols, op. cit., p. 85.
66 See Paula Gunn Allen, *The Sacred Hoop: Recovering the Feminine in American Indian Traditions* (Boston: Beacon Press, 1992), p. 213. A related critique has appeared

in the works of American authors, for example in M. A. Jaimes Guerrero, "Savage Hegemony: From 'Endangered Species' to Feminist Indiginism," in Ella Shohat, ed., *Talking Visions: Multicultural Feminism in a Transnational Age* (MIT Press in collaboration with the New Museum, 1998); and M. Guerrero, "'Patriarchal Colonialism' and Indigenism: Implications for Native Feminist Spirituality and Native Womanism," *Hypatia*, Vol. 18, No. 2 (2003), pp. 58–69.

67 Ibid., p. 212.
68 Cited in Sandy Grande, *Red Pedagogy: Native American Social and Political Thought* (Lanham, MD: Rowman and Littlefield, 2004), p. 241.
69 Ibid.
70 Ibid.
71 Ibid., p. 207.
72 See John Mohawk, "Subsistence and Materialism," in Mander and Tauli-Corpuz, op. cit., p. 26.
73 Ibid., p. 27.
74 See Sandy Grande, *Red Pedagogy* (London: Rowman and Littlefield (2015), 10th Anniversary edition), p. 5.
75 Sandy Grande, "Accumulation of the Primitive: The Limits of Liberalism and the Politics of Occupy Wall Street," *Settler Colonial Studies*, Vol. 3, No. 3–4, 369–80, Published online: September 13, 2013.
76 See Eve Tuck and K. Wayne Yang, "Decolonization Is Not a Metaphor," *Decolonization, Indigeneity, & Society*, Vol. 1, No. 1 (2012), pp. 1–40.
77 Ibid., p. 7.
78 Ibid., p. 3.
79 Ibid., p. 16.
80 Ibid., p. 23.
81 Ibid., p. 24. At the same time one might question the stigmatization of metaphor, which has played such a rich role in indigenous thought and art, and the finalization of identity as fixed, with little room for transformation, disidentification, and reaffiliation.
82 Leanne Betasamosake Simpson, op. cit., p. 25.
83 See Glen Sean Coulthard, *Red Skin White Masks: Rejecting the Colonial Politics of Recognition* (Minneapolis: University of Minnesota Press, 2014), p. 153.
84 Quoted in Byrd, op. cit., p. xxxiii.
85 Eric Cheyfitz, "The (Post)Colonial Predicament of Native American Studies," *Interventions*, Vol. 4, No. 3 (2002), p. 406.
86 Ella Shohat and I, both together and individually, have endorsed and ourselves taught many aspects of postcolonial theory while critiquing its blind spots vis-à-vis indigenous peoples since 1992, beginning with Shohat's "Notes on the 'Post-Colonial,'" *Social Text*, Vol. 31–32, Spring 1992, pp. 99–113; continued in *Unthinking Eurocentrism* (first published in 1994), 20th Anniversary 2nd edition, with a co-authored new Afterward Chapter, "Thinking about Unthinking: Twenty Years After," London: Routledge, 2014, pp. 363–436; as well as in "Whence and Whither Postcolonial Theory?" Special focus, "The State of Postcolonial Studies continued—Responses to Dipesh Chakrabarty and Robert Young," *New Literary History*, Vol. 43, No. 2 (Spring 2012), pp. 371–90.
87 See Patrick Wolfe, "The Settler Complex: An Introduction," *American Indian Culture and Research Journal*, Vol. 37, No. 2 (2013), p. 10.

88 See Arif Dirlik, "The Past as Legacy and Project: Postcolonial Criticism in the Perspective of Indigenous Historicism," in Troy Johnson, ed., *Contemporary Native American Political Issues* (Walnut Creek, CA: AltaMira Press, 1999).
89 Sandy Grande, op. cit., p. 145.
90 Dirlik cited in Coulthard, op. cit., p. 98.
91 Dale Turner, *This Is Not a Peace Pipe: Towards a Critical Indigenous Philosophy* (University of Toronto Press, 2006), p. 36.
92 Taiaiake Alfred, *Wasáse: Indigenous Pathways of Action and Freedom* (Peterborough, ON: Broadview Press, 2005), p. 42.
93 Sheryl Lightfoot, op. cit., p. 200.
94 Ibid., p. 201.
95 Ibid., p. 202.
96 See Robert Stam and Ella Shohat, *Race in Translation: Culture Wars around the Postcolonial Atlantic*, for a comparative (complete).
97 Sheryl Lightfoot, *Global Indigenous Politics: A Subtle Revolution* (New York: Routledge, 2016), p. 204.
98 Ibid.
99 Ibid., p. 210.
100 Ibid., p. 211.
101 Ailton has given scores if not hundreds of interviews and talks available on the internet, usually in Portuguese but occasionally with subtitles.
102 Ailton Krenak, *A Vida Não é Útil* (São Paulo: Companhia das Letras, 2020), pp. 83–4.
103 In *Race in Translation*, Ella Shohat and I critique Walter Benn Michaels on this point.
104 Robin Wall Kimmerer, *Braiding Sweetgrass: Indigenous Wisdom, Scientific Knowledge, and the Teachings of Plants*, op. cit., p. 258.
105 See Viveiros de Castro: Interview in the *Nouvel Observateur* (July 10, 2014), https://bibliobs.nouvelobs.com/essais/20140710.OBS3375/et-si-le-temps-etait-venu-de-devenir-indiens.html.
106 Ailton Krenak, op. cit.
107 In conversation in São Paulo in July 2019.
108 Ailton Krenak, *A Vida Não é Útil* (São Paulo: Companhia das Letras, 2020).
109 Ailton Krenak, op. cit.
110 Ibid.
111 Ailton Krenak, *A Vida Não é Útil*, op. Cit., pp. 14–15 (hope it is from the same book?).
112 Ibid., pp. 12–13.
113 Ibid., p. 82.
114 Ibid., p. 80.
115 For more, consult Fred Di Giacomo, "Eleito intelectual do ano, Aílton Krenak ensina: 'A vida não é útil,'" *Universo Online* (October 1, 2020), https://www.uol.com.br/ecoa/colunas/arte-fora-dos-centros/2020/10/01/eleito-intelectual-do-ano-ailton-krenak-ensina-a-vida-nao-e-util.htm?cmpid=copiaecola.
116 See Eduardo Viveiros de Castro, *Metaphysiques Cannibales* (Paris: PUF, 2009), p. 5.
117 See Robert Nichols, op. cit., pp. 106–7.
118 See Elizabeth Cook-Lynn "Who Stole Native American Studies?," *Wicazo Sa Review*, Vol. 12, No. 1 (Spring 1997), pp. 9–28 and Sara C. Heitshu, Thomas H. Marshall, *Native American Studies: A Guide to Reference and Information Sources* (2nd revised edition, Libraries Unlimited, 2009).

119 Michael Greyeyes, "Inside the Machine: Indigeneity, Subversion, and the Academy," *Studies in American Indian Literatures*, Vol. 26, No. 4 (2015), pp. 1–18.
120 See Helen Gilbert et al., op. cit., p. 38. Greyeyes says of his academic experience at York University that he disliked the acting courses but reveled in the "Studies Courses." We know Greyeyes has charmed audiences but he certainly made two academics very happy when he wrote in celebration of his Studies readings: "Foucault! Baudrillard! Shohat! Stam!"
121 "Remarks concerning the Savages of North America, [before January 7, 1784]," *Founders Online*, National Archives, https://founders.archives.gov/documents/Franklin/01-41-02-0280. [Original source: The Papers of Benjamin Franklin, Vol. 41, September 16, 1783, through February 29, 1784, ed. Ellen R. Cohn. New Haven and London: Yale University Press, 2014, pp. 412–23.]
122 Timeu Assurini, "Manifesto de Decolonizacao" https://marytykwawara.github.io/manifesto_decolonizacao
123 Ibid.
124 Ibid.
125 The academy's sometimes extractivist attitudes toward indigenous culture, for Assurini, exist on a continuum with corporations extracting minerals. Knowledge about indigenous people is sometimes exploited by financial "circles of interest" that perpetuate colonization. Scientific knowledge ends up being "harnessed" for the profit motives of corporations, as occurred with the Belo Monte Dam and other development projects in Awaete/Assurini territories. Assurini became acutely aware of this corrupt relationship when he observed Petrobras and Vale engineers giving praise to the Belo Monte project in talks at UFRJ (Federal University of Rio de Janeiro).
126 Timeu Assurini, op. cit.
127 In a parallel discussion, Sheryl Lightfoot asserts that indigenous approaches to research employ a particular set of ethics, protocols, and methodologies, involving three basic principles—reciprocal and respectful relationships, trustworthiness and integrity, and accountability to indigenous communities.
128 Timeu Assurini, op. cit.
129 Jose Jorge de Carvalho and Juliana Flórez-Flórez, "The Meeting of Knowledges: a project for the decolonization of universities in Latin America," *Postcolonial Studies*, Vol. 17, No. 2 (April 2014), pp. 122–39: Decoloniality, Knowledges, and Aesthetics, https://www.tandfonline.com/doi/abs/10.1080/13688790.2014.966411.
130 Ibid.
131 Ibid.
132 In *Race in Translation* (New York: New York University Press, 2012) Ella Shohat and I trace the pattern of Eurocentric academic disciplines which were questioned beginning in the 1960s by what we call the "seismic shift," i.e. the attempted decolonization of various academic disciplines in the United States, France, and Brazil in the wake of decolonization struggles outside of the West and anti-racist struggles within the three zones that we discuss.
133 Jose Jorge de Carvalho and Juliana Florez-Florez, op. cit.
134 Ibid.
135 Ibid.
136 Ibid.
137 Ibid.

138 Leanne Betasamoksake Simpson, *As We Have Always Done* (Minneapolis: University of Minnesota Press, 2017), p. 159.
139 Ibid., p. 171.
140 *Pacificando O Branco: Cosmologias do contato no norte-Amazonico*, Bruce Albert and Alcida Rita Ramos, eds (Marseille: IRD Éditions, 2002).
141 Ibid.
142 Ibid., p. 10.
143 Ibid.
144 Marc Augé, *Le Sens des autres: Actualité de l'anthropologie or Pour une anthropologie des mondes contemporains 1994* (Paris: Aubier, 1994), p. 10.
145 See Sean Cubitt, *Finite Media: Environmental Implications of Digital Technologies* (Durham, NC: Duke University Press, 2017), p. 65.
146 Robin Wall Kimmerer, *Braiding Sweetgrass: Indigenous Wisdom, Scientific Knowledge, and the Teaching of Plants* (Minneapolis: Milkweed, 2013), p. 94.
147 Arturo Escobar, "Latin America at a Crossroads," Lecture at the Center for Latin American and Caribbean Studies at NYU (October 29, 2009).
148 See "U.S. Delegation Disrupts Accord on Breast Milk," *New York Times* (July 9, 2018), and the follow-up article in the NYT on July 10, 2018. The *Times* article pointed out that the marketing of milk substitutes had led to more than 60,000 deaths in low and middle-income countries in the single year of 1981 alone, because the mothers would mix the formula with contaminated water. In the present, the same administration that has separated immigrant mothers from their children, also tries to separate infants from their own mother's milk.
149 Peter Linebaugh, op. cit.
150 While indigenous people speak of "forest islands" or special places within nature, classical European literature spoke of the *locus amoenus,* a beautiful forest utopia.
151 Qouted in Adauto, ed., *A outra margem do Ocidente*, op. cit., p. 20.
152 Ibid.
153 Ibid., p. 480 (please review because I found a similar quote in the falling sky, p. 393).
154 Ibid., pp. 20–1.
155 Ibid., p. 329.
156 Ibid., p. 413.
157 Ibid., p. 429.
158 Ibid., p. 355.
159 Ibid., p. 357.
160 Naomi Klein, *This Changes Everything: Capitalism vs. the Climate* (New York: Simon and Schuster, 2014).
161 Arundhati Roy, "The Trickledown Revolution," *Outlook*, September 20, 2010.
162 Cited Klein, p. 291.
163 Ibid., p. 419.
164 Ibid., p. 345.
165 Ibid., p. 380.
166 Ibid., p. 383.
167 Ibid., p. 398.
168 Ibid., p. 443.
169 Ibid., p. 443.
170 Coulthard, op. cit., p. 12.
171 Naomi Klein, op. cit., p. 444.

172 John Mohawk in Jose Barreiro, op. cit., p. 205.
173 Robert Nichols, op. cit., p. 9.
174 Ibid., p. 29.
175 Simpson, op. cit.
176 See G. Coulthard, "For Our Nations to Live, Capitalism Must Die," *Nations Rising* (November 5, 2013), http://nationsrising.org/for-our-nations-to-live-capitalism-must-die/
177 Leanne Betasamosake Simpson, op. cit., pp. 67–73.
178 Ibid., p. 77.
179 Ibid.
180 See Robert Nichols, op. cit., p. 109.
181 When I was a Fellow at SUNY Buffalo I would occasionally run into Oren Lyons, who was part of the faculty. One time, he was carrying a suitcase and I asked him where he was going, and got an amazing response; "I'm going to the Vatican to ask the Pope to take the word 'pagan' out of Church documents, because that was the word they used to disqualify us."
182 Sheryl Lightfoot, op. cit., p. 72.
183 Ibid., p. 77.
184 Ibid., p. 89.
185 Ibid., p. 200.
186 Georges Sioui, in Gerald McMaster and Lee-Ann Martin, eds., op. cit., p. 67.
187 Luis Macas, in Mander op. cit., p. 42.
188 Taiaiake Alfred, *Peace, Power, Righteousness: An Indigenous Manifest* (Oxford: Oxford University Press, 1999), p. 2.
189 Ibid.
190 Lightfoot, op. cit., p. 33.
191 Johansen, op. cit., p. 85.
192 Ibid., p. 93.
193 Ibid., p. 94.
194 Cited in Mann, op. cit., p. 334.
195 Johansen, op. cit., p. 112.
196 For what it is worth, perhaps because of such perverse view of what constitutes freedom, statistics suggest that the American "pursuit of happiness" has recently been less than successful since the United States now ranks number 19 on the list of happy nations, according to a report produced by the Sustainable Development Solutions Network, a UN initiative. The top three spots this year were occupied by social democratic states—Finland, Denmark and Norway. At the bottom were Afghanistan, Central African Republic and South Sudan.
197 Cited in Johansen, op. cit., p. 123.
198 Research has suggested that Marx's ideas about indigenous people were becoming more nuanced subsequent to these statements. See Lawrence Krader, *The Ethnological Notebooks of Karl Marx* (Assen: The Netherlands, 1974).
199 Glen Sean Coulthard, *Red Skin White Masks* (Minneapolis: University of Minnesota Press, 2014), p. 8.
200 Macarena Gómez-Barris, *The Extractive Zone: Social Ecologies and Decolonial Perspectives* (Durham, NC: Duke University Press, 2017), p. xvi.
201 See Eduardo Viveiros de Castro, "Etnologia Brasileira," in Sergio Miceli, ed., *O Que Ler na Ciencia Social Brasileira (1970–1995)* (São Paulo: Anpocs, 2002), p. 152.

Bibliography

Adam Gilders, "Ich Bin Ein Indianer: Germany's Obsession with a Past It Never Had," *The Walrus* (October 12, 2003), https://thewalrus.ca/ich-bin-ein-indianer/, Accessed April 4, 2022.

Adam Loften and Emmanuel Vaughan-Lee, "Counter Mapping," in *Emergence Magazine* (California, EUA: Kalliopeia Foundation, 2018), https://emergencemagazine.org/story/counter-mapping/.

Adauto Novaes ed., *A Outra Margem do Ocidente* (São Paulo: Companhia das Letras, 1999).

Adrian Tanner, *Bringing Home Animals: Religious Ideology and Mode of Production of the Mistassini Cree Hunters* (New York: St. Martin Press, 1979).

Afonso Arinos de Melo Franco, *O Indio Brasileiro e a Revolucao Francesa: As Origens Brasileiras da Teoria da Bondade Natural* (Rio de Janeiro: Topbooks, 2002).

Afonso Arinos de Melo Franco, *L'Indien Bresilien et la Revolution Francaise*, trans. Monique de Moing (Paris: La Table Ronde, 2005).

Ailton Krenak, *A Vida Não é Útil* (São Paulo: Companhia das Letras, 2020).

Alan Gallay, *The Indian Slave Trade: The Rise of the English Empire in the American South, 1670–1717* (New Haven: Yale University Press, 2002).

Alan Moorhead, *The Fatal Impact: An Account of the Invasion of the South Pacific* (Harmondsworth: Penguin, 1987).

Alberto Mussa, *Meu Destino e Ser Onca* (Rio: Editora Record, 2009).

Alcida Rita Ramos, "Reflecting on the Yanomami: Ethnographic Images and the Pursuit of the Exotic," *Cultural Anthropology*, Vol. 2, No. 3 (1987), pp. 284–304.

Alcida Rita Ramos, "Vozes indígenas: o contato vivido e contado," in *Anuário Antropológico*, 87 (Brasília: Ed. UNB: Tempo Brasileiro, 1990).

Alcida Rita Ramos and Kenneth I. Taylor, "The Yanoama in Brazil," in *Document no. 37* (Copenhagen: International Work Group for Indigenous Affairs, 1979).

Alessandra Santos, "Review of Itão Kuêgü—As Hiper Mulheres—The Hyperwomen," *E-misférica*, Vol. 11, No. 1 (2014), http://archive.hemisphericinstitute.org/hemi/en/emisferica-111-decolonial-gesture/santos, Accessed March 31, 2022.

Alexandre Nodari and Maria Carolina de Almeida Amaral, "A Revista Antropofago," *Direito e Práx*, Vol. 9, No. 4 (Rio de Janeiro, 2018).

Alice Fátima Martins, "As hiper mulheres kuikuro: apontamentos sobre cinema, corpo e performance," *Sociedade e Estado*, Vol. 29, No. 3 (Brasília, September–December, 2014), pp. 747–66.

Amalia Córdova, "After-Effects: Mapping the Experimental Ethnography of Juan Downey in the Invisible Architect," *Brooklyn Rail* (June 2012).

Amalia Córdova, "Reenact, Reimagine: Performative Indigenous Documentaries of Bolivia and Brazil," in *New Documentaries in Latin America*, eds. Vinicius Novarro and Juan Carlos Rodrigues (New York: Palgrave, 2014).

Amalia Cordova, "Healing through Curation: A Conversation between Three Indigenous Image Curators in the Abya Yala Movement," *Senses of Cinema* (December 2018), https://www.sensesofcinema.com/author/amalia-cordova/.

Amy Lonetree, *Decolonizing Museums: Representing Native America in National and Tribal Museums* (Chapel Hill: University of North Carolina Press, 2012).

Ana Gabriela Morim de Lima, *Hoxwa: Imagens do Corpo, do Riso e do Outro Uma Abordagem Etnografica dos Palhacos Ceremoniais Kraho* (Masters thesis for UFRJ, Rio de Janeiro, 2010).

André Brasil, "Bicicletas de Nhanderu: lascas do extracampo," *Devires: Cinema e Humanidades*, Vol. 9, No. 1 (2012), pp. 101–117.

Andre Brasil, "Tikmũ'ũn's Caterpillar-Cinema: Off-Screen Space and Cosmopolitics in Amerindian Film," in *Space and Subjectivity in Contemporary Brazilian Cinema*, eds. Antônio Márcio da Silva and Mariana Cunha (Belo Horizonte, Brazil: Palgrave Macmillan, 2017), pp. 23–39.

André Brasil and Bernard Belisario, "Desmanchar o Cinema: Variações do fora-de-campo em Filmes Indígenas," *Sociologia and Antropologia*, Vol. 6, No. 3 (Rio de Janeiro September/December 2016), https://www.scielo.br/scielo.php?script=sci_arttext&pid=S2238-38752016000300601&lng=pt&tlng=pt, Accessed April 4, 2022.

André Breton, "Second Manifesto of Surrealism (1930)," in *Manifestoes of Surrealism*, trans. Richard Seaver and Helen R. Lane (Ann Arbor: University of Michigan Press, 1972).

André Gaudreault, *Du littéraire au filmique: Système du récit* (Paris and Quebec City: Armand Colin/Nota bene, 1999, revised and expanded 2nd edition, with afterword entitled "Le cinéma: entre littérarité et intermédialité").

Anibal Quijano, "Coloniality of Power, Eurocentrism and Latin America," in *Nepantla: Views from the South*, No. 3 (Durham, NC: Duke University Press, 2000), pp. 533–80.

Annette Kolodny, *The Lay of the Land: Metaphor as Experience and History in American Life and Letters* (Chapel Hill: University of North Carolina Press, 1975).

Antônio Brand, "'Quando Chegou esses que são Nossos Contrários': A Ocupação Espacial e o Processo de Confinamento dos Kaiowá/Guarani no Mato Grosso do Sul," *Multitemas*, Vol. 12 (1998), pp. 21–51.

Antonio A. R. Ioris, "Political Agency of Indigenous Peoples: The Guarani-Kaiowá's fight for Survival and Recognition," in *Vibrant: Virtual Brazilian Anthropology*, Vol. 16 (Brasília, 2019) (Epub October 17, 2019).

Antonio Callado, *The Montaigne Expedition* (Rio de Janeiro: Nova Fronteira, 1982).

Antonio Negri and Michael Hardt, *Declaração: Isto Não É Um Manifesto* (São Paulo: SIP, 2016).

Aparecida Vilaca, "Fazendo corpos: reflexões sobre morte e canibalismoentre os Wari' à luz do perspectivismo," *Revista de Antropologia*, Vol. 41, No. 1 (São Paulo, 1998).

Arif Dirlik, "The Past as Legacy and Project: Postcolonial Criticism in the Perspective of Indigenous Historicism," in *Contemporary Native American Political Issues*, ed. Troy Johnson (Walnut Creek, CA: AltaMira Press, 1999), pp. 73–92.

Aristóteles Barcelos Neto, Danilo Ramos, Maíra Santi Buhler, Renato Sztutman, Stelia Marras, Valeria Macedo, "Abaeté, rede de antropologia simétrica: entrevista com Marcio Goldman e Eduardo Viveiros de Castro," *Cadernos de Campo*, Vol. 15, No. 14–15 (2006).

Arthur Rimbaud, *Rimbaud: The Works, A Season in Hell; Poems & Prose; Illuminations*, trans. Dennis Carlile (Indiana, U.S.: Xlibris, 2001).

Arturo Escobar, "Latin America at a Crossroads," Lecture at the Center for Latin American and Carribean Studies at NYU (October 29, 2009).

Arturo Escobar, *Pluriversal Politics: The Real and the Possible* (Durham: Duke University Press, 2020).
Arturo Escobar, *Designs for the Pluriverse: Radical Interdependence, Autonomy, and the Making of Worlds* (Durham, NC: Duke University Press, 2018).
Arundhati Roy, "The Trickledown Revolution," *Outlook* (September 20, 2010).
Audra Simpson, *Mohawk Interruptus: Political Life across the Borders of Settler States* (Durham: Duke University Press, 2014).
Augusto de Campos, *Pagu—Vida e obra* (São Paulo: Companhia das Letras, 2014).
Barbara Browning, *Caetano Veloso's A Foreign Sound* (London: Bloomsbury, 2017).
Barbara Christian, paper presented at the Gender and Colonialism Conference at the University of California, Berkeley (October, 1989).
Beatriz Azevedo, *Antropofagia—Palimpsesto Selvagem* (São Paulo: CosacNaify, 2016).
Beatriz Azevedo and Laura Francis, "Será esse o futuro do século XXI ?" *Das Questoes*, Vol. 11, No. 1 (UNB Universidade de Brasília, April 2021).
Beatriz Miranda, "'The way I am is an outrage': The Indigenous Brazilian Musicians Taking Back a Burning Country," *The Guardian* (October 26, 2020), https://www.theguardian.com/music/2020/oct/26/brazil-music-indigenous-tribes-environment-bolsonaro, Accessed March 31, 2022.
Beatriz Perrone-Moises, "Relacoes Preciosas: Franceses e Ameríndios no Seculo xvii" (Doctoral Thesis, University of São Paulo, 1996).
Benedito Nunes, *Oswald Cannibal* (São Paulo: Perspectiva, 1979).
Beth A. Conklin, *Consuming Grief: Compassionate Cannibalism in an Amazonian Society* (Austin: University of Texas, 2001).
Benoît de L'Estoile, *Le Goût des Autres: De L'exposition coloniale aux Arts Premiers* (Paris: Flammarion, 2007).
Bernard Belisario, "As Hipermulheres: cinema e ritual entre mulheres, homens e espíritos," (M.A. thesis for Belo Horizonte: Universidade Federal de Minas Gerais, Faculdade de Filosofia e Ciências Humanas, 2014).
Bernard Belisario, "Resonancias entre cinema, cantos e corpos no filme: As Hipermulheres," *Galáxia*, Vol. 32 (São Paulo, May–August 2016), https://doi.org/10.1590/1982-25542016223451, Accessed March 31, 2022.
Bernard Belisario's doctoral thesis on Xavánte film, 'Desmanchar o cinema: pesquisa com filmes Xavante no Waia Rini" (Universidade Federal de Minas Gerais, Faculdade de Filosofia e Ciências Humanas, 2018), http://hdl.handle.net/1843/BUBD-AWFLDS, Accessed April 4, 2022.
Binot Paulmier de Gonneville, *Le Voyage e Gonneville (1503–1505): et la decouvere de la Normandie par les Indiens du Bresil*, trans. Ariane Witkowski (Paris: Chandeigne, 1995).
Brian R. Ferguson, *Yanomami Warfare: A Political History* (Santa Fe, NM: School of American Research Press, 1995).
Bruce Albert and Alcida Ramos eds., *Pacificando os Brancos: Cosmologias do contato no norte-Amazonico* (IRD Éditions, São Paulo: Emprensa Oficial SP/Unesp, 2002).
Bruce E. Johansen, *Forgotten Founders: Benjamin Franklin, the Iroquois, and the Rationale for the American Revolution* (Ipswich, MA: Gambit Incorporated Publishers, 1982).
Bruno Franchetto, "O que se Sabe Sobre as Linguas Indigenas no Brasil," in *Povos Indígenas no Brasil 1996/2000*, ed. Carlos Alberto Ricardo (São Paulo: Instituto SocioAmbiental, 2000).
Caetano Veloso, *Verdade Tropical* (São Paulo: Companhia das Letras, 1997).

Caetano Veloso, *Tropical Truth: A Story of Music and Revolution in Brazil*, trans. Isabel de Sena (New York: Da Capo Press, 2003).
Caio de Salvi Lazaneo, "Produção Partilhada do Conhecimento: Uma experiência comas comunidades indígenas Xavante e Karajá," Masters Dissertation with the School of Communications at University of São Paulo, https://www.teses.usp.br/teses/disponiveis/27/27152/tde-21052013-120828/pt-br.php, Accessed April 4, 2022.
"Can Our Culture Survive Climate Change?" in a special section "The Amazon Has Seen Our Future," *New York Times* (October 3, 2020), https://www.nytimes.com/2020/10/02/opinion/amazon-indigenous-people-brazil.html. Accessed March 31, 2022.
Carlo Severi, *The Chimera Principle: An Anthropology of Memory and Imagination*, trans. Janet Lloyd (Chicago: HAU Books, 2015).
Carlos Fausto, "A Inimizade: Forma e Simbolismo da Guerra Indigena," in *A Outra Margem do Ocidente*, ed. Adauto Novaes (São Paulo: Companhia das Letras, 1999).
Carlos Fausto, *Warfare and Shamanism in Amazonia*, trans. David Rodgers (Cambridge: Cambridge University Press, 2001).
Carlos Fausto, *Art Effects: Image, Agency, and Ritual in Amazonia*, trans. David Rodgers (Lincoln: University of Nebraska Press, 2020).
Cássio dos Santos Tomaim and Valquiria Rodrigues Reis Tomaim, "O estranhamento como matriz estética em Brava Gente Brasileira, de Lúcia Murat," *Diálogos* (Maringá. Online), Vol. 17, No. 3 (Maringá, Brasil: Universidade Estadual de Maringá, September-December, 2013), https://www.redalyc.org/pdf/3055/305529845017.pdf, Accessed March 31, 2022.
César Guimaraes and Ruben Caixeta, "Apresentação," *Devires: Cinema e Humanidades*, Vol. 1, No. 1 (Belo Horizonte, July/December 2003), pp. 6–9.
Chadwick Allen, *Blood Narrative: Indigenous Identity in American Indian and Maori Literary and Activist Texts* (Durham: Duke University Press, 2000).
Chadwick Allen, *Trans-Indigenous: Methodologies for Global Native Literary Studies* (Minneapolis: University of Minnesota, 2012).
Christian F. Feest ed., *Indians and Europe: An Interdisciplinary Collection of Essays* (Lincoln and London: University of Nebraska Press, 1999).
Christopher Frayling, *Spaghetti Westerns: Cowboys and Europeans from Karl May to Sergio Leone* (Revised paperback edition) (London and New York: I.B. Tauris, 2006).
Cibele Tenório, "Indígenas inspiradoras: conheça a história de cinco mulheres," *EBC* (April 19, 2016), https://memoria.ebc.com.br/cidadania/2016/04/dia-do-indio-cinco-historias-de-mulheres-inspiradoras, Accessed March 22, 2022.
Clarisse Alvarenga, *Da Cena do Contato ao Inacabamento da história* (From the Scene of Contact to the Unfinishedness of History) (Salvador, Bahia: UDUFBA, 2017).
Clarisse Alvarenga and Bernard Belisário, "O cinema-processo de Vincent Carelli em Corumbiara," in *Limiar e partilha: uma experiência com filmes brasileiros*, eds. Roberta Veiga, Carla Maia and Victor Guimarães (Belo Horizonte: PPGCOM UFMG, 2015).
Claude Lévi-Strauss, *Tristes Tropiques* (Librairie Plon, 1955; New York: Penguin, 1973; São Paulo: Companhia das Letras, 1996).
Claude Lévi-Strauss, *The View from Afar*, trans. Joachim Neugroschel and Phoebe Hoss (New York: Basic Books, 1984).
Claude Lévi-Strauss, "New York Post et Prefiguratif," in *Le Regard Eloigne* (Paris: Plon, 1955, new edition 1993).
Claude Lévi-Strauss, *O pensamento selvagem* (Campinas, São Paulo: Papirus, 1997).
Claude Lévi-Strauss, *Loin de Bresil* (Paris: Chandeigne, 2005).
Claude Lévi-strauss and D. Eribon, *De près et de loin* (Paris: Odile Jacob, 1988).

Cláudia Mesquita, "Retratos em diálogo: notas sobre o documentário brasileiro recente," *Revista Novos estudos—Cebrap* (March 2010).

Cláudia Mesquita, "Obra em processo ou processo como obra?" in *Cinema Brasileiro Anos 2000: 10 questões*, eds. Cleber Eduardo (Eduardo Valente and João Luiz Vieira, 2011).

Colleen Connolly, "The True Native New Yorkers Can Never Truly Reclaim Their Homeland," *Smithsonian Magazine* (October 5, 2018), https://www.smithsonianmag.com/history/true-native-new-yorkers-can-never-truly-reclaim-their-homeland-180970472/, Accessed March 31, 2022.

Corinn Columpar, *Unsettling Sights: The Fourth World on Film* (Carbondale: Southern Illinois University Press, 2010).

Dakshana Bascaramurty, "The Modern Touch of an Old Master." *The Globe and the Mail* (December 1, 2017), https://www.theglobeandmail.com/arts/inside-the-process-behind-kent-monkmans-art/article37126241/, Accessed April 4, 2022.

Dale Turner, *This Is Not a Peace Pipe: Towards a Critical Indigenous Philosophy* (Toronto: University of Toronto Press, 2006).

Damien Short, *Redefining Genocide: Settler Colonialism, Social Death and Ecocide* (London: Zed Books, 2016).

Daniel Coleman, "Canadian White Civility and the Two Row Wampum of the Six Nations," in *Narratives of Citizenship: Indigenous and Diasporic Peoples Unsettle the Nation State*, eds. Aloys N. M. Fleischmann, Nancy Van Styvendale and Cody McCarroll (Edmonton: University of Alberta Press, 2011).

Daniel Defoe, *Robinson Crusoe* (London and Cambridge: Macmillan & Co., 1866).

Daniela Fernandes Alarcon, *O retorno da terra: as retomadas na aldeia Tupinambá da Serra do Padeiro, sul da Bahia* (São Paulo: Elefante Editora, 2019).

Darcy Ribeiro, *Kadiwéu: Ensaios Etnológicos sobre o Saber, o Azar e a Beleza* (Rio de Janeiro: Global Editora, 2019).

Darlene J. Sadler, *Nelson Pereira dos Santos* (Urbana: University of Illinois Press, 2003).

Davi Kopenawa, "A Yanomami Leader Speaks: A Message from Davi Kopenawa Yanomami," *Anthropology Newsletter*, transcribed by Bruce Albert and translated by Terry Turner (September 1991).

Davi Kopenawa and Bruce Albert, *La chute du ciel: Paroles d'un chaman yanomami* (Paris: Plon, 2010).

Davi Kopenawa and Bruce Albert, *The Falling Sky: Words of a Yanomami Shaman*, trans. to English by Nicholas Elliott and Alison Dundy (Cambridge: Harvard University Press, 2013).

Davi Kopenawa and Bruce Albert, *A queda do céu: Palavras de um xamã yanomami*, trans. to Portuguese by Beatriz Perrone-Moisés (São Paulo: Companhia das Letras, 2015).

David Graeber and David Wengrow, *The Dawn of Everything: A New History of Humanity* (New York: Farrar Strauss and Giroux, 2021).

David Hajdu, "His Kind of River," *New York Times* (20 March 2009), http://www.nytimes.com/2009/03/22/nyregion/thecity/22rive.html?_r=0, Accessed March 31, 2022.

David Wallace Adams, *Education for Extinction: American Indians and the Boarding School Experience, 1875–1928* (Lawrence: University Press of Kansas, 1997).

Debora Herszenhut's Masters Dissertation at the Federal University of Rio de Janeiro, defended in 2014, and entitled "Militância, performance e devires imagéticos: o cinema indígena brasileiro através das três décadas do projeto vídeo nas aldeias," https://www.academia.edu/39198587/MILIT%C3%82NCIA_PERFORMANCE_E_DEVIRES_IMAG%C3%89TICOS_O_CINEMA_IND%C3%8DGENA_

BRASILEIRO_ATRAV%C3%89S_DAS_TR%C3%8AS_D%C3%89CADAS_DO_PROJETO_V%C3%8DDEO_NAS_ALDEIAS, Accessed April 4, 2022.
Deborah Danowski and Eduardo Viveiros de Castro, *Ha Mundo por Vir? Ensaio sobre os Medos e os Fins* (Is there a World to Come? Essay on Fears and Ends) (São Paulo and Florianópolis: Cultura e Barbárie and Instituto Socioambiental, 2014).
Diana Taylor, *The Archive and the Repertoire* (Durham: Duke University Press, 2003).
Djelal Kadir, *Columbus and the Ends of the Earth: Europe's Prophetic Rhetoric as Conquering Ideology* (Berkeley: University of California Press, 1992).
Don Philips, 'We are Facing Extermination: Brazil Losing a Generation of Indigenous Leaders to Covid-19,' *New York Times* (June 21, 2020).
Donald Grinde Jr. and Bruce E. Johansen, *Exemplar of Liberty: Native America and the Evolution of Democracy* (Los Angeles: American Indian Study Center, University of California, 1991).
Doris Sommer, *Foundational Fictions: The National Romances of Latin America* (Berkeley: University of California Press, 1991).
Dustin Tahmahkera, *Tribal Television: Viewing Native People in Sitcoms* (Chapel Hill: University of North Carolina Press, 2014).
Edward Shanken, "Broken Circle &/Spiral Hill?: Smithson's Spirals, Pataphysics, Syzygy and Survival," *Technoetic Arts: A Journal of Speculative Research*, Vol. 11, No. 1 (2013).
Édouart Glissant, *The Poetics of Relation* (Ann Arbor: University of Michigan, 1997).
Eduardo Kohn, *How Forests Think: Toward an Anthropology Beyond the Human* (Berkeley: University of California Press, 2013).
Eduardo Victorio Morettin, *Humberto Mauro, Cinema, História* (São Paulo: Alameda, 2013).
Eduardo Viveiros de Castro, *Araweté: Os Deuses Canibais* (Rio de Janeiro: Jorge Zahar, 1986).
Eduardo Viveiros de Castro, *Cosmological Perspectivism in Amazonia and Elsewhere, Four Lectures given in the Department of Social Anthropology*, University of Cambridge, February–March 1998 (HAU Masterclass Series, 2012).
Eduardo Viveiros de Castro, *From the Enemy's Point of View: Humanity and Divinity in an Amazonian Society*, trans. Catherine V. Howard (Chicago: University of Chicago Press, 1992).
Eduardo Viveiros de Castro, "Os pronomes cosmológicos e o perspectivismo ameríndio," *Mana*, Vol. 2, No. 2 (1996).
Eduardo Viveiros de Castro, "Etnologia Brasileira," in *O Que Ler na Ciencia Social Brasileira (1970–1995)*, ed. Sergio Miceli (São Paulo: Anpocs, 2002).
Eduardo Viveiros de Castro, "No Brasil todo mundo é índio, exceto quem não é," in *Povos indígenas no Brasil 1996/2000*, ed. Carlos Alberto Ricardo (São Paulo: Instituto Socioambiental, 2006).
Eduardo Viveiros de Castro, *Metaphysiques Cannibales* (Paris: PUF, 2009).
Eduardo Viveiros de Castro, *Cannibal Metaphysics*, ed. and trans. Peter Skafish (Minneapolis: Minnesota University Press, 2014).
Eduardo Viveiros de Castro, "Eduardo Viveiros de Castro: Landed Natives against State and Capital," *Autonomies* (May 8, 2017), https://autonomies.org/2017/05/eduardo-viveiros-de-castro-landed-natives-against-state-and-capital/ republished and translated from the published text on raiz.org 26/07/2016.
Edwin G. Burrows and Mike Wallace, *Gotham: A History of New York City to 1898* (New York: Oxford, 1999).
Elizabeth Bird, "Gendered Construction of the American Indian in Popular Media," *Journal of Communication*, Vol. 49, No. 3 (September 1999).

Elizabeth Cook-Lynn, "Who Stole Native American Studies?" *Wicazo Sa Review*, Vol. 12, No. 1 (Spring 1997).
Elizabeth Pochoda, "A Native Perspective at the Met," *New York Times* (July 11, 2021).
Ella Shohat, *Israeli Cinema: East/West, and the Politics of Representation* (Austin: University of Texas Press, first published in 1989 and reprinted with a new Afterward in 2010).
Ella Shohat, "Ethnicities-in-Relation: Toward a Multi-Cultural Reading of American Cinema," *Unspeakable Images: Ethnicity and the American Cinema*, ed. Lester Friedman (University of Illinois Press, 1991).
Ella Shohat, "Notes on the 'Post-Colonial,'" *Social Text*, Vol. 31–32, Spring 1992.
Ella Shohat and Robert Stam, *Unthinking Eurocentrism: Multiculturalism and the Media* (New York: Routledge, 1994, and 20th Anniversary 2nd edition, with a co-authored new Afterward Chapter, "Thinking about Unthinking: Twenty Years After," London: Routledge, 2014).
Ella Shohat and Robert Stam eds., *Multiculturalism, Postcoloniality, and Transnational Media* (New Brunswick: Rutgers University Press, 2003).
Ella Shohat and Robert Stam, *Race in Translation: Culture Wars in the Postcolonial Atlantic* (New York: New York University Press, 2012).
Ella Shohat and Robert Stam, "Whence and Whither Postcolonial Theory?" Special focus, The State of Postcolonial Studies continued—Responses to Dipesh Chakrabarty and Robert Young, *New Literary History*, Vol. 43, No. 2 (Spring 2012).
Els Lagrou, "Rir do poder e o poder do riso nas narrativas e performances Kaxinawa," in *Revista da Antropologia*, Vol. 49. No. 1 (São Paulo: USP, 2006).
Els Lagrou, *A fluidez da forma: arte, alteridade e agência em uma sociedade amazônica* (Rio De Janeiro: Topbooks, 2007).
Emannuel Bento, "Coletivo de cinema indígena de Pernambuco faz campanha para contar histórias sem estereótipos," *Diario de Pernambuco* (Published April 27, 2019 and updated August 6, 2020), https://www.diariodepernambuco.com.br/noticia/viver/2019/04/coletivo-de-cinema-indigena-de-pernambuco-faz-campanha-para-contar-his.html, Accessed March 31, 2022.
Emma LaRocke, *When the Other Is Me: Native Resistance Discourse, 1850–1990* (Winnipeg: University of Manitoba Press, 2010).
Emma Marris, *Wild Souls: Freedom and Flourishing in the non-Human World* (New York: Bloomsbury, 2021).
Emma Mitchell, "Seeing Blue: Negotiating the Politics of Avatar Media Activism," originally a thesis submitted in partial fulfillment of the requirement for an Honours degree in the Department of Gender and Cultural Studies, University of Sydney, October 2011. https://core.ac.uk/download/pdf/41235981.pdf.
Eric Aeschimann, "Et si le temps était venu de 'devenir indiens'?" *Nouvel Observateur* (July 10, 2014), https://bibliobs.nouvelobs.com/essais/20140710.OBS3375/et-si-le-temps-etait-venu-de-devenir-indiens.html, Accessed April 4, 2022.
Eric Cheyfitz, "The (Post)Colonial Predicament of Native American Studies." *Interventions* Vol. 4, No. 3 (2002).
Eric Michaels, "How to Look at Us Looking at the Yanomami Looking at Us," in *A Crack in the Mirror: Reflexive Perspectives in Anthropology*, ed. Jay Ruby (Philadelphia: University of Pennsylvania Press, 1982).
Eric Sanderson, *Manahatta: A Natural History of New York* (New York: Abrams, 2013).
Eve Tuck and K. Wayne Yang, "Decolonization Is Not a Metaphor," *Decolonization, Indigeneity, Education & Society*, Vol. 1, No. 1 (2012), pp. 1–40.

"Evo Morales Praises Avatar," *Huffington Post* (January 12, 2010), http://www.huffingtonpost.com/2010/01/12/evo-morales-praises-avata_n_420663.html, Accessed March 7, 2010.

Faye Ginsburg, "Indigenous Media: Faustian Contract or Global Village," *Cultural Anthropology*, Vol. 6, No. 1 (1991).

Faye Ginsburg, "Aboriginal Media and the Australian Imaginary," *Public Culture*, Vol. 5, No. 3 (Spring 1993).

Faye Ginsburg, "Australia's Indigenous New Wave: Future Imaginaries in Recent Aboriginal Feature Film," (Adrian Gerbrands Lecture, May 29, 2012).

Faye Ginsburg, "Indigenous Media from U-matic to YouTube," *Sociologia and Anhtropologia*, Vol 6, No. 3 (2016).

Federico Ferretti, "Tropicality, the Unruly Atlantic and Social Utopias: The French Explorer Henri Coudreau (1859–1899)," *Singapore Journal of Tropical Geography*, Vol. 38, No. 3 (September 2017).

Felipe Fernández-Arnesto, *1492: The Year the World Began* (New York: Harper One, 2010).

Félix S. Cohen, "Americanizing the White Man," *The American Scholar*, Vol. 21, No. 2 (1952).

Félix S. Cohen, *Handbook of Federal Indian Law* (Washington, DC: Department of the Interior, 1942 reissue of the original by Albuquerque: University of New Mexico Press, 1968).

Ferdinand Denis, "Resumo da História Literária do Brasil," in *Paradise Betrayed: Brazilian Literature of the Indian*, ed. David Brookshaw (Amsterdam: CEDLA, 1988).

Fernao Ramos, *Historia do Cinema Brasileiro* (Porto Alegre: Martins Livreiro, 1987).

Florent Guenard, "Rousseau, l'homme sauvage et les Indiens d'Amérique," in *Un continent en partage: Cinq siècles de rencontres entre Amérindiens et Français*, eds. Gilles Havard and Mickaël Augeron (Paris: Les Indes Savantes, 2013).

Florestan Fernandes, *A Organização Social dos Tupinambá* (São Paulo: Instituto Progresso Editorial, 1949).

Frank Lestringant, "Tristes tropistes: Du Brésil à la France, une controverse à l'aube des guerres de religion," *Revue de l'histoire des religions*, Vol. 202, No. 3 (1985), https://www.persee.fr/doc/rhr_0035-1423_1985_num_202_3_2710, Accessed March 31, 2022.

Frank Lestringant, *Jean de Léry ou l'invention du sauvage: Essai sur l'Histoire d'un voyage faict en la terre du Bresil* (Paris: Honoré Champion, 1991).

Frank Lestringant, "The Myth of the Indian Monarchy: An Aspect of the Controversy between Thévet and Léry (1575–1585)," in *Indians and Europe: An Interdisciplinary Collection of Essays*, ed. Christian F. Feest (Lincoln and London: University of Nebraska Press, 1999).

Frank Lestringant, *Le Huguenot et le Sauvage: L'Amérique et la controverse coloniale, en France, au temps des guerres de Religion (1555–1589)* (Geneva: Librarie Droz, 2004).

Frank Lestringant, "La mémoire de la France Antarctique," *História* (São Paulo), Vol. 27, No. 1, Franca (2008), http://dx.doi.org/10.1590/S0101-90742008000100007.

Franz Kafka, "The Wish to Be a Red Indian," in *Meditations, 1904–1912* (Leipzig: Rowohlt, 1913).

Fred Di Giacomo, "Eleito intelectual do ano, Aílton Krenak ensina: 'A vida não é útil,'" *Universo Online* (October 1, 2020), https://www.uol.com.br/ecoa/colunas/arte-fora-dos-centros/2020/10/01/eleito-intelectual-do-ano-ailton-krenak-ensina-a-vida-nao-e-util.htm?cmpid=copiaecola, Accessed April 4, 2022.

Freya Schiwy, *Indianizing Film: Decolonization, the Andes, and the Question of Technology* (New Brunswick: Rutgers University Press, 2009).
Friedrich Nietzche, "On the Uses and Disadvantages of History for Life," in *Untimely Meditations*, eds. Daniel Breazeale, trans. R. J. Hollingdale (Cambridge: Cambridge University Press, 1997; 2012), pp. 57–124.
Gabriel Garcia Marquez, *One Hundred Years of Solitude* (New York: Avon, 1971).
Gabriel Leao, "Brazil's Indigenous Gaming Scene Is On," *Wired* (March 12, 2022) https://www.wired.com/story/brazil-indigenous-gaming-arani/, Accessed March 31, 2022.
Gerald Vizenor, "Transethnic Anthropologism: Comparative Ethnic Studies at Berkeley," *Studies in American Indian Literatures*, Vol. 7, No. 4 (University of Nebraska Press, 1995), http://www.jstor.org/stable/20736879, Accessed March 31, 2022.
Gerald Vizenor, *Fugitive Poses: Native American Scenes of Absence and Presence* (Lincoln: University of Nebraska Press, 1998).
Gerald Vizenor, *Manifest Manners: Narratives on Postindian Survivance* (Lincoln and London: University of Nebraska Press, 1999).
Gerald Vizenor and Jill Doerfler, *The White Earth Nation* (Lincoln: University of Nebraska Press, 2012).
Georg W. F. Hegel, *The Philosophy of History* (Mineola, NY: Dover, 1956).
Georg W. F. Hegel, *Lectures on the Philosophy of World History*, translated from the German edition of Johannes Hoffmeister from Hegel papers assembled by H. B. Nisbet (New York: Cambridge University Press, 1975).
Georges E. Sioui, *Pour Une Auto-Histoire Amerindienne* (Quebec City: Presse de l'Universite Laval, 1989).
Georges E. Sioui, *For an American Auto-History*, trans. Sheila Fischman (Montreal: McGill-Queen's University Press, 1992).
Georges E. Sioui Wendayete, "1992: The Discovery of Americity," in *Indigena: Contemporary Native Perspectives in Canadian Art*, eds. Gerald McMaster and Lee-Ann Martin (Vancouver: Craftsman House, 1992), pp. 59–70.
Gilles Havard, *L'Amerique Fantome: Aventuriers Francophones en Amerique* (Paris: Flamarion, 2019).
Gilles Havard and Mickaël Augeron eds., *Un continent en partage: Cinq siècles de rencontres entre Amérindiens et Français* (Paris: Les Indes Savantes, 2013).
Giorgio Mariani, "Was Anybody More of an Indian than Karl Marx?: The 'Indiani Metropolitani' and the 1977 Movement," in *Indians and Europe: An Interdisciplinary Collection of Essays*, ed. Christian F. Feest (Lincoln and London: University of Nebraska Press, 1999).
Giorgio Mariani, "The Red and the Black: Images of American Indians in the Italian Political Landscape," *Studia Anglica Posnaniensia*, Vol. 53, No. S1 (December 2018).
Glen Coulthard, "For Our Nations to Live, Capitalism Must Die," *Nations Rising* (November 5, 2013), http://nationsrising.org/for-our-nations-to-live-capitalism-must-die/, Accessed April 4, 2022.
Glen Sean Coulthard, *Red Skin White Masks: Rejecting the Colonial Politics of Recognition* (Minneapolis: University of Minnesota Press, 2004).
Gordon Brotherston, *Book of the Fourth World: Reading the Native Americas through Their Literature* (Cambridge: Cambridge University Press, 1992).
Grace L. Dillon ed., *Walking the Clouds: An Anthology of Indigenous Science Fiction* (Phoenix: University of Arizona Press, 2012).
Gregory Bateson, *Steps to an Ecology of Mind* (New York: Ballantine, 1972).

Gregory Cajete, *Native Science: Natural Laws of Interdependence* (Santa Fe: Clear Light, 2000).
Guilherme Leite Gonçalves and Sérgio Costa, *Um Porto no Capitalismo Global: Desvendando a acumulação entrelaçada no Rio de Janeiro* (São Paulo: Boitempo, 2020).
Guillermo Gómez-Peña, *Conversations across Borders* (London: Seagull, 2011).
Gustavo Furtado, *Documentary Filmmaking in Contemporary Brazil* (New York: Oxford University Press, 2019).
H. Glenn Penny, *Kindred by Choice* (Durham: The University of North Carolina Press, 2013).
Hartmut Lutz, "German Indianthusiasm: A Socially Constructed German National(ist) Myth," in *Germans and Indians: Fantasies, Encounters, Projections*, eds. Colin G. Calloway, Gerd Gemunden, and Susanne Zantop (Lincoln: University of Nebaskra Press, 2000).
Hartmut Lutz, Florentine Strzelczyk, and Renae Watchman eds., *Indianthusiasm: Indigenous Responses* (Waterloo, ON: Wilfrid Laurier University Press, 2019).
Heike Paul, *The Myths That Made America: An Introduction to American Studies* (Transcript Verlag, 2014), pp. 115–16 JSTOR, www.jstor.org/stable/j.ctv1wxsdq, Accessed March 31, 2022.
Hélène Clastres, *Terra sem Mal* (São Paulo: Brasiliense, 1978).
Helena Salem, *Nelson Pereira dos Santos: O Sonho Possivel do Cinema Brasileiro* (Rio de Janeiro: Nova Fronteira, 1987).
Henri Coudreau, *La France équinoxiale, Vol. I* (Paris: Challemel, 1886).
Henri Coudreau, *La France équinoxiale, Vol. II* (Paris: Challemel, 1887).
Henri Coudreau, *Chez nos Indiens: Quatre Années Dans La Guyane Francaise (1887–1891)* (Nabu Press, 2011).
Henry Jenkins, "Avatar Activism: Pick Your Protest," *The Globe and Mail* (September 18, 2010), https://www.theglobeandmail.com/opinion/avatar-activism-pick-your-protest/article4190179/, Accessed November 23, 2020.
Herbert Marcuse, *Eros and Civilization: A Philosophical Inquiry into Freud* (Boston: Beacon Press, 1955).
Herman Melville, *Moby Dick* (New York: Penguin Classics, 2002).
Hūfanga "Okusitino Māhina, 'Our Sea of Islands,'" *The Contemporary Pacific*, Vol. 6, No. 1 (1994).
"Interview: Jeff Barnaby Talks Blood Quantum," *Scream Horror Mag* (May 12, 2020), https://www.screamhorrormag.com/interview-jeff-barnaby-talks-blood-quantum/, Accessed April 4, 2022.
Ivana Bentes, "Vídeo e cinema: rupturas, reações e hibridismos," in *Made in Brasil: três décadas de vídeo brasileiro*, ed. Arlindo Machado (São Paulo: Iluminuras: Itaú Cultural, 2007).
Ivana Bentes, "Eu vejo você: antropologia reversa em Avatar, ciber-índios, pós-cinema ou como arrancar um pensamento complexo dos clichés," in *Avatar: o futuro do cinema e a ecologia das imagens digitais*, eds. Erick Felinto and Ivana Bentes (Porto Alegre: Sulina, 2010).
Ivana Bentes, *Midia-Multidao: Esteticas da Communicacao e Biopoliticas* (Rio de Janeiro: Mauad, 2015).
Ives Goddard, *Handbook of North American Indians: Northeast*, Vol. 15, ed. William Sturtevan (Wahsington, DC: Smithsonian Institution, 1978).
Jace Weaver, *The Red Atlantic: American Indigenes and the Making of the Modern World, 1000–1927* (North Carolina Press, 2014).

Jack D. Forbes, *Columbus and Other Cannibals* (New York: Autonomedia, 1992).
Jack D. Forbes, *The American Discovery of Europe* (Urbana: University of Illinois Press, 2007).
Jack Weatherford, *Indian Givers: How the Indians of the Americas Transformed the World* (New York: Fawcett, 1988).
Jack Weatherford, *Native Roots: How the Indians Enriched America* (New York: Fawcett, 1991).
Jacques Derrida, *De la Grammatologie* (Paris: Minuit, 1967).
Jacques Derrida, "The Violence of the Letter," in *Of Grammatology*, trans. Gayatri Spivak (Baltimore and London: The Johns Hopkins University Press, 1974).
Jacques Lizot, *Tales of the Yanomami* (Cambridge: Cambridge University Press, 1985).
Jacques Ranciere, *La Fable Cinematographique* (Paris: Le Seuil, 2001).
Jacques Ranciere, *Dissensus: On Politics and Aesthetics* (New York: Continuum, 2019).
Jamaias DaCosta, "Interview with Filmmaker Jeff Barnaby On Rhymes For Young Ghouls," *Muskrat Magazine* (February 1, 2014), http://muskratmagazine.com/interview-with-filmmaker-jeff-barnaby-on-rhymes-for-young-ghouls/, Accessed April 4, 2022.
James Clifford, *Returns: Becoming Indigenous in the Twenty First Century* (Cambridge: Harvard University Press, 2013).
James F. Cooper, *The Deerslayer* (New York: Signet, 1963).
James F. Weiner, Howard Morphy, Joanna Overing, Jeremy Coote, and Peter Gow, "1993 Debate: Aesthetics is a cross-cultural category," in *Key Debates in Anthropology*, ed. Tim Ingold (New York: Routledge, 1996).
James Tully, *Strange Multiplicity: Constitutionalism in an Age of Diversity* (Cambridge: Cambridge University Press, 1995).
Jane Griffith, "Hoover Damn: Land, Labor, and Settler Colonial Cultural Production," in *Cultural Studies ↔ Critical Methodologies*, Vol. 17, No. 1 (First pub. April 6, 2016).
Jason W. Clay, "People, Not States, Make a Nation," in *Mother Jones* (November/December 1990).
Jean de Léry, *History of a Voyage to the Land of Brazil* (Berkeley: University of California Press, 1992).
Jean-Louis Comolli, *Ver e Poder: A Innocencia Perdida: Cinema, Television, Ficcao, Documentario* (Belo Horizonte: UFMG, 2008).
Jean-Louis Comolli, *Corps et Cadre: Cinema, Ethique, Politique* (Paris: Editions Verdier, 2012).
Jean-Yves Merian, *Les Aventures des Bretons au Brésil l a L'Epoque Coloniale* (Rennes: Portes duLarge, 2007).
Jeanette Armstrong, "Community: 'Sharing One Skin,'" in *Paradigm Wars: Indigenous People's Resistance to Globalization*, eds. Jerry Mander and Victoria Tauli-Corpuz (San Francisco: Sierra Club Books, 2006).
Jeff Barnaby, "Director's Statement," in *Press Kit* (Montreal: Prospector Films, 2013).
Jerry Mander and Victoria Tauli-Corpuz eds., *Paradigm Wars: Indigenous People's Resistance to Globalization* (San Francisco: Sierra Club Books, 2006).
Jimmy Chi and Kuckles, *Bran Nue Dae: A Musical Journey* (Sydney: Currency Press, Magabala Books, 1991).
João Cezar de Castro Rocha, *Culturas Shakespearianas: Teoria Mimética e os Desafios da Mímesis Em Circunstâncias Não Hegemônicas* (É Realizações, 2017).
João Cezar de Castro Rocha, *Shakespearean Cultures: Latin America and the Challenges of Mimesis in Non-Hegemonic Circumstances*, trans. Flora Thomson-DeVeaux (Michigan State University Press, 2019).

João Pedro Turri, "Espelho Ofuscante: Xapiri e a etnografia digital," "Bachelor's Thesis presented in the Dept. of Cinema, Radio and Television (ECA), at University of São Paulo, under guidance of Dr. Eduardo Victorio Morettin," http://www3.eca.usp.br/sites/default/files/form/biblioteca/acervo/textos/tc3683-turri.pdf, Accessed April 4, 2022.

Joanna Hearne, *Native Recognition: Indigenous Cinema and the Western* (Albany: State University of New York Press, 2012).

Joana Oliveira, "O canto tikuna é muito espiritual, você escreve com a alma," *El País* (May 16, 2019), https://brasil.elpais.com/brasil/2019/05/13/cultura/1557783452_873253.html, Accessed March 31, 2022.

Joanna Overing and Alan Passes eds., *The Anthropology of Love and Anger: the Aesthetics of Conviviality in Native Amazonia* (London: Routledge, 2000).

Joanne Barker ed., *Critically Sovereign: Indigenous Gender, Sexuality, and Feminist Studies* (Durham: Duke University Press, 2017).

Joanne Barker, "Territory as Analytic: The Dispossession of Lenapehoking and the Subprime Crisis," *Social Text 135*, Vol. 36 No. 2 (June 2018).

Joaquim de Sousândrade, *O Guesa* (Sao Luiz: Edicoes SIOGE, 1979).

Jodi A. Byrd, *The Transit of Empire: Indigenous Critique on Colonialism* (Minneapolis: University of Minnesota, 2011).

John Hemming, *Die if You Must* (London: Macmillan, 2004).

John Hemming, *People of the Rainforest: The Villas Boas Brothers, Explorers and Humanitarians of the Amazon* (London: Hurst and Company, 2019).

John H. Bodley, *Victims of Progress* (Mountain View, CA: Mayfield, 1990).

John Manuel Monteiro, *Negros da terra: índios e bandeirantes nas origens de São Paulo* (São Paulo: Companhia das Letras, 1994).

John Murray Cuddihy, *The Ordeals of Civility: Freud, Marx, Levi-Strauss and the Jewish Struggle with Modernity* (Boston: Beacon, 1974).

John P. Foley ed., *The Jefferson Encyclopedia* (New York: Harper and Row, 1900).

José Barreiro ed., *Thinking in Indian: A John Mohawk Reader* (Golden, CO: Fulcrum, 2010).

Jordan Crucchiola, "Jeff Barnaby Made an Apocalypse Movie to Watch the System Fall. Then a Pandemic Hit," *The Vulture* (May 6, 2020), https://www.vulture.com/2020/05/jeff-barnaby-is-worried-white-people-wont-get-blood-quantum.html, Accessed April 4, 2022.

José de Alencar, *Ubirajara* (Rio de Janeiro: Jose Olympio, 1965).

Jose Jorge de Carvalho and Juliana Flórez-Flórez, "The Meeting of Knowledges: A Project for the Decolonization of Universities in Latin America," *Postcolonial Studies*, Vol. 17, No. 2: Decoloniality, Knowledges, and Aesthetics (April 2014) https://www.tandfonline.com/doi/abs/10.1080/13688790.2014.966411, Accessed April 4, 2022.

Julian Burger, *The Gaia Atlas of First Peoples: A Future for the Indigenous World* (New York: Doubleday, 1990).

Kaka Werá Jecupé, *Oré Awé Roiru´a Ma: Todas as vezes que dissemos adeus, Whenever we said goodbye* (Triom 2nd edition, 2002).

Karl Marx, *Capital, Volume I,* trans. Ben Fowkes (London: Penguin Books, 1990, first published 1867).

Karl Marx, *Capital: A Critique of Political Economy*, Vol. 1 (New York: Cosimo, 2007, originally published 1867).

Kerstin Knopf, *Decolonizing the Lens of Power: Indigenous Films in North America* (Leiden, The Netherlands: Brill, 2008).

Kathryn Lehman, "Beyond Academia: Indigenous Media as an Intercultural Resource to Unlearn Nation-State History," *Revistas Tempos e Espacos em Educacao*, Vol. 10 (January–April 2017).

Kelly J. Madison, "Legitimation, Crisis and Containment: The 'anti-racist-white-hero' film," *Critical Studies in Mass Communication*, Vol. 16, No. 4 (1999).

Kenneth Good, *Into the Heart: One Man's Pursuit of Knowledge among the Yanomama* (New York: Simon and Schuster, 1991).

Kerstin Knopf, *Decolonizing the Lens of Power: Indigenous Films in North America* (Brill, 2008).

Kester Dyer, "Anticipating the Colonial Apocalypse: Jeff Barnaby's Blood Quantum," *Pandemic Media* (2020), https://pandemicmedia.meson.press/chapters/activism-sociability/anticipating-the-colonial-apocalypse-jeff-barnabys-blood-quantum/, Accessed April 4, 2022.

Kim Beauchesne and Alessandra Santos eds., *Performing Utopias in the Contemporary Americas* (New York: Palgrave Macmillan, 2017).

Kirkpatrick Sale, *The Conquest of Paradise: Christopher Colombus and the Columbian Legacy* (New York: Alfred A. Knopf, 1990).

Kirsten Acuna, "James Cameron Swears He Didn't Rip Off The Idea For 'Avatar,'" *Business Insider* (April 28, 2010), http://www.businessinsider.com/james-camerons-45-page-declaration-proving-avatar-was-his-idea-2012-12?page=1, Accessed April 4, 2022.

Laura Mulvey, "*Xala*, Ousmane Sembene (1974): The Carapace That Failed," *Camera Obscura*, Vol. 11, No. 1 (31) (1993).

Leanne Betasamosake Simpson, *Dancing on Our Turtle's Back: Stories of Nishnaabeg Recreation, Resurgence, and a New Emergence* (Winnipeg: Arbeiter Ring Press, 2011).

Leanne Betasamoksake Simpson, *As We Have Always Done* (Minneapolis: University of Minnesota Press, 2017).

Leonardo Sakamoto, "Modern-Day Slavery in the Amazon," *News International* (Jan 20, 2020), https://newint.org/features/2020/01/20/modern-day-slavery-amazon, Accessed March 31, 2022.

Leslie Fiedler, *Love and Death in the American Novel* (New York: Criterion, 1960).

Leslie Marmon Silko, "Language and Literature from a Pueblo Indian Perspective," in *Nothing but the Truth: An Anthology of Native American Literature*, eds. John L. Purdy and James Ruuppert (Upper Saddle River, NJ: Prentice Hall, 1998).

Leslie Marmon Silko, "Videomakers and Basketmakers," *Aperture*, No. 119 (Summer 1990).

Jessé Souza ed., *A Invisibilidade da Desigualdade Brasileira* (Belo Hirozonte: UFMG, 2006).

Jessica Lee, "'Avatar' Activism: James Cameron Joins Indigenous Struggles Worldwide," *The Indypendent* (April 26, 2010), https://indypendent.org/2010/04/avatar-activism-james-cameron-joins-indigenous-struggles-worldwide/#:~:text='AVATAR'%20ACTIVISM%3A%20James%20Cameron%20Joins%20Indigenous%20Struggles%20Worldwide,-Jessica%20Lee%20Apr&text=While%20he%20said%20that%20he,helping%20illuminate%20these%20struggles%20worldwide, Accessed April 4, 2022.

Leyla Perrone-Moisés, *Vinte Luas: Viagem de Paulmier de Gonneville ao Brasil: 1503–1505* (São Paulo: Companhia das Letras, 1992).

Leyla Perrone-Moisés, "Essmoricq: O Venturoso Carijo," in *Aoutra margem do Ocidente*, eds. Adauto Novaes (São Paulo: Companhia das Letras, 1999).

Linda Tuhiwai Smith, *Decolonizing Methodologies: Research and Indigenous Peoples* (Chicago: University of Chicago Press, 1999).

Lucio Paiva Flores, *Adoradores do Sol* (Petropolis: Vozes, 2003).

Lucia Sa, *Rain Forest Literatures: Amazonian Texts and Latin American Culture* (Minneapolis: University of Minnesota Press, 2004).

Lucia Sa, "Part II: "Macunaíma and the Native Trickster," Woodrow Wilson International Center for Scholars, Special Report (November 2008).

Luther Standing Bear, *The Land of the Spotted Eagle* (Boston: Houghton Mifflin, 1933).

M. A. Jaimes Guerrero, "Savage Hegemony: From 'Endangered Species' to Feminist Indiginism," in *Talking Visions: Multicultural Feminism in a Transnational Age*, ed. Ella Shohat (MIT Press in collaboration with the New Museum, 1998).

M. A. Jaimes Guerrero, "Patriarchal Colonialism," *Hypatia: A Journal of Feminist Philosophy*, Special Issue: Indigenous Women in America Spring, Vol. 18, No. 2 (2003).

M. Elise Marubbio, "Decolonizing the Western: A Revisionist Analysis of Avatar with a Twist," in *The Post-2000 Film Western*, eds. M. Paryz and J.R. Leo (London: Palgrave Macmillan, 2015).

Macarena Gómez-Barris, *The Extractive Zone: Social Ecologies and Decolonial Perspectives* (Durham: Duke University Press, 2017).

Manuela Carneiro da Cunha, *Cultura com aspas e outros ensaios* (São Paulo: Cosac Naify, 2009).

Manuela Lavinas Picq, "Spreading Faith and Disease," *The New York Times* (October 2, 2020), https://www.nytimes.com/2020/10/02/opinion/amazon-missionaries-tribes-disease.html, Accessed April 4, 2022.

Manuela Penafria, "O ponto de vista no filme documentário," (Universidade da Beira Interior, 2001), http://www.bocc.ubi.pt/pag/penafria-manuela-ponto-vista-doc.pdf, Accessed March 31, 2022.

Marc Augé, *Pour une anthropologie des mondes contemporains* (Paris: Aubier, 1994).

Marcel Trudel, *L'Esclavage au Canada Français* (Montréal: Les Éditions de l'Horizon, 1963).

Marcel Trudel, *Deux siècles d'esclavage au Québec* (Montréal: Hurtubise HMH, 2004).

Marcelo Fiorini, "Desire in music: Soul-speaking and the power of secrecy," in *Burst of Breath: Indigenous Ritual Wind Instruments in Lowland South America*, eds. Jonathan David Hill and Jean-Pierre Chaumeil (Lincoln: University of Nebraska Press, 2011), pp. 171–98.

Marcio Souza, "Teatro sem Palavras," in *A Outra Margem do Ocidente*, ed. Adauto Novaes (São Paulo: Companhia das Letras, 1999).

Margarida Maria Adamatti, "As Duas Faces de Gustavo Dahl em Uira: entre o realizador e o critico," *Revista Fronteiras: Estudos Midiaticos*, Vol. 21, No. 1 (January/April 2019).

Maria Josefina Saldaña-Portillo and María Eugenia Cotera, "Indigenous but Not Indian? Chicana/os and the Politics of Indigeneity," in *The World of Indigenous North America*, ed. Robert Warrior (Abingdon: Routledge, 2015), pp. 549–68.

Marier-Claude Strigier, "Andre Breton et les Hopis: La Fascination de l'Autre," in *Un continent en partage: Cinq siècles de rencontres entre Amérindiens et Français*, eds. Gilles Havard and Mickaël Augeron (Paris: Les Indes Savantes, 2013).

Mario Carelli, *Brasil-França: cinco séculos de sedução* (Rio de Janeiro: Espaço em Tempo, 1989).
Mario Carelli, *Culturas Cruzadas: Intercâmbios culturais entre França e Brasil* (Campinas, São Paulo: Papirus, 1994).
Marshall Sahlins, "The National Academy of Sciences: Goodbye to All That," *Anthropology Today.*, Vol. 29, No. 2 (2013), pp. 1–2.
Martin Nakata, *Discipling the Savages: Savaging the Disciplines* (Canberra: Aboriginal Studies Press, 2007).
Mary Louise Pratt, *Imperial Eyes: Travel Writing and Transculturation* (New York: Routledge, 1992).
Mary del Priore, "Dans le Apaguer des Lumières: Francophilia e Lusofobia na Capital do Brasil Oitocentista," in *Enciclopedia da Brasilidade: Auto-Estima em Verde e Amarelo*, ed. Carlos Lessa (Rio de Janeiro: Casa da Palavra, 2005).
Mary Louise Pratt, "Concept and Chronotope," in *Arts of Living on a Damaged Plane: Ghosts and Monsters of the Anthropocene*, eds. Anna Lowenhaupt Tsing, Elaine Gan, Heather Anne Swanson and Nils Bubandt (Minneapolis: University of Minnesota Press, 2017), pp. 169–74.
Matt Wade, "Indian Hill Tribe Scores 'Avatar' Victory," *The Sydney Morning Herald* (August 28, 2010), https://www.smh.com.au/environment/conservation/indian-hill-tribe-scores-avatar-victory-20100827-13vym.html, Accessed April 4, 2022.
Matthew Restall, *Seven Myths of the Spanish Conquest* (Oxford: Oxford University Press, 2004).
Maximillian C. Forte, "Amerindian@Caribbean," in *Native on the Net*, ed. Kyra Landzelius (London: Routledge, 2006).
Melissa K. Nelson, *Original Instructions: Indigenous Teachings for a Sustainable Future* (Rochester, VT: Bear and Company, 2008).
Melissa K. Nelson, "Getting Dirty," in *Critically Sovereign: Indigenous Gender, Sexuality, and Feminist Studies*, ed. Joanne Barker (Durham: Duke University Press, 2017), pp. 229–60.
Melissa L. Tatum et al., *Structuring Sovereignty: Constitutions of Native Nations* (Los Angeles, UCLA: American Indian Studies Center, 2014).
Michael Greyeyes, "Inside the Machine: Indigeneity, Subversion, and the Academy," *Studies in American Indian Literatures*, Vol. 26, No. 4 (2015).
Michael Taussig, *Shamanism, Colonialism, and the Wild Man: A Study in Terror and Healing* (Chicago: University of Chicago Press, 1987).
Michael Taussig, "A Lesson in Looking and Laughter," in *Juan Downey: The Invisible Architect*, ed. Valerie Smith (New York: Bronx Museum of the Arts, MIT List Visual Arts Center, 2011).
Michel De Certeau, *Writing of History* (New York: Columbia University Press, 1988).
Michel de Montaigne, "'Of Cannibals' [1590] and 'Of Coaches' [1590]," in *The Complete Essays of Montaigne*, trans. Donald Frame (Stanford, CA: Stanford University Press, 1957).
Michel de Montaigne, *Ensaios I*, Chapter XXXI, trans. Sérgio Milliet (São Paulo: Editora Nova Cultural, 1996).
Michelle H. Raheja, "Reading Nanook's Smile: Visual Sovereignty, Indigenous Revisions of Ethnography, and Artarnajuat (The Fast Runner)," *American Quarterly*, Vol. 59, No. 4 (2007).

Michelle H. Raheja, *Reservation Reelism: Redfacing, Visual Sovereignty, and Representations of Native Americans in Film* (Lincoln: University of Nebraska Press, 2010).
Mikhail Bakhtin, *The Dialogic Imagination*, trans. Caryl Emerson & Michael Holquist (Austin: University of Texas Press, 1981).
Mikhail Bakhtin, *Problems of Dostoevsky's Poetics* (Minneapolis: University of Minnesota Press, 1984).
Mikhail Bakhtin, *Rabelais and His World* (Bloomington: Indiana University Press, 1984).
Moacir Francisco de Sant'ana Barros, "Tava: Cenas da Caminhada e da Conversacao no Cinema Mbya-Guarani," in *Povos Indígenas no Brasil*, eds. Paulo Sergio Delgado and Naine Terena de Jesus (Curitiba: Brazil Publishing, 2018).
Monica Frota, "Taking Aim: The Video Technology of Cultural Resistance," in *Resolutions: Contemporary Video Practices*, eds. Michael Renov and Erika Suderburg (Minneapolis: The University of Minnesota Press, 1996).
"Mostra audiovisual com produções de mulheres indígenas promove debates sobre arte, interculturalidade e gênero," *Universidade Federal do Sul da Bahia* (July 30, 2018), https://ufsb.edu.br/ultimas-noticias/1016-mostra-audiovisual-com-producoes-de-mulheres-indigenas-promove-debates-sobre-arte-interculturalidade-e-genero, Accessed March 31, 2022.
Nan O'Sullivan, "Walking Backwards into the Future: Indigenous Wisdom within Design Education," *Educational Philosophy and Theory*, Vol. 51, No. 4 (2019).
Naomi Klein, *This Changes Everything: Capitalism vs. the Climate* (New York: Simon and Schuster, 2014).
Napoleon Chagnon, *Yanomamö: The Fierce People* (New York: Holt, Rinehart and Winston, 1968).
Neil Kent, *The Sámi Peoples of the North: A Social and Cultural History* (London: Hurst & Company, 2014).
Noam Chomsky, *Year 501: The Conquest Continues* (Boston: South End Press, 1993).
Olga Obry, *Catherine du Bresil: Filleule de Saint Malo* (Paris: Nouvelles éditions latines, 1953).
Oliver Basciano, "Shamans, Spirits, Survival; How Claudia Andujar Fought for the Yanomami Tribe," *The Guardian* (January 29, 2020), https://www.theguardian.com/artanddesign/2020/jan/29/claudia-andujar-photography-yanomami-brazil-jair-bolsonaro, Accessed April 4, 2022.
Olivier Maligne, *Les Nouveaux Indiens: Une Ethnographie du Mouvement Indianophile* (Québec: L'Universite Laval: CELAT, 2006).
Oren Lyons and John Mohawk eds., *Exiles in the Land of the Free: Democracy, the Iroquois Nation and the U.S. Constitution* (Santa Fe: Clearlight Publishers, 1992).
Oswald de Andrade, "Do Pau-Brasil à Antropofagia e às Utopias," in *Obras Completas*, Vol 6. (Rio de Janeiro: Civilização Brasileira, 1978).
Oswald de Andrade, *Poesia, Antipoesia, Antropofagia* (São Paulo: Cortez & Morães, 1978).
Oswald de Andrade, "Cannibalist Manifesto," trans. Leslie Bary, *Latin American Literary Review*, Vol. XIX, No. 38 (July–December 1991).
Oswald de Andrade, *A Utopia Antropofágica* (São Paulo: Globo, 2011).
Patricia Limerick, *The Legacy of Conquest: The Unbroken Past of the American West* (New York: Norton, 1987).
Patrick Petitjean, "As Missoes Universitarias Francesas na Criacao da Universidade de São Paulo (1934–1940)," in *A Ciencia nas Relacoes Brasill-Franca (1850–1950)*, eds. Amelia

Imperio Hamburger, Maria Amélia M. Dantes, Michel Paty and Patrick Petitjean (São Paulo: EDUSP, 1986).

Patricia Seed, *Ceremonies of Possession in Europe's Conquest of the New World, 1492–1640* (Cambridge: Cambridge University Press, 1995).

Patrick Wolfe, "Settler Colonialism and the Elimination of the Native," *Journal of Genocide Research*, Vol. 8, No. 4 (2006).

Patrick Wolfe, "The Settler Complex: An Introduction," *American Indian Culture and Research Journal*, Vol. 37, No. 2 (2013).

Patrick Tierney, *Darkness in El Dorado: How Scientists and Journalists Devastated the Amazon* (New York: Norton, 2002).

Paul Chatt Smith and Robert Allen Warrior, *Like a Hurricane: The Indian Movement from Alcatraz to Wounded Knee* (New York: New Press, 1997).

Paula Gunn Allen, *The Sacred Hoop: Recovering the Feminine in American Indian Traditions* (Boston: Beacon Press, 1986).

Paula Gunn Allen, *Pocahantas: Medicine Woman, Spy, Entrepreneus, Diplomat* (New York: HarperCollins, 2004).

Paula Morgado, "Cinéma amérindien brésilien et utilisation du cyberspace. Pour qui?" *Anthrovision*, Vol. 2, No. 2 (2014), http://journals.openedition.org/anthrovision/1448, Accessed April 4, 2022.

Paulo Emilio Salles Gomes, *Uma Situação Colonial?* (Companhia das Letras 1st edition, 2016).

Peggy Sanday, *Divine Hunger: Cannibalism as a Cultural System* (Cambridge: Cambridge University Press, 1986).

Penelope Myrtle Helsey, *Reading the Wampum: Essays on Hodinöhsö:ni' Visual Code and Epistemological Recovery* (Syracuse: Syracuse University Press, 2014).

Peter Hulme, *Colonial Encounters: Europe and the Native Caribbean, 1492 to 1797* (London: Metheun, 1986).

Peter Hulme and Neil L. Whitehead eds., *Wild Majesty: Encounters with Caribs from Columbus to the Present Day* (Oxford: Clarendon, 1992).

Peter Limbrick, "The Australian Western, or a Settler Colonial Cinema par excellence," *Cinema Journal*, Vol. 46, No. 4 (Summer, 2007), https://www.jstor.org/stable/30137720, Accessed April 4, 2022.

Peter Linebaugh, *The Magna Carta Manifesto: Liberties and Commons for All* (Berkeley: University of California Press, 2008).

Philip J. Deloria, *Playing Indian* (New Haven and London: Yale University Press, 1998).

Philippe Descola, "Selvageria Culta," in *A outra margem do Ocidente*, eds. Adauto Novaes et al. (Companhia das Letras, 1999), pp. 107–24.

Pierre Clastres, *Society against the State: Essays in Political Anthropology*, trans. Robert Hurley and Abe Stein (New York: Zone Books, 1987).

Pierre Clastres, *A Sociedade contra o Estado* (São Paulo: Cosas & Naify, 2003).

Pierre Clastres, *Arqueologie da Violencia: Pesquisas de Antopologia Politica*, trans. Paulo Neves (São Paulo: Cosac and Naify, 2004).

Randal Johnson and Robert Stam eds., *Brazilian Cinema* (first published by Associated University Presses, 1982 and republished by New York: Columbia University Press, 1995).

Raúl Ruiz, *Poetics of Cinema*, trans. Brian Holmes (Paris: Editions Dis Voir, 1995).

Ray Allen Billington, *Land of Savagery, Land of Promise: The European Image of the American Frontier in the Nineteenth Century* (Norman: University of Oklahoma Press, 1981).

'Remarks concerning the Savages of North America, [before 7 January 1784],' *Founders Online*, National Archives, https://founders.archives.gov/documents/ Franklin/01-41-02-0280. [Original source: The Papers of Benjamin Franklin, vol. 41, September 16, 1783, through February 29, 1784, ed. Ellen R. Cohn. New Haven and London: Yale University Press, 2014, pp. 412–23.]

Renata R. Maautner Wasserman, *Exotic Nations: Literature and Cultural Identity in the United States and Brazil, 1830–1930* (Ithaca: Cornell University Press, 1994).

Renato Rosaldo, "Imperialist Nostalgia," *Representations*, No. 26, Special Issue: Memory and Counter-Memory (Spring, 1989).

Renato Sztutman, *O Profeta e o Principal: A Ação Política Ameríndia e Seus Personagens* (São Paulo: EDUSP, 2012).

Renato Sztutman, "Cosmopolíticas transversais: a proposta de Stengers e o mundo ameríndio," Lecture presented at the Museu Nacional, Rio de Janeiro, November 29, 2013. Unpublished.

Renato Sztutman, "The Return of the Anthropophagites: Reconnecting Oswald de Andrade's Proposal to Amerindian Art-Thought," in *Cultural Anthropophagy: The 24th Bienal de São Paulo 1998*, ed. Lisette Lagnado (London: Afterall Books in association with the Center for Curatorial Studies, Bard College, 2015).

René Girard, *Violence and the Sacred* (Baltimore: Johns Hopkins, 1972).

Richard A. Gordon, *Cannibalizing the Colony: Cinematic Adaptations of Colonial Literature in Mexico and Brazil* (West Lafayette: Purdue University Press, 2009).

Richard Pena, "How Tasty Was My Little Frenchman," in *Brazilian Cinema*, eds. Randal Johnson and Robert Stam (first published by Associated University Presses, 1982 and republished by Columbia University Press, 1995).

Richard Slotkin, *Regeneration through Violence: The Mythology of the American Frontier* (Durham: Duke University Press, 1973).

Rivka Galchen, "Wild West Germany: Why Do Cowboys and Indians so Captivate the Country?" *The New Yorker* (2012), https://www.newyorker.com/magazine/2012/04/09/wild-west-germany, Accessed April 4, 2022.

Robert F. Berkhofer, *The White Man's Indian* (New York: Vintage Books, 1979).

Robert J. Miller, *Native America, Discovered and Conquered: Thomas Jefferson, Lewis and Clark, and Manifest Destiny* (Lincoln: University of Nebraska Press, 2008).

Robert Nichols, *Theft Is Property! Dispossession and Critical Theory* (Durham: Duke University Press, 2020).

Robert Stam, *Subversive Pleasures: Bakhtin, Cultural Criticism, and Film* (Baltimore: Johns Hopkins University Press, 1989).

Robert Stam, *Tropical Multiculturalism: A Comparative History of Race in Brazilian Cinema* (Durham and London: Duke University Press, 1997).

Robert Steven Gromet, *Native American Place Names in New York City* (New York: Museum of the City of New York, 1981).

Robert S. Tilton, *Pocahontas: The Evolution of an American Narrative* (Cambridge: Cambridge University Press, 1994).

Robin Wall Kimmerer, *Braiding Sweetgrass: Indigenous Wisdom, Scientific Knowledge and the Teachings of Plants* (Minneapolis, MN: Milkweed Editions, 2013).

Rogerio Budasz, "Of Cannibals and the Recycling of Otherness," *Music & Letters*, Vol. 87 No. 1 (January 2006).

Roger Odin, *De la Fiction* (Brussels: De Boeck, 2000).

Sabrina Furminger, "Fierce Girls Web Series Empowers Indigenous Girls," *Vancouver Is Awesome* (June 12, 2018), https://www.vancouverisawesome.com/courier-archive/

general-archive/fierce-girls-web-series-empowers-indigenous-girls-3077317, Accessed April 4, 2022.
Saddruddin Aga Khan and Hassan Bin Talal, *Indigenous Peoples: A Global Quest for Justice* (London: Zed, 1987).
Sally Price, *Primitive Art in Civilized Places* (2nd edition, Chicago: University of Chicago Press, 2001).
Sally Price, *Paris Primitive: Jacques Chirac's Museum on the Quai Branly* (Chicago: University of Chicago Press, 2007).
Sally Roesch Wagner, *The Untold Story of the Iroquois Influence on Early Feminists* (NY: Sky Carrier Press, 1996).
Sandro de Oliveira, "A Alegoria da Barbárie no filme O Homem que Matou Deus (2013)," *Anais do VIII Seminário Nacional de Pesquisa em Arte e Cultura Visual: arquivos, memorias, afetos*, S. Jesus De (Goiânia, GO: UFG/Núcleo Editorial FAV, 2015), https://files.cercomp.ufg.br/weby/up/778/o/2015.GT1_sandrooliveira.pdf.
Sandy Grande, *Red Pedagogy: Native American Social and Political Thought* (New York: Rowman and Littlefield, 1964).
Sandy Grande, "Accumulation of the Primitive: The Limits of Liberalism and the Politics of occupy Wall Street," *Settler Colonial Studies*, Vol. 3, No. 3–4 (September 13, 2013).
Sankar Muthu, *Enlightenment against Empire* (Princeton: Princeton University Press, 2003).
Sara Ahmed, "Phantasies of Becoming the (Other)," *European Journal of Cultural Studies*, Vol. 2, No. 1 (1999).
Sara Ahmed, *Strange Encounters: Embodied Others in Postcoloniality* (New York: Routledge, 2000).
Sara C. Heitshu and Thomas H. Marshall, *Native American Studies: A Guide to Reference and Information Sources* (2nd revised edition; Libraries Unlimited, 2009).
Sarah Shamash, "Utopic Cannibalism in Carlos Fausto, Leonardo Sette, and Takumã Kuikuro's As Hiper Mulheres," in *Performing Utopias in the Contemporary Americas*, eds. Kim Beauchesne and Alessandra Santos (U.S.: Palgrave Macmillan, 2017).
Scott Richard Lyons, *X-Marks: Native Signatures of Assent* (Minneapolis: University of Minnesota Press, 2010).
Sean Cubitt, *Finite Media: Environmental Implications of Digital Technologies* (Durham, NC: Duke University Press, 2017).
Shari M. Huhndorf, *Going Native: Indians in the American Cultural Imagination* (Ithaca and London: Cornell University Press, 2001).
Sharon W. Tiffany and Kathleen J. Adams, "Anthropology's 'Fierce' Yanomami: Narratives of Sexual Politics in the Amazon," *NWSA Journal*, Vol. 6, No. 2 (Summer, 1994).
Sheila Schvarzman, *Humberto Mauro e as imagens do Brasil* (São Paulo: Edusp, 2004).
Sheryl Lightfoot, *Global Indigenous Politics: A Subtle Revolution* (New York: Routledge, 2016).
Shoshana Zuboff, *The Age of Surveillance Capitalism* (London: Profile Books Ltd, 2019).
Sigurjón Baldur Hafsteinsson and Marian Bredin eds., *Indigenous Screen Cultures in Canada* (Winnepeg: University of Manitoba Press, 2010).
Silvio Back, *República Guarani* (Rio de Janeiro: Paz e Terra, 1982).
Slavoj Žižek, "Avatar: Return of the Natives," *New Statesman* (March 4, 2010).
"Sônia Guajajara desmonta discurso de senadora do PSL no Senado," *Rede Brasil Atual* (April 4, 2019), https://www.redebrasilatual.com.br/politica/2019/04/sonia-guajajara-desmonta-discurso-de-senadora-do-psl-no-senado/, Accessed March 22, 2022.
Stephen Greenblatt, *Marvelous Possessions* (Chicago: University of Chicago Press, 1991).

Stephen Haycox, "Felix S. Cohen and the Legacy of the Indian New Deal," *The Yale University Library Gazette*, Vol. 68, No. 3/4 (April 1994), http://www.jstor.com/stable/40859096, Accessed March 31, 2022.

Steven Leuthold, *Indigenous Aesthetics: Native Art, Media, and Identity* (Austin: University of Texas Press, 1998).

Sunera Thombani, *Exalted Subjects: Studies in the Making of Race and Nation in Canada* (Toronto: University of Toronto Press, 2007).

Susan Dunne, "Film Director Crystallizes Mi'gMaq Perspective," *Hartford Courant* (October 24, 2010), https://www.courant.com/hc-xpm-2010-10-24-hc-jeff-barnaby-1024-20101024-story.html, Accessed April 4, 2022.

Susanne Zantof, "Close Encounters: Deutsche and Indianer," in *Germans and Indians: Fantasies, Encounters, Projections*, eds. Colin G. Calloway, Gerd Gemunden, and Susanne Zantop (Lincoln: University of Nebaskra Press, 2000).

Taiaiake Alfred, *Wasáse: Indigenous Pathways of Action and Freedom* (Peterbrough, ON: Broadview Press, 2005).

Taiaiake Alfred, *Peace, Power, Righteousness: An Indigenous Manifesto* (Oxford: Oxford University Press, 2009).

Terence Turner, "Defiant Images: The Kayapo Appropriation of Video," *Anthropology Today*, Vol. 8, No. 6 (1992).

Terry Turner, "Anthropology and Multiculturalism: What Is Anthropology That Multiculturalists Should Be Mindful of It?" *Cultural Anthropology*, Vol. 8, No. 4 (1993), http://www.jstor.org/stable/656475, Accessed April 4, 2022.

Thelma Wills Foote, *Black and White in Manhattan: The History of Racial Formation in Colonial New York City* (Oxford: Oxford University Press, 2004).

Theodor Koch-Grunberg, *Do Roraima ao Orinoco*, Vol. 1, trans. Cristina Alberts-Franco (São Paulo: EUSP, 2005).

Thomas Hobbes, *Leviathan*, ed. A. P. Martinich (Broadview Literary Texts, 2002).

Thomas Hobbes, *Leviathan*, ed. C. B. Macperson (Middlesex: Penguin, 1968).

Thomas King, *The Inconvenient Indian* (Minneapolis: University of Minnesota Press, 2013).

Thomas Morton, *New English Canaan* (Stoneham, MA: Digital Scanning, 2000. First published Amsterdam, 1637).

Timeu Assurini, "Manifesto de Decolonizacao," https://marytykwawara.github.io/manifesto_decolonizacao.

Todd Woody, Garry Blight, Chris Michael, and Lydia McMullan, "Beneath the Blue: Dive into a Dazzling Ocean under Threat—Interactive," *The Guardian* (February 23, 2021), https://www.theguardian.com/environment/ng-interactive/2021/feb/23/beneath-the-blue-dive-into-a-dazzling-ocean-under-threat-interactive, Accessed April 4, 2022.

Tracy Devine Guzmán, *Native and National in Brazil: Indigeneity after Independence* (Durham: University of North Carolina Press, 2013).

Tzvetan Todorov, *On Human Diversity: Nationalism, Racism, and Exoticism in French Thought*, trans. Catherine Porter (Cambridge: Harvard University Press, 1993).

Tzvetan Todorov, *The Conquest of America: The Question of the Other*, trans. Richard Howard (Norman: University of Oklahoma Press, 1999).

Vandana Shiva, *Monocultures of the Mind: Perspectives on Biodiversity and Biotechnology* (London: Zed Books, 1993).

Vandana Shiva, "Biodiversidade, Direitos de Propriedade Intelectual e Globalização," in *Semear Outras Soluções: Os Caminhos da Biodiversidade e dos Conhecimentos Rivais*,

ed. Boaventura de Sousa Santos (Rio de Janeiro: Civilização Brasileira, 2005), pp. 317–40.
Valerie Trouet, "What Turned California Forests into a Tinderbox? Fire Suppression, Paradoxically," *The Guardian* (September 14, 2020), https://www.theguardian.com/commentisfree/2020/sep/14/california-fire-suppression-forests-tinderbox.
Veronika Bennholdt-Thomsen and Maria Mies, *The Subsistence Perspective: Beyond the Globalized Economy* (London: Zed, 1999).
Viola Cordova, *How It Is: The Native American Philosophy of V.F. Cordova*, eds. Kathleen Dean Moore, Kurt Peters, Ted Jojola and Amber Lacy (Tucson: University of Arizona Press, 2007).
Veronica Eloi de Almeida, "A Muralha e a representação indígena na televisão, na literatura e nas ciências sociais," *PROD Revista de antropologia e artes*, No. 4 (2012).
Vianna Moog, *Bandeirantes and Bandeirantes* (New York: George Braziller, 1956).
Vincent Grégoire, "Jean de Léry: Un Monde non Cannibale est-il possible?" *Sens-Dessous*, Vol. 12, No. 2 (2013), https://www.cairn.info/revue-sens-dessous-2013-2-page-75.html, Accessed March 31, 2022.
Vine Deloria Jr., *Custer Died for Your Sins: An Indian Manifesto* (Norman: University of Oklahoma Press, 1988).
Vine Deloria Jr., *God Is Red: A Native View of Religion* (Golden, Colorado: Fulcrum Publication, 1994).
Vine Deloria Jr., *Red Earth, White Lies: Native Americans and the Myth of Scientific Fact* (Golden Colorado: Fulcrum, 1997).
Vine Deloria Jr., "Comfortable Fictions and the Struggle for Turf," in *Natives and Academics: Researching and Writing about American Indians*, ed. Devon A. Mihesuah (Lincoln: University of Nebraska Press, 1998), pp. 65–83.
Vivian Sobchack, *Carnal Thoughts: Embodiment and the Moving Image* (Berkeley: University of California, 2004).
Wai Chee Dimock, *Through Other Continents: American Literature across Deep Time* (Princeton and Oxford: Princeton University Press, 2006).
Ward Churchill ed., *Marxism and Native Americans* (Boston: South End Press, 1983).
Ward Churchill, "Deconstructing the Columbus Myth: Deconstructing the Columbus Myth: Was the 'Great Discoverer' Italian or Spanish, Nazi or Jew?" *Anarchy: A Journal of Desire*, No. 33 (Summer 1992).
Weeʼena Tikuna, "Overcoming the Odds to Reach My Dreams: An Indigenous Artist's Story," *Langscape Magazine*, Vol. 8 (Sep 2, 2019), https://medium.com/langscape-magazine/overcoming-the-odds-to-reach-my-dreams-an-indigenous-artists-story-9a25050b9b31, Accessed March 22, 2022.
William Brandon, *The American Heritage of Indians* (New York: Dell, 1961).
William Shakespeare, *The Merchant of Venice* (Longmans, Green, and Company, 1899).
Yakuy Tupinamb, "A Ordem da Desordem," *Combate Racismo Ambiental* (June 13, 2018), https://racismoambiental.net.br/2018/06/13/a-ordem-da-desordem-por-yakuy-tupinamba/, Accessed March 31, 2022.
Zoe Graham, PhD thesis proposal at NYU Cinema Studies, provisionally entitled "Transnational Pedagogy: Film School without Borders."

Index

Aboriginal Peoples Television Network (APTN) 184
Achuar 43, 94
Across the Wide Missouri 125
Adams, David Wallace 198
Adams, Evan 191
Adams, John 77
Adams, Kathleen, "Anthropology's 'Fierce' Yanomami: Narratives of Sexual Politics in the Amazon" 288
Africa/African 12, 14–15, 17, 32, 46 n.24, 73, 101, 117, 120, 169, 216–17, 223, 229, 235, 319–20, 341, 345
Afro-Brazilian 141, 184, 224, 243, 248, 256, 267, 302, 319, 345
Agamben, Giorgio 30, 241
   states of exception 151
   bare life 30
al Ahmad, Jalal 19
Aimard, Gustave 179
Ainu 7
Akuntsu 249
Alarcon, Daniela Fernandes, *The Return of the Earth: The Land Recuperation in the village Tupinamba da Serra do Padeiro, in the South of Bahia* 161–2
Albert, Bruce 18, 42, 64, 96–7, 286, 302, 306
   inter-ontological tension 296
   Pacificando o Branco: Cosmologias do contato no norte-Amazonico (Pacifying the White Man: Cosmologies of Contact in the Northern Amazon) 346
   Yanomami: The Fierce Controversy and What We Can Learn from It 278
Alexie, Sherman 190
Alfred, Taiaiake 9, 336, 354, 356
   "Indigenous Manifesto" 5–6
Algonquin 59, 76, 116, 123, 215, 352

Allen, Chadwick
   native/settler indigeneity 26, 171
   trans-Indigenous research 43
Allende, Isabel, *House of the Spirits* 291
Allen, Woody, *Zelig* 191, 319
Alma Gemea (Soul Twin) telenovela 130–1, 231
Almeida, Tatiana, *Martírio* 259–60
Alvarenga, Clarisse 220, 245, 249–51
Alvarenga, Paulo, *O guardado* (The Saved) 261
Amaouche, Nassim, *Des Apaches* (The Apaches) 184
Amazon/Amazonian 11, 15, 24, 34, 37–8, 40–1, 43, 64, 75, 111 n.139, 120, 130, 133–7, 141, 148, 150, 152, 178, 220, 222, 225–6, 233–5, 247–8, 263–4, 267, 283–4, 288, 291–3, 297–8, 300–2, 310–11, 319, 324, 327–8, 340, 358
American Indian Movement (AIM) 8, 91, 175, 238
American Revolution 6, 53, 75–82, 109 n.96, 174, 198, 322
Amerindians 28, 42, 94, 132, 177, 235, 289
Anaconda film 141
anarchism/anarchist 78, 89–94, 179, 356–7
ancestors/ancestry 9, 22, 32, 35, 46 n.24, 96, 102–3, 109 n.87, 119, 125–6, 129–30, 132–3, 138, 144, 149, 151, 154–6, 161, 183, 200, 204, 214, 216–17, 224, 229–31, 235, 243, 252, 255, 257–9, 261, 266–7, 279, 284, 292, 297, 300, 309, 319, 322, 327, 333, 335, 340, 345, 347–9, 352
Anderson, Anthony 277
Andrade, Joaquim de Sousa (Sousandrade) 116, 119
   "O Guesa" 116
Andujar, Claudia 282, 286, 303–4, 310
Angeconeb, Ahmoo Allen 183

Anglo-American 131, 181, 221
Anglo-Saxons 92, 112 n.150, 119, 183, 215
animation 127, 134, 175, 220, 262, 290, 297
Anishinaabe/Anishnaabeg 31, 34, 100, 198, 296, 323–4, 327, 336, 351
Anthropocene 18, 26, 28, 207, 295
anthropology/anthropologists 1, 3, 10, 17, 28, 32, 34–6, 40–2, 49 n.91, 82, 94, 101, 138, 177, 278–80, 288, 303, 304, 315, 341–2, 346
anthropophagy 69–72, 128–9, 156, 163 n.34, 213, 247, 249, 268, 284, 329–30
anti-indigenism 16–22, 121, 124, 251, 337, 358
anti-infidelism 13
anti-Semitism 13, 84, 334
anti-war movement 174–5, 278
Antonio and Pitti film 126
Antonio das Mortes 230
Apache 180–1, 184, 188, 319
Apes, William, *A Son of the Forest* 96, 341
Apocalypse Now film 274 n.102
Arabs 90, 186
Arana, Julio César 133, 137, 226
Arandu Arakuaa band 267
Araní (Brazilian game) 157
The Arara film 261
Arawak people 119, 218
A Arca dos Zo'é (Zo'é's Ark/Meeting Ancestors) 242–3
archives (materials/footage) 33, 38–9, 86–7, 161, 187, 192, 198, 222, 229, 244–9, 251, 260–1, 316, 341 343
Argentina 214, 252
Aritana novela 131, 231
Armstrong, Jeanette 5
Arraes, Guel 126
Artaud, Antonin 64, 283, 291
Arte Eletronica Indigena (Indigenous Electronic Art) 267
Articles of the Constitution (U.S.) 29, 81, 236, 237, 324, 331
Aryanization of Brazil 223
Asch, Tim 281, 286, 311 n.12
  The Axe Fight 279–80, 306
  A Father Washes his Children 279
  A Man and His Wife Weave a Hammock 279

Ashaninka people 126, 149, 241, 254
Asia/Asian 12, 46 n.24, 93, 103, 169, 214, 223, 235, 319–20
assimilation/assimilationist 22–3, 62, 71, 84, 87, 122, 129–31, 138, 162, 205, 223, 225, 252, 260, 263, 311, 319, 337, 342
Assurini, Timeu 343–4, 364 n.125
  decolonial manifesto 342–3
  Indigenous Academic Bill of Rights 344
  marytykwawara 343
Atanarjuat: The Fast Runner film 37–8
The Atomic Bomb Casualty Commission 280
Atomic Energy Commission 278
Augé, Marc 346
avant-garde 61, 69, 71–2, 112 n.152, 120, 147, 195, 248, 261, 284, 305–7, 314 n.106, 333
Awaete 342–3, 364 n.125
ayahuasca 153, 267–8, 291, 319
Aymara people 2, 268
Azevedo, Beatriz 325, 330
Aztec empire 9, 12, 84, 214

Babau, Cacique 156, 161
Babenco, Hector, *At Play in the Fields of the Lord* 233–4
Back, Silvio
  Indio do Brasil 271 n.41
  República Guarani 235
Bakhtin, Mikhail 4, 31, 39, 44, 76, 143, 145, 147–8, 190, 202, 223, 248, 297
  Chronotope of the Road 253
  culture of laughter 190, 262
  gay relativity 197
bandeirantes 15, 65, 216–17, 219, 227–8, 358
Bannon, Steve 356
Baptiste, Marilyn 350
barbarian/barbarism 22, 48 n.67, 61–2, 224, 227, 229
Barclaw, Dean, *Warrier Chiefs in a New Age* 38
Barclay, Barry 4
Barker, Joanne 21, 159, 332
Barnaby, Jeff 203–7, 212 n.104, 308
  Blood Quantum 204–6

positivity porn 204
postcolonial Indian 205–6
Barreto, Lima
   O Cangaceiro 229
   The Sad End of Policarpo Quaresma 215
Barthes, Roland 338
Bastide, Roger 82
Bateson, Gregory 144
Baudelaire, Charles 116
   Les Paradis Artificiels 292
Baudrillard, Jean 72
Bauer, Wolf, *Iracema: Uma Transa Amazônica* 135–6
Beagan, Tara 187
Becaud, Gilbert, "*L'Indien*" music video 91–2
becomings 34, 133, 171, 175, 353
   becoming Christian 98, 183, 220, 292, 319–20
   becoming White 98, 174, 265, 320, 322
   becoming animal 34, 318, 321
   becoming anthropological 241
   becoming Indian 34, 173–5, 251, 315–59
   becoming-other 100, 319–20, 333
   becoming Navi 177
   minoritarian becoming 321
   transformational becomings 315–59
Beirão, Vicentinho 113 n.162
Belisário, Bernard 148, 245, 250, 272 n.58
Belo Monte dam 8, 178, 240, 260, 343, 364 n.125
Benais, Wahwahay 198–9
Bengell, Norma 125
Benites, Germano, *Mokoi Tekoá Petei Jeguatá* (Two Villages One Path) 254
Benjamin, Walter 242, 296, 333
Bentes, Ivana 36, 241, 177
Beresford, Bruce, *Black Robe* 234
Bering Strait theory 193
Berkhofer, Robert F. 169, 188
Berman, Andrew, *We're in the Money: Depression America and Its Films* 146
Bernhardt, Sarah 153
Bhabha, Homi 126
Biard, Pierre 173, 203

Bicycles of Nhanderu 253
Biel, Jessica 216
Billington, R. A. 188
Binet, Laurent, *Civilizations* 12
Biocca, Ettore, *Yo Soy Napëyoma – Relato de Una Mujer Raptada Por Los Indígenas Yanomami* 283
biodiversity 8, 14, 38, 150, 351
Bio-Piracy film 15
Bitter Springs film 185
Black Mesa Water Coalition 350
Blackstone, William, "Commentaries on the Laws of England" 325
Blake, Philip 25
Bloch, Ernst 182, 253
Bloch, Sergio, *Tainá: An Adventure in the Amazon* 141
blood quantum 175, 204, 217, 234
Bodansky, Jorge, *Iracema: Uma Transa Amazônica* 135–6
Bolivia/Bolivians 14, 161, 252, 260, 268, 336, 351
Bollain, Iciar, *Tambien la Lluvia* (Even the Rain) 220–1
Bolognesi, Luiz 309
   Ex-pajé (Ex-shaman) 263, 307–8
   Return to Laughter 308
Bolsonaro, Jair 121, 142, 150, 156, 237, 286, 309, 349
Borofsky, Robert, *Yanomami: The Fierce Controversy and What We Can Learn from It* 278, 280
Bororo 85, 154, 214
Botocudo (Krenak) 64, 138, 340
Bourdieu, Pierre 322–3
Bragança, Felipe
   Don't Swallow My Heart, Alligator Girl! 153
   Zahy: A Tale of Maracanã 152
Brandão, Joana, *New York: Just Another City* 120–1, 155
Brando, Marlon 238
Brandon, William, *American Heritage Book of Indians* 78–9
Bran Neu Day 38
Brasil, Andre 42, 244, 256, 258, 299
Brazil/Brazilian
   affirmative action policies 131, 345

Brazilian Television 127, 130, 231, 247, 318
Brazil and the French 11, 53–4, 56, 58–9, 62–3, 65, 71–2, 74–5, 82–8, 90, 95, 214, 216
  Northeasterns 6, 154, 230, 267
  quincentennial celebration in 126, 218–20
Brazilian Council of Indian Peoples and Organizations (Capoib) 218
Brecht, Bertolt 39, 92, 147, 191, 338–9
  verfremdungeffekt 291
  "A Worker Reads History" 255
Breton, André 55, 64, 74, 104 n.6, 291
Briglia, Thiago, *Nas Trilhas de Macunaíma* 135
Broken Arrow film 125, 184
Brotherston, Gordon 18, 45 n.15
  Book of the Fourth World 84
Brown, Carlinhos 141
Browning, Barbara 312 n.36
  Caetano Veloso's A Foreign Sound 163 n.15
Buck, Sadie 198
Buffalo Bill, "Wild West Show" 4, 169, 185–6
Bureau of Indian Affairs (BIA) 194, 352
Bush, George 99, 199, 293
Byrd, Jodi A. 169–70, 334
  The Transit of Empire 321–2

Cabeza de Vaca film 173
caboclos 136, 184, 217, 227, 319
Cabral, Pedro Alvarez 7, 54, 129, 218–20, 222, 252, 358
  "Discovery" 126, 141, 220
cacicas (women tribal leaders) 153, 196
caciques (indigenous leaders) 56, 60, 86, 89, 130, 137, 141, 157, 161, 173, 224, 228, 237–8, 345
Caetano Veloso 6, 39, 115, 159, 214
  "Manyata" 115–16
  Verdade Tropical (Tropical Truth) 116, 118–19, 163 n.13
The Caetes 106 n.33, 235
Cage, Mathilda Joslyn 330
Caiçara film 229
Cajete, Gregory 24
Calamity Jane 171

Caldeira, Oswaldo
  Ajuricaba: O Rebelde da Amazônia (Ajuricaba: The Rebel of the Amazon) 232–3
  Aukê 232
Callado, Antonio 234
  The Montaigne Expedition 113 n.162
Call Her Savage film 124
Calloway, Colin 180
Calvin, Jean 54, 59, 61–2
Cameron, James 176, 178
  Avatar film 175–8, 294, 297, 301
  A Message from Pandora documentary 178
Caminha, Pero Vaz de 130, 147
  "Birth Certificate of Brazil" letter 221–2
The Canandaigua Treaty Belt (1794) 201
Canassatego 80
Candido, Antonio, *A Formação da Literatura Brasileira* (Formation of Brazilian Literature) 64
candomblé 256, 302, 319
Canevacci, Massimo 268
cangaceiros 228–30
cannibals/cannibalism 7, 10, 13, 19, 56, 59, 65–72, 92–5, 112 n.152, 129, 144, 173, 194, 242, 330
  endo-cannibalism 282, 284
capitalism 7, 14–16, 18, 32, 55, 73, 92, 158, 189, 225, 234, 263–4, 315, 332, 335, 347–8, 358
  outside of capitalism 350–2
  vs. planet 350–5
Caramuru 122–3
Caramuru: The Invention of Brazil 95, 126–31, 138, 223
Carapiru 261
caravela 13, 127, 219, 222, 358
Cardia, Gringo, *Hotxua* 248
Cardinal, Lome 187
Cardoso, Henrique Fernando 219
Carelli, Mario 63, 106 n.37
Carelli, Vincent 47 n.55, 240–5, 250–1, 259, 261
  Corumbiara: They Shoot Indians, Don't They? 249–51
  Eu jáfui seu irmão (*I Was Already Your Brother*) 242–3

Martírio 259–60
Segredos da Mata (Secrets of the Forest) 242
Signs Don't Speak 47 n.55
Yaokwa: Image and Memory 40
Yaokwa: Neglected Patrimony 40
Carib/Caraiba Revolution 68–75, 83, 218, 315, 322–31, 324, 329
Carijo culture 105 n.16, 142
Carlos, Roberto, "*E Papo Firme*" 134
Carpentier, Alejo
  "*lo real maravilloso americano*" 291
  The Lost Steps 291
Carrière, Jean-Claude 85, 233
Caruso, Enrico 153
Cash, Johnny 216
Castaneda, Carlos, *Don Juan: A Yaqui Way of Knowledge* 97
Castro Rocha, João Cezar de 70–1, 108 n.68
  Les Origines de la culture 70
Catholics/Catholicism 59, 87, 112 n.160, 183, 196, 213, 215, 221, 234, 248, 295, 344
Catitu 148
caucus 215, 352
Cavaliers. *See* Kadiweu (Guaicuru)
Cawelti, John 169
Cayuga 78, 202
Cecil B. De Mille Indians 192
Celso Oro Eu 93
censor/censorship 78, 120, 135, 146, 232–3, 345
Centennial commemorations 218–26
Cesaire, Aime 71
Cesar, Amaranta 299
Cesar, Chico 225
  "Demarcation Now!" 156
CGI effects 126–8, 300–1
Chagnon, Napoleon 3, 277, 279–80, 283, 285–90, 308
  The Feast 279
  The Fierce People 1, 278
Chartered West India Company (*Geoctroyeerde Westindische Compagnie*) 117
Cheechoo, Shirley, *Bearwalker* 38
Cherokee 9, 169, 187, 216, 224, 233, 334, 336

Cheyenne people 173, 184
Cheyfitz, Eric 334
Chicanos 194, 198, 216
Chingachgook die Grosse Schlange (Chingachgook the Great Serpent) film 179
Chippewa 46 n.24
Chirac, Jacques 31, 64, 210 n.54, 240
Chiriguanos 252
Christian, Barbara 27
Christian/Christianity 12, 20, 22–3, 32, 38, 59, 66, 75, 83, 98–9, 101, 125, 172, 182–3, 190–1, 220, 227–8, 235, 248, 252–3, 255, 292–3, 316–17
  Christianization 105 n.24, 227, 263
  Providentialism 225
Cinema Novo 36, 229–31
class system 67–8, 76, 103
Clastres, Hélène 64, 238
  A terra sem Mal (The Land without Evil) 252–3, 256
Clastres, Pierre 18, 55, 64, 89–94, 247, 280, 283–5, 309, 328
  Arqueologia da Violência (The Archeology of Violence) 89
  Society against the State 41
Clay, Jason W. 45 n.18
Clifford, James 37, 162
climate change 1–2, 18, 150, 207, 227, 315, 350, 354
Cobo, José Martínez, Study of the Problem of Discrimination against Indigenous Populations 9
Cocteau, Jean 292
Cody, William Frederick. *See* Buffalo Bill
Coelho, Rafael Franco 268
Cohen, Felix S. 79, 172
  Handbook of Federal Indian Law 79, 110 n.107
Colden, Cadwallader 356
Coleman, Daniel 201
colonial/colonialism/colonization
  ambivalence 315–18
  colonial conquest 7, 22, 100, 136, 169, 219, 324
  coloniality 19, 29, 72, 197, 342–3
  colonial mimicry 98, 220
  double colonization 45 n.20

settler-colonialism (*see* settler-colonialism)
Columbus, Christopher (and the Conquest of Americas) 2–3, 7, 9, 11–16, 18, 29, 72–3, 75, 81, 85, 119, 159, 180, 193–5, 218–19, 221, 321, 347
and Queen Isabella 16
Columbus Didn't Discover Us 218
The Columbus Invasion: Colonialism and the Indian Resistance 218
Columbus on Trial 218
Comanches 184
commodity/commodification 26, 101, 170, 189, 254, 259, 331, 347
communal/communalism 22, 25–6, 36, 60, 67, 69, 73–4, 78, 81, 90, 116, 128, 131, 146, 149, 246–8, 277, 282, 284, 299, 305, 308, 311, 324–5, 330, 335, 347–8, 351, 357
communication 18, 35, 43, 59, 135, 155, 215, 250, 268, 285, 299. See also language
communism 26, 73, 89, 330, 342, 350, 352–3
communitas 60, 189, 348
Como Irmaos (Like Brothers) 242
Comolli, Jean-Louis 148, 241, 249, 251
Comte, Auguste 225
"Conference of the Indigenous Peoples and Organizations of Brazil" 219
Congresso Indigenista Americana 29
Conklin, Alice 93
conquest fiction genre 169, 228, 230
Conrad, Joseph, "redeeming idea" of civilization 126
Conselheiro, Antonio 230–1
consensus societies 10, 16, 30, 59, 80, 118, 325, 353–4, 357
Constituent Assembly in Brazil 215, 237
constitutionalism 30–1, 81, 315
contrapuntal narration 252–8
Conversas de Maranhao film 261
convivencia 36, 241, 296
Cooper, James Fenimore 124–5, 179–81
The Last of the Mohicans (*Der Letzte de Mohikanes*) 171, 179
Cordova, Amalia 35, 223, 285
Cordova, Viola Faye 44

Corntassel, Jeff 9
Corrêa, Mari 148–9, 243, 245
Encontro das Mulheres Yanomami (A Meeting with Yanomami Women) 150
Mulheres Cineastas Indigenas (Indigenous Women Filmmakers) 150
Quentura 150
cosmopolitics and cosmopolitanism 58, 71, 258, 283, 299, 334
Costa, Sergio 14, 55
Costner, Kevin, *Dances with Wolves* 34, 174–5, 177, 191, 319
Coudreau, Henri 328, 361 n.45
Coulthard, Glenn Sean 14, 25, 30, 334, 351–2, 357
"For Our Nations to Live, Capitalism Must Die" 352
grounded normativity 31, 206
The Courage Brothers novela 231
coureurs de bois (trackers) 54, 58
Covid-19 pandemic (Coronavirus) 2, 9, 151, 154, 206, 237, 266, 309, 338, 340–1, 355
Crane, Stephen 228
"The Crazy Queen" novela 231
Cree 34, 37, 46 n.24, 94, 196, 214, 248
Cronenberg, David 205
crossed gazes 5–6, 17, 22, 25, 38, 255, 285–90, 307, 310–11
Crusoe, Robinson 107 n.52, 181, 317
Cruze, James 179
Cubitt, Sean 347
Cuddihy, John Murray 85
cultural reciprocity 7, 18, 43, 75, 90, 126–7, 201, 315, 336, 343, 351
cultural relativism 61, 66–7, 286, 298
"Culture Shock" event (2008) 184
Cunhambebe 59–60, 64, 69, 94–6, 105 n.26, 131, 160
Confederação dos Tamoios 236
cunhã (Tupi "young woman") 115–62, 310–11, 318. See also *specific women*
as activist/artist 151–9
degraded 135–7
ecological 148–50
filmic and televisual 130–5

as filmmaker 120–1
as forest princess 141–2
as hyper-woman 143–8
as myth 121–6
as warrior 138–41

da Cunha, Euclides, *Rebellion in the Backlands* 230
da Cunha, Manuela Carneiro 88
   Mortos e os outros 263
   "Xamanismo e tradução" (Xamanism and translation) 296
Dahl, Gustavo, *Uirà: Um Índio a Procura de Deus* (Uirà: An Indian in Search of God) 232
Dakota Bible drawings 33
Dakota people 46 n.24, 143, 181, 215
Dali, Salvador 73
DaMatta, Roberto 214
Dançando com cachorro (Dancing with the Dog) 244
Daniel, João 214
Daniels, Victor (Chief Thunderbird) 192
Danowski, Deborah 207
Da-Rin, Maya, *A Febre* (*The Fever*) 263–5
Darwin, Charles (Darwinism) 43, 169, 278, 297, 302, 355
Darwish, Mahmoud, "The Speech of the Red Indian" 91
Das Criancas Ikpeng para o Mundo (From the Ikpeng Children to the World) 247
Database of Indigenous Slavery in the Americas (DISA) 217, 269 n.14
Dawes Act of 1887 170
Dawson, Rosario 216
de Alencar, Jose 65, 125, 179
   Iracema 124, 126–7, 130, 137
   O Guarani 124–5, 130, 224
   Ubirajara 65, 224
de Almeida Amaral, Maria Carolina 329
de Anchieta, José 60, 105 n.26, 214–15
de Andrade, Carlos Drummond 133
de Andrade, Joaquim Pedro 133–4
   The Brazil-wood Man 164 n.36
de Andrade, Mário 83, 290–1
   Macunaíma: The Hero without Character 83, 127, 132–5, 141, 248, 290, 319

de Andrade, Oswald 54, 56, 69–70, 72–3, 79, 82–3, 90, 94, 129, 156, 159–60, 164 n.34, 164 n.36, 194, 222, 229, 280–1, 291, 325–30, 354–5
   Anthropophagic Manifesto 68–9, 73
   "Cannibalist Manifesto" 71
   on colonialism/post-colonialism 72–3
   Creative Commons License 325
   A Crise da Filosofia Messianica (The Crisis of Messianic Philosophy) 72–3, 326–7
   critical whiteness studies 72
   "*De*-Cabralization" 72, 129
   "*De*-Columbusization" 72
   "*De-*Vespuccization" 72
   "high-tech Indian" (*indio tecnizado*) 56, 74, 82, 129, 156, 157, 238, 266, 268, 311, 317, 326, 329
   "Manifesto of Brazilwood Poetry" 71
   matriarchy 326–7
   "meager Rights of Man" 325, 330, 337
   Messianism 72–3, 326
   praise of *sacer-docio* (sacred leisure) 73, 173
   "Remarks Concerning the Savages of North America" 355–6
   Serafim Ponto Grande 325
de Beauvoir, Simone 4
Debret, Jean-Baptiste, *Voyage Pittoresque et Historique au Brésil, ou Séjour d'un Artiste Français au Brésil* 82
de Brito Alves, Alvaro Renan Jose 299
de Bry, Johann Theodor 56, 121
de Buffon, Comte 66–7
de Carvalho, Ernesto Ignacio 111 n.139
de Carvalho, Jose Jorge 344
de Castro, Eduardo Viveiros 18, 27, 32, 41–2, 55, 69, 97, 103, 177, 207, 247–8, 251, 295–300, 315, 329, 338–9, 341, 346, 359
   equivocation 250
   on first contact 250
de Certeau, Michel 22, 67, 94
Deer, James Young 179
Deer, Tracey, *Club Native* 205
Defoe, Daniel 291
   Robinson Crusoe 181, 317

de Gonneville, Paulmier 54, 56
de Holanda, Chico Buarque, "Iracema" song 137
Delacroix, Eugène, *Christ on the Sea of Galilee* 197
de la Drevetiere, Delisle, *Arlequin Sauvage* 75
Delaware 77, 116, 159, 162 n.5
de Lemos, Gaspar 55
de Léry, Jean 58, 60, 63, 67–8, 74, 82–3, 85, 88, 94–6, 105 n.28, 139, 247, 328, 353
  on cannibalism 66
  Histoire d'un voyage faict en la terre du Brésil 55, 65–6, 76, 85
de L'Estoile, Benoit 32
  Le Gout des Autres: De L'exposition coloniale aux Arts Premiers 31
Deleuze, Gilles 5, 36, 64, 69, 89, 94, 241, 248, 285, 318, 320–2, 359
  deterritorialization 258, 335
  nomadology 258
  A Thousand Plateaus 34, 318, 321
  What Is Philosophy 34
d'Elia, Andre, "Demarcation Now!" 156
de Lima, Ana Gabriela Morim 248
de Lom d'Arce, Louis-Armand (Baron de Lahontan) 76, 327
  New Voyages to North America 76
Deloria, Philip J. 185, 318
  hobbyism 174, 210 n.54
  Playing Indian 174, 210 n.54, 319
Deloria, Vine, Jr. 4, 83, 99, 126, 128–9, 169, 174, 193–4, 293
  Behind the Trail of Broken Treaties 337
  Custer Died for Your Sins: An Indian Manifesto 189
  Indian-grandmother Complex 224
del Toro, Guillermo 205
de Magalhães, Gonçalves. *See also* romanticism
  "A Confederação dos Tamoyos" 64
  "Suspiros Poéticos e Saudades" 64
demarcation 47 n.55, 156, 161, 219, 231, 235–6, 249, 261, 267, 286, 335
de Medici, Catherine 56–7, 122, 125

de Melo Franco, Afonso Arinos 75, 79, 82–3, 109 n.85, 109 n.87, 325
  The Brazilian Indian and the French Revolution: The Brazilian Origins of the Theory of Natural Goodness 74
De Mille, Cecil B. 192
democracy 2, 7, 13, 18–20, 53, 76–7, 81, 227, 258, 260, 315, 322, 325, 331, 347, 350, 352, 354–5
  pseudo-democracy 329, 352
Dene people 14, 25, 30, 46 n.24, 65, 214
Denis, Ferdinand 64–5
  Lês Machakalis 65
  Resume de l'Histoire Litteraire du Bresil 65
  Scènes de la Nature sous les Tropiques 65
de Nobrega, Manuel 60
de Oliveira Andrade, Catarina Amorim 299
de Oliveira, Andre Luis, *Ubirajara: O Senhor da lança* (Ubirajara: Lord of the Spear) 232
de Oliveira, Benjamin 130, 224
de Oliveira, Jovita Maria 153
de Oliveira, Sandro 92
de Queiroz, Dinah Silveira 228
de Queiroz, Ruben Caixeta 243–4, 255, 299
Deren, Maya 291, 305
Derrida, Jacques 27, 31–2, 84–5, 235
de Santos, Boaventura Souza, epistemicide 20
Descola, Phillipe 64, 88, 94
  "Cultivated Savagery" 43
Desejo Proibido novela 131, 231
de Souza, Márcio 231
Devine, Bonnie 184
Dias, Goncalves 125
  "I-Juca Pirama" ("A Worthy Death") 57
Diawara, Manthia, *Opera of the World* 302
Diderot, Denis 17, 27, 53, 74, 83, 92
  Supplement to Bougainville's voyage 16
Die Sohne der Grossen Barin film 182
Digital Village Ecosystem 268
Dillon, Grace L.
  Indigenous Futurism movement 154–5, 266–7

Walking the Clouds: An Anthology of Indigenous Science Fiction 275 n.113
dime novels 169, 228
Dimock, Wai Chee 43–4
Dinis, Renata Otto 299
Diogo Álvares 122–3, 126, 128
Dirlik, Arif 335
discourse of Indian radicalism 18
Disney Corporation 14, 47 n.40, 93, 125
dispossession 2, 8, 22, 25, 58, 77, 80, 190, 205, 215, 220–1, 226–7, 231, 248, 259, 268, 334, 336–7, 351
divide-and-conquer strategy 76, 205
Dixie Chicks band, "Not Ready to Make Nice" song 199
do Amaral, Tarsila 72
"Doctrine of Conquest and Discovery" 12–16, 23, 30, 121, 169, 215, 218, 220, 222, 258, 316, 337
documentaries 3, 15, 86, 148, 186, 198, 232, 235, 240–1, 246, 271 n.41. *See also specific documentaries*
Dois Irmão mini-series 152
Dongria Kondh tribe 178
Donovan, Mishi 198
dos Santos, Laymert Garcia, "Transcultural Amazonas as Shamanism: Technoscience in the Opera" 302
dos Santos, Nelson Pereira 106 n.34, 160
  Como Era Gostoso o Meu Francês (*How Tasty Was My Little Frenchman*) 60–2, 131, 160, 180, 264
  Vidas Secas (Barren Lives) 230
Douglas, Keesic 184
Downey, Juan
  The Abandoned Shabono 283–4
  Cordova on 285
  Guahibos 283
  The Laughing Alligator 283–5
Drinnon, Richard 169
Duarte, Leandro Tadashi, *Naia e a lua* (Naia and the Moon) 262
Dunbar, John 34, 174–5, 321
Dunham, Katherine 109 n.85
Dunne, Susan 203–4
Dunye, Cheryl, *Watermelon Woman* 191
Durão, José de Santa Rita, *Caramuru* 122

Dussel, Enrique 19
The Dutch 116, 118, 159, 201, 204, 216
Dutch West Indies Company 14
Dutilleux, Jean-Pierre, *Raoni* 238
Dyer, Kester, on *Blood Quantum* 206, 212 n.106
Dyer, Richard, "Entertainment and Utopia" 146

ecology 8, 18, 176, 260, 323–4, 348
ecriture 97, 239, 241, 250
Ecuador 351, 354
egalitarian/egalitarianism 20–1, 28, 53, 56, 60, 63, 75, 79, 90, 282, 299, 352–3
Eliot, John 215
Elmalan, Serge, *Nicolas Durand de Villeganon ou L'Utopie Tropciale* 94
Eluard, Paul 64
eminent domain policy 24, 316
Enauene people 40, 247–8
enclosures (land ownership) 8, 14–15, 101, 324, 332, 347–8, 351–3
Engels, Friedrich 18, 73, 90–1, 330, 352, 357
England 8, 12, 118, 123, 181, 226, 359
Enlightenment 16, 18, 28, 68–9, 71, 74–5, 103, 117, 139, 225, 273 n.64, 306, 348
Erasmus, *In Praise of Folly* 67
Erdrich, Louise 184
Escobar, Arturo 19, 347
Essomericq 56, 62
ethnocentric/ethnocentrism 12, 21, 31, 46 n.24, 71, 74, 84, 138, 155, 173, 176, 178, 193, 234
ethnocide 214
Eucharist 59, 70, 105 n.24, 296
Eureka Stockade film 185
European Union 110 n.105
Europe/European 3, 8–17, 19–20, 23, 27–30, 44, 53, 56–63, 65–8, 74–9, 81, 85, 87, 89, 100–1, 103, 104 n.1, 116, 118, 121, 123, 141, 164 n.35, 173, 177, 182–3, 214, 216–17, 220–1, 229, 247, 253, 302, 308, 319–21, 324, 328, 331–2, 336–7, 339, 344, 348–9, 353, 356
  avant-gardes 69, 71–3

Euro-Americans 10, 12, 17, 30, 124, 201, 332
Euro-Brazilian 6, 94, 128, 225, 236–7, 263, 318
Euro-Canadian 196
Eurocentric/Eurocentrism 15, 19, 22, 27, 73, 76, 78–80, 84, 86, 122, 127–8, 201, 213–14, 222, 283, 342, 345–6, 354, 364 n.132
Euro-colonial discourses 20–1
European Enlightenment 55
European Indians 124, 186
European-indigene 72, 124, 129 (*see also specific groups*)
European Renaissance 55, 67
European Wars of Religion 59, 66, 95
European Westerns/Euro-westerns 179 and land 170
evangelical/evangelicalism 58, 135, 160, 173, 247, 263, 287
Expert Mechanism Council 336
extractivism 15
Eyre, Chris, *Smoke Signals* 37, 191

"Falas da Terra" series 157
Falsas Historias (False Histories) 218
Fanon, Frantz 20, 96
　Black Skin, White Masks 98
　The Wretched of the Earth 4, 92, 256
Fantin, Priscila 130, 231
Farmer, Gary 195
Fausto, Carlos 28, 32, 34, 40–1, 88, 240, 247
　consummation 70
　on *Iamarikuma* rituals 41
　Itai Kuegu: As Hiper Mulheres (The Hyperwomen) 143–8
Feest, Christian F. 180, 185
feitiço 101
feminism 21, 71, 73, 323, 326, 330, 332
Ferguson, Brian 278
Fernandes, Florestan 55
　The Social Organization of the Tupinamba 59
Ferreira, Patricia 120–1, 151, 292, 310
　Bicicletas de Nhanderú (The Divine Spirit's Bicycles) 256–7
　Desterro Guarani 258
　Nós e a Cidade (The City and Us) 120

Ferretti, Federico 328
　on Coudreau 361 n.45
"Festa da Onca" (Jaguar Festival) 244
fetish/fetishism/fetishization 101–2, 147, 176, 215, 225
fiction feature film 3, 38, 141, 182, 226, 233
Fiedler, Leslie 181
　"Come Back to the Raft Ag'in, Huck Honey" 163 n.24
Filho, Kleber Medonza, *Bacurau* 231
Fiorini, Marcelo 41, 86–7, 111 n.136, 252
first contacts (films) 6, 9, 53–4, 116, 159, 197, 218–26, 236, 242, 247, 249–50, 267, 358
First Nations in Canada 178, 183, 187
fishing 8, 87, 143–4, 205, 212 n.104, 239, 274 n.94
Fletcher, Alice 330
Flores, Lucio Paiva 297
Flórez-Flórez, Juliana 344
Floyd, Jacob, *Tonto Plays Himself* 191–2
Foner, Eric 356–7
Forbes, Jack D. 159, 342
　Columbus and Other Cannibals 94
Ford, John 170
Fort Apache the Bronx film 184
Foucault, Michel 4, 19, 36, 64, 241, 340
foundational fictions (Doris Summer) 62, 124, 126, 128, 133, 139–40, 224, 311
Founding Fathers of the United States 54, 77–81, 199, 215
Fourth World 45 n.15
France Antartique 53–4, 58–9, 63, 67, 73–4, 94–6, 104 n.2, 106 n.29, 112 n.160, 159–60, 180, 214, 253
　filming 60–5
　and Tupi theory 54–60
France/French 1, 3, 6, 12, 54–7, 59–60, 62–3, 68, 76, 78, 80, 90, 115, 129, 164 n.35, 179, 204, 214, 216, 323
　dissemination 63–4
　"Droits de L'homme" 323, 325
Franco-Brazilian 63–4, 82, 94–104, 106 n.37

Franco-indigenous 6, 11, 55–6, 58, 63–4, 67, 89, 96
Franco-Tupinambá 56
French Connection 69, 92, 112 n.152
French Enlightenment 53–4, 71, 80, 92, 139
French missions 82–8
French Revolution 4, 53, 58, 67, 71, 73–5, 82, 322, 323–4, 328, 337
Franchetto, Bruna 143, 247
Franklin, Benjamin 3, 53, 77, 79–81, 356
  Albany Plan for colonial Union 80
  letter to Parker 80
  "Remarks Concerning the Savages of North America" 342
Frayling, Christopher 179
Freedberg, David, *The Power of Images: Studies in the History and Theory of Response* 32
Freire, Gilberto 223
Freud, Sigmund 101–2, 326
Freyre, Gilberto 128, 214
frontier/frontiersmen/frontier Western 6, 13, 25, 124–5, 162, 169, 179, 185–8, 230, 236
  Hollywood 2, 5–6, 21, 33, 36–7, 39, 186, 228
  and land 170–2
Frost, Robert 171
Frotta, Monica, "Taking Aim: The Video Technology of Cultural Resistance" 239
"Full Speed to Adventure" TV series 283
Fulni-O, Edivan 157
Furtado, Gustavo 209 n.34, 222, 251
Furtado, Jorge 126
  Isle of Flowers 127

Gabriel, Teshome 258
Gallois, Dominique 240, 242, 247
Galvão, Patrícia (Pagu) 326
  Parque Industrial 326
Ganga Zumba film 231
Garcia Marquez, Gabriel, *One Hundred Years of Solitude* 290–1
Gates, Bill 15
Gell, Alfred, *Art and Agency: An Anthropological Theory* 32
"generic Indian" 9, 39, 63, 229

genocide 1–2, 10–11, 13, 16–17, 22, 58, 67, 93, 101, 106 n.34, 124, 141, 151, 171, 183, 189, 196, 213, 216, 221, 225–6, 231, 232, 235, 238–9, 247, 251, 259, 270 n.26, 274 n.99, 286–7, 330–1, 358
Géricault, Théodore, *The Raft of the Medusa* 197
Germany/Germans 6, 23, 36, 48 n.67, 60, 124, 136, 179–85, 189, 210 n.46, 223, 316
  Indianthusiasm 23, 183
gift economy 349
Gil, Gilberto 156, 243, 259
Gilliam, Terry, *Lost in La Mancha* 244
Ginsberg, Allen 175, 179
Ginsburg, Faye 5, 35, 37–8, 212 n.93, 311 n.13
Girard, René 55, 94, 108 n.68
  on cannibalism 70
  Violence and the Sacred 69
Glissant, Édouart 327
  circular nomadism 254
Godard, Jean-Luc
  Bande a Part 90
  Notre Musique 91
  Une Femme est une Femme 90
Goddard, Ives, *Handbook of North American Indians: Northeast* 162 n.5
Gomes, Carlos, *Il Guarani* 125
Gomez-Barris, Macarena 357
  on damned landscapes 8
Gómez-Peña, Guillermo 320, 333
Goncalves, Guilherme Leite 14, 55
"good Indian" 23, 71, 125, 139, 182, 224–5, 229, 247, 260, 318
Good, David, "The Good Project" 310–11
Good, Kenneth 40, 278, 280–1, 310–11
  Into the Heart: One Man's Pursuit of Love and Knowledge among the Yanomama 281–2
Goodman, Amy, *Democracy Now?* 1, 349
Gordon, Richard A. 127
Graeber, David 18, 32, 76, 139, 325–6
  The Dawn of Everything: A New History of Humanity 27
Graham, Zoe, sustainable documentary ecosystem 272 n.56

Gramsci, Antonio 115
   organic intellectual 162 n.1
Grande, Sandy
   authenticity 336
   critical pedagogy 331–2
   recognition liberalism 332
   Red Pedagogy: Native American Social and Political Thought 331
   whitestream feminism 332
Greco-Roman 76–7
The Green Inferno film 141
Grégoire, Victor 65–6
Greyeyes, Michael 364 n.120
   "Inside the Machine: Indigeneity, Subversion and the Academy" 342
Griffith, Jane 8
   Birth of a Nation 223–4
Grinde, Donald A., Jr. 80
   The Iroquois and the Founding of the American Nation 78
Guaicuru people 138–40
Guajajara, Kaê
   "*Essa Rua e Minha*" (This Street in Mine) 154
   "*Wiramiri*" (Birdie) 154
Guajajara, Sônia 134, 156–8
Guajajara, Zahy 152–3
   Don't Swallow My Heart, Alligator Girl! 153
   The Society of Nature 153
   Zahy: A Tale of Maracanã 152
Guaraní 22, 89, 119–21, 152, 180, 229, 235–6, 241, 252–8, 266–8, 336
   Guaraní-Caiowá 151
   Guaraní Collective films 253–6, 266
   Guaraní-Kaiowá 151, 155, 252, 258–65, 336
   Guaraní Mbyá Collective 252, 254
   mobile sovereignty 254
Guarani, Graciela 153, 155
   Mão de barro 155
   "Olhar da Alma" (Gaze of the Soul) 155
   Tempo circular 155
   Terra Nua 155
Guaraní, Mauricio 218
Guatarri, Félix 64, 94, 241, 318, 322
   A Thousand Plateaus 34, 318, 321
   What Is Philosophy 34

Guerra, Rui
   Kuarup 234
   Os Fuzis 230
Guerrero, Gonzalo 173
Guimarães, César 225, 250
Gunn Allen, Paula 5, 122, 331
   Pocahontas: Medicine Woman, Spy, Entrepreneur, Diplomat 122–3
   The Sacred Hoop: Recovering the Feminine in American Indian Traditions 122, 330
   on situation of indigenous women 28–9
Guzman, Tracy Devine 10, 124, 213, 233
gynocracy. *See* matriarchy

Haaland, Deb 2
Haircrow, Red, *Forget Winnetou! Loving in the Wrong Way* 183
Haitian revolution 323
Hajdu, David 162 n.3
Hakiy, Tiago 96
hallucinogen 15, 99, 277, 282, 285, 291, 294, 301–2
Hamburger, Cao, *Xingu* 235
Haraway, Donna 43
Hardt, Michael 323
Harjo, Joy 198
Harvey, David, "accumulation by dispossession" 55
Hatoom, Milton 152
   "Great Law of Peace" (Gayaneshakgowa) 78
Hearne, Joanna 169–70
   The Chief's Daughter film 125
   Comata The Sioux film 125
Hegel, Georg W. F. 16, 21–2, 32, 38, 53, 84, 89, 171, 213, 326
   The Philosophy of History 5, 17, 213, 221
hegemonic/hegemony 19–20, 58, 61, 82, 113 n.162, 136, 155, 178, 195, 213, 335, 351
Heide, Adelberto 244, 316–18
Hemmings, John, architectural masterpieces 277
Henderson, Youngblood 334
Hendrix, Jimi 216
Herder, Johann Gottfried 27

Herszenhut, Debora 243
Herzog, Amy 321
Herzog, Vladimir
    Fitzcarraldo 153
    murder of 106 n.32
heterosexuality 121, 124, 126, 129, 181, 186, 188
heyoka 248
Hiawatha 107 n.46
Hicks, Bob 190–1
"high arts" 71, 128, 134, 147, 153, 195
Highway, Tomson 184
Hill, Charlie 171, 192–3, 203
    Harold of Orange 193–4
Hispaniola 218, 220
A história do monstro Khátpy (The Story of the Khatpy Monster) 262
Hitler, Adolf 181–2, 218, 270 n.26
Hobbes, Thomas 3, 17, 53, 88, 102, 289–90, 327, 354
    bellicose savages 278
    Leviathan 117–18, 279
Hobsbawm, Eric 126, 230
Hollande, Francois 240
Hollywood 124, 145, 169–71, 173, 176, 178, 182, 184, 190–2, 197, 222, 228, 239, 255, 258, 308, 318
    Classical Hollywood films 5, 223
    Hollywood Western 6, 169, 171, 179, 185, 223, 228, 230–1
homoerotic/homoeroticism 181–2, 188
homophobia/homophobic 4, 13, 21, 226
homosocial 13, 181, 317
Hoods, Robin 229
Hopi people 33, 38, 183–4, 192, 198, 350
Hopkins, Gerard Manley 297
horror genre 136, 141, 173, 198, 226, 285, 287
    indigenization of 203–7
Huguenot Corpus 54, 61, 72, 89
Huhndorf, Shari 169, 175–6
Huku, Zandhio 267
Hulme, Peter 218
Huni Kuin 245–6, 254
Huron 3, 59, 63–4, 75–6, 83, 93, 215, 291
Hutukara 302, 314 n.100
hybridity/hybridization 33–4, 84–5, 132, 138, 148, 171, 222, 240, 297, 320, 333, 341

"Icamiabas" animated series 165 n.49
Icamiabas (Amazons) 134, 141
"ideology of whitening" 136, 216, 223, 270 n.34
Idlout, Lucie 198
Igloolik people 37
Ikpeng, Natuyu 242
Ikpeng people 222–3, 240–2, 247
imagineNATIVE Film + Media Arts Festival 184
Imperatriz Rio Samba School group 56
imperialism 9, 17, 21, 23, 73, 179, 226, 231, 235, 322–3, 334
impressionism (in painting) 305, 314 n.106
Incas empire 9, 12, 84–5, 116, 214
India 7–8, 38, 178, 185, 324, 334
Indian hobbyists in Germany 182–6, 318
Indiani Metropolitani (the Urban Indians of Milan) 179
Indianism/Indianist (*Indianismo*) movement 64–5, 124–5, 224–5
Indians on TV series 247
Indian Test Pattern (1983) 217
The Indian Wars film 172
indigenous films. *See specific films*
Indigenous generosity 12, 27, 132, 197, 229, 278
"Indigenous Holocaust" rap music video 198–9
indigenous media (IM) 2, 5–6, 35–43, 144, 148, 186, 198, 200, 221, 223, 232, 236–40, 245, 268, 295, 299, 302, 315, 321 and passim
Indigenous people *See also specific peoples/ groups*
    Australia 25–6, 29, 35, 37–8, 178, 185–6, 304
    Canada 3, 6, 25, 29, 63, 76, 95, 159, 173, 178, 184, 200, 205, 217, 319, 329, 336, 338, 347
    First Peoples 7–8, 22, 30, 152, 161, 184, 196, 200–3, 214, 255, 288, 268, 335
    Plain Indians 33, 180, 183
Indigenous Peoples of Brazil Organization (APIB) 237
indigenous social thought 3, 6–7, 27, 44, 53–4, 58, 73–4, 142, 154, 323, 352–3

Indigenous storytelling 37–9, 43, 165 n.53, 200, 284, 296
"Indigenous Women's Gaze" ("Olhares das Mulheres Indígenas") event 155
Indio-educa (Indians Educate) 161
Indios Online 8, 153, 161, 267
indio tecnizado (high-tech Indian) 56, 82, 157, 238
inheritance 37, 66–7, 134, 145, 189, 294, 349
"Injun" 23, 174, 223, 318
Institute of the National Historical and Artistic Patrimony (IPHAN) 145
intellectual property rights 14–15, 141, 353
International NGO Conference on Discrimination against Indigenous Populations 35
internet 1–3, 35, 38, 62, 160, 175, 186, 191, 200, 266–8, 295, 299, 363 n.101
Ipavu, Kamaiurá 113 n.162
Iraq 177, 287, 355
Irish 8, 46 n.24, 99, 162, 226, 293
"*Irmãos Coragem*" series 130
Iroquois (Haudesaunee) 7, 19, 30, 59, 63, 64, 77–81, 83, 85, 90–2, 102, 107, n.46, 118–19, 200–2, 258, 330–1, 334, 339, 342, 357
    Iroquois Confederacy 80–1, 202
    Iroquois League 77–8
Islam. *See* Muslims
Israel 112 n.149, 169, 173, 186, 234

Jackson, Samuel L. 202
Jakupe, Olivio 96
James, David, "allegory of cinema" 193
James, Henry 247, 298
Jamunkumalu (super-women) Kuikuro festival 143
JB the First Lady 198
Jefferson, Thomas 53, 77–8, 81, 124, 329
    letter to Adams 77
    Notes on the State of Virginia 77, 356
Jeguatá (sacred walk) 258
Jekupé, Olívio Kaka Wera
    "Twenty-First Century" 266
    Whenever We Said Goodbye 266
Jenkins, Henry, on Avatar activism 178
Jennings, Francis 169

Jensen, Doreen 40
Jerico (Jericho) film 173
Jesuits 11, 82, 87, 99, 160, 173, 216, 224, 233–5, 252, 254–5, 258
Jesus da Silva, Gliceria 161
Jews/Jewish 12–13, 32, 59, 84, 90, 105 n.23, 162, 186, 189, 204, 218, 222, 227, 234, 293, 319, 337, 355
Joannette, Odile 339
Jodelle, Etienne 53, 62, 64
Joffe, Roland, *The Mission* 235, 258
Johansen, Bruce E. 78, 80–1
    Forgotten Founders: Benjamin Franklin, the Iroquois, and the Rationale for the American Revolution 78
Johnson vs. M'Intosh case 12
Jolie, Angelina 216
The Journals of Knud Rasmussen film 37
Joyce, James 99, 293
    Ulysses 202
Juruna, Mário 237

Kadir, Djelal 14
Kadiweu (Guaicuru) 85–6, 89, 138–40, 164 n.43, 261
Kafka, Frantz, "Wish to become an Indian" (*Wunsch, Indianer zu werden*) 180
Kambeba, Márcia Wayna 96, 153
Kanienkehaka (Mohawk Nation) 200
Kanoê 249
Kant, Immanuel 17, 27
Karaí 253–4, 256
Karaja 142, 233
Karané 242
Kautokeino Opproret film 8
Kaxinawa 245–6
Kayapo 8, 37, 64, 129, 156, 238–41
Kayapo: Out of the Forest documentary 239
Keats, John 126
Kellog, Laura Cornelius, *Our Democracy and the Indian* 341–2
Kelly, Gene 146–7
Kelsey, Penelope Myrtle 201
Kennedy, John F. 78
Kesey, Ken, *Merry Pranksters* 193
Keys, Alicia
    "Mother Earth" song 166 n.85
    at *Rock in Rio* Festival 157–8

Kilpatrick, Jacquelyn 169
Kimmerer, Robin Wall 78, 90, 143, 149, 339, 347
   Windigo 100
King Charles IX 67
King Henry II 56-7
King Leopold 133, 226
King, Thomas 19, 24, 81, 187-8, 216
   "*Godzilla vs. Postcolonial*" 334
   inconvenient Indian 331, 333
   "Not the Indian you had in mind" 187-9
Kisedje, P. T., *Txêjkhõ Khãm Mby* (Mulheres Guerreiras) 262
Klein, Naomi 18, 348, 351
   "Save the Fraser Declaration" 350
   This Changes Everything: Capitalism vs. the Climate 350
Klotzel, André, *Capitalismo Selvagem* (Savage Capitalism) 235
Kluge, Alexander 333
Koch-Grunberg, Theodor 132, 164 n.37, 180, 290
   Aus Dem Leben der Taulipang 132
Kohn, Eduardo 150
Kolditz, Gottfriend, *Apachen* 184
Kolodny, Annette, *The Lay of the Land: Metaphor as Experience and History in American Life and Letters* 170
Krahô 206, 235, 240, 242, 248, 263, 267
Krenak, Ailton 2, 11, 72, 83, 96, 129, 156-7, 247, 274 n.90, 322, 338-41, 354, 359, 363 n.101
   "The Eternal Return of the Encounter" 90
   "Indigenous Cosmologies" 360 n.19
   Some Ideas for Postponing the End of the World 359
   A Vida Não é Útil (Life Is Not Useful) 340
Krenak, Edson 96
Kreta, Angelo 96
Krukutu subgroup 266
Kuikuro 32, 34, 38, 40, 143-7, 240-1, 254
Kuikuro, Mutuá 143
Kuikuro, Takumã 38
Kulina people 245
Kumaré 242
Kuna people 183, 331

Kunstler, William 319, 359 n.6
Kunuk, Zacharias 37
Kunumi (Werá Jeguaka Mirim), "Xondaro Ka'aguy Reguá" (Forest Warrior) 266

LaDuke, Winona 45 n.21
Lafitau, Joseph-Francois, *Meours des Sauvages Americains* 63
Lagrou, Els 246
Laguna Pueblo 84, 122-3, 331
Lahontan, Baron Louis Armand de 292
   Nouveaux Voyages dans l'Amerique Septentrionale, Memoires de l'Amerique Septentrionale 63
   Supplement aux Voyages ou Dialogues avec le sauvage Adario 63
Lakota 33, 46 n.24, 98, 174, 182, 184, 198-9, 238, 248, 319, 340
Lamarca, Tania, *Tainá: An Adventure in the Amazon* 141
Langton, Marcia, ab-originality 38
language 18, 34, 46 n.24, 62-3, 85-7, 97, 119, 122, 127, 133-4, 151, 159, 170, 173, 181, 191, 215, 229, 233, 236, 242, 250, 264, 293, 296-8, 339. See also communication
Lanzmann, Claude 251
La Otra Conquista film 121
LaRocque, Emma, cultural teaser 195
Latin America 22-3, 35, 119, 124, 132, 173, 181, 183, 263, 283, 332, 337, 342, 344-5
"Laughter and Resilience: Humor in Native American Art" exhibition 194
Lauzon, Jani 198
Law of Peace (Haudenosaunee) 78, 81, 201-2
Lehman, Kathryn 316
Lenape people 94, 116, 118-20, 159, 311
Lenine 127, 153, 156
   "*Tubi Tupy*" song 129
Lescarbot, Marc, *L'Histoire de la Nouvelle France* 27
les Fetes de Rouen case 23, 56-7, 60
Lestringant, Frank 54-5, 60, 83, 94, 112 n.160
"Letter Repudiating the 500 Years of the Discovery" 218

Leuthold, S. M. 169
Leuthold, Steven M. 169
Leutze, Emanuel, *Washington Crossing the Delaware* 197
Levi-Strauss: Aupres de l'Amazonie (Lévi-Strauss, Close to the Amazon) documentary 85, 256
Lévi-Strauss, Claude 3, 15, 32, 59, 64, 79, 82–9, 94, 98, 111 n.136, 111 n.139, 241, 247, 282, 298, 325
  La Pensée Sauvage 84, 88
  on Léry's history 67
  mimics 84, 86, 88
  Mythologiques 55, 88
  savage thinking 177
  Tristes Tropiques 68, 82–7, 103, 139, 250
  The View from Afar 83
  visit to Kadiweu 138
  "The Way of the Masks" 33
Lévi-Strauss, Dina 83, 86
LGBTQ+ 13, 154, 267, 320
Liberation Theology 335
Lightfoot, Sheryl 29, 43, 325–6, 334, 336–8, 353–4, 364 n.127
Lima, Leandro 302–3
Limbrick, Peter 185–6
Limerick, Patricia 170
limpieza de sangre 204
Linebaugh, Peter 47 n.42, 346, 348
  Magna Carta Manifesto 324
Lipschutz, Alejandro, pigmentocracy 49 n.91
Little Big Man film 173, 177
Littlefeather, Sacheen 238
Lizot, Jacques 286–7
  on gender relations 281
  Tales of the Yanomami 280
Locke, John 23, 26, 53, 329, 336
Longfellow, Henry Wadsworth, "The Song of Hiawatha" 181
longue-durée 192, 202, 249, 266
Lopes, André, *New York: Just Another City* 120–1
Lopez-Portillo, Miguel 18
Lorde, Audre 39
Löwy, Emanuel 33
Lucia Sa, *Rain Forest Literatures: Amazonian Texts and Latin American Culture* 290

Lukacs, Martin 350
Lula Presidency (2003–10) 237, 243
Luther Standing Bear 4, 21, 79
Lutz, Hartmut 180, 183
Luxembourg, Rosa 55
Lyons, Oren 258, 353, 366 n.181
Lyons, Scott Richard 354
  X-Marks: Native Signatures of Assent 85

Macas, Luis 354
Macdonald, David, *Christopher Columbus* 220–1
Madison, Kelly J. 178
Mad Maria mini-series 231
Magalhães, Antônio Carlos 218
The Magnificent Savages film 191
Mãhoroẽ̈ö, Domingos 268
Malfatti, Anita 72
mameluco 216–17
A Man Called Horse film 173
Mander, Jerry 16
  paradigm wars 5
Manichean dichotomy 28, 139–40, 142, 170, 174, 220, 317
Manifest Destiny 23, 169, 176, 186, 215, 226–7
Marcondes, Caito 87
Marcuse, Herbert, leisure society 72–3
Margulies, Lyn 43
Mariani, Giorgio 179
Marin, Nadja 285
Marker, Chris, *Les Statues Meurent Aussi* 120
Marris, Emma, *Wild Souls: Freedom and Flourishing in the non-Human World* 43
Martins, Alice Fátima 145
Marubbio, M. Elise 176
Marxism/Marxist 71, 73, 89, 100–1, 326, 331–2, 338, 347, 354, 357
Marx, Karl 14–15, 18, 71, 73, 89, 91, 102, 268, 330–1, 338, 352, 357, 366 n.198
Marzo, Claudio 131, 231
Masayesva, Victor, *Itam Hakim, Hopiit* (We, Someone, the Hopi People) 36
Master Race ideology 137, 191, 215
Materezio Filho, Edson Tosta 40
  What Levi-Strauss Owes to the Amerindians 88

matriarchy 72–4, 164 n.36, 315, 325–7, 331. *See also* patriarchal/patriarchy
Mattheissen, Peter 233
Mauro, Humberto
   Bandeirantes 227
   O Descobrimento do Brasil (The Discovery of Brazil) 221–2, 227
Mauss, Marcel 64
Mayas/Mayan empire 9, 12, 214
May, Karl 53, 124, 179–85, 187, 317
Mbya/Mbya-Guaraní 121, 252, 256
Means, Russel 97–8
"Meeting of Knowledges Project" 344
Meirelles, Renata, *Waapa* (Medicine) 262
Meirelles, Victor, "The First Mass" painting 221
Mekaron Opoi D'joi ("He Who Creates Images") project 239
Melatti, Delvair Montagnet 248
Melville, Herman, *Moby Dick* 181, 317
Mem de Sa 60, 214
Mencken, H. L. 341
Mendes, Chico 245–6
Mendes, Ilda 94
Mendez, Leo, *Cipo Tupi* 161
Mendonça, Paula, *Waapa* (Medicine) 262
Mercer, Kobena 258
merchandise, indigenous view of 55, 98, 100–2, 176, 264, 287, 298, 310, 348–50, 355
Meritororeu, Kleber 268
Mesquita, Claudia 143, 245, 251, 316
Messora, Renée Nader, *The Dead and the Others* 263
mestizo 119, 123–4, 217, 229–31
Metis 34, 122, 195, 200, 216
Metraux, Alfred 55
Metuktire, Raoni 64, 238–40, 334
Metz, Christian 39, 148
Mexico/Mexicans 6, 29, 33, 109 n.96, 121, 161, 172–3, 216, 228, 247, 273, 336, 347
Michiles, Aurélio
   David against Goliath 287
   The Secrets of Putumayo 226, 246
Mignolo, Walter 18–19
migration/migrants 8, 90, 118–19, 137, 197, 253, 258, 260, 336
Miguel, Muriel 183

Miguel, Padre 228
Mi'kmaq people 203, 205, 212 n.104
Miller, Huron 201
Milliken, William 277
Minhaj, Hasan Patriot Act 1, 158
minority/minorities 20–1, 28, 58, 103, 207, 261, 299, 321, 355
Miranda, Marlui 87
Mirim, Katu 154
mistikôsiwak (wooden boat people) 196–7
Mitchell, Emma 178
Mitterand, François 64, 240
mixed-race 62, 129, 133, 197, 222–3, 225, 230–1, 233
mockumentary 92, 190–1
modernism/modernists 68, 72–3, 83, 127–8, 164 n.36, 215, 229–30, 232, 235, 247–8, 291, 302, 354
   archaic modernism 13, 31, 38–9, 88, 132, 144, 191, 200, 266, 333
   Brazilian modernism (*Modernistas*) 6, 20, 31, 42, 53–4, 68–9, 71–4, 83, 89, 127–9, 132, 144, 156, 164 n.36, 215, 229–30, 232, 235, 247–8, 284, 291, 302, 333, 343, 354
Mohawk, John 8, 38, 92, 258, 331, 351
   on Pax Iroquoia 30
Mohawks 78, 92, 174–5, 192, 200, 202, 214, 258, 319, 336, 350–1, 356
Mohicans 118, 159
Monkman, Kent 191, 195–8
   at Great Hall of Metropolitan Museum of Art 196
   Resurgence of the People 197
   The Scream 196
   Shooting Geronimo 191
   Welcoming the Newcomers 197
Monroe, Marilyn, *The Seven Year Itch* 200
Monster from the Black Lagoon film 141
Montaigne, Michel de 3–4, 7, 17–18, 44 n.5, 53, 56, 61, 70, 76, 79, 83, 86, 88–9, 95–6, 99, 113 n.162, 139, 210 n.54, 287, 291, 294, 315, 325, 328, 356
   "Des Cannibales" 67
   "Des Coches" 67
   and Tupi theory 65–8, 75
Montesquieu 74
Montileaux, Donald 33

Monture-Angus, Patricia 351
Moog, Vianna 214
Moore, Michael 251
Morales, Evo 2, 176, 178
Moreira, Renato Neiva, *Esses e outros bichos* (Assorted Animals) 261
Moreno, Soni 198
More, Thomas, *Utopia* 67
Morettin, Eduardo Victorio 227, 270 n.38
Morgan, Henry Lewis 330
  Ancient Society 357
Morinico, Jorge Ramos, *Mokoi Tekoá Petei Jeguatá* (Two Villages One Path) 254
Morton, Thomas 197
  The New Canaan 172–3, 211 n.86
Mother Earth 152, 159, 166 n.85, 174, 338–9, 347, 351
Motta, Gisela 302–3
Moyngo, o sonho de Maragareum (Moyngo, the Dream of Maragareum) 242
Mulvey, Laura 4
Munduruku, Daniel 25, 96
munitions 54, 56, 62
Muniz, Olinda, *Retomar Para Existir* 155
A Muralha (The Wall) mini-series 228
Murat, Lucia 164 n.47
  Brava Gente Brasileira 138, 140
music/music videos 3, 5–6, 26, 29, 34, 38, 43, 57, 61–2, 66, 68, 87–8, 91, 95–6, 116–17, 127, 130, 137, 141, 144–6, 153, 156, 171, 186, 198–200, 203, 215, 220, 222, 265, 266–7, 293, 306, 309, 317
Muslims 12–13, 32, 59, 222, 337
  Moriscos 162
Mussa, Alberto 252
Muthu, Sankhar 27, 76
myths 227, 260, 297–8
  creation myths 307–9, 330, 348
  of extinction (the "vanished indigene") 159–62
  mythology 65, 125, 138–9, 144, 175–6, 197, 216, 233, 253, 277, 296

NacLean, Edna Ahgeak 40
Nagel, Joanne 359 n.7
Nagib, Lucia 235

Nakata, Martin
  Disciplining the Savages: Savaging the Disciplines 5
  indigenous standpoint theory 5
Nambikwara 41, 68, 84–7, 214, 256, 270 n.34
Nambikwara, Alberto 86
Nando, Padre 234
Nanini, Marco 126–8
narcissism/narcissistic 17, 23, 27, 92, 102, 183, 190, 215, 234
Nascimento, Beatriz 163 n.34
The National Institute of Cinematic Education (INCE) 270 n.38
The National Museum (Brazil) 270 n.34
nation-states, critique of 2, 7–9, 11–12, 20, 23, 25, 30, 32, 44, 81, 89, 118, 129, 171, 182, 196, 279, 315–59, 360 n.21
Native American Counter-Cinema 190
Native American Music Association 119
native arts and aesthetics 31–4
native informants 68, 343–4
Native Medicine 345
Navajo (Dine) 9, 37, 46 n.24, 85, 206
Na'vi people (*Avatar*) 175–8
Neel, James V. 277, 279, 283
Negri, Antonio 323
negros da Terra (Blacks from the Land) 162, 217
negros de Guinee (Africans) 217
Nelson, Melissa K. 34
Nepinak, Darryl 184
Netflix programs 1, 11, 158, 307
New Age 38, 183–4
New Amsterdam 116, 118–19, 159, 216
New France Company 14
New Israel 58, 169, 173
New Tribes Mission 242, 263
New World 12–14, 21, 55, 63, 65, 67, 95, 123, 141, 214, 220. *See also* Old World
Ngune Elu film 38
nheengatu 215
Nichols, Robert 8, 33, 76, 351
Nietzsche, Friedrich 24
  fröhliche wissenschaft (joyful knowledge) 262
Nimuendajú, Curt Unckel 180

Niro, Shelley
  500 Year Itch 200
  Kissed by Lightning 200–2
  This Land Is Mime Land 200
noble savage 19, 26–8, 49 n.87, 89, 128, 139, 177, 181, 188, 218, 224, 234
No caminho com Mário (On the Road with Mario) film 257
Nodari, Alexandre 329
nomadic/nomadism 8, 23, 37, 126, 253–4, 258, 284, 286, 322, 354
Norby, Patricia Marroquin 159
No tempo das chuvas (In the Rainy Season) 243
Novaes, Adauto, *A Outra Margem do Ocidente* 95, 113 n.161
Novaes, Washington 329
nudity 61, 66–7, 106 n.31, 147, 188, 232, 243
Nunez, Alvar, *Relacion de los Naufragios* (Story of the Shipwrecked), 173
Nyn, Joao 266–7
  Peerless Android band 267

Obomsawin, Alanis 198
  Incident at Restigouche 212 n.104
Obry, Olga, *Catherine du Bresil: Filleule de Saint Malo* (Catherine of Brasil: God-daughter of Saint Malo) 164 n.35
Occom, Samson 96
Occupy Wall Street (OWS) movement 332
Odin, Roger 148
  documentary effects 93
O Espirito da TV (The Spirit of Television) film 242
Ofelas (Pathfinder) film 8
Oglala Sioux 9, 206
Ojibwe 33, 36, 46 n.24, 181, 183, 248, 254, 319, 336
Okanagan 5
The Oklahoman film 124
Oldroyd, Benjamin 293
Old World 63, 77. *See also* New World
Omama 99–101, 164 n.45, 262, 290, 292–4, 309, 335, 348
O Mestico novela 131, 231
Oneida 78, 192, 341
One Night the Moon 25–6
Onondaga 78, 80, 102, 201
On the Road with Mario film 253
O Relogio e a Bomba film 219
Orientalist 7, 130, 220
orixa 256, 304
Ortega, Ariel
  Bicicletas de Nhanderú (The Divine Spirit's Bicycles) 256–7
  Desterro Guarani 258
  Mokoi Tekoá Petei Jeguatá (Two Villages One Path) 254
Os Sertões de Mato Grosso (The Backlands of Mato Grosso) film 225
Ostern ("Eastern") genre, Soviet films 185
ostrenanie 291
Outros Quinhentos (Another Five Hundred Years) 218
The Overlanders film 185
Oz Guaranís indigenous rap group 267

Padilha, Jose
  Elite Squad 286
  Secrets of the Tribe 286
Paine, Thomas (Tom) 18, 77–8
painterly tricksterism 195–8
paintings 1, 5–6, 33, 38, 40, 56, 72, 126, 134, 147, 154, 194–8, 200, 203, 221, 246, 300, 304–5, 314 n.106, 358
Paĭ-Tavyterã 252
Palacios, Alfredo, *I Married a Xavante* 130
Panara, Komoi, *Priara Jo* (After the Egg, the War) 262
pan-Indian movements 7–8, 35, 157, 236, 268
Pankararu, Alexandre, *Mão de Barro* 155
Papal Bull (by Pope Nicholas) 12
Paraguassu, Tupi Princess 62, 121–31, 138–9, 164 n.35, 175
Paraguay 41, 119, 252, 268
Pareci Indians 87
Parker, James 80
Pastor, Gilbert, *Le Valet d'Aventure* 94
Pataxó 153, 155, 219, 262
patents 14–15, 353
patriarchal/patriarchy 80, 293, 326–7, 330–2. *See also* matriarchy
Paul, Heike 122

Pawnee 174, 182, 217
Pax Iberica 73
Payako, Benki, collective cure 267
Paz, Octavio 121
Peace Treaties 10, 105 n.26, 174
Peck, Raoul, *Exterminate all the Brutes* 13, 215
Peele, Jordan 205
Pelosi, Nancy 158
Peltier, Leonard 189, 319
Pena, Richard 60
Penn, Arthur, *Little Big Man* 173
Penny, H. Glenn 180
 Kindred by Choice 183
Penom 290
People's Palace Projects 38
Pereio, Paulo Cesar 135–6
Pereira, Renato 239
Perkins, Rachel 25–6
Perrone-Moises, Beatriz 11, 59, 97, 105 n.16
Perrone-Moises, Leila 58, 106 n.37
Pessoa, Fernando 133
peyote (plant medicine) 268, 283
philo-indigenism 69, 71, 77, 326
Pindorama 72, 164 n.36, 326
Picasso, Pablo 31, 291
pigmentocracy 49 n.91
Pinhanta, Isaac, *A gente luta mas come fruta* (We Fight, but We Eat Fruit) documentary 149
Piõnhitsi, mulheres xavante sem nome (Xavante Women without Names) documentary 244
Pitanga, Antonio 129
Pitanga, Camilla 129–30
Piyãko, Wewito, *A gente luta mas come fruta* (We Fight, but We Eat Fruit) documentary 149
Plato/Platonic/ Platonism 87, 299–300
Pocahantas/Pocahontas 121–5, 135, 175, 216
Pocahontas film 175, 177
Poltergeist film 192
Pope John Paul II 218
popular culture 3, 6, 117, 169, 218
 transmediatic indigene of 266–8
Portugal 12, 63, 95, 115, 127, 214, 216, 219

Portuguese 10–11, 23, 54, 56, 58, 62–4, 95–6, 100–1, 103, 116, 119, 125–30, 135, 137–8, 140–1, 147, 157, 161, 213–17, 219, 221–2, 224, 227, 230, 233, 236, 261, 267, 340, 363 n.101
Posey, Daryl 24, 238
positive image model 3, 28, 60, 89, 142, 186, 189, 194–5, 203–6, 224, 229, 317
possessive individualism 3, 325, 354
postcolonial theory/postcolonialism 27, 72–3, 204–6, 334–5, 338–41, 353, 362 n.86
postmodernity/postmordernism 19, 31, 72, 128, 163 n.34, 254, 257, 333, 335
post-structuralist theory 31, 322, 335, 338, 354
Potiguara, Eliane Lima dos Santos 153
Powhatan Alliance (Dream-Vision People) 123
Powhatan Confederacy 122–3
Prance, Ghillean 277
Pratt, Mary Louise 19
 Arts of Living on a Damaged Planet 43
Pratt, Scott, native pragmatism 5
primitive accumulation 14, 55, 89
"primitive arts" 31, 64
primitive communism 26, 73, 89
primitive socialism 90, 102, 330
Prinop: My First Contact film 222
process films 143, 245, 249, 251, 272 n.60, 316
Promised Land 170, 186, 232
Protestants 54, 58–9, 87, 112 n.160, 215, 234, 248, 326
 Protestant Huguenots 59
 Weberian 90
protest/protestors
 Alcatraz protest 91, 238, 323
 anti-quincentennial protest (1992) 35
 Belo Monte project 8, 178, 240, 260, 343, 364 n.125
 "Brasil: Outros 500" 219
 Dakota Access Pipeline project 197
 English Only protests 216
 Standing Rock protests 24, 197, 260, 323, 347
 "The Longest March" 238
 Wounded Knee protest 91, 172, 188, 238, 319, 323

proto-indigenist cinema in Brazil 231–6
Proudhon, Pierre-Joseph 78, 328
Pueblo people 44, 64, 84–5, 331
Pura Fe 198
Purepecha 268
Puritans/Puritanism 28, 58, 73, 98, 138, 169, 172–3, 197, 233, 281, 292, 341, 347
Puri, Zelia 96

Quebec 11, 37, 59, 63, 197, 200, 203, 205, 212 n.104, 216
Quebec Provincial Police (QPP) 212 n.104
Quechua people 331–2, 336, 347, 354
queer theory 4, 21, 44, 191, 357
Queiroz, Dulce, *Terras Brasileiras* (Brazilian Lands) 261
Quijano, Anibal 19
Quilombo film 231
quipu 32, 85, 143

radical/radicalism 3, 13, 18, 27, 71, 90, 129, 183–4, 187–8, 218, 238, 315, 321–2, 325, 332–3, 336, 352, 354, 357
Radio Yande (Facebook post) 155
Raheja, Michelle H. 169, 198, 203
  "Transnational Indigenous Media" 39
  visual sovereignty 35
"*A Rainha Louca*" novela 131
Rama, Angel, "Lettered City" 22
Ramos, Alcida Rita 220, 289
  Pacificando o Branco: Cosmologias do contato no norte-Amazonico (Pacifying the White Man: Cosmologies of Contact in the Northern Amazon) 346
Ramos, Graciliano 230
Ranciere, Jacques 64, 148, 256, 321
reahu festival 282, 297
Realpolitik 76–7, 322
rebels/rebellion 7, 29, 54, 61, 63–4, 92, 125, 174, 179, 184, 194, 197, 220, 224, 228, 230–1, 233, 267, 323, 330
Red Atlantic 59, 115, 182
Redbone rock band 172, 198
Reeks, David, *Waapa* (Medicine) 262
Rego, José Lins do 230
Reinega, Fausto, *La Revolución India* 330

Reini, Harald 179
Reis, Luis Thomaz 87, 132, 225
  Ao Redor do Brasil 225–6
replacement theory 355
republican constitutionalism/revolutions 30, 79, 322–31, 337, 355
requerimiento (requisition) 23, 220, 222
Reservation Dogs TV series 1, 195
residential schools 196, 198, 200, 320, 344
resistance 5–6, 8, 29, 31, 35, 176, 178, 183, 197, 220, 228, 233, 236, 259, 267, 337, 350, 353 and passim
resistant readings 187
Resnais, Alain 307
  Les Statues Meurent Aussi 120
Restall, Matthew 16
Return of the Country film 190
Revere, Paul 81
Reynal, Abbe Guillaume 74
  Les Deux Indes 16
Reynolds, Debbie 146–7
Ribeiro, Darcy 138, 232, 328
  Os Índios e a Civilização (Indians and Civilization) 234
Ribeiro, Marcelo, cosmopoetica 299
Ricard, Jolene 151, 269 n.1
Ricelli, Carlos Alberto 131, 231
Rieder, Hans Rudolf 182
Rios, Luiz Henrique 239
Ritual Ticuna da Iniciacao Feminina (Ticuna Ritual of Female Initiation) short film 40
Rituas e Festas Borôro (Bororo Rituals and Feasts) film 225
A River Runs through It film 274 n.94
Robertson, Robbie 198, 216
Rocha, Castro 70–1, 108 n.68
Rocha, Glauber 32, 306
  Deus e Diabo na Terra do Sol (God and the Devil in the Land of the Sun) 230
  Terra em Transe 234
Rodrigues, Aryon 215
Rogin, Michael 169
Rohrbach, Paul 48 n.67
Rolfe, John 122–3, 125, 216
romanticism 26–7, 64, 124–6, 129–30, 182, 228–9, 232, 260, 289
Romero, George 205
  Night of the Living Dead 203

Rondon, Coronel 225, 235
  Rondon Commission 87, 225, 252, 270 n.34
Roosevelt, Teddy 270 n.34
Roquette-Pinto, Edgard 227
Rosaldo, Renato, imperial nostalgia 171, 349
Rouanet, Sergio Paulo, seismograph 75, 109 n.87
Rouch, Jean 145, 148, 258, 272 n.56, 283, 306
  anthropologie partagée 346
  Chronique d'un Ete 274 n.103
  cine-transe 304
Rouen festivities (1550) 56–8, 60
Rousseau, Douanier 61
Rousseau, Jean-Jacques 17–18, 27, 53, 66, 74, 79, 83–4, 88–9, 139, 179, 290, 326, 356
  "Discourses on Inequality" 75
  les sauvages 262
Roussef, Djilma 167 n.91
royal letters (*litterae patents*) 14
Roy, Arundhati 350
Rufin, Jean-Christophe
  Rouge Brésil (novel) 64, 95
  Rouge Brésil (Tele-film), 95
Ruiz, Raul 42
Rutherford Falls TV series 1

Sabatella, Letícia 131, 156, 231
  Hotxua 248
sacred flutes (*kagutu*) 32, 41, 70, 120, 144
sacred land 22–31 and passim
sacred plants 267, 291, 295, 300–1, 304–5, 319
Sahlins, Marshall 18, 90, 203, 278, 280, 309
Said, Edward 44
  traveling theory 53
Sainte-Marie, Buffy 193, 198
Sakamoto, Leonardo 137
Salaviza, João, *The Dead and the Others* 263
Saldanha, Luiz Carlos, *Raoni* 238
Salvat, Joan, *Brasil, la guerre de l'or* (Brazil, the Gold War) 262
Sami people 8
Sampaio, Marcelo Felipe, *O guardado* (The Saved) 261
Sanday, Peggy, on cannibalism 70
Sanderson, Eric W. 119
  Manahatta: A Natural History of New York 119, 162 n.2
Santos, Marcelo 249
Santos, Silvino 141, 226, 250, 270 n.37
Sartre, Jean-Paul 4
  Anti-Semite and Jew 334
Satan/Satanic 13, 98–9, 292
Sauvage (savages) 7, 13, 17, 26–7, 62–4, 84, 88, 90, 118, 125, 140, 250, 356
scheduled tribes of India 7
Schiwy, Freya, *Indianizing Film: Decolonization, the Andes, and the Question of Technology* 165 n.53
Schoolcraft, Henry 33
Schultes, Richard 277
Schultz, Harold 246
Schvartzman, Sheila 222
Schwarz, Roberto, out-of-place ideas 103
Schweitzer, Albert 182
Scott, James C. 4
Second International Decade of the World's Indigenous People (2005–15) 176
Seed, Patricia 11, 222
  Ceremonies of Possession in Europe's Conquest of the New World, 1492–1640 23
  rituals of possession 56
The Seed Wars film 15
Seeger, Pete, "This land is my land" 171
Segreto, Affonso 225
seismic shift 48 n.66, 342, 345, 364 n.125
Sellos, Rodrigo, *Por Onde vai Macunaíma* (Where Is Macunaíma Going?) 135
Seminole 214, 319, 336
Seneca 78, 169, 202, 330–1
Senghor, Léopold Sédar, *Anthologie de la Nouvelle poésie Nègre et Malgache de Langue Française* 4
Senna, Orlando, *Iracema: Uma Transa Amazônica* 135–6
Senra, Stella 302–3
seringueiros (rubber tappers) movement 245

Serras da Desordem film 261
Sette, Leonardo, *Itai Kuegu: As Hiper Mulheres* (The Hyperwomen) 143–8
settler-colonialism 2–3, 8, 24, 29–30, 91, 125, 129, 185, 189, 192, 196, 216, 254, 331–4, 336
Severi, Carlo 32–4, 88
  Aby Warburg archive analysis 33
  The Chimera Principle: An Anthropology of Memory and Imagination 32
  Oral/written dichotomy 32–4
shabono 277, 281–2, 284–5, 301, 305, 309, 358
Shakespeare, William 102, 131, 147
  The Merchant of Venice 102
  Tempest 67
shamans/shamanism 1, 3–5, 8, 13, 34, 38, 42, 44, 90, 96–7, 99–100, 102, 123, 161, 183–4, 207, 263, 285, 292–302, 319, 328
  cinematizing 302–7
  power of critique 346–50
Shamash, Sarah 144
Shanken, Edward 285
Shenandoah, Joanne 198
Shephard, Glenn 209 n.34
Shiva, Vandana 14–15, 19, 47 n.41
Shohat, Ella 104 n.8, 112 n.149, 162 n.1, 178, 186
  "Goodbye Columbus" Conference 269 n.17
  Race in Translation: Culture Wars in the Postcolonial Atlantic 47 n.56, 48 n.66, 112 n.150, 345, 364 n.132
  Unthinking Eurocentrism: Multiculturalism and the Media 3, 12, 19
Shomōtsi 244
Silko, Leslie Marmon 38, 44, 84
Simpson, Leanne Betasamosake 21, 25, 39, 149, 206, 296, 319, 321, 327, 333, 345, 351–2
  As We Have Always Done 5, 106 n.40
Singer, Beverly 169
Singin' in the Rain film 145–7
Sioux 33–4, 46 n.24, 172
Sivan, Eyal (Montage Interdit website) 90

Six Nations Iroquois Confederation 78, 80, 201
slaves/slavery (trade) 12–14, 16–17, 28, 77, 124, 137, 204, 224–5, 227, 231, 233, 321
  abolition of 11
  transatlantic 218
  virtual 136–7, 344, 349
Slotkin, Richard 169
Smith, John 121–3, 125, 163 n.22
Smith, Linda Tuhiwai 3, 7
Smith, Paul Chaat 169, 322
Smithsonian National Museum of the American Indian 119
Sobchack, Vivian
  The Address of the Eye 305
  Carnal Thoughts 305
social evolution (Positivist law of three stages) 225
socialism 75, 90, 102, 252, 330, 352
social media 2, 151, 159, 200, 267
Socrates, *The Odyssey* 99, 202, 294
Solano 256
Soros, George 13
soul (*wakan*) 43, 60, 99, 174, 180, 233, 235, 277, 317
Souza, Jessé 214
Souza, Marcio 67, 108 n.63
sovereign/sovereignty 7, 9, 12, 14, 22–4, 29–30, 78, 81, 88, 92, 116, 151, 157, 176, 221, 236, 254, 260, 289, 325, 336–7, 351, 360 n.21
Spain 12, 14, 18, 162, 185, 204, 218, 227, 337
  Spanish 16, 18, 23, 45 n.20, 46 n.24, 53, 55, 59, 67, 138, 141, 173, 214, 216, 220–1, 227, 288, 347
  Spanish Inquisition 59
  Spanish Monarchy 215
Spiderwoman theater troupe 183
spirituality 8, 182, 246, 252–3, 256, 260, 262, 293–4, 300–1, 304, 335, 337
SPI (Service of the Protection of the Indian) 225, 259
Spivak, Gayatri, "strategic essentialism" 335
The Squaw Man film 125
Staden, Hans 60, 69, 74, 94, 180
  Brasilien: Die wahrhaftige Histoire der wilden nacken, grimmigen

Menschenfresser-Leute (The Brazilians: The True History of the late Wild, Grim Man-Eaters) 55
True History 61
stand-up comedy 3, 6, 171, 186, 192–3, 198
Stanton, Elizabeth Cady 330
"state of nature" 6, 17, 78, 102, 117–18, 278, 288–9, 327
Stoic/Stoicism 190, 228
subsistence cultures 40
Sulpiciens organization 11
Sun, Moon, and Feathers film 183
Surrealist/Surrealism 64, 71–3, 295
Survival organization 178
Surviving Columbus 218
Sustainable Development Solutions Network 366 n.196
Suya, Kambriti 262
Suya, Kokoyamaratxi 262
Suya, Whinti 262
Suya, Yaiku 262
Syberberg, Hans-Jurgen, *Karl May* 182
Sztutman, Renato 10–11, 88, 253, 296
  elective affinity 88
  self-metamorphosis 69

Tainá trilogy films 141–2
Tainos 16, 29, 159, 194, 218, 222, 270 n.26, 347
Tamoio Confederation 96
Tarantino, Quentin 195, 204
  Django 206
  Inglorious Basterds 182
Tate, Greg 321
Tatum, Melissa A, *Structuring Sovereignty: Constitutions of Native Nations* 360 n.21
Tauli-Corpuz, Victoria, paradigm wars 5
Taulipang (Taurepang) people 132, 290
Taunay, Affonso D'Escaglione 227
Taussig, Michael 280, 284
  Shamanism, Colonialism, and the Wild Man 137
Taylor, Diana 18, 22
  The Archive and the Repertoire 21
Taylor, Drew Hayden 184
Teosi (Christian God) 99, 292–4
tepees (Dakota) 33, 215

Terena, Naine 155
Terra Nullius 25, 186, 218, 251
Thatcher, Margaret 30, 170, 352
theoretical indigene 315–59
Thévet, Andre 60, 64, 67, 74, 94–5, 253
  Cosmographie Universelle 54–5
  Les Singularites de la France Antartique 54
Thobani, Sunera, exaltation 23
Thompson, Robert Farris, *Flash of the Spirit* 32
Thomson, Charles 77
Thor (god of Iron) 183
1491s comedy group 195
1492 Revisited 218
Thronicke, Soraia 157
Tibaji Indians 84
Tierney, Patrick 283
  Darkness in El Dorado: How Scientists and Journalists Devastated the Amazon 278
Tiffany, Sharon W., "Anthropology's 'Fierce' Yanomami: Narratives of Sexual Politics in the Amazon" 288
Tikuna, Djuena 156
  Tchautchiüãnein 153
Tikuna, We'e'ena 153–4
  We'e'ena: Indigenous Enchantment 154
Todd, Loretta, *Fierce Girls* 200
Todorov, Tzvetan, hecatomb 9, 111 n.125
Tonacci, Andrea 236, 241, 261
To Protect Mother Earth documentary 208 n.8
Torres, Antonio, *Meu Querido Cannibal* (My Beloved Cannibal) 95–6
Torres-Campos, Tiago, *O Mestre e o Divino* (*The Master and the Divine*) 244, 315–18
Touratier, Jean-Marie, *Bois Rouge* 94
trade/traders 11–12, 23, 54, 58, 63, 66, 101, 117–18, 137, 197, 278, 286, 349
Trans-Amazonian Highway 61, 135–6, 156, 227, 261, 343
transAtlantic 12, 56, 218
transdisciplinary/transdisciplinarity 2, 43–4, 342, 344 and passim
transgenerational 36, 38, 43, 144, 223, 332–3, 349
transhistorical 43–4, 56, 115, 117, 127

transmedial indigeneity 186–9, 192, 200
    of popular culture 266–8
transnational 2, 6–8, 13–14, 25, 36, 43, 55, 103, 115, 117–18, 187, 233, 243, 336
    and indigenous happiness 355–7
transnational gaze 315–18
trans-species 34, 296–7, 305
transtextuality 3, 43, 54, 70, 176, 197
transubstantiation, Catholics 59
Treaty of Fort Laramie (1851) 24
Treaty of Madrid (1750) 252
Treaty of Tordesillas (1493–4) 11, 20, 54, 215, 227, 252
Trismegistus, Hermes 42
Tropicalia Movement 39, 232
truchements (translators) 54, 58, 63, 95, 296, 319
Trudell, John 191, 198
Trump, Donald 99, 292, 347
Tsereptsé, Divino Tserewahú 268
Tsere'ruremé, Natal Anhahö'a 268
Tserewahú, Divino
    Wai'a Rini (The Power of Dream) 244
    Wapté Munhõnõ: iniciação do jovem xavante (Initiation of a Young Xavante) 244
Tuck, Eve 19, 24
    "Decolonization Is Not a Metaphor" 332
Tukano, Daiara 71, 151, 153
    "Ted Talk" 152
Tukano people 151–2, 264
Tully, James 31, 81, 323, 325
    Strange Multiplicity 30
Tupa (god of thunder) 13, 65, 183, 256
Tupinambá, Celia, *Cipo Tupi* 161
Tupinambá, Gliceria 134
"Tupinamba in Rouen" samba pageant 56
Tupinambá, Renata 267
Tupinamba: The Return of the Land documentary 161
Tupinambá, Yakuy 160
    letter to Roussef 167 n.91
    "The Order of Disorder" 160
    "A Proposal for Life" 160–1
Tupiniquim people 56, 63–4, 128, 214, 217
Tupi people 9, 11, 18, 41, 47 n.42, 54–5, 58–9, 62, 68, 80, 83, 128, 134, 162, 214–15, 217, 222, 224, 233, 252, 263
    cannibalism 66–70, 93–4
    childcare 66
    to France 63
    matriarchy 72, 74, 164 n.36, 315
    nakedness of 66
    suffrage 65
Tupi-Guaraní 138, 142, 152, 215, 252–3, 259, 274 n.90
Tupinamba 4, 7, 53, 55–7, 59–68, 72, 94, 99, 105 n.28, 147, 159–62, 184, 228, 291, 294, 315, 349
Tupinization of Manhattan 115–20
Tupi theory 54–60, 104 n.8, 324, 360 n.30
    and Montaigne 65–8
Turner, Dale 18
Turner, Frederick Jackson 322
Turner, Nat 96
Turner, Terence 240
    Yanomami: The Fierce Controversy and What We Can Learn from It 278
Turri, João Pedro 307
    "Obfuscating Mirror" 306
Turtle Island 30, 44, 94, 143
Tuscarora 78, 269 n.1
Txêjkhõ Khãm Mby (Mulheres Guerreiras) 262
Txicao group 222

"*Uga Uga*" telenovela 131, 247
Umbanda Afro-Brazilian religion 184
Um dia na aldeia (A Day in the Village) 244
U.N. Declaration of the Decade of the World's Indigenous Peoples 29
U.N. Declaration of the Rights of Indigenous Peoples 8, 29, 176, 336, 338, 350
Underground Cinema in Brazil (Udigrudi) 298
UNESCO World Patrimony (1983) 255
U.N. Indigenous Human Rights Declaration 353
The United Nations 2, 29, 81, 176
The United States 2–3, 6, 11–12, 23, 25, 29–30, 45 n.20, 77, 79–80, 100, 102, 112 n.150, 115, 124–5, 131, 136–7, 156–7, 159, 170, 179, 181, 185, 213–18, 220, 236, 238, 259, 267, 323, 326, 329, 332–4, 336, 354, 366 n.196
    Americanization 172, 215

Declaration of Independence 80, 323
Tupinization of Manhattan 115–20
Wall Street, New York 116–19, 332
Universal Declaration on the Rights of Mother Earth (2010) 176
Unrepresented Peoples' Organization (UNPO) 261
urban Indians 37, 154, 156, 179, 188, 264, 266
Urubu people 232
Usbeck, Frank 180

Valadão, Virgínia 247, 250
  Yaokwa: Banquet of the Spirits 40
Valades, Franciscan Diego 33
Valero, Helena 282–3
Varda, Agnès 306
Vargas, Getulio, New State period 227, 234, 270 n.38
Vargas, Rafaela 57
Venezuela 1, 6, 135, 173, 218, 268, 283, 336
Verissimo, Paulo, *Exu- Pia: Heart of Macunaíma* 135
Vernet, Horace, "Messe em Kabylie" (Catholic Mass in Kabylie) painting 221
Vertov 306
Veyre, Gabriel, *Repas d'Indien* ("Indian Banquet") 179
Viana, Zelito
  Avaeté: Semente de Vingança (Avaeté: Seeds of Vengeance 234
  Terra dos Índios (Indian Land) 235
Victorian Massacres 133, 226
Victor, Masayesva, *Itam Hakim, Hopiit* (We, Someone, the Hopi People) 38
Vidalin, Maurice 91
Video Cannibalism film 247
Video nas Aldeias (VNA) project (Video in the Villages) 126, 146, 148, 240–4, 247, 252, 254, 259–61, 267
Vieira, Padre 214
Vietnam/Vietnamese 174, 177, 274 n.102, 278, 355
Villas-Boas brothers 222–3, 235, 261, 328–9
Villegagnon, Nicolas de 54, 60–2, 64, 69, 94–5
Virgin Land 121, 186

visual sovereignty 2, 35
Vitoux, Noe 112 n.152
  O Homen que Matou Deus (The Man Who Killed God) 92–3
Vizenor, Gerald 2, 18, 109 n.96, 122, 193, 204
  Manifest Manners 7, 31
  survivance 2, 31, 254
  transmotion 254
Voice-of-God narration 279, 303
Voltaire 53, 74, 78, 83
  Candide 291
  L'ingenu 75
von Martius, Carl Friedrich Phillip 180

Waiãpi 240–3
wampum 11, 18–19, 85, 201
Wanderley, Olinda Yawar Muniz, *Kaapora, O Chamado das Matas* (The Call of the Forest) 262
Wannabees 185, 189
Wapikoni Mobile studio 37, 339
Wari 92–3
Warrior, Emma Lee 184
"Wars of Brazil," Netflix series 11
Washington, George 77
Wayne, John 191, 238
Weatherford, Jack 14, 77, 143, 215
Weaver, Jace 334
Weekend film 90
Weffort, Francisco 219
Wehsehkeha 195
Weinreich, Anna 109 n.84
Wendat 10, 64, 76, 92–3, 327
Wendayete, Georges E. Sioui 10, 63, 93–4, 354
  "Amerindian Autohistory" 76
Wenders, Wim 36
Wengrow, David 76, 139, 325–6
  The Dawn of Everything: A New History of Humanity 27
Wente, Jesse 36
Werreria, Narubia 157
wesakaychak 248
Westerman, Floyd Red Crow 193, 198
Whatley, Janet 56
The White Earth Nation Constitution 191, 327

White Earth Nation of Anishinaabeg Natives 323–4
White, Hayden 147
  Metahistory 126
Whitehead, Neil L. 218
"White Indians" 6, 63, 81, 91, 106 n.39, 130–1, 169–207, 247, 316–18
White Indian Treaty (1794) 174
whiteness 72, 113 n.162, 131, 138, 146, 165 n.61, 186, 228, 238
White Savior 177–8, 197
Whitman, Walt 133, 189
"Wholelottabubblegum" YouTube video 112 n.153
Willmott, Kevin, *The Only Good Indian* 198
Wilmott, Kenneth, *C.S.A.: The Confederate States of America* 191
Winnetou's Snake Oil Show from Wigwam City show 183
Winnetou und das Halbblut Apananatschi film 184
Witness, Ehren Bear 184
Woden (Hermes-like God of eloquence) 183
Wolfe, Patrick 216, 334

Xakriabá, Artemisa 158
Xapiri film 302–7
xapiri (forest spirits) 97–9, 123, 290, 294–7, 300–1, 348
Xavante 7, 9, 37, 46 n.24, 130, 237, 241, 244–5, 254, 261, 272 n.60, 316–17, 343
Xavier, Ismail 245, 261
xawara (lethal pestilence) 100, 309, 349
Xingu (Xinguanos) 41, 234, 328, 343
"Xondaro Ka'aguy Reguá" (Forest Warrior) music video 266
Xuxa show 318, 359 n.4

yãkoana 22, 99, 284, 291, 294–7, 299, 301, 304, 306, 309, 319
Yang, K. Wayne 19, 24
  "Decolonization Is Not a Metaphor" 332
Yanomami Association 302
Yanomami, Davi Kopenawa 1, 4, 22, 83, 96–104, 121, 146, 150, 156–7, 176, 178, 277–311, 313 n.55, 322, 331, 334, 336, 340, 346, 348–50, 355–9
  The Falling Sky: Words of a Yanomami 1, 6, 34, 96–104, 157, 290–9, 308, 319, 348, 357
  mourning wars 10
  A Ultimate Floresta (The Last Forest) 307–11
Yanomami, Morzaniel Iramari, *Urihi Haromatipë* or *Curadores da Terra-Floresta* (Healers of the Earth-Forest) 301
Yanomami people 1, 6, 9, 40, 89, 96, 99–100, 138, 150, 164 n.45, 175, 233, 237, 262, 268, 277–311, 336, 340, 348, 352, 355–9
  demonization of 289
  and Downey 283–5
  fierce tribe 286–8, 357
  genetic research/study 277–8
  and Good 282
  married couples of 289
  portrayal in films 279
  revenge killings 286
  utupë 300
  and Valero 282–3
  violence 278–80, 287–8
  visual imaginary of 300–2
Yawalapiti, Ana Terra 153
Yawalapiti, Watatakalu 153
Yawanawa, Putanny 153
YBY Festival 153, 267
Yoasi 164 n.45, 293
Youngblood, Mary 198
Young, Neil, "Honor the Treaties" tour 350
YouTube videos/clips 68, 71, 112 n.153, 119, 132, 151–2, 160, 178, 186, 192, 195–6, 268, 310
Yube, Zezinho
  Kene yuxi: As voltas do Kene (The Return of Kene) 246
  Ma Ê Dami Xina – Já me Transformei em Imagem (I've Already Become Transformed into an Image) 245–6
Yudja people 262

Zantop, Susanne 180
Zapotec language 119
Zemmour, Eric 13
Zionism 112 n.149
Žižek, Slavoj 176

Zoë 240, 242–3, 263, 271 n.53
zombification 205
Zuboff, Shoshana, *The Age of Surveillance Capitalism* 15–16
Zuni 20, 64